# MAKING CONNECTIONS

## *Readings in Relational Communication*

## Fourth Edition

### Kathleen M. Galvin
*Northwestern University*

### Pamela J. Cooper
*University of South Carolina, Beaufort*

Roxbury Publishing Company
Los Angeles, California

**Library of Congress Cataloging-in-Publication Data**

Making connections : readings in relational communication / [edited by] Kathleen M. Galvin, Pamela J. Cooper.—4th ed.
   p.   cm.
Includes bibliographical references and index.
ISBN 1-931719-66-7 (alk. paper)
1. Interpersonal communication. 2. Interpersonal relations.
3. Communication—Psychological aspects. 4. Sex differences (Psychology)
I. Galvin, Kathleen M. II. Cooper, Pamela J.

BF637.C45M33 2006
302.2—dc22                                               2005026133
                                                         CIP

**MAKING CONNECTIONS: Readings in Relational Communication (Fourth Edition)**

Publisher: Claude Teweles
Managing Editor: Dawn VanDercreek
Production Editor: Nina M. Hickey
Copy Editor: Cheryl Adams
Proofreader: Renee Ergazos
Typography: Jeremiah Lenihan
Cover Artist: Marnie Kenney

Printed on acid-free paper in the United States of America. This book meets the standards for recycling of the Environmental Protection Agency.

ISBN 1-931719-66-7

An Instructor's Manual/Testing Program is available.

**ROXBURY PUBLISHING COMPANY**
P.O. Box 491044
Los Angeles, California 90049-9044
Voice: (310) 473-3312 • Fax: (310) 473-4490
Email: roxbury@roxbury.net
Website: www.roxbury.net

## Dedication

*To our relationship—*
*twenty-eight years of making connections,*
*personal and professional,*
*being there for each other*
*through joyous and tough times,*
*and creating a valued friendship.*

# Table of Contents

## Part I: Communication Foundations in Relationships

Galvin and Wilkinson discuss communication as a process, the elements of communication in general, and interpersonal communication in particular.

Wilmot defines the concept of relationship, describing it as a miniculture complete with metaphors, narratives, idioms, and symbols.

Turner and West present an overview of relational theories and their applications that undergird interpersonal interaction and relate to later chapters in the text.

## Part II: Building Blocks

Verderber and Verderber provide an important overview of the nature of language, including usage, meaning, and cultural and gender differences. They apply these findings to appropriate speaking strategies.

---

\* Revised from Third Edition

# Part III: Perceptual Processes and Communication

## A. Perception and Self-Concept

---

\*\* Reinserted from Second Edition

# B. Perceptual Filters

---

\* Revised from Third Edition

# Part IV: Developing Relationships

# Part V: Sustaining Relationships

---

* Revised from Third Edition

# Part VI: Struggling in Relationships

# Part VII: The Dark Side of Relationships

---

\*\*\* New to Fourth Edition

# Part VIII: Ending Relationships

# Part IX: Contexts

## *A. Family*

---

\* Revised from Third Edition
\*\*\* New to Fourth Edition

---

*** New to Fourth Edition

---

*** New to Fourth Edition

# Preface

The Fourth Edition of *Making Connections* continues to rely on the root metaphor of lenses—a set of "lenses" through which each of us can view and make sense of our own communication interactions and those we observe in the world around us. We believe human beings are more effective at understanding relationships when they have multiple perspectives through which to view interpersonal interactions. We also believe multiple perspectives lead to alternative ways of managing, and thus sustaining, ongoing relationships. Relying on the research and insights of scholars, theorists, and popular writers, we have assembled a timely and challenging set of perspectives on relational communication. This edition continues to offer a mix of theory and practice designed to clarify the connection between communication and the development of such significant relationships as friends, romantic partners, family members, or colleagues. This text reflects our belief that gender, culture, and family serve as perceptual filters, or lenses, through which human beings view the world; these filters directly affect the ways each of us interprets relational interactions and interacts with others. As you read the articles we hope you will examine your own personal perceptual filters in addition to understanding how others use them.

In *Making Connections*, you will encounter concepts and research findings that will provide you with new ways to consider communication in relationships and, in some cases, give you a new terminology for your intuitive relational knowledge and insights. Finally, you will consider a range of strategies for dealing with communication situations. We hope you will consider insights from these readings when making informed personal choices about your own interpersonal communication and to increase your analytical skill as an observer of relational life.

## New to the Fourth Edition

The Fourth Edition has been updated and expanded to include 10 new articles, 5 of which are original. Six other articles have been updated. Based on reviewer feedback, we have included a new Part VII that explores the dark side of communication, including chapters on lying and irresolvable conflicts; and we have also included new chapters on topics such as friendships in urban tribes, Internet communication, and the discourse dependence of diverse families. We continue to apply the same framework as in earlier editions, using gender, family, and culture as "lenses" through which to view and make sense of relational communication. The articles in *Making Connections* were selected from the recent work of communication scholars, theorists, and popular writers—with a balance between humanistic and social science perspectives. The Fourth Edition continues to:

- offer a well-rounded discussion of the links between communication and relationships, including perception, verbal and nonverbal communication, and listening.
- feature a developmental approach in terms of initiating, sustaining, and ending relationships.
- reflect direct applications of relational issues within contexts of friendships, family, and technology.
- explore issues relating to computer-mediated communication and technology.

Based on feedback from current users, we dropped the "Connecting Points" included in earlier editions.

## Structure

Each part of the text is designed to move you from concepts and theories to applications within specific contexts.

*Part I* provides an introduction to the communication process as well as to the key concepts of relational culture, dialectical processes, and relational development.

*Part II* introduces the basic building blocks of communication, which include language, nonverbal communication, listening, and context.

*Part III* establishes the critical role of perceptual processes in relational communication and presents culture, family, and gender as "lenses" through which we view our relational experiences.

*Part IV* discusses the early stage of relational development, emphasizing established relational standards and various models of relational growth for different types of ties.

*Part V* addresses the issues involved in sustaining relationships, including showing affection, managing rules and rituals, nagging, and forgiving.

*Part VI* explores the inevitable struggles that surface in significant long-term relationships and how these can be managed through negotiation skills, listening strategies, and constructive conflict practices.

*Part VII* introduces the dark side or the dysfunctional, exploitative, or shadowed aspects of human communication, exploring the frailty of human nature and the ongoing struggles to confront coercion, manipulation, and verbal abuse.

*Part VIII* confronts the reality of relational decline as friends or partners move toward greater individuality, confront their differences, and engage in leave-taking communication or consider possibilities of reconnecting.

*Part IX* demonstrates the effect of context on relational interaction and explores the interpersonal communication issues unique to the contexts of families, friendships, and computer-mediated communication, or CMC.

We introduce each section of the text, previewing the concepts that are in the readings that follow. In addition, we provide an introduction to each reading, placing it in a theoretical context, summarizing briefly the chapter highlights, and posing a question to consider as you read the piece. At the end of each reading, you will find a set of questions and challenges to help you integrate and apply key points.

We are very excited about the new articles presented in this edition because they represent emerging areas of research and concern. We hope you find the readings thought-provoking and that you will apply the theoretical insights, concepts, and examples to your own personal relationships. With each edition we have learned more about relational communication and about ourselves as communicators. Our desire is that you will be able to say the same after you have reached the last page. ✦

# Acknowledgments

Revising this book continues to be a relational experience. We appreciate the opportunity to examine the responses of persons familiar with the Third Edition, to talk with authors of academic and trade works about their ideas, and to seek out original pieces from established and emerging scholars.

We are grateful to the users of the First, Second, and Third Editions who provided extremely helpful formal and informal feedback, as well as to our Fourth Edition reviewers who provided in-depth responses to the Third Edition, including concrete suggestions for changes and additions. And they had many suggestions! These individuals include: Marcee Andersen, Anoka Ramsey Community College; Theodore Avtgis, West Virginia University; Jennifer Bieselin, Florida Gulf Coast University; Judy Bowker, Oregon State University; Bryan Crow, Southern Illinois University–Carbondale; Janie Harden Fritz, Dusquesne University; Colleen Garside, Weber State University; James Hasenauer, California State University–Northridge; Stephen Klien, Augustana College; Randall Koper, University of the Pacific; Alan Lerstrom, Luther College; and Claire Sullivan, University of Maine.

In addition, we relied heavily on the assistance of Northwestern University students for manuscript development. Lauren Grill and Katrina Shonbeck provided exceptional assistance with manuscript preparation, computer expertise, and interpersonal support. Roxbury's project editor, Nina M. Hickey, provided clear direction, immediate responses, and reassurance. Scott Carter, the editorial coordinator, managed numerous tasks with competence and responsiveness. Our publisher, Claude Teweles, remains a patient and strong supporter, as well as a helpful and flexible advisor.

As you read the Fourth Edition of *Making Connections*, we hope you will make connections between the readings and your personal life experiences, allowing you to apply these communication concepts to a wide range of relationships. We also hope you will make personal choices that will foster and deepen relational communication in the significant relationships in your life. ✦

# Contributors

**Ronald B. Adler** is a professor in the Department of Communication at Santa Barbara City College.

**Isolde K. Anderson** is an assistant professor in the Department of Communication at Hope College.

**Susan B. Barnes** is an associate professor in the Department of Communication at Rochester Institute of Technology.

**Carol J. S. Bruess** is an associate professor in the Department of Theatre Arts and Communication Studies at the University of St. Thomas.

**Daniel J. Canary** is a professor in the Hugh Downs School of Human Communication at Arizona State University.

**Michael J. Cody** is a professor in the Annenberg School for Communication at the University of Southern California.

**Pamela J. Cooper** is a professor in the Humanities Division at the University of South Carolina, Beaufort.

**William R. Cupach** is a professor in the Department of Communication at Illinois State University.

**Mary Kay DeGenova** is a former professor in the Department of Family Studies at the University of New Hampshire and is currently an independent scholar.

**Anita K. Foeman** is a professor in the Department of Communication Studies at West Chester University.

**Sheryl Friedley** is a professor in the Department of Communication at George Mason University.

**Kathleen M. Galvin** is a professor in the Department of Communication Studies at Northwestern University.

**John Gottman** is a professor emeritus in the Department of Psychology at the University of Washington.

**Judith A. Hall** is a professor of psychology at Northeastern University.

**Dale Hample** is a professor in the Department of Communication at Western Illinois University.

**Thomas E. Harris** is a professor in the Communication Studies Department at the University of Alabama.

**Joyce L. Hocker** is a clinical psychologist in Missoula, Montana.

**Michelle Huston** is a research associate for the Rural Girls in Science Program at the University of Washington.

**Navita Cummings James** is an associate professor in the Department of Communication at the University of South Florida.

**David Johnson** is a professor in the Department of Educational Psychology at the University of Minnesota.

**Douglas L. Kelley** is an associate professor of Communication Studies at Arizona State University West.

**Mark L. Knapp** is the Jesse H. Jones Centennial Professor in the Department of Communication Studies at the University of Texas, Austin.

**Jody Koenig Kellas** is an assistant professor in the Department of Communication Studies at the University of Nebraska, Lincoln.

**Amanda Lenhart** is a research specialist at the PEW Internet and American Life Project.

**Harriet G. Lerner** is a staff psychologist at the Menninger Clinic.

**Oliver Lewis** is a research assistant at the PEW Internet and American Life Project.

**Valerie L. Manusov** is an associate professor in the Department of Communication at the University of Washington.

**Sandra Metts** is a professor in the Department of Communication at Illinois State University.

**Courtney Waite Miller** is an assistant professor in the Communication Arts and Sciences Department at Elmhurst College.

**Scott A. Myers** is an associate professor in the Department of Communication Studies at West Virginia University.

**Teresa Nance** is an associate professor in the Department of Communication at Villanova University.

**James Neuliep** is a professor in the Department of Communication at St. Norbert's College.

**Lee Rainie** is a director at the PEW Internet and American Life Project.

**William K. Rawlins** is a professor in the Department of Communication at Purdue University at West Lafayette.

**F. Philip Rice**, recently deceased, was a professor emeritus in the Department of Human Development at the University of Maine.

**George Rodman** is a professor in the Department of Television and Radio at Brooklyn College of the City University of New York.

**Pepper Schwartz** is a professor in the Sociology Department at the University of Washington.

**John C. Sherblom** is a professor of communication and journalism at the University of Maine.

**Katrina Shonbeck** is a senior in the Department of Communication Studies at Northwestern University.

**Kari P. Soule** is a recent doctoral student at Northwestern University.

**Brian H. Spitzberg** is a professor in the School of Communication at San Diego State University.

**Alan Stewart** is a lecturer in the Department of Communication at Rutgers University.

**Lea P. Stewart** is a professor in the Department of Communication at Rutgers University.

**Elizabeth Stone** is a professor of English communication and media studies at Fordham University.

**Deborah Tannen** is a professor in the Linguistics Department at Georgetown University.

**Lynn H. Turner** is a professor in the Department of Communication Studies at Marquette University.

**Anita L. Vangelisti** is a professor in the Department of Communication Studies at the University of Texas, Austin.

**Kathleen S. Verderber** is a professor emeritus in the Department of Communication at Northern Kentucky University.

**Rudolph F. Verderber** is a professor emeritus in the Department of Communication at the University of Cincinnati.

**Clay Warren** is the Chauncy M. Depew Professor in the Communication Program at George Washington University.

**Ethan Watters** is a journalist who writes about social trends.

**Richard West** is a professor in the Department of Communication at the University of Southern Maine.

**Charles A. Wilkinson** recently retired as a family therapist at the North Shore Center for Counseling and Therapy in Northbrook, Illinois.

**William W. Wilmot** is a professor emeritus in the Department of Communication Studies at the University of Montana.

**Steven R. Wilson** is an associate professor in the Department of Communication at Purdue University.

**Julia T. Wood** is the Lineberger Distinguished Professor of Humanities and a professor in the Department of Communication Studies at the University of North Carolina. ✦

# Part I

## Communication Foundations in Relationships

Relationships are messy, unpredictable, joyful, frustrating, comforting, painful, and necessary! Each of us struggles with the relationships in our lives. This struggle is captured by the philosopher Arthur Schopenhauer in his famous porcupine example:

> On a wintry day a couple of chilled porcupines huddled together for warmth. They found that they pricked each other with their quills; they moved apart and were again cold. After much experimentation, the porcupines found the distance at which they gave each other some warmth without too much sting. (Quoted in Bellak 1970, 3)

Most human beings find themselves in similar situations as they try to manage their relationships with the significant people in their lives. They struggle to find the comfortable distance in each relationship and to adjust to changes in themselves and others over time.

Sustaining relationships is a lifelong concern. You may be surrounded by people during most of your waking hours, but it is the quality of your relationships that significantly influences your state of mind, your personal growth, and even your health. Your circles widen as you age, potentially incorporating partners, children, coworkers, classmates, teachers, friends, or neighbors. Some of these people represent highly significant

relationships, but many of them will engage primarily in functional communication with you. After a certain point most older adults find the circle begins to shrink, making the long-term ties even more critical.

Although everyday conversation contains ritualistic and impersonal interactions such as greetings, small talk, or sharing information, requiring very little personal attention, most of your important relationships involve interpersonal interactions that demand attention and care. Relational maintenance involves everyday talk rituals and narratives, as well as attempts at openness, assurances, or forgiveness (Canary, Stafford, and Semic 2002; Duck 1994). It may also include disagreeing, showing concern, solving a problem, giving or requesting advice, listening to feelings, or planning for the future. These less ritualized interactions demand effort and attention from all persons involved. Relational life also reveals a dark side, the source of difficult and painful interactions. Occasionally you will find yourself in "turning-point" interactions, critical conversations that carry great significance for the relationship. Such events may involve revealing something very personal about yourself, asking for help with a serious problem, responding to a friend who is ill or upset, or planning for a major shared life event.

1

Your psychological well-being depends heavily on managing the relationships in your life in a constructive manner. We believe such effective interactions do not "just happen" and that effective communicators are not "born that way." Although there are some people who appear to manage their relationships effortlessly, when you observe them carefully, however, you will see that most effective communicators consciously work at their relationships. Interpersonally skilled communicators may experience this as natural, but their level of effectiveness was developed with time and effort. We believe each person has the opportunity to develop and improve her or his communication effectiveness through a combination of knowledge and strategies that increase competence.

Because our background influences our thinking and writing, we, the editors, wish to share our key beliefs with you in order to establish a context for understanding this book.

1. There is no "right" way to communicate. Communication patterns reflect the unique interaction of participants, who bring their cultural and personal backgrounds as well as a relational history and their perceptions of each other to the interaction. Each significant relationship creates its own identity, distinguishing it from similar relationships. A relationship that "works" for one set of people may not seem desirable to others.

2. Communication serves to construct as well as reflect relationships. It is through talk that people define their identities and negotiate their relationships with each other. Their talk serves to reflect the state of their relationship to others.

3. Communication is the process by which individuals work out and share their meanings with each other. In close relationships, members develop a relational culture—a shared vision of reality, or worldview—that includes unique communication patterns.

4. Interpersonal relationships shift over time as participants respond to changing circumstances. Relationships develop a life of their own. After the early interactions, relationships reinvent themselves through the amount and type of participant involvement. Relationships experience various stages of development as they deepen and, in some cases, become less vital or die.

5. An individual's communication style is influenced by background factors such as cultural heritage, gender, family interactions, and unique life experiences, each of which affects his or her adult interpersonal relationships.

6. Persons in well-functioning interpersonal relationships nurture their ties. Developing and maintaining strong relationships take effort, or what Duck (1994) calls "relationshipping." Most relational partners are self-aware; they avoid taking their relationships for granted.

The text opens with an overview of communication concepts and processes, followed by an examination of personal factors that influence communication. We have chosen to include a range of readings from scholarly books, journals, trade books, and magazines in order to reflect theory and practice.

In this text we intend to accomplish three tasks. First, we present an introduction to the knowledge base of relational communication. You will encounter concepts and research findings providing you with new ways to consider communication in relationships and, in some cases, providing you with terminology for your intuitive knowledge. Second, we establish the importance of individual perceptions in making sense of communication interactions. You will consider a number of perspectives or "lenses" through which to analyze interpersonal interactions. Finally, we include examples of strategies for dealing with communication situations and application pieces that address everyday communication. This information should help you to make informed choices about how to handle particular interpersonal dilemmas.

Our overall aim is to provide you with a set of lenses for analyzing specific communication situations and examples of strategies for action based on your analysis. If you have ever had an eye examination, you will remember the ophthalmologist inserting different lenses into an eyeglass frame while asking you to indicate which lens helped you see most clearly. Each lens provided a slightly different view of the chart.

The way you view the world affects how you relate to others in your environment. We believe the perceptions you bring to communication situations influence how you will respond and, therefore, affect interaction outcomes.

Think back to situations when you tried to make sense out of a sensitive conversation or problem interaction. For example, consider that a reasonably friendly coworker suddenly falls silent in particular interactions with you. If you try on various relational lenses that help you understand an individual's personal experience, you may conclude the silence to be the result of worrying over a child's illness. If you try on lenses illuminating cultural communication styles, you may determine that the person's silence reflects an attempt to be polite when dealing with a sensitive topic. In a third alternative, you may decide the response reflects a gender pattern. Each lens illuminated a different perspective. Your view of the situation will affect how you respond. Whereas you could ignore what appears to be the frustration of a worried person, you might apply the cultural norm to help yourself feel comfortable. In the third situation, you may decide to rephrase a comment in a less assertive manner. In each case, you analyze the situation to the best of your ability and then act on the basis of your explanation.

This sounds very formal and carefully thought out, yet in many everyday interactions, you instinctively respond in particular circumstances. Your conscious awareness of this process occurs when you are confronted with a confusing situation or when high stakes are involved in your actions. This occurs because most routine interactions are patterned, requiring little reflection; however, when the patterns shift, attention is refocused on them. In the diverse world in which we find ourselves, these processes are significant. We cannot assume we all view interactions the same way and that "when Person X says 'beautiful,' it means the same thing as when I say 'beautiful.'"

Significant interpersonal relationships must be nurtured. In one case, this may mean sharing personal problems and "being there" for each other; in another case, it may mean getting together on a regular basis to swap work stories and banter about sports. The goal is to create ways in which both persons feel recognized and connected.

We hope you will find the readings in our fourth edition thought provoking, so that when you put the book down, you will find everyday situations in which to apply the concepts and strategies.

## References

Bellak, L. (1970). *The Porcupine Dilemma.* New York: Citadel Press.

Canary, D. J., Stafford, L., and Semic, B. (2002). A panel study of the associations between maintenance strategies and relational characteristics. *Journal of Marriage and the Family* 64:395–406.

Duck, S. (1994). Steady as (s)he goes: Relational maintenance as a shared meaning system. In D. J. Canary and L. Stafford (eds.), *Communication and Relational Maintenance*, 45–59. San Diego, CA: Academic Press. ✦

# 1
# The Communication Process

## Impersonal and Interpersonal

*Kathleen M. Galvin and*
*Charles A. Wilkinson*

Communication is a complex, ongoing process that brings us into contact with the people
in our world. Often communication is viewed
as a straightforward exchange of messages between a speaker and a listener, but this is a
naïve view. As indicated in this chapter, communication is a symbolic process of sharing
meanings.

A key to interpreting communication is to
find the meanings of messages, and those
meanings are found in people, not in words.
Your friend's meaning of trust or happiness
may be quite different than yours. Even a presumably simple, concrete word can cause
misunderstandings. You may think of vacation as personal time spent away from the
workplace with no thought of your job. Your
boss may think vacation implies that employees will be away from the office but continuously available to discuss work-related problems via cell phone or e-mail. The closer both
meanings are, the easier it is for you to communicate effectively.

Communication is a continuous process
that begins with a first encounter between people and does not end until the last encounter in
their lives. These encounters may involve
functional messages that serve practical purposes, or, in cases of close ties, the encounters
may also involve nurturing messages that
convey a sense of caring and personal connection. Over time, members of a relationship develop increasingly predictable communica-

tion patterns and, if they become close, create
a relational culture or similar worldview.

In the following pages, Galvin and Wilkinson
address this complex issue, discussing the communication process as a constant symbolic interaction of sharing, exchanging, and coordinating meanings. Through various examples,
they apply this understanding of the communication process to explain the difference between
specific types of communication, like interpersonal, impersonal, functional, and nurturing
communication. Finally, they explore relational
culture, a very specific and unique type of interpersonal communication, and discuss the communication dynamics involved. The analysis in
this chapter answers the question "How does
communication work?" and establishes a basis
of knowledge that prepares the reader for the
chapters to follow. As you read this chapter,
begin to formulate your answer to the question:
What is communication?

\* \* \*

How often have you heard someone say,
"We just can't communicate," or "We are having communication problems"? These expressions appear regularly in everyday conversations as people struggle to solve a problem,
start a relationship, manage a conflict, or find
a new way of connecting in an established relationship. Such struggles occur in all areas of
life, in classrooms and offices, at kitchen ta-
bles, and on athletic fields. In our society people of different backgrounds come together to
solve problems or make things happen, and in
those situations they can find themselves frustrated because of "communication breakdowns." Although these dissatisfactions are
not new, they are heightened by the fact that
we live in an information age in which effective communication is expected and valued in
all areas of life.

Over time we have had the opportunity to
listen to many different people discuss their
interpersonal frustrations as we lead communication workshops for family members,
organizational employees, and community
groups. In all these cases participants are invested in improving their handling of certain
situations, in analyzing their relationships,
and in developing new relational skills.

As we discuss interpersonal communication in our workshops, we also describe the communication process and its elements as well as the specific characteristics of *inter*personal communication that distinguish it from *im*personal communication. We also address the concept of relational culture, or the development of a highly unique interpersonal relationship characterized by a unique system of meanings created and maintained by the partners. Our hope is to encourage participants to develop their knowledge and skills in relationship development and relationship maintenance in various contexts. We will introduce these issues in the following pages.

## The Communication Process

Whenever we ask workshop participants how they would define *communication*, we hear responses such as "transmitting ideas," "talking and listening," or "sending messages using words and movements." Each person has some notion of what it means to communicate with another and knows how it feels when communication attempts are successful or unsuccessful, yet they have not thought deeply about the communication process itself. People seem to assume that communication works or it does not work, more as a matter of fate than as a process that can be changed or improved.

Because communication itself is so complex, we could list multiple elaborate and highly technical definitions of it. For our purposes, however, a simple phrase is an appropriate starting point. As we view it, communication is *the symbolic process of sharing meanings*. Because this definition is almost deceptively simple, each of these key words needs to be developed.

### Symbolic

By saying that communication is symbolic, we mean that symbols are used to transmit messages. Symbols are representations of a person, event, place, or object. Words, or verbal expressions, are the most commonly understood symbols, but symbolic actions also include the whole range of nonverbal behaviors: facial expressions, vocal tone, eye contact, gestures, movement, body posture, appearance, context, and spatial distance. In addition, objects and ideas can be used as symbols. For example, friends often exchange gifts, food, or e-mails as symbols of connectedness.

You have learned to use verbal and nonverbal symbols both as a message creator and as a message interpreter. As a speaker (or sender), you create messages by selecting the most appropriate symbols from a range of options in order to reach your intended receivers most effectively. As a listener (or receiver), you attempt to interpret the symbols others convey to you. Although exchanging appropriate symbols appears rather simple and straightforward, we are constantly amazed at the communication breakdowns that occur as symbols are misinterpreted.

Effective communicators are those who are able to select the most appropriate symbols or messages for specific other persons and who are able to interpret the intended message symbols of other speakers. As a child you learned to encode one type of message to ask your father for money and another to request a loan from your best friend. You learned to interpret your brother's gestures indicating if he is feeling sad, worried, or exhausted. You have learned who will be enraged if you roll your eyes at them, and who will decode your nonverbal cue as humorous. For effective communication to occur, the speaker and listener must share the same meanings for the symbolic messages they exchange.

### Process

Relational communication involves a process, a dynamic and continuous process.

Each relationship develops its own communication history, a history that cannot be rewritten. Someone once said, "It's unfortunate you only get one chance to make a first impression." A relationship's communication pattern begins at the first moment of contact—at a party, in a classroom, in a meeting. The relationship may start in any number of ways: a question, a glance, an introduction, or a smile. Once contact is made, the relationship begins to develop its history, which is constructed and reflected by its communication patterns. A relationship's ongoing development may be interrupted by physical or psychological distance; relational partners may move in and out of each others' lives over many years, but the history of the relationship continues from that first meeting. Sometimes people say they wish to wipe out a time period of their relationship or forget a painful argument that occurred. Individuals may choose to emphasize or deemphasize certain communication events throughout their relationship history, but they can never go back to "how things used to be," or delete a piece of that history.

Although some models of the communication process portray it as a circular process, our preferred model for understanding this process comes from the thinking of Frank Dance (Dance and Larson 1976; Dance and Zak-Dance 1986), who proposed a helical representation. Imagine the form of a helix, in which the continuousness of the process is represented by the infinity sign (Figure 1-1). This model depicts the ever-widening scope of the relationships as participants continuously reencounter each other, a process that continues indefinitely.

**Figure 1-1**

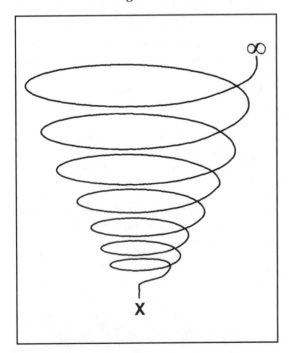

Whereas a circular model suggests that communication returns to the same place, the helical model implies the ever-changing, progressive, and evolving nature of relational interactions. The helix representation provides support for the concept that "you can't put a relationship into reverse and erase a difficult period of time." We have stopped counting the times workshop participants say, "If only things could go back to the way they were two years ago," or, "I want to wipe out the last six months of our marriage." In reality each encounter has inalterably added to their relationship, and this history cannot be denied. People in relationships cannot wipe out a huge hurtful fight, long periods of verbal aggression or silence, or, in romantic situations, the affair. Yet most friends, partners or colleagues can learn to manage their history in effective ways: through emphasizing positives, talking through the conflicts, and behaving in ways that affirm their ties.

A conflictual father and son cannot pretend they never hurt one another with words or fists; friends cannot erase sarcastic comments. All they can do is work through the issues that currently keep them from dealing with each other in constructive or caring ways, and attempt to change their present communication patterns as they continue in their relational process. People can always *choose* to change, to do things differently. Such choices represent one of the most exciting parts of the relational development process.

### Sharing

Even though the words *speaker* and *listener* are commonly used in communication terminology, communication is not a process of trading messages. It does not resemble a poor tennis match in which one Player A hits the ball and then just stands there until the Player B hits the return. Symbolic messages do not travel from Person One to Person Two and back to Person One again in some turn-taking ritual. Rather, at its most basic level, communication requires mutual and continuous involvement, sometimes referred to as *the transactional nature of communication*. This mutual influence process is similar to a skilled tennis match in which both players are always in motion based on what they anticipate the other will do. Similarly, in communication encounters both parties remain actively involved in the process. For example, even though Michael may appear more talkative, Vanessa conveys nonverbally that she is bored or pleased or annoyed, thus influencing Michael's choice of future message symbols. Both are actively and continuously involved in every moment of the interactions; thus, the mutual influence process that characterizes interpersonal interaction. Diagrammed, the transactional nature of communication looks like Figure 1-2.

### Figure 1-2

| Person One | Person Two |
|---|---|
| Speaking<br>Listening   ⟵⟶   | Speaking<br>Listening |

As relationships develop over time, the transactional process becomes more complex. Your perception of another person and that individual's perception of you combine to form a context for your interactions. If you see Person X as warm and supportive, you will relate to him or her in an open manner. Person X is then likely to see you as open and friendly and relate to you with increasing warmth or support. Thus, your perceptions of each other affect each interaction as well as the overall perception of the relationship. The situation can also be reversed, creating a negative context. If you see another person as judgmental or sarcastic, this may lead you to interact in a defensive or combative manner. You may be caught up in a type of negative spiral. Each communication exchange occurs within the context of a mutually constructed relationship.

If the definition of a relationship remains relatively unchanged, for example boss and employee, romantic partners, and parent and child, the nature of the communication process becomes fixed. Each new encounter reinforces the good or the bad. A boss who constantly relates to staff members as incompetent may stifle their attempts to be innovative. A parent who treats children as responsible persons fosters their ability to

handle new situations. This process is captured in the statement "Over time we create an image of another person and relate to the image we create." Individuals construct a reality of themselves and of others through their interactions, and relate to those realities they constructed. The attempt to understand and adapt to another represents a communication challenge.

### Meanings

Although verbal and nonverbal symbols permit us to transmit thoughts and feelings, the symbols must be mutually understood for the meanings to be truly shared. *Common meanings make it possible for us to communicate.* Since there is no absolute standard for all symbols, we are constantly trying to connect with people, even our family members, who do not share exactly the same meanings for the symbols that we use. Therefore it is important to remember the expression "Words don't mean; people do."

Each person's background, including physiological state, family and cultural background, and unique experiences, influences how he or she perceives the world and attaches meanings to symbols. The experience of being nearsighted, athletic, extraverted, dyslexic, artistic, or shy affects how you perceive the world and relate to others. Your family of origin (the family or families in which you were raised) served as your first communication classroom, teaching you how to interpret messages and how to use communication to manage key relational issues such as intimacy and conflict. In addition, your cultural background, socioeconomic level, and educational experiences influence your perceptions. Based on your culture, you may interpret big hugs, multiple-course meals, and shouting voices as symbols of caring. If you grew up in a lower-middle-class neighborhood, you will have different meanings for money and security than someone who grew up in an affluent community.

Finally, your own unique circumstances influence how you assign meanings. A painful custody battle affects how you discuss divorce. Early school experiences influence how you participate in college classes. Living abroad affects how willing you are to interact with people of different cultures.

Fortunately, most people report many similar experiences, but no two people develop the same set of meanings. Each is a unique entity with particular meanings for certain symbols. Ninety dollars may represent a *large* purchase to one person, but her partner assumes that only purchases above $500 are *large*. A nickname may seem funny to you and insulting to your friend. Screaming may be viewed as an acceptable or terrible way to resolve conflicts. Breakdowns in communication often occur because of missed meanings. Only with knowledge and empathy can you walk in someone else's shoes, experience the world from a different perspective, and create messages that reflect that point of view.

Frequently, focus is placed on the words rather than on the entire range of verbal and nonverbal symbols that are constantly being used to create and interpret the meanings of messages. Therefore, at any point in time each person involved in communication is contributing to the process—and experiencing the transactional nature of the communication process. Effective communication requires the psychological presence of both parties—attention and connectedness are indicators that both parties are focused on the encounter.

We find the following simple exercise very useful for demonstrating how individuals may differ in translating the meaning of everyday terms. Imagine yourself saying these phrases to a particular person. Think about exactly what you would hope that other person would do if you said these words to him or her.

I need more *respect* from you.

I feel there is a lack of *trust* in our relationship.

Each of the italicized words receives many different responses. Depending on the person responding, more *respect* may be indicated by (1) listening to me, (2) asking for my opinion, or (3) following my advice. *Trust* may be indicated by (1) keeping what I say confidential, (2) telling me your real feelings, or (3) telling

me when a painful event happens. These are only examples of the many meanings that people have for the two common terms *respect* and *trust*. Shared meanings are critical because they help to create the context for a relationship in which participants learn to predict how the other will react to particular verbal and nonverbal messages.

## Interpersonal Communication

Not all communication should be considered interpersonal communication. Frequently, you are engaged in impersonal interactions. When you ask for directions, pay for a purchase, or call for a doctor's appointment, you are not automatically involved in interpersonal communication. If you ask a teacher for clarification, discuss a project with a boss, or plan a family reunion with a distant cousin, you may be involved in necessary, functional interactions but you do not share a strong, significant relationship.

Interpersonal communication occurs when two or more people engage in voluntary, ongoing, interdependent interactions that involve meaningful interpretation of their verbal and nonverbal behaviors. In short, this implies a perception of the relationship as positive, reflecting a choice to continue to relate to each other over time in order to deepen the relationship and make it increasingly unique. There may be exceptions to this description, such as when you interact involuntarily with particular teachers or managers for a long period of time, learn how to communicate effectively with them, and eventually develop a voluntary interpersonal relationship. In the case of involuntary but required relationships, it is likely that the person with the less power is adapting to the person with greater power, setting up a one-up/one-down interaction pattern. Such relationships tend to remain impersonal, although, on occasion, these persons develop a friendship.

Relationships move from impersonal to increasingly personal as closeness develops. Therefore, you need to think about relationships on a continuum from impersonal to interpersonal, understanding that a particular relationship may move forward and backward at different times.

**Figure 1-3**

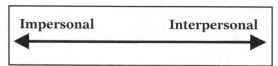

## Patterns

In ongoing relationships, communication becomes patterned and predictable. As you relate with another person, you begin to create increasingly predictable interaction patterns. The more intense and personal the relationship becomes, the more unique the relational patterns. Relational patterns involve verbal and nonverbal communication acts that are (1) recurring and (2) relationship defining. Over time, while people in a relationship develop their own ways of interacting, they evoke certain responses from each other and play off them. For example, you may know that you and Tony will joke around when you see each other, whereas you and Alberto will talk about poker. You may share your romantic problems with Sarah but never with Gail, who you know equally well. Observing an ongoing significant relationship, you may see a remarkably complex pattern, similar to a dance, emerge. For example:

X makes a statement; Y answers with a complaint.

X responds with a kidding remark; Y counters with sarcasm.

X retorts angrily; Y suggests talking is useless.

One or the other stomps away.

In his book *Couplehood* (1994, 202), Paul Reiser describes numerous examples of everyday patterns between partners.

Like all businesses, couples engage in endless meetings to discuss areas of management concern and division of labor.

"You know, we really should call the post office and tell them to hold our mail while we're away."

"*We*? You mean *me*, don't you?"

"No, I mean *we*. I didn't say '*you*.' I said '*we*.' You *or* me."

"Oh, really? Are *you* going to ever call the post office?"

A moment to think. "No."

"Then you mean 'me,' don't you?"

"Yeah."

As in many other areas of life, relationships become predictable; these patterns tend to create or constitute the relationship.

# Functional and Nurturing Communication

In many relationships, the bulk of everyday communication tends to be functional rather than nurturing. *Functional communication* involves managing day-to-day necessities and exchanging impersonal information such as getting plans coordinated, meals fixed, schedules arranged, and group projects finished—all the details that keep life running smoothly. We estimate that 90 percent of the communication that goes on between friends or colleagues, parents and children, and even spouses or partners tends to be functional communication. If the only communication between closely connected persons is functional, that relationship is severely limited. If the necessary and desirable functional interactions are not accompanied by communication that is *more personal*, distance will characterize their ties, limiting their relationship.

*Nurturing communication* occurs when participants send messages that are caretaking of the relationship—messages that indicate that the other person and the relationship are valued. Such nurturing communication may include a hug, a special birthday celebration, a thinking-of-you phone call or IM, a deep conversation about feelings, or a direct personal statement such as "I'm glad we're friends." Nurturing communication involves emotional closeness and carries the "I care about you" messages. People who nurture each other confirm the other's existence—"You are there; I recognize you; I care about you."

Through our work with partners and families, we have developed an informal guideline that states the following: If there is 10 percent nurturing communication going on in any relationship, that relationship is healthy. When 10 percent of the behaviors in a relationship are nurturing, we believe the people involved will feel cared for and valued. In our experience, when individuals in relationships come for counseling, functional messages account for about 95 percent of their communication and the remaining 5 percent is negative, often openly hostile. Nurturing messages disappeared from their relational life.

Nurturing takes different forms in different relationships, but no matter what the form of expression, everyone needs to experience it. Coworkers, friends, and family members can all be involved in levels of nurturing communication. Individuals who have been nurtured are likely to be good nurturers; those who have not been nurtured can learn to nurture others, but often this takes conscious effort and hard work. Nurturing communication serves as the lifeblood of any relationship. Without it, the relationship remains static and functional; with it, the relationship renews itself through continual growth.

## Relational Culture

Persons in strong, highly developed interpersonal relationships eventually create their own relational culture. *Relational culture* describes a jointly constructed worldview, a personally developed set of understandings that affect the attitudes, actions, and identities of the relational partners. Over time many partners or best friends adapt to each other until they experience an evolving, unique set of meanings that are reflected in their relational culture. These private meanings, conveyed verbally and nonverbally, separate the partnership from other relationships; nicknames, joint storytelling, inside jokes, and code words contribute to the creation of a "world built for two." We find Julia Wood's description captures the essence of a relational culture: "processes, structures and practices that create, express and sustain personal relationships and the identities of partners" (2000, 77). Communication patterns serve as the basis for relational cultures as they are constructed, maintained, or changed through communication. A strong relational culture is the hallmark of an intense, intimate interpersonal relationship.

In a world of many stresses and changes, we need our relationships to sustain us and nourish us as human beings. Communication is central to the process of constructing meaningful and fulfilling relational support. The ability to build and nurture such relationships is a critical life skill, one to be learned and valued.

## References

Dance, Frank E. X., and Larson, Carl. (1976). *The Functions of Human Communication: A Theoretical Approach*. New York: Holt, Rinehart & Winston.

Dance, Frank E. X., and Zak-Dance, Carol. (1986). *Public Speaking*. New York: Harper & Row.

Reiser, Paul. (1994). *Couplehood*. New York: Bantam Books.

Wood, Julia. (2000). *Relational Communication*. 2nd ed. Belmont, CA: Wadsworth.

## Questions

1. Describe a relationship you have observed that exhibits functional and nurturing messages. Give examples of each.

2. Think about a communication situation in which the symbols used caused misunderstanding. Describe the communication breakdown, and imagine what the communicators might have done to avoid such a breakdown.

3. Think about the communication in a significant relationship in your life according to the helical model. According to this model, you cannot forget or ignore difficult experiences. Describe how you and the other person have managed to deal with painful or conflictual times in your relational history.

# 2
# The Relational Perspective

*William W. Wilmot*

Metaphors provide a lens for viewing relationships. In his writings, communication scholar William A. Wilmot frequently uses a dance metaphor to capture the dynamics of relational communication. In the following piece, he suggests that "a relationship exists when the participants construct a mental view of it." Without the relational conceptions of both people, there is no way to know what type of relationship exists or even if one exists at all. These perceptions contribute to the creation of a relational world.

One of the ways to understand relationships is to think about the language people use to describe and discuss them. Wilmot writes about relational minicultures in ways that will remind you of the concept of relational culture. He stresses the importance of metaphors, narratives, and idioms as tools for understanding relationships.

Metaphors provide a way of talking about very complex and abstract ideas. A relationship depicted as a "rock" conveys a very different message from one described as a "house of cards." Relationship narratives or stories help participants and outsiders to make sense of their world. Stories reflect where the relationship has been; they also have an impact on the future of the relationship. The use of idioms reinforces the special nature of the relationship and conveys this to the outside world. Finally, participants in a relationship can understand that relationship better by examining the symbols of relational identity, for example, activities, places, or artifacts.

In this chapter Wilmot discusses what relationships are, how one can learn to define them, and ways in which to conceptually think of them. He describes relationships as "private minicultures," which, through metaphors, narratives, idioms, and symbols of identity, take shape and provide meaning for the individuals involved. Combining theory with examples, Wilmot illustrates the complex role that the relationship plays in relational communication. As you read this chapter, consider the following question: What is a metaphor or mental image that you would use to describe each of three relationships in your life?

* * *

Relationships are like a dance. The two partners dance close some times, far apart at others. When they are doing the same dance (like cowboy swing) it works fine. And, similarly to a dance, each relationship has its own form, flow, challenges, disruptions, and recoveries. With relationship partners in synchrony, the flow and synergistic energy elevate both. The dance becomes a thing of beauty to watch, and it looks easy. Often, however, one partner wants to do cowboy swing while the other insists on the foxtrot. And if both insist on doing their own dance, they will struggle, flounder, and fall.

For most of us, our personal relationships with family, friends, work colleagues, and romantic partners sometimes flow and sometimes trip us up—they are among the most fulfilling and frustrating events of our lives. This is reflected by college students, for example, in that the most frequent topic of conversation is romantic relationships (Haas & Sherman, 1982). Our personal relationships ebb and flow throughout our entire life span, yet our knowledge about them is often not equal to the challenges they bring us. . . .

## What *Is* a Relationship?

In the 1800s, not much time was spent by people discussing the "state of our relationship," whereas these days relationships are discussed over coffee and lunch, in college courses, and in the mass media. Just scan the magazines in the grocery store and you'll see articles on "how to make love last," "moving from lovers to friends," and "getting your family to talk to you." Whether people openly discuss relationships or not, participants are in a relationship when they have a "sense of

11

being in a relationship" (Duck, 1988, p. 2). The crucial difference isn't whether some outside social scientist thinks you are in a relationship by some academic criteria (Hinde, 1979), but *a relationship exists when the participants construct a mental view of it*. Those mental images of the relationship occur on many levels.

At the most basic level, Level I, a relationship occurs when there is a mutual recognition of being perceived. Whether it is someone across the aisle in a theatre, or having coffee with a best friend, we become aware of being in a relationship when communication processing is reciprocal. At this first level, a "relationship" is formed when:

1. You and another are behaving;

2. You are aware of his/her behavior, and at the same time

3. The other is aware of your behavior;

4. As a result,
   a. you are aware that the other is aware of you
   b. the other is aware that you are aware of him/her.

People are in a relationship when each *has the perception of being perceived*—when both persons can say "I see you seeing me."

At the more complex level, Level II, relationship awareness occurs over and above the specific cues being sent and received—you treat the relationship as having a *past, present, and future*. As Leatham and Duck (1990) say, "You have a relationship when the partners believe in the *future* of it." A relationship emerges from its history and continually reemerges and transforms over time—continually changing. Thus, you may not be sending messages to your parents, nor they to you, but you would say that you are "in a relationship" with them. You name the relationship by things such as "I am her son" or some other relationship marker to signify its existence. Level II awareness arises from cumulative interactions with a particular person so that you "name" the relationship—it becomes a reality that transcends the particular communication messages being sent. At Level II, people speak of relationships "declining,"

"improving," and "being flat"—clearly relationships are conceptual realities.

Understanding a relationship is much like reading a short story or novel. As we move through time, new information is integrated into our interpretation of the events of the past and makes a difference in the present and our projections about the future. Relationship processing, however, is much more complex, because our interpretations of ongoing events affect how we respond and how others respond to us. As Fletcher and Fincham (1991a) say, "Thus, participants' interpretations of events are part of the changing flux of events as individuals mutually influence each other" (p. 79).

When we enter into a relational world, it is no longer exclusively our own—the other person is considered in the acts we do; there is no such thing as individual behavior not influenced by the relational context from which it springs. Each person's perceptions influence the relationship, because each participant affects and is affected by the other. At Level II, we integrate previous communication exchanges by constructing a view of them and projecting into the future. Thus, while relationships are derived from previous communicative exchanges, it is our mental images of them that create their reality for us. One young man who lives alone has a girlfriend in a small town out of state. She is an incredibly good shopper who can find bargains. When he goes to the local discount store to buy food, as he cruises the aisles looking for bargains and comes upon an item, he can imagine her saying, "Now, *that* is a good value." He brings his past experiences of shopping with her and pushes them forward in time to the current shopping trip. An example of this sort of "carrying the relationship with you" occurs when you imagine the reaction of parents or friends to something you have done. Whenever you think about someone's reaction, you are drawing upon past experience and pulling it forward in time.

## Relationships as Minicultures

Relationships are "private minicultures" where participant perceptions of the relationship are its reality (Fitzpatrick & Indvik,

1982). The perceived reality of relationships builds over time for the participants. And, further, as we move to new relationships, different aspects of ourselves are activated. In a true sense, each relationship is unique, calling forth diverse elements from each participant.

Relationship participants need to "make sense" of their relationships, because relationships are more than the sum of the individual parts. When two people have a relationship, there is a "third party"—the relationship itself—which has a life of its own. This synergistic creation is built by the participants yet goes beyond them. As Humphreys says, "There is no such thing as two, for no two things can be conceived without their relationship, and this makes three" (Humphreys, 1951).

Each relationship is a "miniculture," with its own norms and rules (Morton & Douglas, 1981). In all pairings, such as teacher-student, mother-son, friend-friend, or doctor-patient, the participants have their own conception of the relationship, their own "relational miniculture" that encompasses what they do and who they are to one another. These created "relational minicultures" are particular to the relationship and are more rich and complex than the general labels we all learn (such as "friend," "romantic partner," "family member"). The relationship partners develop a label, or metaphor, for their relationship, replete with its own system of obligations and rights (Hinde, 1979). There are times, of course, when one partner sees the relationship one way and the other another way—and these contrasting or *asymmetric* definitions also comprise the miniculture (Neimeyer & Neimeyer, 1985). Sometimes, a continual disagreement about the nature of a relationship (I want to be friends/I want to be lovers) may be a central feature of the relationship.

## Metaphors for Relationships

People's metaphors about relationships supply meaning for those relationships. We use metaphors when we compare one thing to something else. For example, if you are in a "stormy" romantic relationship, you are comparing the relationship to the weather, emphasizing the bad weather at times. Describing a work relationship or marriage as a "battleground" conveys a different image than the metaphor "game" or "partnership."

When an ongoing relationship does *not* have an agreed-upon definition, it brings conflict and discord. Jackson says that "in a pathologic relationship we see . . . a constant sabotaging or refusing of the other's attempts to define the relationship" (Jackson, 1959). And Weick notes the same effects in organizations: "One of the major causes of failure in organizations is a shortage of images concerning what they are up to, a shortage of time devoted to producing these images, and a shortage of diverse actions to deal with changed circumstance" (Weick, 1979). Some overlap in the definitions is necessary so the participants can have coordinated action, a sense of common purpose, and agreement about "who they are."

The choice of metaphor or image for a relationship evokes a feel for the dynamics of a relationship. If a man describes his marriage as an "endangered species," it conveys a fragile, close-to-extinction nature of the relationship. Themes that emerge in ongoing relationships have been explored by Owen. He notes that thematic interpretation becomes a way to understand "relational life." For instance, "A male and female meet as 'friends,' become 'daters,' then 'lovers,' perhaps finally becoming a 'married couple' making transitions to the different relationship states or definitions primarily through communication." In his study composed of married couples, romantic dating partners, sets of relatives, sets of live-in friends, and groups of friends not living together, Owen identified some central determinants that participants use to make interpretative sense of relationships (Owen, 1984a). The participants saw their relationships illustrating the following:

1. *Commitment*—dedication to this particular relationship in spite of difficult times.

2. *Involvement*—some relationships, such as marriage and family relationships, demand more involvement than others.

3. *Work*—relationships require more "work" to keep them functioning in a healthy manner.

4. *Unique-Special*—this bolsters the belief that the participants have "beat the odds" and survived a "breakup."

5. *Fragile*—for dating couples, the fragile nature of the relationship is paramount, whereas for married couples it helps them feel they have "held it together."

6. *Consideration-Respect*—married couples primarily saw respect as an important gauge of the relationship, whereas others did not.

7. *Manipulation*—women who were dating especially noted that the person might be "playing games" or "using others" in dates (Owen, 1984a).

Owen notes that relationships vary according to these themes—they are the dimensions the participants use to make "sense" out of the relational experience. And it has been suggested by Wilmot and Hocker (1993) that actively working to alter couples' metaphors can help bring change into a married relationship.

One other piece of work on metaphors for relationships has been offered by Baxter (1992b). She classified people's descriptions of heterosexual couples into four root metaphors. People saw their relationships as (1) work-exchange, (2) journey-organism, (3) force-danger, and (4) game. If you characterize your cross-sex romance as work-exchange, it connotes a process of effort and coordination, whereas seeing it as journey-organism suggests an ever-changing process of growth. Characterizing a relationship in terms of force-danger implies that it is a risky undertaking where you can be hurt and have limited control, whereas seeing it as a game suggests that romance is a set of scripts where you can win or lose (Baxter, 1992).

The parties to a relationship also reflect their "miniculture" by manifesting (1) narratives, (2) relationship idioms, and (3) symbols of relationship identity.

## Relationship Narratives

People share narratives or stories about their relationships. Whether a fellow is complaining about his boss, celebrating his newfound love, or wanting to be closer to his brother, he talks about relationships in many ways. When you say, "Gee, she sure isn't the friend I thought she was. When she left me downtown, I had to walk home," you are providing a story or a narrative about a relationship.

What is a narrative? It is a story, telling about a unique event or series of events (Van Kijk, 1985). Narratives organize and synthesize a jumbled set of events into an understandable sequence and come in many forms. Narrative texts are such things as short stories, diaries, and even novels or biographies. For our purposes here, however, we will focus on oral narrative—when you talk about a relationship to someone else. The relationship narratives we share with others usually are conversational stories about important events (Polanyi, 1985)—the struggle with your sister, the special time with your parents, the exhilaration of a new love relation, the fun times you had with your friends over spring break, or the breakup of a love affair. I would guess (since there is scant research on it right now) that most narratives are about turmoil and trouble—how to deal with the difficult boss, how to get freedom from your parents (or children), what to do when you fall out of love, or how to cope when someone you love suddenly stops seeing you without any explanation. . . .

Narratives not only reflect your reaction to a relationship, they also impact the future course of it. When you say, "It was a fine vacation—we love going to the North Fork," it tends to reinforce the positive features of the relationship. Similarly, if one spends a great deal of time criticizing a love relationship partner, that tends to further solidify your negative view of it. In the most dramatic cases, when an ex-spouse says, "My ex-husband and I are enemies since the divorce," it not only reflects the current reality but reinforces this view each time she complains about him.

Not only do our experiences of the relationship change, our accounts and representations of it also change. Relationships tend to flow like the wind—ever changing. To bring some order to the ever-fluctuating reality, people activate "memory structures" about their relationships. They can generate and write down typical communication events and order their relationships across time (Honeycutt, Cantril, & Greene, 1989). Further, the narratives about the relationship change across time. The person who has fallen wildly in love gives you a far different picture of the relationship today than he or she [will] a year following the breakup. We reformulate our memories about our relationships quite dramatically (Duck, 1988). In the Duck and Miell (1986) studies comparing contemporary accounts of first meetings with subsequent retrospective accounts, they found people giving different accounts of where they first met. And as Duck (1988, p. 112) says, "Surra reports that about 30 percent of one of her samples of married couples were in disagreement with their own partner by more than one year about when they first had sexual intercourse together!" And, of course, when a breakup occurs people tend to alter their representation of the entire history of the relationship. . . .

Narratives, being so commonplace, obviously serve important functions for the participants. First, they serve functions *for the storyteller.* By "telling our story" we come to understand our own confusing experiences (Surra, 1987; Veroff, 1993). In fact, some people state, "I don't know what I feel until I talk about it!" In a sense, *all* stories can be seen as "narratives of the self." Telling a story (1) reinforces your view of yourself, (2) contrasts you to others ("he is such a scumbag; I can't believe he stole money from his mother"), and (3) allows you to transform yourself by talk. It is well known that people in crisis "need to talk"—they have to tell their story, to "let it out" and start the process of adjustment to the changes. . . .

Second, in addition to "saving face" for the storyteller, narratives create "*acceptable public and private accounts*" of the events. In the case of romantic breakups, Duck (1982) argues that verbal accounts serve as "grave dressing." When the relationship is over, one of the last stages you go through is "telling a story," a narrative, about the relationship. You do that to both save face and bring further changes for yourself, *and* to create public versions of the relationship for the consumption of others.

Farrell (1984) suggests that the narratives are designed to "delight, instruct, or move the listener" (p. 174). Grandparents who tell stories to their grandchildren can be seen as passing on family values and history. The tried-and-maybe-true story of the parents or grandparents walking through the blizzard to make it to the schoolhouse is a way to tell the progeny about the importance of getting an education—even in a blizzard. My father used to tell me about "going to town" when he was a child twice a year from the homestead in Wyoming and having five cents to spend on candy. Clearly, relationship narratives (or "accounts," as the social science researchers prefer to call them), are "presentational"—they serve as a way to present an event (Duck & Pond, 1991).

As a listener to a narrative, you too have a communication role to perform. You need to (1) agree to hear the story, (2) refrain from taking a turn except to make remarks about the relationship under discussion, and (3) at the end of the storytelling, demonstrate your understanding of it (Polanyi, 1985). In a sense, the active listener ("Yeah, I see; then what did he say to you?") participates as a "co-author," urging the other on (Mandelbaum, 1989).

What about the accuracy of narratives? Rather than ask about accuracy, it is more informative to focus on the degree of overlap in the two people's narratives. If Russell and Susan tell similar stories about their romantic relationship, that is evidence that they have some agreement about important relationship marker events. If both, for example, tell about the time they went winter camping and didn't take enough food and both laugh about it, then it indicates how they are "together" in this view. If the story is a "collaborative effort" (Veroff et al., 1993), it indicates the cooperation between the two. On the other hand, if they have relational difficulties or break up, you can rest assured that Russell will tell one story and Susan another. The "narrative overlap" is an indicator of the "we-ness" of the relationship; conjoint stories indicate more closeness and agreement, while divergent stories indicate people who are defining themselves as more separate and independent. One of the differences between men and women is that, in recalling past events in relationships, women tend to have more vivid memories, which, of course, makes it difficult to have conjoin[t] stories that are perfectly in tune (Ross & Holmberg, 1993). In sum, narratives can be seen as varying between these two poles: (1) individual, divergent accounts; and (2) conjointly agreed-upon accounts. . . .

Listening closely to others' narratives will give you a window into [their] desire to save face and be seen as acceptable, and will also give you information about how they got [to] the state of their relationship. The narrative serves as both a reflection of the relationship and a force for the future of the relationship. And, finally, listen to your own narratives—and see where you are in your own relationships. Are you stuck and frustrated? Do you tell the same story over and over, unable to change over time? Does the narrative correspond with what the other would say? These and related questions about how you talk about your own relationships can give you insight into your reactions to the current situation.

## Idioms in Relationship

Part of the narrative of a relationship involves personal idioms. They tend to develop in concert with the intimacy of a relationship (Bell, Buerkel-Rothfuss, & Gore, 1987) and are part of the "personalized" language used in close relationships. For example, saying "my honey" or "sweetykins" for your romantic partner cues both you and outsiders to the idea that the relationship is something special. Idioms are used both in private and in public, and come into being only after there is a certain degree of intimacy in the couple pairing (Hopper, Knapp, & Scott, 1981). Once used, they tend to both (1) reflect the degree of intimacy and (2) facilitate continued escalation of intimacies (Bell, Buerkel-Rothfuss, & Gore, 1987). Idioms are used in many types of close relationships, for example, among friends and family members, and between romantic partners.

Couples' idioms can be discussed as falling into the following categories (the categories and examples come from Hopper, Knapp, & Scott, 1981, and Bell, Buerkel-Rothfuss, & Gore, 1987):

*Partner Nicknames*: Where the partners refer to one another by special names only fully understood by the couple. . . .

*Expressions of Affection*: These idioms express love, reassurance or praise to one's partner. . . .

*Labels for Others Outside the Relationship*: These are nicknames for specific people who are not in the relationship. . . . The labels allow the couple to discuss others in public, usually in pejorative ways.

*Confrontations*: These idioms show criticism of the partner or displeasure about him or her. . . .

*Requests and Routines*: These are ways to signal the partner. One common situation is when you let the other know you want to leave a party. . . .

*Sexual References and Euphemisms*: Idioms that make a reference to sexual techniques, birth control, intercourse, breasts, or genitals. . . .

*Sexual Invitations*: These idioms become code words for proposing sexual intercourse.

*Teasing Insults*: These idioms are used to derogate our partner, but in a spirit of play. . . .

In the Hopper et al. (1981) study and the Bell et al. (1987) studies, respectively, 57 percent and 43 percent of the idioms were used exclusively in private. About half the idioms used by couples, therefore, are not used or understood by outsiders. Friends, however, more often use idioms in public, and in the research by Bell and Healey (1992), friends' idioms were used 65 percent of the time by their other friends. So friends' idioms are less private and more public than those of couples.

Research has not yet uncovered the specific use of idioms in other close relationships, but we know they exist. One daughter, for example, used to send electronic mail (e-mail) to her father and address it to "Poppy." He picked up on this and started addressing her e-mail to "poppyseed," and they now refer to one another with these interlocked idioms. If this father-daughter relationship parallels those used by friends, other family members may soon learn of the new form of address.

## Symbols of Relational Identity

Baxter (1987b) probed how participants construct relationship meanings. She found that relationship symbols are "concrete metacommunicative 'statements' about the abstract qualities of intimacy, caring, solidarity, etc. which the parties equate with their relationships. The symbols give the parties a sense of 'history' about the relationship; they serve to link the past to the 'forces of novelty and change' " (Baxter, 1987b). In addition, the symbols allow them to test their common conception of their experience and see if the two of them have agreement on the relationship. Baxter found five types of relational symbols, listed in the order of frequency, for same-sex friendships and opposite sex romantic relationships.

1. *Behavioral actions* are actions the participants do. They have three subtypes:

   a. Jointly enacted activities—such as hiding Valentine's Day stuffed hearts from one another, playing sports, or other things jointly created.
   b. Interaction routines unique to the pair, such as jokes and teasing.
   c. Others such as nicknames, affection terms, or code words to refer to sexual matters.

2. *Events or times that held special meaning* were very diverse but all "held special meaning as distinguishing the relationship as unique." Many of them represented "firsts"—first meeting, first time they "really go[t] to know one another," and so on.

3. *Physical objects* include an even more diverse set of examples. Everything from "strawberries, to a stuffed buffalo, to a broken string from a violin, to assorted pieces of jewelry" (Baxter, 1987b, p. 269).

4. *Symbolic places* were of two types. Some were symbolic because they were visual metaphors of the partner or something in the history of the relationship, such as a restaurant or coffee shop. Others were symbolic because they served as a meeting place for the partners, such as Kalispell, Montana.

5. *Symbolic cultural artifacts* were things such as songs, music, books, and films that are part of the surrounding culture that have symbolic meaning for the two people.

Baxter then assessed the symbolic functions of the relationship symbols. She asked the participants what meaning these symbols had that made them feel the relationship was unique and special. The following nine functions [e]merged in order of frequency:

1. *Recollection Prompt*—to remind them about past events or thinking about the other in her/his absence.

2. *Intimacy Indicators*—signs of closeness, trust, or affection.

3. *Communication Mechanism*—promoting togetherness or sharing between the two.

4. *Stimulation/Fun*—offsetting boredom or excessive seriousness.

5. *Seclusion Mechanism*—to physically separate themselves from others.

6. *Exclusivity Indicator*—providing psychological seclusion for the relationship.

7. *Management of Difference/Conflict*—using locations that were conducive to discussion or joking or teasing as a way to deal with difficult issues.

8. *Public Tie-Sign*—giving others a signal that the parties were in a relationship.

9. *Endurance Index*—testifying to the relationship's endurance or strength in withstanding adversity.

This research establishes what we already know intuitively—that relationships contain symbolic elements. The meanings of events in a relationship, while showing some general patterns, are seen as unique and special by the two people involved. Once a symbolic marker begins being used in the relationship, people can make shorthand references to it. A romantic couple, for example, only need say, "Ah, Kalispell," to serve as a symbolic remembrance of events important to them.

One final finding is worthy of note. Baxter found that, even though males and females did not differ in the type or quantity of relationship symbols, "females regarded their relationship symbols more positively than was the case for males. Further, there was a trend towards females finding their relationship symbols more important than was the case for relationship symbols reported by men" (Baxter, 1987b, p. 279). This is consistent with the often-noted finding that females value their close relationships more than do men. . . .

## References

Baxter, L. A. (1987b). Symbols of relationship identity in relationship cultures. *Journal of social and personal relationships*, 4, 261–280.

———. (1992a). Forms and functions of intimate play in personal relationships. *Human communication research*, 18, 336–363.

———. (1992b). Root metaphors in accounts of developing romantic relationships. *Journal of social and personal relationships*, 9, 253–275.

Bell, R. A., Buerkel-Rothfuss, N. L. & Gore, K. E. (Fall, 1987). Did you bring the yarmulke for the Cabbage Patch Kid? The idiomatic communication of young lovers. *Human communication research*, 14, No. 1, 47–67.

Bell, R. A. & Healy, J. G. (1992). Idiomatic communication and interpersonal solidarity in friends' relational cultures. *Human communication research*, 18, 307–335.

Duck, S. W. (1982). A topology of relationship disagreement and dissolution. In Duck, S. W. (Ed.) *Personal relationships, Vol IV: Dissolving personal relationships*. New York: Academic Press, 1–30.

———. (1988). *Relating to others*. Chicago, IL: The Dorsey Press.

Duck, S. W. & Miell, D. E. (1986). Charting the development of personal relationships. In R. Gilmour and S. W. Duck (eds.), *Emerging field of personal relationships*, 133–144. Hillsdale, NJ: LEA.

Duck, S. & Pond, K. (May, 1991). On public display of private intimacy: An analysis of Valentine's day messages. Paper presented to third conference of the International Network on Personal Relationships. Normal/Bloomington, IL.

Farrell, T. B. (1984). Narrative in natural discourse: On communication and rhetoric. *The journal of communication*, 34, 109–127.

Fisher, W. R. (1987). *Human communication as narration: Toward a philosophy of reason, value, and action*. Columbia, SC: University of South Carolina Press.

Fitzpatrick, M. A. & Indvik, J. (1982). Implicit theories in enduring relationships: Psychological gender differences in perceptions of one's mate. *Western journal of speech communication*, 46, 311–325.

Fletcher, G. J. O. & Fincham, F. D. (eds.) (1991a). *Cognition in close relationships*, 7–35. Hillsdale, NJ: Lawrence Erlbaum Associates.

Haas, A. & Sherman, M. A. (1982). Reported topics of conversation among same-sex adults. *Communication quarterly*, 30, 332–342.

Hinde, R. A. (1979). *Towards understanding relationships*. London: Academic Press.

Hollihan, T. A. & Riley, P. (1987). The rhetorical power of a compelling story: A critique of a "toughlove" parental support group. *Communication quarterly*, 35, 12–35.

Honeycutt, J. M., Cantrill, J. G. & Greene, R. W. (1989). Memory structures for relational escalation: A cognitive test of the sequencing of relational actions and stages. *Human communication research*, 16, 62–90.

Hopper, R., Knapp, M. L. & Scott, L. (1981). Couples' personal idioms: Exploring intimate talk. *Journal of communication*, 31, 23–33.

Humphreys, C. (1951). *Buddhism*. Harmondsworth, England: Penguin Books.

Jackson, D. D. (1959). Family interaction, family homeostasis and some implications for conjoint family psychotherapy. In J. H. Masserman (ed.), *Individual and familial dynamics*. New York: Grune and Stratton.

Leatham, G. & Duck, S. (1990). Conversations with friends and the dynamics of social support. In S. Duck (ed.), *Personal relationships and social support*, 1–29. London: Sage.

Mandelbaum, J. (1989). Interpersonal activities in conversational storytelling. *Western journal of speech communication*, 53, 114–126.

Morton, T. L. & Douglas, M. A. (1981). Growth of relationship. In Duck, S. & Gilmour, R. (eds.), *Personal relationships*, 9, 563–584.

Neimeyer, G. J. & Neimeyer, R. A. (1985). Relational trajectories: A personal construct contribution. *Journal of social and personal relationships*, 2, 325–349.

Owen, W. F. (1984a). Interpretive themes in relational communication. *Quarterly journal of speech*, 70, 274–287.

Polanyi, L. (1985). Conversational storytelling. In T. A. van Kijk (ed.), *Handbook of discourse analysis*, vol. 3, 183–201. New York: Academic Press.

Ross, M. & Holmberg, D. (1993). Are wives' memories for events in relationships more vivid than their husbands' memories? *Journal of social and personal relationships*, 9, 585–604.

Surra, C. A. (1987). Reasons for changes in commitment: Variations by courtship type. *Journal of social and personal relationships*, 4, 17–33.

Van Kijk, T. A. (ed.) (1985). *Handbook of discourse analysis*. New York: Academic Press.

Veroff, J., Sutherland, L., Chadiha, L. & Ortega, R. M. (1993). Newlyweds tell their stories: A narrative method for assessing marital experiences. *Journal of social and personal relationships*, 10, 437–457.

Weick, K. E. (1979). *The social psychology of organizing* (2nd edition). Reading, MA: Addison-Wesley.

Wilmot, W. W. & Hocker, J. L. (1993). Couples and change: Intervention through discourse and images. In N. Coupland & J. F. Nussbaum (eds.), *Discourse and lifespan development*, 262–283. Hillsdale, NJ: Lawrence Erlbaum Associates.

# Questions

1. Choose two important relationships in your life. How would you describe the miniculture of each relationship?

2. Choose one of the relationships from your answer to Question 1. Keep a journal about this relationship for one week. Based on your journal entries, would you still use the same mental image and metaphor to describe it? What new insights did you gain about the miniculture of this relationship?

Reprinted from William W. Wilmot, "The Relational Perspective." In *Relational Communication Reader*, 4th ed., pp. 1–12. Published by McGraw Hill. Copyright © 1995 by William W. Wilmot. Reprinted with permission. ✦

# 3

# Theories of Relational Communication

*Lynn H. Turner and Richard West*

**R**elational theories grow out of the questions we ask about the interactions of others or the issues we confront in our own interactions with another. If you have ever been puzzled about someone's behavior and asked yourself, "Why did he say or do that?" and then tried to figure out the answer to the question, you have engaged in theory building. Theories serve several functions. They organize and explain our experience. Because we cannot focus on every detail of every event, a theory suggests which details are the most important. Toulmin (1961, 104) calls theories "intellectual spectacles." Like a pair of tinted sunglasses, the theory we use to explain a communication event colors that event. Depending on which theory is used, the explanation for events may differ.

In addition to organizing our experience, theories extend our knowledge. They enable us to go beyond what we observe and extend our knowledge to events we have not yet encountered. If we observe a friend in one situation when arguing with another person, we can make predictions about how our friend will react in similar situations. Finally, theories stimulate and guide future research. This function is called the heuristic function of theory. As we test our theories, we modify them in order to better explain the events we observe.

A good theory meets certain criteria. First, it is logically consistent; it cannot contain contradictory propositions. For example, social exchange theory suggests that we desire relationships that benefit our self-interest, or relationships in which our rewards are greater than our costs. To be logically consistent, the theory cannot suggest that we desire relationships in which the costs outweigh the rewards.

Second, the theory needs to be consistent with accepted facts. If we observe that people generally do not stay in costly relationships, then social exchange theory makes sense. If, on the other hand, we observe that individuals generally do maintain costly relationships, the theory is not consistent with fact.

Third, as is often said, nothing is as practical as a good theory. In other words, theories need to be useful—relevant to your life. You need to be able to use the theory to explain and, if necessary, change your own behavior. The theory's advice should be helpful to your own life.

This is the lynchpin chapter because its content directly affects many other chapters. In this chapter, Turner and West introduce several theories alluded to throughout this reader. You will encounter a description and application of the following theories: symbolic interaction, uncertainty reduction, social penetration, social exchange, and relational dialectics. As you consider these theories, apply the criteria of a good theory to each. In addition, try to imagine the application of these theories to your everyday life by answering the question: What is one example of how each theory plays out in a familiar relationship?

### Reference

Toulmin, S. (1961). *Foresight and understanding: An inquiry into the aims of science.* New York: Harper Torchbooks.

* * *

**C**ommunicating with relational partners can be exciting, complex, and confusing. Even though we spend so much time talking and listening to others, we are often perplexed by what they say, how they react to what we say, or what happens as a result of our conversations. Researchers believe that theories offer help in clarifying these complexities. In 1986, Jonathan H. Turner defined theory as "a process of developing ideas that can allow us to explain how and why events occur" (p. 5). Theoretical thinking can be applied to any question: how the world began, how people develop their personalities, what causes cancer, or why we communicate the way we do, to list a few. The theories discussed in this chapter help us make sense of questions about our own communication behavior and the behavior of our relational partners.

We are discussing theory as professional researchers use it in their work, yet all of us in daily life think like researchers, using implicit theories to help us understand confusing questions concerning communication. Fritz Heider (1958) used the term "naive psychologists" to describe people puzzling over theoretical issues in their everyday life. Whenever we think about our relational communication and question its direction and meaning, we are engaging in theoretical thinking; that is, we are applying theoretical concepts to make sense of relational communication.

Researchers struggle to develop and agree on explanations for communication behavior. But this process is complicated and people make so many different assumptions about others, that there is no one definitive theory that all researchers use. In fact, there is not even a short list of interpersonal communication theories. The possibilities for theorizing about the communication process remain extensive. Further, most researchers don't try to come up with a theory for all of interpersonal communication. Many theories only attempt to explain a small segment of the process, such as attraction, listening, conflict, or relational development.

In this chapter, the following theories are reviewed: symbolic interaction, uncertainty reduction, social penetration, social exchange, and relational dialectics. You will see the variety in what they attempt to explain, their format, and their assumptions about human behavior. As you read the other chapters in the book, you should see where each of the theories might be applied to explain a part of relational communication. You should remember, however, that these theories are only a few among many that we could use in explaining communication practices. Nonetheless, the five theories reviewed here offer a useful introduction to how theory can help us unravel communication questions. We begin with Symbolic Interaction Theory, which tries to explain the general question of how people make meaning.

## Symbolic Interaction Theory (SI)

### Overview

Symbolic Interaction Theory (SI) originated in the works of the sociologist George Herbert Mead, although he did not publish much about his ideas himself. After he died, his students put together a book, *Mind, Self, and Society* (1934), based on his lectures detailing SI's theoretical framework. As its name suggests, Symbolic Interaction Theory centers on symbols and interactions. Ralph LaRossa and Donald C. Reitzes (1993) state that Symbolic Interactionism is "essentially . . . a frame of reference for understanding how humans, in concert with one another, create symbolic worlds and how these worlds, in turn, shape human behavior" (p. 136). This statement echoes Mead's belief in individuals as active, reflective beings.

### Assumptions

LaRossa and Reitzes (1993) examined SI as it relates to families. They note that seven central assumptions ground the theory. These assumptions include the following:

1. Humans act toward others on the basis of the meanings those others have for them.

2. Meaning is created in interaction between people.

3. Meanings are modified through an interpretive process.

4. Individuals develop self-concepts through interaction with others.

5. Self-concepts provide an important motive for behavior.

6. People and groups are influenced by cultural and social processes.

7. Social structure is worked out through social interaction.

The first assumption focuses on people as choice makers, rejecting the notion that human behavior is predestined. The second assumption stresses Mead's belief that meaning only exists when people share common interpretations of the symbols they exchange in interaction. According to SI, meanings are "social products" or "creations that are formed in and through the defining activities of people as they interact" (Blumer 1969, 5). Therefore, two people from different cultures, or even different regions, have difficulty creating shared meaning.

The third assumption, that meanings are modified through an interpretive process, has two parts. First, people notice the things that have meaning. This involves people in conversation with themselves. When you mull over the possible meanings your friend might have had for canceling a dinner with you, you are engaging in this part of the process. The second step consists of selecting, checking, and transforming the meanings in a particular context. The contextual cues such as your culture, your idiosyncratic knowledge of your friend, and so forth will aid you as you decide why you think your friend canceled. The same behavior practiced by two different friends may have different meanings for you.

The fourth assumption states that it is only through contact with others that we develop a sense of self. We are not born with self-concepts, we learn them through interactions and in relationship with others. The fifth assumption focuses on the importance of the self-concept as a motive for behavior. This assumption relates to the process of self-fulfilling prophecy, or the expectations of self that cause a person to behave in such a way that the expectations are realized. Your prediction that you will have fun at a party, for example, often results in behaviors on your part that ensure you do have a good time.

The sixth assumption recognizes that social norms constrain individual behavior. For instance, when you meet your significant other's parents for the first time, you probably choose clothing that is appropriate for the occasion, not necessarily what you would most prefer wearing. The context and your desire to make a good impression influence your choices. Additionally, culture influences our choices. Thus, what would be appropriate clothing to wear for meeting your future in-laws in India differs from what it would be in the United States. Yet,

people are able to adopt a multicultural perspective and learn to value traits not endorsed by their own culture of origin. When people attend college in a new country they might begin to value attitudes and behaviors of their host country, for instance.

The last assumption of SI acknowledges that although our choices are influenced by social structure, as the previous assumption states, the opposite is true as well. Individuals can modify social situations through interactions. For example, even though you might want to make a good first impression, you might justify wearing jeans to meet the parents by noting that is just how you are and people need to accept your individuality. You could tell your significant other to explain that to the parents.

## Key Concepts

Mead's book title, *Mind, Self, and Society*, reflects the three key concepts of SI. Mead defined *mind* as the ability to use symbols that have common meanings. According to Mead, one of the most critical activities that people accomplish with their minds is role-taking, or the ability to symbolically place oneself in someone else's situation. Whenever we try to imagine how another person might view something or when we try to behave as we think another would, we are role-taking. Mead suggested that role-taking helps us develop our self-concept and allows us to develop empathy with others.

Mead defined *self* as the ability to reflect on ourselves as others would. For Mead, the self developed from a particular kind of role-taking, that is, imagining how we look to others. This is described as the looking-glass self, or our ability to see ourselves in the reflection of another (Cooley 1972). Further, Mead argued that people have the ability to be both subject and object to themselves. As subject we act and as object we observe ourselves acting. Mead called the subject or acting self "I," and the object or observing self "ME." The "I" is spontaneous, impulsive, and creative while the "ME" is more reflective and socially aware. The "I" might want to scream and yell during an argument with a roommate, while the "ME" realizes that this would be counterproductive and offers some reasoned arguments instead. Mead saw the self as a process that integrated the "I" and the "ME."

Mead defined *society* as the network of social relationships humans establish. People engage in society through behaviors that they choose actively and voluntarily. Society and the individual exist in a reciprocal relationship. First, society exists prior to the individual and so exerts influence on individuals. But society is also shaped and influenced by the individual acting in concert with others. Mead thought that two specific parts of society affect the mind and the self: particular others, or the individuals in society who are significant to us, and the Generalized Other, which refers to social standards as a whole. We look to particular others to get a sense of social acceptability and a sense of self. The Generalized Other provides information about roles, rules, and attitudes shared by the community; this information is influential in developing a social conscience.

## Application

Because Symbolic Interaction Theory is such a broad explanation, providing an understanding of how people develop a sense of self, many studies have used its tenets. Recently, Margie Edwards (2004) examined how women work to create a sense of family identity using principles of SI. Edwards interviewed working class women from two rural trailer park communities and she also observed their family routines and interactions.

She concluded that, as SI predicts, women's work consists, in large part, of managing and developing family identity. Further, women in these rural trailer parks believed that an important part of their work was connecting their family's identity with the community. In this way they were able to link the family to the larger community and secure help for the family when it was needed. Edwards stated that SI helped to understand the meanings that women assign to their labor within the family as well as how women's work supports the family.

SI provides a starting point for understanding relational communication. It explains how people see themselves and others and how they make meaning of their obser-

vations. It is a general, broad theory that explores the intersection of the self and its relationship to others. We now turn to a much more specific theory, which focuses the uncertainty that occurs in the beginning of relational development.

## Uncertainty Reduction Theory (URT)

### Overview

Uncertainty Reduction Theory (URT) was conceptualized by Charles Berger and Richard Calabrese in 1975. Their goal was to explain how communication reduces uncertainties between strangers engaging in initial interactions. URT is a theory geared toward understanding the very beginning stages of a relationship. Berger and Calabrese thought that people want to predict and explain what goes on in their initial interactions with strangers. Prediction is the ability to define in advance what we or a relational partner will do or say. Explanation refers to our interpretation of these behaviors. These two concepts—prediction and explanation—comprise the major subprocesses of uncertainty reduction.

After Berger and Calabrese (1975) originated their theory, it was later elaborated (Berger 1979; Berger and Bradac 1982). The final version added the idea that there are two types of uncertainty in initial encounters: cognitive and behavioral. Cognitive uncertainty refers to the degree of uncertainty associated with one's own beliefs and attitudes. (Do I like her?) Behavioral uncertainty, on the other hand, pertains to the extent of certainty associated with behavioral practices: what people do and say. (Why did she interrupt me?) Because we have cultural rituals for small talk, strangers have some certainty about how to behave when they first meet. If these rituals are violated by engaging in inappropriate self-disclosure (revealing intimate information about one's self to another), for example, then behavioral uncertainty increases.

URT has been described as an example of original theorizing in the field of communication (Miller 1981) because it centers on concepts like information seeking and nonverbal behaviors that are specifically relevant to studying communication.

## Assumptions

1. People experience uncertainty in interpersonal settings.

2. Uncertainty is an aversive state, generating cognitive stress.

3. When strangers meet, their primary concern is to reduce their uncertainty or to increase predictability.

4. Interpersonal communication is a developmental process that occurs through stages.

5. Interpersonal communication is the primary means of uncertainty reduction.

6. The quantity and nature of information that people share change through time.

## Axioms and Theorems

URT is an axiomatic theory, which means that it begins with a series of truisms drawn from past research and common sense. These axioms require no further proof as they are accepted as truth. Each axiom presents a relationship between uncertainty (the central theoretical concept) and one other concept. URT rests on seven axioms.

**Axiom 1:** As the amount of verbal communication between strangers increases, the level of uncertainty for each person in the relationship will decrease. As uncertainty is further reduced, the amount of verbal communication will increase. (The more two strangers talk, the more certainty they will feel.)

**Axiom 2:** As nonverbal expressiveness increases, uncertainty levels will decrease and vice versa. (The more you and your partner do things like smile, the more certainty you will both feel.)

**Axiom 3:** High levels of uncertainty cause increases in information-seeking behavior. As uncertainty levels decline, information-seeking behavior decreases. (The more two strangers feel uncertain, the more questioning they will do.)

**Axiom 4:** High levels of uncertainty in a relationship cause decreases in the intimacy level of communication content. Low levels of uncertainty produce high levels of intimacy. (The more two strangers feel uncertain, the less intimate their conversation will be.)

**Axiom 5:** High levels of uncertainty produce high rates of reciprocity. Low levels of uncertainty produce low levels of reciprocity. (High uncertainty brings with it a concern to reciprocate what the other does, such as exchange like information: "What's your major?" "Biology. What's yours?" "English.")

**Axiom 6:** Similarities between persons reduce uncertainty, while dissimilarities produce increases in uncertainty. (The more similar two strangers appear to each other, the less uncertainty they will feel.)

**Axiom 7:** Increases in uncertainty level produce decreases in liking; decreases in uncertainty produce increases in liking. (The more uncertainty you feel around a stranger, the less you like him or her.)

Axiomatic theories proceed by pairing two axioms together to produce a theorem. While the axioms are assumed to be true, the resulting theorems are theoretical and have to be tested. The process follows deductive logic: If A = B, and B = C, then A = C. Berger and Calabrese combined all seven axioms in every possible pairwise combination to derive 21 theorems. For instance, because verbal communication is negatively related to uncertainty (Axiom 1) and intimacy is also negatively related to uncertainty (Axiom 4), verbal communication and intimacy levels are positively related (resulting theorem). You can generate the other 20 theorems by combining the axioms using the deductive formula above. You need to use the rule of multiplication for multiplying positives and negatives:

> If two variables have a positive relationship with a third, they have a positive relationship with each other. If one variable has a positive relationship with a third while the other has a negative relationship with the third, they should have a negative relationship with each other. Finally, if two variables have a negative relationship with a third they should have a positive relationship with each other.

## Application

Although many studies investigate how uncertainty operates in initial interactions, as Berger and Calabrese (1975) intended the theory to be applied, newer research attempts to expand URT. For instance, a recent study (Powell and Afifi 2005) tested how well URT could explain the process of uncertainty management that adoptees engage in about their birth parents. First, the researchers note that adoptees may experience different levels of uncertainty about their birth parents, although 70 percent of their respondents expressed moderate to high levels of uncertainty.

In 21 face-to-face interviews and 32 telephone interviews, the researchers generated data about how adoptees managed uncertainty in this situation which they termed the ambiguous loss of their birth parents. This was the case, because for most of the respondents, the birth parents were presumed to be still living. Although they were not currently in the adoptees' lives, it was theoretically possible to locate them and engage in contact. Thus, their loss was termed ambiguous.

The study concludes that URT may treat uncertainty too simplistically, not acknowledging that in some cases, people would rather remain uncertain. The researchers note that ignorance of potentially unpleasant information may be bliss for some people and reducing uncertainty is only one strategy that people employ.

URT takes a narrow, but common, experience in relational life—uncertainty—and attempts to clearly and completely explain how communication is used to manage it. We will now discuss a theory that examines a much larger aspect of relational communication, the process of relationship development.

# Social Penetration Theory (SPT)

## Overview

Social Penetration Theory (SPT), articulated by Irwin Altman and Dalmas Taylor (1973) moves beyond the initial encounters that URT tries to explain, and attempts to understand overall relational development. The term *social penetration* refers to the movement from superficial communication to more intimate communication during the process of relationship development. In their discussion of SPT, Altman and Taylor utilize an onion metaphor. They believe that the layers of an onion represent various aspects of a person's personality. On the outer layer is an individual's public image. As more and more layers are revealed through interaction, the private self is revealed.

Altman and Taylor (1973) acknowledge that relationships vary. From married couples to supervisor-employee to business partners to friends, relationships "involve different levels of intimacy of exchange or degree of social penetration" (p. 3). Regardless of variation, however, Altman and Taylor believed that all relationships follow some predictable trajectory, or pathway.

## Assumptions

1. Relationships progress from non-intimate to intimate.

2. Relational development is generally systematic and predictable.

3. Relational development includes de-penetration and dissolution.

4. Self-disclosure is at the core of relationship development.

The first assumption presumes that relational communication begins at a non-intimate level and then moves along a continuum to a more intimate level. Initial conversations may at first appear trivial, yet such conversations allow individuals to size each other up and give them a chance to think about prospects for a future. Not all relationships are simply nonintimate or intimate. In fact, most of our relationships fall somewhere in the middle. Many times, we want only a moderately close relationship. The theory does not argue that all relationships have to move to an intimate stage.

The second assumption of SPT pertains to predictability. Specifically, social penetration theorists argue that relationships progress fairly systematically and predictably. Some people may have difficulty with this assertion because they know that relationships are dynamic and ever-changing. Yet, according to SPT, even dynamic relationships follow some standard pattern of development. Social penetration processes are rather organized and predictable. Of course, a number of other events and variables (time, personality, and so forth) affect the way relationships progress so relationships are never completely predictable.

The third assumption of SPT is that relational development includes depenetration and dissolution. Altman and Taylor (1973) liken the process to a film shown in reverse. Just as communication allows a relationship to move forward toward intimacy, communication can also move a relationship back toward nonintimacy. Some researchers refer to this depenetration process as the return of the stranger. Social penetration theorists think that depenetration—like the penetration process—is systematic. If a relationship depenetrates, it does not mean that it will inevitably dissolve. Niall Bolger and Shannon Kelleher (1993), for example, note that stress may cause depenetration, but most couples manage the stress before the relationship dissolves.

The final assumption contends that self-disclosure is at the core of relationship development. According to Altman and Taylor (1973), the way that nonintimate relationships progress toward intimacy is through self-disclosures. Self-disclosure allows people get to know each other. Self-disclosure helps shape a relationship, and, as Altman and Taylor observe, "making self accessible to another person is intrinsically gratifying" (p. 50).

## The Social Penetration Process

The social penetration [process] has two dimensions: breadth and depth. Breadth refers to the number of topics discussed in the relationship and depth refers to the degree of intimacy guiding topic discussions. In the initial stages, most relationships have narrow breadth and shallow depth. As relationships move toward intimacy, a wider range of topics is discussed (more breadth), with several of those topics marked by depth.

Breadth and depth issues affect relationship development. For instance, shifts or changes in central layers (of the onion) have more of an impact on relationships than

shifts in outer or peripheral layers. For example, if you change your hair color, your relationship with a significant other would be less affected than if you changed your opinion about a core value, such as the importance you place on money.

SPT asserts that the process of relationship development follows a stage model consisting of four stages: orientation, exploratory affective exchange, affective exchange, and stable exchange.

The earliest stage of interaction, orientation, occurs at the public level. During this stage, comments usually reflect superficial aspects of individuals. People act in socially desirable ways, smile pleasantly, and react politely. Taylor and Altman (1987) note that people tend not to evaluate or criticize during the orientation stage. The second stage, the exploratory affective exchange stage, represents an expansion in which people progress beyond public level information. Taylor and Altman (1987) describe relationships with casual acquaintances and friendly neighbors as being in this stage. In this stage, people use phrases that are idiosyncratic to the relationship, there is more spontaneity in communication, more touch behavior, and more nonverbal expression of emotions. The researchers note that many relationships stay at this stage.

The affective exchange stage includes those interactions that are more "freewheeling and casual" (Taylor and Altman 1987, 259), meaning that communication is spontaneous and individuals say what they think without fearing that it will end the relationship. The affective exchange stage represents further commitment to the other individual; both interactants are comfortable with one another. The stage includes those aspects of a relationship that make it unique, for example the use of personal idioms (Hopper, Knapp, and Scott 1981), which are private ways of expressing a relationship's intimacy—through words, phrases, and/or behaviors. Idiomatic expressions—such as "rabbit running" or "honey bubbles"—carry unique meaning for two people in a relationship.

The final stage, stable exchange, is reached in few relationships. It involves open expression of thoughts, feelings, and behaviors, which result in much spontaneity and relational uniqueness. Social penetration theorists believe that there are relatively few misinterpretations in communication meaning at this stage because both partners have had numerous opportunities to clarify any previous ambiguities and have established their own personal system of communication. As a result, communication—according to Altman and Taylor—is efficient.

## Application

Social Penetration Theory has been used to frame many studies. For instance, Zhong, Myers, and Buerkel (2004) examined the central variable in Social Penetration Theory: Self-disclosure. They surveyed 123 sons and 118 of their fathers investigating relational intimacy between the pairs. They presented participants a number of surveys that examined perceptions of self-disclosure and trust. Among their conclusions were two relevant to SPT: First, there were no significant differences in perceptions of relationship intimacy between fathers and sons. Second, with respect to self-disclosure, fathers were found to self-disclose more intentionally than their sons.

Zhong and associates (2004) suggest that the differences in self-disclosure may be the result of fathers wanting to maintain positive relationships with their sons. Second, the researchers contend that children are usually not accustomed nor willing to self-disclose, particularly to their fathers. Therefore, a willingness to self-disclose on the part of fathers seems to be an effort to establish closeness with sons. The study concludes with a call for research on the implications of self-disclosure (among other communication traits) in mother-child relationships to assess whether similar findings exist.

SPT approaches relationships as a series of exchanges. It borrows that notion from another theoretical framework called social exchange, which we will now discuss.

# Social Exchange Theory (SET)

## Overview

Social Exchange Theory (SET) is based on the notion that people think about their relationships in economic terms, adding up the

costs involved and comparing those costs to the available rewards. Costs are those aspects of relational life that provide negative value to a person, like having to listen to your best friend talk at length when you need to do other things. Rewards are those things providing positive value to a person, like having your best friend listen to your problems when you need to talk them through. Social exchange theorists argue that people assess their relationships in terms of costs and rewards. The social exchange perspective argues that people calculate the overall worth of a relationship by subtracting its costs from the rewards it provides.

Positive relationships are those in which the rewards exceed the costs. Relationships where the worth is a negative amount (i.e., with greater costs than rewards) tend to be negative ones. Social exchange theory predicts that the worth of a relationship influences whether people will continue the relationship or terminate it. Positive relationships are expected to endure while negative relationships probably will not. The situation is a bit more complex than this simple explanation implies, but it does reveal essentially what exchange theorists argue. As Ronald Sabatelli and Constance Shehan (1993) note, the social exchange approach views relationships through the metaphor of the marketplace, where each person acts out of a self-oriented goal of profit-taking.

So far, we have been talking in general about exchange theories or the overall framework of social exchange, but there are several distinct theories of social exchange. Michael Roloff (1981) discusses five different theories in his book, *Interpersonal Communication: The Social Exchange Approach*. Roloff observes that while these theories differ in several significant respects, they are connected by the central argument that relational partners act on the basis of their self-interest. Additionally, he notes that these theories do not assume that self-interest is a negative thing but, rather, that it may actually enhance a relationship. It is beyond our purposes here to distinguish among all social exchange theories. We will concentrate on explicating what may be the most popular version of social exchange, the theory of interdependence created by John Thibaut and Harold Kelley in 1959.

## Assumptions

All social exchange theories are built upon common assumptions about human beings and about the nature of relationships. Some of these assumptions are probably quite clear to you after the introduction to this theory. Many of these assumptions flow from the notion that people view life as a marketplace. More specifically, Thibaut and Kelley (1959) focused on human nature and the social exchange (or relationship) between two people. Thus, the assumptions they make also fall into these two categories.

The assumptions that social exchange theory makes about human nature include the following:

1. Humans seek rewards and avoid punishments.

2. Humans are rational beings.

3. The standards that humans use to evaluate costs and rewards vary over time and from person to person.

The assumptions that social exchange theory makes about the nature of relationships include these:

1. Relationships are interdependent.

2. Relational life is a process.

## Evaluating Relationships

As we mentioned earlier, SET is more complex than the simple equation stating that worth = rewards minus costs. When people calculate the worth of their relationships and make decisions about staying in them, they are concerned with a few other issues as well. One of the most interesting parts of Thibaut and Kelley's theory (1959) is their explanation of how people evaluate whether or not to leave a relationship. Thibaut and Kelley stated that this evaluation rests on two types of comparisons, which they call comparison level and comparison level for alternatives. The comparison level (CL) is a standard representing what rewards people feel they should receive and what costs they expect to pay in a specific relationship. Your CL is shaped by all past relationships, by family members' advice, and

by popular culture such as TV and film representations of relationships.

Comparison levels vary among individuals because they are subjective assessments. Yet, because we often interact with people who are subjected to similar messages about relationships from the popular culture, we have many relational expectations in common (Rawlins 1992). Thus, people in the same culture overlap somewhat in their general expectations for relationships, and their CLs may not be totally different from each other's.

Thibaut and Kelley's theory (1959) asserts that our satisfaction with a relationship derives from comparing its rewards and costs to our CL. If the relationship meets or exceeds our CL, the prediction is that we will be satisfied with it. Yet people sometimes leave relationships that meet their CL and stay in ones that do not seem to meet it. Thibaut and Kelley explain this type of situation with their second standard of comparison, the comparison level for alternatives (CLalt). This standard refers to how people evaluate a relationship compared to the realistic alternatives to that relationship. CLalt provides a measure of stability rather than of satisfaction. Thus, if you felt you had few chances to make new friends, you might evaluate your current friends more positively than you would if you thought it would be relatively easy to make new friends. If people see no alternatives to an existing relationship, and fear being alone more than being in the relationship, SET predicts they will stay. Some who have written about women in abusive relationships have used this theoretical reasoning to explain why women stay with violent men (Walker 1984).

In addition to these calculations based on comparisons, Thibaut and Kelley (1959) were also interested in how people adjust their behaviors when interacting with their relational partners. Thibaut and Kelley suggested that people are goal directed in their interaction behaviors. This fits with their assumption that human beings are rational. According to Thibaut and Kelley, people engage in what they termed *behavioral sequences*, or a series of actions designed to achieve a goal. These sequences are at the core of what Thibaut and Kelley consider social exchange. Behavioral sequences depend on issues of interdependence and power.

All interpersonal relationships are interdependent and their interdependence results in two types of power: fate control and behavior control. Fate control is the ability to affect another person's outcomes. For example, if your friend normally helps you study and then decides that she no longer has time to do so, she controls, to an extent, how well you may do on your next exam. Behavior control is the power to change a partner's behavior by changing one's own behavior. If you are talking to a friend who suddenly stops talking, you will probably change your behavior in response. You may stop talking too or you might question your friend to find out if something is wrong.

To cope with power differentials and to deal with the costs associated with exercising power, Thibaut and Kelley (1959) state that people develop patterns of exchange. These patterns, made up of behavioral rules or norms, indicate how people attempt to maximize rewards and minimize costs. Thibaut and Kelley describe three different matrices that exist in social exchange: the given matrix, the effective matrix, and the dispositional matrix. The given matrix represents the behavioral choices and outcomes that are determined by a combination of factors external to the relationship (like the environment) with factors that are internal (like the specific skills the relational partners possess). When two people engage in an exchange, the environment may make some options more difficult than others. Romeo and Juliet's love was doomed by their families' feud, for instance. Further, the given matrix depends on the skills people bring to the social exchange. If people lack skills for downhill skiing, for example, that makes it unlikely that they will spend time skiing together.

To some extent people are restricted by the given matrix, but they are not completely trapped by it. By changing their behaviors, acquiring new skills, and creatively managing their environment, they can transform the given matrix into the effective matrix, which expands possible behaviors and/or outcomes. If two people did not know how to

ski, for example, they could take lessons and learn how, transforming their given matrix into the effective matrix. If a couple found that their families were restricting their relationship too much, they could engage in conflict with them until they changed their families' minds. Or they could stop talking about each other at home and keep their affair secret so that they could avoid their families' negative sanctions.

The final matrix, the dispositional matrix, represents how people believe rewards ought to be exchanged. If one member of a couple thought that it was critical for family to approve of their romance, that would affect their dispositional matrix. Some people view exchanges as competition, and this belief would be reflected in their dispositional matrix.

Thibaut and Kelley's Social Exchange Theory (1959) states that knowing the kinds of dispositions a person has (the dispositional matrix) and the nature of the situation (the given matrix) in which they are relating will allow us to predict the transformations they will make (the effective matrix) to affect the social exchange. The dispositional matrix guides the transformations people make to their given matrix, which leads to the effective matrix, which determines the social exchange.

In their theory, Thibaut and Kelley (1959) do not explicitly deal with communication behaviors, yet some of their discussion about the three matrices implies that self-disclosure plays an important role in social exchange. Michael Roloff (1981) observes:

> Self-disclosure would seem to imply the communication of two things: (1) the dispositions one has, and (2) the transformations (strategy) one is going to employ in this exchange. Since dispositions affect a person's strategy, we might assume that knowledge of dispositions might well allow us to predict the transformations. (p. 77)

If people know how their partner transforms the given matrix, that could give them an edge in social exchanges. An understanding of how the matrices affect communication behavior is an important reason why communication researchers are interested in SET.

## Application

Social exchange principles frame many studies. For instance, Kramer (2005) explored two volunteer groups involved in community theatre musicals. The researcher was interested in knowing what benefits and costs (two Social Exchange concepts) people obtain by participating in the groups. Over 50 participants completed a questionnaire asking about their summer productions. Several categories of benefits emerged from the analysis, including Social Interaction, Peer Support, Playfulness, and Performing for an Audience (Response). Among the costs cited were Complaints about a lack of Organization, Personality Conflicts, and Challenging Roles (or Parts). The experiences articulated by theatre group members were discussed employing the "sometimes overlooked" (p. 177) aspects of Social Exchange Theory, namely cost benefit ratios. Kramer concludes that social exchange theorists have often looked at tangible exchanges of costs and rewards. This study provides less-tangible evidence such as "the exchange of affect and status" and its relationship to commitment and satisfaction.

SET supposes a rational, even calculating, side to interpersonal relationships. The final theory we will discuss, Relational Dialectics, takes a much different perspective on the life of a relationship.

# Relational Dialectics Theory (RDT)

## Overview

This theory maintains that what characterizes relational life is ongoing tensions between contradictory desires. While that sounds messy, researchers who use Relational Dialectics Theory (RDT) believe it accurately depicts people's experience. RDT claims that although we are not always able to resolve contradictions, we can be comfortable believing inconsistent things about relationships. For example, the old folk adage that "opposites attract" seems to coexist easily with its opposite, "birds of a feather flock together."

Leslie Baxter and Barbara Montgomery (1996) formulated a complete statement of the theory in their book, *Relating: Dialogues and Dialectics*. Baxter and Montgomery's work was influenced by Mikhail Bakhtin, a Russian philosopher. Social life for Bakhtin was a dialogue among many voices espousing different perspectives and viewpoints. According to Bakhtin, the self was only possible in context with another. Bakhtin's ideas relate to Symbolic Interaction Theory because they both focus on the importance of interaction for meaning making.

Dialectic thinkers maintain that in all contradictions multiple points of view interact. Although we think of a contradiction as involving polar opposites, dialectics states that the resulting situation expands beyond these two poles. As Baxter and Montgomery (1996) observe, "dialectical thinking is not directed toward a search for the 'happy mediums' of compromise and balance, but instead focuses on the messier, less logical, and more inconsistent unfolding practices of the moment" (p. 46).

## Assumptions

RDT is grounded in four main assumptions about relational life:

1. Relationships are not linear.

2. Relational life is characterized by change.

3. Contradiction is the fundamental fact of relational life.

4. Communication is central to organizing and negotiating relational contradictions.

The most significant assumption that grounds this theory is the first one. Rather than being linear (as Social Penetration Theory implies with its stages), dialectical researchers think that relationships consist of oscillations between contradictory desires. Baxter and Montgomery (1996) suggest rethinking the phrase "relational development" because it connotes linear movement or forward progress. Progress implies "either/or" thinking. Relationships that progress are pictured as having more of certain elements such as intimacy, self-disclosure, certainty, and so forth than relationships that do not progress. Either/or thinking frames a relationship as *either* intimate, open, certain *or* not. In the dialectic perspective, the concept of "both/and" replaces either/or.

The second assumption of RDT focuses on the notion of process or change while not necessarily framing change as linear progress. Thus, you and your friend are different today than you were when you first met. But that difference is not a linear move toward intimacy as much as it is simply changes in the way you express togetherness and independence.

The third assumption states that these tensions between opposing desires never go away. People manage to live with tensions and oppositions, and they are constants in relational life. This approach differs from other types of relational theories in that it considers stability to be unnatural—change and transformation are characteristic of relational life in the dialectic perspective (Montgomery 1992).

The final assumption of RDT gives a central position to communication. The communicative practices enacted in relational life organize the three central dialectics that are discussed in the following section: autonomy and connection; openness and protection; and novelty and predictability (Baxter 1990).

### Central Dialectical Tensions

The dialectic between autonomy and connection refers to our simultaneous desires to be independent and to be bonded with significant others. Relational life is filled with conflicting desires to be both close to and separate from relational partners. Baxter and Montgomery (1996) discuss how couples' private communication codes illustrate the presence of both connection and autonomy in relationships. For instance, nicknames celebrate something inherently individual and also indicate a relational closeness in that casual friends do not call each other by affectionate "pet" names.

A second important tension pervading relational life has to do with openness and protection. The openness and protection dialectic focuses on our conflicting desires to be open and vulnerable to our partners while at the same and self-protective in

Katherine Dindia (1994) argues for what she calls an "intrapersonal dialectic" of disclosure. This involves a gradual and incremental process of disclosure, ranging from concealment to full revelation. We do not have much research focusing on the actual communication practices that allow relational partners to simultaneously disclose personal information and to protect themselves from hurt that might arise from their partners' knowledge of their vulnerabilities.

The dialectic between novelty and predictability refers to our desire for both the comfort of stability and the excitement of change. Uncertainty Reduction Theory assumes that people move toward certainty and away from uncertainty as their relationship develops. The dialectic position sees the interplay of certainty and uncertainty in relationships. A couple's planning behavior illustrates this interplay. When they make a plan together, they are accomplishing at least two things with reference to predictability. First, their plan self-defines them as in a relationship, because planning is a relational activity. It also establishes a routine so they know what they will be doing in the short-term future. Yet if they leave the plan a bit open-ended, they can also allow for creativity and novelty. As with the openness/protection dialectic, not much research has uncovered the specific communication behaviors used to manage novelty and predictability.

### Coping With Dialectical Tensions

While dialectical tensions are always present in relationships, people do find ways to manage them. Baxter (1988) identified four main management strategies: (1) cyclic alternation, (2) segmentation, (3) selection, and (4) integration. In cyclic alternation people alternate between two opposites at different times in their relationship. For instance, when brothers are very young they may be inseparable, highlighting their closeness. As adolescents they may favor autonomy in their relationship, seeking separate identities,

*"On our knees we are the most powerful force on earth."*

—*Billy Graham*
—*Source Unknown*

Segmentation means identifying separate arenas for emphasizing each of the opposites. For example, a married couple who work together might stress predictability in the working relationship, but novelty while at home. The third strategy, selection, refers to making a choice between the opposites. Friends who choose to be close at all times, ignoring their needs for autonomy, use selection.

Finally, integration involves a synthesis. Integration takes three forms: neutralizing, disqualifying, or reframing the polarities. Neutralizing means compromising between the polarities. People who choose this strategy find "a happy medium" between opposites. Disqualifying neutralizes the dialectics by exempting certain issues from the general pattern. If you are very open with your best friend on all topics but one, that exemplifies disqualifying.

Reframing refers to transforming the dialectic so that it no longer seems to contain an opposition. Julia Wood and her colleagues (1994) discuss how couples in their study reframed. These couples defined connection as including differences, stating that they felt closer to their partner when they could share their different perspectives on life. Thus, they reframed what it meant to be close so they could incorporate distance in the definition.

## Application

In an interpretive study, Leslie Baxter, Dawn Braithwaite, and Leah Bryant (2004), examined children's perceptions of the contradictions that framed their interactions with stepparents who lived with them in their primary household. Baxter, Braithwaite, and Bryant were interested in seeing how Relational Dialectics Theory helped to understand the relationship between stepchildren and their stepparents. They begin by noting that step relationships are well suited to an analysis guided by RDT because they are relationships freighted with tensions.

In fact, after conducting in depth interviews with stepchildren resulting in 802 pages of double-spaced interview transcripts, the authors found that three dialectics characterized the relationship. These dialectics are similar to the central dialectics we discussed previously, but they are tailored a bit more specifically to the stepchild-stepparent relationship. The researchers found that stepchildren spoke about tensions of integration, status, and expression. Integration referred to their simultaneous desires for closeness and distance while status concerned the tension between labeling the stepparent as a legitimate or an illegitimate authority for them. Finally expression focused on stepchildren's desires for candor and concurrent concerns for discretion in what they told their stepparent.

## Conclusion

We live in relationship with others and interact with them in myriad ways. These interactions create many questions about why things occur the way they do. The five theories discussed in this chapter help us see patterns in relational communication and provide a starting place for answering our questions and posing new questions. Two critical aspects in using theory should be clear from the chapter. First, some theories are more suited to our personal outlooks than others. This is the case because of the underlying assumptions of the theories. Thus, some researchers may not be comfortable using Social Exchange Theory because they do not agree with the calculating picture of humans that it posits. Second, fitting the right theory to a communication question is also a matter of understanding the boundaries and limits of each theory. A theory like Uncertainty Reduction Theory may be better suited for questions about initial encounters between strangers than to marital interaction, although some researchers have tried to extend the theory's axioms to developed relationships (Planalp and Honeycutt 1985; Turner 1989). As we gain experience with theoretical thinking, we can use it to help us answer many perplexing questions about communication in relational life.

### References

Altman, I., and Taylor, D. A. (1973). *Social Penetration: The Development of Interpersonal Relationships*. New York: Holt, Rinehart and Winston.

Baxter, L. A. (1988). A dialectical perspective on communication strategies in relationship development. In S. Duck (ed.) *Handbook of Personal Relationships* (pp. 257–273). New York: Wiley.

———. (1990). Dialectical contradictions in relationship development. *Journal of Social and Personal Relationships*, 7, 69–88.

Baxter, L. A., Braithwaite, D. O., and Bryant, L. (2004). Stepchildren's perceptions of the contradictions in communication with stepparents. *Journal of Social and Personal Relationships*, 21, 447–467.

Baxter, L. A., and Montgomery, B. M. (1996). *Relating: Dialogues and Dialectics*. New York: The Guilford Press.

Berger, C. R. (1979). Beyond initial interaction: Uncertainty, understanding, and the development of interpersonal relationships. In H. Giles and R. St. Clair (eds.), *Language and Social Psychology* (pp. 122–144). Oxford: Blackwell.

Berger, C. R., and Bradac, J. J. (1982). *Language and Social Knowledge: Uncertainty in Interpersonal Relations*. London: E. E. Arnold.

Berger, C. R., and Calabrese, R. J. (1975). Some explorations in initial interaction and beyond: Toward a developmental theory of interpersonal communication. *Human Communication Research*, 1, 99–112.

Blumer, H. (1969). *Symbolic Interactionism: Perspective and Method*. Englewood Cliffs, NJ: Prentice Hall.

Bolger, N., and Kelleher, S. (1993). Daily life in relationships. In S. Duck (ed.), *Social Context and Relationships* (pp. 100–108). Newbury Park, CA: Sage.

Cooley, C. H. (1972). *Human Nature and Social Order*. Glencoe, IL: Free Press.

Dindia, K. (1994). The intrapersonal-interpersonal dialectical process of self-disclosure. In S. Duck (ed.), *Dynamics of Relationships* (pp. 27–56). Thousand Oaks, CA: Sage.

Edwards, M. L. K. (2004). We're decent people: Constructing and managing family identity in rural working class communities. *Journal of Marriage and Family*, 66, 515–529.

Heider, F. (1958). *The Psychology of Interpersonal Relations*. New York: Wiley.

Hopper, R., Knapp, M. L., and Scott, L. (1981). Couples' personal idioms: Exploring intimate talk. *Journal of Communication*, 31, 23–33.

Kramer, M. W. (2005). Communication and social exchange processes in community theatre groups. *Journal of Applied Communication Research*, 33, 159–182.

LaRossa, R., and Reitzes, D. C. (1993). Symbolic interactionism and family studies. In P. G. Boss, W. J. Doherty, R. LaRossa, W. R. Schumm, and S. K. Steinmetz (eds.), *Sourcebook of Family Theories and Methods: A Contextual Approach* (pp. 135–163). New York: Plenum.

Mead, G. H. (1934). *Mind, Self and Society: From the Standpoint of a Social Behaviorist*. Chicago, IL: The University of Chicago Press. (Edited and with an introduction by Charles W. Morris).

Miller, G. R. (1981). Tis the season to be jolly: A yuletide 1980 assessment of communication research. *Human Communication Research*, 7, 371–377.

Montgomery, B. M. (1992). Communication as the interface between couples and culture. *Communication Yearbook*, 15, 475–507.

Planalp, S., and Honeycutt, J. M. (1985). Events that increase uncertainty in personal relationships. *Human Communication Research*, 11, 593–605.

Powell, K. A., and Afifi, T. D. (2005). Uncertainty management and adoptee's ambiguous loss of their birth parents. *Journal of Social and Personal Relationships*, 22, 129–151.

Rawlins, W. K. (1992). *Friendship Matters: Communication, Dialectics, and the Life Course*. New York: Aldine de Gruyter.

Roloff, M. E. (1981). *Interpersonal Communication: The Social Exchange Approach*. Beverly Hills, CA: Sage.

Sabatelli, R. M., and Shehan, C. L. (1993). Exchange and resource theories. In P. G. Boss, W. J. Doherty, R. LaRossa, W. R. Schumm, and S. K. Steinmetz (eds.), *Sourcebook of Family Theories and Methods: A Contextual Approach* (pp. 385–411). New York: Plenum.

Taylor, D. A., and Altman, I. (1987). Communication in interpersonal relationships: Social penetration processes. In M. E. Roloff and G. R. Miller (eds.), *Interpersonal Processes: New Directions in Communication Research* (pp. 257–277). Newbury Park, CA: Sage.

Thibaut, J., and Kelley, H. (1959). *The Social Psychology of Groups*. New York: John Wiley.

Turner, J. H. (1986). *The Structure of Sociological Theory*, 4th edition. Chicago: Dorsey.

———. (1989). The relationship between communication and marital uncertainty. Unpublished doctoral dissertation, Northwestern University, Evanston, IL.

Walker, L. (1984). *The Battered Woman Syndrome*. New York: Springer.

Wood, J. T., Dendy, L. L., Dordek, E., Germany, M., and Varallo, S. M. (1994). Dialectic of difference: A thematic analysis of intimates' meanings for differences. In K. Carter and M. Prisnell (eds.), *Interpretive Approaches to Interpersonal Communication* (pp. 115–136). New York: SUNY Press.

Zhong, M., Myers, S. A., and Buerkel, R. (2004). Communication and intergenerational differences between Chinese fathers and sons. *Journal of Intercultural Communication Research*, 33, 15–27.

## Questions

1. What are three beliefs you hold about how human beings function in their relationships? Identify any of the five theories that appear to help explain your beliefs.

2. Identify and explain two questions or two of your personal theories that were not addressed in the five theories covered by this chapter.

# Part II

## *Building Blocks*

The ability to speak and hear does not ensure communicative success. Effective communication depends on the knowledge, skill, and sensitivity of the speakers and listeners. People who communicate well are referred to as *competent communicators*; they appear to know what to say or do in almost every situation. Competent communicators do not possess a secret formula or magical power; they follow a set of steps that allows them to increase their effectiveness with each important encounter. One of the goals of this section is to help you understand what it means to be a competent communicator and to increase your communication competence.

The term *communication competence* refers to a person's knowledge of how to use verbal and nonverbal language appropriately in a range of communication situations. When people work to develop communication competence, they are concerned with "putting language to work" in the following ways (Wood 1977; Galvin and Terrell 2001).

1. Enlarging a personal repertoire of communication strategies. Reviewing these options.

2. Selecting criteria and making choices from the repertoire. Analyzing and determining the best option.

3. Implementing the communication strategies chosen. Acting on the chosen option.

4. Evaluating the effectiveness of the strategies used. Reviewing the results of the encounter.

## Stages of Competence Development

### Enlarging the Repertoire of Communication Strategies

Communication strategies are the verbal and nonverbal messages created to reach a certain goal. To be effective, communicators must be able to imagine and perform a range of communication strategies appropriate to the conversation, the people, the setting, and the task at hand. The older you get, the more ways you develop to cope with communication difficulties or unforeseen interactions. For example, as a student you may have five strategies for requesting an extension on an assignment, although a few years ago you only had one or two strategies. You enlarge your repertoire by observing others as models for handling certain situations, and reflecting on ways you might have handled difficult situations more effectively. A competent communicator considers a number of possible ways he or she might deal with a situation; alternatives are crucial to this process.

## Selecting a Strategy

Communication effectiveness is based on the appropriateness of the alternative chosen from the repertoire. The competent communicator carefully weighs the factors of the situation, including the following:

1. **Who:** What do you know about the people involved in the interaction? Think about your past relationship and the possible future relationship with them.

2. **Where:** How does the setting—the time, privacy, and place of the communication—affect your interaction?

3. **What:** How important is the topic or subject matter to the other person or yourself? Who is highly knowledgeable about the topic?

4. **Task:** What is the purpose of the interaction? To solve a problem, reduce interpersonal tensions, or enjoy yourselves?

Competent communicators select from their extensive repertoires of communication strategies those that they perceive to be the most appropriate, given the situational factors. The goal of the selection step is to provide an opportunity to identify and sharpen the criteria used in choosing communication strategies.

## Acting on the Choice

How often have you known what you should say or do in a particular situation, but you didn't act on this knowledge? Once people have made communication choices for a particular situation, they must possess skills and the willingness to carry their choices into action. Selecting a strategy does not do much good unless you act on it. It is one thing to plan to tell a friend that she hurt your feelings and another thing to actually talk to the person about it. Just as skilled athletes spend time visualizing their every move on the field, skilled communicators visualize difficult situations in their minds and mentally rehearse how to handle them. Often, they may try out strategies with a "safe" person before confronting the "difficult" person. These planning procedures help build confidence to implement the selected strategy.

## Evaluating the Effects

The final step involves making a judgment about the effectiveness of the strategy you implemented. You need to evaluate your communication in terms of its outcome. As people develop competence, they make more informed judgments about their message effectiveness. These judgments rely on feedback from others, as well as from your personal experiences.

By evaluating each encounter in terms of appropriateness and satisfaction, communicators gain valuable information and develop new criteria for future interactions. Your goal is to sharpen critical awareness of self and others ("Did my plan work?" "What is the effect of my chosen strategy?" "How did the other person appear to feel?" "What would I do in a future similar situation?"). When you communicate in important situations, you need to examine the interaction's effect in order to decide whether you would repeat the strategy in a similar situation or try something different.

Communication competence contributes to successful and satisfying personal relationships. Competent communicators are more likely to reach their goals (Canary, Cody, and Manusov 2003). As later readings in this text suggest, there is little question that communication competence is an important ingredient in the development of friendship, family, and workplace relationships.

In this section, we'll discuss the building blocks, the foundation of the communication process—verbal communication, nonverbal communication, and listening. As you read each of the articles, consider how an understanding of each can help you become a more competent communicator.

### References

Canary, D. J., Cody, M. J., and Manusov, V. L. (2003). *Interpersonal Communication: A Goals-Based Approach*, 3rd ed. Boston: Bedford/St. Martin's.

Galvin, K. M., and Terrell, J. (2001). *Communication Works!* Columbus, OH: Glencoe Press.

Wood, B., ed. (1977). *Development of Functional Communication Skills: Grades 7–12*. Urbana, IL: ERIC and Speech Association. ✦

# 4
# Elements of Language

*Rudolph F. Verderber and
Kathleen S. Verderber*

**A** *word is a symbol but, as these authors indicate, it is not a thing. Stop reading for a moment and write down your description for the word* frog. *What did you write? A tailless amphibian? A small holder placed in a vase to hold flower stems in position? A hoarseness in your throat? A mass of elastic substance found in the middle of a horse's foot? An ornament for fastening the front of a coat? All these are correct definitions of* frog. *It all depends on the meaning you had in mind.*

*Words, in addition to being symbolic, are also arbitrary. They derive their meaning from the people who use them. Linguists Ogden and Richards (1923) created the "semantic triangle," or "triangle of meaning," to graphically illustrate this symbolic, arbitrary nature of words:*

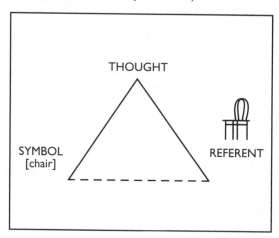

*The symbol (lower left-hand corner) is a word. The apex of the triangle is the thought—the concept you have of an object, idea, or event. The referent (lower right-hand corner)*

*is the actual object or thing being perceived. For example, you see a chair and say "chair." The word you speak is the symbol, the thought is your image of the chair, and the referent is the actual chair. Notice that the line connecting the symbol and the referent is broken. This indicates that the symbol and the referent have no connection except that which you make in your mind—in your thoughts.*

In this chapter on language, the authors describe the importance of meaning and how meanings change across time and subgroups. In addition, they suggest ways to speak more clearly and to be sensitive to cultural and gender differences. Excellent guidelines for language use are included. Research on verbal aggression between spouses (Stamp and Sabourin 1995) reveals that men who abuse their wives experience their spouses' verbal aggression as having physical force, such as by stating, "It was a real blow." In some cases, they responded to this attack with physical force. Other research reveals the negative effects of hostile parent messages on children (Vissing and Baily 1996). Such aggression, often called verbal abuse, included disparaging terms, insults, belittling, ridiculing, sarcasm, and threats.

On a lighter note, think about the words that are used in everyday language but that derive from the game of poker. For example, you talk about being "in the hole," "passing the buck," and "standing pat" without thinking about the gaming origin of the words. Consider how you use words strategically to affect relationships, and how others do the same to you.

*Through careful definitions and examination of how words shape meaning depending on culture and context, this chapter looks at communication from a technical standpoint: highlighting uses of grammar, syntax, connotation, and denotation in everyday speech. First illustrating the universal purposes of language, authors Verderber and Verderber describe how someone's use of language can sometimes change or confuse meanings, and they offer strategies for speaking more clearly, precisely, and accurately. As you read this chapter, consider this question: How conscious are you of changing your language as you move from one circumstance to another, such as from a class-*

*room to an athletic field or from an office to a family dinner?*

## References

Ogden, C. K., and Richards, I. A. (1923). *The Meaning of Meaning.* New York: Harcourt Brace.

Stamp, G., and Sabourin, T. (1995). Accounting for violence: An analysis of male spousal abuse narratives. *Journal of Applied Communication Research* 23: 284–307.

Vissing, Y., and Baily, W. (1996). Parent-to-child verbal aggression. In D. Cahn and S. Lloyd, *Family Violence From a Communication Perspective.* Thousand Oaks, CA: Sage.

\* \* \*

# The Nature of Language

*Language* is the body of words and the systems for their use that are common to the people of the same language community.

## Uses of Language

Although language communities vary in the words that they use and in their grammar and syntax systems, all languages serve the same purposes.

1. *We use language to designate, label, define, and limit.* Thus, when we identify a house as a "Tudor," we are differentiating it from another that may be identified as an "A-frame."

2. *We use language to evaluate.* Through language we give positive or negative slants. For instance, if you see Hal taking more time than others to make a decision, you could describe Hal positively as "thoughtful" or negatively as "dawdling."

3. *We use language to discuss things outside our immediate experience.* Language enables us to speak hypothetically, to talk about past and future events, and to communicate about people and things that are not present. Thus, we can use language to discuss where we hope to be in five years, to analyze a conversation two acquaintances

had last week, or to learn about the history that shapes the world we live in.

4. *We can use language to talk about language.* We can use language to discuss how someone phrased a statement and whether better phrasing would have resulted in a clearer meaning or a more positive response. For instance, if your friend said she would see you "this afternoon," but she didn't arrive until 5 o'clock, when you ask her where she's been, the two of you are likely to discuss the meaning of "this afternoon."

## Language and Meaning

On the surface, the relationship between language and meaning seems perfectly clear: We select the correct word, and people will interpret our meaning correctly. In fact, the relationship between language and meaning is not nearly so simple for two reasons: Language must be learned, and the use of language is a creative act.

First, we are not born knowing a language. Rather, each generation within a language community learns the language anew. We learn much of our language early in life from our families; much more we learn in school. But we do not all learn to use the same words in the same way.

A second reason the relationship between language and meaning is complicated is that even though languages have systems of syntax and grammar each utterance is a creative act. When we speak, we use language to create new sentences that represent our meaning. Although on occasion we repeat other people's sentence constructions to represent what we are thinking or feeling, some of our talk is unique.

A third reason language and meaning is so complicated is that people interpret the meaning of words differently. Words have two kinds of meaning: denotative and connotative. Thus, when Melissa tells Trish that her dog died, what Trish understands Melissa to mean depends on both word denotation and connotation.

***Denotation.*** The direct, explicit meaning a language community formally gives a word is its *denotation.* Word denotation is the meaning found in a dictionary. So, denotatively, when Melissa said her dog died, she meant that her domesticated canine no longer demonstrates physical life. In some situations the denotative meaning of a word may not be clear. Why? First, dictionary definitions reflect current and past practice in the language community; and second, the dictionary uses words to define words. The end result is that words are defined differently in various dictionaries and often include multiple meanings that change over time.

Moreover, meaning may vary depending on the context in which the word is used. For example, the dictionary definition of *gay* includes both having or showing a merry, lively mood and homosexual. Thus, *context*, the position of a word in a sentence and the other words around it, has an important effect on correctly interpreting which denotation of a word is meant. Not only will the other words and the syntax and grammar of a verbal message help us to understand the denotative meaning of certain words, but so will the situation in which they are spoken. Whether the comment "He's really gay" is understood to be a comment on someone's sexual orientation or on his merry mood may depend on the circumstances in which it is said.

*Connotation.* The feelings or evaluations we associate with a word represent the *connotation and may be even more important to our understanding of meaning*.

C. K. Ogden and I. A. Richards (1923) were among the first scholars to consider the misunderstandings resulting from the failure of communicators to realize that their subjective reactions to words are based on their life experiences. For instance, when Melissa tells Trisha that her dog died, Trisha's understanding of the message depends on the extent to which her feelings about pets and death—her connotations of the words—correspond to the feelings that Melissa has about pets and death. Melissa, who sees dogs as truly indispensable friends, may be trying to communicate a true sense of grief, but Trish, who has never had a pet and doesn't particularly care for dogs, may miss the sense of Melissa's statement.

Word denotation and connotation are important because the only message that counts is the message that is understood, regardless of whether it is the message you intended.

## Meaning Varies Across Subgroups in the Language Community

As we mentioned earlier, within a larger language community, subgroups with unique cultures are sometimes formed. These subgroups develop variations on the core language that enable them to share meanings unique to their subcultural experience. People from different subcultures approach the world from different perspectives, so they are likely to experience some difficulty sharing meaning when they talk with each other. . . .

In addition to subgroups based on race, religion, and national origin, there are also subgroup cultures associated with generation, social class, and political interests. The need for awareness and sensitivity in applying our communication skills does not depend on someone's being an immigrant or from a different ethnic background. Rather, the need for being aware of potential language differences is important in every type of communication. Developing our language skills so that the messages we send are clear and sensitive will increase our communication effectiveness in every situation.

## Speaking More Clearly

Regardless of whether we are conversing, communicating in groups, or giving speeches, we can speak more clearly by reducing the ambiguity and confusion. Compare these two descriptions of a close call in an automobile: "Some nut almost got me with his car a while ago" versus "An older man in a banged-up Honda Civic crashed the light at Calhoun and Clifton and came within inches of hitting me last week while I was waiting to turn left at the cross street." The differences are in clarity. In the second example, the message used language that was specific, concrete, and precise as well as statements that are dated and indexed.

### Specificity, Concreteness, and Precision in Language Use

*Specific words* clarify meaning by narrowing what is understood from a general category to a particular item or group within that category. Thus saying "It's a Honda Civic" is more specific than saying "It's a car." *Concrete words* are sense-related. In effect we can see, hear, smell, taste, or touch concrete words. Thus we can picture that "banged up" Civic. Abstract ideas, such as justice, equality, or fairness, can be made concrete through examples or metaphors. *Precise words* are those that most accurately express meaning—they capture shades of difference. It is more precise to note that the Civic came "within inches of hitting me" than it is to say "some nut almost got me."

Often, as we try to express our thoughts, the first words that come to mind are general, abstract, and imprecise. The ambiguity of these words makes the listener choose from many possible images rather than picturing the single focused image we have in mind. The more listeners are called on to provide their own images, the more likely they are to see meanings different from what we intend. . . .

As we move from general to specific, we also move from abstract to concrete. Consider the word *speak*. This is a general, abstract term. To make it more concrete, we can use words such as *mumble, whisper, bluster, drone, jeer,* or *rant*. Say these words aloud. Notice the different sound of your voice when you say *whisper* as opposed to *bluster, jeer,* or *rant*.

Finally, we seek words that are precise—those that most accurately or correctly capture the sense of what we are saying. In seeking the most precise word to describe Phillip's speech, at first we might say, "Phillip blustered. Well, to be more precise, he ranted." Notice that we are not moving from general to specific; both words are on roughly the same level of abstraction. Nor are we talking about abstract versus concrete; both words are concrete. Rather, we are now concerned with precision in meaning. *Blustering* means talking in a way that is loudly boastful; *ranting* means talking in a way that is noisy or bombastic. So, what we are considering here is shades of meaning: Depending on how the person was talking, *blustering* or *ranting* would be the more precise word. . . .

Although specific, concrete, and precise words enable us to reduce ambiguity and sharpen meaning through individual words, sometimes clarity is best achieved by adding a detail or an example. For instance, Linda might add, "He never criticizes a friend behind her back." By following up her use of the abstract concept of loyalty with a concrete example, Linda makes it easier for her listeners to "ground" their idea of this personal quality in a concrete or "real" experience. . . .

## Developing the Ability to Speak More Clearly

Being able to speak more clearly requires us to build our working vocabulary and to brainstorm to generate word choices from our active vocabulary.

***Vocabulary building.*** As a speaker, the larger your vocabulary, the more choices you have from which to select the word you want. As a listener, the larger your vocabulary, the more likely you are to understand the words used by others.

One way to increase your vocabulary is to study one of the many vocabulary building books on the shelves of most any bookstore, such as *Merriam Webster's Vocabulary Builder* (Cornog, 1998). You might also study magazine features such as "Word Power" in the *Reader's Digest*. By completing this monthly quiz and learning the words with which you are not familiar, you could increase your vocabulary by as many as twenty words per month.

A second way to increase your vocabulary is to make note of words that you read or that people use in their conversations with you and look them up. For instance, suppose you read or hear, "I was inundated with phone calls today!" If you wrote inundated down and looked it up in a dictionary later, you would find that "inundated" means *overwhelmed* or *flooded*. If you then say to yourself, "She was inundated—overwhelmed or flooded—with phone calls today," you are likely to remember that meaning and apply it the next time you hear the word. If you follow this practice, you will soon notice the increase in your vocabulary.

***Mental brainstorming.*** Having a larger vocabulary won't help your speaking if you do not have a procedure for using it. One way to practice accessing choices from your memory is to brainstorm during practice sessions and later in conversation. *Brainstorming* is an uncritical, nonevaluative process of generating alternatives. Suppose someone asked you about how well preregistration was working. You might initially say, "Preregistration is awful." If you don't think that *awful* is the right word, you might be able to quickly brainstorm the words *frustrating, demeaning, cumbersome,* and *annoying.* Then you could say, "What I really meant to say is that preregistration is overly cumbersome.". . .

## Dating Information

Because nearly everything changes with time, it is important that we *date* the information we communicate by telling when it was true. Not dating leads to inaccuracies that can be dangerous. For instance, Parker says, "I'm going to be transferred to Henderson City." Laura replies, "Good luck—they've had some real trouble with their schools." On the basis of Laura's statement, Parker may worry about the effect his move will have on his children. What he doesn't know is that Laura's information about this problem in Henderson City is five years old! Henderson City still may have problems, but then, it may not. Had Laura replied, "Five years ago, I know they had some real trouble with their schools. I'm not sure what the situation is now, but you may want to check," Parker would look at the information differently.

Let's consider two additional examples:

| Undated: Professor Powell brings great enthusiasm to her teaching. | Dated: Professor Powell brings great enthusiasm to her teaching—at least she did *last quarter* in communication theory. |
| --- | --- |
| Undated: You think Mary's depressed? I'm surprised. She seemed her regular high-spirited self when I talked with her. | Dated: You think Mary's depressed? I'm surprised. She seemed her regular high-spirited self when I talked with her *the day before yesterday.* |

To date information, (1) consider or find out when the information was true and (2) verbally acknowledge it. We have no power to prevent change. Yet we can increase the effectiveness of our messages through verbally acknowledging the reality of change if we date the statements we make.

## Indexing Generalizations

*Generalizing*—drawing a conclusion from particulars—enables people to use what they have learned from one experience and apply it to another. For instance, when Glenda learns that tomatoes and squash grow better if the ground is fertilized, she generalizes that fertilizing will help all of her vegetables grow better. Glenda has used what she learned from one experience and applied it to another.

*Indexing* generalizations is the mental and verbal practice of acknowledging that individual cases can differ from the general trend while still allowing us to draw on generalization. For instance, we may have a generalized concept of "men." But we must recognize that although Fred, Darnell, and William are all men, they are likely to have individual differences. So, how do we index in ordinary speaking? Let's consider two examples:

| Generalization: Because men are stronger than women, Max is stronger than Barbara. | Indexed Statement: In general men are stronger than women, so *Max is probably stronger* than Barbara. |
| --- | --- |
| Generalization: Your Chevrolet should go 50,000 miles before you need a brake job; Jerry's did. | Indexed Statement: Your Chevrolet may well go 50,000 miles before you need a brake job; Jerry's did, *but of course,* all Chevrolets aren't the same. |

To index, (1) consider whether what you want to say is about a specific object, person, or place, or whether it is a generalization about a class to which the object, person, or place belongs. (2) If what you want to say is a generalization about the class, qualify it appropriately so that your assertion does not go beyond the evidence that supports it. All people generalize at one time or another, but by indexing statements we can avoid the problems that hasty generalization sometimes creates.

## Cultural Differences in Verbal Communication

Cultures vary in how much meaning is embedded in the language itself and how much meaning is interpreted from the context in which the communication occurs.

In *low-context cultures*, such as in Northern Europe or the United States, meaning (1) is embedded mainly in the messages transmitted and (2) is presented directly. In low-context cultures, people say what they mean and get right to the point (Gudykunst & Matsumoto, 1996, pp. 29–30). So, in a low-context culture, "Yes" means "Affirmative, I agree with what you have said." In *high-context cultures*, such as Asian or Middle Eastern countries, meaning is interpreted based on the physical, social, and relational context. High-context culture people expect others to use context cues to interpret meaning. As a result, they present meanings indirectly. In a high-context culture, "Yes" may mean "Affirmative, I agree with what you have said," or it may mean "In this setting it would embarrass you if I said 'No,' so I will say 'Yes,' to be polite, but I really don't agree and you should know this, so in the future don't expect me to act as if I have just agreed with what you said." People from high-context cultures expect others to understand unarticulated feelings and subtle nonverbal gestures that people from low-context cultures don't even process. As a result, misunderstandings often occur.

The United States has a low-context national culture, as described previously. But the United States is a country of immigrants, and we know that individual Americans differ in whether they are high or low context in their approach to language. So, although knowing the characteristics of a national culture or culture of origin may be useful, we still need to be aware that people may or may not behave in line with their ethnic cultures (Adamopoulos, 1999, p. 75). Then why mention these differences at all? Because they give us a clue to how and why people and cultures may differ. An essential aspect of communication is being sensitive to needs and differences among us, so we must be aware of what the nature of those differences might be.

## Gender Differences in Verbal Communication

Over the last two decades, stirred by such book titles as *Men Are from Mars, Women Are from Venus*, people have come to believe gender differences in verbal messages are genetic. Yet research strongly states that differences in gender behaviors are learned rather than biological and that the differences are not nearly as large as portrayed (Wood & Dindia, 1998, pp. 34–36).

There is no evidence to suggest that the differences that have been identified between women's message construction patterns and those of men cause "problems" for either group (Canary & Hause, 1993, p. 141). Nevertheless, a number of specific differences between women's and men's speech patterns have been found, and understanding what has led to them has intrigued scholars. Mulac (1998) notes two differences in language usage between men and women that seem to have the greatest support (pp. 133–134):

1. *Women tend to use both more intensifiers and more hedges than men*. Intensifiers are words that modify other words and serve to strengthen the idea represented by the original word. So, according to studies of the actual speech practices of men and women, women are more likely to use words such as *awfully, quite*, and *so* (as in "It was quite lovely" or "This is so important"). Hedges are modifying words that soften or weaken the meaning of the idea represented by the original word. According to the research, women are likely to make greater use of such words as *somewhat, perhaps*, or *maybe* (as in "It was somewhat interesting that. . ." or "It may be significant that. . .").

2. *Women ask questions more frequently than men*. Women are much more likely to include questions like "Do you think so?" and "Are you sure?" In general, women tend to use questions to gain more information, get elaboration, and determine how others feel about the information.

But are these differences really important? Mulac goes on the report that "our research has shown that language used by U.S. women and men is remarkably similar. In fact, it is so indistinguishable that native speakers of American English cannot correctly identify which language examples were produced by women and which were produced by men" (p. 130). If this is so, then why even mention differences? Even though the differences are relatively small, they have judgmental consequences: "Observers perceive the female and male speakers differently based on their language use" (p. 147). Female speakers are rated higher on *socio-intellectual status* and *aesthetic quality*. Thus people perceive women as having high social status, being literate, and being pleasant as a result of perceived language differences. Men rated higher on *dynamism*. That is, people perceive men to be stronger and more aggressive as a result of their language differences. These judgments tend to be the same whether observers are male or female, middle-aged or young (p. 148).

Julia Wood (1997) explains these differences in language usage as resulting from differences in the basic psychological orientation each sex acquires in growing up. Women establish gender identity by seeing themselves as "like" or connected to mother. They learn to use communication as a primary way of establishing and maintaining relationships with others (p. 167). Men establish their gender identity by understanding how they are different or "separate" from mother. Thus they use talk as a way to "exert control, preserve independence, and enhance status" (p. 173).

## Speaking Appropriately

During the last few years, we have had frequent discussions and disagreements in the United States about "political correctness." Colleges and universities have been on the forefront of this debate. Although several issues germane to the debate on political correctness go beyond the scope of this chapter, at the heart of this controversy is the question of what language behaviors are appropriate—and what language behaviors are inappropriate.

*Speaking appropriately* means choosing language and symbols that are adapted to the needs, interests, knowledge, and attitudes of listeners in order to avoid language that alienates them. Through appropriate language, we communicate our respect and acceptance of those who are different from us. In this section, we discuss specific strategies that will help you craft appropriate verbal messages.

### Formality of Language

Language should be appropriately formal for the situation. Thus, in interpersonal settings, we are likely to use more informal language when we are talking with our best friend and more formal language when we are talking with our parents. In a group setting, we are likely to use more informal language when we are talking with a group of our peers and more formal language when we are talking with a group of managers. In a public-speaking setting, we are likely to use more formal language than in either interpersonal or group settings. . . .

### Jargon and Slang

Appropriate language should be chosen so that *jargon* (technical terminology) and *slang* (informal, nonstandard vocabulary) do not interfere with understanding. We form language communities as a result of the work we do, our hobbies, and the subcultures with which we identify. But we can forget that people who are not in our same line of work or who do not have the same hobbies or are not from our group may not understand language that seems to be such a part of our daily communication. For instance, when Jenny, who is sophisticated in the use of cyberlanguage, starts talking with her computer-illiterate friend Sarah about "Social MUDs based on fictional universes," Sarah is likely to be totally lost. If, however, Jenny recognizes Sarah's lack of sophistication in cyberlanguage, she can work to make her language appropriate by discussing the concepts in words that her friend understands. In short, when talking with people outside your language community, you need to carefully explain, if not abandon, the technical jargon or slang.

### Profanity and Vulgar Expressions

Appropriate language does not include profanity or vulgar expression. There was a time when uttering "hell" or "damn" would have resulted in severe punishment for children and social isolation for adults. Today we tend to tolerate commonplace profanities and vulgarities, and there are many subcultures where the use of profanity and vulgarity are commonplace. Under the influence of film and television writers who aim to scintillate and entertain, we have become inoculated to these expressions. In fact, it is common to hear elementary schoolchildren utter strings of "four letter" words in school hallways, lunchrooms, and on playgrounds. . . .

## Sensitivity

Language is appropriate when it is sensitive to usages that others perceive as offensive. Some of the mistakes in language that we make result from using expressions that are perceived to be sexist, racist, or otherwise biased—that is, any language that is perceived as belittling any person or group of people by virtue of their sex, race, age, handicap, or other identifying characteristics. Two of the most prevalent linguistic uses that communicate insensitivity are generic language and nonparallel language.

***Generic language.*** Generic language uses words that may apply only to one sex, race, or gender as though they represent both sexes, races, or genders. Such use is a problem because it linguistically excludes part of the group of people it ostensibly includes. Let's consider some examples.

Traditionally, English grammar called for the use of the masculine pronoun *he* to stand for the entire class of humans regardless of sex. So, in the past, standard English called for such usage as, "When a person shops, *he* should have a clear idea of what *he* wants to buy." Even though these statements are gramatically correct, they are now considered sexist because they inherently exclude females. Despite traditional usage, it would be hard to maintain that we picture people of both sexes when we hear the masculine word *he*.

One way to avoid this problem is to recast the sentence using plurals. Instead of "Because a doctor has high status, his views may be believed regardless of topic," you could say "Because doctors have high status, their views may be believed regardless of topic." Alternatively, you can use both male and female pronouns: "Because a doctor has high status, his or her views may be believed regardless of topic." These changes may seem small, but they may mean the difference between alienating and not alienating the people with whom you are speaking. Stewart, Cooper, Stewart, and Friedly (1998) cite research to show that using "he and she," and to a lesser extent "they," gives rise to listeners' including women in their mental images, thus increasing gender balance in their perceptions (p. 63).

A second problem results from the traditional reliance on the use of the generic *man*. Many words have become a common part of our language that are inherently sexist because they seem to apply to only one gender. Consider the term *manmade*. What this really means is that a product was produced by human beings, but its underlying connotation is that a male human being made the item. Some people try to argue that just because a word has "man" within it does not really affect people's understanding of meaning. But research has demonstrated that people usually visualize men (not women) when they read or hear these words. Moreover, when job titles end in "man," their occupants are assumed to have stereotypically masculine personality traits (Gmelch, 1998, p. 51). . . .

***Nonparallel language.*** Nonparallel language occurs when terms are changed because of the sex, race, or other characteristic of the individual. Because it treats groups of people differently, nonparallel language is also belittling. Two common forms of nonparallelism are marking and unnecessary association.

Marking means adding sex, race, age, or other designations unnecessarily to a general word. For instance, saying "female" doctor or "black" lawyer would be marking. Marking is offensive to some people because the speaker appears to be trivializing the person's role by emphasizing an irrelevant characteristic. For instance, this usage seems to imply that Jones is a good doctor for a woman or Smith is a good lawyer for a black person. Because you would be very unlikely to ever say "Jones is a good male doctor" and "Smith is a good white lawyer," leave sex, race, age, and other markers out of your labeling.

Another form of nonparallelism is to emphasize one person's association with another when you are not talking about the other person. Very often you will hear a speaker say something like this: "Gladys Thompson, whose husband is CEO of Acme Inc., is the chairperson for this year's United Way campaign." In response to this sentence, you might say that the association of Gladys Thompson with her husband gives further credentials to Gladys Thompson. But using the association may be seen to imply that Gladys Thompson is important not because of her own accomplishment but because of her husband's. If a person has done or said something noteworthy, you should recognize it without making unnecessary associations.

Very few people can escape all unfair language. By monitoring your usage, however, you can guard against frustrating your attempts to communicate by assuming that others will react to your language the same way you do, and you can guard against saying or doing things that offend others and perpetuate outdated sex roles, racial stereotypes, and other biased language.

How can you speak more appropriately? (1) Assess whether the word or phrase used is less appropriate than it should be; (2) pause to mentally brainstorm alternatives; and (3) select a more appropriate word. . . .

## Summary

Language is a system of symbols used for communicating. Through language, we designate, label, and define; evaluate; talk about things outside our immediate experience; and talk about language itself.

You will be a more effective communicator if you recognize that language symbols are arbitrary, that language is learned and is creative, and that language and perception are interrelated. . . .

### References

Adamopoulos, J. (1999). The emergence of cultural patterns of interpersonal behavior. In J. Adamopoulos & Y. Kashima (Eds.), *Social psychology and cultural context* (pp. 63–76). Thousand Oaks, CA: Sage.

Canary, D. J., & Hause, K. (1993). Is there any reason to research sex differences in communication? *Communication Quarterly, 41*, 129–144.

Cornog, M. W. (1998). *Merriam Webster's vocabulary builder*. Springfield, MA: Merriam Webster.

Gmelch, S. B. (1998). *Gender on campus: Issues for college women*. New Brunswick, NJ: Rutgers University Press.

Gudykunst, W. B., & Matsumoto, Y. (1996). Cross-cultural variability of communication in personal relationships. In W. B. Gudykunst, S. Ting-Toomey, & T. Nishida (Eds.), *Communication in personal relationships across cultures* (pp. 19–56). Thousand Oaks, CA: Sage.

Mulac, A. (1998). The gender-linked language effect: Do language differences really make a difference? In D. J. Canary & K. Dindia (Eds.), *Sex differences and similarities in communication: Critical essays and empirical investigations of sex and gender in interaction* (pp. 127–154). Mahwah, NJ: Erlbaum.

Ogden, C. K., & Richards, I. A. (1923). *The meaning of meaning*. London: Kegan, Paul, Trench, Trubner.

Stewart, L. P., Cooper, P. J., Stewart, A. D., & Friedley, S. A. (1998). *Communication and gender* (3rd ed.). Boston, MA: Allyn & Bacon.

Wood, J. T. (1997). *Gendered lives: Communication, gender, and culture* (2nd ed.). Belmont, CA: Wadsworth.

Wood, J. T., & Dindia, K. (1998). What's the difference? A dialogue about differences and similarities between women and men. In D. J. Canary & K. Dindia (Eds.), *Sex differences and similarities in communication: Critical essays and empirical investigations of sex and gender in interaction* (pp. 19–40). Mahwah, NJ: Erlbaum.

## Questions

1. List as many meanings of the words *student* and *teacher* as you can. Compare your list with some of your classmates'. How are the definitions similar? Different? How would those similarities and differences affect communication?

2. What have you learned about adjusting your language across subgroups?

3. Write a paragraph describing language choices and use by someone you consider highly skilled. Include two or three examples of that person's effectiveness in sensitive situations.

# 5
# Listening and Feedback

## The Other Half of Communication

*Thomas E. Harris and*
*John C. Sherblom*

**A**uthor and diarist James Boswell once said that talking isn't everything. It's only half of a communication skill—the other half is listening. In reality, research indicates that listening is actually more than half. As early as 1926, researchers found that adults spend 70 percent of their waking time communicating. Writing occupied 9 percent, reading 16 percent, speaking 30 percent, and listening 45 percent of the total communication time (Rankin 1926). Put in a different way, people listen a book a day, speak a book a week, read a book a month, and write a book a year. In fact, some research suggests that executives spend 60 percent of their communication time listening (Steil 1991). Yet for all its importance, you spend little time learning to listen. No parent waits eagerly for a child to learn to listen. Rather, the emphasis is on learning to talk. Thus, listening is the least taught but the most used. Listening is like physical exercise. Everyone knows it is important, but many find it difficult to do on a regular basis. Listening is hard work. Listening is a complex activity involving four elements:

- *Hearing—the physiological process of receiving aural stimuli.*
- *Interpretation of sound waves—leading to understanding or misunderstanding.*
- *Evaluation—deciding how to use the information.*
- *Response—reacting to information.*

*If any of these steps is missing, listening has not occurred. There are no shortcuts to effec-*tive listening. It is an active, difficult, time-consuming process.

*One of the reasons why listening is difficult is physiological in origin. Although we are capable of understanding speech rates up to 500 or 600 words per minute, the average speaker speaks between 100 and 140 words per minute. Thus, we have a lot of "spare time" to spend thinking while the other person is talking. Too often, rather than spending this time focusing on the other person, we allow ourselves to be distracted. These distractions may be physical (a hot room, uncomfortable clothing, or loud or annoying noises), mental (focusing on ourselves—what we'll say next, our own needs—or allowing our preconceived attitudes to prematurely determine the value of what the other person is saying), semantic (reacting emotionally to the words), and factual (listening for facts rather than the main ideas and feelings of the message).*

*Listening is part of the transactional process of communication. The receiver's responses have a direct impact on the direction of the conversation. The key is to become active listeners rather than passive ones. Active listening involves providing feedback that clarifies and extends a speaker's message. Active listening attempts to reflect rather than direct another's message. As an active listener, you seek to draw out the speaker's feelings and thoughts rather than focusing on adding your own ideas.*

*A variety of studies suggest that active listening is essential for parents, couples, teachers, managers, and supervisors (Wolvin and Coakley 1991). In short, active listening enhances both personal and professional relationships. It is an approach to listening that involves suspending judgment, withholding evaluation, and striving to hear both the surface message and underlying meanings.*

*In this chapter, Harris and Sherblom discuss the importance of listening in communication. After laying out the four components of listening—sensing (hearing the message), interpretation, evaluation, and response—they explain strategies for becoming a more active listener, and subsequently, a better communicator. Finally, they discuss styles of feedback and response, including how to both provide feedback constructively, and receive feedback from others. As you read this chapter, consider the following question: To what extent is listening an innate talent or a skill that can be improved?*

### References

Rankin, P. T. (1926). The measurement of the ability to understand spoken language. Doctoral dissertation, University of Michigan. *Dissertation Abstracts*, 12 (1952): 847–848.

Steil, L. K. (1991). Listening training: The key to success in today's organizations. In D. Boriscoff and M. Purdy (eds.), *Listening in Everyday Life*. Lanham, MD: University Press.

Wolvin, A., and Coakley, C. G. (1991). A survey of the status of listening training in some Fortune 500 corporations. *Communication Education*, 40: 152–164.

\* \* \*

In any human communication process, effective listening is equally as important as clear, articulate speaking. Sensitive, articulate expression of ideas is one half of communication; careful, effective listening is the other. Receiving the message being sent by the other person and accurately assigning meanings to that message are required for understanding and for any real communication to take place. Abbott and Costello's "Who's on First?" misunderstanding can bring a smile to your face, but small group misunderstandings are not usually as funny. . . .

Research indicates . . . that while about half of our communication time is spent listening (Johnson, 1996), most of us are not very good listeners (Alessandra & Hunsaker, 1993). Many physicians, for example, do not listen carefully enough to their patients' stories to make accurate diagnoses (Nyquist, 1996). It has been argued that the average college student listens effectively to only about 50 percent of what is said and remembers only 25 percent of that content after two days (Wolvin & Coakley, 1985). Indeed, most individuals listen at about 25 percent effectiveness level. In addition, the 50 percent I hear may not be the 50 percent you thought was the most important, and the 25 percent I remember is unlikely to be the 25 percent you intended as your main message.

Why are we such poor listeners? Some scholars have suggested that, while we have all been encouraged to talk, few of us have been taught how to listen. As Johnson (1996, p. 91) puts it, "No parent waits eagerly for a child to learn to listen. Rather, the emphasis is on learning to talk." We tend to believe that talking is the same thing as communicating. Yet, as the expression goes, "God gave you two ears and one mouth."

We incorrectly identify talking with leading and following with listening. Often, listening is the more important skill (Ray, 1999). A transcript from an actual radio conversation of a U.S. Navy ship with Canadian authorities off the coast of Newfoundland in October 1995—released by the Chief of Naval Operations on October 10, 1995—makes the point.

> **CANADIANS:** Please divert your course 15 degrees to the South to avoid a collision.
>
> **AMERICANS:** Recommend you divert your course 15 degrees to the North to avoid a collision.
>
> **CANADIANS:** Negative. You will have to divert your course 15 degrees to the South to avoid a collision.
>
> **AMERICANS:** This is the Captain of a U.S. Navy ship. I say again, divert YOUR course.
>
> **CANADIANS:** No, I say again, divert YOUR course.
>
> **AMERICANS:** This is the aircraft carrier USS *Lincoln*. The second largest ship in the United States 92 Fleet. We are accompanied by three destroyers, three cruisers, and numerous support vessels. I demand that you change YOUR course 15 degrees north. I say again, that is one five degrees north, or countermeasures will be taken to ensure the safety of this ship.
>
> **CANADIANS:** This is a lighthouse. Your call.

Listening can be a critical leadership skill.

Mediators, negotiators, and other individuals who are trained to work through problems must first learn to listen effectively. In negotiator training seminars, for example, the negotiator trainees are reminded that they never learned anything while they were talking and that they cannot succeed in a negotiating session until they fully understand the other side (Asherman & Asherman, 1990). When they are talking, they are sending messages but are not developing much insight into how other people think or feel.

In *The Seven Habits of Highly Effective People*, Covey (1989) identifies one of the seven habits as: "Seek first to understand, and only then to be understood." Ineffective people, he explains, are eager to be heard but often do not take the time to understand the other person's perspective before speaking. Highly effective people place understanding the other person first, and that understanding comes only through listening.

## Motivation

No one becomes a better listener without the motivation to do so. Essentially, we all ask, "What's in it for me?" . . .

Listening has been shown to be a vital skill for successful managers, supervisors, and professional employees, taking over 60 percent of their average day on the job (Peters, 1987; Wolvin & Coakley, 1985). In addition, the rewards of good listening include many life-enhancing experiences, such as learning, building relationships, being entertained, making intelligent decisions, saving time, enjoying conversations, settling disagreements, getting the best value, preventing accidents and mistakes, asking intelligent questions, and making accurate evaluations (Bone, 1988). Finally, good listeners get a great deal more out of small group membership and are more appreciated by their fellow members. . . .

## Four Components of Listening

Listening involves four sequential components experienced in rapid succession. We must sense or hear the message, interpret or provide meaning to the message, evaluate the content of the message, and retain and respond to the message in the context of an ongoing communication event. Each of these components is in itself a complex pro-

cess. For this reason, a more detailed examination of each follows.

### Sensing (Hearing the Message)

Hearing the sounds, and even being able to repeat the words, is not the same thing as sensing, or hearing, the message. Hearing is the involuntary "physiological process of receiving aural stimuli" (Johnson, 1996, p. 91). Thus, the act of hearing the sounds is nonselective. Sensing or hearing the message, on the other hand, is a voluntary act whereby we choose certain sounds and noises to pay attention to, while avoiding others. This is an important part of listening and happens as a result of our decision to attune to certain messages. Hearing and listening to the message are influenced by selective attention and the amounts of external and internal noise.

***Selective attention***. Choosing one message over another is called *selective attention*. The messages we attune to are the ones that have some "pre-programmed" importance for us. If I am an avid football fan, for example, I will be drawn toward football-related messages. If I am a quilter, I will selectively attend to messages related to quilting. If I am committed to social justice, I am more likely to pay attention when civil rights issues are discussed. On the other hand, if I don't follow the soap operas on TV, I am not likely to pay attention to someone discussing the latest gossip about one of the stars.

There are several reasons we engage in this practice of selective attention. To start, some things are simply more important to us. For example, when someone calls our name, we are more likely to respond. With the barrage of stimulation that assaults us from all directions in our daily lives, we must learn to discriminate those stimuli that are necessary either to our survival or to our well-being from those that make little difference to us in our ongoing lives. Because we cannot possibly process all the stimulation that surrounds us, we have learned to pay attention to those stimuli that are familiar to us and that have particular significance for us. These can range from issues of crucial importance to those that appear trivial. They can include basic survival, our jobs, our relationships, popular cultural icons, or any number of other stimuli in our environments. . . .

When messages contradict or challenge our way of thinking, we may tend to reject them. Prejudices, stereotypes, and preconceived ideas can prevent us from fully hearing issues and alternative viewpoints on topics. If, for example, we hold preconceived ideas about the place of women in our society, assume that older people have little to contribute to the economic base of our society, make assumptions about the general characteristics of people based on their racial or ethnic backgrounds, hold stereotypes about gay people, or believe adamantly in one side of an issue, such as the right to die or the right to choice, then it becomes difficult for us to hear other people's views on these topics when they oppose or even question our own.

In addition, we make conscious decisions to pay attention to some messages and ignore others. As we become more expert in a particular subject we may tend to dismiss what we consider unsophisticated viewpoints. . . .

Finally, difficult material may discourage us from listening carefully. If we feel we don't understand the issue in question, we may simply drop out of the discussion, assuming we have nothing to offer to it anyway. . . .

*Noise.* Noise is a useful term for the interference that occurs between the spoken message and hearing. There are two types of noise: external and internal. External noise includes distractions that make it difficult to hear the other person. . . . [T]hese can include extraneous sounds, a telephone ringing, bad acoustics, poor visibility between the speaker and the listener, an uncomfortable physical environment, other people talking, coughing, or moving around, or any number of other physical distractions. . . .

Internal noise includes a preoccupation with personal issues, charged-up emotional states, stereotyping and prejudice toward the sender or toward his or her message, or distractions from other aspects of our lives. All of these interfere with our hearing. We are not blank slates that unconditionally accept all incoming verbal and nonverbal message. If we do not make a conscious effort or are not trained in active listening, we frequently allow noise to interfere with our hearing.

## Interpreting the Message

Assigning meaning to someone's message is a complex task. In hearing the message and choosing to pay attention, we accept the message into our memory system. Interpreting the message is the next step. Our goal in this should be to understand the other person's meaning. We are all limited in our perspective and understanding, however, by our perceptions of others' verbal and nonverbal communication. As I listen to someone else, I filter my interpretation of their message through my own attitudes, assumptions, needs, values, past and present experiences, knowledge, expectations, fears, goals, educational background, and emotional involvement. Thus, we each bring our own particular limitations to hearing and accurately interpreting someone else's message.

A much cited story provides an example of the preconceptions we frequently bring to our interpretations. A little boy is involved in a serious automobile accident in which his father, who was driving the car, is killed instantly. The boy is rushed to the hospital in critical condition. The emergency room doctor takes one look at the boy and shouts: "Oh my God, it's my son!" How is this possible? For some of us, the answer is not immediately apparent. Our implicit assumption that doctors are ordinarily men can make the interpretation process difficult. In this case, the doctor is the boy's mother. Recognizing our assumptions are interpretations can be tricky business. . . .

## Evaluating the Message Content

This stage involves forming an opinion or making a judgment regarding the messages. We are asking ourselves if the "facts" support the points being made or justify the positions being taken. It is a quality-control step, which poor listeners frequently overlook in their rush to judgment. Too often we don't stop to make certain that all the information is carefully gathered and weighed.

When we are asked to serve on a jury, we are admonished by the judge to refrain from making any final decision until all the evidence has been heard. This is a reminder of the importance of the evaluation stage of listening. Evaluation is the process of taking in various inputs, filtering out those that we consider unimportant, interpreting those that are important in our schema, and then making decisions about how to deal with them. In the decision-making process, it is important not to evaluate before collecting enough information. . . .

## Active Listening

Active, effective listening is hard work. When we engage in active listening, we respond verbally and nonverbally to the other group members, letting them know we are paying attention. We become part of the transaction and take responsibility for understanding their meanings. These active listening behaviors and skills are not intuitive and do have barriers to their effective achievement. We present eight of those barriers (Golen, 1990).

### Barriers to Active Listening

*Lack of interest*. The first barrier has to do with lack of interest in the subject matter, either because we find it inherently uninteresting or because we have determined it is too difficult for us to understand. . . . This can lead to boredom, impatience with the speaker, daydreaming, or becoming preoccupied with something else instead of listening.

*Distracting delivery*. A second barrier to good listening is our tendency to judge the speaker's personal characteristics. If someone fidgets, refuses to be efficient in his or her comments, seems disorganized, speaks in an accent or cadence different from our own, dresses in an unusual way, or behaves in any number of other ways distracting to us, we may become impatient and inattentive, or begin concentrating on the speaker's mannerisms or delivery, rather than on the message (Pearson & Davilla, 1993). . . .

*External and internal noise*. In line with distracting delivery is the third barrier—external and internal noise. As we discussed earlier under "Noise," this can prevent us from hearing the messages conveyed during a small group session. During any conversation, a phone ringing, a lawn mower running, or someone hammering nearby is a distraction. Whether the noise is external or internal, it is up to each of us to make an effort to hear past it—to concentrate on the message. . . .

*Arrogance and disrespect*. The fourth barrier relates to our emotional responses to behaviors that show arrogance or disrespect. People with know-it-all attitudes or who use generalizations such as "you always," or "you never" may create hostility in us. If we are attacked personally or treated with disrespect, we are less likely to listen carefully to what is being said. . . .

*Pre-programmed emotional responses*. A fifth barrier to effective listening comes when a group member touches on an issue to which we have a strong emotional reaction. Frequently, the more important the topic, the more likely group members are to respond from a pre-programmed point of view than from a rational response to the issue at hand. . . .

*Listening for facts*. A sixth barrier to effective listening is getting past our training in school, which was to listen only for the facts in order to recall them for a test. . . . Deliberative listening, or listening only for facts, can actually blind us to the overall point being made by the sender. Understanding comes from sensing the other person's point, not just from developing a catalog of the facts presented. . . .

*Faking attention*. The seventh barrier to effective listening—faking attention—may also have its genesis in our school training. Usually some time around second or third grade, we are singled out by a teacher who admonishes us to "Pay attention!" After that, we become quite adept at faking attention, and before long we fake more than we listen. . . .

*Thought speed*. Thought speed is the eighth barrier to careful listening. Because we can think three to four times faster than anyone can talk, our temptation is to make use of the "free" time by allowing ourselves to wander around mentally. We may formulate our responses to what we think is being said; we may be triggered into thoughts on totally unrelated subjects; or we may simply feel bored and stop listening altogether. . . .

*Other barriers*. Other barriers to active listening are: laziness or tiredness (avoiding a subject because it is complex or difficult or because it takes too much time); and insincerity (avoiding eye contact while listening and paying attention only to the speaker's words, rather than to the speaker's meaning).

## Active Listening Response Methods

Active listeners take advantage of the opportunity to listen carefully and understand each person.... Four response methods that active listeners use are paraphrasing, expressing understanding, asking questions, and using nonverbal communication.

*Paraphrasing*. Considered one of the secrets of effective listeners, paraphrasing is stating in our own words what we think the speaker intended to say. The description should be objective. Essentially, we are responding to the verbal and nonverbal signals given by the speaker.

Among other things, paraphrasing is an excellent way to fight daydreaming. If we are concentrating on developing an internal summary of another individual's thoughts and ideas, we do not have time to daydream (Wolvin & Coakley, 1985). We can paraphrase verbally to the speaker or simply paraphrase internally by mentally summarizing the other person's points....

*Expressing understanding*. At times, it may seem more appropriate to focus on the feelings of the speaker, rather than to restate the content of the message. This type of statement of understanding allows the group to assess more accurately how well the speaker's feelings have been perceived and understood, and this may permit the speaker to view her or his own feelings more accurately, as well....

*Asking questions*. Part of paraphrasing and expressing understanding is the effective use of questions. This is a skill rarely taught and frequently used in ways that discourage, rather than enhance, discussion. Questions can be seen as challenges to our honesty or position on an issue, or they can be seen as manipulative. A question such as: "You don't really believe those people, do you?" does not invite an open discussion of the respondent's point of view.... [T]he goal of questioning should be to clarify the other person's perspective, open up the discussion, or follow up on a previous idea....

*Using nonverbal communication*. Since more than 50 percent of all meaning is communicated nonverbally, effective listeners make use of nonverbal gestures. Making eye contact, nodding our heads, and sitting in an attentive manner all indicate that we are interested and listening, and they encourage the speaker to continue talking. Fidgeting, frowning, looking at our watches, reading our own notes, or behaving in other distracting ways gives the opposite message.

# Feedback: Responding to the Message

Listening is an active process. Feedback is built on and requires this active process of listening to be effective. Since we cannot not communicate, no response is nonetheless a response. After carefully listening to the message as openly and completely as we can, we are in a position to respond to what was communicated. Feedback plays an important role in the effective listening process, but it is intricately tied to the first three components: hearing the message, interpreting it, and evaluating its content. The most effective feedback should indicate to the sender that we are listening to the content of the message, interpreting it accurately, and understand it....

## Providing Constructive Feedback

When offering feedback, use descriptive statements without judgment, exaggeration, labeling, or attribution of motives. State the facts as specifically as possible. Tell how the behavior affects you. Say why you are affected that way and describe the connection between the facts you observed and your feelings. Let the other person respond. Describe the change you want the other person to consider. Describe why you think the change will alleviate the problem. Listen to the other person's response. Be prepared to discuss options and to compromise to arrive at a solution, rather than argue specific points. For example: "When you are late for meetings, I get angry because I am a busy person and dislike wasting time sitting and waiting for you to arrive. Is there another time that we could schedule our meetings so that you could get here on time?" will probably be more effective than: "You are always late for meetings. I'm tired of you being so irresponsible and wasting my time like that. When will you ever grow up, learn to take your commitments seriously, and take some responsibility for being places on time?"

*Talk first about yourself*, not the other person. Use "I" not "you" as the subject of your feedback statement. . . .

*Phrase the issue as a statement, not a question*. Questions appear controlling and manipulative and can cause people to become defensive and angry. Consider the difference between: "Can you stop that so we can get down to business?" and "I would like to get on with our meeting and business."

*Restrict your feedback to things you know for certain*. Don't present opinions as facts. Speak only of what you saw and heard and what you feel and want.

*Provide positive feedback as well as negative*. Many people take good work for granted and give feedback only when there are problems. People are more likely to pay attention to your complaints if they have also received your compliments. It is important to remember to tell people when they have done something well. . . .

*Understand the context*. An important characteristic of feedback is that it is always in a context. You never simply walk up to a person, deliver a feedback statement, and then leave. Before you give feedback, review the actions and decisions that led to that moment. Determine if the moment is right. You must consider more than your own need to give feedback. Constructive feedback can happen only within a context of listening to and caring about the person. Do not give feedback when you don't know much about the circumstances of the behavior or will not be around long enough to follow up on your feedback. "Hit and run" feedback is not fair.

*Don't use labels*. Describe the behavior. Be clear, specific and unambiguous. Calling someone a "Fascist"; a "Male Chauvinist Pig!"; or an "Unthinking Politically Correct Clone" are labels that are likely to be taken as insults rather than as legitimate feedback.

*Be careful not to exaggerate. Be exact*. An exaggeration will invite an argument from the

feedback receiver rather than dealing with the real issue. Saying "You're always late for meetings" invites a defensive response of "Well, not always," or "I'm not usually very late," rather than a thoughtful one.

*Don't be judgmental*. Evaluative words like "good," "bad," and "should" make implicit judgments that make the content of the feedback difficult to hear.

### Receiving Feedback

When you are receiving feedback, the first thing to do is to breathe. Receiving feedback is stressful, and our bodies react by getting tense. Taking slow, full, deep breaths helps our body relax and allows our brain to maintain greater alertness. Listen carefully. Don't interrupt. Don't discourage the feedback-giver. Ask questions for clarity or for specific examples. Acknowledge the feedback. Paraphrase the message in your own words to let the person know you heard and understood what was said. Acknowledge the valid points and agree with what is true. Acknowledge the other person's point of view and try to understand his or her reaction. Then take time to sort out what you have heard. . . .

### References

Alessandra, T., & Hunsaker, P. (1993). *Communicating at work*. New York: Simon & Schuster.

Asherman, I., & Asherman, S. (1990). *The negotiation sourcebook*. Amherst, MA: Human Resource Development Press.

Bone, D. (1988). *The business of listening*. Los Altos, CA: Crisp.

Covey, S. R. (1989). *The seven habits of highly effective people*. New York: Simon & Schuster.

Furmanek, B., & Palumbo, R. (1991). *Abbott and Costello in Hollywood*. New York: Putnam.

Golen, S. (1990). A factor analysis of barriers to effective listening. *The journal of business communication*, 27, 25–36.

Johnson, D. (1996). Helpful listening and responding. In K. M. Galvin & P. J. Cooper (Eds.), *Making connections: Readings in relational communication*. Los Angeles: Roxbury Publishing Company.

McIntyre, R. M., & Salas, E. (1995). Measuring and managing for team performance: Emerging principles from complex environments. In R. A. Gauzzo, E. Salas, & Associates

(Eds.), *Team effectiveness and decision making in organizations*. San Francisco: Jossey-Bass.

Nyquist, M. (1996). Learning to listen. In K. M. Galvin & P. J. Cooper (Eds.), *Making connections: Readings in relational communication*. Los Angeles: Roxbury Publishing Company.

Pearson, J. C., & Davilla, R. A. (1993). The gender construct. In L. P. Arliss & D. J. Borisoff (Eds.), *Women & men communicating: Challenges and changes*. Orlando, FL: Harcourt Brace Jovanovich.

Peters, T. (1987). *Thriving on chaos*. New York: Knopf.

Ray, R. G. (1999). *The facilitative leader*. Upper Saddle River, NJ: Prentice-Hall.

Sashkin, M., & Kiser, K. J. (1993). *Putting total quality management to work*. San Francisco: Berrett-Koehler.

Scholtes, P. R. (1988). *The team handbook*. Madison, WI: Joiner Associates.

Stewart, J., & Thomas, M. (1990). Dialogic listening: Sculpting mutual meanings. In J. Stewart (Ed.), *Bridges not walls* (5th ed., pp. 192–210). New York: McGraw-Hill.

Wheelan, S. A. (1999). *Creating effective teams*. Thousand Oaks, CA: Sage.

Wolvin, A. D., & Coakley, C. G. (1985). *Listening* (2nd ed.). Dubuque, IA: Brown.

Zemke, R., & Schaaf, D. (1989). *The service edge*. New York: New American Library.

## Questions

1. Write a description of an interpersonal experience in which a breakdown in listening played an important part. Then write an analysis of how the problem could have been avoided through effective listening.

2. Keep a one-day journal of your listening behavior. How would you describe the times you spend listening in various contexts?

3. How can you tell when someone is listening to you? Recount a conversation you've had with someone when you *knew* you were being heard. What did that person do to let you know he or she was listening?

# 6
# Helpful Listening and Responding

*David Johnson*

**E**ffective listening is a critical life skill that impacts your personal and work life on a daily basis. Improving your listening skills is hard work. Cooper and Simonds (2003) suggest several ways to improve listening:

1. **Remove, if possible, the physical barriers to listening**. You might simply move to another room or move the furniture in the room, turn the thermostat up or down, or close the door to your classroom. Manipulate your environment to fit your needs.

2. **Focus on the speaker's main idea**. You can always request specific facts and figures later. Your initial purpose as a listener should be to answer the question, What is this person's main idea?

3. **Listen for the intent, as well as the content, of the messages**. Ask yourself, Why is this person saying this?

4. **Give the other person a full hearing**. Do not begin your evaluation until you have listened to the entire message. When a student tells you that his homework is not finished, allow the student to complete his explanation before you respond. Too often, as listeners we spend our listening time creating our messages rather than concentrating on the content and intent of the other's message.

5. **Remember the saying that meanings are in people, not in words**. Try to overcome your emotional reactions to words. Focus on what you can agree with in the message, and use this as common ground as you move into more controversial issues.

6. **Concentrate on the other person as a communicator and as a human being**. All of us have ideas, and we have feelings about those ideas. Listen with all your senses, not just with your ears. The well-known admonition "Stop, look, and listen" is an excellent one to follow when listening. Focus on questions such as these: What does she mean verbally? Nonverbally? What's the feeling behind the message? Is this message consistent with those she has expressed in previous conversations?

*Listening to another person discuss his or her problems is something that almost everyone does in their relationships, but, according to author David Johnson, not everyone does it in a way that facilitates growth and open communication in the relationship. In this chapter, types of listening and responding styles are discussed in great detail, illustrating the ways in which each can be potentially misinterpreted, or ineffectively delivered. Through multiple examples, Johnson then indicates the ways in which to use conversational skills—after thorough listening—like probing responses, supportive responses, and interpretive responses to help another sort out his or her difficulties in a way that is most beneficial to the development of the relationship. Finally, a detailed discussion of how to phrase such responses wraps up the section. As you read this chapter, think about the following questions. Think about the last time a friend came to you with a serious problem with which you tried to help. Which types of Johnson's response styles did you tend to rely on? Which types might have been more helpful?*

### Reference

Cooper, P. J., and Simonds, C. (2003). *Communication for the Classroom Teacher*, 7th ed. Boston: Allyn & Bacon.

\* \* \*

## Responding to Another Person's Problems

**W**hen someone is talking to you about something deeply distressing or of a real concern to her, how should you listen and respond in order to be helpful? How do you answer in ways that will both help the person solve her problem or clarify her feelings and at the same time help build a closer relationship between that person and yourself?

Perhaps the most important thing to remember is that you cannot solve other people's problems for them. No matter how sure you are of what the right thing to do is or how much insight you think you have into their problems, the other people must come to their own decisions about what they should do and achieve their own insights into the situation and themselves. So how do you listen and respond to ensure that other people will make their own decisions and gain their own insights?

In listening and responding to other people's messages, there are two basic things that determine the effectiveness of your help:

1. Your intentions and attitudes as you listen and give your response

2. The actual phrasing of your response.

. . . Your intentions are the most important single factor in helping other people to solve their problems. The appropriate phrasing of your response involves considerable skill, but skill alone is not enough. It is only when the skills in phrasing responses reflect your underlying attitudes of acceptance, respect, interest, liking, and desire to help that your response will be truly helpful. Your response is helpful when it helps the other person explore a problem, clarify feelings, gain insight into a distressing situation, or make a difficult decision. . . .

## Intentions Underlying the Responses

When other people want to discuss a problem or concern of theirs with you, there are at least five ways in which you can listen and respond:

1. Advising and evaluating

2. Analyzing and interpreting

3. Reassuring and supporting

4. Questioning and probing

5. Paraphrasing and understanding

Each of these alternative ways of responding communicates certain intentions. All of them, at one time or another, will be helpful. None of the responses can be labeled as good or bad, effective or ineffective. All have their place in helping other people solve their problems and gain insight into their difficulties. But some of the above responses are more helpful than others in building friendships and helping people explore further their feelings and thoughts. In exploring the intentions underlying the responses . . . the person with the problem will be called the sender and the person giving the response will be the receiver.

### Advising and Evaluating (E)

Giving advice and making a judgment as to the relative goodness, appropriateness, effectiveness, and rightness of what the sender is thinking and doing are among the most common responses we make when trying to help others. These responses communicate an evaluative, corrective, suggestive, or moralizing attitude or intent. The receiver implies what the sender *ought* or *might* do to solve the problem. When advice is timely and relevant, it can be helpful to another person. Most often, however, when you give advice and evaluation you build barriers that keep you from being helpful and developing a deeper friendship.

For one thing, being evaluative and giving advice can be threatening to other people and make them defensive. When people become defensive they may closed-mindedly reject your advice, resist your influence, stop exploring the problem, and be indecisive. Why? Because giving advice and passing judgment often communicate that the receiver is assuming that her judgment is superior to that of the sender's. When a person has a problem, she does not want to be made to feel inferior. For another thing, being evaluative often seems to be a way of avoiding involvement with another person's concerns and conflicts. While it is quick, fast, and easy, it also allows the receiver to generalize about the sender's problems, and this communicates that the receiver does not care to take the time to understand the sender's problems fully. In addition, advice can encourage people not to take responsibility for their own problems. Even when praise is used to influence others, it can communicate that the sender must meet certain expectations before she is of value. Finally, advice and evaluation often tell more about the giver's values, needs, and perspectives than about the receiver's problems. Thus, if you wish to be helpful and further a relationship, you should usually avoid such phrases as "If I were you. . . ," "One good way is. . . ," "Why don't you. . . ?" "You should. . . ," "You ought to. . . ," "The thing to do is. . . ," and "Don't you think. . . ?"

It is important to avoid giving advice and evaluation in the early stages of helping other people understand and solve their problems and difficulties. There is a place for advising and evaluating, but there are other responses that are usually more helpful.

## Analyzing and Interpreting (I)

When analyzing or interpreting the sender's problems and difficulties, the receiver's intentions are to teach, to tell the sender what his or her problem means, to inform the sender how the sender really feels about the situation, or to impart some psychological knowledge to the sender. In interpreting the sender's problems, the receiver implies what the sender might or ought to think. Analyzing or interpreting attempts to point out some deep hidden reason that makes the sender do the things he or she does. It attempts to give the person some additional insight through an explanation. Through such statements as, "Ah, ha! Now I know what your problem is," or, "The reason you are upset is. . . ," the receiver tries to teach the sender the meaning of the sender's behavior and feelings.

This suggestion will often make the sender defensive and will discourage her from revealing more thoughts and feelings for fear that these will be also interpreted or analyzed. Most of us react negatively when someone else implies that he knows more about us than we do.

When the receiver tries to analyze or interpret the sender's behavior, thoughts, and feelings, the receiver may communicate "I know more about you than you know yourself." People will usually respond better when you help them think about themselves and their

feelings than if you try to figure out what causes them to do the things they do. It also frees you from being an "expert" on human behavior.

## Reassuring and Supporting (S)

Supportive and reassuring responses indicate that the receiver wants to reassure, be sympathetic, or reduce the intensity of the sender's feelings. When the receiver rushes in with support and reassurance, this often denies the sender's feelings. Statements such as, "It's always darkest just before the dawn," and "Things will be better tomorrow," frequently end up communicating a lack of interest or understanding. Supportive statements are, however, frequently used by people trying to help a friend, student, or child. It's distressing to see a friend depressed, so all too often a person will communicate, "Don't be depressed," rather than listening carefully and helping clarify the causes and potential solutions for the depression. While there are times when other people need to be reassured as to their value and worth or supported in their reactions and feelings, reassurance and support are often ways of saying, "You should not feel as you do."

## Questioning and Probing (P)

Probing by asking questions indicates that the receiver wants to get further information, guide the discussion along certain lines, or bring the sender to a certain realization or conclusion the receiver has in mind. In asking a question, the receiver implies that the sender ought or might profitably develop or discuss a point further. Questioning is, however, an important skill in being helpful to people who wish to discuss their problems and concerns with you. In using questions skillfully, it is necessary to understand the difference between an open and closed question and the pitfalls of the "why" question. An *open question* encourages other people to answer at greater length and in more detail. The *closed question* usually asks for only a simple yes or no answer. An example of an open question is, "How do you feel about your job?" while an example of a closed question is, "Do you like your job?" Because open questions encourage other people to share more personal feelings and thoughts, they are usually more helpful.

When you intend to deepen a relationship or help other people understand and solve their problems, it is usually recommended that you avoid why questions. To encourage people to give a rational explanation for their behavior may not be productive because most people do not fully know the reasons they do the things they do. Being asked why can make people defensive and encourages them to justify rather than explore their actions. Why questions are also often used to indicate disapproval or to give advice. For example, the question, "Why did you yell at the teacher?" may imply the statement, "I don't think you should have yelled at the teacher." Because criticism and advice tend to be threatening, people may feel less free to examine the reasons that led them to a particular action or decision. Instead of asking people to explain or justify their actions through answering why, it may be more helpful to ask what, where, when, how, and who questions. These questions help other people to be more specific, precise, and revealing. . . .

Asking questions skillfully is an essential part of giving help to other people who are discussing their problems and concerns with you. But questions, while they communicate that you are interested in helping, do not necessarily communicate that you understand. It may sometimes be more effective to change questions into reflective statements that encourage the person to keep talking. An example is changing the questions, "Do you like swimming?" to a reflective statement, "You really like swimming." Reflective statements, which are discussed in the next section, focus on clarifying and summarizing without interrupting the flow of communication because they don't call for an answer.

### Paraphrasing and Understanding (U)

An understanding and reflecting response indicates that your intent is to understand the sender's thoughts and feelings. In effect, this response asks the sender whether you, the receiver, have understood what the sender is saying and how she is feeling. . . . There are three situations in which you will want to use the understanding response. The first is when you

are not sure you have understood the sender's thoughts and feelings. Paraphrasing can begin a clarifying and summarizing process that increases the accuracy of understanding. The second is when you wish to ensure that the sender hears what he has just said. This reflection of thoughts and feelings often gives the sender a clearer understanding of himself and of the implications of his present feelings and thinking. Finally, paraphrasing reassures the sender that you are trying to understand his thoughts and feelings.

In order to be truly understanding, you may have to go beyond the words of the sender to the feelings and underlying meanings that accompany the words. It is the true meaning of the statement and the sender's feelings that you paraphrase.

## Helping People Solve Their Problems

There are many times when a friend or acquaintance will wish to discuss a problem or concern with you. People do not often get very far in understanding their experiences and deciding how to solve their problems unless they talk things over with someone else. There is nothing more helpful than discussing a problem with a friend who is an effective listener. The first rule in helping other people solve their problems and understand distressing situations is to remember that all insights, understandings, decisions, and solutions occur within the other people, not within you. No matter how convinced you are that you know what the other people should do, your goal in helping must be to assist them in reaching their own decisions and forming their own insights.

The second rule in helping others solve their problems is to differentiate between an internal frame of reference (how the other person sees and feels about the situation) and an external frame of reference (how you see and feel about the other person's situation). You are able to give help to the extent that you understand and respond to the sender's frame of reference rather than imposing your frame of reference on the problem situation. It is not what makes you angry that is important, it is what makes the other person angry. It is not how you see things that matters, it is how the other person sees things. Your ability to be helpful to another person is related directly to your ability to view the situation from the other person's perspective.

Listening and responding in ways that help you understand the other person's perspective or frame of reference is always a tentative process. Many times the other person will not fully understand or be able to communicate effectively her perspective. While you are clarifying your own understanding of the other person's perspective, you will also be helping the other person understand herself better.

## Listening and Responding Alternatives

The exercise on listening and responding alternatives is based on the work of Carl Rogers, a noted psychologist. Several years ago he conducted a series of studies on how individuals communicate with each other in face-to-face situations. He found that the categories of evaluative, interpretative, supportive, probing, and understanding statements encompass 80 percent of all the messages sent between individuals. The other 20 percent of the statements are incidental and of no real importance. From his observations of individuals in all sorts of different settings—businessmen, housewives, people at parties and conventions, and so on—he found that the responses were used by individuals in the following frequency: (1) evaluative was most used, (2) interpretative was next, (3) supportive was the third most common response, (4) probing the fourth, and (5) understanding the least. Finally, he found that if a person uses one category of response as much as 40 percent of the time, then other people see him as *always* responding that way. This is a process of oversimplification similar to stereotyping.

The categories of response are in themselves neither good nor bad. It is the overuse or underuse of any of the categories that may not be functional or the failure to recognize when each type of response is appropriate that interferes with helping the sender and

building a better friendship. If, [in analyzing your own listening behavior], you use only one or two of the responses, it may be that you overuse some types of responses while you underuse others. You can easily remedy that by becoming more aware of your responses and working to become proficient in using all five types of responses when they seem appropriate.

When is each response appropriate? From your own experience and from listening to the discussion of your group, you may have some good ideas. In terms of what is appropriate in the early stage of forming a friendship, two of the possible responses to be most sensitive to are the understanding and the evaluative responses. Basically, the understanding response revolves around the notion that when an individual expresses a message and that message is paraphrased in fresh words with no change of its essential meaning, the sender will expand upon or further explore the ideas, feelings, and attitudes contained in the message and achieve a recognition of previously denied meanings or feelings or move on to express a new message that is more meaningful to him. Even when the receiver has misunderstood and communicated a faulty understanding of the sender's ideas and feelings, the sender will respond in ways that will clarify the receiver's incorrect response, thus increasing the accuracy and clarity of communication between the two individuals.

It is the understanding response that is most likely to communicate to the sender that the listener is interested in the sender as a person and has an accurate understanding of the sender and of what he is saying, and it is this same response that most encourages the sender to go on and elaborate and further explore his problem. The understanding response may also be the most helpful for enabling the receiver to see the sender's problem from the sender's point of view. Many relationships or conversations are best begun by using the understanding response until a trust level is established; then the other categories of response can be more freely used. The procedures for engaging in the understanding response are rather simple . . . and anyone who takes the time and effort can become quite skillful in their use.

. . . [T]he major barrier to mutual understanding is the very natural tendency to judge, evaluate, approve, or disapprove of the messages of the sender. For this reason you should usually avoid giving evaluative responses in the early stages of a relationship or of a conversation about the sender's problems. The primary reaction to a value judgment is another value judgment (for example, "You say I'm wrong, but I think I'm right and you're wrong"), with each person looking at the issue only from his own point of view. This tendency to make evaluations is very much heightened in situations in which feelings and emotions are deeply involved, as when you are discussing a personal problem. Defensiveness and feelings of being threatened are avoided when the listener responds with understanding rather than with evaluative responses. Evaluative responses, however, may be helpful when you are specifically asked to make a value judgment or when you wish to disclose your own values and attitudes.

There will be times when another person tries to discuss an issue with you that you do not understand. *Probing responses* will help you get a clear definition of the problem before you respond. They may also be helpful if you do not think the sender is seeing the full implications of some of her statements. *Supportive responses* are useful when the person needs to feel accepted or when she needs enough support to try to engage in behavior aimed at solving her problem. Finally, *interpretive responses* are sometimes useful in confronting another person with the effect of her behavior on you. . . . Interpretation, if carried out with skill, integrity, and empathy, can be a powerful stimulus to growth. Interpretation leads to insight, and insight is a key to better psychological living. Interpretation is one form of confrontation. . . .

## Phrasing an Accurate Understanding Response

The second important aspect of listening with understanding is the phrasing you use to paraphrase the message of the sender. The phrasing of the response may vary in the following ways:

1. *Content.* Content refers to the actual words used. Interestingly enough, responses that are essentially repetitions of the sender's statements do not communicate the receiver's understanding to the sender. It seems that repeating a person's words actually gets in the way of communicating an understanding of the essential meaning of the statement. It is more effective if the receiver paraphrases the sender's message in the receiver's own words and expressions.

2. *Depth.* Depth refers to the degree to which the receiver matches the depth of the sender's message in his response. You should not respond lightly to a serious statement, and correspondingly, you should not respond seriously to a shallow statement. In general, responses that match the sender's depth of feeling or that lead the sender on to a slightly greater depth of feeling are most effective.

3. *Meaning.* In the receiver's efforts to paraphrase the sender's statements, he may find himself either adding meaning or omitting meaning. Some of the obvious ways in which meaning can be added are (1) completing a sentence or thought for the sender, (2) responding to ideas the sender has used for illustrative purposes only, and (3) interpreting the significance of a message. Perhaps the most obvious way meaning can be omitted is by responding only to the last thing the sender said.

4. *Language.* The receiver should keep the language he uses in his response simple in order to ensure accurate communication.

## Questions

1. Think about the last time you had a problem that you tried to discuss with someone to gain some help, but they simply were no help whatsoever. What made their efforts to help ineffective? What could they have changed in their

style that would have been more help-ful for you?

2. Select the response style that you find most difficult to implement, and indicate why you believe this is the case. What keeps you from being effective at that style?

3. Interview someone whose career involves high-level listening skills. Ask that person to describe his or her listening style, the conscious choices he or she makes while listening at work, and how this person has improved his or her listening skills over time.

---

# 7

# Elements of Nonverbal Communication

*Mark L. Knapp and Judith A. Hall*

**A**lbert Mehrabian (1972), a psychologist working in the area of nonverbal communication, claims that 93 percent of the emotional impact of a message comes from a nonverbal source. Anthropologist Roy Birdwhistell (1970) describes a 65–35 percent split between nonverbal and verbal. Thus, the nonverbal portion of any message is extremely important. Although scholars have disputed the exact percentages, there is overall agreement that nonverbal messages are critical to conveying meaning accurately.

Nonverbal communication has multiple functions. It can repeat the verbal message (a wave while saying "goodbye"), substitute for the verbal (a silent wave goodbye), regulate the verbal (a vocal intonation), or complement and accent the nonverbal (a finger circling the ear to signal that "he's crazy"). It is primarily the nonverbal message that contains the relational portion of the message. For example, a woman tells her husband, "We need to talk," and the husband says, "Okay," but continues to e-mail a friend. In other words, the nonverbal message contradicts the verbal message and carries the moment. It is important to note that in general, when the nonverbal message contradicts the verbal, people tend to put great emphasis on what is done rather than what is said.

What are the differences between verbal and nonverbal messages? Verbal messages use a single channel—you cannot say two words simultaneously. Nonverbal messages do not arrive in a sequential manner. Rather, they bombard you simultaneously through a variety of channels. You observe people's facial expressions, how they are dressed, and their gestures as you hear their vocal intonation and quality. Verbal messages are discrete—they have clear beginnings and endings. Unlike the spoken word, nonverbal messages are continuous. While you usually think about what you are going to say, most nonverbal messages are not deliberate. They are often unconscious. For example, although you might smile because you want to appear happy, your slumped shoulders might "give it away." There are just too many nonverbal channels to be able to think about and control all of them. Finally, verbal and nonverbal messages differ in their degree of ambiguity. In general, nonverbal messages are more ambiguous. What does it mean when the teacher smiles at your answer in class? Is the smile a signal of approval, or is your answer wrong but amusing? The best way to find out is to ask for verbal clarification.

In the article that follows, Knapp and Hall describe the three primary types of nonverbal communication that provide a continuous flow of messages. They stress the importance of physical context as well as the physical characteristics of communicators and their behaviors. Finally, they elaborate on how each of these types of nonverbals can contradict, repeat, substitute for, regulate, and complement the verbal messages. In addition, remember that nonverbal messages vary across cultures, so crossed fingers in one culture may have a very different meaning in another one. As you read this chapter, ask yourself the following questions: Am I satisfied with my skills at interpreting others' nonverbal messages? If not, how can I begin to improve my competence?

### References

Birdwhistell, R. (1970). *Kinesics and Context*. Philadelphia: University of Pennsylvania Press.

Mehrabian, A. (1972). *Nonverbal Communication*. Chicago: Aldine-Atherton.

* * *

## Classifying Nonverbal Behavior

. . . $\mathrm{T}$he theory and research associated with nonverbal communication focus on three primary units: the environmental structures and conditions within which

61

communication takes place, the physical characteristics of the communicators themselves, and the various behaviors manifested by the communicators. A detailed breakdown of these three features follows.

## The Communication Environment

### Physical Environment

Although most of the emphasis in nonverbal research is on the appearance and behavior of the persons communicating, increasing attention is being given to the influence of nonhuman factors on human transactions. People change environments to help them accomplish their communicative goals; conversely, environments can affect our moods, choices of words, and actions. Thus this category concerns those elements that impinge on the human relationship but are not directly a part of it. Environmental factors include the furniture, architectural style, interior decorating, lighting conditions, colors, temperature, additional noises or music, and the like, amid which the interaction occurs. Variations in arrangements, materials, shapes, or surfaces of objects in the interacting environment can be extremely influential on the outcome of an interpersonal relationship. This category also includes what might be called *traces of action*. For instance, as you observe cigarette butts, orange peels, and wastepaper left by the person you will soon interact with, you form an impression that will eventually influence your meeting. Perceptions of time and timing comprise another important part of the communicative environment. When something occurs, how frequently it occurs, and the tempo or rhythm of actions are clearly a part of the communicative world even though they are not a part of the physical environment per se.

### Spatial Environment

*Proxemics* is the study of the use and perception of social and personal space. Under this heading is a body of work called *small group ecology*, which concerns itself with how people use and respond to spatial relationships in formal and informal group settings. Such studies deal with seating and spatial arrangements as related to leadership, communication flow, and the task at hand. On an even broader level, some attention has been given to spatial relationships in crowds and densely populated situations. Personal space orientation is sometimes studied in the context of conversation distance and how it varies according to sex, status, roles, cultural orientation, and so forth. The term *territoriality* is also used frequently in the study of proxemics to denote the human tendency to stake out personal territory (or untouchable space) much as wild animals and birds do.

## The Communicators' Physical Characteristics

This category covers things that remain relatively unchanged during the period of interaction. They are influential nonverbal cues that are not visibly movement bound. Included are physique or body shape, general attractiveness, height, weight, hair, skin color or tone, and so forth. Odors (body or breath) associated with the person are normally considered part of a person's physical appearance. Further, objects associated with the interactants also may affect their physical appearance. These are called *artifacts* and include things such as clothes, lipstick, eyeglasses, wigs and other hairpieces, false eyelashes, jewelry, and accessories such as attaché cases.

## Body Movement and Position

Body movement and position typically includes gestures, movements of the body (limbs, hands, head, feet, and legs), facial expressions (smiles), eye behavior (blinking, direction and length of gaze, and pupil dilation), and posture. The furrow of the brow, the slump of a shoulder, and the tilt of a head are all considered body movements and positions. Specifically, the major areas are gestures, posture, touching behavior, facial expressions, and eye behavior.

### Gesture

There are many different types of gestures (and variations of these types), but the most frequently studied are the following:

***Speech independent***. These gestures are not tied to speech, but they have a direct verbal translation or dictionary definition, usually consisting of a word or two or a phrase. There is high agreement among members of a culture or subculture on the verbal "translation" of these signals. The gesture used to represent "A-OK" or "Peace" (also known as the "V-for-Victory" sign) are examples of speech-independent gestures for large segments of the U.S. culture.

***Speech related***. These gestures are directly tied to, or accompany, speech—often serving to illustrate what is being said verbally. These movements may accent or emphasize a word or phrase, sketch a path of thought, point to present objects, depict a spatial relationship, depict the rhythm or pacing of an event, draw a picture of a referent, depict a bodily action, or serve as commentary on the regulation and organization of the interactive process.

## Posture

Posture is normally studied in conjunction with other nonverbal signals to determine the degree of attention or involvement, the degree of status relative to the other interactive partner, or the degree of liking for the other interactant. A forward-leaning posture, for example, has been associated with higher involvement, more liking, and lower status in studies where the interactants did not know each other very well. Posture is also a key indicator of the intensity of some emotional states, for example, the drooping posture associated with sadness or the rigid, tense posture associated with anger. The extent to which the communicators mirror each other's posture may also reflect rapport or an attempt to build rapport.

## Touching Behavior

Touching may be self-focused or other focused. Self-focused manipulations, not usually made for purposes of communicating, may reflect a person's particular state or a habit. Many are commonly called *nervous mannerisms*. Some of these actions are relics from an earlier time in life—times when we were first learning how to manage our emotions, develop social contacts, or perform some instructional task. Sometimes we perform these manipulations as we adapt to such learning experiences, and they stay with us when we face similar situations later in life, often as only part of the original movement. Some refer to these types of self-focused manipulation as *adaptors*. These adaptors may involve various manipulations of one's own body such as licking, picking, holding, pinching, and scratching. Object adaptors are manipulations practiced in conjunction with an object, as when a reformed male cigarette smoker reaches toward his breast pocket for the nonexistent package of cigarettes. Of course, not all behaviors that reflect habitual actions or an anxious disposition can be traced to earlier adaptations, but they do represent a part of the overall pattern of bodily action.

One of the most potent forms of nonverbal communication occurs when two people touch. Touch can be virtually electric, but it also can irritate, condescend, or comfort. Touch is a highly ambiguous form of behavior whose meaning often takes more from the context, the nature of the relationship, and the manner of execution than from the configuration of the touch per se. Some researchers are concerned with touching behavior as an important factor in the child's early development; some are concerned with adult touching behavior. Subcategories include stroking, hitting, greetings and farewells, holding, and guiding another's movements.

## Facial Expressions

Most studies of the face are concerned with the configurations that display various emotional states. The six primary affects receiving the most study are anger, sadness, surprise, happiness, fear, and disgust. Facial expressions also can function as regulatory gestures, providing feedback and managing the flow of interaction. In fact, some researchers believe the primary function of the face is to communicate, not to express emotions.

## Eye Behavior

Where we look, when we look, and how long we look during interaction are the primary foci for studies of gazing. *Gaze* refers to the eye movement we make in the general direction of another's face. *Mutual gaze* occurs when interactants look into each other's eyes. The dilation and constriction of our pupils also has interest to those who study nonverbal communication because it is sometimes an indicator of interest, attention, or involvement.

### Vocal Behavior

Vocal behavior deals with *how* something is said, not what is said. It deals with the range of nonverbal vocal cues surrounding common speech behavior. Generally, a distinction is made between two types of sounds:

1. The sound variations made with the vocal cords during talk that are a function of changes in pitch, duration, loudness, and silence.

2. Sounds that result from physiological mechanisms other than the vocal cords, for example, the pharyngeal, oral, or nasal cavities.

Most of the research on vocal behavior and its effects on human interaction has focused on the pitch level and variability; the duration of sounds (clipped or drawn out); pauses within the speech stream and the latency of response during turn exchanges; loudness level and variability; resonance; precise or slurred articulation; rate; rhythm; and intruding sound during speech such as "uh" or "um." The study of vocal signals encompasses a broad range of interests, from questions focusing on stereotypes associated with certain voices to questions about the effects of vocal behavior on comprehension and persuasion. Thus even specialized sounds such as laughing, belching, yawning, swallowing, moaning, and the like, may be of interest to the extent that they may affect the outcome of interaction.

## Nonverbal Communication in the Total Communication Process

Even though this [chapter] emphasizes nonverbal communication, don't forget the inseparable nature of verbal and nonverbal signals. Ray Birdwhistell, a pioneer in nonverbal research, reportedly said that studying only *nonverbal* communication is like studying *noncardiac* physiology. His point is

well taken. It is not easy to dissect human interaction and make one diagnosis that concerns only verbal behavior and another that concerns only nonverbal behavior. The verbal dimension is so intimately woven and subtly represented in so much of what has been previously labeled *non*verbal that the term does not always adequately describe the behavior under study. Some of the most noteworthy scholars associated with nonverbal study refuse to segregate words from gestures and hence work under the broader terms of *communication* or *face-to-face interaction* (McNeill, 2000). Kendon (1983, pp. 17, 20) puts it this way:

> It is a common observation that, when a person speaks, muscular systems besides those of the lips, tongue, and jaws often become active. . . . Gesticulation is organized as part of the same overall unit of action by which speech is also organized. . . . Gesture and speech are available as two separate modes of representation and are coordinated because both are being guided by the same overall aim. That aim is to produce a pattern of action that will accomplish the representation of a meaning.

Because verbal and nonverbal systems operate together as part of the larger communication process, efforts to distinguish clearly between the two have not been very successful. One common misconception, for example, assumes nonverbal behavior is used solely to communicate emotional messages, whereas verbal behavior is for conveying ideas. Words can carry much emotion—we can talk explicitly about emotions, and we also communicate emotion between the lines in verbal nuances. Conversely, nonverbal cues are often used for purposes other than showing emotion; as examples, people in conversation use eye movements to help tell each other when it is time to switch speaking turns, and people commonly use hand gestures while talking to help convey their ideas (McNeill, 2000).

Argyle (1988) has identified the following primary functions of nonverbal behavior in human communication as follows:

1. Expressing emotion.

2. Conveying interpersonal attitudes (like/dislike, dominance/submission, etc.).

3. Presenting one's personality to others.

4. Accompanying speech for the purposes of managing turn taking, feedback, attention, and so on.

Argyle also notes that nonverbal behaviors are important in many rituals, such as greeting. Notice that none of these functions of nonverbal behavior is limited to nonverbal behavior alone; that is, we can express emotions and attitudes, present ourselves in a particular light, and manage the interaction using verbal cues, too. This does not suggest, however, that in any given situation we might not rely more heavily on verbal behavior for some purposes and on nonverbal for others.

We also need to recognize that the ways we attribute meanings to verbal and nonverbal behavior are not all that different either. Nonverbal actions, like verbal ones, may communicate more than one message at a time—for example, the way you nonverbally make it clear to another person that you want to keep talking may simultaneously express your need for dominance over that person and, perhaps, your emotional state. When you grip a child's shoulder during a reprimand, you may increase comprehension and recall, but you may also elicit such a negative reaction that the child fails to obey. A smile can be a part of an emotional expression, an attitudinal message, part of a self-presentation, or a listener response to manage the interaction. And, like verbal behavior, the meanings attributed to nonverbal behavior may be stereotyped, idiomatic, or ambiguous. Furthermore, the same nonverbal behavior performed in different contexts may, like words, receive different attributions of meaning. For example, looking down at the floor may reflect sadness in one situation and submissiveness or lack of involvement in another. Finally, in an effort to identify the fundamental categories of meaning associated with nonverbal behavior, Mehrabian (1970, 1981) identified a threefold perspective resulting from his extensive testing:

1. **Immediacy**. Sometimes we react to things by evaluating them—positive or negative, good or bad, like or dislike.

2. **Status**. Sometimes we enact or perceive behaviors that indicate various aspects of status to us—strong or weak, superior or subordinate.

3. **Responsiveness**. This third category refers to our perceptions of activity—slow or fast, active or passive.

In various verbal and nonverbal studies over the past three decades, dimensions similar to Mehrabian's have been reported consistently by investigators from diverse fields studying diverse phenomena. It is reasonable to conclude, therefore, that these three dimensions are basic responses to our environment and are reflected in the way we assign meaning to both verbal and nonverbal behavior. Most of this work, however, depends on subjects translating their reactions to a nonverbal act into one identified by verbal descriptors. This issue has already been addressed in our discussion of the way the brain processes different pieces of information. In general, then, nonverbal signals, like words, can and do have multiple uses and meanings; like words, nonverbal signals have denotative and connotative meanings; and like words, nonverbal signals play an active role in communicating liking, power, and responsiveness. With these in mind, we can now examine some of the important ways verbal and nonverbal behavior interrelate during human interaction. Ekman (1965) identified the following: repeating, contradicting, complementing, substituting, accenting/moderating, and regulating.

### Repeating

Nonverbal communication can simply repeat what was said verbally. For instance, if you told a person he or she had to go north to find a newspaper stand and then pointed in the proper direction, this would be considered repetition.

### Conflicting

Verbal and nonverbal signals can be at variance with one another in a variety of ways. They may communicate two contradictory messages or two messages that seem incongruous or in conflict with one another. In both instances two messages that do not appear to be consistent with one another are perceived. It is quite common (and probably functional) to have mixed feelings about some things. As a result, incongruous verbal and nonverbal messages may be more common than we realize. But it is the more dramatic contradictions we are more likely to notice. Perhaps it is the parent who yells to his or her child in an angry voice, "Of course I love you!" Or the public speaker, who, with trembling hands and knees and beads of perspiration on the brow, claims, "I'm not nervous."

Why do these conflicting messages occur? In some cases it is a natural response to a situation in which communicators perceive themselves in a bind. They do not want to tell the truth, and they do not want to lie. As a result, their ambivalence and frustration produce a discrepant message (Bavelas et al., 1990). Suppose you have just given a terrible presentation, and you ask me how you did. I may say you did fine, but my voice, face, and body may not support my words. In other situations, conflicting messages occur because people do an imperfect job of lying. On still other occasions, conflicting messages may be the result of an attempt to communicate sarcasm or irony, saying one thing with words and the opposite with vocal tone and/or facial expression. The term *coy* is used to describe the display of coexisting signals that invite friendly contact with those that signal rejection and withdrawal. We live in a complex world that makes feelings of ambivalence or mixed emotions a much more common experience in everyday life than we sometimes acknowledge (Weigert, 1991).

These displays of incongruous or conflicting signals may occur in a variety of ways. Sometimes two nonverbal signals may manifest the discord (e.g., vocal with visual), but verbal and nonverbal signals can combine in several ways: positive voice/negative words, negative voice/positive words, positive face/negative words, negative face/positive words.

When confronted with conflicting verbal and nonverbal messages that matter to us, how do we react? Leathers (1979) has identified a common three-step process:

1. The first reaction is confusion and uncertainty.

2. Next, we search for additional information that will clarify the situation.

3. If clarification is not forthcoming, we will probably react with displeasure, hostility, or even withdrawal.

Responses to conflicting messages are often ambiguous themselves. Some believe a constant barrage of inconsistent messages can contribute to a psychopathology for the receiver. This may be particularly true when people have a close relationship and the receiver has no other people he or she can turn to for discussion and possible clarification of the confusion. Some research finds that parents of disturbed children produce more messages with conflicting cues (Bugental, Love, Kaswan, & April, 1971). Other work suggests that the differences are not in conflicting cues but in negative messages; that is, parents with disturbed children send more negative messages (Beakel & Mehrabian, 1969). The combination of negativity, confusion, and punishment can be very harmful if it is a common style of communication directed toward children. Date rape is another situation in which testimony often centers around the extent to which the signals of rejection were unequivocal.

We do not wish to give the impression that all forms of discrepancy are harmful. Our daily conversations are probably peppered with instances where gestures and speech do not exactly match one another—for example, a speaker telling a story about someone climbing up a pipe while simultaneously gesturing like he or she was climbing a ladder (McNeill, Cassell, & McCullough, 1994). Sometimes these discrepancies go unnoticed, and many are cognitively "resolved" without overtly discussing the mismatch. Even contradictions with more important implications for the conversants may not, in some situations, be considered very harmful. Moreover, as stated earlier, discrepancy is *required* for achieving certain effects: Sarcasm occurs when the words are pleasant and the voice quality is unpleasant; when the words are unpleasant but the tone of voice is pleasant, we are likely to communicate the message "just joking."

Finally, some discrepancies may be helpful in certain situations. In an experiment, teachers used mixed messages while teaching a lesson to sixth-grade pupils. When the teachers combined positive words with a negative nonverbal demeanor, pupils learned more than with any other combination (Woolfolk, 1978). Similarly, a study of doctors talking with patients found that the combination of positive words said in a negative voice tone was associated with the highest levels of patient satisfaction with the visit (Hall, Roter, & Rand, 1981). Possibly the positive verbal/negative nonverbal combination is perceived in classrooms and doctors' offices as serious and concerned and, therefore, makes a better impression.

Some research has questioned whether we trust and believe nonverbal signals more than verbal when we are confronted with conflicting messages (Bugental, 1974; Mehrabian, 1972; Stiff, Hale, Garlick, & Rogan, 1990). Burgoon (1980, p. 184), after surveying numerous studies in this area, concluded, "the nonverbal channels carry more information and are believed more than the verbal band, and . . . visual cues generally carry more weight than vocal ones."

Burgoon goes on to discuss some important reservations about this general conclusion. It is often assumed that nonverbal signals are more spontaneous, harder to fake, and less likely to be manipulated—hence, more believable. It is probably more accurate to say, however, that some nonverbal behaviors are more spontaneous and harder to fake than others and that some people are more proficient than others at nonverbal deception. With two conflicting cues (both of which are nonverbal) we predictably place our reliance on the cues we consider harder to fake. One research team found that people tended to rely primarily on visual cues in visual/auditory discrepancies, but when the discrepancy was great, people tended to rely on the audio signals (DePaulo, Rosenthal, Eisenstat, Rogers, & Finkelstein, 1978).

Credibility of the information presented is also an important factor in determining which cues to believe most in inconsistent messages. If the information being communicated in one channel lacks credibility, we are likely to discount it and look to other channels for the "real" message (Bugental, 1974). Sometimes we are faced with the difficult dilemma of perceiving the meaning communicated by hard-to-fake cues that do not seem credible. If a person says, "This is really great" with a sad tone of voice upon receiving a gift you know was long desired, you are likely to search for other explanations—for example, something else may be bothering the person.

Interestingly, young children seem to give less credence to certain nonverbal cues than adults do when confronted with conflicting verbal and nonverbal messages (Bugental, Kaswan, Love, & Fox, 1970; Bugental, Love, & Gianetto, 1971; Volkmar & Siegel, 1982). Conflicting messages in which the speaker smiled while making a critical statement were interpreted more negatively by children than adults, particularly when the speaker was a woman.

Other work casts a further shadow on the "reliance on nonverbal cues in conflicting message situations" theory. Shapiro (1968) found that student judges differed as to whether they relied on linguistic or facial cues when asked to select the affect being communicated by incongruent sketched faces and written messages and to be consistent in their choices. Vande Creek and Watkins (1972) extended Shapiro's work by using real voices and moving pictures. The stimulus persons were portraying inconsistencies in the degree of stress in verbal and nonverbal channels. Again, they found some respondents tended to rely primarily on verbal cues, some tended to rely on nonverbal cues, and some responded to the degree of stress in general regardless of the channels manifesting it. The cross-cultural research of Solomon and Ali (1975) suggests that familiarity with the verbal language may affect our reliance on verbal or nonverbal cues. They found, for instance, that persons who were not as familiar with the language used to construct the contradictory message relied on the content for judgments of affective meaning. Those who knew the language well were more apt to rely on the vocal intonation for the affective meaning. So it appears some people rely more heavily on the verbal message, whereas others rely on the nonverbal.

We do not know all the conditions that affect which signals people look to for valid information. As a general rule, people tend to rely on those signals they perceive harder to fake, but this will most likely vary with the situation; so the ultimate impact of verbal, visual, and vocal signals is best determined by a close examination of the people involved and the communication context.

## Complementing

Nonverbal behavior can modify, or elaborate on, verbal messages. When the verbal and nonverbal channels are complementary, rather than conflicting, our messages are usually decoded more accurately. Some evidence suggests that complementary nonverbal signals also may be helpful in remembering the verbal message. A student who reflects an attitude of embarrassment when talking to a professor about a poor performance in class assignments is exhibiting nonverbal behavior that complements the verbal. When clarity is of utmost importance (as in a job interview or when making up with a loved one after a fight), we should be especially concerned with making the meanings of verbal and nonverbal behavior complement one another.

## Substituting

Nonverbal behavior can substitute for verbal messages. It may indicate more permanent characteristics (sex, age), moderately long-lasting features (personality, attitudes, social group), and relatively short-term states. In the latter case, we may find a dejected and downtrodden executive (or janitor) walk into his or her house after work with a facial expression that substitutes for the statement, "I've had a rotten day." With a little practice, people soon learn to identify a wide range of these substitute nonverbal displays—all the way from "It's been a fantastic, great day!" to "Oh, God, am I miserable!" We do not need to ask for verbal confirmation of our perception.

Sometimes, when substitute nonverbal behavior fails, the communicator resorts to the verbal level. Consider the woman who wants her date to stop trying to become physically intimate with her. She may stiffen, stare straight ahead, act unresponsive and cool. If the suitor still does not stop, she might say something like, "Look, Larry, please don't ruin a nice friendship."

## Accenting/Moderating

Nonverbal behavior may accent (amplify) or moderate (tone down) parts of the verbal message. Accenting is much like underlining or *italicizing* written words to emphasize them. Movements of the head and hands are frequently used to accent the verbal message. When a father scolds his son about staying out too late, he may accent a particular phrase with a firm grip on the son's shoulder and an accompanying frown. In some instances, one set of nonverbal cues can accent or moderate other nonverbal cues. The intensity of a facial expression of emotion, for example, may be revealed by observing other parts of the body.

## Regulating

Nonverbal behavior is also used to regulate the verbal behavior. We do this in two ways:

1. Coordinating our own verbal and nonverbal behavior in the production of our messages

2. Coordinating our verbal and nonverbal messages behavior with those of our interaction partner(s)

We regulate the production of our own messages in a variety of ways. Sometimes we use nonverbal signs to segment units of interaction. Posture changes may demarcate a topic change; a gesture may forecast the verbalization of a particular idea; pauses may help in organizing spoken information into units. When we speak of a series of things, we may communicate discreteness by linear, staccato movements of the arm and hand; for example, "We must consider A, B, and C." When we insert one of these chopping gestures after each letter, it may suggest a separate consideration of each letter; a single chop after C might indicate either a consideration of all three (as a group) or just C in particular.

We also regulate the flow of verbal and nonverbal behavior between ourself and an interactant. This may manifest itself in the type of behavior two interactants elicit from one another (e.g., every time one person gets mad and yells, the other behaves in a solicitous manner) or in less obvious ways (e.g., the signals of initiation, continuation, and termination of interaction). The way one person stops talking and another starts in a smooth, synchronized manner may be as important to a satisfactory interaction as the content. After all, we do make judgments about people based on their regulatory skills (for example, "Talking to him is like talking to a wall" or "You can't get a word in edgewise with her"). When another person frequently interrupts or is inattentive, we may feel this person is making a statement about the relationship, perhaps one of disrespect. There are rules for regulating conversations, but they are generally implicit. It is not written down, but we seem to know that two people should not talk at the same time, that each person should get an equal number of turns at talking if he or she desires, that a question should be answered, and so forth. Wiemann's (1977) research found that relatively minute changes in these regulatory behaviors (interruptions, pauses longer than 3 seconds, unilateral topic changes, etc.) resulted in sizeable variations in how competent a communicator was perceived to be. As listeners, we are apparently attending to and evaluating a host of fleeting, subtle, and habitual features of another's conversational behavior. There are probably differences in the actual behaviors used to manage conversational flow across cultures. As children are first learning these rules, they use less subtle cues, for example, tugging on clothing, raising a hand, and the like. Children are also less skilled in accomplishing smooth turn taking, as you will have noticed if you have conversed with a young child on the telephone.

Conversational regulators involve several kinds of nonverbal cues. When we want to indicate we are finished speaking and the other person can start, we may increase our eye contact with the other person. This is often accompanied by the vocal cues associated with ending declarative or interrogative statements. If the other person still does not figuratively pick up the conversational ball, we

might extend silence or interject a "trailer," for example, "you know . . ." or "so, ah . . ." Keeping another from speaking in a conversation means we have to keep long pauses from occurring, decrease eye contact, and perhaps raise the volume if the other tries to speak. When we do not want to take a speaking turn, we might give the other some reinforcing head nods, maintain attentive eye contact, and, of course, refrain from speaking when the other begins to yield. When we do want the floor, we might raise our index finger or enact an audible inspiration of breath with a straightening of the posture as if ready to take over. Rapid nodding may signal the other to hurry up and finish, but, if we have trouble getting in, we may have to talk simultaneously for a few words or engage in stutter starts that, we hope, will be more easily observed cues to signal our desire.

Conversational beginnings and endings also act as regulatory points. When we are greeting others, eye contact indicates that the channels are open. A slight head movement and an *eyebrow flash* of recognition (a barely detectable but distinct up-and-down movement of the eyebrows) may be present. The hands are also used in greetings for salutes, waves, handshakes, handslaps, emblematic signals such as the peace or victory sign, a raised fist, or thumbs-up. Hands may also perform grooming activities (running fingers through one's hair) or be involved in various touching activities such as kissing, embracing, or hitting another on the arm. The mouth may form a smile or an oval shape, as if one were ready to start talking (Krivonos & Knapp, 1975).

Saying good-bye in semiformal interviews was shown, in one study, to elicit many nonverbal behaviors. The most common included the breaking of eye contact more often and for longer periods of time, positioning one's body toward an exit, leaning forward and nodding. Less frequent, but very noticeable, were accenting behaviors that signaled, "This is the termination of our conversation, and I don't want you to miss it!" These accentors included explosive hand and foot movements such as raising the hands and/or feet and bringing them down with enough force to make an audible slap while simultaneously using the hands and feet as leverage to catapult the interactant out of his or her seat. A less direct manifestation was placing hands on thighs or knees in a leveraging position (as if one was preparing to catapult), hoping that the other person picked up the good-bye cue (Knapp, Hart, Friedrich, & Shulman, 1975).

## References

Argyle, M. (1988). *Bodily communication* (2nd ed.). London: Methuen.

Bavelas, J. B., Black, A., Chovil, N., & Mullett. J. (1990). *Equivocal communication*. Newbury Park, CA: Sage.

Beakel, N. G., & Mehrabian, A. (1969). Inconsistent communications and psychopathology. *Journal of Abnormal Psychology*, 74, 126–130.

Bugental, D. E. (1974). Interpretations of naturally occurring discrepancies between words and intonation: Modes of inconsistency resolution. *Journal of Personality and Social Psychology*, 30, 125–133.

Bugental, D. E., Kaswan, J. W., Love, L. R., & Fox, M. N. (1970). Child versus adult perception of evaluative messages in verbal, vocal, and visual channels. *Develelopmental Psychology*, 2, 367–375.

Bugental, D. E., Love, L. R., & Gianetto, R. M. (1971). Perfidious feminine faces. *Journal of Personality and Social Psychology*, 17, 314–318.

Bugental, D. E., Love, L. R., Kaswan, J. W., & April, C. (1971). Verbal-nonverbal conflict in parental messages to normal and disturbed children. *Journal of Abnormal Psychology*, 77, 6–10.

Burgoon, J. K. (1980). Nonverbal communication research in the 1970s: An overview. In D. Nimmo (Ed.), *Communication yearbook 4*. New Brunswick, NJ: Transaction.

DePaulo, B. M., Rosenthal, R., Eisenstat, R., Rogers, P. L., & Finkelstein, S. (1978). Decoding discrepant nonverbal cues. *Journal of Personality and Social Psychology*, 36, 313–323.

Ekman, P. (1965). Communication through noverbal behavior: A source of information about an interpersonal relationship. In S. S. Tomkins & C. E. Izard (Eds.), *Affect, cognition, and personality*. New York: Springer.

Hall, J. A., Roter, D. L., & Rand, C. S. (1981). Communication of affect between patient and physician. *Journal of Health and Social Behavior*, 22, 18–30.

Kendon, A. (1983). Gesture and speech: How they interact. In J. M. Wiemann & R. P. Harrison (Eds.), *Nonverbal interaction*. Beverly Hills, CA: Sage.

Knapp, M. L., Hart, R. P., Friedrich, G. W., & Shulman, G. M. (1975). The rhetoric of goodbye: Verbal and nonverbal correlates of human leave-taking. *Speech Monographs*, 40, 182–198.

Krivonos, P. D., & Knapp, M. L. (1975). Initiating communication: What do you say when you say hello? *Central States Speech Journal*, 26, 115–125.

Leathers, D. G. (1979). The impact of multichannel message inconsistency on verbal and nonverbal decoding behaviors. *Communication Monographs*, 46, 88–100.

McNeill, D. (Ed.). (2000). *Language and gesture*. New York: Cambridge University Press.

McNeill, D., Cassell, J., & McCullough, K. E. (1994). Communicative effects of speech-mismatched gestures. *Research on Language and Social Interaction*, 27, 223–237.

Mehrabian, A. (1970). A semantic space for nonverbal behavior. *Journal of Consulting and Clinical Psychology*, 35, 248–257.

———. (1981). *Silent messages*, 2nd ed. Belmont, CA: Wadsworth.

———. (1972). Inconsistent messages and sarcasm. In A. Mehrabian (Ed.), *Nonverbal communication*. Chicago: Aldine-Atherton.

Shapiro, J. G. (1968). Responsivity to facial and linguistic cues. *Journal of Communication*, 18, 11–17.

Solomon, D., & Ali, F. A. (1975). Influence of verbal content and intonation on meaning attributions of first-and-second language speakers. *Journal of Social Psychology*, 95, 3–8.

Stiff, J. B., Hale, J. L., Garlick, R., & Rogan, R. G. (1990). Effect of cue incongruence and social normative influences on individual judgments of honesty and deceit. *Southern Communication Journal*, 55, 206–229.

Vande Creek, L., & Watkins, J. T. (1972). Responses to incongruent verbal and nonverbal emotional cues. *Journal of Communication*, 22, 311–316.

Volkmar, F. R., & Siegel, A. E. (1982). Responses to consistent and discrepant social communications. In R. S. Feldman (Ed.), *Development of nonverbal behavior in children*. New York: Springer-Verlag.

Weigert, A. (1991). Ambivalence as a social reality. In A. J. Weigert (Ed.), *Mixed emotions: Certain steps toward understanding ambivalence* (pp. 33–58). Albany: SUNY Press.

Wiemann, J. M. (1977). Explication and test of a model of communicative competence. *Human Communication Research*, 3, 195–213.

Woolfolk, A. (1978). Student learning and performance under varying conditions of teacher verbal and nonverbal evaluative communication. *Journal of Educational Psychology*, 70, 87–94.

## Questions

1. Interview someone from a culture different from your own to learn how nonverbal codes differ between the two cultures. Together, develop a list of ways you could violate unstated but important rules about nonverbal communication in each of the following categories:

   a. gestures
   b. eye contact
   c. touch
   d. personal space

2. Interview a close friend to find out what nonverbal cues he or she uses to interpret your feelings when you talk. How can that person tell when you are

   a. sad?
   b. angry?
   c. depressed?
   d. happy?

3. In the last week, think of a time when you deliberately relied on nonverbal communication to send a message. Explain what you did and the effect it had on your ability to communicate with others. Did it help? Did it make it more difficult? Did it contradict what you were saying verbally?

Adapted from Mark L. Knapp and Judith A. Hall, "Elements of Nonverbal Communication." In *Nonverbal Communication in Human Interaction*, 5th ed., pp. 7–18. Copyright © 2002 by Wadsworth, an imprint of the Wadsworth Group, a division of Thomson Learning. Fax (800) 730-2215. Reprinted with permission. ✦

# Part III

## *Perceptual Processes and Communication*

# A. Perception and Self-Concept

How many confusing conversations have you experienced in the past week? Why did these communication breakdowns occur? As discussed in Chapter 1, communication involves the negotiation of shared meanings; if meanings are not held in common, confusion and misunderstanding occur.

But how do you gain meaning? Your set of meanings develops through your perceptual processes. *Perception* is the process by which you filter and interpret what your senses tell you in order to create a meaningful picture of the world. The process of perception involves how your mind interacts with the physical and social world. Remember the lenses metaphor: each person has a set of lenses or filters through which he or she views the world. No two people see the world exactly the same, nor do people see absolutely everything differently (see Figure III-1). The degree of shared or common meanings affects how accurately we can communicate with another person (Cooper and Simonds 1999).

Meanings emerge as information passes through your physical and social filter systems. Your physical state and sensory processes, such as sight, hearing, touch, smell, and taste, constitute the first set of filters. Perceptions are also filtered through your so-cial system, including the way you use language and the socially constructed conventions of your society, such as gender, culture, and family experiences.

### Figure III-1
#### How People See the World

| All people see things exactly the same way. | People have shared or in-common meaning. | All people see things differently. |

Your language limits and shapes the ways in which you construct messages and the meanings you are able to interpret. The current pressure to use inclusive language reflects a belief that those persons excluded by some language forms, such as women or minorities, develop less powerful images of themselves arising from their experiences with noninclusive linguistic cues. For example, proponents of nonsexist language believe that the self-perceptions of women are altered positively by the use of inclusive language.

Your sense of yourself affects your perceptions and, therefore, your communication effectiveness. How you communicate depends to a great extent upon how you define yourself (self-concept) and how you evaluate yourself (self-esteem). Your definitions and evaluation emerge from your communication with others. In Figure III-2, Kinch (1963) provides a model of the relationships between self-concept and communication.

### Figure III-2
*Kinch's Model of the Relationship Between Self-Concept and Communication*

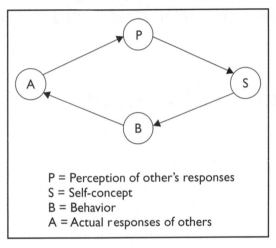

P = Perception of other's responses
S = Self-concept
B = Behavior
A = Actual responses of others

One can begin to examine this model using any of the four circles. Your perception of how others see you (P) influences your self-concept (S). Your self-concept influences your behavior (B). Your behavior (B), in turn, influences the actions of others toward you (A). These actions influence your perception of how others see you; hence, a return to the starting point.

As a student, you can impact the self-concepts of teachers and classmates by the nature of the communication you direct toward them. As a parent or child you influence the self-concepts of other family members, just as they influence yours. In general, the way you perceive the communication you receive from others influences your self-concept and your subsequent communication (Cooper and Simonds 1999).

One of the major ways self-concept affects communication is through self-fulfilling prophecies. *Self-fulfilling prophecies* are predictions that come true because, consciously or not, an individual believes in the prediction and acts on that belief over a period of time. For example, if Martin perceives himself as having difficulty getting to know others, he sees himself as more introverted than extroverted. Before attending a party, he says to himself, "I'm going to have a lousy time tonight." Because he fears meeting new people, he is reluctant to introduce himself to others. As a result, he spends most of his time standing by himself observing others having fun. He does indeed have a miserable time. He tends to fulfill his own prophecy in this situation and many other ones.

Perception is a powerful factor in our communication effectiveness. It undergirds our self-concept development and our ability to construct and interpret messages effectively. In this section, you will read about perception processes and self-concept. In the second section of Part II, you will encounter the role of culture, gender, and family experiences in shaping our worldviews and our communication patterns.

### References

Cooper, P., and Simonds, C. (1999). *Communication for the Classroom Teacher*, 6th ed. Boston: Allyn & Bacon.

Cooper, P., Stewart, L., and Gudykunst, W. (1982). Relationship with instructor and other variables influencing evaluation of instruction. *Communication Quarterly*, 30: 308–315.

Kinch, J. (1963). A formalized theory of self-concept. *American Journal of Sociology* 68: 481–486. ✦

# 8
# Perceiving the Self

*Ronald B. Adler and*
*George Rodman*

I am me.

In all the world, there is not one exactly like me.

There are people who have some parts like me but no one adds up exactly like me. Therefore, everything that comes out of me is authentically mine because I alone choose it.

—Virginia Satir (1988, 28)

*How people communicate depends to a great extent on how they define themselves (self-concept) and how they evaluate themselves (self-esteem). In this piece on self-perception and communication, communication scholars Adler and Rodman explore how people perceive themselves and how those perceptions affect their communication with others.*

*As adults, this connection may be difficult to recognize, since fully formed self-concepts do not always appear to be terribly vulnerable to communication. If someone insults your intelligence, for instance, and you have always thought of yourself as smart, you are not likely to question this concept of yourself. Yet, as the authors illustrate, children are not born with a self-concept, and therefore they must use the influence and feedback from others to conceive an understanding of themselves. In this way, people learn to depend upon others to reinforce a certain self-image.*

*The authors develop an argument for understanding how the communication of others influences how you see yourself. The concept of reflected appraisal describes how you develop an image of yourself from the way you think others view you; in other words, relationally, other people construct your sense of self. Therefore,*

*self-concept comprises the physical and social perception individuals have of themselves that they have gained through their interactions with others. Yet the key point involves the interactive nature of building self-concept. An individual selectively incorporates the feedback of others; the messages that really count come from significant others, those whose opinions are valued.*

*By first defining the complex nature of the self-concept, Adler and Rodman explain why and how we form the image of ourselves, concluding with the role of personality in shaping both the self-concept and the degree of influence that communication plays in its development and maintenance. As you read this article, consider this question: What person or persons have significantly impacted my image of myself, and what messages did I receive that I incorporated into my view of myself?*

### Reference

Satir, V. (1988). *The New Peoplemaking*. Mountain View, CA: Science and Behavior Books.

* * *

## Self-Concept Defined

The *self-concept* is a set of relatively stable perceptions each of us holds about ourselves. The self-concept includes our conception about what is unique about us and what makes us both similar to, and different from, others. To put it differently, the self-concept is rather like a mental mirror that reflects how we view ourselves: not only physical features, but also emotional states, talents, likes and dislikes, values, and roles.

We will have more to say about the nature of the self-concept shortly, but first you will find it valuable to gain a personal understanding of how this theoretical construct applies to you. You can do so by answering a simple question: "Who are you?"

How do you define yourself? As a student? A man or woman? By your age? Your religion? Occupation?

There are many ways of identifying yourself. Take a few more minutes and list as many ways as you can to identify who you are. You'll need this list later in this [chapter], so be sure to complete it now. Try to include all the characteristics that describe you:

- your moods or feelings
- your appearance and physical condition
- your social traits
- talents you possess or lack
- your intellectual capacity
- your strong beliefs
- your social roles

Even a list of twenty or thirty terms would be only a partial description. To make this written self-portrait complete, your list would have to be hundreds—or even thousands—of words long.

Of course, not every item on such a list would be equally important. For example, the most significant part of one person's self-concept might consist of social roles, whereas for another it could consist of physical appearance, health, friendships, accomplishments, or skills.

You can begin to see how important these elements are by continuing this personal experiment. Pick the ten items from your list that describe the most fundamental aspects of who you are. Rank these ten items so that the most fundamental one is in first place, with the others following in order of declining importance. Now, beginning with the tenth item, imagine what would happen if each characteristic in turn disappeared from your makeup. How would you be different? How would you feel?

For most people, this exercise dramatically illustrates just how fundamental the self-concept is. Even when the item being abandoned is an unpleasant one, it's often hard to give it up. And when they are asked to let go of their most central feelings or thoughts, most people balk. "I wouldn't be *me* without that," they insist. Of course, this proves our point: The self-concept is perhaps our most fundamental possession. Knowing who we are is essential, for without a self-concept it would be impossible to relate to the world.

# Communication and Development of the Self

So far we've talked about what the self-concept is; but at this point you may be asking what it has to do with the study of human communication. We can begin to answer this question by looking at how you came to possess your own self-concept.

Newborn babies come into the world with very little sense of self. In the first months of life infants have no awareness of their bodies as being separate from the rest of the environment. At eight months of age, for example, a child will be surprised when a toy grabbed from the grip of another child "resists." Not until somewhere between their first and second birthday are most children able to recognize their own reflections in a mirror. The lack of self-concept in very young children helps explain why toddlers are so difficult to control. Since they lack any sense of individuality, they don't recognize themselves as the target of disapproval by their caretakers. Neither do they experience emotions such as remorse, guilt, or shame that come from being criticized. We can amuse very young children through play; frighten them by speaking loudly and harshly; and comfort them with hugs, songs and soft speech; but we can't influence self-esteem until children have a sense of self.

How do we develop the kind of rich, multidimensional self-concept described in the preceding section? Our identity comes almost exclusively from communication with others. As psychologists Arthur Combs and Donald Snygg put it:

> The self is essentially a social product arising out of experience with people. . . . We learn the most significant and fundamental facts about ourselves from . . . "reflected appraisals," inferences about ourselves made as a consequence of the ways we perceive others behaving toward us.

The term *reflected appraisal*, coined by Harry Stack Sullivan, is a good one, for it metaphorically describes the fact that we develop an image of ourselves from the way we think others view us. This notion of the "looking-glass self" was first introduced in 1902 by Charles H. Cooley, who suggested that we put ourselves in the position of other people and then, in our mind's eye, view ourselves as we imagine they see us.

As we learn to speak and understand language, verbal messages—both positive and negative—also contribute to the developing self-concept. These messages continue later in life, especially when they come from what social scientists term *significant others*—people whose opinions we especially value. A teacher from long ago, a special friend or relative, or perhaps a barely known acquaintance who you respect can all leave an imprint on how you view yourself. To see the importance of significant others, ask yourself how you arrived at your opinion of you as a student . . . as a person attractive to the opposite sex . . . as a competent worker . . . and you will see that these self-evaluations were probably influenced by the way others regarded you.

Research supports the importance of reflected appraisals. One study identified the relationship between adult attitudes toward children and the children's self-concepts. The researcher first established that parents and teachers expect children from higher socioeconomic backgrounds to do better academically than socioeconomically disadvantaged youngsters. In other words, parents and teachers have higher expectations for socioeconomically advantaged students. Interestingly, when children from a higher socioeconomic class performed poorly in school their self-esteem dropped; but children from less advantaged backgrounds did not lose self-esteem. Why was there this difference? Because the parents and teachers sent messages about their disappointment to the higher status children, whereas no such messages went to their less-advantaged counterparts.

Later in life the influence of significant others is less powerful. The evaluations of others still influence beliefs about the self in some areas, such as physical attractiveness and popularity. In other areas, however, the looking glass of the self-concept has become distorted, so that it shapes the input of others to make it conform with our existing beliefs. For example, if your self-concept includes the element "poor student," you might respond to a high grade by thinking "I

was just lucky" or "The professor must be an easy grader."

You might argue that not every part of one's self-concept is shaped by others, insisting there are certain objective facts that are recognizable by self-observation. After all, nobody needs to tell you that you are taller than others, speak with an accent, can run quickly, and so on. These facts are obvious.

Though it's true that some features of the self are immediately apparent, the *significance* we attach to them—the rank we assign them in the hierarchy of our list and the interpretation we give them—depends greatly on the opinions of others. After all, there are many of your features that are readily observable, yet you don't find them important at all because nobody has regarded them as significant.

Recently we heard a woman in her eighties describing her youth. "When I was a girl," she declared, "we didn't worry about weight. Some people were skinny and others were plump, and we pretty much accepted the bodies God gave us." Compare this attitude with what you find today: It's seldom that you pick up a popular magazine or visit a bookstore without reading about the latest diet fads, and television ads are filled with scenes of slender, happy people. As a result, you'll find many people who complain about their need to "lose a few pounds." The reason for such concern has more to do with the attention paid to slimness these days than with any increase in the number of people in the population who are overweight. Furthermore, the interpretation of characteristics such as weight depends on the way people important to us regard them. We generally see fat as undesirable because others tell us it is. In a society where obesity is the ideal (and there are such societies), a heavy person would feel beautiful. In the same way, the fact that one is single or married, solitary or sociable, aggressive or passive, takes on meaning depending on the interpretation society attaches to those traits. Thus, the importance of a given characteristic in your self-concept has as much to do with the significance you and others attach to it as with the existence of the characteristic. . . .

## The Self-Concept, Personality, and Communication

While the self-concept is an internal image we hold of ourselves, the personality is the view others hold of us. We use the notion of *personality* to describe a relatively consistent set of traits people exhibit across a variety of situations. We use the notion of personality to characterize others as friendly or aloof, energetic or lazy, smart or stupid, and in literally thousands of other ways. In fact, one survey revealed almost 18,000 trait words in the English language that can be used to describe a personality. People do seem to possess some innate personality traits. Psychologist Jerome Kagan reports that ten percent of all children appear to be born with a biological disposition toward shyness. Babies who stop playing when a stranger enters the room, for example, are more likely than others to be reticent and introverted as adolescents. Likewise, Kagan found that another ten percent of infants seem to be born with especially sociable dispositions. Research with twins also suggests that personality may be at least partially a matter of physical destiny. Biologically identical twins are much more similar in sociability than are fraternal twins. These similarities are apparent not only in infancy but also when the twins have grown to adulthood, and are noticeable even when the siblings have had different experiences.

Despite its common use, the "personality" is often an oversimplification. Much of our behavior isn't consistent. Rather, it varies from one situation to another. You may be quiet around strangers and gregarious with friends and family. You might be optimistic about your schoolwork or career and pessimistic about your romantic prospects. The term "easygoing" might describe your behavior at home, while you might be a fanatic at work. This kind of diversity isn't only common; it's often desirable. The argumentative style you use with friends wouldn't be well received by the judge in traffic court when you appeal a citation. Likewise, the affectionate behavior you enjoy with a romantic partner at home probably wouldn't be appropriate in public. . . . [A] wide range of behaviors is an important ingredient of communication competence. In this sense, a consistent personality can be more of a drawback than an asset—unless that personality is "flexible."

**Figure 8-1**
*The Self-Concept and Communications: A Cyclic Process*

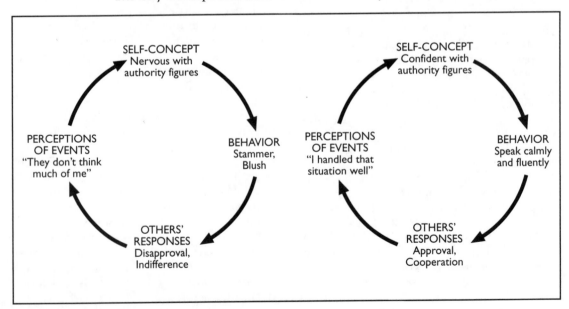

Figure 8-1 pictures the relationships between the self-concept and behavior. It illustrates how the self-concept both shapes much of our communication behavior and is affected by it. We can begin to examine the process by considering the self-concept you bring to an event. Suppose, for example, that one element of your self-concept is "nervous with authority figures." That image probably comes from the evaluations of significant others in the past—perhaps teachers or former employers. If you view yourself as nervous with authority figures like these, you will probably behave in nervous ways when you encounter them in the future—in a teacher-student conference or a job interview. That nervous behavior is likely to influence how others view your personality, which in turn will shape how they respond to you—probably in ways that reinforce the self-concept you brought to the event. Finally, the responses of others will affect the way you interpret future events: other job interviews, meeting with professors, and so on. This cycle illustrates the chicken-and-egg nature of the self-concept, which is shaped by significant others in the past, helps to govern your present behavior, and influences the way others view you.

### References

Allport, G. W., and Odbert, H. W. (1936). Trait names, a psychological study. *Psychological Monographs*, 47.

Combs, A. W., and Snygg, D. (1959). *Individual behavior*, rev. ed. New York: Harper & Row.

Cooley, C. H. (1902). *Human nature and the social order*. New York: Scriber's.

Kagan, J. (1989). *Unstable ideas: Temperament, cognition, and self*. Cambridge: Harvard University Press.

Keltikangas, J. (1990). The stability of self-concept during adolescence and early adulthood: A six-year follow-up study. *Journal of General Psychology*, 117: 361–369.

Lewis, M., and Brooks, J. (1978). Self-knowledge and emotional development. In M. Lewis and L. A. Rosenblum (Eds.), *The development of affect*. New York: Plenum.

McCroskey, J. C., and Richmond, V. (1980). *The quiet ones: Communication apprehension and shyness*. Dubuque: Gorsuch Scarisbrick.

Ryce-Menuhin, J. (1988). *The self in early childhood*. London: Free Association Books.

Smith, M. D., Zingale, A., and Coleman, J. M. (1978). The influence of adult expectations/child performance discrepencies upon children's self-concepts. *American Educational Research Journal*, 15: 259–266.

Steinfatt, T. M. (1987). Personality and communication: Classical approaches. In J. C. McCroskey and J. A. Daly (Eds.), *Personality and interpersonal communication*. Newbury Park: Sage.

Stipek, D. J., Gralinski, J., and Kopp, C. B. (1990). Self-concept development in the toddler years. *Developmental Psychology*, 26: 972.

Sullivan, H. S. (1953). *The interpersonal theory of psychiatry*. New York: W. W. Norton.

## Questions

1. Number a piece of paper from 1 to 5 (or 10). Then answer this question: Who am I? List the characteristics that you think define you. Then, take a moment to rank the top three that you think are most important or crucial to your self-concept. Why are these most important to you? What feedback have you received from others on these characteristics?

2. Identify three people who have contributed to the development of your self-concept, positively or negatively, through the process of reflected appraisal. Why are these individuals important to you, and what have they helped you to understand about yourself?

3. Using the authors' suggestions, develop a list of the many ways you identify yourself. Star the ones that are most important to you. Identify three characteristics you would like to add to this list in the next few years, and note one way to work on each of those characteristics.

# 9

# Four Important Cognitive Processes

*Daniel J. Canary, Michael J. Cody, and Valerie L. Manusov*

Social cognition is the study of mental processes and structures used to make sense of, remember, and think about people and interactions—that is, cognitive structures and processes that influence our perceptions of people and events. These perceptions in turn affect our communication. Social cognition enables you to categorize individuals and make sense of social interactions. Trenholm and Jensen (2000) indicate that there are four key social cognition questions for any given communication:

1. *How does each participant view the situation?*

2. *What impressions do the participants have of each other?*

3. *What kind of relationship have the participants enacted? Do they both view the relationship as having the same status (for example, friends or casual acquaintances)?*

4. *What explanations do the participants provide to account for their own and each other's behavior?*

*Every person sees the world differently and therefore has a slightly different process of perception, remembering, and thinking about others' interactions. In this chapter, authors Canary, Cody, and Manusov explain social cognition, starting with a discussion of different knowledge structures, or* schemata, *and elaborate upon the four specific cognitive processes that determine how you react and re-*spond to different situations. Citing relevant research and examples, they depict each of the four processes—interpersonal expectancies, attributions, person perception, and stereotypes—revealing their impact on communication. As you read this chapter, explore this question: How do my social cognition processes appear to be similar to and/or different from those of my close friends?*

### Reference

Trenholm, S., and Jensen, A. (2000). *Interpersonal Communication*, 4th ed. Belmont, CA: Wadsworth.

* * *

In the film *He Said/She Said*, two directors portray the relationship of Lorie Bryor and Dan Hanson, one from the perspective of Lorie and the other from the perspective of Dan. The portrayal follows the opening scene in which Lorie throws a coffee mug at Dan on their TV show, "He Said/She Said." Dan, who believes that the mug-throwing incident is "just the way we are," presents a very positive "almost perfect" view of their relationship. Lorie, who feels their relationship is over, gives a less glowing view; she talks about Dan as an unreliable womanizer and herself as an insecure individual who thinks marriage will help quiet her fears. At the end of the film, the audience is left guessing whose version of events is more accurate.

. . . Most researchers believe that people are relatively strategic in their communication with others. To better understand the dynamics of interpersonal communication, it is helpful to know more about how the mind works when people interact with others and when they think about their own behavior. To do this, we focus . . . on several processes that are part of **social cognition** (the mental processes and structures used to make sense of, remember, and think about people and interactions). . . .

In the [above] example, the two characters were looking back on their relationship in very different ways. Dan, who did not want the relationship to end, remembered events in one way. Lorie, who was very unhappy at the time, remembered the same events quite differently. Their memories "one of the cognitive processes important to interpersonal communication" were affected by their feelings, backgrounds, personalities, and fears. Each had memories of a very different reality.

What "really" happened was probably not exactly what either of the characters recalls—because we tend to remember very selectively. Indeed, we remember only certain parts of events or only some events and not others. In addition, what we do remember tends to be in a different form than what may have happened originally. We may do this because we are not able to notice everything, so we (usually unconsciously) make choices about what, and where, we will focus attention. This is known as *selective attention*.

The operation of **selectivity** in perception is important, because it shows that we each interact with others and with the world in a way that is different from others. This is natural yet inherently problematic: Because no two people will ever perceive events or situations in exactly the same way, the discrepancy has the potential to increase communication errors. Our goal in this chapter is to explain some of the perception processes that we all use in our interpersonal interactions as we attempt to achieve our communication goals. We hope that a better understanding will make the influences of those processes more apparent.

## · Knowledge Structures and Communication

When people communicate with others or try to make sense of their own behavior, they do so within the constraints of a certain way of viewing the world. Over their lifetimes, people develop knowledge structures, or **schemata**, that they carry with them, and these structures help them interpret, remember, and organize new information. Schemata are influenced by the culture in which people live . . . and the personal experiences people have. So, when you see someone act in a certain way, you process the observations through existing schemata. You are likely to take something that was potentially ambiguous (i.e., the observed behav-

ior) and make sense of it with an already established way of viewing the world.

One the first day of class, for example, you probably entered your classroom, sat down in a seat, and waited for the instructor. You may have talked to others in the class whom you knew already or asked other students you did not know brief questions about the class. It is likely that your instructor distributed a syllabus and talked about what the class would involve. Without knowledge structures, you would not have known how to act, and little of what your instructor did would have made any sense. Instead, however, you relied on established schemata to help you process the situation and communicate with others.

Different types of schemata exist. Fiske and Taylor (1984) discuss four:

1. *Self-schemata* reflect peoples' views of themselves and guide how they process information about themselves. These are discussed later in this chapter.

2. *Event schemata*, also called scripts, help people recognize the typical ways in which a sequence of actions tends to unfold (e.g., the particular events that are likely to occur on the first day of a class and the order in which they occur).

3. *Role schemata* provide information about appropriate behavior based on social categories (e.g., age, race, sex, and occupation) (Fiske & Taylor, 1984). Scholars often refer to these as stereotypes.

4. *Person schemata* reflect peoples' understanding of individuals they know (e.g., "my husband Chuck") and/or particular "types" of people (e.g., happy people). This knowledge guides interactions with others.

Planalp (1985) argues that people also have a fifth schemata, a *relational schemata* to make sense of their love, friendship, family, and work bonds. Relational schemata help predict, interpret, expect, and remember things for these different types of relationships. Fitzpatrick and Ritchie (1994) describe some of the relational schemata that are particular to families and their communication patterns. According to Fitzpatrick and Ritchie, people form one of the following schemata about what families are or should be like: *pluralistic* families, in which communication is open and discussion is encouraged; *consensual* families, in which there is strong pressure toward agreement and children are supposed to be involved in the family without disturbing the family's power structure; *laissez-faire* families, in which little direction comes from parents to children and children are influenced more by people outside the family; and *protective* families, in which obedience is highly valued and the family is focused internally. Like other types of knowledge structures, these family schemata are thought to affect the ways in which people think and communicate.

## Four Important Cognitive Processes

Researchers have identified some important processes involved when people communicate that are all connected to knowledge structures. Four particularly important processes for understanding how people communicate and ultimately achieve their interpersonal goals are (1) interpersonal expectancies, (2) attributions, (3) person perception, and (4) stereotyping.

### Interpersonal Expectancies

When people communicate with others, they usually bring along a set of *interpersonal expectancies* for how they think the interaction (or the relationship they have or hope to have with another) will proceed. Like relational schemata, expectancies guide our communication with others; but expectancies focus particularly on how we think people will or ought to communicate with us. They may also be reflected in our behavior as we act in ways that adapt to the expectations we have for others. In turn, our behaviors may affect others' communication.

One of the best-known interpersonal expectancies is the *self-fulfilling prophecy*, discussed originally by Merton in 1948. "[A] self-fulfilling prophecy is, in the beginning, a *false* definition of the situation evoking a new behavior which makes the originally false conception come *true*" (Merton, 1948, p. 195). Thus, if you

believed, incorrectly, that another student was not likely to be friendly, you may have acted toward him or her *as if* he or she were unfriendly. A self-fulfilling prophecy would have occurred if that student reacted in an unfriendly way *rather than* how he or she might have otherwise. Because of your actions, you brought about what you had expected would occur. Merton also discussed the *self-disconfirming prophecy*. This happens when the beliefs that we have about others make them act in ways that would counter the expectancy (e.g., they would act particularly friendly). If another responds to our friendliness with friendliness—and this is not how he or she would have behaved had we not acted as we did—a self-disconfirming prophecy would have occurred. Our "opposite" behaviors helped bring about behaviors that went against how we expected the other to act.

Another type of prophecy effect is the *Pygmalion effect*. According to this prophecy, if people believe something will take place, they behave in ways that ensure that it will occur. Rosenthal and Rubin (1978) first used the term to define the potential influence of teachers' expectancies on students' performance. According to Miller and Turnbull (1986), in Rosenthal and Rubin's initial study,

> Teachers in an elementary school were told that a new IQ test administered to their students indicated that certain students, "bloomers," should show a marked increase in intellectual competence over the course of the school year. In actuality, the label "bloomer" was assigned randomly by the researchers. All students were given an IQ test at both the beginning and the end of the school year. The results indicated that students labeled "bloomers" showed a significantly greater gain in IQ than other pupils. (p. 235)

Rosenthal and Rubin concluded that the expectancies the teachers had for the students affected how the teachers treated the students. This treatment in turn had significant outcomes: higher IQ. Although subsequent studies have found mixed support for the Pygmalion effect (and for the other types of prophecies), there has been enough research to document and sometimes expectancies have an effect on another's behavior.

Expectancies can take different specific forms. One such type of expectancy entails how a romance develops. Honeycutt and his colleagues concluded that people have a knowledge structure that reflects their expectations for how they think a relationship is likely to grow. . . .

Honeycutt (1995) found that people's awareness of how they think relationships ought to progress affects the ways in which they practice or "imagine" future interactions with their partner. A recent study shows that people also use their expectancies of a romance to determine what compliance-gaining strategies they might use to convince their partner to move forward to another stage (Honeycutt, Cantrill, Kelly, & Lambkin, 1998).

People in relationships also develop expectancies for the actual and desired behaviors they think or want their romantic partners to use with them. Kelley and Burgoon (1991) proposed that people enter relationships with *relational expectancies*, beliefs about what behaviors their partners will and should use. . . . [P]eople's communication reflects the kind of relationship that they have with one another. For example, if a relationship is defined to be unequal (i.e., one person has more power), this inequality may be shown through the behaviors used (e.g., one person may speak more and control the conversation in other ways). Relational expectancies are those knowledge structures that mirror the beliefs we have for how our interaction partner will (or should) act.

Like the imagined interactions discussed earlier, relational expectancies become particularly important for communication, because they may influence how we act with others. A recent study by Manusov, Trees, Liotta, Koenig, and Cochran (1999) showed, for example, that relational expectancies affected whether married couples reciprocated or compensated their partners' behaviors. . . . Specifically, when one couple member expected the other to act dominantly, he or she was more likely to compensate (act different from) the partner. When high levels of intimacy were expected, some reciprocity of intimacy cues was most likely. This is a clear case of how expectancies can affect communication behavior.

The preceding studies demonstrate that we have expectancies and that we act in ways that are influenced by our expectancies for others. Of course, those others do not always act as we expect them to. When people notice that someone has violated their beliefs about how they thought the other would act (e.g., acted more or less involved in the conversation than they would expect normally), they try to make sense of the violation (Burgoon & Hale, 1988). One way that people do this is to consider the person who committed the violation. If they judge that person to be "high reward" (e.g., they think well of that person or that person is attractive or has power), people assume that he or she violated their beliefs for a good reason. This judgment actually makes others evaluate the "violator" better than if he or she had acted "normally." Those who are judged to be "low reward," however, are thought to have less positive reasons for violating beliefs. In that case, the violation of expectations results in a lower evaluation than would have occurred if she or he had not committed the violation. . . .

## Attributions

When we perceive others and make judgments about them or about ourselves, we are making **attributions** about their behavior. The term *attribution* refers to assessments of the *cause* of an action or behavior (i.e., our thoughts about why someone acted as he or she did or what caused us to act in a certain way).

Fritz Heider (1958) was one of the first researchers to study attributions in any depth. He asserted that people act as "naïve scientists" (i.e., untrained but active psychologists) who study others' (and their own) actions in order to determine why people behave in certain ways. Finding a cause (even an incorrect one) helps put unexpected behavior in order and make sense of the world.

Causes can be either *internal* to a person (e.g., a person's disposition, mood, or other character trait), *external* to him or her (e.g., environmental or situational factors), or both. Heider called these dimensions of attributions **causal loci** or the *sources* of observed behavior. For example, if you see someone who is walking across campus suddenly trip, you may attribute the cause to the person ("She fell because she's clumsy"), to something outside of the person ("A crack in the pavement must have caused her to fall"), or to a combination ("There must be a crack, but only clumsy people would trip on cracks"). Other dimensions besides causal locus differentiate attributions (e.g., responsibility for the stability of the cause), and these factors help reflect the great variety of causes that can be found for any communication behavior.

In an extension of Heider's work, Jones and Davis (1965) argued that human behavior has the potential to be more or less meaningful depending on the *level of intention* inferred for a behavior. Accordingly, one of the most important considerations for making an attribution is deciding whether or not another person acted with intent. Those behaviors judged to be intended are thought to say more about the person (i.e., to be more meaningful) than those thought to have occurred without intent (i.e., on a whim or under conditions that could not have been controlled). Importantly, Jones and Davis argued that people will judge a behavior to be intended under specific conditions: (1) the other had *knowledge* about the potential effects of his or her action, and (2) he or she had the *ability to enact the actions*.

What else beyond level of intention determines our attributions of actions to internal or external causes? Three features of observing others may influence such judgments: distinctiveness, consistency, and consensus (Kelley, 1973). *Distinctiveness* is whether or not a person's behavior is clearly different in one situation than in other situations. For example, if a friend of yours got good grades in all of her classes but one, you are likely to make an external attribution: the one class is too difficult or is taught poorly. However, if your friend received poor grades in all her classes, you would be more likely to make an internal attribution: she is not very smart and/or she is not very motivated.

*Consistency* is the extent to which a person's behavior is the same over time. Highly consistent behavior means, using the preceding example, that your friend has always received high grades or has always received low grades. If your friend has in the past demonstrated the ability and motivation to get good grades, you would probably look for external causes for a recent bout of bad grades. Perhaps this semester she had tough professors, or other things going on in her life are distracting her from her coursework.

*Consensus* is the perception of similar others in similar situations (e.g., how well your friend is doing in one class relative to other similar students in the same class). High consensus means that all students in particular classes receive poor grades. When all students get poor grades, you would probably attribute your friend's poor grades to an external cause, such as the professor's grading or the difficulty of the material. Consensus is low, however, when other students are receiving high marks, but your friend is one of the few who are not. Overall, according to Kelley, people are likely to believe that a person's behavior is caused by external factors when distinctiveness, consistency, and consensus are high. . . .

The *fundamental attribution error*, for instance, suggests that people are more likely to assume that another's actions were caused by something internal rather than external (Ross, 1977). Rather than going through the steps of one of the attribution models listed earlier, a person may just believe that some personality trait or intention was the cause of the action. This may occur because it is earlier to find an internal cause—there are fewer of them and the observer is already focused on the person. The *ultimate attribution error* asserts that peoples' tendency to assume another's actions were caused by something internal is particularly likely when another's behavior is negative. Conversely, people are less likely to assume an internal explanation with positive behaviors. So, if a stranger acted nice to you, you might assume that he was just following social rules (i.e., an external explanation). If he acted rudely, you would be more likely to think that his actions were due to something about him (e.g., "he's a snob").

Other errors or biases depend on our "place" in an interaction. The *actor-observer bias* refers to people's tendency to see their own behaviors as less negative overall than others' actions (Jones & Nisbett, 1972). For example, if you decided to turn down a job, you could easily say that the cause of your behavior was your belief that taking the job would hurt your school performance. If someone else had done the same thing, however, you might attribute his or her actions to laziness ("He or she didn't want to have to work hard").

The *negativity and positivity biases* (Kellermann, 1984) are also due to one's perspective in an interaction. If people are watching someone from afar, they tend to make relatively negative judgments of the other's actions (the negativity bias) at least when compared to what they do when they try to make sense of the same behavior while interacting with that person. It appears that having a chance to actually talk with another person helps us focus on more positive attributes (positivity bias). Some researchers say that we do this because *we* can now be seen as the cause of the other's actions ("She acted that way because she likes me"). We may label other people and/or their behavior positively (rather than negatively as we do with strangers) because we want to think that we would cause others to take only positive actions.

Attributions may also be biased by people's feelings for each other. In one study, Manusov (1990) had couples play the game "Trivial Pursuit." One of the couple members had been asked to become a part of the study, and his or her cards were marked. About a third of the way into the game, he or she received a marked card that told him or her to start acting unusually positive or negative. Watching the videotape of the interactions after they were complete, the "naïve" partner was asked to explain any unusual behaviors. Manusov found that, for most couples, negative behaviors were more likely to prompt attribution-making than were positive behaviors (not all behaviors make us think about their causes). For positive behaviors, however, the nature of the attributions differed based on couples' satisfaction level. Couples who were happy with one another attributed positive behaviors to something internal to their partner, whereas unhappy couples made more external attributions.

Manusov's study was only one of many that have looked for biases in the attributions made by couples. Indeed, it is so common for unhappy couples to assume that their partners are responsible for negative actions and for happy couples to attribute internal causes for positive behaviors that these tendencies have names. The tendency for unhappy couples to "see the worst" is known as the *distress-maintaining bias*; whereas the inclination for happy couples to "see the best" is called the *relationship-enhancing bias* (Holtzworth-Munroe & Jacobson, 1985). . . .

Attributions are important for understanding interpersonal communication in that the causes we give for behaviors are part of the *meaning* we derive from them. This meaning is a fundamental part of what is communicated in an interpersonal interaction. As well, the attribution we decide on for another's behavior helps influence how we communicate with him or her.

### Person Perception

The positivity and negativity biases just discussed reflect a larger social cognition process: **person perception**. Every day as we communicate with others, we attempt to determine what those others are like and whether we like them. Person perception is therefore a communicative goal in itself and/or it is used as we attempt to pursue other goals (e.g., we try to figure out what someone is like in order to know best how to ask them to comply with a request).

As noted earlier, people create person schemata that guide their actions and thoughts regarding (1) people they know, and (2) certain "types" of people (i.e., people who are in particular groups with characteristics people think they can identify). Thus schemata for *specific* friends, family, and co-workers (e.g., the authors have schemata for one another) and for "types" of people such as friends, family, and co-workers (e.g., the authors have schemata for what "co-authors" are like) are part of person perception. People also have general person schemata that are based in personality traits such as shyness, humorousness, and kindness. These are called *prototypes*.

Sometimes general perception categories are very broad and influenced by factors out of our awareness. Monahan (1998) argues that people make quick and often automatic judgments of whether another person is good or bad. Interestingly, these views of others can be instigated in a number of ways. Monahan had her participants watch some slides prior to viewing a videotape of a young man whom they were going to judge. Some of the participants saw presentations that included subliminal (quickly shown, out of awareness) slides of the young man smiling. Those participants who had been "primed" to see the young man positively evaluated him as more attractive and more likeable than did those who did not receive the subliminal slides. Further, those who saw the slides evaluated *others* more positively as well. This suggests that person perception processes may be affected by factors unknown to the perceiver (e.g., mood, temperature, and even time of year). . . .

In addition to the perceptions we form of others, we also have *self-perceptions* and generally work equally hard to maintain them. Swann (1987) explains that, as part of their primary task of making sense of the world, children watch their own behavior and how others react to them and form a view of self. As their self-views become clearer, children try to find ways to maintain them, even if the self-perceptions are negative. According to Swann (1990), "people want to confirm their self-views *not* as an end in itself, but as a means of bolstering their perception that the world is predictable and controllable" (p. 414). We tend to seek out, notice, and remember those things that are consistent with our self-views. These "stabilizing processes" cause us often to have what Swann calls a "chronic view of self," one that is particularly unlikely to change.

How we view ourselves is important for several reasons. First, who we see ourselves to be and how we evaluate ourselves (i.e., self-esteem) likely influence what goals we set and whether or not we pursue them. Second, self-views affect the choices of others with whom we wish to interact or form relationships. Third, the way we see ourselves is also likely to influence how we interpret others' behaviors in regard to us and our relationship with them. So, in *He Said/She Said*, the example at the beginning of this chapter,

Lorie's view of her relationship with Dan was made more negative by her own belief that she was largely unlovable. As was seen, however, Dan's view reflected a very different reality (i.e., that Lorie was interesting and dynamic and a person whom he could love).

The processes of person perception are key to our communication. Our perceptions of others affect how we will communicate with them—or even if we will communicate with them at all. Our perceptions of self also influence how we will communicate and in what contexts as well as the types of relationships we develop.

## Stereotypes

In addition to creating a view of ourselves (and of those around us), we also tend to use categories for others. Lakoff (1987) states that,

> [T]here is nothing more basic than categorization to our thought, perception, action, and speech. Every time we see something as a *kind* of thing, for example, a tree, we are categorizing. Whenever we reason about *kinds* of things—chairs, nations, illnesses, emotions, any kind of things at all—we are employing categories. (pp. 5–6)

When categories are about people and are based on their group membership, they are called **stereotypes**. "People categories" may include ethnic or cultural groups, gender groups, and social groups, and stereotypes include beliefs about the characteristics common to all members of that group (e.g., "All basketball players are tall"). As Lakoff suggests, stereotypes, as a type of categorization, are a common way to make sense of people and objects and in this regard are thought of as important to communication. Stereotypes are also, however, sometimes incorrect and always only partially reflect the complexities of the group; thus they may hurt our ability to communicate with others.

As a type of category or knowledge structure, stereotypes help people process information. When one person sees another person act in a particular way, the observer may do so in light of a stereotype of the other person's group. But using a stereotype, like any other form of perception, means that people see things *in a certain way*, and that way is usually consistent with the stereotype they hold. For example, if you notice someone from another group (e.g., you are a college student, and you are watching someone who is not a student), and that person is doing something that does not fit your stereotype (e.g., reading a textbook), you probably will not even notice the behavior because it doesn't fit with your image of things. If you do pay attention to it (and sometimes this is actually *more* likely because the behavior may seem so extraordinary), you probably will try to make it fit with your existing stereotype. Thus you may say that the person you observed was an "exception" or that he or she was enacting the behavior for a reason that allows it to fit with your view (e.g., you may offer an external attribution that means something else besides the person was responsible for the behavior). In other words, you will usually try to make what you observe fit with your preexisting views if possible.

We do, of course, change our stereotypes or even let go of them completely in favor of other categorizations. As noted earlier, a person's behaviors (i.e., "individuating information") can often become more important than expectancies in judging that person. If enough people from a group act inconsistently with our preconceptions, we may change our stereotypes for the group. Having the opportunity to interact with people from an "out-group" (i.e., a group that is not our own) may allow us to see more similarities than differences with their group and thus no longer categorize them.

More commonly, however, an individual's behaviors do not affect views of a group as a whole, but they do influence how he or she is judged and how we communicate with him or her (Jussim, 1990). Manusov, Winchatz, and Manning (1997), for instance, paired up students from the United States with students from other countries. Before interacting, the authors asked the participants to evaluate how positively or negatively they viewed people from the other group. After talking for ten minutes, some "residual," or leftover, effects of the initial stereotype remained (e.g., if participants expected a positive interaction, they judged their partner more positively no matter how the partner behaved). Still, it was clear

that in the majority of the evaluations people made, how their partner *actually acted* more strongly influenced particpants' assessments. So, even if the initial stereotype led them to think they would *not* enjoy the conservation, if they thought their partner acted positively, the study participants were likely to evaluate their partners well (or if they had high expectations that were not met, they judged their partners more negatively than their initial stereotype would have led them to do). . . .

# Suggested Reading

## Schemata and Expectancies

Fitzpatrick, M. A., & Ritchie, L. D. (1994). Communication schemata within the family: Multiple perspectives on family interaction. *Human Communication Research, 20,* 275–301.

Kelley, D. L., & Burgoon, J. K. (1991). Understanding marital satisfaction and couple type as functions of relational expectations. *Human Communication Research, 18,* 40–69.

Planalp, S. (1985). Relational schemata: A test of alternative forms of relational knowledge as guides to communication. *Human Communication Research, 12,* 3–29.

Rosenthal, R., & Rubin, D. B. (1978). Interpersonal expectancy effects: The first 345 studies. *Behavioral and Brain Sciences, 3,* 377–415.

## Attributions

Heider, F. (1958). *The psychology of interpersonal relations.* New York: John Wiley.

Kelley, H. H. (1973). The processes of causal attribution. *American Psychologist, 28,* 107–128.

Manusov, V. (1990). An application of attribution principles to nonverbal behavior in romantic dyads. *Communication Monographs, 57,* 104–118.

## Stereotypes and Person Perception

Jussim, L. (1990). Social reality and social problems: The role of expectancies. *Journal of Social Issues, 46,* 9–34.

Manusov, V., Winchatz, M. R., & Manning, L. M. (1997). Acting out our minds: Incorporating behavior into models of stereotype-based expectancies for cross-cultural interactions. *Communication Monographs, 64,* 119–139.

Swann, W. B. (1987). Identity negotiation: Where two roads meet. *Journal of Personality and Social Psychology, 53,* 1038–1051.

# References

Burgoon, J. K., & Hale, J. L. (1988). Nonverbal expectancy violations: Model elaboration and application to immediacy behaviors. *Communication Monographs*, 55, 58–79.

Cooper, P. (1995). *Communication for the classroom teacher* (5th ed.). Scottsdale, AZ: Gorsuch Scarisbrick.

Dansereau, F., & Markham, S. E. (1987). Superior-subordinate communication: Multiple levels of analysis. In F. M. Jablin, L. L. Putnam, K. H. Roberts, & L. W. Porter (Eds.), *Handbook of organizational communication: An interdisciplinary perspective* (pp. 343–388). Newbury Park, CA: Sage.

Fiske, S. T., & Neuberg, S. L. (1990). A continuum of impression formation, from category-based to individuating processes: Influences of information and motivation on attention and interpretation. In M. P. Zanna (Ed.), *Advances in experimental psychology* (Vol. 23, pp. 1–74). San Diego, CA: Academic Press.

Fiske, S. T., & Taylor, S. E. (1984). *Social cognition*. New York: Random House.

Fitzpatrick, M. A., & Ritchie, L. D. (1994). Communication schemata within the family: Multiple perspectives on family interaction. *Human Communication Research*, 20, 275–301.

Gross, B., & O'Hair, H. D. (1988). *Communicating in interpersonal relationships*. New York: Macmillan.

Heider, F. (1958). *The psychology of interpersonal relations*. New York: Wiley.

Holtzworth-Munroe, A., & Jacobson, N. S. (1985). Causal attributions of married couples: When do they search for causes? What do they conclude when they do? *Journal of Personality and Social Psychology*, 48, 1398–1412.

Honeycutt, J. M. (1995). Predicting relational trajectory beliefs as a consequence of typicality and necessity rating of relationship behaviors. *Communication Reports*, 12, 3–14.

Honeycutt, J. M., Cantrill, J. G., & Greene, R. W. (1989). Memory structures for relational escalation: A cognitive test of the sequencing of relational actions and stages. *Human Communication Research*, 16, 62–90.

Honeycutt, J. M., Cantrill, J. G., Kelly, P., & Lambkin, D. (1998). How do I love thee? Let me consider my options: Cognition, verbal strategies, and the escalation of intimacy. *Human Communication Research*, 25, 39–63.

Johnson, D. (1996). Helpful listening and responding. In K. M. Galvin & P. Cooper (Eds.), *Making connections: Readings in relational communication* (pp. 91–97). Los Angeles: Roxbury.

Jones, E. E., & Davis, K. (1965). From acts to dispositions: The attribution process in person perception. In L. Berkowitz (Ed.), *Advances in experimental social psychology* (Vol. 2, pp. 219–267). New York: Academic Press.

Jones, E. E., & Nisbett, R. E. (1972). The actor and the observer: Divergent perceptions of the causes of behavior. In E. E. Jones, D. E. Kanouse, H. H. Kelley, R. E. Nisbett, S. Valins, & B. Weiner (Eds.), *Attributions: Perceiving the causes of behavior* (pp. 79–94). Morristown, NJ: General Learning Press.

Jussim, L. (1990). Social reality and social problems: The role of expectancies. *Journal of Social Issues*, 46, 9–34.

Kellermann, K. (1984). The negativity effect and its implications for initial interaction. *Communication Monographs*, 51, 37–55.

Kelley, D. L., & Burgoon, J. K. (1991). Understanding marital satisfaction and couple type as functions of relational expectations. *Human Communication Research*, 18, 40–69.

Kelley, H. H. (1973). The processes of causal attribution. *American Psychologist*, 28, 107–128.

Kelly, L. (1972). Empathic listening. In J. Stewart (Ed.), *Bridges not walls: A book of interpersonal communication* (pp. 222–227). Reading, MA: Addison-Wesley.

Kirtley, M. D., & Honeycutt, J. M. (1996). Listening styles and their correspondence with second guessing. *Communication Research Reports*, 13, 174–182.

Lakoff, G. (1987). *Women, fire, and dangerous things: What categories reveal about the mind*. Chicago: University of Chicago Press.

Manusov, V. (1990). An application of attribution principles to nonverbal behavior in romantic dyads. *Communication Monographs*, 57, 104–118.

Manusov, V., Trees, A. R., Liotta, A., Koenig, J., & Cochran, A. T. (1999, May). *I think therefore I act: Interaction expectations and nonverbal adaptation in couples' conversations*. Paper presented to the Interpersonal Division of the International Communication Association, San Francisco.

Manusov, V., Winchatz, M. R., & Manning, L. M. (1997). Acting out our minds: Incorporating behavior into models of stereotype-based expectancies for cross-cultural interactions. *Communication Monographs*, 64, 119–139.

McComb, K. B., & Jablin, F. M. (1984). Verbal correlates of interviewer empathic listening and employment outcomes. *Communication Monographs*, 51, 353–371.

Merton, R. K. (1948). The self-fulfilling prophecy. *Antioch Review*, 8, 193–210.

Miller, D. T., & Turnbull, W. (1986). Expectancies and interpersonal processes. *Annual Review of Psychology*, 37, 233–356.

Monahan, J. L. (1998). I don't know it but I like you: The influence of nonconscious affect on person perception. *Human Communication Research*, 24, 480–500.

Nyquist, M. (1996). Learning to listen. In K. M. Galvin & P. Cooper (Eds.), *Making connections: Readings in relational communication* (pp. 98–100). Los Angeles: Roxbury.

Planalp, S. (1985). Relational schemata: A test of alternative forms of relational knowledge as guides to communication. *Human Communication Research*, 12, 3–29.

Rosenthal, R., & Rubin, D. B. (1978). Interpersonal expectancy effects: The first 345 studies. *Behavioral and Brain Sciences*, 3, 377–415.

Ross, L. (1977). The intuitive psychologist and his shortcomings: Distortions in the attribution process. In L. Berkowitz (Ed.), *Advances in experimental social psychology* (Vol. 10, pp. 173–220). New York: Academic Press.

Stiff, J. B., Dillard, J. P., Somera, L., Kim, H., & Sleight, C. (1988). Empathy, communication, and prosocial behavior. *Communication Monographs*, 55, 198–213.

Swann, W. B. (1987). Identity negotiation: Where two roads meet. *Journal of Personality and Social Psychology*, 53, 1038–1051.

———. (1990). To be adored or to be known: The interplay of self-enhancement and self-verification. In E. T. Higgins & R. M. Sorrentino (Eds.), *Handbook of motivation and cognition: Foundations of social behavior* (Vol. 2, pp. 408–448). New York: Guildford.

Thompson, T. (1994). Interpersonal communication and health care. In M. L. Knapp & G. R. Miller (Eds.), *Handbook of interpersonal communication* (pp. 696–725). Beverly Hills, CA: Sage.

## Questions

1. Think of a situation in which you and a friend have viewed the exact same event or situation in two very different ways. Why did this happen? List three reasons why you think your perceptions and opinions differed.

2. How do stereotypes help people process information? How do they hinder information processing? Give an example.

3. What role do interpersonal expectancies have in the perception process?

# B. Perceptual Filters

Social experience frames your world. The groups with which you are affiliated create a perceptual filter used to view the world. Three powerful social perceptual influences are your culture, your gender, and your family. These three factors will be addressed in the articles in this section; we chose them with the hope that you will think about your personal experiences as you read about the experiences of others.

Culture is "that set of values and beliefs, norms and customs, rules and codes, that socially define groups of people, binding them to one another and giving them a sense of commonality" (Trenholm and Jensen 2000, 368). Culture represents a collective answer to such fundamental questions as: "Who am I?" "Where do I fit in this world?" "How should I live my life?" and "How do I make sense out of the behaviors of others?" Although each person ultimately answers these questions individually, your personal viewpoints are affected by your culture.

How does this happen? First, culture affects perceptions; it influences what we see and how we see. It affects whether we view the world as an individual or as part of a collective society. For example, the typical Westernized family is often portrayed as parent(s) and children, a highly individualized unit. This is unlike the typical Chinese family that is more communal, including extended family members and ancestors. In the latter case, the behavior of specific members reflects directly on the entire family, a reality that influences many decisions. Ancestors are honored and counted as members of the family when the concept of family is discussed. What one says or does reflects directly on many other people because one is part of a collective society. In more Western-ized societies, one's communication acts are thought to reflect the individual rather than an entire family system.

Second, culture affects verbal and nonverbal language codes. Language is the primary tool a culture uses to transmit its values and beliefs. The Sapir-Whorf hypothesis suggests that your language determines how you view the world. If this is true, then people who speak different languages will experience the world differently. For example, English speakers use "you" regardless of the status or age of the person addressed. In German, however, there are two words: *du* for informal use and *Sie* for formal use—for strangers, those of high status, and older persons. Some cultures have no words for illnesses recognized in other cultures; what are symptoms in one culture may have different meanings in another one (Fadiman 1997). Cross-cultural speakers often display nonverbal language differences, particularly in their use of space. Natives of the Middle East tend to stand much closer to one another while speaking than persons raised in the United States, who prefer a greater spatial distance.

Third, culture affects role identity. The value placed on birth order, gender, or titles affects communication. In addition, the roles of children or elders vary across cultures. In some cultures children are expected to remain unobtrusive when adults are talking; in other cultures children are the center of attention for the adults and are welcomed into conversation.

Fourth, culture affects goal achievement. Some cultures emphasize social goals, while others emphasize task goals; whether business or friendship comes first will vary according to cultural norms. In some cultures individuals believe that they have little control over their future, that God controls their fate; in other cultures individuals are considered responsible for "making" their own destinies.

In order to communicate effectively with people from other cultures, it is necessary to be aware of and sensitive to cultural differences. Culture and communication are interdependent. Your culture teaches you how to communicate effectively, and culture is transmitted and maintained through communication. Persons raised in multiple cultures have greater potential to see the world through multiple cultural lenses.

A second major perceptual filter is gender. Males and females tend to be socialized differently, although the differences tend to be less sharp. For example, in our society males are socialized to be successful, aggressive, sexual, and self-reliant, whereas females are socialized to be nurturing, sensitive, interdependent, and concerned with appearance (Stewart et al. 2003; Wood 2005). Because of these differing socializations, males and females view the world somewhat differently; this is reflected in their communication styles. Until recently, men were discouraged from expressing feelings directly, whereas women were permitted to express theirs. Wood and Inman (1993) have developed masculine models of closeness, which emphasize sharing joint activities or doing things for others, approaches that differ from the more feminine pattern of self-disclosure.

In several of the articles in this text, you will read about gender issues related to relationship development and to various contexts such as friendship and marriage. As you read these pieces, recognize that you may respond in a particular manner based on your gender.

In addition to culture and gender, families and what you learn in them act as perceptual filters. All families have rules, themes, roles, and boundaries that influence members' communication. The family you grew up in—your "family of origin"—taught you a great deal about sharing affection, expressing anger, making decisions, and trusting others. These beliefs, in turn, affect your perceptions and communication. For example, if you grew up in a family with prescribed and rigid gender roles, your perception of what constitutes appropriate mother-child interaction will differ from someone raised in a family with flexible gender roles. You may be amazed at the way a friend argues with his mother, or confides in her, because that may not be comfortable for you. In addition, the family lessons about expressing emotions carry into all parts of your life. If your family taught you to express anger directly, you may have difficulty with a roommate who learned to keep anger inside or express it indirectly.

These three powerful forces—culture, gender, and family—are among those that shape your worldview and, hence, your communication patterns. The more fully you understand your own cultural, gendered, and family background, the more effectively you will be able to understand your current communication experiences.

## References

Fadiman, A. (1997) *The Spirit Catches You and You Fall Down*. New York: Farrar, Straus & Giroux.

Stewart, L., Cooper, P., Stewart, A., and Friedley, S. (2003). *Communication Between the Sexes*, 4th ed. Boston: Allyn & Bacon.

Trenholm, S., and Jensen, A. (2000). *Interpersonal Communication*. Belmont, CA: Wadsworth.

Wood, J. (2005). *Gendered Lives*, 5th ed. Belmont, CA: Wadsworth.

Wood, J., and Inman, C. (1993). In a different mode: Masculine styles of communicating closeness. *Journal of Applied Communication*, 21(3): 279–295. ✦

# 10
# The Necessity of Intercultural Communication

*James Neuliep*

If you have lived or traveled in different parts of the world, you know the joys and frustrations of intercultural communication. In a diverse society such as the United States, you regularly encounter individuals and groups with strong cultural traditions different from your own. Because most people view the world through the labels, categories, and concepts that are products of their culture, it can be difficult to communicate effectively outside that culture.

Several dimensions have been used to discuss cultural characteristics that might affect intercultural communication (Samovar and Porter 2001). The first dimension concerns ways in which members of a particular culture deliver messages. A low-context culture, such as that found in the United States, relies primarily on language to express thoughts, feelings, and ideas as clearly and logically as possible. Verbal fluency is admired, and a direct statement of opinions and desires is valued. In high-context cultures, such as that found in China or Japan, important information is carried in contextual and nonverbal cues (such as time, place, relationship between speakers, and situation). Relational harmony is valued, so communicators rely on a less direct verbal style. They rely heavily on contextual, nonverbal messages to convey important messages.

A second dimension involves the difference between individualistic and collectivistic cultures. A culture that values the individual believes that each person is a separate, unique individual who should be independent and self-sufficient. Such is the case in the United States, where value is placed on autonomy, youth, individual security, equality, and personal achievement. Many cultures in Latin America and Asia are collective. These cultures have a "we" rather than an "I" orientation. A high value is placed on order, duty, traditions, age, group security, and hierarchy. People are identified by their membership in extended families, and sometimes in their workplaces, and are expected to reflect a "we" orientation. High value is placed on acting as a group member rather than as an individual.

The third dimension, power distance, refers to the degree to which members of a society accept an unequal distribution of power. Cultures with low power distance believe in minimizing the differences between social classes. The culture of the United States is generally considered a low power distance culture. Low power distance cultures believe that challenging authority is acceptable, even desirable. High power distance cultures honor a strong hierarchy and the role of authority.

The word culture is a highly complex term, which, like communication, is easily recognized for what it is, but not as easily defined. You may very easily be able to identify an example of American culture, for instance, but not be able to define the term culture. Because culture plays a large role in shaping communicative practices, author James Neuliep uses the first half of this chapter to break down four different components of a definition of culture. Next, he explains a model for understanding the contexts in which intercultural communication take place, including cultural, microcultural, environmental, perceptual, and sociorelational contexts. Overall, this chapter provides further explanation for the occurrence of varying, and sometimes conflicting, perceptions on the part of different people, especially in situations involving intercultural participants with different backgrounds, values, beliefs, rules, and practices.

As you read this article, consider your own intercultural communication experiences and address this question: How do my cultural experiences affect my interactions with people from backgrounds different from my own?

### Reference

Samovar, L., and Porter, R. (2001). *Communication Between Cultures*. Belmont, CA: Wadsworth.

* * *

# The Benefits of Intercultural Communication

Although the challenges of an increasingly diverse world are great, the benefits are even greater. Communicating and establishing relationships with people from different cultures can lead to a host of benefits, including healthier communities; increased international, national, and local commerce; reduced conflict; and personal growth through increased tolerance. Joan England (1992) argues that genuine community is a condition of togetherness in which people have lowered their defenses and have learned to accept and celebrate their differences. England contends that we can no longer define equality as "sameness" but instead must value our differences with others, whether they be differences of race, gender, ethnicity, lifestyle, occupation, or professional discipline. Healthy communities are made up of individuals working collectively for the benefit of everyone, not just their own group. Through open and honest intercultural communication people can work together to achieve goals that benefit everyone, regardless of group or cultural orientation. According to M. Scott Peck (1987), the overall mission of human communication is (or should be) reconciliation. He argues that effective communication can ultimately lower or remove the walls and barriers of misunderstanding that separate human beings from one another. Peck states that the rules for community building are the same as the rules for effective communication. Communication is the foundation of all human relationships. Moreover, argues Peck, the principles of community are applicable to any situation in which two people are gathered together, including the global community, the home, business, or neighborhood. Healthy communities support all community members and strive to understand, appreciate, and acknowledge each member. . . .

As you communicate with people from different cultures, you learn more about them and their way of life, including their values, history, habits, and the substance of their personality. As your relationships with people from other cultures develop, you start to understand them better, perhaps even empathizing with them. One of the things you will learn eventually is that although your cultures are different, you have much in common. As humans we all have the same basic needs and desires—we just have different ways of achieving them. As we learn that our way is not the only way, we develop a tolerance for difference. . . .

# The Nature of Culture

Like communication, culture is ubiquitous and has a profound effect on humans. Culture is simultaneously invisible and pervasive. As we go about our daily lives, we are not overly conscious of our culture's influence on us. How often have you sat in your dorm room or classroom and consciously thought about what it means to be an American? As you stand in the lunch line, do you say to yourself, "I am acting like an American?" As you sit in your classroom do you say to yourself, "The professor is really acting like an American?" Yet most of your thoughts, emotions, and behaviors are culturally driven. One need only step into a culture different from one's own to feel the immense impact of culture.

Culture has a direct influence on the physical, relational, and perceptual environment. The next time you enter your communication classroom, consider how the room is arranged *physically*, including where you sit and where the professor teaches, the location of the chalkboard, windows, and so forth. Does the professor lecture from behind a podium? Do the students sit facing the professor? Is the chalkboard used? Next, think about your *relationship* with the professor and the other students in your class. Is the relationship formal or informal? Do you interact with the professor and students about topics other than class material? Would you consider the relationship personal or impersonal? Finally, think about your *perceptual disposition*—that is, your attitudes, motivations, and emotions about the class. Are you happy to be in the class? Do you enjoy attending? Are you nervous when the instructor asks you a question? To a great extent, the answers to these questions are contingent on your culture. The physical arrangement of classrooms, the social relationship between students and teachers, and the perceptual profiles of the students and teachers vary significantly from culture to culture.

Like communication, culture is difficult to define. Australian anthropologist Roger Keesing (1974, p. 73) argues that:

> Culture does not have some true and sacred and eternal meaning we are trying to discover, but that like other symbols, it means whatever we use it to mean; and that as with other analytical concepts, human users must carve out—and try to partly agree on—a class of natural phenomena it can most strategically label.

Just about everyone has a definition of culture. To be sure, over forty years ago two well-known anthropologists, Alfred Kroeber and Clyde Kluckhohn (1993), found and examined three hundred definitions of culture, none of which were the same. . . .

Although there may not be a universally accepted definition of culture, there are a number of properties of culture upon which most people agree describe its essence. In this textbook, *culture* is defined as *an accumulated pattern of values, beliefs, and behaviors, shared by an identifiable group of people with a common history and a verbal and nonverbal symbol system.*

## Culture as an Accumulated Pattern of Values, Beliefs, and Behaviors

Cultures can be defined by their value and belief systems and by the actions of their members. People who exist in the same culture generally share similar values and beliefs. . . . In the United States, individuality is highly valued. An individual's self-interest takes precedence over group interests. Americans believe that people are unique. Moreover, Americans value personal independence. Conversely, in Japan, a collectivistic and homogeneous culture, a sense of groupness and group harmony is valued. Most Japanese see themselves as members of a group first, as individuals second. Where Americans value independence, Japanese value interdependence. Norwegians value conformity. Norwegian children are taught to put the needs of society above their own. Cultural aspects of confor-

mity are embodied in what Norwegians call *Janteloven*, which denotes the fear of individuality, of standing out in a crowd. Although the Norwegian literacy rate is among the highest in the world, Norwegian schools do not have accelerated programs for gifted and talented students. Norwegians believe that to divide students on the basis of intellectual ability would disrupt the social cohesion (Yurkovich and Halverson, 1993).

The values of a particular culture lead to a set of expectations and rules prescribing how people should behave in that culture. Although many Americans prefer to think of themselves as unique individuals, most Americans behave in similar ways. Most work forty hours a week, receive some form of payment for their work, and pay some of their earnings in taxes. Most spend their money on homes and cars. Almost every home in the United States has a television. Observe the students around you in your classes. Although you may think that you are very different from your peers, you are really quiet similar to them. Most of them follow a daily behavioral pattern very similar to your own, attending classes, taking examinations, going to lunch, studying, partying, writing papers, and so forth.

## Culture as an Identifiable Group of People With a Common History

Because the members of a particular culture share similar values, beliefs and behaviors, they are identifiable as a distinct group. In addition to their shared values, beliefs, and behaviors, the members of a particular culture share a common history. Any culture's past inextricably binds it to the present and guides its future. At the core of any culture are traditions that are passed on to future generations. In many cultures, history is a major component of the formal and informal education systems. To learn a culture's history is to learn that culture's values. One way children in the United States develop their sense of independence is by learning about the Declaration of Independence, one of this country's most sacred documents. Elementary school children in Iran learn of the historical significance of the political and religious revolution that took place in their culture in the 1970s and 1980s. Russian children are taught about the arts in Russian history, including famous Russian composers such as Tchaikovsky, Rachmaninoff, and Stravinsky. The arts of the past help Russians remember their culture as they face the disrupting social and political crises of the present. Such historical lessons are the glue that binds people to one another (Westfahl, Koltz, and Manders, 1993).

## Culture as a Verbal and Nonverbal Symbol System

One of the most important elements of any culture is its communication system. The verbal and nonverbal symbols with which the members of a culture communicate are culture bound. To see the difference between the verbal codes of any two cultures is easy. The dominant verbal code in the United States is English whereas the dominant verbal code in Mexico is Spanish. Two cultures that share the same verbal code may have dramatically different verbal styles, however. Most white Americans use a very direct, instrumental, personal style in speaking English. Many Native Americans use an indirect, impersonal style in speaking English and may prefer the use of silence instead of words (Basso, 1990).

Nonverbal code systems vary significantly across cultures also. Nonverbal communication includes the use of body language, gestures, facial expressions, the voice, smell, personal and geographical space, time, and artifacts. Body language can communicate a great deal about one's culture. When adults interact with young children in the United States, it is not uncommon for the adult to pat the head of the child. This nonverbal gesture is often seen as a form of endearment and is culturally acceptable. In Thailand, however, where the head is considered the seat of the soul, such a gesture is unacceptable. Belching during or after a meal is viewed by most Americans as rude and impolite, perhaps even disgusting. But in parts of Korea and the Middle East, belching after a meal might be interpreted as a compliment to the cook (Axtell, 1991). . . .

## Microcultural Groups

Within most cultures there are groups of people, or *microcultures*, that coexist within the mainstream society. Microcultures exist within the broader rules and guidelines of the dominant cultural milieu but are distinct in some way, perhaps racially, linguistically, or through their sexual orientation, age, or even occupation. In some ways, everyone is a member of some microcultural group. Often microcultures may have histories that differ from the dominant cultural group. In many cases, microcultural groups are subordinate in some way, perhaps politically or economically. . . .

# A Contextual Model of Intercultural Communication

Intercultural communication occurs whenever a minimum of two persons from different cultures or microcultures come together and exchange verbal and nonverbal symbols. A central theme throughout this book is that intercultural communication is contextual. A contextual model of intercultural communication is shown in Figure 10-1.

According to the model, intercultural communication occurs within a variety of contexts, including (1) cultural, (2) microcultural, (3) environmental, (4) perceptual, and (5) sociorelational contexts. A context is a complex combination of a variety of factors, including the setting, situation, circumstances, background, and overall framework within which communication occurs. The largest, outer circle of the model in Figure 10-1 represents the *cultural context*. This is the largest circle because the dominant culture permeates every aspect of the communicative exchange, even the physical geography. All communicative exchanges between persons occur within some culture. . . .

The next-largest circle in the model is the *microcultural context*. As mentioned earlier, within most cultures, separate groups of people coexist. These groups, called microcultures, are in some way different from the larger cultural milieu. Sometimes the difference is ethnicity, race, or language. Often microcultures are treated differently by the members of the larger culture. . . .

The next-largest circle in the model is the *environmental context*. This circle represents the physical, geographical location of the in-

**Figure 10-1**
*A Contextual Model of Intercultural Communication*

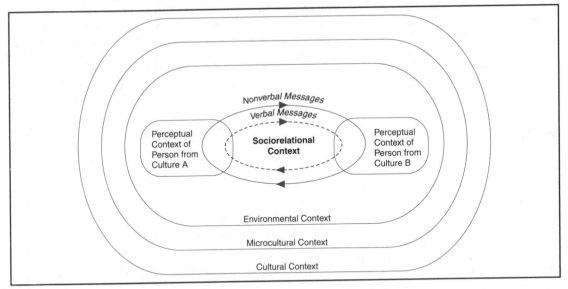

teraction. While culture prescribes the overall rules for communication, the physical location indicates when and where the specific rules apply. For example, in the United States there are rules about yelling. Depending on the physical location, yelling can be prohibited or encouraged. In church, yelling is generally prohibited, whereas at a football game, yelling is the preferred method of communicating. The physical environment includes the physical geography, architecture, landscape design, and even the climate of a particular culture. All of these environmental factors play a key role in how people communicate. . . .

The two circles in the model on either side of the sociorelational context represent the *perceptual* contexts of the individuals interacting. The perceptual context refers to the individual characteristics of the interactants, including their cognitions, attitudes, dispositions, and motivations. How an individual perceives the environment and gathers, stores, and retrieves information is uniquely human but also culturally influenced. How an individual develops attitudes about others, including stereotypes, varies from culture to culture. . . .

The circle intersecting the perceptual contexts in the model is the *sociorelational con-*

*text*—that is, the relationship between the interactants. Whenever two people come together and interact, they establish a relationship. Within this relationship each person assumes a role. Right now, you are assuming the role of student. The person teaching your communication class is assuming the role of teacher. Roles prescribe how people should behave. Most of the people with whom you interact are related to you through your role as student. The reason you interact with so many professors is because you are a student. What you interact about—that is, the topic of your interaction—is also defined by your role as student. You and your professors interact about courses. How you interact with your professor—that is, the style of talk (for example, polite language)—is also prescribed by your role as student. The language and style of your talk with your professor is probably very different from the language and style of talk you use when you go back to your dorm room and interact with your friends. Probably the last ten people with whom you interacted were directly related to you through your role as student. When you go back to your hometown during semester break and step into the role of son or daughter, or brother or sister, you are assuming a different role, and your interaction changes accordingly. Your interaction varies as a function of the role you assume.

Roles vary from culture to culture. Although in just about every culture there are student/teacher role relationships, how those roles are defined varies significantly. What it means to be a student in the United States is very different from what it means to be a student in Japan. In Japan, students go to school six days a week. Japanese teachers are highly respected and play a very influential role in the Japanese student's life. What it means to be a mother or father also varies considerably from one culture to another. In the Masai culture of Kenya, a woman is defined by her fertility. To be defined as a mother in Masai culture, a woman must endure circumcision (clitoridectomy), an arranged marriage, and wife beating (Angeloni, 1995). One's roles prescribe the types of verbal and nonverbal symbols that are exchanged.

In the model in Figure 10-1, the sociorelational context is graphically represented by two circles labeled "nonverbal messages" and verbal "messages." The nonverbal circle is larger of the two and is represented by a continuous line. The verbal circle is smaller and is represented as a series of dashes. The nonverbal-message circle is larger than the verbal-message circle because the majority of our communicative behavior is nonverbal. Whether we are using words or not, we are communicating nonverbally though eye contact, bodily stance, and space. In addition, our nonverbal behavior is ongoing—we cannot not behave. The verbal message circle is portrayed as a series of dashes to represent the *digital* quality of verbal communication. By digital, we mean that, unlike our nonverbal communication, our verbal communication is made up of words that have recognizable and discrete beginning and ending points. A word is like a digit. We can start and stop talking with words. Our nonverbal behavior goes on continuously, however. . . .

## References

Angeloni, E., ed. (1995). *Mystique of the Masai.* Guilford, CT: Dushkin.

Axtell, R. (1991). *Gestures: Do's and taboos of body language around the world.* New York: Wiley.

Basso, K. (1990). To give up on words: Silence in western Apache culture. In D. Carbaugh (Ed.), *Cultural communication and intercultural contact* (pp. 303–320). Hillsdale, NJ: Erlbaum.

England J. T. (1992). Building community for the 21st century, *ERIC Digest*, ED347489. www.ed.gov/databases/ERIC_Digests/ed347489.html.

Keesing, R. (1974). Theories of culture. In B. J. Siegel (Ed.), *Annual review of anthropology.* Palo Alto, CA: Annual Reviews.

Kroeber, A. I., and Kluckhohn, C. eds. (1954). *Culture: A critical review of concepts and definitions.* New York: Random House; H. N. Seelye. (1993). *Teaching culture: Strategies for intercultural communication.* Lincolnwood, IL: National Textbook Company.

Peck, M. S. (1987). *The different drum: Community making and peace.* New York: Touchstone.

Westfahl, G., Koltz, R., and Manders, A. (1996). "Ethnic Russian culture and society". Unpublished student manuscript, St. Norbert College, De Pere, WI; A. Resnick. (1993). *The commonwealth of independent states.* United States: Childrens Press.

Yurkovich, D., Pliscott, K. and Halverson, R. (1996). "The Norwegian culture". Unpublished student manuscript, St. Norbert College, De Pere, WI; A. R. Gayle and Knutson, K. P. (1993). Understanding cultural differences: Jenteloven and social conformity in Norway," *Et Cetera*, 50, 449.

## Questions

1. Define the word *culture*. Ask 10 other people to define *culture*. What are the similarities and differences in the definitions? What does this suggest about intercultural communication?

2. Think about an intercultural interaction you have had that was difficult. After reading this article, what things might you do differently if you found yourself in a similar situation?

3. An old adage suggests, "When in Rome, do as the Romans do." Based on this article, is that sound advice? Why or why not?

# 11
# When Miss America Was Always White

*Navita Cummings James*

You need not travel to another country to experience "culture shock,"—anxiety that results from losing all our familiar signs and symbols of social intercourse. Ethnic identity, social class, role, and regional identity can all lead to cultural misunderstanding. In the United States, differences in communication between members of the African American and white communities have been the subject of research for over 30 years.

In their book on interracial communication, Orbe and Harris (2001) suggest that one of the primary barriers to interracial friendships is stereotypes. Most people resist developing relationships across racial lines due to societal stereotypes. It is only when people meet as individuals, begin to recognize the uniqueness of each other, and listen to each other's stories that the potential for friendship emerges. Today, barriers are breaking down as more members of various ethnicities experience prolonged contacts through school, sports, jobs, and neighborhoods. The number of interracial friendships, romantic relationships, and marriages are growing. In addition, transracial and international adoption is creating mixed-race families. Given these growing changes, communication about similarities and differences is less threatening than it was when communication research in this area began. Yet, struggles still occur as stereotypes remain salient and persona stories remain untold.

Members of each culture experience family stories that pass on family values and prepare children for the world of adulthood. Race and culture directly or indirectly permeate such stories. Each individual has his or her own stories, often passed on by older family members, as well as beliefs and stereotypes about others.

In this chapter, communication scholar James develops her own life history and personal narrative to illustrate how the family stories about race that she heard as a child influenced her racial identity. The author first looks at the ways in which we define people in American culture, using gender, race, age, and social class as mechanisms through which we create roles and labels for both ourselves and others. She further emphasizes the importance of stories and personal narratives in this process of understanding one's identity and learning about others'. Through the sharing of several stories and discussing their significance in her own life, beliefs, and identity, she demonstrates how we can use our own stories and backgrounds to do the same.

As you read James' article, consider how your upbringing might have influenced the personal stories you relate. Think about the culture(s) in which you were raised. Consider this question: How much emphasis was placed on stories when you were growing up, and what did you learn from these stories?

### Reference

Oberg, K. (1985). Culture shock: Adjustment to new cultural environments. *Practicing Anthropology*, 7: 170–179.

Orbe, M. P. and Harris, T. M. (2001). *Interracial Communication: Theory Into Practice*. Belmont, CA: Wadsworth/Thomson Learning.

\* \* \*

I am a child of the American baby boom. I am a person of color, and I am a woman. All of these factors have influenced the creation of the person I am today, just as the time and place of each of our births, our genders, races, and ethnicities influence the people we are today. On some level, we all know that the configurations of these factors are intertwined with the unique life stories we each have to tell. But some stories are not as well known as others. For example, the lived experiences of everyday Black[1] women are not reflected very well in the academic knowledge base. Any student of the Black female experience in the United States, who is interested in how this female and racial identity has emerged, would be better served by studying the music written and performed by Black women, their novels, short stories, essays, and poems, or their oral and written life histories—rather than relying on traditional social scientific research.

In this [chapter], I will use my own life history and personal narrative to illustrate how family stories about race that I heard as a child influenced the development of my racial identity. These family stories were a powerful counterforce to the negative images of Blacks in the dominant culture, and they helped me to grow up believing that I could be a doctor, a lawyer, or whatever I wanted to be, assuming that I had the talent and that I worked hard. Nevertheless, I also knew a "colored girl" in the 1950s, no matter how smart, talented, or attractive she was, could never grow up to be President of the United States or Miss America.

Two related conceptual frameworks for studying the human experience inform my analysis of racial identity. The first framework assumes that individuals take an active role in constructing themselves within particular cultural contexts. The second framework assumes that one's personal story is a powerful way to gain insight into the way people construct their lives and social worlds. Each of these approaches is briefly addressed here.

The first framework undergirds much contemporary thinking on human behavior and is sometimes labeled social constructivism. It is based on the works of Berger and Luckman (1967), who argued that reality, culture, and personal identity are socially constructed by humans. The construction of personal identity, they suggest, is a dialectic between the self and the culture in which it evolves. Individual personal identities or selves evolve differently in given cultures, in part because those cultures provide different scripts and experiences for different people. What script one receives is based on socially significant constructs in the culture. For example, in the United States, gender, race, age, and class are socially significant. In other cultures, other social constructs

might be important. Because cultures change over time, the scripts and resulting meanings of gender, race, class, and age in a given culture may also change. So the meanings of gender, race, and class are not only culturally but historically bound. Another way to phrase this is that being a "colored" middle-class girl in the 1950s was not the same as being an "African American" middle-class girl in the 1990s.

The second framework of this essay addresses the role of narrative or personal story in social inquiry. The personal story is an important research strategy that gives us new insights into how people construct their lives. Anthropologist Mary Catherine Bateson in *Composing a Life* (1990) studied the personal stories of five extraordinary women. She revealed how women of significant achievement constructed their lives in a society that did not provide role models for female success outside the family.

Stories are memorable in ways that statistical studies are not. As they are recalled and given meaning, stories are not "right" or "wrong." Facts can be challenged, but a person's story *just is*. Also, as individuals and their life experiences are products of particular socio-cultural milieus, no one story is so unique or idiosyncratic that it cannot provide us insight into the overall human experience. One of the most powerful ways to gain an understanding of "the other" (e.g., a person from a culture other than one's own) is to hear or read the story of "the other" in *his or her own words*.

## Family Stories

The telling of family stories not only informs children about their past, but also passes on family values and helps prepare them to live in the world beyond the family. I was born in 1952 in Columbus, Ohio. One of the duties of my parents in the 1950s and 1960s was to help prepare my sister and me for a world that would attempt to put limitations on what we could achieve because of our race. Our family always refuted the dominant culture's message of what it meant to be "colored" or "Negro." Race was a frequent topic of discussion in our family, especially among the adults.

The most vivid race-related stories of my youth were about the treachery and violence of White men, how Whites could get away with any crime committed against Black people. These stories led me to believe that Black life was not highly valued by White people and that, in the eyes of White society, Black women had no virtue worth respecting or protecting.

The single most upsetting story I can recall, related to me by an aunt, happened to a young Black girl in Georgia in the 1920s. Two young school girls were walking down a road and met a drunken White man carrying a gun. He pulled one of the girls aside, put the gun in her mouth, and began to play a form of Russian roulette. One of the chambers was loaded, and he blew the back of the girl's head off. I expected my aunt to say that the man was punished and sent to jail. But *nothing* happened to him. Instead, White people felt pity on the man because he was drunk and had to witness his own folly, rather than for the murdered child and her family. I remember my horror that such a man could get away with killing a little Black girl *like me*.

The story taught me that White men were violent and not to be trusted. Other stories I heard about lynchings only served to reconfirm this for me. I was horrified when I learned about the practice of castrating Black men during lynchings and placing their genitals in their mouths or in jars to be displayed in community stores as trophies or warnings.

The other family stories I vividly recall were about the Cummings family from my father's side and the Pearson family from my mother's.

## The Cummings Family

According to my father, my great-grandfather "Gramps" was a slave in his youth and always carried the scars of the beatings he received as a child. One of the stories I recall was about Gramps' mother. She was the child of a slave woman and a White Virginian plantation owner. Apparently she resembled her father so much that the owner's wife became upset and had the child sold off. Because of her father's betrayal, the child hated Whites so intensely that she married the darkest man she could find.

There were several interesting stories about Gramps himself. At the age of 16 he was freed from slavery. As an adult he became a land owner in Laurens County, Georgia. He learned to read and passed his love of reading on to his children and grandchildren. He gave his daughters an education so they would not have to work in "Miss Anne's"[2] kitchen, and he gave his sons land. Gramps was one of the first people in his county to own a car. As the story goes, the Whites did not like the idea of a Black man owning a car when the vast majority of Whites could not afford them. So Gramps had to carry a shotgun with him to protect himself from jealous Whites.

The stories about Gramps and his family reinforced what I had been told about the evil of White men. I was shocked that a father would sell his own flesh and blood. As I grew up, I came to believe that being White was nothing to be proud of and that the light skin color of some Blacks (including myself) was a badge of shame. It seemed to me that Whites would resort to any means—even murder—to keep Blacks beneath them.

I later learned other families in the Black community educated their women so that daughters would not have to work in the homes of Whites. This strategy helps to explain, in part, why Black women often had more education than Black men and why this difference did not create tension in the Black community.

My father's stories about his own life also influenced me. Among the most vivid were those of his experiences during World War II. My father was a Tuskeegee Airman. He was very proud to have been part of a U.S. Army experiment to test whether Black men were intelligent enough to fly airplanes. The Tuskeegee Airmen units that ultimately served in Europe and North Africa had one of the most distinguished records of the war. After the war, however, Black pilots were not hired by the airlines unless, perhaps, they were interested in being janitors.

Some of the most painful memories of my childhood revolve around my father's business. Since he couldn't get a job as a civilian pilot, he fell back on skills he learned as a boy in Georgia—masonry and carpentry—and started his own contracting business. But racial discrimination followed him here as well. My father often complained that when Whites contracted with him, they would pay him less than what they paid the White contractors for the same work. Even after he finished the work, some would not pay him for weeks or months. However, I began to notice that not all Whites were alike. Jews seemed to be different. They would pay for quality regardless of whether a Black or White man did the work. At least they were more likely to hire and less likely to delay payment.

Perhaps the most important lesson I learned from my father's stories, that would later be reflected in my own life and the lives of my children, was the idea that many Whites fail to see the talents and accomplishments of Black people—even when the evidence is right before their eyes.

## The Pearson Family

The stories about Whites from my mother's family were less violent and shocking. Nat Pearson, my grandfather, was also a land owner. He lived in Wheeler County, Georgia. According to my mother, Whites respected "Mr. Nat" and his children. He was a hard-working and fair man. His wife was also respected in the community. She took food to the sick and the poor, Black or White, in addition to taking care of her nine children.

The Pearson family emphasized the importance of getting a college education. My mother and her eight siblings all attended college and earned degrees. (In my generation it was just expected that all 26 of us would earn at least *one* college degree.) In my mother's generation, the older children helped the younger ones through college by providing financial support. The family stuck together, helping one another. That was very important.

My mother emphasized different things than my father did when she talked about race. For example, she stressed how my grandmother helped poor Whites. My mother did not believe in any way that Blacks were inferior to Whites. She was very proud of her family, and there was no false humility here. However, as the mother of daughters, she did give

us one race-related warning: "There is only one thing a White man wants from a Black woman." She warned that Black women should be wary of White men, because, in the event of rape, the White man would probably go unpunished. We should never think of marrying a White man, because, according to her, a Black woman's virtue meant nothing to Whites.

My Pearson cousins were another source of information about race. While I was going to racially integrated schools in the North, most of them attended segregated schools in the South. I was amazed that they had all Black teachers, just as they were amazed that mine were all White.

My cousins and their friends loved to tease and tell jokes. They sometimes used profanity just out of hearing distance of the adults. During one of our visits to Georgia, I learned an interpretation of the origin of the word "motherfucker." They said it was used by the African slaves in the Old South to describe White men who raped their African slave mothers.

## Beliefs and Stereotypes

From these significant stories of my youth emerged a set of beliefs and stereotypes which provided a backdrop for my own lived experience. These beliefs and stereotypes about Blacks and Whites can be summarized as follows:

*Black People*

- Black people are "just as good" as White people—and in some ways (e.g., morally) better.

- Black people are just as smart and capable as White people, if not more so.

- Black people should always be prepared to fight for fair treatment from Whites.

- Black people have to be twice as good as Whites to be considered half as good.

*White People*

- White people are often violent and treacherous.

- White people probably have some kind of inferiority complex which drives them to continually "put down" Blacks and anyone else who is not White.

- White men often rape Black women. If they say they love a Black woman, they are doing so to gain sexual favors. A White man would never marry a Black woman.

- Most White people do not want to see Blacks rewarded for their abilities and accomplishments.

- Most Whites, especially Northerners, cannot be trusted. They can hardly ever be a real friend to a Black person.

- White men are usually arrogant. White women are usually lazy.

- There are some good White people, but they are the exceptions.

These childhood beliefs and stereotypes, however, did *not* become an intellectual prison of my self-identity or beliefs about Whites. Below, I address how these beliefs and stereotypes blended with my own experiences. From this dialectical interaction, my racial identity emerged.

## The Dialectic of Family Stories, Culture, and Identity

Earlier, I suggested that the construction of personal identity is a dialectic between self and culture. In some circumstances, families may reinforce the messages of the dominant culture, but as we have seen in my case, my family's messages ran counter to it. The social-cultural milieu of the integrated North in the 1950s was rife with overt and covert messages about Blacks. Whites often pretended that there was no prejudice in the North. Yet the dominant culture portrayed Black people as stupid, lazy, dirty, dishonest, ugly—and invisible. We were unwelcome in many public places, even if it was legal for us to be there. If my self-image had relied solely on the messages of the dominant culture, I might have grown up with low self-esteem and seen no value in being Black.

Instead, my family's stories gave me pride in my people and in myself. They encouraged me to reject the dominant culture's scripts and embrace those from my family

and the Black community that said I was a person of value and worth. The stories became a sort of metaphorical shield that protected me from the larger, hostile culture. In high school, I learned that there were many times I did not need the shield, e.g., with some of my White schoolmates. But I also learned that, because racism is a constant feature of our culture, I would be a fool to ever throw that shield away.

Moreover, I had to revise my stereotyped ideas about Whites and Blacks—hence about myself. For example, I learned that race was not a good predictor of violence—gender was; and that race was not a good predictor of intelligence—income and opportunities were. I further came to believe that all people, regardless of color, deserve to be treated with dignity and respect. We are all equal in God's eyes and in principle in American cultural mythology. Finally, I learned that prejudice existed on both sides of the color line, but sometimes for different reasons.

Through this dialectical process, my beliefs and stereotypes changed and evolved. I made definitive choices about how I would relate to others. Unlike some Blacks who preferred to socialize only with Blacks, I chose to have friends of diverse backgrounds, including Whites.

I am now the mother of two girls. What is the role of family stories related to race in *my* family? I have already had to reassure my four-year-old that "brown" people are good and beautiful. I have stressed the importance of reading and education in our family—values which span generations. And I have passed along my parents' stories, along with my own experiences. For example, I have told my twelve-year-old how as children my sister and I used to run excitedly into the living room whenever there was someone Black on TV. In the 1950s, it was a rare occurrence to see someone Black on TV. And I told her how beauty pageants such as the Miss America Pageant celebrated only European standards of beauty, so Miss America was always White.

In the course of my daughters' childhoods, Black women have finally been crowned Miss America. But when I was a child, I secretly yearned for a Black Miss America. To me that would have been a sign that our culture was learning to value Black women—that we could be viewed as beautiful, smart, and virtuous.

As I grew up, I fantasized about what my life might have been like were race not such a socially significant construct in the United States: after World War II my father would have been hired as a commercial airline pilot and our family would have flown the world for free. I would have been able to afford the Ivy League school I could not attend for lack of funds. I would have studied in Paris, become an anthropologist/pilot, and gone to Africa. . . .

As for Miss America? I would have been too busy traveling to have cared about her.

## Notes

1. The use of the upper case "B" in the word "Black," when Black refers to African Americans, is a convention dating back to the 1960s and is still currently utilized by some writers. In the late 1960s and early 1970s, the common usage of the word "Negro" changed to "black." However, since black referred to a people and not just a color, some writers thought the upper case "B" in Black seemed more appropriate and dignifying. (Some of these writers also adopted the equivalent use of the upper case "W" when referring to Whites.) Also, since terms used to describe other ethnic and racial groups utilized upper case first letters, for the major descriptor for Black to appear with a lower case "b" seemed an unfortunate, yet grammatically correct, way to reinforce the stereotypical view of Blacks as less important. Black writers using this convention recognized the subtle power of language and that rules of language and grammar are arbitrary and evolve over time. These writers chose to take an active role in promoting what they viewed as a useful change.

2. "Miss Anne" is an unflattering term referring to White women.

## References

Bateson, M. C. (1990). *Composing a life*. New York: Plume.

Berger, P. L. and Luckman, C. (1967). *The social construction of reality*. Garden City, NY: Anchor Books.

Leeds-Hurwitz, W. (1992). Forum Introduction: Social Approaches to Interpersonal Communication. *Communication Theory*, 2, 131–139.

## Questions

1. How have your family stories about race, or lack of such stories, influenced your ideas about interacting with people of another race?

2. Describe the culture you were raised in. What communication rules are characteristic of your culture? How has this background affected your development of new relationships?

3. What family stories have you or will you tell to your children? What messages are contained in these stories that you wish to convey?

# 12
# Why Examine Family Background?

*Mary Kay DeGenova and
F. Philip Rice*

Your experiences in your family of origin serve as a perceptual filter as you enter into new relationships, close friendships, and romantic partnerships. Family of origin *refers to the family or families in which a person is raised, and is generally thought to be the earliest and most powerful influence in one's personality (Bochner and Eisenberg 1987). Families of origin provide blueprints for the communication of future generations. Initially, communication is learned in the home, and, throughout life, the family setting provides a major testing ground for new communication skills or strategies. Young people leaving families of origin to form new families take with them a set of conscious and unconscious ways of relating to people.*

*Family relationship models act as a guide for children's behavior and become central to their interpretation of others' behavior (Dixson 1995). For instance, if you have lived in a stepfamily, you may have witnessed the stress involved in integrating your stepparent's family of origin influences into a system with communication patterns that already reflected two other families of origin.*

*Although family of origin issues focus on parent-to-child transmissions, recently greater emphasis has been placed on influences across generations. In recent years family scholars and researchers have focused more directly on the effect of multigenerational systems, suggesting, "Evidence indicates a link between the parenting children receive and their subsequent behaviors" (Buerkel-Rothfuss, Fink, and Buerkel 1995, 63). Some of the issues that may* be used to examine multigenerational issues include how gender roles are played out, how families deal with losses, how ethnic patterns affect interactions, how affection is shared, how family boundaries are managed, and how members deal with conflict. These issues are viewed across three or four generations to see how patterns are passed down, consciously or unconsciously.

*Yet, although patterns do move across generations, changes also occur. In their study of grandfather-father-son relational closeness patterns, Buerkel-Rothfuss, Fink, and Buerkel (1995) conclude that "males use communication behaviors similar to those of their fathers, and in many cases, their grandfathers, but father-son relationships may be evolving into a more positive form than they were in the 1940s and 1950s" (p. 80).*

*Many of you may desire a family life different from the one in which you grew up, yet you find yourself re-creating similar patterns in a new relationship. Because parental socialization serves as a major factor in determining children's family-formation behavior (Dixson 1995), children often establish marriages similar to those of their parents, not because of heredity but because they are following family patterns. Yet, in their study of fathers' and sons' patterns of sharing affection, Floyd and Morman (2000) found that some sons modeled their father, whereas others behaved in opposite ways with their children, thus compensating for their upbringing.*

*This chapter discusses the ways in which families shape your self-understanding, values, attitudes, roles, and habits. Through a careful discussion of family influence and impact, the authors also emphasize the need to take personal responsibility for one's own actions and choices. Family background, therefore, can be seen and used as a learning tool and an important resource, not as an excuse for undesirable behaviors or lifestyle choices. As you read this chapter, ask yourself the following: What is one communication-related pattern from your family of origin that you anticipate maintaining in your life?*

## References

Bochner, A. P., and Eisenberg, E. (1987). Family process: System perspectives. In C. Berger and S. Chaffee (Eds.), *Handbook of Communication Science*, pp. 540–563. Beverly Hills, CA: Sage Publications.

Buerkel-Rothfuss, N., Fink, D. S., and Buerkel, R. A. (1995). Communication in the father-child dyad: The intergenerational transmission process. In T. J. Socha and G. H. Stamp (Eds.), *Parents, Children, and Communication*, pp. 63–85. Mahwah, NJ: Lawrence Erlbaum.

Dixson, M. D. (1995). Models and perspectives of parent-child communication. In T. Socha and G. Stamp (Eds.), *Parents, Children, and Communication*, pp. 433–462. Mahwah, NJ: Lawrence Erlbaum.

Floyd, K. and Morman, M.T. (2000). Affection received from fathers as a predictor of the men's affection with their own sons: Tests of the modeling and compensation hypotheses. *Communication Monographs*, 67, 347–361.

*  *  *

Our values, attitudes, and habits are largely molded by our family, although the influence of parents is subject to a number of variables. By being conscious of the positive and negative aspects of our family background, we can make responsible choices about the kind of partner we want to be and, if we choose to become partners, the kind of parent we want to be. Without understanding what influences behavior, it is very difficult to work toward change.

## Understanding the Socializing Influence of the Family

The family is the chief socializing influence on children. In other words, the family is the principal transmitter of knowledge, values, attitudes, roles, and habits from one generation to the next. Through word and example, the family shapes a child's personality and instills modes of thought and ways of acting that become habitual. This process is called *generational transmission* (Peterson and Rollins, 1987).

This learning takes place partly through the formal instruction that parents provide their children and partly through the system of rewards and punishments they use to control children. Learning also takes place through *reciprocal parent-child interaction*, as each influences and modifies the behavior of the other in an intense social process. And learning occurs through *observational modeling*, as children observe, imitate, and model the behavior that they find around them (Bandura, 1976). What parents say is important, but what children perceive parents to believe and do influences them most. As adults, our attitudes toward marital and parental roles are strongly related to the marital and parental role attitudes of our parents (Snyder, Velasquez, and Clark, 1997).

## Determining Differential Effects

Not all children are influenced to the same degree by their families. The degree of influence that parents exert depends partly on the frequency, duration, intensity, and priority of their social contacts with their children. Parents who are emotionally close to their children and who have long-term loving relationships with them exert more influence than do those who are not so close and who relate to their children less frequently. Moreover, family influence may be either modified or reinforced by influences outside the family: the school, church, other social organizations, peer groups, or the mass media. Here again, the extent of influence depends partly on the duration and intensity of the exposure.

Another important factor in determining the influence of the family is the differences among individual children. Not all children react in the same way to the same family environment because children differ in temperament, cognitive perception, developmental characteristics, and maturational levels. Because A happens does not mean that B will inevitably result. When children are brought up in an unhappy, conflicting family, it is more difficult for them to establish happy marriages themselves (Fine and Hovestadt, 1984), but some still do. A person's marital fate is not cast in concrete.

## Developing Self-Understanding

Not all children are influenced by their families to the same degree, and not all react the same way to the same environment. However, background has an effect, whatever it might be. The first task in developing self-understanding is determining what effects our families have had on us and evaluating them and the dynamics of their development.

What we have learned in our family of origin may be either helpful or detrimental to subsequent group living. Thus, a family may instill qualities of truth or deceit, of kindness or cruelty, of cooperation or self-centeredness, or of tolerance or obstinacy (Elliot, 1986). In relation to marriage and family living itself, the family may teach flexible or rigid gender roles. It may exemplify and teach democratic or authoritarian power patterns. It may teach rational communication skills or habits of destructive conflict. It may teach children how to express love and affection or how to withhold it. Parents may model responsibility or irresponsibility; they may teach that sex is healthy and pleasurable or that it is dirty and painful. The family helps children develop positive self-images and self-esteem or negative self-images. The family may teach the value of work and the wise management of money or ways to avoid work and mismanage money. The family may teach what a happy marriage can be like or how miserable marriage can be. By examining family background, we can determine how much influence our family of origin had and whether it was positive or negative.

## Assuming Personal Responsibility

Another task in examining family background is to begin to choose the goals and directions we want to take and to assume responsibility for our own selves. We can't continue to blame our parents for our problems if these problems are ever to be solved (Caplan, 1986). Nor can we assume that everything will be all right just because we grew up in a happy home.

When grown children enter into intimate relationships, they bring with them the background of experiences from their own families. They tend to feel that the way they were brought up is either the right way (which they try to duplicate in their own families) or the wrong way (which they try to avoid). By examining our family background, we can

develop insight into what our own attitudes, feelings, and habits are, how these might cause us to respond, and whether we need to change any of them. Consider this example:

One couple in their middle fifties went to a marriage counselor after the wife announced she wanted to divorce her husband. The wife's chief complaint was her husband's authoritarian dominance over the family. The wife explained: "Everything has to be done his way. He never considers my wishes. Several years ago I wanted to remodel the kitchen. It was going to cost five thousand dollars, but I was going to pay for it out of my own salary. He said he didn't want the kitchen remodeled and that was that. Our relationship has always been like that. I never do anything I want to do. So I decided I couldn't stand it any longer. I'm leaving him."

In subsequent counseling sessions, the family backgrounds of the couple were explored. The husband pointed out that his father was a dictator in his family. "I really got so I couldn't stand my father," the husband explained.

"And you're just like him," the wife remarked.

It was difficult for the husband to accept this observation at first, but by talking about his experience with his dad compared to his present role as a father, he was able to determine that he needed to change himself.

He did, and the marriage survived. (Author's counseling notes)

## Making Peace With the Past

Examining family background also enables us to "make peace with our past." For example, if we are afraid of marriage because our parents were unhappily married, examining background experiences helps us to face these anxieties honestly and to rid ourselves of them so that we can dare to marry. Similarly, spouses who become hostile toward their partner because of unhappy experiences with their own parents may have difficulty relating to a partner in a positive, warm way. For example, research has indicated that physical violence witnessed in one's family of origin is predictive of greater psychological distress in adulthood for men and women. Men's reports of symptoms of psychological distress, such as depression or mental illness, in the family of origin indicate that this distress was an important contributor to their own displays of physical and verbal aggression in their marriages (Julian, McKenry, Gavazzi, and Law, 1999). Facing the past squarely, talking about it, and releasing the anger will often help people to change their feelings and behaviors. Similar steps have helped adult children of alcoholics move beyond their damaging histories.

## References

Bandura, A. (1976). *Social Learning Theory.* Englewood Cliffs, NJ: Prentice-Hall.

Caplan, P. J. (1986, October). Take the blame off mother. *Psychology Today*, 20, 70–71.

Elliot, F. R. (1986). *The Family: Change or Continuity?* Atlantic Highlands, NJ: Humanities Press International.

Fine, M., and Hovestadt, A. J. (1984). Perceptions of marriage and rationality by levels of perceived health in the family of origin. *Journal of Marriage and Family Therapy*, 10, 193–195.

Julian, T., McKenry, R., Gavazzi, S., and Law, J. (1999). Test of family of origin structural models of male verbal and physical aggression. *Journal of Family Issues*, 20(3), 397–423.

Peterson, G. W., and Rollins, B. C. (1987). Parent-child socialization. In M. B. Sussman and S. K. Steinmetz (Eds.), *Handbook of Marriage and the Family* (pp. 471–507). New York: Plenum.

Snyder, D. K., Velasquez, J. M., and Clark, B. L. (1997). Parental influence on gender and marital role attitudes: Implication for intervention. *Journal of Marital and Family Therapy*, 23, 191–201.

## Questions

1. To what extent do you believe that individuals enact communication patterns similar to those in their family of origin? Cite two examples to support your position.

2. In what ways do you believe you or your siblings influenced your parents' communication behavior through reciprocal parent-child interaction?

3. What is one communication-related pattern from your family of origin that you hope to carry into your parenting behavior? What pattern would you wish to avoid in your parenting experiences?

---

# 13
# Growing Up Masculine, Growing Up Feminine

*Julia T. Wood*

What does it mean to be masculine or feminine in our society? The family introduces the child to the definitions, meanings, and values of gender in the child's culture. The majority of males and females embody these definitions, meanings, and values in their own communication, thus perpetuating existing social and cultural views of gender.

Gender identity is believed to begin at an early age. Fagot, Leinbach, and O'Boyle (1992) indicate that the year between a child's second and third birthdays is the time during which gendered perceptions of toys, clothing, household objects, games, and work are acquired. During this time period, children learn to label boys and girls accurately and to become aware that they themselves belong in one category or the other.

Today, two approaches dominate understanding of gendered family communication. Historically, scholars conceptualized gender as role bound, with women and men playing distinct parts in response to socialization and particular settings or circumstances in which their roles were embedded. From this role perspective, men and women "are seen as enacting roles that are separable, often complementary, and necessary elements to the integrity of the social settings or structures in which the roles are embedded" (Fox and Murry 2000, 1163). This approach reifies difference between the sexes and suggests that gender-specific socialization of boys and girls both takes place in and reproduces different masculine and feminine

speech communities. Such communities are purported to represent different cultures—"people who have different ways of speaking, acting, and interpreting, as well as different values, priorities, and agendas" (MacGeorge et al. 2004, 144). For example, Martin, Wood, and Little (1990) argue that gender ideologies develop through a series of stages:

> Children in the first stage ... learn what kinds of things are directly associated with each sex, such as "boys play with cars, and girls play with dolls.". ... Around the ages of 4–6, children seem to move to the second stage, where they begin to develop the more indirect and complex associations for information relevant to their own sex but have yet to learn these associations for information relevant to the opposite sex. By the time they are 8, children move to the third stage, where they have also learned the associations relevant to the opposite sex. These children have mastered the gender concepts of masculinity and femininity that link information within and between the various content domains. (p. 1893)

The alternative approach views gender as a social construct that embodies cultural meanings of masculinity and femininity; essentially, gender is conceived as "a constituent element of social structures, intricately interwoven with other elements of social structures such as class and race, and tied to the social distribution of societal resources" (Fox and Murry 2000, 1164). This approach assumes that "gender is disengaged from norms based on heterosexuality and power differences between men and women, and relationships are thought of in terms of equality rather than gender differences" (Knudson-Martin and Laughlin 2005, 110). No matter how you choose to view gender, the rapidly changing world in which you live will present you with increasingly ambiguous data.

Given the increasing diversity of family life, the social construction lens may be an increasingly valuable way to view gender in families. In other words, many children no longer experience a dress rehearsal that prepares them for future family or relational life. Rather, more adults will have to "make it up as they go along" because, as the possibilities expand, so does the nature of gendered family experiences (Galvin in press).

*In the following article, Wood presents themes of growing up for both males and females. She provides the different socially understood expectations for most males and females in this society, and raises the issue of what happens when people do not adapt to these gendered themes. Finally, the question of growing up outside these conventional roles is addressed. Consider your own growing up as you read these themes, and consider this question: To what extent are these gendered themes consistent with your youthful experience?*

## References

Fagot, B., Leinbach, M., and O'Boyle, C. (1992). Gender labeling, gender stereotyping, and parenting behaviors. *Developmental Psychology*, 28:225–230.

Fox, G. L., and Murry, V. M. (2000). Gender and families: Feminist perspectives and family research. *Journal of Marriage and the Family*, 62:1160–1172.

Galvin, K. M. (in press). Gender and family interaction: Dress rehearsal for an improvisation? In B. Dow and J. T. Wood (Eds.), *The SAGE Handbook of Gender and Communication*. Thousand Oaks, CA: Sage Publications.

Knudson-Martin, C. and Laughlin, M. J. (2005). Gender and sexual orientation in family therapy: Toward a postgender approach. *Family Relations*, 54:101–115.

MacGeorge, E. L., Graves, A. R., Feng, B., Gillihan, S. J., and Burleson, B. R. (2004). The myth of gender cultures: Similarities outweigh differences in men's and women's provision of and responses to supportive communication. *Sex Roles*, 50:143–175.

Martin, C. L., Wood, C. H., and Little, J. K. (1990). The Development of gender stereotype components. *Child Development*, 61:1891–1904.

\* \* \*

## Growing Up Masculine

What does it mean to be masculine in the United States in the 21st century? . . .In his book *The Male Experience*, James A. Doyle (1997) identifies five themes of masculinity. . . . We will consider each of these elements of the male role, as well as a sixth that seems to have emerged since Doyle made his analysis.

*Don't be female* seems to be the most fundamental requirement for manhood. Early in life, most boys learn they must not think, act, or feel like girls and women. Any male who shows sensitivity or vulnerability is likely to be called sissy, crybaby, mama's boy, or wimp (Kantrowitz & Kalb, 1998; Pollack, 2000). The antifemale directive is at least as strong for African American men as for European American men. . . . [M]any gay males discover that straight men consider them unmanly.

The second element of the male role is the command to *be successful*. Men are expected to achieve status in their professions, to "make it." Warren Farrell (1991) writes that men are regarded as "success objects," and their worth as marriage partners, friends, and men is judged by how successful they are at what they do. Training begins early with sports, where winning is stressed (Messner, 2000). Peer groups pressure males to be tough, aggressive, and not feminine (Lobel & Bar, 1997; Ponton, 1997).

. . . [T]he theme of success translates not just into being good at what you do but into being better than others, more powerful than peers, pulling in a bigger salary than your neighbors, and having a more expensive home, car, and so on than your friends. Most men today . . . think that being a good provider is the primary requirement for manhood—an internalized requirement that appears to cut across lines of race and economic class (Eagly, 1996; Ranson, 2001).

A third injunction for masculinity is to *be aggressive*. Even in childhood, boys are often encouraged to be roughnecks or at least are seldom scolded for being so (Cohen, 1997). They are expected to take stands and not run from confrontations (Nelson, 1994b; Newburger, 1999; Pollack, 2000). Later, sports reinforce early training by emphasizing aggression, violence, and toughness (Messner, 2000). Coaches psych teams up with demands that they "make the other team hurt, hurt, hurt" or "make them bleed." The masculine code tells men to fight, inflict pain on others, endure pain stoically themselves, and win, win, win. Dr. Michael Miller (2003) says that many men don't seek help when they are depressed because their gender identity is "tied up with strength, independence, efficiency, and self-control" (p. 71).

Men's training in aggression may be linked to violence (Gordon, 1988; Kivel, 1999; Messner, 1997a,b), especially violence against women. Because masculine socialization encourages aggression and dominance, some men think they are entitled to dominate women. This belief surfaces in studies of men who rape (Costin & Schwartz, 1987; Scott & Tetreault, 1987) and men who abuse girl-friends and wives (Gelles & Straus, 1988; Wood, 2001, In press). One study (Thompson, 1991) reports that both college women and men who are violent toward their dates have masculine gender orientations, reminding us again that *gender* and *sex* are not equivalent terms.

A fourth element of the male role is captured in the injunction to *be sexual*. Men should be interested in sex—all the time, anytime. They are expected to have a number of sexual partners; the more partners a man has, the more of a stud he is (Gaylin, 1992; Martin & Hummer, 1989). During rush, a fraternity recently sent out invitations with the notation "B.Y.O.A.", which one of my students translated for me: Bring your own ass. Defining sexual conquest as a cornerstone of masculinity encourages men to view and treat women as sex objects rather than as multidimensional human beings (Brownmiller, 1993; French, 1992; Russell, 1993).

Finally, Doyle says the male sex role demands that men *be self-reliant*. A "real man" doesn't need others, particularly women. He depends on himself, takes care of himself, and relies on nobody. Autonomy is central to social views of manliness. As we noted earlier, male self-development typically begins with differentiation from others, and from infancy most boys are taught to be self-reliant and self-contained (Newberger, 1999; Thompson & Pleck, 1987). Men are expected to be emotionally controlled, not to let feelings control them, and not to need others.

In addition to the five themes of masculinity identified by Doyle, a sixth seems to have emerged. This theme highlights the mixed messages about being men that confront many boys and men today: *Embody and transcend traditional views of masculinity.* . . .

For many men today, the primary source of pressure to be conventionally masculine is other men who enforce what psychologist William Pollack (2000) calls the "boy code." Boys and, later, men encourage each other to be silent, tough, and independent and to take risks. Boys and men who don't measure up often face peer shaming ("You're a wuss," "Do you do everything she tells you to do?"). At the same time, many men feel other pressures—often from romantic partners, female friends, and mothers—to be more sensitive and emotionally open and to be a full partner in running a home and raising children. It's hard to be both traditionally male and not traditionally male. Just as women in the 1960s and 1970s were confronted with mixed messages about being traditionally female and not, men today are negotiating new terrain and new ways of defining themselves.

What happens when men don't measure up to the social expectations of manhood? Some counselors believe men's striving to live up to social ideals of masculinity has produced an epidemic of hidden male depression (Kahn, 1997). Terrence Real is a psychotherapist who specializes in treating depressed men. According to Real (1997), male depression is widespread, and so is society's unwillingness to acknowledge it, because it is inconsistent with social views of masculinity. Whereas depressed women suffer the social stigma of having emotional problems, Real says men who admit they are depressed suffer the double stigma of having emotional problems and being unmanly by society's standards.

The first five themes of masculinity clearly reflect gender socialization in early life and lay out a blueprint for what being a man means. Yet we also see a sixth theme that points out and challenges the contradictions in traditional and emerging views of masculinity. Individual men have options for defining and embodying masculinity, and many men are crafting nontraditional identities for themselves. . . .

## Growing Up Feminine

What does it mean to be feminine in the United States in the 21st century? Casual talk and media offer us two quite different versions of modern women. One suggests that women now have it all. They can get jobs that were formerly closed to them and rise to the top levels of their professions; they can have egalitarian marriages with liberated men and raise nonsexist children. At the same time, our culture sends us the quite different message that women may be able to get jobs, but fewer than 20% will actually be given opportunities to advance to the highest levels of professional life. Crime statistics warn us that the incidence of rape is rising, as is battering of women. We discover that married women may have careers, but more than 80% of them still do most of the housework and child care. And media relentlessly carry the message that youth and beauty are women's tickets to success. Prevailing images of women are conflicting and confusing. . . . We can identify five themes in current views of femininity and womanhood.

The first theme is that *appearance still counts.* . . . [W]omen are still judged by their looks (Greenfield, 2002; Haag, 2000). To be desirable, they are urged to be pretty, slim, and well dressed. The focus on appearance begins in the early years of life, when girls are given dolls and clothes, both of which invite them to attend to appearance. Gift catalogues for children regularly feature makeup kits, adornments for hair, and even wigs so that girls learn early to spend time and effort on looking good. Dolls, like the ever-popular Barbie, come with accessories such as extensive wardrobes so that girls learn that clothes and jewelry are important. Teen magazines for girls are saturated with ads for makeup, diet aids, and hair products. Central to current cultural expectations for women is thinness, which can lead to harmful and sometimes fatal eating disorders (Davies-Popelka, 2000; Pike & Striegel-Moore, 1997). . . .

The ideals of feminine appearance are communicated to women when they enter retail stores. Most manikins in stores are size 2, 4, or 6, which does not reflect the size of most normal, real-life women. Social prescriptions for feminine beauty are also made clear by the saleswomen, who are often hired because of their looks, not their experience or skills. Stores that market to young women like to hire people who are young, sexy, and good-looking. According to Antonio Serrano, a former assistant store manager for Abercrombie and Fitch, he and other employees were told by upper management "to approach someone in the mall who we think will look attractive in our store. But if someone came in who had lots of retail experience and not a pretty face, we were told not to hire them at all" (Greenhouse, 2003, p. 10 YT). Elysa Yanowitz, who was a regional sales manager for L'Oreal stores, says she was pressured to hire physically attractive saleswomen and once told to fire a top-performing employee who was "not hot enough" (Greenhouse, 2003, p. 10 YT). The Equal Employment Opportunity Commission has brought suit against a number of companies for discriminating against people who do not meet the current ideals for attractiveness.

At Abercrombie and Fitch, The Gap, and throughout the culture in general, cultural ideals of feminine beauty continue to reflect primarily White standards (Lont, 2001). Women of color may be unable to meet White standards of beauty on the one hand and, on the other, to reject the standards that the culture as a whole prescribes (Garrod, Ward, Robinson, & Kilkenny, 1999; Haag, 2000). In a critique of Blacks' acceptance of White standards of beauty, bell hooks (1994, 1995) describes the color caste system among Blacks whereby lighter skin is considered more desirable. She also points out that some Black children learn early to devalue dark skin, and many Black men regard biracial women as the ideal. In a society as ethnically diverse as ours, we need to question and challenge standards that reflect and respect only the identities of some groups.

A second cultural expectation of women is to *be sensitive and caring.* Women feel pressure to be nice, deferential, and helpful in general, whereas men are not held to the same requirements (Hochschild, 1975, 1979, 1983; Tavris & Baumgartner, 1983). In addition, girls and women are supposed to care about and for others. It's part of their role as defined by the culture. From assuming primary responsibility for young children to taking care of elderly, sick, and disabled relatives, women do the preponderance of hands-on caring (Aronson, 1992; Cancian & Oliker,

2000; Ferguson, 2000). Caring for others is seen as a requirement for femininity.

. . . When psychologist Barbara Kerr (1997, 1999) asks . . . [what an ideal day would be like for you 10 years in the future] of undergraduates in her classes, she reports a striking sex difference in responses. College men tend to describe their perfect day like this:

> I wake up and get into my car—a really nice, rebuilt '67 Mustang—and then I go to work—I think I'm some kind of manager of a computer firm—then I go home, and when I get there, my wife is there at the door (she has a really nice figure), she has a drink for me, and she's made a great meal. We watch TV or maybe play with the kids. (p. B7)

Contrast the men's perfect day with this typical description from college women:

> I wake up, and my husband and I get in our twin Jettas, and I go to the law firm where I work. Then after work, I go home, and he's pulling up in the driveway at the same time. We go in and have a glass of nice wine, and we make an omelet together and eat by candlelight. Then the nanny brings the children in and we play with them until bedtime. (p. B7)

Note that the typical male scenario features wives who work but who also have drinks and a meal ready for husbands. Fewer and fewer college women see this as an ideal day—or life. Yet, women's fantasy of shared responsibilities for home and family are not likely to be met unless there are major changes in current patterns.

A third persistent theme of femininity is *negative treatment by others*. According to substantial research, this still more or less goes with the territory of being female. Supporting this theme are the differential values our culture attaches to masculinity and femininity. Devaluation of femininity is not only built into cultural views but typically is internalized by individuals, including women. Negative treatment of females begins early and can be especially intense in girl's peer groups (Chesler, 2001; Lamb, 2002; Simmons, 2002; Tavris, 2002). Girls can be highly critical of other girls who are not pretty, thin, and otherwise femi-

nine. Another aspect of negative treatment of women is the violence inflicted on them. They are vulnerable to battering, rape, and other forms of abuse in ways men generally are not (Goldner et al., 1990; Wood, 2001).

*Be superwoman* is a fourth theme emerging in cultural expectations of women. Jana's sense of exhilaration at "being able to have it all" is tempered by the realization that the idea that women *can* have it all appears to be transformed into the command that they *must* have it all. It's not enough to be just a homemaker and mother or to just have a career—young women seem to feel they are expected to do it all.

Women students talk with me frequently about the tension they feel in trying to figure out how to have a full family life and a successful career. They tell me that they want both careers and families and don't see how they can make it all work. The physical and psychological toll on women who try to do it all is well documented (Coltrane & Adams, 2001; Greenberg, 2001; Orenstein, 2000), and it is growing steadily as women find that changes in the workplace are not paralleled by changes in home life. Perhaps it would be wise to remember that superwoman, like Superman, is a comic-book character, not a viable model for real life. Instead of trying to have it all, some young women aim to have some of it all—some career, some family (Greenberg, 2001; Orenstein, 2000).

A final theme of femininity in the 1990s is one that reflects all the others and the contradictions inherent in them: *There is no single meaning of* feminine *anymore*. A woman who is assertive and ambitious in a career is likely to meet with approval, disapproval, and curiosity from some people and to be applauded by others. At the same time, a woman who chooses to stay home while her children are young will be criticized by some women and men, envied by others, and respected by still others. This underlines the excitement and possibilities open to women of this era to validate multiple versions of femininity. . . . [T]here are many ways to be feminine, and we can respect all of them.

Prevailing themes of femininity in North America reveal both constancy and change. Traditional expectations of attractiveness and caring for others persist, as does the greater likelihood of negative treatment by others. Yet today there are multiple ways to define femininity and womanhood, which may allow women with different talents, interests, and gender orientations to define themselves in diverse ways and to chart life courses that suit them as individuals.

## Growing Up Outside Conventional Gender Roles

Not every male and female grows up identifying with the gender society prescribes for him or her. For people who do not identify with and embody the prescribed gender role, growing up is particularly difficult. Gay men are often socially ostracized because they are perceived as feminine, while lesbians are scorned for being masculine. Social isolation also greets many people who are (or are thought to be) transgendered. . . .

Many transsexuals and transgendered and intersexed people want "a society free from the constraints of nonconsensual gender" (Bornstein, 1994, p. 111). In other words, they want the freedom to choose the gender and sex that suits them personally and have society accept them as the people they choose to be. Instead, in the United States they find themselves trapped in a society that rigidly pairs males with masculinity and females with femininity. There are no in-between spaces; there is no room for blurring those rigid lines. For people who do not fit the conventional sex and gender roles, it is hard to find role models and equally difficult to find acceptance from family, peers, and society (Berlant & Warner, 1998; Fausto-Sterling, 2000; Feinberg, 1996; Glenn, 2002).

## References

Aronson, J. (1992). Women's sense of responsibility for the care of old people: "But who else is going to do it?" *Gender and Society*, 6, 8–29.

Berlant, L., & Warner, M. (1998). Sex in public. *Critical Inquiry*, 24, 547–566.

Bornstein, K., (1994). *Gender outlaw: On men, women and the rest of us*. New York: Vintage.

Brownmiller, S. (1993, January 4). Making female bodies the battlefield. *Newsweek*, p. 37.

Cancian, F., & Oliker, S. (2000). *Caring and gender*. Thousand Oaks, CA: Sage.

Chesler, P. (2001). *Woman's inhumanity to woman*. New York: Thunder's Mouth Press/Nation Books.

Cohen, L. (1997, fall). Hunters and gatherers in the classroom. *Independent School*, pp. 28–36.

Coltrane, S., & Adams, M. (2001). Men, women and housework. In D. Vannoy (Ed.), *Gender mosaics* (pp. 145–154). Los Angeles: Roxbury.

Costin, F., & Schwartz, N. (1987). Beliefs about rape and women's social roles: A four-nation study. *Journal of Interpersonal Violence*, 2, 46–56.

Davis-Popelka, W. (2000). Mirror, mirror on the wall: Weight, identity and self-talk in women. In D.O. Braithwaite & J.T. Wood (Eds.), *Case studies in interpersonal communication* (pp. 52–60). Belmont, CA: Wadsworth.

Doyle, J. (1997). *The male experience*. (3rd ed.) Dubuque, IA: William C. Brown.

Eagly, A. H. (1996). Differences between women and men. *American Psychologist*, 51, 158–159.

Farrell, W. (1991, May/June). Men as success objects. *Utne Reader*, pp. 810–884.

Fausto-Sterling, A. (2000). *Sexing the body: Gender politics and the construction of sexuality*. New York: Basic Books.

Feinberg, L. (1996). *Transgender warriors: Making history from Joan of Arc to RuPaul*. Boston, MA: Beacon.

Ferguson, S. (2000). Challenging traditional marriage: New married Chinese-American and Japanese-American women. *Gender and Society*, 14, 136–159.

French, M. (1992). *The war against women*. New York: Summit.

Garrod, A., Ward, J., Robinson, T., & Kilkenny, R. (Eds.). (1999). *Souls looking back: Life stories of growing up Black*. New York: Routledge.

Gaylin, W. (1992). *The male ego*. New York: Viking/Penguin.

Gelles, R., & Straus, M. (1988). *Intimate violence*. New York: Simon & Schuster.

Glenn, D. (2002, November 22). Practices, identities, and desires. *Chronicles of Higher Education*, pp. A20–A21.

Goldner, V., Penn, P., Sheinberg, M., & Walker, G. (1990). Love and violence: Gender paradoxes in volatile attachments. *Family Process*, 19, 343–364.

Gordon, L. (1988). *Heroes of their own lives*. New York: Viking.

Greenberg, S. (2001, January 8). Time to plan your life. *Newsweek*, pp. 54–55.

Greenfield, (2002). *Girl culture*. San Francisco: Chronicle Books.

Greenhouse, S. (2003, July 13). Going for the look, but risking discrimination. *The New York Times International*, p. 10 YT.

Haag, P. (2002). *Voices of a generation: Teenage girls report about their lives today*. New York: Marlowe.

Hochschild, A. (1975). The sociology of feeling and emotion: Selected possibilities. In M. Millman & R. M. Kanter (Eds.), *Another voice* (pp. 180–207). New York: Doubleday/Anchor.

———. (1979). Emotion work, feeling rules, and social structure. *American Journal of Sociology*, 85, 551–595.

———. (1983). *The managed heart: Commercialization of human feeling*. Berkeley: University of California Press.

hooks, b. (1994). *Outlaw culture*. New York: Routledge.

———. (1995, August). Appearance obsession: Is the price too high? *Essence*, 26, 69–71.

Kahn, J. (1997, April 11). Therapist says male depression widespread and widely denied. *Raleigh News and Observer*, p. 5D.

Kantrowitz, B., & Kall, C. (1998, May 11). How to build a better boy. *Newsweek*, pp. 55–60.

Kerr, B. (1997). *Smart girls: A new psychology of girls, women, and giftedness*. Scottsdale, AZ: Gifted Psychology Press.

———. (1999, March 5). When dreams differ: Male-female relations on campuses. *Chronicle of Higher Education*, pp. B7–B8.

Kivel, P. (1999). *Boys will be men: Raising our sons for courage, caring and community*. Gabriola Island, BC: New Society Press.

Lamb, S. (2002). *The secret life of girls: Sex, play, aggression, and their guilt*. New York: Free Press.

Lobel, T., & Bar, E. (1997). Perceptions of masculinity and femininity of kibbutz and urban adolescents. *Sex Roles*, 37, 283–289.

Lont, C. (2001). The influence of media on gender images. In D. Vannoy (Ed.), *Gender mosaics* (pp. 114–122). Los Angeles: Roxbury.

Martin, P. Y., & Hummer, R. A. (1989). Fraternities and rape on campus. *Gender and Society*, 3, 457–473.

Messner, M. (1997a). Boyhood, organized sports, and the construction of masculinities. In E. Disch (Ed.), *Reconstructing gender* (pp. 57–73). Mountain View, CA: Mayfield.

———. (1997b). *Politics of masculinities: Men in movements*. Thousand Oaks, CA: Sage.

———. (2000). Barbie girls versus sea monsters: Children constructing gender. *Gender and Society*, 7, 121–137.

Miller, M. (2003, June 16). Stop pretending nothing's wrong. *Newsweek*, pp. 71–72.

Nelson, M. B. (1994b). *The stronger women get, the more men love football: Sexism and American culture of sports*. New York: Harcourt Brace.

Newberger, E. (1999). *The men they will become: The nature and nurture of male character*. Cambridge, MA: Perseus Books.

Orenstein, P. (2000). *Flux: Women on sex, work, love, kids and life in a half-changed world*. New York: Doubleday.

Pike, K., & Striegel-Moore, R. (1997). Disordered eating and eating disorders. In S. Gallant, G. Keita, & R. Royak-Schaler (Eds.), *Healthcare for women* (pp. 97–114). Washington, DC: American Psychological Association.

Pollack, W. (2000). *Real boys: Rescuing ourselves from the myths of boyhood*. New York: Owl Books.

Ponton, L. (1997). *The romance of risk: Why teenagers do the things they do*. New York: Basic Books.

Ranson, G. (2001). Men at work: Change or no change in the era of the "new father?" *Men and Masculinities*, 4, 3–26.

Real, T. (1997). *I don't want to talk about it: Overcoming the secret legacy of male depression*. New York: Scribner's.

Russell, D. E. H. (Ed.). (1993). *Feminist views on pornography*. Cholchester, VT: Teachers College Press.

Scott, R., & Tetreault, L. (1987). Attitudes of rapists and other violent offenders toward women. *Journal of Social Psychology*, 124, 375–380.

Simmons, R. (2002). *Odd girl out: The hidden culture of aggression in girls*. New York: Harcourt.

Tavris, C. (2002, July 5). Are girls really as mean as books say they are? *Chronicle of Higher Education*, pp. B7–B9.

Thompson, E. H., Jr. (1991). The maleness of violence in dating relationships: An appraisal of stereotypes. *Sex Roles*, 24, 261–278.

Thompson E. H., Jr., & Pleck, J. H. (1987). The structure of male role norms. In M. S. Kimmel (Ed.) *Changing men: New directions in research of men and masculinity* (pp. 25–36). Newbury Park, CA: Sage.

Thompson, L., & Walker, A. J. (1989). Gender in families: Women and men in marriage, work, and parenthood. *Journal of Marriage and the Family*, 51, 845–871.

Wood, J. T. (2001) The normalization of violence in heterosexual romantic relationships: Women's narratives of love and violence. *Journal of Social and Personal Relationships*, 18, 239–262.

## Questions

1. How might you wish to socialize a child born today into what it means to be a male or female in this society? How might this socialization differ from your childhood messages regarding gender?

2. To what extent do you think the themes presented by Wood remain relevant in the social contexts in which you find yourself? Are they more visible in one context than in another?

3. Interview a person from a culture other than your own about her or his culture's views of masculinity and femininity. How are these views similar to those of your culture? How are they different?

---

# 14

# 'Put That Paper Down and Talk to Me!'

## Rapport-Talk and Report-Talk

*Deborah Tannen*

**O**ne of the most prolific writers on gender issues is linguistics scholar Deborah Tannen. In her book You Just Don't Understand, *she discusses at length the differences between the communication of males and females. Discussions of issues in the area of male-female communication are always fraught with tension. Stereotyping may create negative responses. It is important to remember, when discussing gender and communication, that gender and sex are not the same. Sex is a biological characteristic. Gender is socially and psychologically constructed. Each person has some characteristics that our culture labels feminine and some characteristics that your culture labels masculine. How much one has of each determines gender within the culture. Essential gender results from how individuals view masculine and feminine characteristics. In general, men are considered masculine and women are considered feminine. However, it is not uncommon for a male to be more feminine than most males or for a female to be more masculine than most females. The point is that the terms* sex *and* gender *are not interchangeable.*

*Countless popular books, certain studies, and individual personal experiences describe men and women as holding different perspectives on most issues. As Tannen illustrates in this chapter, the value and purpose of talk comprise one such issue. Stereotypes often lead to the conclusion that women ultimately talk more than men, which seems, at first, to be at the heart of the problem. However, Tannen demonstrates that it is not necessarily the quantity of*

*talk that differentiates women from men, but rather the type of talk: women tend to prefer "rapport-talk" or "private talk" and men prefer "report-talk" or "public talk." She suggests that for most men "talk is primarily a way of preserving independence, negotiating, and maintaining status in a hierarchical social order." Hence, the label* report-talk. *On the other hand, for women "the language of conversation is primarily a language of* rapport, *a way of establishing connections and negotiating relationships." Tannen creates this distinction in order to emphasize her points. She does not suggest that individuals cannot use both types of talk. As you read Tannen's ideas, remember that she is discussing communication differences between males and females in general terms. Not all males and not all females will fit her description.*

*The following article cites the difference in perspective regarding the purpose of talk for men and women, the environmental influences, and social conditioning as reasons why men and women are more or less talkative in different situations. Finally, the author suggests ways to avoid conflicts that often arise out of this issue, and to come to a mutual understanding of the others' perspective and the others' needs. As you read this article, ask yourself this question: In my experience, what characterizes differences between male and female speech, and how closely are my observations related to the author's position?*

\* \* \*

**I** was sitting in a suburban living room, speaking to a women's group that had invited men to join them for the occasion of my talk about communication between women and men. During the discussion, one man was particularly talkative, full of lengthy comments and explanations. When I made the observation that women often complain that their husbands don't talk to them enough, this man volunteered that he heartily agreed. He gestured toward his wife, who had sat silently beside him on the couch throughout the evening, and said, "She's the talker in our family."

Everyone in the room burst into laughter. The man looked puzzled and hurt. "It's true," he explained. "When I come home from work,

I usually have nothing to say, but she never runs out. If it weren't for her, we'd spend the whole evening in silence." Another woman expressed a similar paradox about her husband: "When we go out, he's the life of the party. If I happen to be in another room, I can always hear his voice above the others. But when we're home, he doesn't have that much to say. I do most of the talking."

Who talks more, women or men? According to the stereotype, women talk too much. Linguist Jennifer Coates notes some proverbs:

A woman's tongue wags like a lamb's tail.

Foxes are all tail and women are all tongue.

The North Sea will sooner be found wanting in water than a woman be at a loss for a word.

Throughout history, women have been punished for talking too much or in the wrong way. Linguist Connie Eble lists a variety of physical punishments used in Colonial America: Women were strapped to ducking stools and held underwater until they nearly drowned, put into the stocks with signs pinned to them, gagged, and silenced by a cleft stick applied to their tongues.

Though such institutionalized corporal punishments have given way to informal, often psychological ones, modern stereotypes are not much different from those expressed in the old proverbs. Women are believed to talk too much. Yet study after study finds that it is men who talk more—at meetings, in mixed-group discussions, and in classrooms where girls or young women sit next to boys or young men. For example, communications researchers Barbara and Gene Eakins tape-recorded and studied seven university faculty meetings. They found that, with one exception, men spoke more often and, without exception, spoke for a longer time. The men's turns ranged from 10.66 to 17.07 seconds, while the women's turns ranged from 3 to 10 seconds. In other words, the women's longest turns were still shorter than men's shortest turns.

When a public lecture is followed by questions from the floor, or a talk show host opens the phones, the first voice to be heard asking a question is almost always a man's. And when they ask questions or offer comments from the audience, men tend to talk longer. Linguist Marjorie Swacker recorded question-and-answer sessions at academic conferences. Women were highly visible as speakers at the conferences studied; they presented 40.7 percent of the papers at the conferences studied and made up 42 percent of the audiences. But when it came to volunteering and being called on to ask questions, women contributed only 27.4 percent. Furthermore, the women's questions, on the average, took less than half as much time as the men's. (The mean was 23.1 seconds for women, 52.7 for men.) This happened, Swacker shows, because men (but not women) tended to preface their questions with statements, ask more than one question, and follow up the speaker's answer with another question or comment.

I have observed this pattern at my own lectures, which concern issues of direct relevance to women. Regardless of the proportion of women and men in the audience, the men almost invariably ask the first question, more questions, and longer questions. In these situations, women often feel that men are talking too much. I recall one discussion period following a lecture I gave to a group assembled in a bookstore. The group was composed mostly of women, but most of the discussion was being conducted by men in the audience. At one point, a man sitting in the middle was talking at such great length that several women in the front rows began shifting in their seats and rolling their eyes at me. Ironically, what he was going on about was how frustrated he feels when he has to listen to women going on and on about topics he finds boring and unimportant.

## Rapport-Talk and Report-Talk

Who talks more, then, women or men? The seemingly contradictory evidence is reconciled by the difference between what I call *public* and *private speaking*. More men feel comfortable doing "public speaking," while more women feel comfortable doing "private" speaking. Another way of capturing these differences is by using the terms *report-talk* and *rapport-talk*.

For most women, the language of conversation is primarily a language of rapport: a way of establishing connections and negotiating relationships. Emphasis is placed on displaying similarities and matching experiences. From childhood, girls criticize peers who try to stand out or appear better than others. People feel their closest connections at home, or in settings where they *feel* at home—with one or a few people they feel close to and comfortable with—in other words, during private speaking. But even the most public situations can be approached like private speaking.

For most men, talk is primarily a means to preserve independence and negotiate and maintain status in a hierarchical social order. This is done by exhibiting knowledge and skill, and by holding center stage through verbal performance such as storytelling, joking, or imparting information. From childhood, men learn to use talking as a way to get and keep attention. So they are more comfortable speaking in larger groups made up of people they know less well—in the broadest sense, "public speaking." But even the most private situations can be approached like public speaking, more like giving a report than establishing rapport.

## Private Speaking: The Wordy Woman and the Mute Man

What is the source of the stereotype that women talk a lot? Dale Spender suggests that most people feel instinctively (if not consciously) that women, like children, should be seen and not heard, so any amount of talk from them seems like too much. Studies have shown that if women and men talk equally in a group, people think the women talked more. So there is truth to Spender's view. But another explanation is that men think women talk a lot because they hear women talking in situations where men would not: on the telephone; or in social situations with friends, when they are not discussing topics that men find inherently interesting; or, like the couple at the women's group, at home alone—in other words, in private speaking.

Home is the setting for an American icon that features the silent man and the talkative woman. And this icon, which grows out of the different goals and habits I have been describing, explains why the complaint most often voiced by women about the men with whom they are intimate is "He doesn't talk to me"—and the second most frequent is "He doesn't listen to me."

A woman who wrote to Ann Landers is typical:

> My husband never speaks to me when he comes home from work. When I ask, "How did everything go today?" he says, "Rough . . ." or "It's a jungle out there." (We live in Jersey and he works in New York City).
>
> It's a different story when we have guests or go visiting. Paul is the gabbiest guy in the crowd—a real spellbinder. He comes up with the most interesting stories. People hang on every word. I think to myself, "Why doesn't he ever tell me these things?"
>
> This has been going on for 38 years. Paul started to go quiet on me after 10 years of marriage. I could never figure out why. Can you solve the mystery?
>
> —The Invisible Woman

Ann Landers suggests that the husband may not want to talk because he is tired when he comes home from work. Yet women who work come home tired too, and they are nonetheless eager to tell their partners or friends everything that happened to them during the day and what these fleeting, daily dramas made them think and feel.

Sources as lofty as studies conducted by psychologists, as down to earth as letters written to advice columnists, and as sophisticated as movies and plays come up with the same insight: Men's silence at home is a disappointment to women. Again and again, women complain, "He seems to have everything to say to everyone else, and nothing to say to me."

The film *Divorce American Style* opens with a conversation in which Debbie Reynolds is claiming that she and Dick Van Dyke don't communicate, and he is protesting that he tells her everything that's on his mind. The doorbell interrupts their quarrel, and husband and wife compose themselves before opening the door to greet their guests with cheerful smiles.

Behind closed doors, many couples are having conversations like this. Like the character played by Debbie Reynolds, women feel men don't communicate. Like the husband played by Dick Van Dyke, men feel wrongly accused. How can she be convinced that he doesn't tell her anything, while he is equally convinced he tells her everything that's on his mind? How can women and men have such different ideas about the same conversations?

When something goes wrong, people look around for a source to blame: either the person they are trying to communicate with ("You're demanding, stubborn, self-centered") or the group that the other person belongs to ("All women are demanding"; "All men are self-centered"). Some generous-minded people blame the relationship ("We just can't communicate"). But underneath, or overlaid on these types of blame cast outward, most people believe that something is wrong with them.

If individual people or particular relationships were to blame, there wouldn't be so many different people having the same problems. The real problem is conversational style. Women and men have different ways of talking. Even with the best intentions, trying to settle the problem through talk can only make things worse if it is ways of talking that are causing trouble in the first place.

## Best Friends

Once again, the seeds of women's and men's styles are sown in the ways they learn to use language while growing up. In our culture, most people, but especially women, look to their closest relationships as havens in a hostile world. The center of a little girl's social life is her best friend. Girls' friendships are made and maintained by telling secrets. For grown women too, the essence of friendship is talk, telling each other what they're thinking and feeling, and what happened that day: who was at the bus stop, who called, what they said, how that made them feel. When asked who their best friends are, most women name other women they talk to regularly. When

asked the same question, most men will say it's their wives. After that, many men name other men with whom they do things such as play tennis or baseball (but never just sit and talk) or a chum from high school whom they haven't spoken to in a year.

When Debbie Reynolds complained that Dick Van Dyke didn't tell her anything, and he protested that he did, both were right. She felt he didn't tell her anything because he didn't tell her the fleeting thoughts and feelings he experienced throughout the day—the kind of talk she would have with her best friend. He didn't tell her these things because to him they didn't seem like anything to tell. He told her anything that seemed important—anything he would tell his friends.

Men and women often have very different ideas of what's important—and at what point "important" topics should be raised. A woman told me, with lingering incredulity, of a conversation with her boyfriend. Knowing he had seen his friend Oliver, she asked "What's new with Oliver?" He replied, "Nothing." But later in the conversation it came out that Oliver and his girlfriend had decided to get married. "That's nothing?" the woman gasped in frustration and disbelief.

For men, "Nothing" may be a ritual response at the start of a conversation. A college woman missed her brother but rarely called him because she found it difficult to get talk going. A typical conversation began with her asking, "What's up with you?" and his replying, "Nothing." Hearing his "Nothing" as meaning "There is nothing personal I want to talk about," she supplied talk by filling him in on her news and eventually hung up in frustration. But when she thought back, she remembered that later in the conversation he had mumbled, "Christie and I got into another fight." This came so late and so low that she didn't pick up on it. And he was probably equally frustrated that she didn't.

Many men honestly do not know what women want, and women honestly do not know why men find what they want so hard to comprehend and deliver.

# 'Talk to Me!'

Women's dissatisfaction with men's silence at home is captured in the stock cartoon setting of a breakfast table at which a husband and wife are sitting: He's reading a newspaper; she's glaring at the back of the newspaper. In a *Dagwood* strip, Blondie complains, "Every morning all he sees is the newspaper! I'll bet you don't even know I'm here!" Dagwood reassures her, "Of course I know you're here. You're my wonderful wife and I love you very much." With this, he unseeingly pats the paw of the family dog, which the wife has put in her place before leaving the room. The cartoon strip shows that Blondie is justified in feeling like the woman who wrote to Ann Landers: invisible.

Another cartoon shows a husband opening a newspaper and asking his wife, "Is there anything you would like to say to me before I begin reading the newspaper?" The reader knows that there isn't—but that as soon as he begins reading the paper, she will think of something. The cartoon highlights the difference in what women and men think talk is for: To him, talk is for information. So when his wife interrupts his reading, it must be to inform him of something that he needs to know. This being the case, she might as well tell him what she thinks he needs to know before he starts reading. But to her, talk is for interaction. Telling things is a way to show involvement and listening is a way to show interest and caring. It is not an odd coincidence that she always thinks of things to tell him when he is reading. She feels the need for verbal interaction most keenly when he is (unaccountably, from her point of view) buried in the newspaper instead of talking to her.

Yet another cartoon shows a wedding cake that has, on top, in place of the plastic statues of bride and groom in tuxedo and gown, a breakfast scene in which an unshaven husband reads a newspaper across the table from his disgruntled wife. The cartoon reflects the enormous gulf between the romantic expectations of marriage represented by the plastic couple in traditional marriage costume, and the often disappointing reality represented by the two sides of the newspaper at the breakfast table—the front,

which he is reading, and the back, at which she is glaring.

These cartoons, and many others on the same theme, are funny because people recognize their own experience in them. What's not funny is that many women are deeply hurt when men don't talk to them at home, and many men are deeply frustrated by feeling they have disappointed their partners, without understanding how they failed or how else they could have behaved.

Some men are further frustrated because, as one put it, "When in the world am I supposed to read the morning paper?" If many women are incredulous that many men do not exchange personal information with their friends, this man is incredulous that many women do not bother to read the morning paper. To him, reading the paper is an essential part of his morning ritual, and his whole day is awry if he doesn't get to read it. In his words, reading the newspaper in the morning is as important to him as putting on makeup in the morning is to many women he knows. Yet many women, he observed, either don't subscribe to a paper or don't read it until they get home in the evening. "I find this very puzzling," he said. "I can't tell you how often I have picked up a woman's morning newspaper from her front door in the evening and handed it to her when she opened the door for me."

To this man (and I am sure many others), a woman who objects to his reading the morning paper is trying to keep him from doing something essential and harmless. It's a violation of his independence—his freedom of action. But when a woman who expects her partner to talk to her is disappointed that he doesn't, she perceives his behavior as a failure of intimacy: He's keeping things from her; he's lost interest in her; he's pulling away. A woman I will call Rebecca, who is generally quite happily married, told me that this is the one source of serious dissatisfaction with her husband, Stuart. Her term for his taciturnity is *stinginess of spirit*. She tells him what she is thinking, and he listens silently. She asks him what he is thinking, and he takes a long time to answer, "I don't know." In frustration she challenges, "Is there nothing on your mind?"

For Rebecca, who is accustomed to expressing her fleeting thoughts and opinions as they come to her, *saying* nothing means *thinking* nothing. But Stuart does not assume that his passing thoughts are worthy of utterance. He is not in the habit of uttering his fleeting ruminations, so just as Rebecca "naturally" speaks her thoughts, he "naturally" dismisses his as soon as they occur to him. Speaking them would give them more weight and significance than he feels they merit. All her life she had practice in verbalizing her thoughts and feelings in private conversations with people she is close to; all his life he has had practice in dismissing his and keeping them to himself.

## What to Do With Doubts

In the above example, Rebecca was not talking about any particular kind of thoughts or feelings, just whatever Stuart might have had in mind. But the matter of giving voice to thoughts and feelings becomes particularly significant in the case of negative feelings or doubts about a relationship. This difference was highlighted for me when a fifty-year-old divorced man told me about his experiences in forming new relationships with women. On this matter, he was clear: "I do not value my fleeting thoughts, and I do not value the fleeting thoughts of others." He felt that the relationship he was currently in had been endangered, even permanently weakened, by the woman's practice of tossing out her passing thoughts, because, early in their courtship, many of her thoughts were fears about their relationship. Not surprisingly, since they did not yet know each other well, she worried about whether she could trust him, whether their relationship would destroy her independence, whether this relationship was really right for her. He felt she should have kept these fears and doubts to herself and waited to see how things turned out.

As it happens, things turned out well. The woman decided that the relationship was right for her, she could trust him, and she did not have to give up her independence. But he felt, at the time that he told me of this, that he had still not recovered from the wear and tear of coping with her earlier doubts. As he

put it, he was still dizzy from having been bounced around like a yo-yo tied to a string of her stream of consciousness.

In contrast, this man admitted, he himself goes to the other extreme: He never expresses his fears and misgivings about their relationship at all. If he's unhappy but doesn't say anything about it, his unhappiness expresses itself in a kind of distancing coldness. This response is just what women fear most, and just the reasons they prefer to express dissatisfactions and doubts—as an antidote to the isolation and distance that would result from keeping them to themselves.

The different perspectives on expressing or concealing dissatisfactions and doubts may reflect a difference in men's and women's awareness of the power of their words to affect others. In repeatedly telling him what she feared about their relationship, this woman spoke as though she assumed he was invulnerable and could not be hurt by what she said: perhaps she was underestimating the power of her words to affect him. For his part, when he refrains from expressing negative thoughts or feelings, he seems to be overestimating the power of his words to hurt her, when, ironically, she is more likely to be hurt by his silence than his words.

These women and men are talking in ways they learned as children and reinforced as young adults and then adults, and in their same-gender friendships. For girls, talk is the glue that holds relationships together. Boys' relationships are held together primarily by activities: doing things together, or talking about activities such as sports or, later, politics. The forums in which men are most inclined to talk are those in which they feel the need to impress, in situations where their status is in question.

## Making Adjustments

Such impasses will perhaps never be settled to the complete satisfaction of both parties, but understanding the differing views can help detoxify the situation, and both can make adjustments. Realizing that men and women have different assumptions about the place of talk in relationships, a woman can observe a man's desire to read a morning paper at the breakfast table without interpreting it as an unreasonable demand or a manipulative attempt to prevent him from doing what he wants to do.

A woman who had heard my interpretations of these differences between women and men told me how these insights helped her. Early in a promising relationship, a man spent the night at her apartment. It was a weeknight, and they both had to go to work the next day, so she was delighted when he made the rash and romantic suggestion that they have breakfast together and report late for work. She happily prepared breakfast, looking forward to the scene shaped in her mind: They would sit facing each other across their small table, look into each other's eyes, and say how much they like each other and how happy they were about their growing friendship. It was against the backdrop of this heady expectation that she confronted an entirely different scene: As she placed on the table an array of lovingly prepared eggs, toast and coffee, the man sat across her small table—and opened the newspaper in front of his face. If suggesting they have breakfast together had seemed like an invitation to get closer, in her view (or obstructing her view) the newspaper was now erected as a paper-thin but nonetheless impenetrable barrier between them.

Had she known nothing of the gender differences I discuss, she would simply have felt hurt and dismissed this man as yet another clunker. She would have concluded that, having enjoyed the night with her, he was now availing himself of her further services as a short-order cook. Instead, she realized that, unlike her, he did not feel the need for talk to reinforce their intimacy. The companionability of her presence was all he needed, and that did not mean that he didn't cherish her presence. By the same token, had he understood the essential role played by talk in women's definition of intimacy, he could have put off reading the paper—and avoided putting her off.

## The Comfort of Home

For everyone, home is a place to be offstage. But the comfort of home can have opposite and incompatible meanings for women and men. For many men, the comfort of home means freedom from having to prove themselves and impress through verbal display. At last, they are in a situation where talk is not required. They are free to remain silent. But for women, home is a place where they are free to talk, and where they feel the greatest need for talk, with those they are closest to. For them, the comfort of home means the freedom to talk without worrying about how their talk will be judged.

This view emerged in a study by linguist Alice Greenwood of the conversations that took place among her three preadolescent children and their friends. Her daughters and son gave different reasons for their preferences in dinner guests. Her daughter Stacy said she would not want to invite people she didn't know well because then she would have to be "polite and quiet" and put on good manners. Greenwood's other daughter, Denise, said she would like to have her friend Meryl over because she could act crazy with Meryl and didn't have to worry about her manners, as she would with certain other friends who "would go around talking to people probably." But Denise's twin brother, Dennis, said nothing about having to watch his manners or worry about how others would judge his behavior. He simply said that he would like to have over friends with whom to joke and laugh a lot. The girls' comments show that for them being close means being able to talk freely. And being with relative strangers means having to watch what they say and do. This insight holds a clue to the riddle of who talks more, women or men.

## Public Speaking: The Talkative Man and the Silent Woman

So far I have been discussing the private scenes in which many men are silent and many women are talkative. But there are other scenes in which the roles are reversed. Returning to Rebecca and Stuart, we saw that when they are home alone, Rebecca's thoughts find their way into words effortlessly, whereas Stuart finds he can't come up with anything to say. The reverse happens when they are in other situations. For example, at a meeting of the neighborhood council or the parents' association at their children's school, it is Stuart who stands up and speaks. In that situation, it is Rebecca who is silent, her tongue tied by an acute awareness of all the negative reactions people could have to what she might say, all the mistakes she might make in trying to express her ideas. If she musters her courage and prepares to say something, she needs time to formulate it and then waits to be recognized by the chair. She cannot just jump up and start talking the way Stuart and some other men can.

Eleanor Smeal, president of the Fund for the Feminist Majority, was a guest on a call-in radio show, discussing abortion. No subject could be of more direct concern to women, yet during the hour-long show, all the callers except two were men. Diane Rehm, host of a radio talk show, expresses puzzlement that although the audience for her show is evenly split between women and men, 90 percent of the callers to the show are men. I am convinced that the reason is not that women are uninterested in the subjects discussed on the show. I would wager that women listeners are bringing up the subjects they heard on *The Diane Rehm Show* to their friends and family over lunch, tea, and dinner. But fewer of them call in because to do so would be putting themselves on display, claiming public attention for what they have to say, catapulting themselves onto center stage.

I myself have been the guest on innumerable radio and television talk shows. Perhaps I am unusual in being completely at ease in this mode of display. But perhaps I am not unusual at all, because although I am comfortable in the role of invited expert, I have never called in to a talk show I was listening to, although I have often had ideas to contribute. When I am the guest, my position of authority is granted before I begin to speak. Were I to call in, I would be claiming that right on my own. I would have to establish my credibility by explaining who I am, which might seem self-aggrandizing, or not explain who I am and risk having my comments ignored or not valued. For similar reasons, though I am comfortable lecturing to groups numbering in the thousands, I rarely ask questions following another lecturer's talk, unless I know both the subject and the group very well.

My own experience and that of talk show hosts seems to hold a clue to the difference in women's and men's attitudes toward talk: Many men are more comfortable than most women in using talk to claim attention. And this difference lies at the heart of the distinction between report-talk and rapport-talk.

## Report-Talk in Private

Report-talk, or what I am calling public speaking, does not arise only in the literally public situation of formal speeches delivered to a listening audience. The more people there are in a conversation, the less well you know them, and the more status differences among them, the more a conversation is *like* public speaking or report-talk. The fewer the people, the more intimately you know them, and the more equal their status, the more it is like private speaking or rapport-talk. Furthermore, women feel a situation is more "public"—in the sense that they have to be on good behavior—if there are men present, except perhaps for family members. Yet even in families, the mother and children may feel their home to be "backstage" when Father is not home, "onstage" when he is: Many children are instructed to be on good behavior when Daddy is home. This may be because he is not home often, or because Mother—or Father—doesn't want the children to disturb him when he is.

The difference between public and private speaking also explains the stereotype that women don't tell jokes. Although some women are great raconteurs who can keep a group spellbound by recounting jokes and funny stories, there are fewer such personalities among women than among men. Many women who do tell jokes to large groups of people come from ethnic backgrounds in which verbal performance is highly valued. For example, many of the great women stand-up comics, such as Fanny Brice and Joan Rivers, came from Jewish backgrounds.

Although it's not true that women don't tell jokes, it is true that many women are less likely than men to tell jokes in large groups, especially groups including men. So it's not surprising that men get the impression that women never tell jokes at all. Folklorist Carol Mitchell studied joke telling on a college campus. She found that men told most of their jokes to other men, but they also told many jokes to mixed groups and to women. Women, however, told most of their jokes to women, fewer to men, and very few to groups that included men as well as women. Men preferred and were more likely to tell jokes when they had an audience: at least two, often four or more. Women preferred a small audience of one or two, rarely more than three. Unlike men, they were reluctant to tell jokes in front of people they didn't know well. Many women flatly refused to tell jokes they knew if there were four or more in the group, promising to tell them later in private. Men never refused the invitation to tell jokes.

All of Mitchell's results fit in with the picture I have been drawing of public and private speaking. In a situation in which there are more people in the audience, more men, or more strangers, joke telling, like any other form of verbal performance, requires speakers to claim center stage and prove their abilities. These are the situations in which many women are reluctant to talk. In a situation that is more private, because the audience is small, familiar, and perceived to be members of a community (for example, other women), they are more likely to talk.

The idea that telling jokes is a kind of self-display does not imply that it is selfish or self-centered. The situation of joke telling illustrates that status and connection entail each other. Entertaining others is a way of establishing connections with them, and telling jokes can be a kind of gift giving, where the joke is a gift that brings pleasure to receivers. The key issue is asymmetry: One person is the teller and the others are the audience. If these roles are later exchanged—for example, if the joke telling becomes a round in which one person after another takes the role of teller—then there is symmetry on the broad scale, if not in the individual act. However, if women habitually take the role of appreciative audience and never take the role of joke teller, the asymmetry of the individual joke telling is diffused through the larger interaction as well. This is a

hazard for women. A hazard for men is that continually telling jokes can be distancing. This is the effect felt by a man who complained that, when he talks to his father on the phone, all his father does is tell him jokes. An extreme instance of a similar phenomenon is the class clown, who, according to teachers, is nearly always a boy.

## Rapport-Talk in Public

Just as conversations that take place at home among friends can be like public speaking, even a public address can be like private speaking: for example, by giving a lecture full of personal examples and stories.

At the executive committee of a fledgling professional organization, the outgoing president, Fran, suggested that the organization adopt the policy of having presidents deliver a presidential address. To explain and support her proposal, she told a personal anecdote: Her cousin was the president of a more established professional organization at the time that Fran held the same position in this one. Fran's mother had been talking to her cousin's mother on the telephone. Her cousin's mother told Fran's mother that her daughter was preparing her presidential address, and she asked when Fran's presidential address was scheduled to be. Fran was embarrassed to admit to her mother that she was not giving one. This made her wonder whether the organization's professional identity might not be enhanced if it emulated the more established organizations.

Several men on the committee were embarrassed by Fran's reference to her personal situation and were not convinced by her argument. It seemed to them not only irrelevant but unseemly to talk about her mother's telephone conversations at an executive committee meeting. Fran had approached the meeting—a relatively public context—as an extension of the private kind. Many women's tendency to use personal experience and examples, rather than abstract argumentation, can be understood from the perspective of their orientation to language as it is used in private speaking.

A study by Celia Roberts and Tom Jupp of a faculty meeting at a secondary school in

England found that the women's arguments did not carry weight with their male colleagues because they tended to use their own experience as evidence, or argue about the effect of policy on individual students. The men at the meeting argued from a completely different perspective, making categorical statements about right and wrong.

The same distinction is found in discussions at home. A man told me that he felt critical of what he perceived as his wife's lack of logic. For example, he recalled a conversation in which he had mentioned an article he had read in *The New York Times* claiming that today's college students are not as idealistic as students were in the 1960s. He was inclined to accept this claim. His wife questioned it, supporting her argument with the observation that her niece and her niece's friends were very idealistic indeed. He was incredulous and scornful at her faulty reasoning; it was obvious to him that a single personal example is neither evidence nor argumentation—it's just anecdote. It did not occur to him that he was dealing with a different logical system, rather than a lack of logic.

The logic this woman was employing was making sense of the world as a more private endeavor—observing and integrating her personal experience and drawing connections to the experiences of others. The logic the husband took for granted was a more public endeavor—more like gathering information, conducting a survey, or devising arguments by rules of formal logic as one might in doing research.

Another man complained about what he and his friends call women's "shifting sands" approach to discussion. These men feel that, whereas they try to pursue an argument logically, step by step, until it is settled, women continually change course in midstream. He pointed to the short excerpt from *Divorce American Style* quoted above as a case in point. It seemed to him that when Debbie Reynolds said, "I can't argue now. I have to take the French bread out of the oven," she was evading the argument because she had made an accusation—"all you do is criticize"—that she could not support.

This man also offered an example from his own experience. His girlfriend had told him of a problem she had because her boss wanted her to do one thing and she wanted to do another. Taking the boss's view for the sake of argumentation, he pointed out a negative consequence that would result if she did what she wanted. She countered that the same negative consequence would result if she did what the boss wanted. He complained that she was shifting over to the other field of battle—what would happen if she followed her boss's will—before they had made headway with the first—what would happen if she followed her own.

## Speaking for the Team

A final puzzle on the matter of public and private speaking is suggested by the experience I related at the opening of this [chapter], in which a woman's group I addressed had invited men to participate, and a talkative man had referred to his silent wife as "the talker in our family." Following their laughter, other women in the group commented that this woman was not usually silent. When their meetings consisted of women only, she did her share of talking. Why, then, was she silent on this occasion?

One possibility is that my presence transformed the private-speaking group into a public-speaking event. Another transformation was that there were men in the group. In a sense, most women feel they are "backstage" when there are no men around. When men are present women are "onstage," insofar as they feel they must watch their behavior more. Another possibility is that it was not the presence of men in general that affected this woman's behavior, but the presence of *her husband*. One interpretation is that she was somehow cowed, or silenced, by her husband's presence. But another is that she felt they were a team. Since he was talking a lot, the team would be taking up too much time if she spoke too. She also may have felt that, because he was representing their team, she didn't have to, much as many women let their husbands drive if they are in the car, but do the driving themselves if their husbands are not there.

Obviously, not every woman becomes silent when her husband joins a group; after all, there were many women in the group who talked a lot, and many had brought spouses. But several other couples told me of similar experiences. For example, when one couple took evening classes together, he was always an active participant in class discussion, while she said very little. But one semester they decided to take different classes, and then she found that she was a talkative member of the class she attended alone.

Such a development can be viewed in two different ways. If talking in a group is a good thing—a privilege and a pleasure—then a silent woman will be seen as deprived of her right to speak, deprived of her voice. But the pleasures of report-talk are not universally admired. There are many who do not wish to speak in a group. In this view, a woman who feels she has no need to speak because her husband is doing it for her might feel lucky that she doesn't have to when her husband is there—and a man who does not like to drive might feel unlucky that he has to, like it or not.

## Avoiding Mutual Blame

The difference between public and private speaking, or report-talk and rapport-talk, can be understood in terms of status and connection. It is not surprising that women are most comfortable talking when they feel safe and close, among friends and equals, whereas men feel comfortable talking when there is a need to establish and maintain their status in a group. But the situation is complex, because status and connection are bought with the same currency. What seems like a bid for status could be intended as a display of closeness, and what seems like distancing may have been intended to avoid the appearance of pulling rank. Hurtful and unjustified misinterpretations can be avoided by understanding the conversational styles of the other gender.

When men do all the talking at meetings, many women—including researchers—see them as "dominating" the meeting, intentionally preventing women from participating, publicly flexing their higher-status muscles.

But the *result* that men do most of the talking does not necessarily mean that men *intend* to prevent women from speaking. Those who readily speak up assume that others are as free as they are to take the floor. In this sense, men's speaking out freely can be seen as evidence that they assume women are at the same level of status: "We are all equals," the metamessage of their behavior could be, "competing for the floor." If this is indeed the intention (and I believe it often, thought not always, is), a woman can recognize women's lack of participation at meetings and take measures to redress the imbalance, without blaming men for intentionally locking them out.

The culprit, then, is not an individual man or even men's styles alone, but the difference between women's and men's styles. If that is the case, then both can make adjustments. A woman can push herself to speak up without being invited, or begin to speak without waiting for what seems a polite pause. But the adjustment should not be one-sided. A man can learn that a woman who is not accustomed to speaking up in groups is not as free as he is to do so. Someone who is waiting for a nice long pause before asking her question does not find the stage set for her appearance, as do those who are not awaiting a pause, the moment after (or before) another speaker stops talking. Someone who expects to be invited to speak ("You haven't said much, Millie. What do you think?") is not accustomed to leaping in and claiming the floor for herself. As in so many areas, being admitted as an equal is not in itself assurance of equal opportunity, if one is not accustomed to playing the game in the way it is being played. Being admitted to a dance does not ensure the participation of someone who has learned to dance to a different rhythm.

### References

Coates, Jennifer. (1986). *Women, men, and language*. London: Longman.

Eakins, Barbara Westbrook, and Eakins, R. Gene. (1978). *Sex Differences in Communication*. Boston: Houghton Mifflin.

Eble, Connie C. (1976). Etiquette books as linguistic authority. In Peter A. Reich (Ed.), *The Second LACUS Forum 1975*, pp. 468–475. Columbia, SC: Hornbeam.

Goffman, Erving. (1959). *The Presentation of Self in Everyday Life*. Garden City, NY: Doubleday.

Maltz, Daniel N., and Borker, Ruth A. (1982). A cultural approach to male-female miscommunication. In John J. Gumperz (Ed.), *Language and Social Identity*, pp. 196–216. Cambridge: Cambridge University Press.

Mitchell, Carol. (1985). Some differences in male and female joke-telling. In Rosan A. Jordan and Susan J. Kalcik (Eds.), *Women's Folklore, Women's Culture*, pp. 163–186. Philadelphia: University of Pennsylvania Press.

Spender, Dale. (1980). *Man Made Language*. London: Routledge and Kegan Paul.

Swacker, Marjorie. (1976). Women's verbal behavior at learned and professional conferences. In Betty Lou Dubois and Isabel Crouch (Eds.), *The Sociology of the Languages of American Women*, pp. 155–160. San Antonio: Trinity University.

## Questions

1. Explain the difference between report-talk and rapport-talk and its relationship to gender. Indicate the extent to which you agree with the author's categories of report-talk and rapport-talk.

2. Think of your mother and father, or of a close friend's mother and father. In certain situations, who seems to talk more, Mom or Dad? For two of the following situations, offer a suggestion or explanation for why you think Mom or Dad tended to be more talkative.

   a. At the breakfast table
   b. At the dinner table
   c. At family parties
   d. During family downtime (like weekends or vacations)
   e. When you had your friends visit your home

3. Conduct a mini-study of your professors. Are males or females more likely to use personal examples and stories in their teachings?

Adapted from Deborah Tannen, "'Put That Paper Down and Talk to Me!': Rapport-Talk and Report-Talk." In *You Just Don't Understand*, pp. 74–95. Copyright © 1990 by Deborah Tannen. Reprinted by permission of HarperCollins Publishers, Inc. ✦

# Part IV

## *Developing Relationships*

Every new face holds the potential for a connected relationship, yet only a small number of people you meet will become a significant part of your life. Friends and romantic pairs collaboratively create unique relational cultures that represent their understandings of each other and the world. Relational culture is fundamentally a product of communication—it arises out of communication, is maintained and altered through communication, and is dissolved through communication. Within these relational cultures, intimacy and closeness develop at levels consistent with the individuals' previous relational, cultural, and family-of-origin experiences.

All developing relationships reflect history-building processes. There are multiple perspectives on these processes, the most common of which involves stage models. These models are developed on the assumption that all relationships exhibit points of initiation, maintenance, and possible dissolution. However, issues raised by the dialectical perspective have called into question some of the assumptions of stage models.

## Stage Models

Numerous scholars have proposed models of relationship development based on stages through which the partners move as they draw closer (Knapp and Vangelisti 2005; Altman

and Taylor 1973). These are called *linear models*. Psychologists Altman and Taylor created a linear model, *social penetration*, which depicts the stages of relational development. They hypothesize that interpersonal exchange gradually progresses from superficial, nonintimate topics to more intimate, deeper layers of the self; people assess the interpersonal costs and rewards gained from their interactions. Altman and Taylor propose a four-stage model of relational movement, relying on eight characteristics of a developed relationship; each dimension becomes more apparent as the relationship moves through stages toward the highest point. Movement through these stages also depends on the perceived costs or rewards of interactions as estimated by each person in the relationship.

The model is best understood by picturing a continuum (Figure IV-1) with guidelines for movement through these stages. The levels represent where the relationship is at a given time, even if one or the other person involved wishes it were different.

The *orientation stage* represents the first meeting, when strangers tend to follow traditional social rules, try to make a good first impression, and attempt to avoid conflict. In short, they try to reduce uncertainty about the other person and increase their ability to imagine future reactions. Adult family relationships, such as partners or in-laws, start

**Figure IV-1**

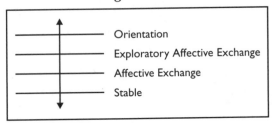

at this point, although some previous information may be known about the "other."

The second stage, *exploratory affective exchange*, is characterized by the relationship between casual acquaintances or friendly neighbors. By this point, the relationship contains some honest sharing of opinions or feelings that are not too personal, but no real sense of commitment exists. Most relationships do not go beyond this second casual exploratory stage.

The third stage, *affective exchange*, is characterized by close friendships or dating relationships, in which people know each other well and have a fairly extensive history of association based on reciprocity. This association may be built over a long period of time or through intense short meetings. Communication includes sharing positive and negative messages, including evaluations. Many marriages exist at the affective exchange level, and partners remain either satisfied or frustrated, depending on their spouses. Numerous people find this level of intimacy sufficient.

Finally, some relationships enter the fourth, or *stable*, stage, which is characterized most often by committed, intimate friendships or familial relationships. This stage is characterized by high symbolic interdependence and a strong "relationship worldview." Yet even these relationships require extensive effort if they are to be maintained. Individuals who share a stable relationship are very aware of each other's needs and changes; they are willing to work to actively maintain their relationship.

Relationships do not follow the four stages easily and simply. Some relationships may speed through certain stages; others may remain at one stage for years. Certain relationships move up and down the levels as the part-

ners' lives change. Relationships that proceed too quickly to the core area may have to retrace their steps through beginning stages. Altman and Taylor suggest that the stages are reversed as a relationship dissolves.

Other stage models provide variations on the theme. For example, in a following article, Knapp and Vangelisti (2005) propose a model of interaction stages in relationships that details five coming together and coming apart stages. This model has a unique "bonding" stage, which occurs when the partners undergo a public ritual announcing to the world a contract or commitment.

## The Dialectical Perspective

Theorists who question stage models believe that they appear too linear and static; that is, they include predictable moves while implying that relationships may remain in the same place for a long time. A dialectical approach recognizes that relationships begin, develop, and deteriorate, but it stresses the ongoing "background noise" or the struggles that characterize the overall life of a relationship rather than a linear, step-by-step approach (Baxter and Montgomery 1996). This perspective highlights the continual tensions that relationships must manage, or the nonlinear nature of relational life. This approach does not mean that a relationship experiences constant struggle or tension, but suggests that relationships are constantly at some level of flux; the movement may be very slight. Although at critical times relational struggles move to the forefront of a relationship's life, there are more times when the dialectical tension serves as the background of an ongoing relationship. In other words:

> Dialectics may work backstage in a relationship beyond partners' mindful awareness or ability to identify and describe them, but still contribute a sense of unsettledness or instability in the relationship. (Montgomery 1993, 206)

Yet the initiation and maintenance of relationships rest entirely in the premise that people acknowledge each other as human beings. This means that they fully acknowledge and respond relevantly to each other, a process called *confirmation* (Sieburg 1985).

The chapters in this section provide you with a description of a particular relationship development model and two examples of relational stage models in particular types of relationships. As you read these chapters, remember that each new relationship represents a potential adventure, a chance to discover new parts of yourself and to connect with a significant other person.

## References

Altman, I., and Taylor, D. (1973). *Social Penetration*. New York: Holt, Rinehart and Winston.

Baxter, L. A., and Montgomery, B. M. (1996). *Relating: Dialogues and Dialectics*. New York: The Guilford Press.

Knapp, M., and Vangelisti, A. (2005). *Interpersonal Communication and Human Relationships*, 5th ed. Boston: Allyn & Bacon.

Montgomery, B. (1993). Relationship maintenance versus relationship change: A dialectical dilemma. *Journal of Social and Personal Relationships*, 10: 205–233.

Sieburg, E. (1985). *Family Communication: An Integrated Systems Approach*. New York: Gardner Press. ✦

# 15
# Relationship Stages

## A Communication Perspective

*Mark L. Knapp and
Anita L. Vangelisti*

**R**elationships are not static; they change and shift slightly or greatly over the years. An intense relationship may become more distant; a superficial relationship may deepen. In this chapter, Knapp and Vangelisti create a stage model for developing, maintaining, and terminating relationships. As you read this article, it is important to remember that movement through the stages is somewhat predictable. The following generalizations will help you see the underlying assumptions of such a stage model.

1. **Movement through stages is generally systematic and sequential**. This is true, according to Knapp and Vangelisti, because each stage contains groundwork for the following stage. Progressing in sequence makes predicting behavior in the next stage easier, and skipping steps is an uncertain gamble caused by a lack of information that would have been learned in the skipped step. Sometimes it is easier to think about the stages as points on a continuum so you can imagine the early intensifying point and the late intensifying point.

2. **Movement may be forward**. As people "come together," they evaluate the rewards and costs in moving the relationship forward. Any movement toward greater intimacy is a move forward within the coming together stages.

3. **Movement may be backward**. A movement toward less intimacy is a movement backward. Two people might decide to "step back" from intensifying to experimenting, such as when one person gets involved with an all-consuming interest that the other does not share.

4. **Movement is always to a new place**. Once something has been talked through, the relationship is different. The continuous nature of communication implies that friends or partners cannot go back to the way they were. This is because communication is a process—irreversible and unrepeatable. This concept is best represented by the helical model of communication that you found in the Part 1 introduction.

5. **Movement may be rapid or slow**. If there is daily positive interaction with a new person, the relationship's movement will be more rapid than if there is weekly or monthly contact. In addition, movement is usually faster during the early stages or when time is short (for example, summer romances or week long retreats). Movement will be slower when only one person desires to move forward.

6. **Dialectical tensions serve as background to each stage**. At all times, ongoing tensions or struggles between goals such as autonomy-connection or openness-closedness will be present in each stage.

The ideas presented in this chapter are based upon the notion that there are separate stages in the development and decline of relationships. Authors Knapp and Vangelisti elaborate upon five stages of relationship growth: initiating, experimenting, intensifying, integrating, and bonding. Within each description, they cite examples for the types of communication behavior expected. (In Chapter 28, you will encounter their stages of decline.) As you read this chapter, consider this question: At what stage would you locate a highly significant relationship in your life, and how does your relationship display characteristics of that stage?

\* \* \*

# A Model of Interaction Stages in Relationships

Scientists are forever seeking to bring order to a seemingly chaotic world of overlapping, interdependent, dynamic, and intricate processes. Frequently, the process of systematizing our life and environment is discussed in terms of stages of growth, stages of deterioration, and the forces that shape and act on this movement through stages. For instance, developmental psychologists recount regularized patterns of behavior accompanying stages of infancy, childhood, adolescence, maturity, and old age. Anthropologists and geologists plot the evolutionary stages of human beings and human environments. Biologists note similarities in the life processes of such seemingly diverse organisms as trees and fish. Physical and social scientists talk about affinity and attraction, weak and strong interactions, friction, repulsion, and splitting-up as basic forces acting on matter and people. Rhetorical critics often dissect spoken messages by noting patterns regularly occurring during the introduction, development toward the main points, transitions, and conclusion.

The idea that there are stages in the development of relationships that are characterized by certain patterns of communication is not new.[1] We tried to synthesize as well as expand on this previous work in the development of the model presented in Table 15-1.

Before each stage is described in greater detail, several preliminary remarks about the model are in order. First, we should resist the normal temptation to perceive the stages of coming together as "good" and those of coming apart as "bad." It is not "bad" to terminate relationships nor is it necessarily "good" to become more intimate with someone. The model is descriptive of what seems to happen—not what should happen.

We should also remember that in the interest of clarity the model simplifies a complex process. For instance, the model shows each stage adjacent to the next—as if it was clear when a communicating couple left one stage and entered another. To the contrary. Each stage contains some behavior from other stages. So *stage identification becomes a matter of emphasis*. Stages are identified by the proportion of one type of communication behavior to another. This proportion may be the frequency with which certain communication acts occur, or proportion may be determined by the relative weight given to certain acts by the participants. For example, a couple at the Intensifying Stage may exhibit behaviors that occur at any of the other stages, but their arrival at the Intensifying Stage is because: (1) the most frequent communication exchanges are typical of the Intensifying Stage and/or (2) the exchanges that are crucial in defining the couple's relationship are statements of an intensifying nature. The act of sexual intercourse is commonly associated with male-female romantic couples at the Intensifying or Integrating Stages, but it may occur as an isolated act for couples at the Experimenting Stage. Or it may occur regularly for a couple at the Experimenting Stage, but remain relatively unimportant for the couple in defining the closeness of their relationship. Thus, interaction stages involve both overt behavior and the perceptions of behavior in the minds of the parties involved. During the formation of a romantic relationship, the couple's overt behavior (to each other and in front of others) may be a good marker of their developmental stage. During periods of attempted rejuvenation of a relationship, we may find that the overt behavior is an effective marker of the stage *desired*. However, in stable or long-established relationships, overt behavior may not be a very accurate indicator of closeness. Instead it is the occasional behavior or memories of past behaviors that are perceived by the couple as crucial in defining their relationship. For example, the married couple of fifteen years may spend much of their interaction time engaging in small talk—behavior typical of an early developmental stage. And even though the small talk does play an important role in maintaining the relationship, it is the less frequent but more heavily weighted behavior that the couple uses to define their relationship, as at the Integrating Stage. Similarly, close friends may not engage in a lot of talk that outside ob-

***Table 15-1***
*A Model of Interactive Stages*

| Process | Stage | Representative Dialogue |
|---|---|---|
| | Initiating | "Hi, how ya doin"<br>"Fine. You?" |
| | Experimenting | "Oh, so you like to ski . . . So do I."<br>"You do? Great, where do you go?" |
| Coming Together | Intensifying | "I . . . I think I love you."<br>"I love you too." |
| | Integrating | "I feel so much a part of you."<br>"Yeah, we are like one person. What happens to you happens to me." |
| | Bonding | "I want to be with you always."<br>"Let's get married." |
| | Differentiating | "I just don't like big social gatherings."<br>"Sometimes I just don't understand you. This is one area where I'm certainly not like you at all." |
| | Circumscribing | "Did you have a good time on your trip?"<br>"What time will dinner be ready?" |
| Coming Apart | Stagnating | "What's there to talk about?"<br>"Right, I know what you're going to say and you know what I'm going to say." |
| | Avoiding | "I'm so busy, I just don't know when I'll be able to see you."<br>"If I'm not around when you try, you'll understand." |
| | Terminating | "I'm leaving you . . . and don't bother trying to contact me."<br>"Don't worry." |

servers would associate with closeness. In some cases, friends are separated for long periods of time and make very little contact with one another. But through specific occasional acts and the memory of past acts, the intimacy of the friendship is maintained.

The dialogue in the model is heavily oriented toward mixed-gender pairs. This does not mean the model is irrelevant for same-gen-der pairs. Even at the highest level of commitment, the model may apply to same-gender pairs. The bonding ceremony, for instance, need not be marriage. It could be an act of becoming "blood brothers" by placing open wounds on each other to achieve oneness. Granted, American cultural sanctions against the direct expression of high-level intimacy between same-sexed pairs often serve to inhibit, slow down, or stop the growth of relationships between same-sexed pairs. But when such relationships do develop, similar patterns are reported.[2]

The model . . . also focuses primarily on relationships where people voluntarily seek contact with, or disengagement from, one another. But the model is not limited to such relationships. All people drawn into, or pulled out of, relationships by forces seemingly outside their control will like or not like such an event and communicate accordingly. For instance, a child's relationship with his or her parent (involuntary) may, at some point, be very close and loving, at another time be cold and distant, and at another time be similar to relationships with other friends.

Our model of relationship development is primarily focused on the interaction patterns of the relationship partners. Nevertheless, we should not forget that these relationships are nested within a network of other social relationships which affect communication patterns manifested by the partners.[3] Friends, co-workers, and/or kin make up the larger social system which influences and is influenced by any single relationship. Sometimes these networks are small, sometimes large; sometimes they are influential on one issue or at one point in time and not so on other issues or at another point in time; sometimes these other relationships tend to serve one relationship partner, and at other times they serve both. What role do social networks play as we develop and maintain a relationship? The people who comprise these networks give us feedback, advice, and support; they act as a sounding board; they help mediate problems; they offer consultation and engage in persuasion. They may, of course, fail to provide these things when they are expected. In short, social networks are comprised of coaches who can dramatically affect our communicative performance as relationship partner. In addition, they are sources of a social identity which extends beyond the pair bond.

Finally . . . we would expect the Initiating and Terminating Stages to be characterized by communication that is more narrow, stylized, difficult, rigid, awkward, public, hesitant, and with overt judgments suspended; the stages of Integrating, Bonding, and Differentiating should show more breadth, uniqueness, efficiency, flexibility, smoothness, personalness, spontaneity, and overt judgments given. In short, it is proposed that we communicate within a prescribed range of content, style, and language at different levels of intimacy. . . .

# Interaction Stages

## Initiating

This stage incorporates all those processes enacted when we first come together with other people. It may be at a cocktail party or at the beach; it may be with a stranger or with a friend. As we scan the other person we consider our own stereotypes, any prior knowledge of the other's reputation, previous interactions with this person, expectations for this situation, and so on. We are asking ourselves whether this person is "attractive" or "unattractive" and whether we should initiate communication. Next, we try to determine whether the other person is cleared for an encounter—is he or she busy, in a hurry, surrounded by others. Finally, we search for an appropriate opening line to engage the other's attention.

Typically, communicators at this stage are simply trying to display themselves as a person who is pleasant, likable, understanding and socially adept. In essence, we are saying: "I see you. I am friendly, and I want to open channels for communication to take place." In addition, we are carefully observing the other to reduce any uncertainty we might have—hoping to gain clarification of mood, interest, orientation toward us, and aspects of the other's public personality. Our conscious awareness of these processes is sometimes very low. "Morning, Bob. How ya doin'?" "Morning, Clayton. Go to hell." "Fine, thanks.". . .

## Experimenting

Once communication has been initiated, we begin the process of experimenting—trying to discover the unknown. Strangers trying to become acquaintances will be primarily interested in name, rank, and serial number—something akin to the sniffing ritual of animals. The exchange of demographic information is frequent and often seems controlled by a norm that says: "If you tell me your hometown, I'll tell you mine." Strangers at this stage are diligently searching for an integrating topic, an area of common interest or experience. Sometimes the strain of this search approaches the absurd: "Oh, you're from Oklahoma. Do you know . . . ?" Obviously, the degree to which a person assists another in finding this integrating topic shows the degree of interest in continuing the interaction and the willingness to pursue a relationship. . . .

Small talk is the *sine qua non* of experimenting. It is like exercising; we may hate it, but we may also engage in large quantities of it every day. If we hate it, why do we do it? Probably because we are vaguely aware of several important functions served by small talk:

1. It is a useful process for uncovering integrating topics and openings for more penetrating conversation.

2. It can be an audition for a future friendship or a way of increasing the scope of a current relationship.

3. It provides a safe procedure for indicating who we are and how another can come to know us better (reduction of uncertainty).

4. It allows us to maintain a sense of community with our fellow human beings.

Relationships at this stage are generally pleasant, relaxed, overtly uncritical, and casual. Commitments are limited. And, like it or not, *most of our relationships probably don't progress very far beyond this stage.*

## Intensifying

When people achieve a relationship known as "close friends," indicators of the relationships are intensified. Active participation and greater awareness of the process typify this stage when it begins. Initial probes toward intensification of intimacy are often exercised with caution, awaiting confirmation before proceeding. Sitting close, for instance, may precede hugging; holding hands will generally precede holding genitals. Requests for physical or psy-

chological favors are sometimes used to validate the existence of intensity in a relationship. . . .

The amount of personal disclosure increases at this stage, and we begin to get a glimpse of some previously withheld secrets—that my father was an alcoholic, that I masturbate, that I pretend I'm a rhino when I'm drunk, and other fears, frustrations, failures, imperfections, and prejudices. Disclosures may be related to any topic area, but those dealing most directly with the development of the relationship are crucial. These disclosures make the speaker vulnerable—almost like an animal baring its neck to an attacker.

Verbally, a lot of things may be happening in the intensifying stage:

1. Forms of address become more informal—first name, nickname, or some term of endearment.

2. Use of the first person plural becomes more common—"*We* should do this" or "*Let's* do this." One study of married couples found that the use of "we" was more likely to be associated with a relationship orientation, while the use of "I" was more likely to be associated with a task orientation or the functional requirements and accomplishments of marriage.[4]

3. Private symbols begin to develop, sometimes in the form of a special slang or jargon, sometimes using conventional language forms that have understood, private meanings. Places they've been together, events and times they've shared; and physical objects they've purchased or exchanged; all become important symbols in defining the nature of developing closeness.[5] Such items or memories may be especially devastating and repulsive reminders if the relationship begins to come apart unless the symbols are reinterpreted ("I like this diamond ring because it is beautiful, not because he gave it to me.") or put in a different perspective ("It really was fun when we did ____, but in so many other ways he was a jerk.").

4. Verbal shortcuts built on a backlog of accumulated and shared assumptions, expectations, interests, knowledge, interactions, and experiences appear more often; one may request a newspaper be passed by simply saying, "paper."

5. More direct expressions of commitment may appear—"We really have a good thing going" or "I don't know who I'd talk to if you weren't around." Sometimes such expressions receive an echo—"I really like you a lot." "I really like you, too, Elmer."

6. Increasingly, one's partner will act as a helper in the daily process of understanding what you're all about—"In other words, you mean you're . . ." or "But yesterday, you said you were. . . ."

Sophistication in nonverbal message transmission also increases. A long verbalization may be replaced by a single touch; postural congruence may be seen; clothing styles may become more coordinated; possessions and personal space may be more permeable.

As the relationship intensifies, each person is unfolding his or her uniqueness while simultaneously blending his or her personality with the other's.

## Integrating

The relationship has now reached a point where the two individual personalities almost seem to fuse or coalesce, certainly more than at any previous stage. Davis discusses this concept, which he calls *coupling*:

> The extent to which each intimate tries to give the other his own self-symbols or to correct the other's self-symbols measures the degree to which he wants to increase their communion.[6]

The experience of former Florida State Senator Bruce Smathers and his fiancée provides one example of movement toward this interpersonal fusion. He switched from Methodist to Presbyterian; she switched from Republican to Democrat. The wire service report indicated this was "a compromise they say will help pave the way for their wedding."

Verbal and nonverbal manifestations of integrating may take many forms:

1. Attitudes, opinions, interests, and tastes that clearly distinguish the pair from others are vigorously cultivated—"We have something special; we are unique."

2. Social circles merge and others begin to treat the two individuals as a common package—one present, one letter, one invitation.

3. Intimacy "trophies" are exchanged so each can "wear" the other's identity—pictures, pins, rings.

4. Similarities in manner, dress, and verbal behavior may also accentuate the oneness.

5. Actual physical penetration of various body parts contributes to the perceived unification.

6. Sometimes common property is designated—"our song," a joint bank account, or a co-authored book.

7. Empathic processes seem to peak so that explanation and prediction of behavior are much easier.[7]

8. Body rhythms and routines achieve heightened synchrony.[8]

9. Sometimes the love of a third person or object will serve as glue for the relationship—"Love me, love my rhinos."

Obviously, integration does not mean complete togetherness or complete loss of individuality. Maintenance of some separate and distinct selves is critical, and possible, due to the strength of the binding elements. One married woman of ten years told us: "I still hold some of myself back from John because it's the only part of me I don't share, and it's important to have something that is uniquely mine."

Thus, we can see that as we participate in the integration process we are intensifying and minimizing various aspects of our total person. Consequently, when we commit ourselves to integrating with another, we also agree to become another individual.

## Bonding

Bonding is a public ritual that announces to the world that commitments have been formally contracted. It is the institutionalization of the relationship. There are many kinds of bonding rituals and they characterize several stages of the mixed-sex relationship—going steady, engagement, and ultimately marriage. American society has not sanctioned similar rituals for same-sexed romantic pairs, although some exist.

Since bonding is simply the contract for the union of the pair at any given stage of the relationship, one might question why it has been designated as a separate stage. It is because the act of bonding itself may be a powerful force in changing the nature of the relationship "for better or for worse." The institutionalization of the relationship hardens it, makes it more difficult to break out of, and probably changes the rhetoric that takes place without a contract. The contract becomes, either explicitly or implicitly, a frequent topic of conversation. Communication strategies can now be based on interpretation and execution of the commitments contained in the contract. In short, the normal ebb and flow of the informal relationship can be, and often is, viewed differently. . . .

### Notes

1. Representative works include: F. Lacoursiere, *The Life Cycle of Groups* (New York: Human Sciences Press, 1980); R. Thornton and P. M. Nardi, "The Dynamics of Role Acquisition," *American Journal of Sociology* 80 (1975): 870–885; I. Altman and D. A. Taylor, *Social Penetration: The Development of Interpersonal Relationships* (New York: Holt, Rinehart, & Winston, 1973); B. W. Tuckman, "Developmental Sequence in Small Groups," *Psychological Bulletin* 63 (1965): 384–399; S. W. Duck, *Personal Relationships and Personal Constructs: A Study of Friendship Formation* (New York: John Wiley & Sons, 1973); M. S. Davis, *Intimate Relations* (New York: Free Press, 1973); T. M. Newcomb, *The Acquaintance Process* (New York: Holt, Rinehart, & Winston, 1961); C. B. Broderick, "Predicting Friendship Behavior: A Study of the Determinants of Friendship Selection and Maintenance in a College Population" (Doctoral diss. Cornell University, 1956); G. M. Phillips and N.

J. Metzger, *Intimate Communication* (Boston: Allyn & Bacon, 1976), pp. 401–403; C. R. Berger and R. J. Calabrese, "Some Explorations in Initial Interaction and Beyond: Toward a Developmental Theory of Interpersonal Communication," *Human Communication Research* 1 (1975): 99–112; C. R. Rogers, "A Process Conception of Psychotherapy," *American Psychologist* 13 (1958): 142–149; G. Simmel, *The Sociology of George Simmel*, trans. K. Wolff (New York: Free Press, 1950); K. Lewin, "Some Social Psychological Differences Between the United States and Germany," *Character and Personality* 4 (1936): 265–293; J. T. Wood, "Communication and Relational Culture: Bases for the Study of Human Relationships," *Communication Quarterly* 30 (1982): 75–83; D. P. McWhirter and A. M. Mattison, *The Male Couple* (Englewood Cliffs, NJ: Prentice-Hall, 1984); W. J. Dickens and D. Perlman, "Friendship over the Life Cycle." In S. Duck and R. Gilmour, eds., *Personal Relationships: 2. Developing Personal Relationships* (New York: Academic Press, 1981); C. A. VanLear, Jr., and N. Trujillo, "On Becoming Acquainted: A Longitudinal Study of Social Judgment Processes," *Journal of Social and Personal Relationships* 3 (1986): 375–392; J. M. Honeycutt, J. G. Cantrill, and R. W. Greene, "Memory Structures for Relational Escalation: A Cognitive Test of the Sequencing of Relational Actions and Stages," *Human Communication Research* 16 (1989): 62–90; J. M. Honeycutt, J. G. Cantrill, and T. Allen, "Memory Structures for Relational Decay: A Cognitive Test of Sequencing of Deescalating Actions and Stages," *Human Communication Research* 18 (1992): 528–562; and J. M. Honeycutt, "Memory Structures of the Rise and Fall of Personal Relationships." In S. Duck, ed., *Individuals in Relationships* (Newbury Park, CA: Sage, 1993).

2. McWhirter and Mattison, *The Male Couple*. S. M. Haas and L. Stafford, "An Initial Examination of Maintenance Behaviors in Gay and Lesbian Relationships," *Journal of Social and Personal Relationships* 15 (1998): 846–855.

3. T. L. Albrecht, M. B. Adelman, and Associates, *Communicating Social Support* (Newbury Park, CA: Sage, 1987). M. R. Parks and M. B. Adelman, "Communication Networks and the Development of Romantic Relationships: An Expansion of Uncertainty Reduction Theory," *Human Communication Research* 10 (1983): 55–79. R. Klein and R. M. Milardo, "Third-Party Influence on the Management of Personal Relationships." In S. Duck, ed.,

*Social Context and Relationships* (Newbury Park, CA: Sage, 1993), pp. 55–77. G. Allan, *Friendship: Developing a Sociological Perspective* (Boulder, CO: Westview, 1989). M. R. Parks, "Communication Networks and Relationship Life Cycles." In S. Duck, ed., *Handbook of Personal Relationships*. 2nd ed. (New York: John Wiley & Sons, 1997).

4. H. L. Rausch, K. A. Marshall, and J. M. Featherman, "Relations at Three Early Stages of Marriage as Reflected by the Use of Personal Pronouns," *Family Process* 9 (1970): 69–82.

5. L. A. Baxter, "Symbols of Relationship Identity in Relationship Cultures," *Journal of Social and Personal Relationships* 4 (1987): 261–280.

6. M. S. Davis, *Intimate Relations* (New York: The Free Press, 1973), p. 188.

7. W. Ickes, ed., Empathic Accuracy (New York: Guildford, 1997).

8. H. C. Davis, D. J. Haymaker, D. A. Hermecz, and D. G. Gilbert, "Marital Interaction: Affective Synchrony of Self-Reported Emotional Components," *Journal of Personality Assessment* 52 (1988): 48–57; and K. Grammar, K. B. Kruck, and M. S. Magnusson, "The Courtship Dance: Patterns of Nonverbal Synchronization in Opposite-Sex Encounters," *Journal of Nonverbal Behavior* 22 (1998): 3–29.

# Questions

1. Choose a friendship relationship in which you find yourself currently. According to Knapp and Vangelisti, what stage is it in? What predictions would you make concerning movement to the next stage? Why?

2. Watch a movie such as *When Harry Met Sally* or *The Sisterhood of the Traveling Pants*. Discuss the relationships in the movie in terms of Knapp and Vangelisti's stages. Try to indicate how they reached their current stage.

3. Think about which stage into which most of your good relationships fall. Are they closer to the beginning stages? Closer to the more intimate stages? How satisfied are you with the level?

# 16

# From Miscegenation to Multiculturism

## Perceptions and Stages of Interracial Relationship Development

*Anita K. Foeman and Teresa Nance*

In the not-too-distant past, interracial marriages were prohibited in the United States. In fact, it was only in 1967 that the Loving v. Virginia Supreme Court decision abolished all statutes prohibiting interracial marriage. As a result, much of the original research on interracial marital relationships was developed in the 1960s and 1970s. Researchers did not examine interracial marriage again in any depth until the 1990s.

In an article on interracial dialogue, Houston and Wood (1999) overview some of the reasons why marital relationships between whites and African Americans face particular challenges that are not experienced in marital relationships of same-race couples; these are presented as generalizations because each marriage is different and some couples may not encounter these issues. One issue they identify is differing values. For example, whites may emphasize individualism—an emphasis on I rather than we. African Americans are less individualistic, placing greater emphasis on family and community. Such differences in orientation can lead to misunderstanding in the marriage relationship. How much time should be spent with family, how much monetary support should be given to family members, and "who comes first" are all issues to be negotiated. Orbe and Harris (2001) suggest that interracial marriage "may become an option when people have more in common with those from a different racial/ethnic group than their own" (p. 178).

Second, differing communication styles can lead to misunderstandings. For example, African Americans tend to be more confrontational and forceful in conversations among themselves than most whites. Thus, the authors suggest, whites sometimes perceive African Americans as rude, and African Americans sometimes perceive whites as unfeeling. Certainly, all married couples confront issues of differing values and communication styles. However, according to many researchers, these issues are greater in interracial marriages.

Although there are universal challenges that all relationships encounter, interracial couples have a series of extra obstacles to overcome in order to maintain a successful relationship. Assuming these differences, Foeman and Nance present a relationship development model of African American–white couples. The authors suggest that because of the unique issues that interracial couples face, the way the relationship develops may differ from the way the relationships of same-race couples develop.

Based on couples' experiences, the authors developed a "new model" for examining these relationships. Their model identifies four stages of development—racial awareness, coping, identity awareness, and maintenance—which lead to the establishment of long-term commitment. Throughout this chapter, each stage is carefully identified and described, laying out the framework for a new way to understand and view interracial relationships. As you read this chapter, reflect on this question: What communication skills are critical for persons entering an interracial romantic partnership?

## References

Houston, M., and Wood, J. (1999). Difficult dialogues, expanded horizons: Communicating across race and class. In J. Wood (Ed.), *Gendered Relationships*, pp. 39–56 Mountain View, CA: Mayfield.

Orbe, M. P. and Harris, T. M. (2001). *Interracial Communication: Theory Into Practice.* Belmont, CA: Wadsworth/Thomson Learning.

\* \* \*

## A New Model of Interracial Relationship Development

Researchers have begun to look at the success strategies of interracial couples, the ways in which their relationships are functional and the reasons for their steady increase (Hall 1980; Jeter 1982; Poston 1990; Poussaint 1984). These researchers' developing work begins to suggest specific stages of relationship evolution. It is important to know that interracial couples are working through these stages, in addition to all those any other couple must negotiate, as they move toward establishing a long-term commitment to each other. The following framework stems from past work, but evolves theoretically toward a new view of interracial families. Briefly, the stages include (a) racial awareness, (b) coping, (c) identity emergence, and (d) maintenance.

### Stage 1: Racial Awareness

Awareness for an interracial couple is an interpersonal and cultural experience. As any two individuals become acquainted, they must become familiar with the similarities and differences between them and develop a shared belief that a relationship is possible. For same-group couples, growing awareness may require a subtle process of learning individual patterns and idiosyncrasies and making intentions known. To the extent that a couple does not share similar group membership (i.e., religious, socioeconomic, political), the process may be more tentative, even grinding. When the couple is of different races, differences are immediately obvious.

Interracial couples that survive likely learn in this early stage to develop an awareness of at least four concurrently operating sets of perspectives: (a) their own, (b) their partner's, (c) their collective racial group's, and (d) their partner's racial group's. Even if the couple decides not to discuss or even acknowledge one or more of these perspectives, they may influence early decisions that the couple makes (like where or whether to dine out, or which friends to socialize with). Motoyoshi (1990) describes the source of the interracial couple's challenge, stating that "In the United States, the racial stratification system is caste; that is, a person is either white or non-white" (pp. 85–86). This being the case, individuals of two different races will likely experience and respond to the world and each other in different ways (e.g., the majority partner may develop a more trusting nature than the minority one). Furthermore, outsiders will likely view the partners in different ways. The couple may also feel pressure to frame their relationship in terms of traditional social roles and attitudes. At this phase of the relationship, communication functions to bring about and articulate a common perspective on the role of race in their initial interpersonal attraction (e.g., "I liked a man who happened to be Black" versus "I am often attracted to Black men") and to highlight or downplay race as an influencing factor (e.g., "Let's just eat in tonight" versus "I didn't like the way they treated us at the restaurant last night"). Interracial couples work their way through the awareness stage by engaging in communication behaviors related to their mutual attraction and sensitivity.

*Attraction.* Interpersonal attraction for partners of different races may not be unlike attraction for single race couples. Interracial couples, however, have the added dimension of acknowledging the volatility of their interracial attraction in the social context. If, for example, a Black male partner admires his White lover's blond hair, the cultural implications take on an added dimension. If a White man admires aloud a Black woman's full lips, the society may view the statement as offensive. And, of course, in this context the individuals themselves may question their own attraction to one another (e.g., "Is there something wrong with me for being attracted to this person?").

*Sensitivity.* The awareness of this stage is also produced by emerging sensitivity to the racial place of the other. Racial place is the way that members of a racial group are treated in society, what is seen as their natural role and profile. The discovery of the other's racial place may occur in a number of different ways. It may be revealed in discussion as the couple talks directly about race, or revealed indirectly as a couple addresses daily life. For example, the White partner could talk about experiences revealing cultural privilege (the assumption of neutral or positive regard in public places). The minority person may respond in a defensive or suspicious manner to poor treatment in a new situation. Suddenly, each member may find that he or she has to make explicit life-long assumptions (regarding how one deals with new situations, what it means to be a man or woman, how to interact with strangers, how to expect to be treated, etc.). Both partners must explain their thinking and perspective to a sometimes unfamiliar but intimate other. Both must develop sensitivity to a sometimes uncomfortable alternate perspective. In-group patterns, ranging from music and eating habits to ways of talking about the other, come under new scrutiny in this context. Both must learn new sets of public responses they are likely to receive when they are out together.

Emerging racial sensitivity is an important subphase, because it fosters the development of racial consciousness that previously would have been unattainable to either partner in a single race relationship. Such insight will probably change each partner's view of the world, regardless of the future course of the relationship.

Each interracial couple must resolve issues of racial awareness in their own time and manner. And, of course, individual partners' past experience in interracial relationships and mixed race situations will shape the manner in which this phase unfolds. In any case, the couple's communication at this early stage reflects their ability to adequately address awareness that forms the foundation for later stages. Success at this initial stage begins to build a base of trust and dialogue for the interracial couple.

## Stage 2: Coping With Social Definitions of Race

Most people would agree that a couple from different races has additional ongoing challenges, as well as unique benefits to their relationship, both from without and from within.

Should the couple find satisfaction in their initial interactions and choose to move forward, the next task is to manage these challenges. At the end of the awareness stage, interracial couples recognize their attraction for each other and their increased sensitivity to the function of race in their lives. They must now decide how to integrate this new information into their long-term relationship.

It is interesting to note that many couples are actually forced into the coping phase by an unaccepting society. Ironically, whereas a couple from different cultures may need more time to work through their complex attraction, they may be pushed into deeper commitment than they had intended. Those around them may predict negative outcomes or challenge the couple's choices and, in response, the couple may draw together to learn to respond to these assaults.

During the coping stage, the couple develops proactive and reactive strategies. The couple learns to insulate itself when possible from people and situations that are potentially harmful. For example, the couple may chose not to attend a family reunion. They will also learn to negotiate potentially threatening situations when necessary. To appease a parent, one partner might agree to attend a family reunion without the other-race companion.

As the couple begins to become proficient in the process of insulation and negotiation, they begin to work together to establish sets of characteristic responses to a variety of situations. They may select public places that are more diverse and welcoming, or learn to respond to questions about their group loyalty in a deescalating or curtailing manner. For example, in response to a comment like, "You must think you are Black/White," the recipient might say in jest, "Look at me, how could I not know I'm Black/White?" or "If I leave my Black/White spouse, will you marry me?" Or more provocatively, when questioned about the choice to date a White woman, a Black partner might ask, "Do you want to go back to the days when Black men were lynched for dating White women?"

The couple may learn to avoid racially hot issues or language in public settings. They may learn to read the code in phrases like

"What about the children?" as a thin mask for a deeper felt discomfort. They may learn to ignore people who insist that their every problem is because of race. They may learn where to turn for support and common perspective or to develop new networks. They will probably learn that "Not everyone has to like me—and if they dislike me for racist reasons, that is their problem." They may join a support group.

Communication will function at this stage to relay strategies and enact them as necessary. As couples work their way through these issues, they draw closer together. If the couple cannot or will not face these challenges together and to their own satisfaction, they will likely feel pressure to split. It is reasonable to speculate that success in the coping process will build on success in the attraction phase and increase the likelihood for success of the relationship, helping the couple grow stronger. The couple begins to establish a culture common to them.

The coping stage can be summarized as a time for generating sets of reactive strategies to ensure the survival of the relationship. This is essentially a defensive posture. The couple stands ready to protect itself. But whereas safety is important, healthy family life demands more than simple defense from a racially biased culture. Healthy family life requires that restrictive and inaccurate descriptions of interracial couples and individuals be reframed and/or redefined.

Although most of the literature helps us to understand the awareness and coping phases of relationship development, the most positive and transforming ones have yet to be fully explored. We suggest that these are identity emergence and relationship maintenance, and begin to outline them here.

## Stage 3: Identity Emergence

Redefinition occurs as the interracial couple and individual take control over images of themselves. For example, children may learn to answer questions like "Are you Black or White?" with "I am 100% both" or "I am biracial." In the emergence stage, couples begin to develop behaviors that are self-sustaining. Instead of looking at their differences as obstacles to be overcome, interracial couples view the unique racial configuration of their families as a positive source of strength (e.g., "Being biracial is a gift").

Interracial couples are also in a position to reframe their experience for the culture at large. They may learn to deconstruct statements like "I would never date a person outside my race and I think anyone who would is sick" by questioning its foundation: "If you say you would never date a person outside your race, how could you possibly understand the motivations of someone who would?"

Interracial couples or individuals may choose to see themselves as exceptional or different but, ultimately, as existing in their own right and on their own terms rather than as an inadequate subset of what is deemed desirable by others. Communication functions to provide the voice and words to recast their world: We are the inevitable family of a truly multicultural society. Successful interracial couples develop skills to resolve problems that threaten the very foundation of our society. They have perspective that escapes others and the wherewithal to define themselves where no set guidelines exist. These are skills that will be needed in the multicultural society of the future. Interracial families can see themselves as at the head of a trend.

## Stage 4: Maintenance

As couples emerge with effective strategies and perspectives, they may feel energized to share their views. Over a lifetime together, an interracial couple will have more or less need at any given time to focus on race or to evolve as an interracial couple. Literature and experience tell us that the stages suggested here are not lock step. Individuals and couples may revisit steps at different points in their lives.

Although each couple will probably begin with their own awareness, individuals within couples may be at different beginning points. One partner may have addressed issues in earlier interracial relationships and have to revisit them with a new partner. Another couple may enter a relationship with the posture that race is not an issue and only much later be forced to overtly address racial awareness. If and when couples begin to rear interracial children, they may need to recycle through stages in light of their children's experiences as well as their own. Essentially, each phase of a couple's life together brings new opportunities for racial awareness, development of new coping strategies, emergence as a reconstructed unit, and ongoing relationship maintenance. . . .

## References

Hall, C. C. I. (1980). The ethnic identity of racially mixed people: A study of Black-Japanese. Unpublished doctoral dissertation, University of California, Los Angeles.

Jeter, K. (1982). Analytic essay: Intercultural and interracial marriage. *Marriage and Family Review*, 5, 105–111.

Motoyoshi, M. M. (1990). The experience of mixed-race people: Some thoughts and theories. *Journal of Ethnic Studies*, 18, 77–94.

Poston, W. S. C. (1990). The biracial identity development model: A needed addition. *Journal of Counseling and Development*, 69, 152–155.

Poussaint, A. (1984). Study of interracial children presents positive picture. *Interracial Books for Children Bulletin*, 15, 9–10.

## Questions

1. Compare the states of relationship presented by Foeman and Nance to those of Knapp and Vangelisti in Chapter 15. How are they similar? How are they different? What reasons can you posit for the similarities and differences?

2. What media images exist of interracial relationships? Are these images generally positive or negative? What do these images tell us about society's view of interracial relationships?

3. What type of communication situation(s) might members of an interracial couple encounter that same-race partners never face? What communication skills would help them to deal with the situation(s)?

# 17

# The Relationships of Lesbians and of Gay Men

*Michelle Huston and*
*Pepper Schwartz*

Much of the research on interpersonal relationship development assumes a heterosexual relational model. Only in recent years have researchers conducted in-depth and multivariate studies of gay and lesbian relationships. This change is the result of many factors. The sociopolitical climate in the United States is changing. Gay and lesbian committed couples and families are becoming more visible due, in part, to a greater willingness of same-sex partners to identify their lifestyle. Census data do not include gay and lesbian partners, although the 2000 U.S. Census data on unmarried partner households indicated that over half a million households were headed by same-sex partners, representing 1 percent of all coupled households (Simmons and O'Connell 2003). A growing number of same-sex couples report children present in their home: about 21 percent of partnered lesbians and 5.2 percent of partnered gays (Black et al. 2000, 150). Yet, lesbian and gay partners and families are not easily categorized because they come in different sizes, shapes, ethnicities, races, and religions (Stacey 1999).

Many more young adults have come out openly and entered same-sex partnerships as compared to a decade or two ago, when sexual orientation was secretive or was disclosed much later in life, often following a heterosexual marriage. In addition, more gays and lesbians who have been in long-term, satisfying relationships are coming out. Thus, there are role models and norms legitimizing the relationships to the larger society. The study of gay and lesbian relationships tells us a great deal

about committed pairs and the ways in which gender, power, and society affect relationships.

*Although the research on lesbians and gay males is limited, current studies indicate that gay and lesbian couples are similar in many ways, yet different in others (Kurdek 2003). In this chapter, Michelle Huston and Pepper Schwartz identify the key components involved in the development of homosexual relationships and clarify the types of issues, processes, and factors that are important to such couples. The authors discuss the entire relationship cycle, starting with gay and lesbian dating rituals and gendered preferences, incorporating maintenance strategies, and, finally, describing the process of ending the relationship.*

*As you read this article, consider how gay and lesbian partnerships are similar to and different from heterosexual partnerships and what both types of relationships tell us about the effect of gender, power, and society on communication and relationships. Ask yourself this question: What are key communication issues faced by members of gay and/or lesbian partnerships?*

### References

Black, D., Gates, G., Snaders, S. and Taylor, L. (2000). Demographics of the gay and lesbian population in the United States. *Demography*, 37, 139–154.

Kurdek, L. A. (2003). Differences between gay and lesbian cohabiting couples. *Journal of Social and Personal Relationships*, 20, 411–436.

Simmons, T., and O'Connell, M. (2003, February). *Couple and Unmarried Partner Households: 2000.* (CENSR-5) Census 2000 Brief. Washington, DC: U.S. Census Bureau, Department of Commerce.

Stacey, J. (1999). Gay and lesbian families are here; All our families are queer; Let's get used to it. In S. Coontz (with M. Parson, and G. Raley) (Eds.), *American Families: A Multicultural Reader* (pp. 372–405). New York: Routledge.

\* \* \*

Although interest in gays and lesbians has increased and diversified in the last two decades, the majority of research has primarily concentrated on drawing a broad descriptive and demographic picture of this understudied population. Early work in the 1960s and 1970s generally centered on "normalizing" gays as people and providing ethnographic accounts of their lives and sexual preference (e.g., Warren, 1974; Wolf, 1979). In recent years our knowledge has begun to grow more sophisticated, with new attention to relationships, internal states, experiences, community organization and mobilization, and the impact of race and gender differences. . . .

The first issue that must be addressed when studying gays and lesbians is exactly who we are talking about. Over the course of their lives, many men and women who consider themselves to be heterosexual have physically intimate same-sex experiences. Some homosexuals fall in love with members of the opposite sex; some marry early in life before they know or act on their "true" orientation. In short, sexuality is much more fluid and harder to categorize than many researchers and most laypeople assume. This makes researching this topic difficult; definitions become tricky, and we must resist the temptation to make unwarranted assumptions, overgeneralize, or reify data.

We must also realize that traditional models of relationships (all of which assume heterosexuality) may not be the only viable models of intimacy. To apply models derived from and appropriate for heterosexuals to homosexual relationships not only leads to questionable conclusions but also obscures a wealth of information about ways couples organize and conduct their relationships (Harry & DeVall, 1978; Peplau, 1991).

Likewise, notions of "competence" and "success" in relationships are often different for heterosexuals and gays and lesbians. In marriage, "success" is usually (at least partially) defined in terms of endurance. Because homosexuals do not use "lifetime" marriage as their model—nor place the length of the relationship above other factors—gays and lesbians measure "success" by other factors, such as equity, satisfaction, and happiness. This difference has profound effects on how lesbians and gay men conduct their relationships and how they evaluate them.

This chapter introduces issues, processes, and factors that have been identified as important for lesbian and gay relationships. We cover influences on finding partners as well as on the maintenance and dissolution of already established couples.

Throughout, it is important for readers to realize that the data on which most of our conclusions are based are affected by the limitations placed upon any research about a hidden community. It is impossible to get a truly representative sample, and findings may be skewed because they exclude people who are not "out," underrepresent people who live in rural or isolated settings, and usually miss older, more conservative couples who do not want to talk about their private life. These limitations notwithstanding, existing research indicates that gay and lesbian relationships are very similar to heterosexual relationships in some ways, and quite distinct in others.

## Beginning a Relationship

Like most people, the majority of gay men and lesbians value long-term, committed relationships. In the pre-AIDS years, more lesbians than gay men reported being in committed relationships, partially because the gay subculture of that time period endorsed singlehood over couplehood for most gay men (Hoffman, 1968; Silverstein, 1981; Tuller, 1978). Most researchers agree that this finding underrepresents older gay men who did not frequent gay bars and who were probably coupled in marriage-like relationships. More recent work indicates a growing desire among gay men to commit early and monogamously (Davidson, 1991; McWhirter & Mattison, 1984). In this case, when individuals do get ready to look for a committed relationship, how do they find partners? In a society that, in general, stigmatizes homosexuality, how do gays and lesbians identify others who share their sexual preference, and how do they communicate their interest? How is the intricate courtship process leading from casual acquaintance to a more serious involvement negotiated? Furthermore, how is this process affected by gender, sexual preference, community, and ideology?

## Gendered Dating Patterns and Preferences

Traditionally, men and women in Western society grow up having different values about when sex is appropriate. More women than men are taught that only love legitimizes sex. More men than women are taught that it is justifiable to have sex for its own sake. Hence lesbians usually seek emotional connection before having sex with their dating partner (Wolf, 1979), whereas gay men frequently have sex first and develop feelings of attachment and emotional closeness later (Warren, 1974). These gendered styles of viewing love and sex influence the dating styles of lesbians and gay men, just as they shape the styles of heterosexuals. . . .

## Gendered Preferences for Partners

Gender also influences the characteristics that lesbians and gay men look for in partners. Data gathered both from interviews and from personals advertisements lend credence to this assertion (Gonzales & Meyers, 1993; Laner, 1978). Gay men tend to desire a very specific "type" of man for both recreational sex and more serious relationships. This standard includes an extremely attractive face, an athletic body, and a well-groomed appearance. Some men have specific demands that place extreme importance on particular parts of the body—most commonly the buttocks, but also the penis or chest. Gay men also value many of the "status symbols" that go along with "manliness" in this culture: a well-paid or "masculine" career, and the material accoutrements of the "good life" (Davidson, 1991; Silverstein, 1981). Lesbians are much more likely to emphasize socioemotional characteristics, and less likely to concentrate on physical characteristics or dress. However, many lesbians admire an androgynous or "butch" look—which signifies rejection of male derived standards of beauty and weakness. Recently, more traditional standards of female attractiveness have also become acceptable. By virtue of their involvement in the women's movement, many lesbians also value self-sufficiency and strength in a long-term partner; however, job status or prestige is not as important to them as it is for gay men. This is pragmatic as well as ideological: Few women have high-prestige, high-paying jobs, and prioritizing status and money would make finding a partner more difficult.

A more detailed analysis of the gay community helps contextualize the ways in which gender affects the dating relationships of lesbians and gay men. For men, bars have provided a relatively secure pickup spot: a place to meet other men interested in casual sexual encounters. Occasionally these one-night stands result in long-term relationships, but this is the exception rather than the rule (Silverstein, 1981). Indeed, there is some stigma attached to men who go to bars and overromanticize a given sexual encounter. Therefore, men who are interested in finding a potential partner may find little encouragement at gay bars. . . .

Outside the big cities, lesbian bars are even more rare than gay bars, mostly due to the fact that lesbians do not have the large disposable income available to many gay men, but perhaps also due to the fact that more lesbians are "closeted" and infrequently visit bars or other public lesbian places. Hence it is hard to keep lesbian bars financially stable and able to stay in business. Partially because of many women's desire to know a person before having sex, lesbian bars are rarely "pickup" spots. Although it is possible to meet unattached women there, most are already partnered. Therefore, lesbian bars are more oriented to socializing within well-defined acquaintanceship circles than toward finding new love interests. . . .

Although bars are a mainstay of gay culture, it is not surprising that the majority of homosexuals meet their future partner by some other means. For both lesbians and gay men, it is most often mutual friends who do the matchmaking (Peplau, Cochran, Rook, & Padesky, 1978; Tuller, 1978; Vetere, 1982; Warren, 1974). This usually promotes a greater degree of similarity between potential partners in terms of interests and backgrounds. However, this also means that couples who break up have to renegotiate relationships with mutual friends and may have to deal with loyalties. This puts additional pressure on the ex-couple because they are likely to run into each other at social events, dinner parties, and celebrations that bring the friendship circle together (Becker, 1988; Clunis & Green, 1988). . . .

For lesbians, the second most common meeting place is political functions (feminist and/or lesbian). As with matchmaking by mutual friends, this method emphasizes similarities—in this case, political activism. This is extremely important because matching on certain characteristics is highly predictive of lesbian satisfaction and stability (Howard, Blumstein, & Schwartz, 1992). For example, a great deal of research has pointed out that lesbians usually value both dyadic attachment and autonomy. Partners try to balance a high degree of emotional closeness and intimacy with a high degree of independence and freedom. Although these characteristics are not mutually exclusive, tension between needs for intimacy and autonomy causes conflict (Andrews, 1990). Starting out mismatched complicates the beginning of a relationship and lessens the possibility of relationship longevity.

What neither very many young gay men or lesbians can do is court openly. They cannot go to the high school prom (although a few couples have made newspaper headlines trying to do so) or openly discuss their latest crush with their predominantly heterosexual peer group. It is even less likely that they can confide in their parents. Deprived of these early experiences common to heterosexual teens, initial homosexual exploration is generally confined to furtive and hidden impersonal sex or a taboo relationship with a peer that must be concealed. Thus most gay men and lesbians begin courtship and dating experience after high school, sometimes even after college. These days, there are more gay teen clubs or college homosexual associations, but these are usually confined to larger cities and schools or elite smaller high schools and colleges. Many gay students, not yet comfortable with or ready to take on the burdens of social stigma, avoid these places even if they would clearly love to go. Thus, for many gay men and lesbians, serious courtship starts much later than it does for their heterosexual peers. This means that they may have fewer social skills than comparable heterosexuals, less practice at knowing who is right for them, less awareness about available choices, and fewer opportunities to check reality and make social comparisons with peers.

This whole research area of how individuals go about finding other gays and lesbians, as well as what they do once they find them, needs much more attention from researchers. What effect does the smaller pool of eligible people have on relationships? To what extent does the fact that lesbian and gay youth enter serious relationships later than most heterosexuals affect those (and subsequent) relationships? How do homosexuals overcome their more circumscribed set of experience and limited practice at knowing what they want in a partner?

## Maintaining a Relationship

Once begun, which factors contribute to stability and satisfaction in lesbian and gay relationships? In general, relationships of lesbians and gay men are strengthened by a variety of factors. For lesbians, an equitable balance of power, a high degree of emotional intimacy, and high self-esteem all contribute to satisfying relationships (Eldridge & Gilbert, 1990). For gay men, little conflict, high appreciation of partner, stability, and cooperation are important for satisfaction (Jones & Bates, 1978). For both types of couples, the frequency of "destructive arguing" is negatively correlated with satisfaction (Kurdek, 1993b). . . .

### Communication

The large body of literature about communication between men and women suggests several interesting points relevant to relationships of gay men and lesbians. In general, women use conversation as a springboard to intimacy and are skilled at playing a supportive role in communication to further this goal. Men, on the other hand, frequently see conversation as a competitive endeavor, with the most powerful partner "winning" points while asserting his status for his conversational "opponent." These basic styles of communication form the underpinnings on which couples base problem-solving and decision-making efforts: In general, women seek consensus when faced with a hurdle, whereas men tend to expedite decision making by allowing the more powerful partner to get his own way (Kollock, Blumstein, & Schwartz, 1985; Tannen, 1990). . . .

In heterosexual couples, the "dominant-supportive" model of conversing is somewhat preprogrammed. The male, traditionally the more powerful member of a couple, also plays a dominant role in communication. He interrupts more, uses fewer tag questions (a supportive device used to show interest and ask for others' opinions and input), and reveals less of his emotional state than his partner (Blumstein & Schwartz, 1983; Fishman, 1983). Women, on the other hand, tend to play a supportive role in conversations. They interrupt less often and less successfully, use more tag questions, and reveal more of themselves than their male partners (Fishman, 1983; Lakoff, 1975; Thorne & Henley, 1975). . . . Gay and lesbian couples, by virtue of the sex composition of their relationships, are not prompted to automatically fall into this gendered style of communication. Nonetheless, gender socialization does affect the goals and styles of gay and lesbian discourse, and it is not without its own pitfalls and dangers.

Some researchers have argued that it is often power, and not gender, that determines the style of communicating used by partners in intimate couples. A study by Kollock et al. (1985) found that the more powerful partner often uses conversational privileges not available to the less powerful partner. These tactics include using minimal responses ("hmmms" and "uh-huhs" used to avoid having to do the work of formulating a verbal response), interrupting more often, and not seeking other opinions through the use of tag questions. Other elements of conversational style seem related more to the gendered goals of partners than to power alone. For example, women in general desire greater emotional disclosure from themselves and their partners than men do (Tannen, 1990). Also, women often see the use of challenges as running contrary to the intent of conversation (the building of intimacy), whereas men view challenges as an excellent way to spar for dominance (Tannen, 1990).

Communication for lesbians and gay men is thus shaped by power and gender in different ways. Because most lesbians are very conscious of power imbalances in their relationships, they try to avoid most of the dominant conversational techniques discussed above. They usually have a common goal (the creation and maintenance of emotionally close and fulfilling conversations), and the power differentials that are somewhat unavoidable in heterosexual relationships are not usually played out in the communication styles of lesbian partners. For example, for most partners, the less powerful member uses more tag questions; this effect is much smaller in lesbian couples. Although power is an important determinant of the use of questions for all other types of couples, it is not significant for lesbians. They also have the lowest rates of attempted interruptions of all intimate couples (Kollock et al., 1985), and issue few challenges (Clunis & Green, 1988; Tannen, 1990).

Although gay men also tend to share a conception of how conversation is to be used, and what its goals are, this notion is less conductive to the creation of intimacy, at least as it is traditionally defined. Communications, for many men, is a tool by which power is accumulated and displayed. More than any other type of couple, gay men use minimal responses as a way to fill conversational gaps. Unlike heterosexual couples, for whom the use of tag questions is correlated with less power, the most powerful partner in a gay relationship uses the most tag questions. This could be due to an effort on the part of the couple to equalize the power imbalance in the conversation, with the more powerful trying to draw the less powerful into the discussion. Negotiations over power also influence the success of interruptions. Although attempts are made, gay couples have the lowest successful interruption rate of all couples. Furthermore, like most men, gay men perceive challenges as a normal part of dialogue (Tannen, 1990), and use them as a reasonable way to assert their own authority within the conversation. . . .

## The End of the Relationship

In general, gay and lesbian relationships are not as durable as heterosexual marriages. Even though there are a significant minority of couples who break this rule, Blumstein and Schwartz found that nearly 48% of their lesbian respondents and 36% of their gay male respondents (compared to 29% for heterosexual cohabitors and 14% for married couples) broke up within 2 years of the original study (Blumstein & Schwartz, 1983). . . .

Research about the reasons gays and lesbians break up has shown that there are distinct patterns among each group that correlate with relationship dissolution. Among lesbians, couples who argue about sex are more likely to report being dissatisfied with their relationship (Blumstein & Schwartz, 1983; Kurdek, 1991b) and break up more than those who do not. . . . Arguments about money, kin, friends, or unequal power also correlate with higher chances of breaking up (Eldridge & Gilbert, 1990; Peplau et al., 1982). As with heterosexuals, homosexuals who are higher earners—and more powerful partners—are most likely to leave (Blumstein & Schwartz, 1983). Lesbians have no training or affection for the provider role; thus if they have this role, their resentment may push them out of the relationship.

According to therapists who work with lesbian couples, the most common source of strain results from the combination of unrealistic expectations and outside pressures. Women in this society are usually expected to be empathetic and relationship oriented. However, most lesbians also have responsibilities outside the couple, including a career and political involvement. This sets up a no-win situation for some lesbians who expect a great deal from themselves and their partner in terms of time and energy spent on the relationship.

Finally, lesbian relationships are susceptible to affairs and jealousy (Becker, 1988; Wolf, 1979). Usually it is the woman who had the affair who ends the relationship, probably because she has fallen in love with the other woman (Becker, 1988). Also, if one woman moves away to pursue educational opportunities or a career, the couple may break up. Because lesbians need their jobs to survive, the option of following a partner is not always available. Distance makes it hard to maintain the relationship, especially if the couple cannot afford frequent trips or high phone bills. . . .

Gay men often break up over large and unresolvable power differences. Whereas for lesbians this is usually due to the discomfort arising from supporting a partner who is (ideally) supposed to be independent, for gay men it is probably more due to an ego-based tug of war that one partner is losing. Other literature about the dissolution of gay couples simply cites "personality differences," whereas ethnographic accounts point to the trend among gay men that they simply fall out of love and move on.

Although these correlates of dissatisfaction and dissolution are interesting, they tell us nothing about the processes and consequences of terminating a relationship. For most people, ending a relationship is rarely easy, especially if it was long-term and the couple lived together. For gays and lesbians, this process may be aggravated by the fact that they do not have access to the culturally accepted symbols that mark the demise of a marriage or institutional regulations to protect partners' rights: They do not legally separate, sign divorce papers, and so forth. Furthermore, a heterosexual going through a divorce can usually expect sympathy and advice from family, friends, and coworkers. Depending on how closeted they are, lesbians and gay men may not have these outlets and must therefore carry the burden of their turmoil alone (Becker, 1988). . . .

## References

Andrews, C. (1990). *Closeness and satisfaction in lesbian relationships*. Unpublished master's thesis, University of Washington.

Becker, C. S. (1988). *Unbroken ties: Lesbian ex-lovers*. Boston: Alyson.

Blumstein, P., & Schwartz, P. (1983). *American couples*. New York: William Morrow.

Clunis, D. M. & Green, G. D. (1988). *Lesbian couples*. Seattle, WA: Seal.

Davidson, A. G. (1991). Looking for love in the age of AIDS: The language of gay personals, 1978–1988. *Journal of Sex Research, 28,* 125–137.

Eldridge, N. S., & Gilbert, L. A. (1990). Correlates of relationship satisfaction in lesbian couples. *Psychology of Women Quarterly, 14,* 43–62.

Fishman, P. (1983). Interaction: The work women do. In K. Thorne & U. Henley (Eds.), *Language, gender, and society* (pp. 89–100). Rowley, MA: Newbury House.

Gonzales, M. H., & Meyers, S. A. (1993). "Your mother would like me": Self-presentation in the personals ads of heterosexual and homosexual men and women. *Personality and Social Psychology Bulletin*, 19, 131–142.

Harry, J., & DeVall, W. B. (1978). *The social organization of gay males*. New York: Praeger.

Hoffman, M. (1968). *The gay world*. New York: Basic Books.

Howard, J., Blumstein, P., & Schwartz, P. (1992). *Homogamy in intimate relationships*. Unpublished manuscript.

Jones, R. W., & Bates, J. E. (1978). Satisfaction in male homosexual couples. *Journal of Homosexuality*, 3, 217–224.

Kollock, P., Blumstein, P., & Schwartz, P. (1985). Sex and power in interaction: Conversational privileges and duties. *American Sociological Review*, 50, 34–46.

Kurdek, L. A. (1991b). Predictors of increases in marital distress in newly wed couples. *Developmental Psychology*, 27, 627–636.

———. (1993a). The allocation of household labor in gay, lesbian, and heterosexual married couples. *Journal of Social Issues*, 49, 127–139.

Lakoff, R. (1975). *Language and woman's place*. New York: Harper & Row.

Laner, M. R. (1978). Media Mating II: "Personals" advertisements of lesbian relationships. *Journal of Homosexuality*, 4, 41–61.

McWhirter, D. P., & Mattison, A. M. (1984). *The male couple: How relationships develop*. Englewood Cliffs, NJ: Prentice Hall.

Peplau, L. A. (1991). Lesbian and gay relationships. In J. C. Gonsiorek & J. D. Weinrich (Eds.), *Homosexuality: Research implications for public policy* (pp. 177–196). Newbury Park, CA: Sage.

Peplau, L. A., Cochran, S., Rook, K., & Padesky, C. (1978). Loving women: Attachment and autonomy in lesbian relationships. *Journal of Social Issues*, 34, 7–27.

Peplau, L. A., Padesky, C., & Hamilton, M. (1982). Satisfaction in lesbian relationships. *Journal of Homosexuality*, 8, 23–35.

Silverstein, C. (1981). *Man to man: Gay couples in America*. New York: William Morrow.

Tannen, D. (1990). *You just don't understand: Women and men in communication*. New York: Ballantine.

Thorne, B., & Henley, N. (Eds.). (1975). *Language and sex: Difference and dominance*. Rowley, MA: Newbury House.

Tuller, N. R. (1978). Couples: The hidden segment of the gay world. *Journal of Homosexuality*, 3, 331–343.

Vetere, V. A. (1982). The role of friendships in the development and maintenance of lesbian love relationships. *Journal of Homosexuality*, 8, 51–65.

Warren, C. A. B. (1974). *Identity and community in the gay world*. New York: John Wiley.

Wolf, D. G. (1979). *The lesbian community*. Berkeley: University of California Press.

## Questions

1. How is communication in lesbian and gay relationships different from in heterosexual relationships?

2. Using Wood's "Growing Up Masculine, Growing Up Feminine" article (Chapter 13), consider how the themes might affect communication in same-sex pairs.

3. How are gay and lesbian relationships portrayed in the media? How do you think this portrayal affects society's perceptions of gay and lesbian relationships?

Reprinted from Michelle Huston and Pepper Schwartz, "The Relationships of Lesbians and Gay Men." In *Under-Studied Relationships: Off the Beaten Track*, Julia T. Wood and Steve Duck (eds.), pp. 89–118. Copyright © 1995 by Sage Publications, Inc. Reprinted with permission. ✦

# Part V

## *Sustaining Relationships*

Sustaining relationships is not easy. That may sound trite, but it is nonetheless true, because *sustaining* relationships implies proactive efforts to invest emotionally in the relational ties and struggle through major changes and crises. Commitment—financial, emotional, and temporal (time invested)—sustains ongoing relationships. The stronger the commitment level, and the fewer good alternatives that exist, the more likely a relationship will continue (Rusbult, Drigotas, and Verette 1994). People remain in relationships for various reasons. Frequently it is the result of emotional attachment, liking or loving the other person, or gaining something from the connection. However, some relationships are continued due to one person's desire to control the other person or feel responsible for that person.

Some relational ties are maintained through inertia; change seems like too much effort, so partners maintain lifeless relationships. Certain relationships are continued out of convenience. Two people may own a business together and wish to avoid the trouble of finding another business partner. Marital relationships are often maintained "for the sake of the children." Divorces and separations are financially and emotionally costly; therefore, couples stay together to avoid other problems. Fear motivates some people to stay together—fear of being lonely, of social criticism ("What would people say?"), or of violating a religious, cultural, or parental norm.

How do individuals keep relationships vital over the years? According to Werner and Baxter (1994), relationships are maintained by the ways partners manage competing needs and obligations, how they organize and coordinate their activities, how they introduce novelty and pleasure into their relationship, and how they build a place in which to nurture the relationship (pp. 324–325). Several researchers have focused on the strategies that people use to sustain various relationships. For example, Dindia and Baxter (1987) suggest four general types of strategies:

1. *Prosocial behaviors*, such as being friendly and polite, avoiding criticism, and compromising.

2. *Ceremonial behaviors*, such as celebrating birthdays and anniversaries, eating at a favorite restaurant, and discussing past pleasurable times.

3. *Communication behaviors*, such as sharing feelings, talking honestly and openly, and calling just to say, "Hi, how are you?"

4. *Togetherness behaviors*, such as spending time together, visiting friends, and doing specific things as a couple.

In two recent studies (Canary et al. 1993), the researchers identified specific relational maintenance strategies, including the following:

1. sharing joint activities together;

2. sending cards and letters and telephoning one another;

3. sharing tasks, such as cleaning the house;

4. engaging in self-disclosure;

5. apprising the other of the significance of the relationship;

6. attempting to make interactions pleasant and upbeat;

7. making jokes and teasing one another;

8. establishing specific times for talking; and

9. acting affectionately and romantically.

In a study of marital life, Canary, Stafford, and Semic (2002) describe marital resilience as a process in which people purposefully engage in *maintenance strategies* to repair and protect their connections. They discuss the following five relational maintenance strategies: positivity, openness, assurances, social networks, and sharing tasks.

As you read the following articles, keep in mind these general relationship-sustaining behaviors and the concept of relational culture. Consider how these concepts relate to the position of each of the authors. You will notice that many of the articles use the term *maintaining* relationships, a commonly used expression. We have chosen to emphasize the concept of *sustaining* relationships because we were persuaded by Montgomery's (1993) point that "sustaining relationships" is a more desirable term because *maintaining* sounds like an attempt to create a steady state rather than to acknowledge the ongoing inevitable tensions.

This section includes articles that focus on everyday relational life, the issues you confront, and the communication strategies you use to sustain a relationship once you have moved through the early stages of development. These articles should make you consider how much thought and effort you devote to nurturing the relationships in your life.

## References

Canary, D., Stafford, L., Hause, K., and Wallace, L. (1993). An inductive analysis of relational maintenance strategies: Comparisons among lovers, relatives, friends and others. *Communication Research Report*, 10: 5–14.

Canary, D. J., Stafford, L., and, Semic, B. A. (2002). A panel study of the association between maintenance characteristics and relational characteristics. *Journal of Marriage and Family*, 64: 395–406.

Dindia, K., and Baxter, L. (1987). Strategies for maintaining and repairing marital relationships. *Journal of Social and Personal Relationships*, 4: 143–158.

Montgomery, B. (1993). Relationship maintenance versus relationship change: A dialectical perspective. *Journal of Social and Personal Relationships*, 10: 205–223.

Rusbult, C. E., Drigotas, S. M., and Verette, J. (1994). The investment model: An interdependence analysis of commitment processes and relationship maintenance phenomena. In D. J. Canary and L. Stafford (Eds.), *Communication and Relational Maintenance*, pp. 115–140. San Diego: Academic Press.

Werner, C. M., and Baxter, L. (1994). Temporal qualities of relationships: Organismic, transitional, and dialectical views. In M. L. Knapp and G. R. Miller (Eds.), *Handbook of Interpersonal Communication*, 2nd ed., pp. 323–379. Thousand Oaks, CA: Sage. ✦

# 18

# Expressing Affection

## A Vocabulary of Loving Messages

### Charles A. Wilkinson

**A**lthough sharing affection is central to relational maintenance, many well-intended attempts at displaying caring or positivity fail to create their intended result. The intended recipient of the caring message misses the point, wishes for something different, or does not respond in a desirable manner. Randy Fujishin, who believes that body language provides the most powerful form of communicating caring, says that "whether it's the reassuring pat on the back from a friend, the gentle kiss of a mother, or the familiar touch of a lover, body language conveys an important message—the gift of showing you care" (1998, 103).

In the following article, Charles Wilkinson, a marriage and family therapist, discusses the various ways people express affection to others and the difficulty that can arise when you cannot construct loving messages in the way your partners or friends need to hear them. In his work as a counselor, Wilkinson frequently encounters good, well-meaning people who are experiencing relationship problems because they "don't speak the same language." In other words, they do not have shared meanings.

If you think of your family as your first communication classroom, you will realize how much you learned about how to share or withhold affection. This experience, coupled with your cultural heritage, provided a solid base from which to construct your "affection vocabulary" or the ways in which you would express and receive affection. Wilkinson develops a list of varied ways of indicating caring ranging from direct verbal statement to doing favors. He suggests that the key point is the similarity of the relational participants' values; any loving behavior is valid if both parties interpret and value it in similar ways.

Painful relational breakdowns occur when Partner A tries so hard to indicate caring by giving gifts or making special meals while Partner B waits for a hug. The situation becomes even more complex when Partner B reaches out through touch and caring words and Partner A does not really get the message.

After briefly describing the many ways in which people share affection, Wilkinson develops three that he views as critical in the work he does—direct relational statement, self-disclosure, and gifts. Each of these is commonly used to send "I care" messages, with very different effects. As you read this piece, you may wish to consider how participants in a particular relationship try to reach out to each other and evaluate their effectiveness. As you read this chapter, consider this question: How satisfied am I with the ways I share affection in friendships and family relationships, and what changes might I wish to make in how I use relational currencies?

### Reference

Fujishin, R. (1998). *Gifts From the Heart*. San Francisco: Acada Books.

\* \* \*

**H**ow did you know you were loved as a child? Did someone tease you, give you a backrub, surprise you with a present, fix your meals, listen to your troubles, hug you goodnight? Every family implicitly and explicitly teaches its members specific ways to show caring for others and to accept caring from others. Growing up, we all learn specific nurturing behaviors. You learned to use and expect certain behaviors and not to use or to expect others. You were taught the rules for how affection should or should not be shared, and how intensely it should be expressed. In addition, you learned appropriate nurturing messages for males and females, older and younger persons, immediate family, and friends. Some of these lessons reflected your family's cultural background. In short, part of growing up consisted of a series of family lessons on communicating affection. Thus everyone, knowingly and unknowingly, develops a specific set of acceptable ways of sharing affection within his or her family of origin, the first words of your vocabulary of caring. It is important to note that, although many people follow their family of origin patterns, others deliberately choose to alter them. For example, in their study of father-son affection Floyd and Morman (2000) found that men who are most affectionate with their sons had fathers who were either highly affectionate or highly unaffectionate. In such cases, sons either followed their fathers' modeling or compensated for the lack of affection by demonstrating strong affection when they became fathers.

Verbal and nonverbal messages that carry meaning about the caring dimension of human relationships may be called *relational currencies*. Although the concept of "currency" reflects an economic model of investing or trading, within a communication framework, relational currencies can be considered part of a symbolic exchange process. As partners share relational currencies, they form agreements about the meanings of things and either strengthen or limit their relationship worldview (Stephen 1984). When certain currencies are equally valued, communication is clearer.

As you know, the ways you learned to show affection to friends and relatives are not necessarily the ways learned by other people. Growing up, you gradually became aware that others expressed caring differently, and you also learned to appreciate and to use some of the nurturing messages taught to you by others. Occasionally you also have been surprised or angered by the insensitive ways others expressed caring, resisting their intensity or their actions.

Friends from different cultures can value different ways of sharing affection. One may be very expressive, physically hugging and touching; another may be very reserved but brings you wonderful gifts of food. Cross-gender relationships are sources of confusion regarding the most comfortable ways to show affection (Wood and Inman 1993). These differences may have broadened your ways of thinking about affection.

Some of the most frustrating relational experiences occur when a cared-for person does not respond with the intensity you expect or becomes silent or distant. It hurts when another does not understand your attempts to show affection and when you feel unloved by the responses from someone you care about.

The most painful experiences in some partnerships occur when members value different ways of sharing affection. Many husbands and wives feel unloved because their spouses never seem to do the "right thing"—to send the expected or desired caring message. Holidays and special family times become painful events as relatives' loving vocabularies bypass each other. Each grew up learning a different set of behaviors, so the "I care" messages look and feel very different. Naturally, when members move away from their families they carry their relational currency patterns with them. For example, college roommates may experience frustration as one cleans the room to please the other but never gives holiday gifts. The other roommate may miss the positive message entirely.

In their early work on relational communication, Villard and Whipple (1976) discuss intimate and economic relational currencies, or communication behaviors that convey affection. Proponents of transactional analysis also discuss currencies for expressing affection (Berne 1964). In his discussion of communication skills in loving relationships, Fujishin (1998) refers to them as ways of showing caring. Just as children learn verbal language and expand their vocabularies as they encounter new objects, people, and ideas, so too they learn a vocabulary of loving behaviors that should expand as they mature and encounter new people and ideas. The vocabulary learned initially in the family of origin influences greatly any development of a lifetime loving vocabulary.

Being conscious of such a vocabulary helps individuals identify their particular patterns of expressing affection, and examine how those patterns fit or miss the needs of their significant others—partners, parents, children, extended families, and friends. In more emotionally distanced families, each member has a small number of loving behaviors that coordinate with the specific behaviors used or valued by the others. There are many possible patterned messages for conveying affection.

Each of the following (Figure 18-1) represents one way of sharing affection. The use of each must be considered within the contexts of gender, culture, and developmental stage (McGoldrick, Giordano, and Pearce 1996; McGoldrick, Anderson, and Walsh 1989).

### Figure 18-1

| | |
|---|---|
| Direct relational statement | Gifts |
| Positive verbal statements | Money |
| Self-disclosure | Food |
| Listening | Favors |
| Nonverbal expressiveness | Service |
| Touch | Time together |
| Sexuality | Access rights |
| Aggression | |

(Adapted from Villard and Whipple, 1976.)

## Overview of Currencies

### Direct Relational Statements

Such statements include oral and written messages that directly indicate love or caring. In some relationships, people express affection easily, saying "I love you" directly and frequently. In other relationships, members view such directness as unacceptable, preferring to save such words for unusual occasions (weddings, homecomings) or crisis situations. A study of statements of love within birthday cards reveals that the recipients of such affectionate messages are more likely to be female relatives (Mooney and Brabant 1988).

### Positive Verbal Statements

Such statements include oral and written messages that directly or indirectly indicate support, praise, or liking. Compliments, encouragement, indications, pleasure, and involvement (I'm really glad you decided to come, I missed you) may convey liking or affection. A "Thinking of you" card or a phone call or e-mail to "touch base" also conveys involvement.

### Self-Disclosure

Disclosure about self, or voluntarily telling someone personal information about yourself that the other is unlikely to discover from other sources, serves as a means of deepening understanding and trust between people. In such cases, self-disclosure must be intentionally used to show caring and investment in a relationship.

### Listening

A frequently underappreciated communication behavior, listening carries a message of involvement with, and attention to, another person. More than any other currency, it communicates *presence*. True empathetic listening requires focused energy and practice. "It's a mental habit at which one has to work" (Ryan and Ryan 1982, 44). Listening may be taken for granted and the effort discounted unless the speaker is sensitive to the listener's careful attention.

### Staying in Touch

Staying in touch implies efforts to maintain important relational ties, often across significant distances. Traditionally this involved sending cards and gifts or long-distance phone calls. Today many friends and family members remain in close connection through the use of e-mail and the Internet. Dating partners may IM each other 4–5 times a day; parents and college students may check in regularly over e-mail. Many grandparents are getting online in order to participate in the family's round-robin letters or check updates on the family website. The ease of everyday interaction has helped to maintain many friendship or extended family ties that might have frayed in the past. Even if the words are not affectionate, the effort to stay in touch is symbolic of caring.

### Nonverbal Expressiveness

Spontaneous displays of affection, best characterized as love "in that 'eyes lighting up' sense" (Malone and Malone 1987, 14), are referred to as *nonverbal expressiveness*. Nonverbal symbols such as facial expressions, outstretched arms, or general exuberance convey delight at the other's presence.

### Touch

Touch is the language of physical intimacy. Positive physical contact carries a range of messages about friendship, concern, love, or sexual interest. Touch may serve as a significant tie sign (Goffman 1959) indicating interpersonal connection to outsiders. Touching behaviors vary greatly across genders and cultures, and so may be easily misinterpreted.

## Sexuality

For adult partners, sexuality provides a unique opportunity for intimacy. The discourse surrounding intercourse and the act itself combine to create a powerful message of affection as long as both partners interpret the meaning of their sexual exchange in the same way.

## Aggression

Aggression connotes actions usually thought to be incompatible with affection. Yet aggressive actions may serve as the primary emotional connection between members of certain families. Persons who are afraid to express intimacy directly but who wish to feel connected may use verbal or physical aggression as a sign of caring. When persons do not know how to express intimacy in positive ways, their friends and relatives may encounter or experience sarcasm, teasing, tickling, or put downs as attempts at connection. Some conflictual couples may maintain their contact through bickering and disagreements. An individual who avoids conflict may indicate caring by engaging in an argument as a way to stay connected.

## Gifts

Gifts are symbols of affection that may be complicated by issues of cost, appropriateness, and reciprocity. Gifts may read as signals of a person's intentions about future investment in a relationship (Camerer 1988). The process of identifying, selecting, and presenting the gift serves as part of the caring message.

## Money

Dollars and cents symbolize the economic nature of an exchange of currencies. Money must be given or loaned as a sign of affection and not as an obligation if the act is to convey caring.

## Food

A symbol of nurturing in many cultures, food preparation has emerged as a sign of caring in romantic and immediate family relationships, in addition to its historical place in intergenerational methods of affection.

## Favors

Performing helpful acts for another may be complicated by norms of reciprocity and equality. Favors, to be considered signs of affection, must be performed willingly rather than in response to a friend or relative's order. The underlying message of an action may be missed if the effort of the favor is not appreciated.

## Service

Service implies that a favor has evolved into a habitual behavior. Driving the carpool, making the coffee in the morning, or maintaining the checkbook may have begun as favors and moved into routines. Such services frequently go unnoticed or are taken for granted, thus negating the underlying message of affection.

## Time Together

Being together, whether it's just "hanging out" or voluntarily accompanying a person on a trip or errand, carries the message "I want to be with you." This is a subtle message with potential for being overlooked. A variation on being together involves "staying in touch" whereby people make efforts to remain regularly connected through phone calls, e-mail, IM, or other means.

## Access Rights

Allowing another person to use or borrow things you value conveys affection when the permission is intended as a sign of caring. What makes this a relational message is the exclusive nature of the permission, which is given only to persons you care about; not "just anyone" can use your things.

This "vocabulary" list does not represent the last word on the subject. You may add to your vocabulary list based on your cultural heritage, personal experiences, and observations.

Clearly some of these categories overlap. You may also think of something that does not seem to fit into the items on the list. Yet, for most people, some of these specific behaviors represent major ways of showing affection or of receiving affection. Some of these behaviors will send a more direct message than others—not necessarily a more powerful message but a more direct one.

Any or all of these behaviors can be used to manipulate another or to gain power in a relationship. These serve as nurturing messages only when they communicate a genuine attitude that says "I honestly care" and carries the intention of maintaining or deepening the relationship. A closer look at three key aspects of this vocabulary demonstrates the subtleties and complexities of any currency.

## Direct Relational Statements

Verbal statements of affection are not always easy to express. In *Fiddler on the Roof*, Teyve asks his wife Golda, "Do you love me?" Her reply takes the form of a list of all the things she'd done for him over the years. She says: "For twenty-five years I've washed your clothes, cooked your meals, cleaned your house, given you children, milked the cow. After twenty-five years why talk about love right now?" Clearly for Golda such things are not talked about directly. Yet Teyve really wants a statement of caring, and reluctantly Golda finally admits, "I suppose I do." Teyve, to be safe, replies, "And I suppose I love you too."

Each of us can recall wondering about another's affection for us and thinking, "Does he really love me?" or "How much does she really care about me?" Many adults still wonder how much their parents loved them because they never heard words such as "I love you" or "You're very special to me" while they were growing up. In some households direct statements of affection and caring occur with great frequency, and may even lose certain impact through such regularity, whereas in other homes direct verbal affection does not occur or it occurs sparingly during special family occasions. In such families, one seldom hears words such as "I'm glad you are my daughter" or "I missed you." In many relationships, such statements serve to clarify and strengthen the bond between individuals.

If you grew up in a family that was highly verbal about its affection, it may be hard to appreciate just how difficult it is for some other people to put affection into words. Some people think that it isn't necessary to go around talking about how you feel. Others will know it by your actions. Many men have learned that it is "masculine" to withhold feelings. In today's society, greeting card companies have made fortunes by writing the caring messages so all the customer has to do is select the right card. This serves as a buffer for verbalizing deep feelings. Humorous cards often allow people to avoid sharing their feelings directly because the joke serves as a functional remembrance of a day. Sometimes, expressing verbal affection can best be done in writing. One man left love notes on his wife's mirror, even after nineteen years of marriage. A student bemoaned the fact that her parents lived near her college and so she never got letters. The only way her father expressed his feelings was by writing, and he wrote such wonderful letters about how much he missed her when she was away at camp.

One wife said in the presence of her husband, "We've been married eleven years and in all that time, never once, not ONCE has he ever said to me, 'I love you!' " Asked if that was so, he replied, "Well, I take care of her, she's very special." When asked, "But have you ever said the words 'I love you' to her?" he said, "Not really, I guess." And even then he couldn't add, "But I do love you, Hon."

Most people have a deep need to talk about caring. Witness the letters to advice columnists bemoaning the death of a family member with "If only I had told him how much I loved him before he died."

Some people can nurture others through direct, caring statements but cannot accept such statements comfortably. In a society that teaches many people to put themselves down, direct statements of caring can be unsettling and may be met with averted eyes, a flip remark, or some such disclaimer as "Oh, you tell everyone that."

Direct statements of affection, spoken and written, are essential to all healthy relationships, and especially to relationships within families whose primary function is to nurture.

# Self-Disclosure

Carl Sandburg once wrote: "Life is like an onion: You uncover it a layer at a time and sometimes you weep." Relationships are also like onions. The surface, onion-skin stuff is there for all to see. But as layer after layer is peeled away, the deeper truths of any relationship can cause its members to laugh, cry, appreciate, discover, despair, grow, and expand, or cling to the safe and known. People, like onions, grow from the inside out; that growing edge is at the core of one's being. And sharing the growing edge with another, inviting another "in," is a powerful way of saying "I care about you."

Closely related to direct verbal statements of caring, self-disclosure implies voluntarily telling another person private/personal information that person is not likely to discover from another source. This personal/private information may involve your feelings for the other person, or it may involve information about yourself. But what is clearly communicated is: "I am willing to share this information with you as a symbol of my caring for you and for our relationship."

True self-disclosure involves some degree of risk because the other person learns information that, if misused, could be hurtful to you. For example, the person could throw the information back at you in anger or reveal to others what you have shared. Still, despite the risks, many individuals self-disclose to establish bonds between themselves and to deepen their relationships.

Although a verbal statement of caring for another is one type of self-disclosure, statements about yourself constitute the major type of self-disclosure. How often have you heard, "I'm only telling this to you," or "Only a very few people know this about me." Such statements designate the listener as "special" and make the information privileged.

The decision to self-disclose is tied to a history with the other. For example, you may find yourself thinking, "I've reached a point in my relationship with Sarah where I can talk about my mother's illness or my fears of losing my job." Or you may think, "John is a close enough friend to know about the breakup of my first marriage." What this really says is that the relationship is secure enough, and mature enough, to handle such information appropriately. Sarah or John, although they may be surprised or upset by the information, will not withdraw from the relationship based on the disclosure because the growth of the relationship allows risks to be taken.

One of the most intriguing aspects of self-disclosure is how differently it is handled by varied individuals. What one person considers to be deep self-disclosure, another may not. Allen may sit and talk for hours about his sexual exploits and think nothing of it while Rick would never be comfortable discussing his sexual life, except in a very special relationship. Jamie may share her poetry easily but struggles when it comes to talking about her inner feelings. Julie may be just the opposite. Self-disclosure is valued in certain cultures and not in others; women are socialized to value this vocabulary more than men in our society, who may follow an alternative model (Wood 2005; Wood and Inman 1993).

Occasionally self-disclosure conjures up an image of telling another person all the bad stuff—the pain, the negative scary feelings, the dark sides of self. This is partially true since that's where the risk may be perceived as the greatest. In most long-term relationships, there are times when one or both members are too vulnerable to take such risks.

Self-disclosure is not only about planned revelation. It's also about responding to the moment. If you suddenly hear a piece of music that has emotional meaning for you—sharing that meaning. If you accidentally encounter a person who triggers off powerful feelings in you—risking those feelings. It means seizing the moment to tear down walls rather than building them up through silence or distance.

Healthy self-disclosure involves being alive to where a relationship has grown and being willing to take risks to foster future growth. All relationships have the potential for deepening, no matter how old, static, and locked-in they are. Oftentimes all it takes is for one or the other to take the risk of saying, "I need to talk" or "I need you to know."

Finally, self-disclosure is not unidirectional. It doesn't work for one person in a relationship to take all the risks of sharing. Self-disclosure develops through reciprocity. Over time, both parties must share with each other or the relational growth will wither. The deepening of intimacy is incremental and shared.

## Gifts

In some relationships, how much you are loved bears directly on the gifts you receive. At a symbolic level, "Gifts become containers for the being of the donor" (Csikszentmihalyi and Rochberg-Halton 1981, 37). How often have you asked yourself, "Was the gift picked out with me in mind?" or "How much love does this gift symbolize?" In some relationships, gifts are the most commonly used vocabulary for conveying affection; in others, gifts play a minor role. Love letters, cards, or a kiss may substitute adequately for presents.

In some families, holiday gift selection is delegated to the female adult who is expected to decide what her father-in-law likes in shirts, or whether her niece still plays with trains. Usually this delegation of responsibility occurs without discussion and may be gladly taken on or greatly resented. Some men feel unprepared to use the vocabulary of gifting and find themselves haunting the local drugstore or florist the evening before Mother's Day or Valentine's Day, hoping the "right thing" will miraculously appear! Other men spend hours at a Hallmark store looking for the perfect card.

The importance of shared or "recognized as different" attitudes toward gift giving cannot be overestimated. More holidays have been ruined, often annually, because one or the other spouse felt ignored or discounted by the lack of gifts or the type of gift given.

Often gift giving raises the issue of reciprocity. The tit-for-tat social rule is so strong that the gift-giving process becomes filled with scorekeeping. College roommates often encounter differences in gift-giving style, and one or the other may feel uncared for because there isn't an easy reciprocity.

Not an easy thing, this ritual of gifting another! Because it may appear "silly" or "unimportant," many people never express their real wishes around the subject of presents when, if the wishes were known, others would cheerfully change their behavior. Many individuals

expect others to mind read, believing, "If you really loved me, you would know I want." This creates a frustrating and futile trap for both parties.

## Meanings and Currencies

The meanings attached to a specific vocabulary of relational caring have a direct impact on relationship development. Interaction may be viewed as an exchange process in which actors are invested in trading meanings. When meanings are shared, rewards are experienced; when meanings are missed, costs are experienced (Stephen 1984). Therefore, over a period of time, intimate partners will create common assumptions about the importance of parts of a relational vocabulary and will develop high levels of symbolic interdependence.

Although messages of affection may be exchanged with the best intentions, accurate interpretation occurs only when both parties agree upon the meaning of the act. Usually, the meanings you give to another's messages are those you would use in a familiar situation. For example:

> Each of us tends to identify as loving those expressions of love that are similar to our own. I may express my love . . . by touching you, being wonderfully careless with you, or simply contentedly sitting near you without speaking. You may express an equally deep love feeling by buying me a gift, cooking the veal, working longer hours to bring us more monetary freedom, or simply fixing the broken faucet. These are obviously different ways of loving. (Malone and Malone 1987, 74)

In the previous example, the question remains, "Does the contented silent partner know that a veal dinner or a fixed faucet is a way of showing love?" When you think about your relationships, you may find that you are apt to see others as more loving if they express their affection the same way you do. Such a similarity adds to a growing sense of symbolic interdependence.

What happens if family members want to share affection but seem unable to exchange the currencies desired by others? After interviewing married couples, Villard and

Whipple (1976) concluded that spouses with similar affection exchange behaviors were more likely to report (1) high levels of perceived equity and (2) high levels of relationship satisfaction. Thus, they experienced greater relationship rewards. But note that accuracy in predicting (i.e., understanding) the other spouse's choice of vocabulary did not raise relational satisfaction level. Persons who were accurate at predicting how their spouses would respond to certain items still reported low marital satisfaction levels if the couple was dissimilar in their affection behaviors. Unfortunately, this finding, coupled with the finding that wives are more likely to use more intimate communication, suggests that many marriages may face "unhappiness, unfulfillment, conflict and/or divorce because of socialized differences between men and women in how they share 'who they are' and how they manifest 'affection'" (Millar, Rogers-Millar, and Villard 1978, 15). Being able to share affections provides advantages. In recent research Floyd found that high-affection communicators receive advantages in psychological, emotional, mental, social, and relational characteristics compared to low-affection communicators. He reports, "They were more likely to have a secure attachment style and less likely to have a fearful/avoidant style. They received more affection from others" (Floyd 2002, 147). Their higher self-esteem than low-affection communicators rendered them more likely to achieve greater levels of social or economic success.

Personal meaning placed on such vocabularies changes over time. As relationships mature, members may change their ways of sharing affection because of new experiences, pressures, or expectations. Economic conditions also affect how certain currencies are exchanged. A lost job may result in fewer gifts but more sharing and favors within a family. If an unemployed executive is able to share his feelings and frustrations, the self-disclosure may deepen his relationship with his partner. Once employed, he may not have the time or inclination to continue their sharing sessions, and the relationship may revert to former patterns.

The process of exchanging affectionate messages significantly affects relational levels of intimacy. The more similarity in the exchange process, the higher the levels of symbolic interdependence and relational satisfaction. In summary, persons with an expanded vocabulary of loving messages have a greater chance of connecting with others in satisfying ways.

## References

Berne, E. (1964). *Games People Play*. New York: Grove.

Camerer, C. (1988). Gifts as economic signals and social symbols. *American Journal of Sociology*, 94, S180–S214.

Csikszentmihalyi, M., and Rochberg-Halton, E. (1981). *The Meaning of Things: Domestic Symbols and the Self*. Cambridge UK: Cambridge University Press, 37.

Floyd, K. (2002). Human affection exchange: V. Attributes of the highly affectionate. *Communication Quarterly*, 50, 135–152.

Floyd, K & Morman, M.T. (2000). Affection received from fathers as a predictor of men's affection with their own sons: Tests of the modeling and compensation hypotheses. *Communication Monographs*, 67, 347–361.

Fujishin, R. (1998). *Gifts From the Heart*. San Francisco: Acada Books.

Goffman, E. (1959). *The Presentation of Self in Everyday Life*. New York: Doubleday.

Malone, T. and Malone, P. (1987). *The Art of Intimacy*. New York: Prentice-Hall, 14, 74.

McGoldrick, M., Anderson, C., and Walsh, F. (Eds.). (1989). *Women in Families: A Framework for Family Therapy*. New York: W. W. Norton.

McGoldrick, M., Giordano, J., and Pearce, J. (Eds.). (1996). *Ethnicity and family therapy*. 2nd edition. New York: Guildford Press.

Millar, F., Rogers-Millar, L. E., and Villard, K. (1978, April). *A Proposed Model of Relational Communication and Family Functioning*. Paper presented at the Central States Speech Association Convention, Chicago.

Mooney, L. and Brabant, S. (1988). Birthday cards, love, and communication. *Social Science Research*, 72, 106–109.

Ryan, K. and Ryan, M. (1982). *Making a Marriage*. New York: St. Martin's Press, 44.

Stephen, T. (1984). A symbolic exchange framework for the development of intimate relationships. *Human Relations*, 37, 393–408.

Villard, K. and Whipple, L. (1976). *Beginnings in Relational Communication*. New York: John Wiley and Sons.

Wood, J. T. (2005). *Gendered Lives: Communication, Culture and Gender*. 6th edition. Belmont, CA: Thomson/Wadsworth.

Wood, J. and Inman, C. (1993). In a difficult mode: Masculine styles of communicating closeness. *Journal of Applied Communication* 21: 30, 279–294.

## Questions

1. Think about the ways you express affection. Which of the ways discussed here are comfortable for you? Uncomfortable for you? Why?

2. Describe a person you know who tries to reach out to others to be a friend, but who seems to have difficulty "speaking the same language" as those with whom he or she is trying to connect. Indicate what you might suggest to that person in order to be more effective.

3. What relational currencies did you think about that the article did not mention? Describe two of them, and indicate examples of how they are enacted.

# 19

# Face Management in Interpersonal Communication

*William R. Cupach and Sandra Metts*

**S**ociologist *Erving Goffman (1967) defined face as the favorable social impression that a person wants others to have of him or her. In other words, it is the concept of self that each person attempts to display in interaction with others. Thus, face is not what people think of themselves, but what they want others to think of them; face occurs in a relational context. One can only gain or lose face through actions that are known and interpreted by others. The concept of face is meaningful only when considered in relation to others in the social context.*

*Robyn Penman (1994) suggests facework is not something people do some of the time; it is something that they unavoidably do all the time—it is the core of our social selves. What is critical is that the process of face management seems to be as enduring as human social existence. In the very act of communicating, individuals are continuously adapting to others and attempting to influence their impressions.*

*This impression may not be shared by everyone and may differ from a person's own self-image. To maintain face, you engage in facework in order to convince others to act toward you with respect, regardless of their "real" impression of you. Facework is the communication designed to counteract face threats to self or others. In their study of workplace communication, Carson and Cupach (2000) perceived that face threat was negatively correlated with perceptions of the other's interactional fairness and communicative competence. Finally, face relates to the positive social attributes that people want others to acknowledge. Negative attrib-*utes are concealed and protected from judgment. For example, communicators may use euphemisms to avoid negative judgments of others (McGlone and Batchelor 2003).*

*In most relationships, there are moments in which you completely embarrass yourself, and others in which you make yourself proud. These moments of pride or embarrassment are examined in this chapter, in the context of face management, in which* embarrassment *means "losing" face and* pride *means "sustaining" face. In the following article, Cupach and Metts integrate Goffman's facework theories into their discussion of the ways in which people use communication to manage face. Throughout the chapter, they discuss face needs, threats, facework, and, finally, the reasons why managing face is important for the development and maintenance of interpersonal relationships. As you read this article, consider how this concept of face relates to your own interpersonal communication. Ask yourself this question: How do I tend to manage my face in new situations, and how do I adapt to face threats in these circumstances?*

### References

Carson, C. L. and Cupach, W. R. (2000). Facing corrections in the workplace: The influence of perceived face threat on the consequences of managerial reproaches. *Journal of Applied Communication Research*, 28: 215–234.

Goffman, E. (1967). *Interaction Ritual: Essays on Face-to-Face Behavior*. Garden City, NY: Anchor Books.

McGlone, M. and Batchelor, J. A. (2003). Looking out for number one: Euphemism and face. *Journal of Communication*, 53: 251–264.

Penman, R. (1994). Facework in communication: Conceptual and moral challenges. In Stella Ting-Toomey (Ed.), *The Challenge of Facework: Cross-Cultural and Interpersonal Issues*. Albany: State University of New York Press.

\* \* \*

## Face Management in Interpersonal Relationships

"**I** was so embarrassed!" Have you ever found yourself recounting a story of how you stumbled and fell while trying to impress a new date with your dancing talents? Have you ever expressed in much more somber tones a time when you felt great shame because you violated a trust that you and your partner shared about sexual exclusivity? If you have felt embarrassment, or shame, then you have experienced the effects of losing face. If, on the other hand, you have felt pride, or validation, or respect, then you have experienced the effects of sustaining face, even, perhaps, during awkward situations. This [article] is about gaining and losing face in close relationships. The notion of face, and related concepts, is used to explain the role of communication in managing the course of interpersonal relationships.

# Communication and the Management of Face

## Face and Face Needs

The conception of self that each person displays in particular interactions with others is called face. When a person interacts with another, he or she tacitly presents a conception of who he or she is in that encounter, and seeks confirmation for that conception. In other words, the individual offers an identity that he or she wants to assume and wants others to accept. In social scientific terms, face refers to "socially situated identities people claim or attribute to others" (Tracy, 1990, p. 210).

According to Goffman (1967), whatever the context in which communication occurs, and whatever the relationship shared by interactants, it is assumed that each person's face is supported and maintained during interaction. Out of self-respect, communicators are emotionally invested in the presentation and preservation of their own face; out of considerateness, communicators exert effort to save the feelings and maintain the face of other people. Goffman characterizes an individual who can experience his or her own face loss without distress as "shameless" and an individual who can unfeelingly observe others lose face as "heartless."

Under normal circumstances, then, individuals reciprocate face support and cooperate to ensure that each other's face is protected. Indeed, when any person's face is threatened during an interaction, all participants are motivated to restore it because not doing so leaves them open to the discomfort and embarrassment that arises from a disrupted interaction.

This mutual cooperation in the maintenance of face is so ordinary and pervasive that it is considered a taken-for-granted principle of interaction. People do it automatically—unless the intent is to embarrass someone playfully or to discredit someone contemptuously. Generally, face is not a conscious concern of communicators. The everyday goals of expressing one's beliefs, ingratiating others, seeking advice, eliciting information, and so on "are typically pursued in such a way as to be consistent with the maintenance of face" (Goffman, 1967, p. 12).

Thus maintaining face is an underlying motive in all social encounters, but it is not usually a strategic objective. It is only when some event, action, or comment discredits face or threatens to discredit face that strategies to minimize the occurrence and consequences of face threat come into consciousness. The next subsection deals with face threats and ways of coping with them.

## Threats to Face

Face threats occur when a person's desired identity in a particular interaction is challenged. Given that it is virtually impossible to avoid all face threats at all times, any interaction is potentially face-threatening (Tracy, 1990). Even the most skillful and well-intended communicator sometimes finds him- or herself in the position of having spoken an inappropriate comment or having felt diminished by receiving a complaint or criticism from someone else. And as we will see later, some types of interaction episodes, such as terminating a relationship, are by their very nature face-involving situations.

A particularly interesting explication of how face is threatened is offered by Penelope Brown and Stephen Levinson (1987). Drawing from their analysis of 13 societies in various areas of the world, they present a theory based on two types of universal face needs: positive face needs and negative face needs. Positive face refers to the desire to be liked and respected by the significant people in our lives. Positive face is supported when messages communicate value for the things we value, appreciation for us as competent individuals, and solidarity with us (Lim & Bowers, 1991). Positive face is threatened when one's fellowship is devalued or one's abilities are questioned. Negative face pertains to the desire to be free from constraint and imposition. Messages respecting one's autonomy are supportive of negative face, whereas messages interfering with one's desired actions are threatening to negative face.

Brown and Levinson's description of positive and negative face is interesting because of the dilemma it exposes for people trying to meet both types of face needs for themselves and other people. Essentially, the dilemma is that satisfying one type of face need often threatens the other. Consider this just within an individual. Karen Tracy (1990) gives an example of a college professor who values teaching very highly and wants to cultivate his students' potential. However, the cost of this desire is that students make daily demands on his time and drain his energy. His positive face needs are satisfied at the cost of his negative face needs.

To understand this dilemma at the relationship level, think for a moment about what you do when you like someone: You spend time with the person, teasing and complimenting, self-disclosing, borrowing money or clothes; you drop by the person's home unexpectedly, and so forth. You do what comes naturally when you care about and value someone. You are, in these behaviors, showing regard for the individual's positive face. However, consider how these actions might threaten negative face. This other person may feel it an imposition to have to stop his or her activity to visit with you, or may not be comfortable with your self-disclosures, or may find it tiring to entertain you when he or she would prefer to do something else. These responses are natural because your friend's negative face is being constrained at the very same time his or her positive face is being validated. In fact, sometimes your own negative face may feel threatened because you simply don't want to be pleasant, or funny, or supportive toward your friend; you may even want to be free of the

sense of obligation that the friendship implies. Leslie Baxter (1988) eloquently captures the dialectical nature of these competing forces:

> No relationship can exist by definition unless the parties sacrifice some individual autonomy. However, too much connection paradoxically destroys the relationship because the individual identities become lost (Askham, 1976). Simultaneously, an individual's autonomy can be conceptualized only in terms of separation from others. But too much autonomy paradoxically destroys the individual's identity, because connections with others are the "stuff" of which identity is made (Lock, 1986). (p. 259)

The dilemma of satisfying positive and negative face at the same time may seem like a no-win situation, but it is not. It is a matter of balancing the natural tension between being connected to someone and being independent. As we will discuss below, facework and politeness are communication mechanisms that allow us to manage this dilemma.

## Facework

Facework is communication designed to counteract face threats to self and others (Goffman, 1967). On many occasions, face-threatening acts can be avoided or minimized before they occur through the use of preventive facework. On other occasions, face threats are not anticipated and the loss of face must be remediated through corrective facework. We will spend the next few pages discussing each of these types of facework. We then close this chapter with discussion of a third type of facework unique to close relationships that is contained in a couple's personal idioms.

***Preventive Facework***. Avoiding face threat is often accomplished by such tactics as avoiding face-threatening topics, changing the subject of conversation when it appears to be moving in a face-threatening direction, and pretending not to notice when something face-threatening has been said or done. In addition, individuals employ linguistic devices such as "disclaimers" (Hewitt & Stokes, 1975) and "politeness" (Brown & Levinson, 1987) to minimize the negative implications that might be made about them when they know they are about to threaten someone's face.

Disclaimers are statements people use to minimize the negative attributions that might be ascribed to their motives or character because they are about to violate expectations for appropriate behavior. Hewitt and Stokes (1975) identify five types of disclaimers:

1. *hedging*: indicates uncertainty and receptivity to suggestions ("I may be wrong, but. . . .")

2. *credentialing*: indicates that there are good reasons and appropriate qualifications for engaging in a sanctionable action ("I'm your husband; I have every right to read your mail.")

3. *sin license*: indicates that this is an acceptable occasion for rule violation and should not be taken as a character defect ("What the hell, this is a special occasion.")

4. *cognitive disclaimer*: indicates that the impending behavior is reasonable and under cognitive control, in spite of appearances ("I know this sounds crazy, but. . . .")

5. *appeal for suspended judgment*: request to withhold judgment for a possibly offensive act until it has been fully explained ("Hear me out before you get upset.")

In essence, disclaimers are used by speakers to save their own face; they signal a message something like, "Please recognize that I am aware of social appropriateness and I ask your indulgence while I act inappropriately; I am not merely rude or stupid." Politeness strategies, on the other hand, are more directly focused on the face of the recipient of the threat. They signal a message something like, "Please recognize that I regard your face needs very highly and would not threaten them if it were not necessary to do so; I am not merely selfish and insensitive to your needs."

Politeness strategies allow people to walk a fine line between being totally indirect and possibly never getting their point across (e.g., "Gee, there's a great movie playing downtown tonight . . . hmm, well, hope you enjoy it."),

and being unexpectedly blunt and direct (e.g., "Take me to the movie tonight because I want to see it"). Very intimate partners can be a bit more indirect than social acquaintances because they are attuned to each other's hints. And intimate partners can be a bit more direct than social acquaintances because they know that the relationship is based on mutual positive regard even when it is not demonstrated in one or two particular interactions. However, frequent and repeated disregard for each other's face may eventually lead a couple to feel the foundation of mutual regard in their relationship may be weakening.

Thus it is no accident that people have developed an elaborate system of politeness strategies to use when they want to reach a goal efficiently but do not want to appear insensitive to the face concerns of the other person. Brown and Levinson (1987) describe the general strategies of positive and negative politeness that are respectively directed toward the positive and negative face needs of the partner. Positive politeness expresses appreciation for the value of another person and expresses affiliation with that person. Positive politeness includes messages showing that the partner's desires are known and considered to be important, that he or she is viewed as a member of an in-group, a friend, or a valued other. For instance: "Hey buddy! You're really doin' great in calculus class. How 'bout sharing some of your talent with me?" Negative politeness offers assurances that the partner's freedom will not be unnecessarily curtailed and that he or she has options. These messages are characterized by self-effacement and formality, permitting the partner to feel that his or her response was not obligatory or coerced. For example: "John, I hate to bother you, but if you are not too busy, would it be possible to get a lift to campus?"

***Corrective Facework***. In an effort to repair face damage that has occurred because of a transgression, corrective facework is employed. Corrective behaviors may be defensively offered by the actor responsible for creating face threat, may be protectively offered by other people who witness the loss of face, or may be offered by the person who has lost face as he or she attempts to regain lost social identity.

The facts that facework can be performed by observers and participants, that it can be accepted or rejected, and that its effectiveness depends on the features of a particular situation underscore how challenging problematic events can be. The restoration of lost face and the smooth realignment of a disrupted episode are truly cooperative accomplishments. We describe below several types of strategies used during the remediation process.

Although we present them separately, it is important to remember that people often use several of them in various orderings as the process of restoring face unfolds (Cupach & Metts, 1990).

A large class of behaviors intended to contain or control the extent of damage to face is called avoidance. The principle underlying avoidance is that in some face-threatening situations, drawing explicit attention to the face threat may be counterproductive. If only one's own face has been modestly threatened but the face of others remains largely intact, then the benefit of saving one's own face might be at the expense of threatening the face of others (Cupach & Metts, 1990). Belaboring a minor infraction can create inconvenience for others and possibly induce them to feel embarrassment. Similarly, if an observer notes that one has committed an error, he or she may overlook it. People routinely gloss over their own and each other's mistakes when they are relatively minor. This is accomplished by acting as if face has not been threatened. Gracefully continuing with social interaction following a minor predicament demonstrates one's poise and minimizes the extent to which other people become embarrassed or annoyed. Of course, when abashment is intense, one may exhibit an extreme form of avoidance by physically fleeing the embarrassing or shameful encounter (Cupach, Metts, & Hazleton, 1986).

Humor is frequently a response to predicaments, partly because some predicaments are intended to be comical (such as teasing; Argyle, Furnham, & Graham, 1981; Knapp, Stafford, & Daly, 1986; Sharkey, 1991) and some are inherently funny in their consequences. Argyle et al. (1981) found, for example, that rule-breaking episodes are characterized by a fundamental underlying dimension ranging from humorous to irritating. Similarly, affective reactions to rule-breaking episodes are characterized by the dimension of laughter versus anger. If the face-threatening event involves a harmless accident or flub, then laughter allows the release of nervous tension and signals that the problematic circumstances need not be taken too seriously. Making a joke can show that the offending person acknowledges blameworthiness (as with a simple excuse or apology) and can also allow the person to demonstrate poise and social competence (Edelmann, 1985; Fink & Walker, 1977).

Apologies admit blame and seek atonement for untoward behavior (Goffman, 1967; Schlenker, 1980; Tedeschi & Riess, 1981). The form of an apology can range from a simple statement, such as "I'm sorry," to more elaborate forms including one or more of the following elements: (a) expression of regret or remorse, (b) requests for forgiveness, (c) self-castigation, (d) promises not to repeat the transgression in the future, and (e) offers of restitution (Goffman, 1971; Schlenker & Darby, 1981).

The nonverbal display of anxiety or discomfort can function much like an apology insofar as it demonstrates to others that the offending person acknowledges the impropriety of his or her own behavior. Merely appearing to be chagrined (by blushing or grimacing) can show one's self-effacement and thereby mitigate negative attributions that might be ascribed by observers (Castelfranchi & Poggi, 1990; Edelmann, 1982; Semin & Manstead, 1982).

Accounts are verbal explanations given to explain inappropriate or awkward behavior (Buttny, 1985, 1987; Scott & Lyman, 1968). Two general classes of accounts are excuses and justifications. Excuses attempt to minimize the actor's responsibility for an event ("I didn't mean it"; "I couldn't help it"; "It's not my fault"); justifications reframe an event by downplaying its negative implications ("It's not so bad"; "It's for your own good"). There are numerous varieties of excuses and justifications. Several authors have described a wide range of types of excuses and justifications (Schlenker, 1980; Schonbach, 1980,

1990; Scott & Lyman, 1968; Snyder, Higgins, & Stuckey, 1983; Tedeschi & Riess, 1981)....

Physical remediation involves behavioral (nonverbal) correction or repair of physical damage (if any has occurred) associated with a loss of face. This includes such acts as adjusting clothing (zipping up one's pants), cleaning up a spill, and fixing a broken toy (Metts & Cupach, 1989b; Semin & Manstead, 1982; Sharkey & Stafford, 1990).

Most of the remedial facework strategies employed by a person creating face loss can also be utilized by observers on the person's behalf. Observers can offer physical assistance following a pratfall, and can make various types of positive comments to assist a face-threatened individual, including attribution of guilt or responsibility for the occurrence of the event to persons other than the embarrassed person, positive comments on the embarrassed person's conduct during the failure event (e.g., expressing understanding, appeasement, friendly advice), and positive comments on the embarrassed person's liability for the consequences of the failure event (exoneration, waiving of claims, pardon, compassion, offers of help) (Schonbach, 1990). Humor is also a common strategy, although it entails some risk, as the inferred line between laughing "with" the person and laughing "at" him or her can be blurry (Cupach & Metts, 1990). Similarly, attempts to avoid calling attention to an untoward act are expected, particularly for minor infractions. However, such inattention can exacerbate discomfort on some occasions. By not overtly attempting to repair the awkward encounter, individuals remain somewhat uncertain about whether or not they have demonstrated efforts commensurate with expectations to repair face.

Observers also have unique remedial responses at their disposal that can be particularly effective in diminishing the discomfort felt by the person who has lost face. In fact, one study found that observers were much more effective than transgressors in ameliorating the transgressor's embarrassment following a face-threatening predicament (see Cupach & Metts, 1990). In particular, observers can offer help by expressing empathy, communicating to the distressed person

that his or her predicament is not unique or uncommon. They can also offer support through indications of positive regard in spite of the predicament. We found in one study that approximately half of all remedial responses offered by observers were such displays of empathy and support (Metts & Cupach, 1989b).

## The Importance of Facework in Interpersonal Relationships

For several reasons, the management of face is particularly relevant to the formation and erosion of interpersonal relationships. First, the ability to manage one's own and others' face is fundamental to interpersonal competence (Cupach & Imahori, 1993a; Weinstein, 1969; Wiemann, 1977). In order for people to achieve their own goals, they must be able to establish and maintain desired identities for each other when they interact. Succinctly stated, getting ahead ordinarily entails getting along, which in turn necessitates sensitivity to the face needs of others. As Goffman (1967) suggests, in our society, the ability to engage in appropriate facework is tantamount to "tact, *savoir-faire*, diplomacy, or social skill" (p. 13).

Second, face support is identity confirming. Situational identities constitute important sources of rewards and costs for social actors (Weinstein, 1969). The importance of confirmation is magnified as the intimacy of the relationship between partners escalates. Indeed, Weinstein (1969) contends that "it is only in the most impersonal encounters that the situational identities of the parties are not a principal nexus of rewards and costs. Often, they are precisely and completely that" (p. 757).

Third, effective facework fosters mutual respect and buttresses against contempt (see Penman, 1990). This supports the ritual order of social interactions, allowing encounters between people to be relatively smooth and enjoyable, rather than disruptive and distressing. Moreover, facework is integral to managing the challenges and dilemmas of relationships. At its best, effective face support permits us to achieve (however fleeting) relationship nirvana. At its worst, persistent face loss can create bitter enmity and personal agony.

## References

Argyle, M., Furnham, A., & Graham, J. A. (1981). *Social Situations*. Cambridge: Cambridge University Press.

Baxter, L. A. (1988). A dialectical perspective on communication strategies in relationship development. In S. Duck (Ed.), *Handbook of personal relationships: Theory, research, interventions* (pp. 257–273). London: John Wiley.

Brown, P., & Levinson, S. (1987). *Politeness: Some universals in language usage*. Cambridge: Cambridge University Press.

Buttny, R. (1985). Accounts as a reconstruction of an event's context. *Communication Monographs*, 52, 57–77.

———. (1987). Sequence and practical reasoning in accounts episodes. *Communication Quarterly*, 35, 67–83.

Castelfranchi, C., & Poggi, I. (1990). Blushing as discourse: Was Darwin wrong? In W. W. Crozier (Ed.), *Shyness and embarrassment: Perspectives from social psychology* (pp. 230–251). Cambridge: Cambridge University Press.

Cupach, W. R., & Imahori, T. T. (1993a). Identity management theory: Communication competence in intercultural episodes and relationships. In R. L. Wiseman & J. Koester (Eds.), *Intercultural communication competence* (pp. 112–131). Newbury Park, CA: Sage.

Cupach, W. R., Metts, S., & Hazleton, V. (1986). Coping with embarrassing predicaments: Remedial strategies and their perceived utility. *Journal of Language and Social Psychology*, 5, 181–200.

Cupach, W. R., & Metts, S. (1990). Remedial processes in embarrassing predicaments. In J. A. Anderson (Ed.), *Communication yearbook 13* (pp. 323–352). Newbury Park, CA: Sage.

Edelmann, R. J. (1985). Social embarrassment: An analysis of the process. *Journal of Social and Personal Relationships*, 2: 195–213.

———. (1987). *The psychology of embarrassment*. Chichester, UK: John Wiley.

Fink, E. L., & Walker, B. A. (1977). Humorous responses to embarrassment. *Psychological Reports*, 40: 475–485.

Goffman, E. (1967). *Interaction ritual: Essays on face-to-face behavior*. New York: Pantheon.

———. (1971). *Relations in public*. New York: Basic Books.

Hewitt, J., & Stokes, R. (1975). Disclaimers. *American Sociological Review*, 40: 1–11.

Knapp, M. L., Stafford, L., & Daly, J. (1986). Regrettable messages: Things people wish they hadn't said. *Journal of Communication*, 36: 40–58.

Lim, T. S., & Bowers, J. W. (1991). Facework: Solidarity, approbation, and tact. *Human Communication Research*, 17: 415–450.

Lock, A. J. (1986). The role of relationships in development: An introduction to a series of occasional articles. *Journal of Social and Personal Relationships*, 3: 89–100.

Metts, S., & Cupach, W. R. (1989b). Situational influence on the use of remedial strategies in embarrassing predicament. *Communication Monographs*, 56: 151–162.

Penman, R. (1990). Facework and politeness: Multiple goals in courtroom discourse. *Journal of Language and Social Psychology*, 9: 15–38.

Schlenker, B. R. (1980). *Impression management: The self-concept, social identity, and interpersonal relations*. Monterey, CA: Brooks/Cole.

Schlenker, B. R., & Darby, B. W. (1981). The use of apologies in social predicaments. *Social Psychology Quarterly*, 44: 271–278.

Schonbach, P. (1980). A category system for accounts please. *European Journal of Social Psychology*, 10: 195–200.

———. (1990). *Account episodes: The management or escalation of conflict*. Cambridge: Cambridge University Press.

Scott, M. B., & Lyman, S. M. (1968). Accounts. *American Sociological Review*, 33: 46–62.

Semin, G. R., & Manstead, A. S. R. (1982). The social implications of embarrassment displays and restitution behavior. *European Journal of Social Psychology*, 12: 367–377.

———. (1983). *The accountability of conduct: A social psychological analysis*. London: Academic Press.

Sharkey, W. F. (1991). Intentional embarrassment: Goals, tactics, and consequences. In W. R. Cupach & S. Metts (Eds.), *Advances in interpersonal communication research, 1991* (Proceedings of the Western Speech Communication Association Interpersonal Communication Interest Group) (pp. 105–128). Normal: Illinois State University, Personal Relationships Research Group.

Sharkey, W. F., & Stafford, L. (1988, November). *I've never been so embarrassed: Degree of embarrassment and its effect upon communicative responses*. Paper presented at the annual meeting of the Speech Communication Association, New Orleans.

Synder, C. R., Higgins, R. L., & Stuckey, R. J. (1983). *Excuses: Masquerades in search of grace*. New York: John Wiley.

Tedeschi, J., & Riess, M. (1981). Verbal strategies in impression management. In C. Antaki (Ed.), *The psychology of ordinary explanations of social behavior* (pp. 271–309). New York: Academic Press.

Tracy, K. (1990). The many faces of facework. In H. Giles & W. P. Robinson (Eds.), *Handbook of language and social psychology* (pp. 209–226). New York: John Wiley.

Weinstein, E. A. (1969). The development of interpersonal competence. In D. A. Goslin (Ed.), *Handbook of socialization theory and research* (pp. 753–775). Chicago: Rand McNally.

Wiemann, J. M. (1977). Explication and test of a model of communicative competence. *Human Communication Research*, 3: 195–213.

## Questions

1. Consider a relationship in which you are very conscious of personally engaging in facework. What characterizes this relationship, and what are examples of your facework efforts?

2. Describe two relationships in which you do not experience a strong need to manage your face. What type of communication characterizes these relationships?

3. Describe a relationship in which you observe one person's regular attempt to conduct preventive facework. Give two examples, and indicate under what conditions such preventive facework is likely to occur.

# 20

# Belly Button Fuzz and Wicky-Wacky Cake

## Rituals in Our Personal Relationships

*Carol J. S. Bruess*

**R**ituals serve as a powerful way to bond individuals in developing or established relationships. Although generations of scholars in varied fields have studied rituals, only recently have communication scholars turned their attention to the role of rituals in sustaining and deepening interpersonal relationships. Most people think of rituals as major ceremonial acts or events such as weddings, birthdays, or holiday celebrations. Such a view is correct but narrow. Another way to conceptualize rituals is to see them as customary, repeated acts that are commonplace. Therefore, patterned greetings or leavetaking, ways of expressing affection, and unique conversational expressions may be considered rituals. Such acts serve as the focus for communication scholars. This approach is in keeping with Duck's (1994) call for a focus on everyday or mundane interactions, Baxter's (1987) suggestion that communication rituals are linked to the development of relational cultures, and Gottman's (Gottman and Silver 1999) assertion that rituals are one of the primary ways in which couples develop shared meanings.

In the following piece, Carol Bruess presents her perspective on the role of rituals within interpersonal relationships, including friendships and romantic pairs. Beginning with a story about a ritual from her childhood, Bruess depicts the importance of rituals in relationships. She defines relational rituals, discusses their form and function, and describes some partner rituals. She stresses the com-

monplace and everyday aspect of rituals that may be taken for granted but that serve an important function in sustaining interpersonal relationships. As you read this chapter, consider this question: How would you explain the link between relational rituals and relational currencies?

## References

Baxter, L. (1987). Symbols of relationship identity in relationship cultures. *Journal of Social and Personal Relationships*, 4: 261–280.

Duck, S. (1994). Steady as (s)he goes: Relational maintenance as a shared meaning system. In D. Canary and L. Stafford (Eds.), *Communication and Relational Maintenance*. New York: Academic Press.

Gottman, J. M. and Silver, N. (1999). *The Seven Principles for Making Marriage Work*. New York: Three Rivers Press.

\* \* \*

## Introduction

**M**y name is Carol Bruess (pronounced "breece"), and I'm 29 years old. I started teaching communication studies at a small college in Minnesota after receiving my Ph.D. in interpersonal communication when I was 25. I know this is an unusual way to begin a book chapter, but I think it's important to know that the research you are reading about in this book was done by real people, not too different from yourself. My research, for instance, is about something that I have experienced in my own marriage of six years and in my family growing up. It's about my experiences with my life-long friend Sarah and my other friends, Cory, Suzy, and Russell. It also reflects something that I'm just plain old interested in—communication in our marriages, families, and friendships, and how that communication creates a unique and special "culture" all our own. I've done most of this research, particularly the stuff you're about to read in this chapter, with my friend and graduate school advisor Dr. Judy Pearson. She deserves much credit for the research and stories I'm about to share with you. So, with that background in mind, I'd like us to explore the concept of ritual and interpersonal communication in the next couple of pages.

When I was growing up, my entire family (my mom, dad, sister Lynn, and brother Greg—both older than me) would go to my grandmother's house every Sunday. It was always the same routine. The repetition has etched very vivid memories in my mind. About an hour or so after returning from church Sunday morning, we would all load into our brown Chevy station wagon and take the six-mile trip out to Grandma's farm. The farm was a great place of adventure for kids. My three cousins lived on the adjoining farm, just a mile down the road. They'd greet us in the yard or on Grandma's sofa where we'd begin our afternoon of exploring the woods, the barn, the hay loft, the pond, and the muddy cow trails, as well as searching Grandma's attic and closets for unknown treasures like dolls and hats and old buttons and beads. We'd play basketball with the hoop attached to the red wooden barn, and my uncle would often have us feeding calves, washing cars, or raking leaves and clearing cross-country ski trails for winter. In the winter, we would sled down the massive hill (which for some reason now seems tiny when I visit it again), ski through the woods (trading boots and skis each time around so the next kid could give it a try), and we would ice skate on the pond if it were a lucky year when the pond had frozen with a smooth and glassy finish. When our feet were frozen and our noses feeling like our feet, we would each, usually in pairs or as a whole group, trek back up to Grandma's kitchen table for hot cocoa overflowing with tiny marshmallows. Grandma never limited our marshmallow intake. Then, winter or summer—no matter the season—we all convened (3 cousins, 3 uncles/aunts, Grandma, Grandpa, and our family of 5) in Grandma's kitchen for a familiar feast. Every Sunday, without exception, we ate barbecue on burger buns, Pringles chips, peanut butter (for my cousin Jeff), lemonade, ice cream, and Grandma's homemade chocolate chip cookies (always with mini-chips) for dessert. By that time, my grandma was pretty much ready for all of us to go home. And we did. Every Sunday. Without question. That was our ritual.

## What's the Point?

I'll bet each and every one of you reading this chapter could tell a similar story about a ritual in your family. Maybe it wasn't a weekly ritual. Maybe it was a dinnertime ritual, or one that your family had at a certain holiday, or during a certain time of year. Maybe it was a bedtime ritual you and your siblings shared, or a summer vacation ritual. Whatever its shape or form, what you may not realize is that those rituals—the ones you remember from your childhood, the ones you currently share in your families, as well as those you share with friends, and with spouses or partners, and with your own children—played and continue to play very important roles in your relationships. You probably already intuitively know that rituals are important. But the purpose of this chapter is to try to help you understand exactly how important rituals are, what rituals actually are, and what we know about the nature of having and sharing rituals in your personal relationships.

My goal is to raise your awareness to this very important aspect of interpersonal communication, a kind of daily interaction that we often take for granted. To do this, I'm going to share with you the results of some of my own research on rituals, conducted by interviewing and surveying married couples about the rituals in their relationships and the rituals they shared with their friends. I think you'll find the stories of these people funny and interesting. You'll also find that you have a new understanding of what the term "ritual" means, and what it means to you and in your relationships.

Are you familiar with an author named Robert Fulghum? You probably are. He wrote that very popular book, *Everything You Ever Needed to Know You Learned in Kindergarten*. Recently, Robert Fulghum (1995) wrote another book, called *From Beginning to End: The Rituals of Our Lives*. He makes a very brief but insightful statement in this book that I'd like to use to begin our discussion of ritual. Fulghum writes:

> Nobody lives without rituals. Rituals do not live without somebody. (Fulghum, 1995, p. 113)

One thing we know about rituals is that they are valuable dynamics in relationships. We all have them. And we need them. Without them, we would be alone (or at least lonely). With and through them, we develop and maintain relationships: our families and friendships. They serve so many positive functions that there is an entire section below which addresses their worth (see "What Good Are They?"). It might seem that their "good" is quite obvious or just common sense. But we actually haven't been studying rituals in relationships for all that long, and are just starting to understand the intricate and delicate ways rituals serve us and our relationships. Rituals were originally in the domain of anthropologists, particularly those anthropologists who studied and were interested in religious rituals (Durkheim, 1965). Ritual in this form, however, often connotes magic, myth, taboo, or other mystical practices (Bossard and Boll, 1950). However, we know from decades of research that rituals are common in our personal relationships, especially family and friendships (Bossard and Boll, 1950; Wolin and Bennett, 1984). But what exactly is a ritual? What does "ritual" mean in the relational context?

## What Are They? Rituals Defined

Ritual, in many ways, is a mysterious concept. It is, at first glance, an easily understood concept. However, people in relationships and the people who study relationships define and understand rituals variously. Two researchers who have studied ritual extensively note: "Ritual itself is an elusive concept, on the one hand transparent and conspicuous in its enactment, on the other, subtle and mysterious in its boundaries and effects on participants" (Wolin and Bennett, 1984, p. 401). Most often, rituals have been defined as repetitive, symbolic behaviors or practices shared by members of a relationship (Allen, 1993; Wolin and Bennett, 1984).

Some authors offer distinctions between rituals and other repetitious patterns of interaction. For instance, Wise (1986) distinguishes between routines and rituals: Routines are activities or behaviors predictably enacted by family members; rituals are routines which take on symbolic meaning. For example, routines are generally characterized by their functional aspect, such as eating breakfast, washing the dishes every evening, or taking weekly trips to the grocery store. Rituals have significance beyond the activity itself, such as dining out on Friday evenings without the children, baking someone's favorite cake every year for his or her birthday, meeting friends for coffee on Saturday mornings at a local restaurant, or taking summer family vacations. However, Wise (1986) notes that any routine behavioral pattern (e.g. eating) can become a ritual when the routine is viewed by the participants as somehow relationally or symbolically significant (i.e., when dinner time is not simply for feeding, but is cherished as a time to talk with children and to share the day's events). According to Goffman (1967), rituals are communicative enactments that pay homage to a person or object which is sacred. Goffman's definition is the one I used in my study of rituals. It is useful because it acknowledges the nature of rituals as "symbolically" significant; no ritual is special until it is ascribed meaning or value (even implicitly) by members of the relationship who develop and/or enact the ritual. For instance, is taking your friend out to lunch for her birthday a ritual? It depends. It depends on the meaning this lunch has for you and your friend. To you, of course, the lunch is a "ritual"—it has been taking place for 15 years, and you have accorded this lunch with much meaning by its long history and what the lunch symbolizes in your friendship. In other words, the lunch ritual probably pays homage to—or symbolically reinforces the importance of—the unique character of your friendship. To another set of friends, that lunch is a one-time event, which is indeed important, but probably not yet a ritual. As you can see, the question of what "counts" as ritual is not entirely a clear one. But the nature of symbolic significance and repetition are two key concepts to keep in mind when defining ritual.

## How Do I Know One? Ritual Forms

At this point in the chapter I hope you are already trying to think of some of the rituals in your own relationships. If not, this section should inspire your thoughts. When I first started my own research on the topic of rituals, I had a hunch that people in relationships—particularly in marriages and friendships—had a variety of kinds of rituals. I guessed they ranged in form and type from the daily to the annual to the periodic. What I didn't realize, however, is just how many or how diverse (and how amusing) they would be . . . that people would tell me about their belly button fuzz, their "tough guys night," or their exchanges of flamingo lawn art with neighbors. The list of ritual types and forms is almost endless. Read on.

Indeed, rituals take on various forms. Earlier researchers such as Wolin and Bennett (1984) suggested that family rituals come in three varieties: celebrations, traditions, and patterned family interactions. Family celebrations are family rituals created and enacted in conjunction with more standardized culture celebrations such as holidays or rites of passage. Included would be Thanksgiving, New Year's Eve, weddings, funerals, and bar mitzvahs. Family traditions are more idiosyncratic to each family and less culturally influenced. Annual family vacations, family reunions, customary birthday celebrations, family meetings, and visits to extended family members are a few common examples of family traditions. Often, family traditions are created to serve a special family need or solve problems (e.g., family meetings) (Wolin and Bennett, 1984). Of the three types of family rituals, patterned family interactions are "the least deliberate and the most covert" (Wolin and Bennett, 1984, p. 406). Such are the rituals that organize daily life. They are the highly frequent daily routines, which typically involve little conscious planning. Dinnertime, bedtimes, general evening or morning routines, and other patterned family rules for interaction (e.g., seats at the table) are examples. Wolin and Bennett (1984) note that such rituals are often not recognized as ritualistic because of their mundane and routine nature.

In my own research (see Bruess and Pearson, 1997) of married couples and of friendship rituals, individuals and couples reported ritualizing many aspects of their daily married lives, everything from sharing romance to sharing household tasks to sharing in annual outings and get-togethers. I was primarily interested in two questions: What kinds of rituals did they have, and what purpose did they serve? I'll answer the first of these questions here. The second question is answered in a later section of this chapter ("What Good Are They?"). To answer the questions, I interviewed and/or surveyed 99 married couples (25 were interviewed, the rest were sent open-ended surveys) and asked them to tell me about the rituals in their own marriages. I also asked each spouse to tell me about the rituals in their separate (and possibly joint) friendships. Just to give you some background, the couples I interviewed were mostly from the Midwest, and they had been married an average of 19 years, ranging from one month to 53 years. The average age of participants was about 49. The 25 interviews I conducted lasted between 20 minutes and 4½ hours. The biggest news was that the 198 individuals in the study reported over 1000 different types of rituals in their marriages and friendships.

To help make sense of all these ritual examples, I grouped similar rituals into categories. For married couples, for instance, rituals mostly fell within seven types (or categories), including (1) Enjoyable Activities, Togetherness Rituals, and Escape Episodes; (2) Favorites, Private Codes, Play Rituals, and Celebration Rituals; (3) Daily Routines and Tasks; (4) Intimacy Expressions; (5) Communication Rituals; (6) Patterns/Habits/Mannerisms; and (7) Spiritual Rituals. I won't elaborate on each one of these categories here, but will give you some examples from a variety of the types.

One woman, for example, explained a ritual which represents the category Favorites. She was describing a ritual in her marriage which is a long-standing ritual paying homage to her husband via one of his "favorites." She explained:

> His favorite cake is wicky-wacky chocolate. It's a chocolate-out-of-scratch cake, an old family recipe. . . . So when I really,

really, really, really, like him, and he's really, really, really, really, made me happy, I bake him a wicky-wacky cake. He knows I'm really happy with him when he gets a wicky-wacky cake.

Another couple shared details of their Play Rituals called "A Game of Elephants" which includes two players: "Marco" (husband) and "Simba" (wife), and involves "quick trunk movements made with the arms accompanied by appropriate elephant noises." They reveal: "[it] is used to indicate private playfulness." Samples of other couple rituals include the married couples who developed Private Code Rituals. One couple reported ritualistically saying to each other "Honey, you make me hotter than Georgia asphalt," a line from a movie they saw together. Another couple explained their idiomatic ritual for indicating how they are feeling about one another on any given day:

> Whoever goes in and brushes their teeth first always puts toothpaste on the other's toothbrush. . . . If we're upset with one another we might set the tube next to the brush, not put paste on it. This is sort of a sign of "how ya feeling today about one another?"

Couples reported many creative, playful rituals. An example is this couple's ritual:

> I would check my husband's belly button for fuzz on a daily basis at bedtime. It originated when I noticed some blanket fuzz in his belly button one day and thought it was funny. . . . We both found it funny and teased often about the fuzz. If there wasn't any fuzz for a few days my husband would put some in his belly button for me to find. It's been happening for about 10 years now.

Idiomatic games and contests are also ritualized by couples, as in the example of one couple's game called the "Happy Anniversary Contest." They explained:

> We were married on the 26th day of May. We have a monthly contest to see who says 'Happy Anniversary' first on the 26th day of every month. Rules are: no waking spouse, said anytime after midnight, and must be person to person (in other words no written messages or answering machine messages). This originated the first month after we were married. It is on going since 1968 (305 months), we never missed a month, and we don't keep score.

Not all rituals were necessarily as playful and fun, yet were equally important. For instance, many couples reported celebration rituals for holidays, birthdays, or anniversaries. Often the rituals were simple yet important sites for symbolic value, paying homage to the relationships or relational members. For instance, one couple reports a ritual for celebrating their relationship by returning to the same restaurant where they had their first date. Other rituals included those of daily tasks and routines. One couple, for instance, explained their daily ritual of "Usually one washes and one dries the dishes." These examples are just a few of the hundreds married couples reported in my studies.

What I also discovered by talking to these couples is that rituals play a large part in their friendships, too. People reported that they ritualize many of their friendship activities, everything from annual celebrations to daily phone calls. Similar to the marriage ritual categories, six types, or categories, of friendship rituals emerged in our study, including: (1) Enjoyable Activities, Getting Together Rituals, Established Events, and Escape Episodes, (2) Celebration Rituals, Play Rituals, and Favorites, (3) Communication Rituals, (4) Share/Support/Vent Rituals, (5) Tasks/Favors, and (6) Patterns/Habits/Mannerisms.

Regular phone calls were common among friends, representing a kind of Communication Ritual. A good example is the monthly calling ritual one woman reported she and her friend have maintained "for 21 years and over 5 continents." They call one another every month, and have done this for over two decades as they have each moved around the world. Rituals among friends were often mundane and even spontaneous, as in the Getting Together ritual explained by one male. He said he simply has a ritual of regularly "having a beer with my neighbor." Others represented rituals of shared activities, such as the female who reported her ritual of meeting with friends once a month for a "Stitch and Bitch Club" where "we learn crafts, work on some holiday gifts, visit, and have dessert." Often friends, especially adult friends who have demands of family and work, develop annual rituals which help them pay homage to their shared interests as friends. One man explained a ritual developed among some of his male friends. They call the event "Tough Guys' Night Out." Once a year during the Golden Gloves Tournament the men in the group enjoy a steak dinner and cigars, and watch the boxing match together.

Similar to marriage rituals, some friendship rituals were playful, silly, and/or represented "inside jokes" or private codes. Illustrative is the ritual shared among the couple-friends in one neighborhood. They explain: "We have a collection of flamingo lawn art that we put in the neighbors' yard when they least expect it. Then eventually the items return!" They talked about this ongoing game as a ritual which has lasted for many years, and one which provides a playfulness which promotes the group's closeness as friends.

The examples and stories of rituals reported by people in these studies are endless. The point is, however, that rituals take a variety of forms. Our studies (Bruess and Pearson, 1997) were an attempt to further sort out some of the questions about ritual forms and functions. Recall, the two questions which guided this research were (1) What kinds of rituals did they (friends and couples) have? And (2) What purpose or function do they serve? I'll try to answer the second question next.

## What Good Are They? Ritual Functions

You start to get the sense, based on just the few examples above, that rituals are important in relationships for a number of reasons. Most obviously, you probably can conclude that rituals provide, in any relationship, a chance to "connect" or be together, to develop a sense of "we-ness" or a private culture, and that many provide opportunities for fun and play. If you are thinking that these are what rituals are good for, you are right. But that's not all. Based on years of research, we know that rituals serve a whole

host of functions in our relationships, some of which might surprise you.

For instance, rituals create intergenerational bonds and preserve a sense of meaningfulness (Schvaneveldt and Lee, 1983). They transmit family values, attitudes, and beliefs (Bossard and Boll, 1950), are related to family strength (Meredith et al., 1989), provide members with a sense of belonging (Wolin, Bennett, Noonan, and Teitelbaum, 1980), serve to bond and promote closeness (Meredith, 1985), help families maintain and perpetuate a paradigm or shared belief systems (Reiss, 1982), create and maintain family cohesion (Wolin and Bennett, 1984), and provide means for maintaining family contact (Meredith, 1985). They even protect alcoholic families from the generational recurrence of alcoholism (Wolin et al., 1980). Bossard and Boll (1950) best capture the importance of family rituals:

> Just as those religions with the most elaborate and pervasive rituals best retain the allegiance of their members, so families that do things together prove to be the most stable ones. (Foreword)

We also know that the importance of ritual extends beyond the family. Rituals are important in all kinds of our interpersonal relationships. For friends, for instance, rituals can help develop a shared understanding of what is important in the friendship and provide a shared history (Oring, 1984). Leslie Baxter (1987) found in her research that rituals among friends provide fun and stimulation, opportunities for sharing, and express closeness or intimacy. In all, we know that rituals play a role in sustaining and maintaining relationships. Bossard and Boll, two ritual researchers, in 1950 made the poignant suggestion that ritual is "the core of family culture." Rituals are central to relational cultures in all types of relationships, functioning to transmit relational goals, attitudes, and values.

In my own research the multivocal and multilayered meanings of rituals were evident in reports by individuals of their marriage and friendship rituals. Interviews revealed rich insights into the many ways rituals contribute to both personal and relational well being. In the words of one couple: "A relationship needs rituals and routines to function properly. In this day and age with our fast-moving society, rituals are the one constant." In marriages, rituals appear to function as masons by building and cementing the marriage, in the management of everyday life, in providing enjoyment and fun, togetherness, and communication among partners. Rituals among adult friends function in the maintenance and affirmation of the friendship, and as important events of personal support and self-affirmation, as well as personal improvement and escape.

First, I discovered that rituals in marriage function in Relational Masonry, or in the building and cementing of a bond, commitment, and a sense of security in marriage. Couples reported that rituals "reinforce our love and commitment," "help us build a solid relationship," and "bond a couple together." Rituals also function in Relational Maintenance, contributing to marital satisfaction and representing the core of the relationship culture. As one couple said: "Sometimes I think they [rituals] are what makes our marriage work and what makes us special." Another individual succinctly observed: "Rituals are the foundation of a marriage."

The third ritual function we discovered by talking with the married couples was Life Management, which represented the ability of rituals to make married life easier, provide organization, and define roles in marriage. Couples observed that rituals: "provide a sense of control over the random happenings of the week," and "simply make life easier." One couple noted: "Rituals serve as a clock for our inner lives; they give us a rhythm." Rituals further function as Fun/Enjoyment, as they provide stress-relief, enjoyment, and recreation. As one couple affirmed: "It's communication that builds a relationship, but the rituals which add the spice." Rituals also provide Togetherness, serving to bring couples closer together and provide shared time together. In the words of one couple: "They provide us with structured time together." Couples reported that rituals also function simply as providing time to communicate, or as Talk-Time.

A very small number of couples reported the potentially negative function that rituals serve, such as "making our lives too boring" or "allowing us to be lazy about our relationship." The few negative indications of rituals might be a factor of the positive connotations of the term ritual as it is used in most research and practice. As one couple in our study observed: "I think the rituals in my life are positive. If they weren't, I'd probably call them bad habits."

Similar to marriage rituals, friendship rituals also serve multiple functions, both personal and relational. I uncovered seven different functions from the hundreds of ritual functions reported by participants about their friendships. First, people told us that friendship rituals play a role in Personal and Relational Stimulation. For instance, rituals stimulate and maintain friendships by fostering loyalty and keeping friends in touch, and provide stimulation for relational members in the form of fun, humor, and "something to look forward to." Friends observed: "Without the ritual there is a sense of loss," "Without them we wouldn't be as good of friends," "Rituals establish a reliableness in your friends and a certain amount of trust," and "They provide a sense of security—something to count on and look forward to." According to one woman, the sharing of rituals "has simply made the friendship stronger." According to another, ritual "definitely makes your relationship closer."

According to the participants in the study, rituals among friends also function as Personal Improvement, as arenas of personal enhancement in such forms as time management, spiritual and skill development, and networking. For instance, individuals reported that rituals shared with friends helped them: "grow as a person" and "learn new skills," and that rituals provided needed "relaxation, both mentally and emotionally." One man observed that certain of his friendship rituals "build me spiritually." Others found that rituals function in networking: "Our rituals provide times for meeting new people, and just networking in the community."

Relational Affirmation was another function of friendship rituals, suggesting that rituals reinforce and/or reaffirm the exigencies of friendship such as trust, common interests, and shared experiences. Friends report: "Rituals seem to start friendships and kept them going," "With rituals, you know who your real friends are," "Rituals give you something common forever," and "Rituals seem to serve as anchors during the ups and downs of friendship." Rituals also "create a history" in many friendships. For one woman, "Rituals are reminders of where you began, or what you've shared." According to another, "Rituals kept our friendship alive."

Support was yet another function of friendship rituals; rituals appear to offer opportunities for receiving and giving support and advice from friends. Friends observed that their rituals: "help us realize we're not alone," "provide emotional support," and "provide physical, financial and spiritual support." As one woman reports: "Rituals give me the opportunity to sort out my thoughts." In the words of another: "I need them just to get through my weeks."

Another function of friendship rituals involves Self-Affirmation; friendship rituals are opportunities for individuals, and their ideas, to be affirmed. Rituals are often therapeutic, as they allow friends to share ideas and compare thoughts. One man reported that certain rituals serve as "a kind of therapy session." Another reported that rituals in friendship serve as "a means of finding people with the same ideas and attitudes." One woman stated: "I like my rituals of talk with other women; it makes me realize I'm the only one who has problems."

Friendship rituals also appear to function as Escape, providing freedom and privacy from spouses, family, work, and/or other pressures. One woman reports of her friendship rituals: "They provide my own sort of independence." Others reported that their rituals: "give us a break from the kids," "give you an outlet from the family," and are simply "an escape . . . a time for not dealing with family anything during those moments."

Friendship rituals, like family and couple rituals, are diverse in form and function. They are centralizing forces for friends that serve individuals and their friendships in many important ways. According to Steve Duck (1992), "Taken-for-granted routines build in

ways that we do not always realize until they are removed. Their loss takes away unspoken and unrealized parts of ourselves" (p. 86), and probably our relationships too. The contribution of rituals to our personal lives, as well as our relationships, is significant.

## Conclusion

Hopefully, by reading this chapter, you have begun to recognize some of the rituals in your own relationships and appreciate the potential value they have both for you personally, and for the health and well-being of your relationships. As researchers we have just begun to really understand the dynamics of rituals in our personal relationships. The inherent paradoxes of ritual—as both predictable yet dynamic, individual yet coordinated, as both new yet familiar, as both created from, and expressive of, communication in a relationship—make them inherently interesting questions about interpersonal interactions and relationships. I hope that you have begun to ask some similar questions, to yourself or with your class members, of your own rituals and relationships, and to wonder about the mystery, the power, and the central force of ritual in our many relationships. One of the interesting things about ritual and its study is that rituals are incredibly visible, yet invisible, relational dynamics. Members often take them for granted to the point of not recognizing them. They are so tightly woven into the tapestries of everyday living and relational management, they are what we might call subtly pervasive. Whatever they are, you have them. Hopefully this chapter has helped you further understand them.

### References

Allen, J. (1993, February). The incredible healing power of family rituals. *McCalls*, 120, 68.

Baxter, L. (1987). Symbols of relationship identity in relationship cultures. *Journal of Social and Personal Relationships*, 4, 261–280.

Bossard, J. and E. Boll. (1950). *Ritual in family living*. Philadelphia: University of Pennsylvania Press.

Bruess, C. J. S. and J. C. Pearson. (1997). Interpersonal rituals in marriage and adult friendships. *Communication Monographs*, 61, 25–46.

Duck, S. (1992). *Human relationships* (2nd ed.). London: Sage.

Durkheim, E. (1965). *The elementary forms of religious life.* New York: The Free Press.

Fulghum, R. (1995). *From beginning to end: The rituals of our lives.* New York: Villard.

Goffman, E. (1967). *Interaction ritual.* Garden City, NY: Anchor.

Meredith, W. (1985). The importance of family traditions. *Wellness Perspectives*, 2, 17–19.

Meredith, W., D. Abbott, M. Lamanna, and G. Sanders. (1989). Rituals and family strengths. *Family Perspectives*, 23, 75–83.

Oring, E. (1984). Dyadic traditions. *Journal of Folklore Research*, 21, 19–28.

Reiss, D. (1982). The working family: A researcher's view of health in the household. *American Journal of Psychiatry*, 139, 1412–1428.

Schvaneveldt, J. and R. Lee. (1983). The emergence and practice of ritual in the American family. *Family Perspective*, 17, 137–143.

Wise, G. (1986). Family routines, rituals, and traditions: Grist for the family mill and buffers against stress. In S. Van Zandt (Ed.), *Family strengths 7: Vital connections* (pp. 32–41). Lincoln, NE: Center for Family Strengths.

Wolin, S. and L. Bennett. (1984). Family rituals. *Family Process*, 23, 401–420.

Wolin, S., L. Bennett, D. Noonan, and M. Teitelbaum. (1980). Disrupted family rituals: A factor in the intergenerational transmission of alcoholism. *Journal of Studies in Alcohol*, 41, 199–214.

## Questions

1. Identify and describe two rituals you have developed in a friendship or romantic relationship that are unique to that relationship and that have helped to deepen the relational culture you share.

2. Over time, certain rituals change or disappear because they no longer seem to meet the needs of the relationship. Under what circumstances have your friendship rituals changed, and what has been the effect of the change?

3. Although Bruess' research uncovered rituals that could be considered positive or neutral, what negative rituals have you seen in a relationship with which you are familiar? (These might include unpleasant teasing, name calling, or avoidance.)

# 21

# The What, When, Who, and Why of Nagging in Interpersonal Relationships

*Kari P. Soule*

**A** *particular communication ritual occurs in many relationships, creating responses ranging from humor to exasperation to anger. That interpersonal ritual is nagging. If you read newspaper cartoons or watch sitcoms regularly, you are very familiar with examples of nagging. You may also experience it in your friendships or family relationships, situations in which you may be the nagger or the naggee. Everyone has stereotypical information on who nags or is nagged, how nagging is interpreted, and the function it plays in a relationship; these generalizations are reinforced by popular culture. But few research studies have addressed nagging behaviors.*

*Currently a large body of communication research, including work on self-presentation theory, perceptual contrast theory, and indebtedness theory, attempts to explain why people comply when others make requests of them. Self-presentation theory suggests that, when asked to do something for others, people monitor the image that others will have of them. They may feel bad about not complying. If so, they are motivated to comply in order to avoid being judged negatively.*

*Perceptual contrast theory is based on two principles—anchoring and contrast (Cialdini 1993). When people choose an amount of money, generosity, happiness, or the like, and then expect that amount as typical or normative, they have "adapted" to that level. Essen-*

*tially we anchor our expectations to our experiences. After such an anchor is established, a contrast effect occurs when one judges others against his or her standard for characteristics such as wealth, intelligence, and politeness, and is disappointed. Essentially the other is displaced away from the anchor. Language creates expectations for how people anchor experience to expectations. Contrast effects are common in relationships. Consider the following example:*

> *A: "Honey, could you do me a really big favor?"*

> *B: "What?" (Expecting a really major request to be stated.)*

> *A: "Could you bring in the mail when you come back from the store?"*

*No doubt B will comply with this request. After all, in contrast to what B was expecting to be asked, bringing in the mail is a small favor.*

*Indebtedness theory (Bell et al. 1996) utilizes the idea of reciprocity. This theory is based on the idea that we come to feel indebted (a felt obligation to repay another) when a person has done something for us. If B brings in the mail, perhaps A will feel indebted and comply with B's next request. Obviously, there is a level of equality here. A might feel obligated to get B a soda from the refrigerator but not to buy B a new car. What if the person does not comply with such a request? What are the options then?*

*Research by Kari Soule suggests that one of the options is to nag the other person. She suggests that nagging is a fairly common phenomenon in attempting to gain compliance. In one of the first attempts to examine the pattern of nagging in close relationships, Soule categorizes nagging as "persistent persuasion" and tries to discover how it is similar to or different from other types of ongoing persuasion. She studied nagging experiences of friends and marital partners; her findings are contained in the following piece.*

*As you read this, you will see that some respondents believe nagging indicates caring while others view it as a way to get partner compliance. We have included nagging in this section of the book because it is frequently viewed as a type of caretaking communication. Although nagging might be considered a negative and controlling interpersonal behavior, Soule presents nagging as a method of persuasion, with sequential, logical steps involved. From this perspective, she discusses the circumstances under which nagging occurs and explains that it is a product of the actions of both parties (the nagger and the naggee). The chapter concludes with an emphasis on the function of nagging in relationships, why it occurs, and both its positive and negative impacts.*

*As you read this chapter, think about how you interpret or enact nagging. Consider your general reaction to being nagged. Under what conditions are you more or less likely to comply with a first request? If you wish to avoid complying, you may wish to consider the importance of nondefensive responses to nagging, such as taking responsibility, avoiding the "summarizing-self syndrome," or reframing the message (Gottman 1994). Ask yourself this question: To what extent should I reconsider the messages contained within nagging behavior in my family or friendship relationships?*

### References

Bell, R. A., Cholerton, M., Davison, V., Fraczek, K. E., and Lauter, H. (1996). Making health education self-funding: Effectiveness of pregiving in an AIDS fundraising/education campaign. *Communication Quarterly,* 8: 331–352.

Cialdini, R. B. (1993). *Influence, Science, and Practice,* 3rd ed. New York: Harper-Collins.

Gottman, J. (1994). *Why Marriages Succeed or Fail.* New York: Simon and Schuster.

\* \* \*

"Take out the trash."

"I asked you to take out the trash."

"When are you going to take out the trash?"

*"I need you to take out the trash now."*

Does this sound familiar? Though your experience with this type of communication may not be in the context of taking out the trash, I am sure that you are familiar with its pattern.

In fact, it is probable that someone with whom you share an interpersonal relationship has nagged you just as I have described, or that you may have been the one doing the nagging. While you may be quite familiar with nagging, have you ever really thought much about it, besides perhaps to make jokes or laugh about it? (Just think how many cartoons and comics you have probably been exposed to depicting an aggressive wife nagging a browbeaten husband.) My goal in this essay is to make you more aware of this everyday behavior and the purpose it may serve in your interpersonal relationships. To this end, I am going to answer four basic questions about nagging, particularly the what, when, who, and why of nagging. I turn to "What is nagging?" first.

## What Is Nagging?

As you can tell from the above description of someone nagging another person to take out the trash, the goal of nagging is to persuade someone to perform or, depending on the situation, stop performing some behavior. So an easy way to think of nagging is as a form of persuasion. We can further categorize nagging as an example of persistent persuasion. Persistent persuasion implies that a persuader tries several times to get another to comply. In effect, the person receiving these persuasive attempts is not doing what the persuader wants, so the persuader keeps trying to gain his or her compliance. This may be your experience when you try to persuade someone to do something; people rarely do what we want the first time we try to influence them. Indeed, in this chapter's opening description of a nagging interaction, the persuader made not just one request to get the trash taken out but four.

So what exact form of persistent persuasion does nagging take? Kozloff (1988), a researcher, helps to answer this question by identifying the sequential steps that occur in a nagging interaction. These steps are as follows:

1. A nagger gives a naggee a signal to perform (or stop performing) a specific behavior (such as asking him or her to take out the trash).

2. The naggee does not cooperate or comply with the nagger.

3. In response, the nagger repeats his or her initial signal in a further effort to gain the naggee's compliance.

4. The naggee again responds by being noncompliant.

Kozloff argues that this exchange of the nagger's signal to comply and the naggee's noncompliance continues until either the nagger gives up and stops trying to persuade the naggee or the naggee eventually gives in and does what the persuader wants.

There are several important processes that Kozloff identifies in his description of a nagging interaction. The first is that a naggee does not immediately comply with a nagger. Noncompliance is necessary for a persuader to be persistent, since once a naggee complies there is no need for a persuader to continue trying to influence him or her. The second, as was previously discussed, is that a persuader reacts to this noncompliance by being persistent or continuing to try to influence a naggee; he or she does not at first give up. However it is *how* the persuader is persistent in a nagging interaction that is interesting. Specifically, the nagger repeats the initial message. Now this is not to say that a nagger repeats the previous message word for word. It is likely, as shown in the example of someone nagging another to take out the trash, that subsequent attempts will be worded differently but will still communicate the same essential message. Moreover, a nagger may also change paralinguistic cues, such as beginning to whine or to speak in a pleading tone.

A persuader choosing to be persistent by repeating himself or herself is at odds with research indicating that individuals often become more aggressive when trying to influence someone who will not comply (deTurck 1985, 1987). Particularly, persuaders usually start trying to influence someone using polite strategies, such as asking them to do something. However, when polite strategies are not successful, persuaders may become more aggressive by making threats, harassing the other, or, in rare cases, turning to violence (Pruitt, Parker, and Mikolic 1997). Throughout your life, you have probably seen examples of a persuader "escalating" to more aggressive strategies. Just think of a parent trying to persuade a child to pick up toys. The parent probably starts out by using requests or by asking the child several times to pick up the toys. When this strategy does not work, the parent may threaten the child with a time out or spanking if the child does not cooperate. If the child still does not comply, the parent may then follow through on his or her threat.

Through my research, I sought to determine whether nagging could be differentiated from other instances of persuader persistence by a nagger repeating himself or herself rather than escalating to more aggressive strategies. I asked two different groups of people to complete a questionnaire about nagging. The first group was composed of 103 students at a midwestern university (63 females and 40 males, ranging in age from 19 to 49). The second group included 101 married couples (202 individuals whose ages ranged from 25 to 84 years; the number of years the couples had been married ranged from 1 to 59 years). Consistent with what was expected, both groups described nagging as more repetitious than aggressive (Soule 2001).

Let us turn back to the original question of "What is nagging?" The answer is that nagging is a form of persistent persuasion that involves a persuader repeating himself or herself rather than escalating to a more aggressive persuasive strategy. You may now be asking yourself, why would a persuader choose to be repetitive rather than become more aggressive? It probably seems an annoying and less successful way to try to persuade someone. The answer to why a nagger relies on repetition may lie in the actions of the person being persuaded; when this individual behaves in a specific manner, a persuader replies by nagging. Thus, we next turn to the question "When does nagging occur?"

## When Does Nagging Occur?

You are aware that people's communicative behaviors do not occur in a vacuum; rather, they are affected by and in turn affect the communicative behaviors of others; thus, a persuader may nag in response to the actions of a naggee. Indeed, we already know that a naggee must be noncompliant in order for a persuader to continue nagging. However, just as it is *how* a persuader is persistent that differentiates nagging from other types of persuader persistence, *how* a naggee reacts to a persuader's initial and subsequent influence messages can bring about and continue nagging behavior.

An individual who is not complying with a persuader can enact this noncompliance in one of two ways. The first is that he or she can be verbally noncompliant. Verbal noncompliance involves a persuasive target telling a persuader through words that he or she will not comply. For example, when asked to take out the trash, a verbally noncompliant person could simply say "No," or "It is not my job to take out the trash." On the other hand, this individual could be behaviorally noncompliant. When being behaviorally noncompliant, an individual does not necessarily verbalize an intent not to comply; he or she simply does not do what the persuader wants. For example, when asked to take out the trash, a behaviorally noncompliant person may just calmly say nothing and continue the activity in which he or she was engaged, such as watching TV or reading. Moreover, being behaviorally noncompliant could also be accompanied by a verbal agreement to comply without actually doing so. For example, when asked to take out the trash, a behaviorally noncompliant person might simply say "Okay" or "All right" without doing what the persuader wants. This individual could also communicate a plan to take out the trash in the future (perhaps without intending to do so) by saying "I'll do it in a minute," or "I'll take it out at the next commercial break" when watching TV.

When thinking back to your own experiences with nagging, you can probably guess which type of noncompliance, behavioral versus verbal, most often occurs in nagging interactions. If you said behavioral, your response would be consistent with the results of my research. When I asked the sample of married couples to think about a nagging interaction they have had with their spouse, most of them indicated that the naggee's

most common response was behavioral noncompliance (Soule 2001).

Why do nagging interactions more often entail behavioral rather than verbal noncompliance? The answer to this question may have to do with the repetitive nature of nagging. By not making a verbal refusal to a persuader, a behaviorally noncompliant person makes it difficult for a persuader to use a more aggressive or less polite method of persuasion. Indeed, if a behaviorally noncompliant individual has apparently agreed to do what the persuader wants (e.g., says "I'll do it in a minute"), a persuader may feel that it is inappropriate to use a more aggressive strategy (such as threats or harassment). In effect, the persuader may believe that this person has seemingly done nothing to deserve such a response. Even if a person simply says nothing when being behaviorally noncompliant, a persuader may feel (either consciously or unconsciously) that it is not appropriate to use a more aggressive strategy in response. As a result, since escalating to a more aggressive influence method seems inappropriate, a persuader is left with no choice but to repeat the original message and therefore nag.

Thus, nagging occurs as a product of the actions of both the nagger and naggee. When a naggee responds to a persuader's initial influence attempts with behavioral noncompliance, a persuader is ostensibly left with no other option than to nag. This reasoning suggests that nagging may not always occur because someone is simply a nag or nags because it is his or her personality to do so, but rather as a result of the situation. You may have made this assumption (i.e., that nagging is a personality trait) about some of the people in your life, for example stating that "My husband/wife is such a nag," or "All my mother/father knows how to do is nag." If nagging is in part a result of the actions of a naggee, this would suggest that a variety of people might nag. To further investigate this idea, the next question is "Who nags?"

## Who Nags?

Think for a moment about the numerous interpersonal relationships you share with the variety of people in your life. In which ones do you and/or the other person in the relationship nag? Many of you may think that this behavior only occurs in intimate relationships, such as with a spouse, boyfriend/girlfriend, or your parents. Though this may be the case for some, the results of my research indicate that a large variety of people nag one another.

I asked the sample of students to list the people who nag them and the people they nag, indicating the relationship they share with each. For example, participants could list their father, roommate, friend, and so forth. Surprisingly, the persons in this study listed a large assortment of people. Among those whom they nag, participants included not only the people we would expect, such as significant others (i.e., boyfriends, girlfriends, spouses, ex-boyfriends and ex-girlfriends) but also persons in less obvious relationships. For example, several participants indicated that they nagged superiors (e.g., professors, teachers, bosses at work, and coaches), roommates, friends, best friends, co-workers, siblings, neighbors, and subordinates (e.g., the children they babysit). When participants indicated who nags them, many of the same people were listed, such as roommates, friends, superiors, and significant others. In addition, participants indicated that their parents, grandparents, aunts, and uncles were likely to nag them.

Thus, it appears that nagging occurs in a wide variety of interpersonal relationships. But when you think of nagging, with whom do you most often associate this behavior, men or women? Turning back to the opening of this chapter, which depicts someone nagging another to take out the trash, did you picture a man or woman saying these words? If you pictured a woman as the nagger, your perception may be consistent with that of many people in Western culture. We often stereotype nagging as a feminine behavior and believe that women are more likely to nag than men. To gain a greater understanding of sex differences in nagging, I first examined whether most people really do view nagging as a feminine behavior. The point was not to look at which sex actually nags most but whether society views nagging in general as more feminine or masculine.

Thus, I asked individuals in both of the samples (the married couples and students) whether they perceive or think of nagging as a more feminine or more masculine behavior. Not too surprisingly, both samples viewed nagging as more feminine than masculine (Soule 2001).

Though many people may view nagging as more feminine, I was curious as to whether one sex is more likely than the other to nag. In effect, I wanted to see whether the perception of nagging as a more feminine behavior is accurate; specifically, do women really nag others more than men? An examination of the lists generated by the sample of students concerning whom they nag and who nags them indicated that nagging not only depends on the sex of the nagger but on that of the naggee as well. Specifically, women were found to nag similar numbers of men and women, whereas men were more likely to nag other men than women (Soule 2001). Therefore, it appears that both sexes engage in nagging behavior, but men tend to be more selective than women in that they are more likely to nag other men.

It appears, then, that a variety of people in a variety of interpersonal relationships nag. Moreover, though we may think of nagging as a more feminine than masculine behavior, men do nag, although they are more likely to nag other men than women. Perhaps this is why nagging is perceived to be feminine. Since women nag a greater variety of people, we may tend to stereotypically associate this behavior with them. We now have an idea of who nags; however, we still do not know exactly why nagging occurs in such a diverse group of relationships or why men tend to nag other men rather than women. Thus the last question is, "Why nag?"

## Why Nag?

Think back to the opening of this chapter; why do you think the persuader is nagging another to take out the trash? The persuader's motive may seem obvious—he or she simply wants the trash taken out. Thus, the most apparent answer to the question "Why nag?" is to influence another. Indeed, when asked why they nag their spouse, the majority of subjects in the sample of married couples reported that it was to gain the naggee's (their spouse's) compliance (Soule 2001). However, nagging may serve several other important functions in our interpersonal relationships. Think back to instances where you have nagged someone you care about. Though your primary goal may have been to gain compliance, did you also nag this person out of feelings of concern or love? Perhaps you even used nagging as a means of showing your affection. For example, nagging your significant other about calling you when he or she stays out late may be a way for you to express how you worry about this person's safety and well-being. In the context of parent/child relationships, Youniss and Smollar (1985) found that many children and adolescents view their parents' nagging as annoying and intrusive. Surprisingly, they also view it as a sign of caring, concern, and love. Rosenfeld (1985) interviewed a 17-year-old boy who complained about his mother's nagging but then added that it showed her concern for him, since, "You only nag someone you care about." In my own research, when I asked married participants to describe something about which they nag their spouse, their responses appeared to be motivated by love and a concern for their spouse's well-being (Soule 2001). For example, several of these individuals reported that they nagged their spouse about taking his or her medicine, going to the doctor, stopping smoking, or starting to exercise for health reasons.

In addition to showing affection, another function of nagging may be to avoid becoming aggressive toward a relational partner. As noted earlier, nagging is different from other instances of persuader persistence in that a persuader repeats himself or herself rather than escalating to a more aggressive influence strategy (such as angry and abusive statements, threats, or even physical violence). Though a persuader may not consciously choose to nag in order to avoid hurting a naggee, it might be a way to be a persistent persuader while avoiding conflict, destructive statements, or even violence. This reasoning may explain why men tend to nag other men rather than women. Indeed,

men may choose to nag other men as a way to avoid conflict. Since men are thought to be more aggressive than women (e.g., Clarke-Stewart, Friedman, and Koch 1985; Maccoby and Jacklin 1980), a persistent male persuader who escalates to a more aggressive strategy to try to influence another male could cause a verbal conflict or even a physical fight. Moreover, since women have traditionally held less power than men in society, they may be likely to comply immediately with a male persuader. As a result, men may rarely have to resort to nagging with a female naggee.

Thus, nagging may serve a variety of functions in our interpersonal relationships. It may allow us not only to influence someone but also to show caring and to avoid acting aggressively. These functions indicate that nagging may play an important role in helping to maintain harmony in a variety of relationships. However, it should be noted that interactions involving nagging are not always positive. Repeatedly nagging another person could cause him or her to feel irritation or annoyance. In extreme cases, a naggee could become irritated enough to respond to a nagger with violence (Gelles 1972). Though nagging may be an important part of most healthy relationships, in some cases it can cause problems.

## Conclusion

I trust that this chapter has given you a greater understanding of nagging in your own interpersonal relationships. Though you might not have given much thought to nagging (besides to wish that a nagger would go away or that a naggee would just comply), you may now recognize what constitutes this behavior and how the actions of both the nagger and naggee can cause and continue a nagging interaction. Moreover, not only may nagging occur in a variety of our relationships, but it might also serve several important functions, such as showing affection and helping us to avoid acting aggressively. Therefore, as strange as this idea may have seemed to you at first, everything we do in our interpersonal relationships has meaning and serves a purpose, even nagging.

## References

Clarke-Stewart, A., Friedman, S., and Koch, J. (1985). *Child Development: A Topical Approach*. New York: John Wiley and Sons.

deTurck, M. A. (1985). A transactional analysis of compliance-gaining behavior: Effects of noncompliance, relational contexts, and actors' gender. *Human Communication Research*, 1: 54–78.

———. (1987). When communication fails: Physical aggression as a compliance-gaining strategy. *Communication Monographs*, 54: 106–112.

Gelles, R. J. (1972). *The Violent Home: A Study of Physical Aggression Between Husbands and Wives*. Thousand Oaks, CA: Sage.

Kozloff, M. A. (1988). *Productive Interaction With Students, Children, and Clients*. Springfield, IL: Charles C. Thomas.

Maccoby, E. E., and Jacklin, C. N. (1980). Sex differences in aggression: A rejoinder and reprise. *Child Development*, 51: 964–980.

Pruitt, D. G., Parker, J. C., and Mikolic, J. M. (1997). Escalation as a reaction to persistent annoyance. *The International Journal of Conflict Management*, 8: 252–270.

Rosenfeld, A. A. (1985). Parents who nag. *Human Sexuality*, 19: 133–142.

Soule, K. P. (2001). Persistence in compliance-gaining interactions: The role of nagging behavior. Doctoral dissertation, Northwestern University, 2001.

Youniss, J., and Smollar, J. (1985). *Adolescent Relations With Mothers, Fathers, and Friends*. Chicago: The University of Chicago Press.

## Questions

1. Define *nagging*. Ask five other people to define it as well. What are the similarities in the definitions? The differences?

2. Describe two different patterns of nagging you have witnessed in close friendships or romantic relationships. How do you interpret the goals of the naggers? What is the effect on the relationships?

3. Are there some "nagging principles" or conclusions you can draw from considering who nags you and who you nag? Design your own list of five recommendations to break a nagging pattern.

# 22
# Communicating Forgiveness

*Douglas L. Kelley*

"**I** am sorry." Frequently these words are difficult to speak to another and difficult to accept from another. Forgiveness is not, as Douglas Kelley suggests in this article, an easy thing—whether you are the person who needs to offer forgiveness or the person who needs to be forgiven. Often the first step toward forgiveness is an apology. Children learn at an early age that apologies are necessary to resolve conflicts when the rights of others have been violated (Darby and Schlenker 1982). Apologies can help repair relationships. Cody and McLaughlin (1990) review a number of studies that suggest that apologies help reduce both the punishments the perpetrator receives and the anger the victim experiences. In their study of forgiveness, McCullough, Worthington, and Rachal (1997) stress the importance of empathy because empathizing with a significant other raises the probability of maintaining closeness and lowered the possibility of avoidance and revenge.

Even after the words are spoken and accepted, and time has passed, true forgiveness is difficult. As Smedes (1984) suggests:

> There are some hurts that we can leave behind which float away like debris on rushing water. But, there are others which rivet themselves into our memory. Deep hurts we never deserved flow from a dead past into our living present. A friend betrays us; a parent abuses us; a spouse leaves us in the cold—these hurts do not heal with the coming of the sun. (p. 11)

In the following article, Kelley addresses a significant concept that has received little attention in the communication literature. He suggests: Forgiveness is a concept that most everyone has attempted, but few have actually accomplished. Part of this problem, according to Kelley, is the fact that very few people have a real definition of what forgiveness is. To this end, the first section of this chapter provides a detailed look at different ideas or "types" of forgiveness, subsequently specifying a comprehensive definition. The next section discusses the interpersonal aspects of forgiveness, using several examples to illustrate the complex dynamics involved in the process. The final section reviews the role of communication in forgiveness, assessing both the motivation for forgiveness and strategies for expressing such feelings appropriately. Overall, Kelley places emphasis on the complex and transactional nature of forgiveness, specifically asserting that forgiving is based upon not only the feelings and actions of the forgiver, but also the responses of the offender. Further, he notes that the consequences (both positive and negative) of the decision to forgive (or not to forgive) impact both parties as well. As you read this chapter, think about your experience with forgiveness and ask yourself this question: What criteria do I tend to use when deciding if I need to ask for forgiveness or to expect forgiveness from another person?

## References

Cody, M. J., and McLaughlin, M. L. (1990). Interpersonal accounting. In H. Giles and P. Robinson (Eds.), *Handbook of Language and Social Psychology*. London: Wiley, 227–255.

Darby, B. W., and Schlenker, B. R. (1982). Children's reactions to apologies. *Journal of Personality and Social Psychology*, 43, 742–753.

McCullough, M. E., Worthington, E. L., and Rachal, K. C. (1997). Interpersonal forgiving in close relationships. *Journal of Personality and Social Psychology*, 73, 321–336.

Smedes, L. (1984). *Forgive and Forget: Healing the Hurts we Don't Deserve*. New York: Pocket Books.

\* \* \*

'I cried some, too, then, holding him in my arms, kissing his hair. . . . All the same I knew I was forgiving him. I had that miraculous clarity for an instant and so I understood that the forgiveness itself was strong, durable, like strands of a web, weaving around us, holding us.'

Alice–*A Map of the World*,
(p. 390)

Just last week, as I was preparing to write this chapter, someone in our office said to me, "Forgiveness is tough. If anyone thinks it's easy, then they haven't really tried it." She went on to say, "I realized that at first I didn't really want things to get better. I wanted to hurt the other person like they had hurt me." Her comments made me think about the first marriage workshop I conducted in which I included information about forgiveness. I had completed about ninety minutes worth of material on working through conflict in marriage and was finishing with ten minutes on forgiveness. I actually thought that talking about forgiveness would be a "nice" way to end the session—you know, after we had been talking about the heavy stuff, now each partner could forgive the other and go back to marital bliss. I was very surprised when most of the questions during the question-and-answer period were about forgiveness. "Should you forgive if you think they may do it again?" "Should you forgive if they have apologized?" "How do you forgive someone? I'm trying, but it doesn't seem to be working."

In order to answer these questions, we need to understand something about the nature of forgiveness. Contemporary definitions of forgiveness vary in terms of their complexity and their etiology. For example, Hargrave (1994a), a marriage and family therapist, offers the following general definition of forgiveness: "Generally, the word *forgive* means to cease to feel resentment against an offender" (p. 339). Hargrave's definition is parsimonious and succinct and easy to grasp by couples and family members. On the other side of the coin, Enright et al. (1992) reviewed ancient writings and modern philosophies, in order to provide a more comprehensive understanding of what forgiveness includes. They concluded that the idea of forgiveness generally includes "the casting off of deserved punishments, the abandonment of negative reactions, the imparting of love toward the other person, self-sacrificial nature, the potential restoration of the rela-

tionship, and positive benefits for the forgiver" (p. 88).

Some of you may be thinking, "Whoa, hold the boat! It's one thing to cease having negative feelings toward offenders. It's a whole other thing to feel positively toward them"—and you would be right. Enright et al. provide a very ambitious definition of forgiveness. However, if you think their definition is unrealistic, I invite you to consider the following story about Marietta Jaeger (Jaeger 1998). Marietta and her family (her husband, five children, and her parents) were camping for a full month in Montana. One night, as she tucked the children into bed, she could barely reach Susie, her 7-year-old. Marietta stretched over all of the kids to reach Susie, but could barely reach her cheek to kiss her goodnight. Marietta recalls Susie exclaiming, "'Oh no, Mama,!' and she crawled out of her sleeping bag and over her sister to kneel right in front of me. She hugged me hugely and kissed me smack on the lips. 'There, Mama, that's the way it should be!'" This was the last time Marietta was ever to see her little girl. During the night Susie was discovered missing—a hole had been slashed in the tent next to where she had lain.

I can hardly do justice in this short amount of space to Marietta's emotional journey, but let me summarize her process to forgiveness as well as I can. Shortly after the event she felt that, "Even if the kidnapper were to bring Susie back, alive and well, this very moment, I could still kill him for what he has done to my family. I believed I could have done so with my bare hands and a big smile on my face, if only I knew who he was." I think most of us would agree that Marietta had every right to feel that way. However, she soon realized that this mindset violated her own value system, and that nurturing her hatred was not psychologically healthy. Eventually she made a decision to forgive the kidnapper, whoever he was, and she finally slept soundly for the first time since Susie's abduction.

A year after Susie's kidnapping, after a newspaper article was written in which Marietta expressed her concern for Susie's abductor, the kidnapper called to taunt her. Marietta, ever since her intellectual decision to forgive this man, had been working at her forgiveness. She had repeated, again and again, "that, however I felt about the kidnapper, in God's eyes he was just as precious as my little girl . . . that , even if he wasn't behaving like one, this man was a son of God . . . that, as a Christian, I am called to pray for my enemies." However, now, one year to the day after Susie's disappearance, her forgiveness was put to the test by a phone call. Her response? Marietta looked past his smug taunting and asked him how she could help him. His response? He broke down and wept, "I wish this burden could be lifted from me." During the course of their conversation this broken man revealed enough information to allow the FBI to locate him. After his conviction for kidnapping and murder, Marietta could have asked for the death penalty, yet she believed that she better honored Susie, "not by becoming that which I deplored, but by saying that all life is sacred and worthy of preservation."

Marietta Jaeger's courageous story demonstrates in dramatic fashion that turning negative feelings to positive ones is possible. Yet her story also helps us understand what forgiveness is not. In understanding the forgiveness process, it is crucial to realize that forgiveness is distinct from the concepts of forgetting, condoning, excusing, and denying. Each of these concepts fails to recognize a person's responsibility for a relational transgression and therefore eliminates the need for forgiveness. Forgetting implies that memories of the offense are gone. Yet, as Desmond Tutu (1998) states, "Forgiveness does not mean amnesia" (p. xiv). If we no longer remember the transgression, then there is no longer forgiveness. Similarly, condoning justifies an infraction by denying that any wrong took place. Excusing implies that the wrongdoer had a good reason for the offense and thereby removes responsibility from wrongdoers for their actions. Likewise, denying is a refusal to recognize a transgression.

What seems clear, from analyzing what forgiveness is not, is that for something to count as forgiveness, a wrong must be recognized. In Marietta Jaeger's case, the wrongdoing was not excused, condoned, denied, or forgotten. Rather, the wrong was experienced and acknowledged and was, of course, remembered. But in light of this, Marietta made a decision to move beyond her hatred.

North's (1987) work emphasizes this need to move beyond negative feelings by making a willful decision to forgive. She states, "Forgiveness is a matter of a willed change of heart, the successful result of an active endeavor to replace bad thoughts with good, bitterness and anger with compassion and affection" (p. 506). I like the way that Enright, Freedman, and Rique (1998) put it when they define forgiveness as "a willingness to abandon one's right to resentment, negative judgment, and indifferent behavior toward one who unjustly hurt us, while fostering the undeserved qualities of compassion, generosity, and even love toward him or her" (pp. 46–47). Forgiveness, at its best, is "abandoning" the negative, and "fostering" the positive.

## Interpersonal Aspects of Forgiveness

Stories like Marietta Jaeger's help us realize the powerful reality of forgiveness (many other forgiveness stories can be found by studying conflictual settings around the world, such as the Truth and Reconciliation process in South Africa or the conflict in Northern Ireland). However, as poignant as these stories are, what most of us need is to understand how forgiveness is managed in our day-to-day lives. Studying the communication of forgiveness in daily interactions requires us to focus on the transactional nature of forgiveness interactions, that is, the mutual influence that forgiver and offender exert on one another, and to emphasize the potential of forgiveness to restore hurting relationships.

North (1987) moves forgiveness from a purely intrapersonal experience to an interpersonal experience by placing forgiveness in the role of restoring damaged relationships. She recognizes the importance of internal change but also argues that internal change may lead to outward expression:

Typically an act of wrongdoing brings about a distancing of the wrongdoer from the one he has harmed. . . . Forgiveness is a way of healing the damage done to one's relations with the wrongdoer, or at least a first step towards a full reconciliation. (North 1984, 502–503)

Although little social scientific research has been done to study directly the interpersonal dynamics of the forgiveness process, certain researchers have developed theoretical models that address issues of importance in understanding the interpersonal nature of forgiveness. Enright and the Human Development Study Group (1991) offer a model of forgiveness that includes the need for the forgiver to respond behaviorally to the offender. This model focuses on the forgiver and begins with the initial injury. At this point the injured party experiences negative psychological consequences, such as emotional pain. This leads to the need to resolve the conflict in some way, namely, to choose between two basic strategies: justice and mercy. Justice takes the form of legal action, seeking personal fairness, or revenge. Mercy involves the options we discussed previously, such as condonation, excuse, and denial, or it takes on a more active response, such as forgiveness. Various motives lead the offended party to make the cognitive decision to forgive the injurer, which leads to eventually changing the way the injury or injurer is viewed. Finally, the injured individual recognizes the need for some type of behavioral response that will bring about either reconciliation or release. Both of these options result in less negative, and more positive, affect experienced toward the offender. Release occurs if reconciliation is deemed impossible or unwise.

Similar to Enright et al.'s description of the various ways that mercy can be given is Hargrave's distinction between exonerating and forgiving. Exonerating involves gaining *insight* and *understanding* into the offending person's situation. This perspective change results in the offended party no longer holding the offender accountable for his or her actions. In contrast, forgiveness provides the offender *opportunity to provide compensation*. This means that the offending party is held accountable for his or her wrongdoing. In contrast to Enright et al.'s distinction between justice and mercy, forgiveness is con-

ceptualized as providing the wrongdoer with an opportunity to engage in restorative justice. Hargrave also includes in his discussion an *overt act of forgiving*. This overt act involves renegotiating the relationship to restore a sense of fairness or balance.

One aspect of Hargrave's (1994a, 1994b) perspective that I find particularly interesting is his belief that there are three prerequisites before the two parties renegotiate the relationship covenant. First, both parties must agree about what constituted the infraction. This may seem like an obvious step, but often individuals in conflict do not agree on what the conflict is really about. Second, there has to be a mutual recognition of the damage that the wrongdoing caused. Finally, there must be some type of apology from the offender for the damage caused.

Interestingly, these three prerequisites parallel the phases that individuals go through when giving an account of a wrong action (Cody and McLaughlin 1988; Schonbach and Kleibaumhuter 1990). For example, the account process begins by one party experiencing what is termed a *failure event*. Failure events can involve an action that is viewed as an offense or an omission of a behavior that was expected or required. Once the offended party experiences the offense, they reproach the perceived offender by behaving in some way that indicates that they feel wronged. Some time after experiencing the reproach, the offender responds either by giving a mitigating response, such as conceding or confessing guilt, or by giving an aggravating response, such as denying responsibility for the wrong done. Finally, the offended person assesses the veracity of the account, the offense in light of the account, and the characteristics of the perceived offender.

Hargrave's (1994a, 1994b) suggestion that an apology is needed before the relationship is renegotiated is also consistent with the accounts research indicating that more mitigating strategies, such as concession (of which apology is one type), are more likely to bring mitigating responses (Cody and McLaughlin 1988), such as forgiveness of the offense. Several other studies have also found a close relationship between apology and forgiveness. For example, McCullough, Worthington, and Rachal (1997) tested the relationship between apology, empathy, and forgiveness, and found strong evidence for the relationship between apology and forgiveness. Likewise, Emmers and Canary (1996) conceptualized forgiveness and apology as related constructs. In a study examining the effect of young couples' communication strategies on relational repair, they found that individuals listed forgiveness when asked to describe what was done to repair the relationship after a negative event. Forgive was defined as "forgave" or "accepted apology" (Emmers and Canary 1996, 174). Forgiveness was one of many interactive strategies reported by respondents. Interactive strategies are those that involve directly interacting with the other person (Baxter and Wilmot 1984). Walters (1984) offers an interesting perspective on actually interacting with the one who has hurt us. For Walters, forgiveness often involves "follow-through"; that is, at times you simply need to talk to the person being forgiven.

## Communicating Forgiveness

In order to better understand how forgiveness is communicated day to day, I conducted a study wherein participants were asked to write about three forgiveness stories: a time they were forgiven, a time they forgave, and a time they asked for forgiveness. After collecting 304 stories, my staff and I analyzed them for themes related to forgiveness motivations, forgiveness strategies, and relational consequences. The stories the participants shared were mostly about family relationships, dating relationships, and friendships.

### Forgiver Motivation

Participants' forgiveness stories primarily described five different reasons for forgiving someone: love, well-being, restoring the relationship, strategy of the other, and reframing. The first dimension, *love*, was often mentioned as follows: "I forgave him, primarily because I love him. . . ." Likewise, one of our participants who was on the receiving end of forgiveness stated, "I guess the reason I was forgiven was because he loves me."

The second dimension, *well-being*, included forgiving in order to restore well-being to oneself or to the offender. One individual realized that her negative emotions were damaging to her own self: "I began to realize that this anger was not only torturing him, but myself as well. It was eating me up inside and making me more of an angry person. Why should I suffer for what he has done? So I wrote him. . . ." The following statement demonstrates how motivations were often multifaceted, arising from both the motivations of love and well-being of the other: "I forgave him because I love him and he needed my forgiveness to make himself feel better."

The third dimension focused on *restoring the relationship*. Responses in this dimension were grouped three ways. Sometimes individuals simply mentioned that they desired to forgive the other so that the relationship would continue. Other times, individuals mentioned that the nature of the relationship prompted the giving of forgiveness. Participants who reported this aspect of forgiveness motivation indicated, at times, that there were implicit or explicit obligations because of the relationship type, for example, "I forgave her because she is my friend of 12 years. . . ." The third grouping represented statements that compared the severity of the infraction to the worth of the relationship. For example, "I forgave the person because it was not a major problem that a tape was destroyed. It was not worth risking a friendship over."

The fourth motivation dimension was *strategy of the other*. Here forgivers' motivations were seen to be influenced by how the offender responded to his or her own infraction. Of course, this was no surprise to us given the previous research that demonstrated the close relationship between apology and forgiveness. It was common for individuals to mention the importance of hearing an apology. Additional strategies mentioned were a show of responsibility and a demonstration of remorse. The following example demonstrates both apology and responsibility: "He said he forgave me but only because I apologized and admitted I was wrong."

The final dimension of forgiver motivation was entitled *reframing*. This concept is consistent with several of the more psychologically based models of forgiveness (Cunningham 1985; Enright et al. 1991). Reframing often took the shape of claiming to understand why the other person engaged in the offending behavior; viewing the offender as not responsible for his or her actions; viewing the offender's act as unintentional; or diminishing the perceived significance of the offending behavior. One female participant describes her motivation as based on reframing her boyfriend's character: "I forgave him, primarily because I love him and I know that what occurred was not part of his normal character. He comes from a great family, he's a Christian, and I knew he wasn't the cheating kind." Another respondent was forgiven because his friend reframed the significance of the infraction: "He forgave me because it was a small issue to him."

## Offender (Forgiveness-Seeking) Motivation

While less varied than forgiver motivations, it is clear that not all forgiveness seeking comes from the same motives. The two primary motives for individuals seeking forgiveness were *well-being* and *restoring the relationship*. One respondent described his response to his mother, which was designed to restore *well-being* when things had become too uncomfortable: "When I could not stand this behavior any more, or needed her forgiveness, I started visiting her more frequently. . . ."

Offenders who desired forgiveness in order to *restore the relationship* handled things differently than did their forgiving counterparts. As with forgivers, this dimension represented a sense of obligation to obtain forgiveness in certain relationships. For offenders, however, restoring the relationship was also associated with restoring trust and with a simple desire to maintain the relationship, for example: "I feel that we lost that friendship. . . . After I talked to him, I explained to him that I hoped he could forgive me and we could remain friends."

## Forgiveness-Granting Strategies

Forgiveness was granted using any of three main strategies: direct, indirect, and conditional. Many of our respondents reported giving forgiveness by *directly* addressing the transgression with the offender. Direct strategies included such things as discussing the issue; the forgiver telling the offender that he or she understands; directly telling the other, "I forgive you"; and using a third party to mediate the issue. For example, one respondent reported, "I told him I understood, but would hope he would be more up front with problems. I told him of course I forgave him."

*Indirect* strategies included a wide variety of tactics. For example, some individuals used humor or tried to diminish the perceived effect of the infraction by saying something like, "It was no big deal." Many people used nonverbal behavior such as hugging, touching, eye contact, changes in vocal patterns, and shows of emotion. Sometimes the nonverbal behaviors accompanied a more direct strategy, while at other times the nonverbal elements were meant to carry the whole meaning. A number of narratives reported "returning to normal" as a way of showing the offender they had been forgiven. In these cases nothing was really said, but the return to normal behavior signaled that all had been forgiven. Similarly, some described how the forgiveness was "just understood." For example, one respondent describes forgiving his father: "The forgiveness was spontaneous but not vocalized, it was understood."

A third way in which individuals granted forgiveness was *with conditions*. This could best be described as "forgiveness if. . . ," that is, I will forgive you if you adhere to certain stipulations. One typical narrative describes a child-father discussion, wherein the father asks forgiveness as part of his alcohol recovery; forgiveness is given in the following way: "I told him I would accept his apology; however, we both knew that there was the stipulation that he stay off of the booze."

## Offender (Forgiveness-Seeking) Strategies

Forgiveness-seeking strategies are used by offenders in order to gain forgiveness from the person they injured. The dimensions identified here were the same as for the forgiver; however, specific tactics within each dimension differed when it was forgiveness-seeking rather than forgiveness-granting. For example, *conditions* that were placed on the forgiveness as they related to the offenders' strategies were not set by the forgiver but offered instead by the offender.

*Direct* strategies used by the offender involved discussion, as they did for the forgiver, but the focus was not on the forgiver understanding but rather on the offender explaining. Also, direct requests for forgiveness were reported (e.g., "Will you forgive me?"), as was the use of third parties to help solve the problem. Paralleling the forgiver motivation category, individuals also reported such elements as apologizing, taking responsibility for their actions, and showing remorse. These types of behavior were deemed direct because they focused specifically on dealing with the infraction; for example, "I apologized to him over and over. I told him I didn't deserve him and that I took him for granted." Taking responsibility and apologizing were an effective combination in the following description: "At this time he apologized and explained that he felt responsible for my leaving. . . . At the time I forgave him. . . ."

*Indirect* forgiveness-seeking strategies included such elements as humor, nonverbal displays of acceptance or emotion, using one's social network to communicate remorse or apology (e.g., having a friend tell the injured person that you are sorry), ingratiation, or returning to normalcy. One common example of nonverbal display of emotion was summed up like this: "I was crying because I was truly sorry for my action." In the following quote, the offender sought forgiveness by using a combination of strategies: "After not talking for two days I came home from work one day with a funny belated birthday card for her and a gift certificate to her favorite restaurant. . . . We went to dinner and in a joking manner, I expressed to her how sorry I was. . . ."

*Relational consequences* took place in two basic ways: relational change and return to normalcy. The most common form of relational consequence was to experience some type of change in the relationship. In fact, 72 percent of the narratives reporting relational consequences described some type of change, while 28 percent reported a return to normalcy. Relational change consisted of a variety of responses. Some relationships changed in type, such as from dating partners to "just friends." The following quote from a father-son scenario describes a rather interesting change in type: "The typical father/son relationship we had prior to the separation is gone and has been replaced by one where we exist more as friends rather than father/son."

Some relationships did not change in type but rather strengthened, as is illustrated in this work scenario: "My forgiveness was appreciated. The relationship seemed to improve slightly, as evidenced by more casual talk and sharing of what's going on in our lives." However, other relationships were not so lucky: "I apologized and asked him to forgive me and he did. After a while he did, and we were still friends, but not as good of friends." A final type of relationship change involved behavior or rules. One participant's story demonstrates this well: "No name-calling's become a rule in our relationship and we stand by it. It's helped us fight fairly."

Those individuals who did not report relational change often noted that the relationship required a *return to normalcy*. One of our participants succinctly sums this up: "After I forgave her things returned to normal." Returning to normal included the way the individuals communicated, interacted, or the kinds of tasks they could do (e.g., after a fender bender, Dad still trusts you to take his truck to the store).

### Time

Often the participants described the forgiveness process as taking time. This could be described as taking time to be ready to forgive (motivation), taking time to actually work through the forgiveness (strategy), or taking time for the full effect of the forgiveness to become evident (relational consequences). It was not uncommon for time to play a role in more than one of these aspects of the forgiveness process: "It took probably ten months for her to get over my disappointing her (my mom). She finally forgave me when she found out that I was pregnant with my first child." While it is evident that time is a factor, it is not clear as to whether time is primarily influencing motivation, strategy, relational consequence, or some combination of the three. What is obvious, however, is that time is often an important component of the forgiveness process.

I was also interested in how the forgiveness process might vary depending on the type of relationship. To explore this question I used chi-square analysis which compared my actual data with what I would have expected for each relationship type, if all the relationship types were equal. What I found was that, compared with the expectation that all relationship types are the same, family members were less likely to be motivated by love or to restore the relationship, and were less likely to experience deterioration of the relationship; dating individuals were more influenced by love and friends had a greater tendency to experience a deterioration of the relationship. Other results compared with this expectation showed there was a tendency for family members to be less motivated to forgive because of the strategy of the offender; dating couples were more likely to be motivated by a desire to restore the relationship or by the strategy of the offender when deciding to forgive someone, and as the offender they were more likely to seek forgiveness to restore well-being. Dating couples were the only relationship to experience change in relationship type more than expected; friends were less motivated to forgive by love, but were more motivated than expected by a desire to restore the relationship; in addition, friends were less motivated to seek forgiveness in order to restore well-being.

## Some Final Thoughts on the Forgiveness Process

It is evident that forgiveness, while certainly a psychological process, often has interpersonal dimensions and that these dimensions are important to the overall forgiveness process. For example, the strategy the offenders in the study chose affected the decision to forgive, as individuals noted that they forgave because the other apologized, took responsibility for his or her actions, or showed remorse. Thus, this influence of the offenders' strategies on the decision to forgive demonstrates the need to conceptualize forgiveness as a dynamic interpersonal process.

The dimensions generated as possible motivations in this study both consolidate and build upon previous research. Of particular interest is the concept of reframing. Reframing, in the current investigation, includes such elements as understanding, recognizing that the other person did not mean to hurt you, or realizing that the offender cannot be held responsible for his or her actions. This perspective also represents what Hargrave (1994b) refers to as exoneration. That is, once one reframes the infraction, the incident is no longer viewed as a violation; the offender is no longer held accountable; and subsequently he or she is no longer in need of forgiveness. It is important to realize that while the distinction between exoneration and forgiveness is an important one, the individuals who participated in this study believe that all of the events they reported involved forgiveness. However, understanding the difference between exoneration and forgiveness may account for differences in individuals' forgiveness experiences and relational outcomes.

The important emphasis placed on reframing raises interesting questions regarding attribution and account processes. It can be argued from an attribution theory perspective that the most effective strategies with which to secure forgiveness would involve making external attributions for the cause of a relational transgression ("I was late because of an accident on the freeway"), since individuals are only accountable for an infraction if it can be attributed to internal causes ("You were late because you are insensitive") (Jellison 1990; Sillars 1982). This argument is consistent with current findings indicating that individuals were often motivated to forgive because they reframed the infraction and concluded that the perceived offender was not responsible for his or her actions or did not intend to inflict harm—in other words, the cause of the infraction was located outside of the offending party. This reframing of the infraction from internal to external causes could be the result of the offender offering excuses. As was found by McLaughlin, O'Hair, and Cody (1983), "Excuse was by far the most popular mode of failure management and may simply reflect the fact that most people in judging their own behavior attribute failure to the circumstances of the situation rather than to their own bad intentions" (p. 222). However, although excuses may be quite effective in certain circumstances, concession, including apology, has been conceptualized as a more mitigating strategy than excuse (McLaughlin, O'Hair, and Cody 1983) and therefore could be more effective in achieving forgiveness. Concession can be understood as applying internal causal attributions to the offender's actions. Clearly in the present investigation, apologizing, taking responsibility for one's actions, and expressing remorse were related to the offended party's motivation to forgive. As such, it appears that both internal and external attributions can be effective when seeking to achieve forgiveness or manage a relational failure. This conclusion is consistent with research suggesting that apologies, excuses, or an "excuse-apology" hybrid is most effective when deflecting blame in interpersonal settings (Cody and McLaughlin 1990). In spite of these findings, however, it remains to be seen under what conditions internal and external attributions of behavior may be most effective in securing forgiveness.

Forgiveness strategies, in the present study, were either direct, engaging the other specifically about the issue, or indirect, wherein the issue is never explicitly dealt with. Direct strategies for offenders were characterized by discussion and often by further explanation of the infraction, direct requests for forgiveness, using a third party to intervene, apologies, taking responsibility for one's actions, and showing remorse. Indirect strategies involved humor, nonverbal behaviors and displays of emotion, using the social network to communicate the offender's feelings to the forgiver, and treating the injured party as he or she would normally be treated.

Interestingly, forgiver direct and indirect strategies largely paralleled offender strategies. Offender direct strategies included discussion, which often led to the forgiver understanding the offender's position, statements of forgiveness ("I forgive you"), and use of third-party mediators. Indirect strategies involved the use of humor, diminishing the perceived effect of the infraction ("It was no big deal"), nonverbal behaviors and emotional displays, a return to normalcy, and a sense that the other was forgiven and it was just "understood." These findings are interesting in light of the fact that Hargrave (1994b) believes that forgiveness requires an overt expression. Only a little over one-half of the scenarios in this study that identified a forgiver strategy mentioned the forgiver using direct strategies. If Hargrave is correct, this would mean that "true forgiveness" was not experienced in almost half of the participants' stories. To address this issue, it will eventually be necessary for forgiveness researchers to study dyads where partners' perceptions of forgiveness can be compared and contrasted; however, it is important to note here that our participants considered these stories to be stories of forgiveness.

Two additional strategy issues involve forgiving conditionally and time. Both forgivers and offenders were described as using conditional forgiveness at times. For instance, the forgiver might forgive the other as long as he or she promised that the transgression was never to happen again. Sometimes the offender initiated this condition when they were asking for forgiveness by promising never again to commit such a wrong. Also, both forgiver and offender mentioned that forgiveness took time. That is, while forgiveness can be a one-time act, it often involves a process of discussion and repeated requests for forgiveness. As we saw in Marietta Jaeger's story, it can take time to decide to forgive, and then often, once the decision is made, it takes time and effort to practice acting in a forgiving manner.

This study has also identified a variety of relational consequences that are associated with interpersonal forgiveness. The central dimensions are change and return to normalcy. Participants' narratives revealed that relationships can change in type, strengthen, deteriorate, or develop new behavior or rules in response to forgiveness. A common response that served as both a relational consequence and a type of forgiver indirect strategy was returning the relationship to normal. Many participants indicated that treating each other "normally" was the way that they knew they had been forgiven. Also, respondents noted that time played a role in the relational effects. Time, as it is understood as part of relational consequences, typically referred to the process of relationship healing. Individuals indicated that even after forgiveness was imparted to the other person, it could still take time to restore the relationship.

It was also interesting to find that forgiveness motivations, strategies, and relational consequences vary by relationship type. Possibly because family relationships are not voluntary relationships, family members reported being less motivated to give forgiveness because of love, to restore the relationship, or because of what the other person might do to seek forgiveness. This obligatory quality of family relationships may also account for the fact that family members reported their relationships being weakened fewer times than was expected. This may be because the involuntary nature of these relationships creates a sense of stability and resiliency in the relationship.

In the voluntary relationships, both dating and friendship, there was more of a tendency for individuals to be motivated to forgive in order to restore the relationship. In both of these relationship types there are fewer social constraints to hold individuals in a relationship. However, dating relationships and friendships differed in that dating individuals were motivated to forgive by love, well-being, and the forgiveness-seeking strategy of their partner. Friends, however were less inclined to be motivated by love or well-being, but were more likely to report a deterioration of the relationship. It was interesting that dating individuals were the only ones to show a higher likelihood than expected of changing relationship type as a consequence of the infraction and forgiveness process. Here we are aware of the pro-

verbial "let's just be friends" in response to some violation in the relationship. That is, I may forgive you, but I've also learned through the process that I no longer want to seriously date you. Friendships evidently can also be weakened but do not as often change relationship type.

The information presented here emphasizes the transactional nature of the forgiveness process as it demonstrates that the decision to forgive may be based on how the offender reacts after he or she realizes that the other person has been injured. It is important to consider the role of both the offender and the forgiver. This discussion also highlights the complex nature of the offender/offended relationship and the interrelationships between relationship type, motivation, strategy, and relational consequences. Perhaps most important, it is evident that forgiveness plays an important role in relational repair and personal well-being. As Walters (1984) puts it, "When we have been hurt we have two alternatives: be destroyed by resentment, or forgive. Resentment is death; forgiving leads to healing and life" (p. 366).

## References

Baxter, L. (1991). Content analysis. In B. M. Montgomery and S. Duck (Eds.), *Studying Interpersonal Interaction*, pp. 239–254. New York: The Guilford Press.

Baxter, L. A., and Wilmot, W. W. (1984). 'Secret Test': Social strategies for acquiring information about the state of the relationship. *Human Communication Research*, 11: 171–201.

Cody, M. J., and McLaughlin, M. L. (1990). Interpersonal accounting. In H. Giles and W. P. Robinson (Eds.), *Handbook of Language and Social Psychology*, pp.227–255. Chichester: John Wiley and Sons.

———. (1988). Accounts on trial: Oral arguments in traffic court. In C. Antaki (Ed.), *Analysing Everyday Explanation: A Casebook of Methods*, pp. 113–126. London: Sage.

Cunningham, B. R. (1985). The will to forgive: A pastoral theological view of forgiving. *Journal of Pastoral Care*, 39: 141–149.

Emmers, T. M., and Canary, D. J. (1996). The effect of uncertainty reducing strategies on young couples' relational repair and intimacy. *Communication Quarterly*, 44: 166–182.

Enright, R. D., and the Human Development Study Group. (1991). The moral development of forgiveness. In W. Kurtines and J. Gewirtz (Eds.), *Handbook of Moral Behavior and Development*, Vol. 1, pp. 123–152. Hillsdale, NJ: Erlbaum.

Enright, R. D., Eastin, D. L., Golden, S., Sarinopoulos, I., and Freedman, S. (1992). Interpersonal forgiveness within the helping professions: An attempt to resolve differences of opinion. *Counseling and Values*, 36: 84–103.

Enright, R. D., Freedman, S., and Rique, J. (1998). The psychology of interpersonal forgiveness. In R. D. Enright and J. North (Eds.), *Exploring Forgiveness*, pp. 46–62. Madison, WI: University of Wisconsin Press.

Freedman, S. R., and Enright, R. D. (1996). Forgiveness as an intervention goal with incest survivors. *Journal of Consulting and Clinical Psychology*, 64: 983–992.

Hamilton, J. (1994). *A Map of the World*. New York: Anchor Books/Doubleday.

Hargrave, T. D. (1994a). *Families and Forgiveness*. New York: Brunner/Mazel.

———. (1994b). Families and forgiveness: A theoretical and therapeutic framework. *The Family Journal: Counseling and Therapy for Couples and Families*, 2: 339–348.

Jaeger, M. (1998). The power and reality of forgiveness: Forgiving the murderer of one's child. In R. D. Enright and J. North (Eds.), *Exploring forgiveness*, pp. 9–14. Madison, WI: The University of Wisconsin Press.

Jellison, J. M. (1990). Accounting: Societal implications. In M. J. Cody and M. L. McLaughlin (Eds.), *The Psychology of Tactical Communication*, pp. 283–298. Philadelphia: Multilingual Matters, LTD.

McCullough, M. F., and Worthington, E. L., Jr. (1994). Encouraging clients to forgive people who have hurt them: Review, critique, and research prospectus. *Journal of Psychology and Theology*, 22: 3–20.

McCullough, M. F., Worthington, E. L., and Rachal, K. C. (1997). Interpersonal forgiving in close relationships. *Journal of Personality and Social Psychology*, 73: 321–336.

McLaughlin, M. L., O'Hair, H. D., and Cody, M. J. (1983). The management of failure events: Some contextual determinants of accounting behavior. *Human Communication Research*, 9: 208–224.

North, J. (1987). Wrongdoing and forgiveness. *Philosophy*, 62: 499–508.

Schonbach, P., and Kleibaumhuter, P. (1990). Severity of reproach and defensiveness of accounts. In M. J. Cody and M. L. McLaughlin (Eds.), *The Psychology of Tactical Communication*, pp. 229–243. Philadelphia: Multilingual Matters, LTD.

Sillars, A. L. (1982). Attribution and communication: Are people 'naïve scientists' or just naïve? In M. E. Roloff and C. R. Berger (Eds.), *Social Cognition and Communication*, pp. 73–106. Beverly Hills, CA: Sage.

Tutu, D. (1998). Foreword: Without forgiveness there is no future. In R. D. Enright and J. North (Eds.), *Exploring Forgiveness*, pp. xiii–xiv. Madison, WI: University of Wisconsin Press.

Walters, R. P. (1984). Forgiving: An essential element in effective living. *Studies in Formative Spirituality*, 5: 365–374.

# Questions

1. Do you think the model of forgiveness created by Enright and the Human Development Study Group (p. 191) realistic? Why or why not?

2. Describe an episode of forgiveness in your own life. Which of the forgiveness-granting or forgiveness-seeking strategies described in this article did you use or witness? What was their effect on the relationship?

3. Brainstorm several occasions upon which you have decided to forgive someone, whether a member of your family, a friend, and/or a dating partner. What enabled you to forgive them? To what extent are your strategies or reasons for forgiveness different depending upon the relationship?

# Part VI

## *Struggling in Relationships*

"If you have to work at a relationship, there is something wrong with it." Many people have expressed this "throwaway" response, reflective of a fast-paced environment—"if it doesn't work, throw it away." Fortunately, maturity and a history of relational losses have convinced most people that relational life is not like a worn gym shoe; rather, relationships have to be nurtured and renegotiated over time for them to continue to grow. When discussing relationships, many writers use a gardening metaphor that evokes images of caretaking—seeding, watering, weeding, and so on.

The writings in this section are supported by the concepts of dialectical tension and dialectical management. In the opening of this book, we cited Bellak's porcupine dilemma: "How can we live together without hurting each other too much?" This question is an indicator of the tension that all significant relationships face. As you remember, the term *dialectic* implies opposition, change, and interconnection. As people develop relationships, they encounter struggles that are normal and predictable but that may feel frustrating or frightening. The management of this struggle usually takes attention and effort. Some of the tensions emerge from the natural differences among persons; others develop as a result of individual developmental changes or a crisis, such as illness,

which affects the relationship. No matter what the source, the tensions must be faced and managed. For many people it is hard to realize that conflict is inevitable because no two people see the world in exactly the same way; our needs and goals vary. Even people you love get in your way, just as you get in their way. Persons who are aware of such predictable struggles often attempt to nurture their relationships to reduce or limit the tensions.

One metaphor for discussing relationships is weather. How would you describe an important relationship? Warm? Sunny? Stormy? Cold? Every relationship has a pervasive mood—a climate—about it. Sometimes the climate is warm, and we feel positive and supported. Other times the climate is cold, and we feel negative and defensive.

Many factors compete for attention in your life. Meeting your responsibilities at home, work, and school while maintaining friendships takes tremendous time and effort. The nurturing of friendships, partnerships, and marital or family relationships often gets the time and energy that is "left over," a minimal amount at best. In most cases, this limited attention spells relational disaster. Unless relational ties receive high priority, relationships will "go on automatic pilot" and eventually stagnate or deteriorate (Galvin, Bylund, and Brommel 2004).

The most difficult part of managing a relationship is addressing relational differences. It is easier to avoid a conflict, and remain frustrated or unhappy, than to address the issue directly. Such avoidance places relationships into a pattern of stagnation—creating off-limits topics and predictable silences—that eventually results in relationship dissolution. In her research on hurtful messages, Vangelisti (1994) describes their negative effect on relationships, concluding, "If hurtful messages are sometimes associated with positive relational outcomes, partners must have (or develop) ways to minimize their feelings of hurt" (p. 53). Therefore, learning to manage conflict directly and constructively is part of relational struggle for many individuals.

As you read the following selections, consider your willingness to engage in conflict rather than avoid it, to take responsibility for your part of a problem, and to put forth explicit effort to repair relational difficulties.

## References

Galvin, K. M., Bylund, C. L., and Brommel, B. J. (2004). *Family Communication: Cohesion and Change*, 6th edition. New York: Addison Wesley Longman.

Vangelisti, A. L. (1994). Messages that hurt. In W. R. Cupach and B. H. Spitzberg (Eds.), *The Dark Side of Interpersonal Communication*, pp. 53–82. Hillsdale, NJ: Lawrence Erlbaum. ✦

# 23
# Collaborative Negotiation

*Joyce L. Hocker and*
*William W. Wilmot*

Relational conflict is inevitable. No two people perceive the world in exactly the same way; differences characterize relational life. Hocker and Wilmot define conflict as "an expressed struggle between at least two interdependent parties who perceive incompatible goals, scarce rewards, and interference from the other party in achieving their goals," thus highlighting the interconnection of the communicators. By this definition, one quietly seething individual and a partner who is unaware of the other's anger are not considered to experience interpersonal conflict. Although conflict cannot be eliminated, it can be managed effectively. Hocker and Wilmot suggest that the way to manage conflict effectively is through collaborative negotiation. As you read this article, keep in mind that two important communication behaviors are inherent in the collaborative negotiation process—argumentativeness and confirmation.

Argumentativeness is important in conflict situations. This may seem strange, as often being argumentative is associated with verbal aggression. However, argumentativeness implies your willingness to argue for a point of view, to speak your mind. Infante (1988) suggests several ideas for preventing argumentativeness from turning to aggressiveness:

- Treat disagreements as objectively as possible; avoid assuming that because someone takes issue with your position or interpretation, they are attacking you as a person.

- Avoid attacking the other person (rather than the person's arguments), even if the attack would give you a tactical advantage; center your arguments on issues rather than personalities.

- Reaffirm the other person's sense of competence; compliment the other person as appropriate.

- Avoid interrupting; allow the other person to state her or his position fully before you respond.

- Stress equality and stress the similarities you have with the other person; emphasize areas of agreement before attacking the disagreements.

- Express interest in the other person's position, attitude, and point of view.

- Avoid presenting your arguments too emotionally; using an overly loud voice or interjecting vulgar expressions will prove offensive and eventually ineffective.

- Allow the other person to save face; never humiliate the other person.

Confirmation is critical to collaborative negotiation. A confirming message communicates, "you exist," or, "you matter." Disconfirming messages communicate the opposite—"you don't exist," or "you don't matter." Confirming messages aid conflict management because they convey interpersonal respect even though there is disagreement.

Confirming messages occur on three levels (Cissna and Sieberg 1990):

1. Recognition—the most fundamental confirming message is to recognize the other person. Often we don't do this. When we fail to return a phone message, visit a friend, make eye contact, or approach someone we know, we fail to recognize them.

2. Acknowledgment—when we acknowledge the feelings or ideas of others, we send a stronger confirming message than when we simply recognize them. Listening to another and asking them questions are two ways to acknowledge them. So is paraphrasing—feedback that restates, in your own words, the message you thought the speaker sent.

3. Endorsement—this is an agreement message and is the strongest type of confirming message. Often we don't agree with everything the person said, but we

*can usually find something in the message that we can endorse.*

*In addition, collaborators have dual concerns for themselves and for others, sometimes called an* integrative approach. *Essentially, persons using this style are "assertive and try to find new and creative solutions to problems by focusing both on their own needs and the needs of their partners" (Guerrero, Andersen, and Afifi 2001, 378).*

*In the following article, Joyce Hocker and William Wilmot address the critical topic of collaborative negotiation, a highly valuable approach to problem solving. The authors lay out the assumptions underlying this approach, describe the communication patterns and principles associated with this approach, and then note the difficulty of using it. As you read this chapter, think about your usual pattern for addressing conflicts and ask this question: What approaches are contained in this article that I can use to expand my repertoire of conflict management skills?*

### References

Cissna, K. N. L., and Sieberg, E. (1990). Patterns of interactional confirmation and disconfirmation. In J. Stewart (Ed.), *Bridges not Walls*, 5th ed. New York: McGraw-Hill.

Guerrero, L. K., Andersen, P. A., and Afifi, W. A. (2001). *Close Encounters*. Mountain View, CA: Mayfield Publishing.

Infante, D. A. (1988). *Arguing Constructively*. Prospect Heights, IL: Waveland Press.

\* \* \*

In competitive or distributive negotiations, it is assumed that what one person wins the other loses. Integrative or collaborative bargaining, on the other hand, assumes that the parties have both (1) *diverse interests* and (2) *common interests*, and that the negotiation process can result in both parties gaining something. Whereas the competitive model assumes that "someone loses and someone wins," collaborative negotiation assumes that creativity can be brought to bear to transcend the "win-lose" aspect of competitive negotiations.

The classic example, often repeated in a variety or forms, comes from Mary Parker Follett (1940), who coined the term "integrative." She illustrates an integrative solution to a conflict that at first appears to be competitive.

In the Harvard Library one day, in one of the smaller rooms, someone wanted the window open, I wanted it shut. We opened the window in the next room, where no one was sitting. This was not a compromise because there was no curtailing of desire; we both got what we really wanted. For I did not want a closed room, I simply did not want the north wind to blow directly on me; likewise the other occupant did not want the particular window open, he merely wanted more air in the room. (Follett 1940, 32)

Although she doesn't detail her bargaining process, clearly the result was integrative—it integrated the needs of both parties. Integrative or collaborative negotiations emphasize maximizing joint benefits for both parties, often in creative ways (Bazerman, Magliozzi, and Neale 1985). Such bargaining places value on the relationship between the conflict parties, requires trust, and relies on full disclosure of relevant information (Walker 1988).

Follett (1940) relates yet another story that provides insight into collaborative or integrative negotiations. Two sisters were fighting over an orange and after much acrimony, agreed to split the orange in half—a compromise. Thus, one sister could use her half of the orange for juice. The other sister took her half of the orange and used the peel for a cake. They overlooked the integrative or collaborative elements of negotiations. They each could have had a full orange since they wanted different parts! As Walton and McKersie note, integrative or collaborative negotiators can use negotiations as joint problem-solving, jointly devising solutions that solve problems for the mutual benefit of the parties (Walton and McKersie 1965). This process of joint improvement is called by some "problem solving" bargaining (Karrass 1970).

## Assumptions

Just as the competitive model for negotiations has basic assumptions, so does the integrative-collaborative-problem-solving style of negotiation. At base, it presumes the following:

- The negotiating world is controlled by enlightened self-interest.
- Common interest valued.
- Limited resources with unlimited variation in personal preferences.
- The resource distribution system is integrative in nature (joint).
- The goal: mutually agreeable solution that is fair to all parties and efficient for community. (Murray 1986)

As you can see, the collaborative approach has very different assumptions about the world. Rather than a "dog-eat-dog" view, it presumes that we can, even in the midst of conflict, work from "enlightened self-interest." We then get what we need from others but do it in such a way as to also help them achieve some of their goals. The collaborative bargainer is also interested in preserving the relationship with the other. Therefore, driving a bargain at the expense of the other is not seen as a victory—you maintain some interest in the other while holding out for your own goals. You assume that it isn't "win-lose" but that both of you can come away from the negotiations with an intact relationship willing to trust and work with one another in the next bargaining situation.

## Communication Patterns

The obvious next questions is, "How does one do collaborative negotiations?" The basic principles sound fine, but unless we can specify communication behaviors that can activate a collaborative negotiation set, the basic principles won't take us very far. The following list gives some hints as to communication behaviors that are associated with collaborative negotiations. The negotiator:

- Tries to maximize returns for own client inducing any joint gains available.
- Focuses on common interests of the parties.

- Tries to understand the merits as objectively as possible.
- Uses nonconfrontational debating techniques.
- Is open to persuasion on substance.
- Is oriented to qualitative goals; a fair/wise/durable agreement, efficiently negotiated. (Murray 1986)

. . . There are also some specific techniques that are worthy of note, all of which lead to collaborative outcomes. They are (1) expanding the pie, (2) nonspecific compensation, (3) logrolling, (4) cost cutting, and (5) bridging (Lewicki and Litterer 1985).

*Expanding the pie* builds collaborative outcomes because most conflicts are based on the perception of scarce resources and expanding the resources alters the structure of the conflict. For example, if Jane wants to go to the mountains and Sandy wants to go to the seashore, they might collaborate to find a mountainous seashore. While it won't be the perfect mountain and the shore may have some limitations, they do get to spend their vacations together—they have expanded the pie. Similarly, if there is a dispute over promotion, increasing the number and types of rewards may build a collaborative result. Often children squabble with one another because of the perception that there is not enough parental care and consideration to go around. Thus, they fight, say nasty things to one another, and struggle over the available love. As the parent, if you refuse to "parcel out" the love and attention, giving each child attention and focus without leaving out the other, you have expanded the pie. Whether the "pie" is actual or metaphorical, its expansion alters the conflict.

*Nonspecific compensation* is a process in which one of the parties is "paid off" with some other form of compensation. If two roommates are bargaining over use of the car, one may say, "OK, you can have the car, but I get to have the apartment for an all-night party after graduation." If the deal is sealed, the roommates have created a form of nonspecific compensation. One finds some dimension that is valued by the other and makes an offer to offset what is gained in the negotiations. Another example is the purchase of a house, and discovery that the owner is more interested in moving rapidly than in getting the stated purchase price. Your cousin owns a moving company, so you arrange to have the houseowner moved at no cost, your cousin charges you less than the going rate, and you get the house for less money than was originally asked.

*Logrolling* is similar to nonspecific compensation, only one offers to "trade off" issues that are the top priority for the other. The parties have to find multiple issues in the conflict (for example, time is of the essence to you, money to him). Then you arrange agreements so that each of you gets that top priority item while giving on the lower priority item. You "roll the log" and shuffle issues so the top priority issues come to the top of the pile. In an organization we worked with recently, the supervisor wanted more work from one particular employee. The employee wanted a "fairer" evaluation at the end of the year. With the help of an outsider, they negotiated so that (1) the evaluation process would be changed involving discussion before memos were sent and (2) the employee agreed to take on some extra work. Each got his main concern dealt with and gave on the item that was vitally important to the other.

*Cost cutting* minimizes the other's costs for going along with you. For example, you want to go skiing with your friend. She is overloaded with work, so you offer to ski only half a day and not let her incur the "cost" of missing all her work time. Or, alternatively, you are negotiating with your romantic partner about going on vacation. He is "tied up" and feels he can't just "take off" for so many days, yet you both want to vacation together. So, you offer to pay half his airfare, drive your car to the resort you wish to visit, and he flies to join you two days later. You shorten his total vacation time yet increase your total vacation time together.

*Bridging* invents new options to meet the other side's needs. You want to rent an apartment, but it is too expensive. You discover that your landlord is concerned about the appearance of the property. So you offer her a rent somewhat below what she wants but agree to do fifteen hours of "fix-it-work"

each month. She gets a nice house in good condition, and you get reduced rent. Everyone gains!

In collaborative negotiations, parties brainstorm to invent new and creative options to meet everyone's needs. For example, Sally is negotiating with her work partner. She is frustrated about the job not being done and Chuck is feeling that the work intrudes too much on his personal time. So, she offers to do more of the work on the spreadsheet if he will bring her coffee and sandwiches. Chuck gains more free time, Sally sees the project "moving ahead," and both of them contribute to the task while maintaining their working relationship.

Whatever specific technique or approach is used, the bargainers who employ collaborative approaches see the items as more complex; thus they find more creative ways to "package" the agreements and invent new options (Raiffa 1982). The collaborator moves from "fighting" to "conferring" (Follett 1940), assuming that working with the other will bring joint benefit. Information serves as "fact-finding" material for the bargainers rather than as a "wedge" to drive against the other. With the information, one problem solves, explores causes, and generates alternative solutions (Lewicki and Litterer 1985).

One of the most complete approaches to collaborative negotiations comes from Fisher and Ury (1981). Their four principles can be remembered by the key words: *people*, *interests*, *options*, and *criteria*. Fisher and Ury term this process "negotiation on merits" or "principled negotiation."

(1) *People: Separate the People from the Problem.* The participants should come to see themselves working side by side on a problem, attacking the problem instead of each other. The overarching process goal is "We, working together, can solve this problem that is confronting us." Part of the self-interest of conflict parties is preserving a workable relationship; focusing on the problem instead of the other people assists in relational maintenance. The problem is faced as one would face an enemy, working cooperatively with one's conflict partner to solve the problem. An example would be a divorcing couple who, instead of asking, "Why are

you causing me difficulties?" would ask "What can we, working together, create that will be in the best interest of the children?"

In collaborative negotiations, relational preservation becomes a *superordinate goal* (Sherif and Sherif 1956). In the classic description of "superordinate goals" groups of boys at camp were placed in situations with conflict of interests. The researchers introduced a common enemy, thus stimulating the two groups to work together, which reduced their intergroup hostility. For persons in interpersonal conflicts, long-term relational or content goals can become superordinate goals that reduce conflict over short-term goals, but only if you separate the people from the problem.

(2) *Interests: Focus on Interests, Not Positions*. At the Harvard Negotiations Project, researchers found that when people stated their goals in terms of positions that had to be defended, they were less able to produce wise agreements. The more you clarify your position and defend yourself, the more committed you become to the position. Arguing over positions endangers ongoing relationships, since the conflict often becomes a contest of wills. They found that "Whether a negotiation concerns a contract, a family quarrel, or a peace settlement among nations, people routinely engage in positional bargaining. Each side takes a position, argues for it, and makes concessions to reach a compromise" (Fisher and Ury 1981, 3).

Focusing on interests, not positions, was what the parties in the library did in the earlier example cited in this [article]. Rather than starting with "Do you want the window closed or open?" (a position), each party searched for their own underlying interest. Interests underlie the positions, and many possible positions can be derived from one's interests. But a position is a specific solution to an interest; if you start with the position, you will overlook many creative options for meeting the interest. Interests are more diffuse than positions and sometimes are difficult to identify, but they keep the process of collaboration in motion when you focus on them.

(3) *Options: Generate a Variety of Possibilities Before Deciding What to Do*. Trying to

resolve a conflict in the face of an adversary narrows one's vision. Pressure reduces creative thinking at the very time when creativity is most needed. Searching for the one right solution may be futile. You can get around this problem by setting up time to focus on a new solution instead of defending your prospective goals endlessly. Goal setting continues throughout the period of active conflict management, and afterward as well. A good decision is one that springs from the many options generated from concerned conflict parties.

(4) *Criteria: Insist That the Result Be Based on Some Objective Standard*. One person's will is not enough to justify a conflict solution. Some principle of fairness or judgment should be used. One can develop objective criteria by using fair procedures and/or fair standards. Fair procedures can be used in many cases. In the classic situation of two people dividing a piece of cherry pie, one gets to cut the piece and then the other gets first choice; the procedures guarantee fairness. Or in the case of a marital couple in a divorce mediation, they can decide on the specifics of custody, visitation, and child support before they decide which party will have custody.

Fair standards can be based on the following:

| | |
|---|---|
| market value | costs |
| precedent | what a court would decide |
| scientific judgment | moral standards |
| professional standards | equal treatment |
| efficiency | reciprocity |

(Fisher and Ury 1981, p. 89)

A private individual may effectively use the four principles of collaboration. They may be informally adopted and used even in one-on-one conflicts that arise. The following are some statements that you might use when you are in conflict and are talking about your perceptions of incompatible goals.

From the standpoint of a competitive approach, one can be assumed to be "weak" if one "gives in" to the superior strength and force of one's opponent. Interestingly, the col-

| Collaborative Principle | Sample Statement |
|---|---|
| People | "This is a problem you and I haven't had to face before. I'm sure we can work it out." |
| Interests | "What is it that you are most hoping for?" |
| | or |
| | "Let's figure out where we agree, and that will give us a base to work from." |
| Options | "I'd like to postpone making a decision about filing a grievance until our next meeting. Today I want to explore all the options that are available to us in addition to filing a grievance. Is that all right with you?" |
| Criteria | "I can't be satisfied with getting my way if you're miserable. Let's get an example of the car's current value from an objective source." |

laborative bargainer can be just as "tough" as the competitive bargainer. However, you *get tough about different aspects*. You remain firm about your goals, but flexible regarding how to accomplish them—doing what Pruitt calls *firm flexibility* (Pruitt 1983). You work with the other party, but you don't capitulate; your goals are always firm in your mind but the means you use are flexible and adapted to the other person's needs as well. As Follett (1940, 48) noted, "Mushy people are no more good at this than stubborn people."

## The Downside

As with competitive tactics, collaborative approaches have some disadvantages. Probably the biggest overall difficulty is that they may require "a high order of intelligence, keen perception and discrimination, more than all a brilliant inventiveness" (Follett 1940, 45). Without specific training, or having seen collaboration modeled in the home or on the job, collaboration may require specific training. For the beginning bargainer (whether an attorney, spouse, friend, or coworker) unless one has some level of training, the usual approach is to equate "good" bargaining with competitive tactics.

Murray (1986) has provided a comprehensive listing of some downside risks from collaborative problem-solving, integrative bargaining approaches:

- Strongly biased toward cooperation, creating internal pressures to compromise and accommodate.
- Avoids strategies that are confrontational because they risk impasse, which is viewed as failure.
- Focuses on being sensitive to other's perceived interests; increases vulnerability to deception and manipulation by a competitive opponent; and increases possibility that settlement may be more favorable to other side than fairness would warrant.
- Increases difficulty of establishing definite aspiration levels and bottom lines because of reliance on qualitative (value-laden) goals.
- Requires substantial skill and knowledge of process to do well.
- Requires strong confidence in own assessment powers (perception) regarding interests/needs of other side and other's payoff schedule. (Murray 1986, 184)

Collaborative negotiations, then, are not a panacea to be used in every conflict. They require considerable skill on the part of the negotiator who strives to keep the negotiations from disintegrating into a win-lose approach.

Specific communication phrases that a collaborative negotiator utters are:

"I know this is difficult, but we can work it out."

"I can understand why you want to 'split the difference,' but let's try for some creative alternatives."

"I certainly appreciate your stance. Let's talk also about what I need to be satisfied."

"Your threat tells me how important this issue is to you, but it will work better with me not to threaten. Can we back this up and come at it another way?"

"I don't see any conflict between us both getting more of what we want, but up until now we are acting as if what we each get the other loses."

"I really do want a fair and durable settlement for both of us. That requires, of course, more direct information about what we each want. Let's explore that awhile."

"I will discuss with you as long as it takes to reach a settlement that will work for both of us."

"Yes, I see that you think that is the best solution. Remember, however, that there are two of us here. Let's see if both of us can be satisfied with the outcome."

Most people approach negotiating from a competitive frame of mind—assuming both sides have to lose part of the pie. The competitive or collaborative approaches are more a function of the bargainers than of any other factors. In fact, you can be in a negotiation where one person takes a cooperative and the other a competitive stance—a cooperative negotiation (Walker 1988). If you take a competitive approach, whether you are negotiating about how to spend the evening with a friend or buying a house, the negotiation process will probably be a competitive, win-lose experience. On the other hand, if you stick firmly to a collaborative approach, you will find creative options that someone with a competitive approach simply would not find. Creative options often become available (Follett 1940), but unless the negotiators believe it possible and do the hard work to jointly produce those options, the negotiations will begin and end on a win-lose footing. Having had experience negotiating and serving as third party interveners, we are always amazed at how many creative, jointly satisfying options can occur and how difficult they remain for the parties to initially see.

## References

Bazerman, M. H., Magliozzi, T., and Neale, M. A. (1985). Integrative bargaining in a competitive market. *Organizational Behavior and Human Decision Processes*, 35, 294–313.

Carnevale, P. J. D. and Lawler, E. J. (1986). Time pressure and the development of integrative agreements in bilateral negotiations. *Journal of Conflict Resolution*, 30, 636–659.

Fisher, R. and Ury, W. (1981). *Getting to yes: Negotiating agreement without giving in.* Boston, MA: Houghton Mifflin, Co.

Fogg, R. W. (1985). Dealing with conflict: Repertoire of creative, peaceful approaches. *Journal of Conflict Resolution*, 29, 330–358.

Folger, J. P. and Poole, M. S. (1984). *Working through conflict: A communication perspective.* Glenview, IL: Scott, Foresman and Co.

Follett, M. P. (1940). *Dynamic administration: The collected papers of M. P. Follett.* H. C. Metcalf and L. Urwick (Eds.). New York: Harper and Brothers, Publishers.

Gulliver, P. H. (1979). *Disputes and negotiations: A cross-cultural perspective.* New York: Academic Press.

Jones, T. S. (1988). Phase structures in agreement and no-agreement mediation. *Communication Research*, 15, 470–495.

Karrass, C. (1970). *The negotiating game.* New York: Thomas Y. Crowell.

Lewicki, R. J. and Litterer, J. A. (1985). *Negotiation.* Homewood, IL: Irwin.

Murray, J. A. (April 1976). Understanding competing theories of negotiation. *Negotiation Journal*, 2, 179–186.

———. Understanding competing theories of negotiation. *Negotiation Journal* 2 (April: 179–186).

Pace, R. C. (1988). Communication patterns in high and low consensus discussions: A descriptive analysis. *The Southern Speech Communication Journal*, 53, 184–202.

Popple, P. R. (1984). Negotiation: A critical skill for social work administrators. *Administration in Social Work*, 8, 1–11.

Pruitt, D. G. (1983). Achieving integrative agreements. In M. H. Bazerman and R. Lewicki (Eds.), *Negotiating in organizations.* Beverly Hills, CA: Sage.

Putnam, L. L. (October 21, 1986). Negotiation of intergroup conflict in organizations. A lecture delivered at Baylor University, Waco, TX.

———. (Spring 1988). Reframing integrative and distributive bargaining: A process perspective. Revised manuscript, Purdue University.

Putnam, L. L, Wilson, S. R., Walman, M. S. and Turner, D. (1986). The evolution of case arguments in teachers' bargaining. *Journal of the American Forensic Association*, 23, 63–81.

Raiffa, H. (1982). *The art and science of negotiation*. Cambridge, MA: Belknap Press of Harvard University Press.

Sherif, M. and Sherif, C. W. (1956). *An outline of social psychology*, rev. ed. New York: Harper and Brothers.

Tutzauer, F. and Roloff, M. E. (1988). Communication processes leading to integrative agreements: Three paths to joint benefits. *Communication Research*, 15, 360–380.

Walker, G. B. (1988). Bacharach and Lawler's theory of argument in bargaining: A critique. *Journal of the American Forensic Association*, 24, 218–232.

Wall, J. A. (1985). *Negotiation: Theory and practice*. Glenview, IL: Scott, Foresman and Co.

Walton, R. E. and McKersie, R. B. (1965). *A behavioral theory of labor negotiations: An analysis of a social system*. New York: McGraw-Hill.

## Questions

1. Reconstruct a recent disagreement you had with a close friend. Write down as completely as possible who said what in what sequence. Analyze the conflict using Hocker and Wilmot's ideas. To what extent did you use collaborative negotiation? Which of these strategies did you use, or might you have used?

2. Transcribe an argument from a movie with which you are familiar. Analyze the strategies used by the participants. Prepare a list of suggestions you would make to them in order to develop a more collaborative style.

3. Identify someone you believe demonstrates good communication skills. Carefully listen to that person engage in a problem-solving discussion. What communication principles or skills did he or she employ to help solve the problem?

# 24

# I Can't Talk About It Now

*Julia T. Wood*

**W**hen friends, colleagues, or partners reflect different styles of relational conflict, tension rises the minute a tough subject must be discussed or one party acts a certain way. Many people are raised to believe that conflict should be avoided; however, researchers suggest that conflict in relationships is not only unavoidable but also necessary to effective relationships. For example, Knapp and Vangelisti (2005) suggest that conflict can produce a greater understanding of the two parties and their relationship, clarify the similarities and differences between them, help the two learn better methods for handling future conflict, and reveal areas in which communication can be strengthened. In his classic book, Getting Together: Building Relationships As We Negotiate, *Fisher (1988) suggests that it is how people negotiate conflict that determines whether the conflict will be beneficial or destructive to the relationship.*

*Frequently, males and females are socialized differently toward conflict. Boys may be encouraged to be expressive, aggressive, and active in their responses, girls may learn to be gentle, indirect, and adaptive. Recent research with adult males and females reveals physiological differences in response to conflict. Women are likely to experience more negative physiological changes as a result of negative conflict interactions than men (Jones, Beach, and Jackson 2004). Marital disagreements are associated with women's higher blood pressure and heart rates (Kiecolt-Glaser and Newton 2001) due to the effects of conflict.*

*In the following article, Julia Wood presents a model of conflict response and relates this model to gender differences in conflict response. She presents an example of a difficult discussion in which romantic partners use very different conflict management styles.*

*This is followed by an overview of varied responses to conflict, a consideration of the influence of gender, and suggestions for improving communication.*

*As you read this article, think about the differences discussed between how men and women handle conflict. Consider this question: To what extent does my experience confirm or deny the significance of gender in the development of conflict styles?*

## References

Fisher, R. (1988). *Getting Together: Building Relationships As We Negotiate*. New York: Penguin.

Jones, D. J., Beach, S. R. H., and Jackson, H. (2004). Family influences on health: A framework to organize research and guide intervention. In A. Vangelisti (Ed.), *Handbook of Family Communication* (pp. 647–672). Mahwah, NJ: Lawrence Erlbaum Associates.

Kiecolt-Glaser, J. K., and Newton, T. L. (2001). Marriage and health: His and hers. *Psychological Bulletin*, 127, 472–503.

Knapp, M., and Vangelisti, A. (2005). *Interpersonal Communication and Human Relationships*, 6th ed. Boston: Allyn & Bacon.

\* \* \*

**T**akisha and William are locked into a tense discussion, the latest in a series of arguments about whether they will move to Minnesota. Takisha has been offered the job of her dreams: vice president of a training and development firm located in Minneapolis. William has never lived outside of Virginia, and he has no desire to do so now.

"This job is an excellent opportunity for me," Takisha says, repeating what she has told William before. "Can't you understand that?"

"I see that, but it's not an opportunity for me, and you don't see that," William replies. "You have a good job here. We both do. Why can't you let well enough alone?"

"Because it isn't good enough when I have such a big chance to advance."

"It is good enough, good enough for me, anyway!"

"But you can be a network technician anywhere. Your career doesn't depend on being here, so a move wouldn't damage your career. I can't go any farther in my job here. I can only advance if we move to Minneapolis. Not moving would damage my career."

"You have a fine career here. Why can't you just be satisfied and leave well enough alone?"

"You're not being reasonable."

"I am being reasonable. But life is about more than jobs. We can't live anywhere. This is our home." William paces as he speaks. "We don't belong in Minnesota."

"William, I know you're comfortable here. I know you love Virginia," Takisha says. "I can understand that. But can't you at least try living somewhere else? You might find you like it."

"I wouldn't like it. I don't need to try living there to know I won't like it. I hate snow and cold weather, and I don't like the hassles of a big city."

"So you're saying that a place means more to you than I do?" she demands.

"You said that, I didn't."

"That's the only conclusion I can draw if you refuse to move, knowing what it means to me." She moves closer to him. "Please work with me to make this happen."

"Stop trying to control me," he barks. "You're not going to roll over me just to get what you want."

"I'm not trying to roll over you. I'm trying to figure out how to come to some decision that works for both of us."

"I plan to stay here, with or without you." He clamps his jaw firmly and stares ahead at the wall.

"Sweetheart, you can't mean that," she says softly. "We can work this out if we really try."

William moves away and cradles his head in his hands. He doesn't speak.

"Don't go silent on me, William," she says. "The only way we can work this out is to keep talking."

"I'm talked out," he mumbles.

"But we haven't resolved the issue," she insists. "We have to keep talking until we work it out."

He shakes his head and doesn't speak.

"William, what would it take to persuade you to move to Minneapolis?" she asks.

"What would make the move comfortable for you?"

"Nothing, I don't want to move." His voice is tense and tired.

"Well, that's not good enough. Come on, talk to me about what would make this move good for you."

"Nothing. I don't want to move period."

"Please don't be so inflexible," she asks. "There have to be ways we can work out something that suits both of us. How about an experiment? We'll move to Minnesota and commit to staying there for one year. At the end of that time, if you're not happy, we can reassess our options. How does that sound?"

"Just let me be," he says, moving across the room.

"How can I do that when we aren't through with this discussion?"

"We are through. I'm talked out," he says, his voice strained and his jaw muscles flexing tensely.

"William, not talking doesn't solve anything," she insists. "Please talk to me?"

"I can't talk about this now," he thunders and stomps to the door, opens it, walks out, and slams it behind him.

What is Takisha to think when William walks out on her and the argument? Often people in Takisha's position think the other person is refusing to deal with the conflict. They feel that the other person (William in this case) doesn't care enough about the relationship to work through problems. Takisha may feel that when William stomps out he is dismissing the importance of her career and is disrespecting their relationship.

But Takisha's feelings are only half the picture. What is William feeling? He may feel pressured by Takisha's demands for talk. He may feel she is trying to control him by manipulating him to do what she wants. He may not share Takisha's view that she's inviting him to collaborate. Also, he may not be comfortable talking about deep feelings, such as his attachment to Virginia and his anxiety about moving to an unfamiliar place.

Why does he walk out instead of working with Takisha to resolve the issue? Takisha perceives his departure as a sign that he doesn't care about her or the issue, but that may not be what leaving means to William.

Perhaps he leaves because he cares so strongly about Takisha and the relationship that the discord between them is tearing him up. Perhaps he feels so strongly about not moving he is afraid he'll become belligerent, or even violent, if he doesn't leave. Perhaps he sees leaving as the only way to avoid letting the conflict degenerate into open warfare. Perhaps he sees nothing to be gained by staying and talking more because he doesn't know what else to say.

If Takisha understands how William perceives conflict, she might realize that his leaving is not a sign that he doesn't care about her career or their relationship. If William figures out that Takisha sees talking as a way to make them closer, maybe he will feel less pressured by her requests to talk. And perhaps if each of them learns that people have different ways of responding to conflict, they can better understand how each views conflict and why they both respond as they do.

## Understanding the Misunderstanding

Psychologist Caryl Rusbult and her colleagues have studied how people respond to interpersonal conflict. Rusbult's work shows four basic responses to conflict. These are habitual responses that we learned at some point and now repeat without much thought or contemplation of alternative ways we might respond when tension surfaces in relationships.

### The Exit-Voice–Loyalty-Neglect Model

Rusbult graphs responses to conflict in terms of whether they are active (assertive) or passive (yielding) and whether they affect relationships in ways that are constructive (preserve the possibility of continuing the union) or destructive (undermine the relationship and its future).

The exit response is to leave an argument or even end a relationship when conflict arises. William relied on the exit response when he stomped out on the conversation with Takisha. Another version of the exit response is what marriage counselor John Gottman calls "stonewalling." The person who stonewalls refuses to discuss problems and conflicts. The stonewaller may stick around, but he or she will not talk about problems. Exit, then, may be physical or psychological; either way, the person who exits ceases to be involved in the conflict. Exit is an active response because it is forceful. Because it doesn't allow people to resolve differences, however, it can damage relationships.

The neglect response occurs when a person denies or minimizes problems. When presented with a problem, the neglecter may say, "You're blowing this all out of proportion." William used the neglect response when he told Takisha that her career advancement was less important than other things in life. Neglecters often gloss over tensions and conflicts rather than deal with them. Because neglect is not forceful, Rusbult labels it passive. Because it doesn't address problems fully and with respect for each person's feelings, neglect can be destructive for relationships.

Loyalty responses involve quietly staying loyal to a partner and a relationship. Someone who uses this response may silently hope things will get better. Alternatively, she or he may think, "It could be worse" or "This doesn't matter a whole lot in the big picture." Loyalty may also be expressed by transferring anger or blame from the other person to oneself: "I should have known better." "I expect too much." Because loyalty doesn't assertively engage problems, it is passive. Because it assumes a relationship is worth continuing, it can have a constructive impact on relationships and people's feelings for each other.

The fourth response is voice, which is an active way to manage conflict. The voice response engages the conflict and invites the other person to collaborate in resolving it. "Let's talk about our problem" is a voice response. "I want to work this out with you" and "I'm willing to discuss the issue" are also voice responses. Because voice actively works to resolve problems, Rusbult considers it constructive for relationships.

In the example that opened this chapter, William used the neglect and exit responses, and Takisha relied on voice. According to Rusbult, their responses are typical of their respective sexes. Her research shows that men are more likely than women to respond with neglect or exit. Women, on the other hand, are more likely than men to choose voice and loyalty when conflict arises.

## The Influence of Gender

Some scholars think the different response tendencies of women and men reflect gender socialization. Psychologist Carol Gilligan maintains that women are socialized to value relationships and to use talk as a way of maintaining them. Masculine socialization typically places less emphasis on talk. As a result, many men have little or no training in how to talk about problems, especially problems that involve strong feelings. They may also feel frustrated if they can't fix a problem. Masculine socialization encourages men to fix things, to engage in instrumental activities that solve problems. If men feel they cannot do this when conflict erupts, they may communicate that the problem is unimportant or they may walk out on discussion or even the relationship.

Anne Campbell has studied links between aggression and gender. She reports that boys and girls typically are taught different meanings for conflict. She explains that girls are most often taught to respond to conflicts by talking (voice) and turning anger and disappointment inward (loyalty). Masculine socialization is more likely to encourage aggressive responses to conflict—asserting dominance to maintain control and self-esteem. Many boys are taught not to harm girls, however, so they may not feel able to respond aggressively in conflicts with women. It's not surprising, then, that men might choose to minimize conflicts (neglect) or leave when arguments erupt (exit) rather than risk losing control or acting aggressively toward women.

Further insight into the link between gender and responses to conflict comes from psychologist Eleanor Maccoby, who has studied socialization patterns typically experienced by girls and boys. Maccoby informs us that, at early ages, many boys are taught to derail tense interaction by threatening, inhibiting, contradicting, or topping a partner. William contradicted several of Takisha's statements and he issued a veiled threat to break up their relationship if she insisted on moving. He also showed little empathy with Takisha's feelings and desires. When these measures don't work, boys (and later the men they become) may feel they can't get control, so they exit rather than suffer outright defeat.

Girls, more often than boys, are taught to enable others in conversation. Typically, they learn to try to understand what others need and feel and to support others, even while disagreeing with them. Takisha expressed understanding of William's love of Virginia and his reluctance to move, and she tried to get him to talk with her about what he would need to be comfortable moving to Minneapolis.

John Gottman adds to our understanding of differences in how women and men typically respond to conflict. He maintains that men and women have different physiological reactions to tension and confrontation. During such times, men's blood pressure rises more quickly and stays elevated for longer periods of time than does women's. In other words, many men have a more intense physiological response to conflict than do women. Thus, it may cost [men] more than women to engage in conflict.

Working with his colleague Sybil Carrere, Gottman studied men and women in marriages in which they were in conflict about responsibilities for homemaking and child care.... Husbands often felt flooded by their wives' complaints. The men felt overwhelmed by criticisms and complaints. They felt psychologically and physiologically deluged and this disabled them from responding constructively. The women were less likely to feel flooded when they encountered negative emotions and criticism, and were more likely to feel that they could continue dealing with conflict.

Why do men and women differ so often in initiating and responding to discussions of problems? Carol Tavris, a social psychologist, suggests that women are expected by others and themselves to be "relationship experts," so it is their job to notice problems and to work to address and resolve them. Girls and later women, says Tavris, have the role of identifying and bringing up problems in relationships.

In childhood socialization, many girls learn how to talk about interpersonal tensions. Because they have experience in working through problems, dealing with conflict tends to be less uncomfortable for them psychologically and physiologically than it is for many men.

Psychologist Sharon Brehm extends Tavris's analysis by suggesting that women's socialization tends to make them sensitive to and aware of existing and potential problems in relationships. They may also see as problems events or conditions that men do not perceive or consider significant. In other words, women may feel a need to address issues that men don't perceive as difficulties, disappointments, and failed expectations. Brehm suggests that this difference may reflect women's higher expectations of relationships.

My own research confirms what we've discussed in this chapter. Several years ago I asked heterosexual women and men to describe how they responded to crises in their relationships. Although there weren't differences in the issues men and women cited as precipitating crises, there were clear differences in how they responded to the events. Men were more likely to deny that any difficulty existed (neglect) or to walk out (exit) when an acute problem erupted. Women consistently gave priority to voice as a means of responding to these extreme difficulties. If voice failed, many of the women in my study relied on loyalty—quiet allegiance to the relationship despite its problems.

I later replicated my study with lesbians and gay men. Again, I found that men tended to respond to crises by neglecting problems and especially by walking out of relationships. Again, the women gave priority to talking about problems, to working collaboratively to resolve issues or at least to understand each other. Caryl Rusbult and her colleagues confirm my findings by reporting that gender is more important than sexual orientation in shaping people's responses to conflict in relationships.

## Improving Communication

The first step in dealing effectively with conflicts is to understand that people differ in how they view and respond to problems, tensions, and crisis. Someone who doesn't know how to talk about feelings and fears may not see voice as a useful or helpful response to conflict. A person who experiences substantial physiological discomfort when relationship tension arises may be less willing to engage in conflict than someone who is less physiologically taxed by it. A person who has been socialized to believe people should talk through differences may regard exit as a dismissive and counterproductive response to problems. On the other hand, someone who doesn't feel comfortable talking about problems may regard exit as a reasonable response to conflict.

### Try to Understand Different Views of Conflict

William and Takisha might improve their communication if they realize they don't see conflict in the same way. To her, it's a call to engage, talk, and resolve problems. To him, it's a contest for control and he doesn't want to lose. In other words, they have different constitutive rules for what conflict is, or what it counts as.

The relationship would benefit if William understood that Takisha isn't trying to control him; that's not what arguments are about for her. The relationship would also be helped if Takisha understood that William feels pressured by her needs and her demands for talk and that he views conflict as a competition for power.

People who have different individual ways of responding to conflict can develop a variety of strategies for talking about tense topics without harming their relationships. I know of one couple much like William and Takisha. Like the men in John Gottman's studies, the man in this couple felt emotionally flooded when his wife brought up problems or complaints. He felt that she was trying to control him, to remake him into a person different from who he was. Early in their marriage, he would deny or minimize conflicts or he would stonewall. His wife relied on voice and was hurt continuously when he wouldn't talk with her. She interpreted his behavior as expressing a lack of caring about her and problems in their relationship.

When the couple's efforts to resolve their differences were unsuccessful, they sought therapy. After several months of counseling, each one began to understand how the other viewed conflict and why each of them responded in particular ways when tension arose in their relationship. Now when he feels emotionally flooded and unable to respond, he doesn't just leave. Instead, he says, "I can't talk about it now, but I promise I will later when I've thought it through." This signals his wife that he does care about the issues and will discuss them—but later, after he's calmed down and regained the sense of control he needs. His response gives her the assurance she needs that he will collaborate with her to resolve the problem. It also gives him the time and space he needs to regain his emotional equilibrium.

## Evaluate Your Responses to Conflict

Because our responses to conflict tend to be habituated, we seldom reflect on them. If we think about our ways of dealing with conflict, however, we may discover that they don't always serve us well. Realizing this provides us with an incentive to change how we act and what consequences follow.

An acquaintance of mine realized she was hurting herself and her relationship by not giving voice to her dissatisfactions and frustrations. As she explained to me, "They don't go away. They fester in me." She relied on the loyalty response virtually any time she encountered conflict with friends or romantic partners. Because that response did not enhance her self-esteem or her relationships, she worked to learn to voice her concerns assertively but not aggressively. She now feels that her relationships are more honest and healthy and she has greater self-respect.

## Enlarge Your Response Repertoire

Another way to improve communication during conflict is to broaden your ways of responding to relationship tensions. Most of us have one or two habitual ways of reacting when problems erupt—behaviors for dealing with interpersonal tension that are almost automatic. Some of us consistently respond by trying to talk about the problems; others of us unfailingly react by refusing to discuss the issues or even by walking out on relationships.

Yet habitual ways of reacting to conflict are neither permanent nor absolute, and they may not be the most constructive ways for us to use. With commitment and patience, we can change our usual patterns of dealing with relationship tensions. Takisha might adopt the loyalty response so that William has some time to mull over issues before talking about them. William could commit to talking about his feelings about the move, difficult as that would be for him. The point is that we can choose to move out of the restrictive framework of our habitual responses to conflict. Doing so allows us to communicate in ways that are effective in a range of situations that invite diverse modes of response.

We don't change our habituated responses to conflict easily or immediately. To do so, we must make firm commitments to changing and we must develop patience. The first requirement for change is a serious commitment to learning new ways of viewing and responding to conflict. Unless you really want to change, you can't. You may find the motivation to do so, however, if you realize that your habitual ways of responding to conflict are not serving you or your relationships well.

The second requirement for change is patience. We need to be patient with ourselves and our partners. It's much more realistic to realize that the more we try a new style, the more comfortable and skillful we will be in using it. We also need to be patient with our partners. Like us, they have habituated responses to conflict and to our ways of dealing with it. When we change our approach to conflict, they may not immediately change how they respond to us. Given time and consistent effort to become proficient in new response styles, our partners and we will change the way we communicate about difficult issues.

Conflicts are part of relationships and human interaction. They're inevitable and they can be productive for us as individuals and for our relationships. Their productivity, however, depends on two conditions. First, we should recognize and respect different ways of responding to conflicts. Second, we should reflect on our own responses to conflicts and ask whether they are effective, honest, and respectful of ourselves and others. If not, we have the freedom to choose to become proficient in other modes of responding. We can change how we act and, if we do, we will influence changes in our partners and the relationships we collaboratively create and inhabit.

## References

Brehm, S. (1992). *Intimate relationships*. New York: McGraw-Hill.

Campbell, A. (1993). *Men, women, and aggression*. New York: Basic Books.

Crouter, A. and Helms-Erikson, H. (1997). Work and family from a dyadic perspective: Variations in equality. In S. Duck (Ed.), *Handbook of personal relationships* (2nd ed., pp. 487–503). West Sussex, England: Wiley.

Gilligan, C. (1982). *In a different voice: Psychological theory and women's development*. Cambridge: Harvard University Press.

Gottman, J. (1979). *Marital interaction*. New York: Academic Press.

Gottman, J. and Carrere, S. (1994). Why can't men and women get along? Developmental roots and marital inequities. In D. Canary and L. Stafford (Eds.), *Communication and relational maintenance* (pp. 203–229). San Diego, CA: Academic Press.

Gottman, J. and Levenson, R. W. (1986). Assessing the role of emotion in marriage. *Behavioral Assessment*, 8, 31–48.

Gottman, J., Markman, H., and Notarius, C. (1977). The topography of marital conflict: A sequential analysis of verbal and nonverbal behavior. *Journal of Marriage and the Family*, 39, 461–477.

Heavy, C., Layne, C., and Christensen, A. (1993). Gender and conflict structure in marital interaction: A replication and extension. *Journal of Consulting and Clinical Psychology*, 61, 16–27.

Jones, E. and Gallois, C. (1989). Spouses' impressions of rules for communication in public and private marital conflicts. *Journal of Marriage and the Family*, 51, 957–967.

Klein, R. and Johnson, M. P. (1997). Strategies of couple conflict. In S. Duck (Ed.), *Handbook of personal relationships* (2nd ed., pp. 469–486). West Sussex, England: Wiley.

Maccoby, E. (1990). Gender and relationships: A development account. *American Psychologist*, 45, 513–520.

Rusbult, C. (1987). Responses to dissatisfaction in close relationships: The exit-voice-loyalty-neglect model. In D. Perlman and S. Duck (Eds.), *Intimate relationships: Development, dynamics, and deterioration* (pp. 209–238). London: Sage.

Rusbult, C., Zembrodt, I., and Iwaniszek, J. (1986). The impact of gender and sex-role orientation on responses to dissatisfaction in close relationships. *Sex Roles*, 15, 1–20.

Tavris, C. (1992). *The mismeasure of woman: Why women are not the better sex, the inferior sex, or the opposite sex*. New York: Simon and Schuster.

Wood, J. T. (1986). Different voices in relationship crises: Contrasting reasons, responses, and relational orientations. In J. Ringer (Ed.), *Queer words, queer images: The (re)construction of homosexuality* (pp. 238–264). Albany: New York University Press.

## Questions

1. Using Rusbult's model, which response to conflict do you usually use? After reading Wood's article, do you want to change this response? Why or why not?

2. How does your gender affect your response to conflict? Give a specific example.

3. Watch a film in which romantically paired males and females have ongoing conflicts. To what extent did their chosen styles reflect the gender patterns noted in the article?

---

# 25
# Who's Responsible for What?

*Harriet G. Lerner*

The age-old question "Whose problem is it?" has been used to help individuals consider if and how they should respond to situations that raise their stress levels or engage them in disagreements. Frequently this question leads them to consider areas of differences between parties and to decide whether a problem belongs to another individual or to themselves and whether a problem belongs to the relationship. In the following piece, psychologist Harriet Lerner addresses the issue of "Who is responsible for what?" She published this in a book targeted for female readers, but the question can be asked by either gender profitably. Lerner challenges her readers to take more responsibility for themselves, and less responsibility for the thoughts, feelings, and behaviors of others, when making sense out of problem situations. This excerpt successfully depicts how people blame others for their own behavior or feelings. How often have you said, "She made me mad," or, "It's his fault I was so upset"?

In the following article, Lerner presents a sample argument and analyzes it according to possible points that each person might make while blaming the other. She suggests that when a person is angry with another, a typical response is to try to decide who is to blame, who is at fault for the problem. This anger can often lead to defensiveness on the part of both relational partners. This means you either define the problem as your own, accepting the responsibility to solve it, or you define the problem as the other person's, giving him or her responsibility to solve it. However, since relationships exist between people, both approaches are unrealistic.

Did you grow up believing you had to "win" each disagreement, or did you think you always had to give in or fix things? Sometimes one partner acts as if she or he must be in control at all times; the other may learn to underfunction or give up a strong sense of self. Eventually such positions harden into an unhealthy, predictable pattern for addressing differences or conflicts. Communication patterns for managing anger and conflict can change, but only with careful and conscious efforts to address the issues and the relational patterns clearly and directly. As you read this piece, consider this question: Under what conflict conditions am I likely to lay the blame on another person, and under what conditions do I tend to assume the blame?

* * *

While attending a conference in New York one spring, I rode by bus to the Metropolitan Museum with two colleagues. I had lost my old familiarity with the city, and my companions, Celia and Janet, felt like foreigners in a strange land. Perhaps as a result of our "big-city" anxiety, we reminded the bus driver—once too often—to announce our stop. In a sudden and unexpected fury, he launched into a vitriolic attack that turned heads throughout the crowded bus. The three of us stood in stunned silence.

Later, over coffee, we shared our personal reactions to this incident. Celia felt mildly depressed. She was reminded of her abusive ex-husband and this particular week was the anniversary of their divorce. Janet reacted with anger, which seemed to dissipate as she drummed up clever retorts to the driver's outburst and hilarious revenge fantasies. My own reaction was nostalgia. I had been feeling homesick for New York and almost welcomed the contrast to the midwestern politeness to which I had become accustomed. It was a New York City "happening" that I could take back to Topeka, Kansas.

Suppose we reflect briefly on this incident. We might all agree that the bus driver behaved badly. But is he also responsible for the reactions of three women? Did he cause Celia's depression and Janet's anger? Did he make me feel nostalgic for my past? And if one of us had reacted to this man's surliness by jumping off the Brooklyn Bridge that night, should he be held accountable for a death? Or, viewed from another perspective, were we responsible for his outburst to begin with?

It is tempting to view human transactions in simple cause-and-effect terms. If we are angry, someone else caused it. Or, if we are the target of someone else's anger, we must be to blame; or, alternately—if we are convinced of our innocence—we may conclude that the other person has no right to feel angry. The more our relationships in our first family are fused (meaning the togetherness force is so powerful that there is a loss of the separate "I's" within the "we"), the more we learn to take responsibility for other people's feelings and reactions and blame them for our own. ("You always make Mom feel guilty." "You give Dad headaches." "She caused her husband to drink.") Likewise, family members assume responsibility for causing other people's thoughts, feelings, and behavior.

Human relationships, however, don't work that way—or at least not very well. We begin to use our anger as a vehicle for change when we are able to share our reactions without holding the other person responsible for causing our feelings, and without blaming ourselves for the reactions that other people have in response to our choices and actions. We are responsible for our own behavior. But we are not responsible for other people's reactions; nor are they responsible for ours. Women often learn to reverse this order of things: We put our energy into taking responsibility for other people's feelings, thoughts, and behavior and hand over to others responsibility for our own. When this happens, it becomes difficult, if not impossible, for the old rules of a relationship to change.

To illustrate the point, let's [turn] to Katy's problem with her widowed father, whom she initially described as excessively demanding and guilt-inducing. If Katy perceives her father as unilaterally causing her anger and/or guilt, she is at a dead end. She will feel helpless and powerless because she cannot change him. Similarly, if Katy takes responsibility for causing her father's feelings and reactions, she is also stuck. Why? Because if Katy does make a change in the status quo, her father will become emotionally reactive to her new behavior. If Katy then feels responsible for causing his reactions, she may reinstate the old pattern in order to protect her father (and herself) from uncomfortable feelings and to safeguard the predictable sameness of the relationship. ("My father got so angry and crazy when I said no that there was just nothing I could do.") The situation is then defined as hopeless.

Why is the question "Who is responsible for what?" such a puzzle for women? Women in particular have been discouraged from taking responsibility for solving our own problems, determining our own choices, and taking control of the quality and direction of our own lives. As we learn to relinquish responsibility for the self, we are prone to blame others for failing to fill up our emptiness or provide for our happiness—which is not their job. At the same time, however, we may feel responsible for just about everything that goes on around us. We are quick to be blamed for other people's problems and pain and quick to accept the verdict of guilty. We also, in the process, develop the belief that we can avert problems if only we try hard enough. Indeed, guilt and self-blame are a "woman's problem" of epidemic proportion. A colleague tells the story of pausing on a ski slope to admire the view, only to be knocked down by a careless skier who apparently did not notice her. "I'm s-o-r-r-y," she reflexively yelled after him from her prone position as he whizzed on by.[1]

In this [article] we will see how confusion about "Who is responsible for what?" is one source of nonproductive self-blaming and other-blaming, as well as a roadblock to changing our situation. How can we learn to take more responsibility for the self and less for the thoughts, feelings, and behavior of others? At this point, you should be clearer on the subject than when you started out, but let's continue to try our hand at sorting out the elements of this perplexing question. Remember—assuming responsibility for the self means not only clarifying the "I" but also observing and changing our part in the patterns that keep us stuck. In this chapter we will be looking carefully at the over-functioning-underfunctioning patterns in which we all participate.

## A Crisis at Midnight

Jane and Stephanie have lived together for eight years and have raised a German shepherd who is a much-loved member of their household. One evening the dog woke them in the middle of the night and was obviously quite ill. Stephanie thought that the situation was serious enough to warrant an immediate call to the vet. Jane insisted that it could wait till morning. She accused Stephanie of being excessively worried and overreactive.

When they awoke the next morning, their dog's condition had worsened. When the veterinarian examined him, she said, "You should have called me immediately. Your dog could have died." Stephanie was furious at Jane. "If anything had happened," she said, "you would have been to blame!"

What is your perspective on this situation?

How would you react if you were in Stephanie's shoes at this point?

How do you view the responsibility of each party in contributing to Stephanie's anger?

We may empathize with Stephanie's anger, but she is nonetheless confused about who is responsible for what. Let's analyze the situation in more detail.

It is Jane's responsibility to clarify her beliefs and take action in accord with them. She did this. It was her opinion that the dog did not need immediate medical attention and so she did not call the doctor. Stephanie, too, is responsible for clarifying her beliefs and acting upon them. She did not do this. She was worried that the dog might need immediate attention and still she did not call the vet.

I am not suggesting that Stephanie should not feel angry with Jane. If she is angry, she is angry. She may be angry that Jane put down her fears, minimized her concerns, disqualified her perception of reality, or acted like a know-it-all. Nonetheless, it is Stephanie, not Jane, who has the ultimate responsibility for what Stephanie decides to do or not to do.

### 'But You Don't Know Jane!'

"The reason I didn't call," Stephanie explained later, "is that Jane would never have let me hear the end of it if I was wrong. If I had woken the vet up in the middle of the night for nothing, Jane would have been on my case for weeks and she'd have one more reason to label me a neurotic worrier. I love Jane, but you don't know how difficult she can be! She is so sure of herself that it makes me question my own opinions." In this formulation, Stephanie continues to blame Jane for her (Stephanie's) behavior.

Of course, if Stephanie does begin to assert her own self, Jane may have an intense reaction—especially if Jane has operated as the dominant partner whenever decisions had to be made. But if Stephanie can stick to her position without emotionally distancing or escalating tensions further, chances are that over time Jane will manage her own feelings and reactions just fine.

What are the steps we can take to translate our anger into a clear sense of personal responsibility that will result in more functional relationships with others? Some steps for Stephanie are: observation, clarifying the pattern, and gathering data.

### Observation

Imagine that you are in Stephanie's shoes and feeling angry—not just about the dog incident but also about the relationship pattern that this incident brought to light. What might be your next step?

The first step in the direction of gaining greater clarity about who is responsible for what is to begin to carefully observe the sequences of interaction that lead up to our feeling angry or emotionally intense. For example, Stephanie might observe that the pattern around decision-making often goes like this:

A situation occurs (in this case, a sick dog) that requires a decision. Stephanie tends to respond first by voicing a rather tentative opinion. Jane then states her own opinion, which may be different, in a supremely confident manner. Stephanie then begins to doubt her initial opinion, or simply concludes that "it's not worth the fight." In either case, she defers to Jane. Often this pattern works fine for both of them and things remain calm. But when anxiety and stress are high (as in the present example), Stephanie becomes angry with Jane if the outcome of Jane's decision-making is not to her liking. Stephanie then either withdraws from Jane or criticizes her decision. If she does the latter, a fight ensues, and by the next day things are usually calm again.

## Clarifying the Pattern

Although she might define it differently, Stephanie is beginning to identify an overfunctioning-underfunctioning pattern around decision-making. The more Jane overfunctions (jumps in to make decisions for the two of them; fails to express any doubt or insecurity about her own judgment; behaves as if she does not benefit from Stephanie's help and advice), the more Stephanie underfunctions (spaces out or does nothing when a decision is to be made; relies on Jane to take over; feels lazy or less competent to make important decisions). And the more Stephanie underfunctions, the more Jane will overfunction. Overfunctioners and underfunctioners reinforce each other's behavior in a circular fashion.

Approaching a relationship pattern in this way—gathering the objective data about who does what, when, and in what order—is difficult enough when things are calm. It is next to impossible if we are locked into emotionally intense and blaming behavior. We have seen how women learn to be the emotional reactors in our relationships, especially when stress hits, so we may need to make a conscious effort to become less reactive in order to focus our attention on the task of getting the facts.

## Gathering Data

Stephanie will also benefit from gathering some data about how this pattern of relating to Jane fits with her own family tradition over the generations. For example, how did Stephanie's parents, and their parents before them, negotiate issues of decision-making? In Stephanie's extended family, which relationships were characterized by a balance of power and which marriages had one dominant (overfunctioning) partner who was viewed as having the corner on competence? How is Stephanie's relationship with Jane similar to and different from her parents' relationship with regard to the sharing of decision-making power? What other women in Stephanie's family have struggled to shift away from the underfunctioning position and how successful were they? As we saw with Katy, our current relationship struggles are part of a legacy that began long before our birth. A familiarity with this legacy helps us gain objectivity when evaluating our behavior in relationships.

Birth order is another factor that strongly influences our way of negotiating relationships.[2] In Stephanie and Jane's case, for example, their pattern around decision-making fits their sibling positions. Jane is the older of two sisters. It is characteristic of one in this sibling position to be a natural leader and to believe, in one's heart of hearts, that one truly knows best, not only for oneself, but for the other person as well. Stephanie is the younger of the two sisters in her family, and, in the manner of one in that position, is often comfortable letting other people do things for her. Although she may compete fiercely with the "leader," she may also shun leadership should it be offered her. Simply being aware that one's sibling position within the family affects one's approach to life can be extremely helpful. If Stephanie finds herself having a hard time taking charge of things, and Jane an equally hard time not taking charge, they will both be able to deal with their situation with more humor and less self-criticism if they can appreciate the fact that they are behaving much the way people in their sibling positions behave under stress.

## So Who Has the Problem?

Let us suppose that Stephanie has taken the following steps since the dog incident: First, she has let go of her blaming position ("If anything had happened, you would have been to blame!") and has begun to think about, rather than simply react to, the problem. Second, she has pretty clearly figured out who does what, when, and in what order; when stress hits, Stephanie underfunctions and Jane overfunctions. Third, Stephanie has thought about how this pattern fits with the traditions in her own family. Finally, she has concluded that she is in a de-selfed position and that her anger is a signal that she would like to achieve more balance in her relationship with Jane when it comes to decision-making.

The following dialogues reflect two modes of using our anger: The first assumes that Jane has the problem and it is her responsibility to take care of it. The second assumes that Stephanie has the problem and it is her responsibility to take care of it.

### Dialogue One

"Jane, you are so damned sure of yourself. You're impossible to argue with because you're always right and you don't really listen to my opinions in any open way. You come on so strong that no one can argue with you. I'm really fed up with your know-it-all attitude. When I give my opinion, you pronounce it true or not true, like you're God or something. You make me feel totally insecure about my own thinking. And you always take over and manipulate things to get your way."

### Dialogue Two

"You know, Jane, I've been thinking about the problem that I have in our relationship. I think it has to do with how difficult it is for me to make decisions and take charge of things. I didn't call the vet the other night because when you expressed such confidence in your opinion, I began to doubt my own. And when you were critical of my opinion and put me down for being so worried—which I don't like—I reacted by being even more ready to back down. I'm aware that I do this a lot. And I'm planning to work harder to make my own decisions and stand behind them. I'm sure I'll make mistakes and our relationship might be more tense for a while—but I'm just not satisfied with things as they are. However, I'm also aware that the women in my family haven't done too well making their own decisions—so it may not be easy for me to be a pioneer in this way."

What about Dialogue One? Some relationships thrive on tough confrontation, and feedback of this sort and fighting it out may be viewed by both partners as a valuable and spicy aspect of the relationship. For all we know, Jane might respond to Dialogue One by becoming thoughtful and saying, "You know, I've been told that before by other people in my life. I think you have something there. I'm sorry for coming on so strong and I'll try to watch it."

This dialogue does, however, reflect Stephanie's confusion about the matter of individual responsibility. Can you spot the problem? She holds Jane responsible for Jane's behavior (putting Stephanie down), which is fair enough; but she also holds Jane responsible for Stephanie's behavior (feeling insecure and manipulated and failing to stand firmly behind her own opinion), which is not fair at all. Blaming of this sort blurs the boundaries between self and other in a close relationship.

What about Dialogue Two? Here, Stephanie shares something about herself and does not assume to be an expert on Jane. She talks about her own dilemma in the relationship and takes responsibility for her own participation in the pattern. While Dialogue One might lead to a further escalation of an already stressful situation, Dialogue Two would probably calm things down a bit and foster greater objectivity on both women's parts.

Which dialogue better suits your personal style? For me, it depends on the relationship. With my husband, Steve, I sometimes dissipate tension by fighting Dialogue-One style, although with less frequency and intensity as I get older. At work, however, and during visits from long-distance friends and family, I end up feeling much better if I communicate in Dialogue-Two style, and I find that these relationships do better, too. It all depends on what the circumstances are, what your goals are, and what in the past has left you feeling better or worse in the long run.

Of course, what is most important is not what Stephanie says to Jane but what she does. Next time around, perhaps Stephanie will listen to Jane and consider her perspective but then take responsibility to make her own reasoned decision about what she will and won't do. Stephanie's communication style will make little difference if she does not modify her own underfunctioning position.

As we learn to identify relationship patterns, we are faced with a peculiar paradox: On the one hand, our job is to learn to take responsibility for our thoughts, feelings, and behavior and to recognize that other people are responsible for their own. Yet, at the same time, how we react with others has a great deal to do with how they react with us. We cannot not influence a relationship pattern. Once a relationship is locked into a circular pattern, the whole cycle will change when one person takes the responsibility for changing her or his own part in the sequence.

Assuming this responsibility does not mean we take a self-blaming or self-deprecating position. Learning to observe and change our behavior is a self-loving process that can't take place in an atmosphere of self-criticism or self-blame. Such attitudes frequently undermine, rather than enhance, our ability to observe relationship patterns. They may even be part of the game we learn to play in which the unconscious goal is to safeguard relationships by being one down in order to help the other person feel one up.

In contrast, it is a position of dignity and strength that allows us to say to ourselves or others, "You know, I observe that this is what I am doing in this relationship and I am now going to work to change it." Such owning of responsibility does not let the other person off the hook. To the contrary, we have seen how it brings our "separateness" into bold relief and confronts others with the fact that we alone bear the ultimate responsibility for defining ourselves and the terms of our own lives. It respectfully allows others to do the same. . . .

## Notes

1. Thanks to Meredith Titus for her ski-slope story.

2. How sibling position affects our world view depends on many factors, which include the number of years between siblings, and the sibling position of each parent. Walter Toman in his book *Family Constellation* (New York: Springer, 1976) presents profiles of different sibling positions, which are informative and fun to read despite the author's unexamined biases toward women, which color his presentation.

## Questions

1. Describe a situation in which two partners fall into the overfunctioning-underfunctioning pattern, and provide two examples of each person's behavior.

2. Using the situation described in Question 1 or another situation, write two dialogues depicting opposite ways of handling anger. Dialogue One should reflect X's assumption that Y has the problem and it is Y's job to take care of it. Dialogue Two should reflect X's assumption that the problem belongs to herself or himself and that X has personal responsibility to take care of it.

3. How has your style of placing blame affected your friendships?

Adapted from Harriet G. Lerner, "Who's Responsible for What?" In *The Dance of Anger*, pp. 122–134. Copyright © 1985 by HarperCollins Publishers Inc. Reprinted with permission. ✦

# 26
# Anti-Comforting Messages

*Dale Hample*

No matter how hard you may try, there is absolutely no guaranteed, tried-and-true method for comforting someone when they are upset. Everyone has a different style of coping and responds best to different types of comforting. You were socialized into strategies for comforting others by family members as well as by friends. In some cases gender influenced this socialization, as males often receive messages to avoid being feminine, and therefore sensitive, whereas females are encouraged to express their sensitivity. Therefore some males learned that joking, one-liners, or general avoidance is workable, whereas their female counterparts learned to talk things out and convey sensitivity. By young adulthood such communication rules become less powerful, but, in many situations, individuals have difficulty conveying an appropriate sense of support when others find themselves in emotional need. These are times that call for emotional support, and these are times when an inappropriate response can really make a difference in the relationship. As Burleson (2003) so aptly puts it, "But seeking social support does not guarantee the receipt of sensitive, effective support" (p. 551). In describing how emotional support relates to communication, Burleson (2003) suggests, "it is useful to view emotional support as specific lines of communicative behavior enacted by one party with the intent of helping another cope effectively with emotional distress" (p. 552). Yet, some attempts at providing emotional support fail miserably because they tend to reflect the respondents' discomfort with direct sensitivity and lack of an appropriate communication repertoire to bring to an emotionally charged situation. Therefore, the response to another's bid for support results in distance and frustration instead of a sense of comfort and understanding.

*According to Dale Hample, there are very specific strategies that are almost guaranteed to make another feel worse, not better. Even with the best intentions, these "anti-comforting" styles often serve to discount, disregard, or diminish the feelings of someone in emotional distress, under the guise of words of support or assistance. Using the underlying tenets of face theory, confirmation, disconfirmation, and rejection, Hample frames this unusual communication circumstance and demonstrates how certain attempts at supportive messages can be hurtful. Further, Hample depicts multiple examples of the differences between content-level anti-comforting and relationship-level anti-comforting. Through the descriptions of each type of anti-comforting, the ways to recognize and avoid anti-comforting in one's own interactions are made clear. Overall, this chapter offers a very interesting and detailed discussion of a pervasive yet illusive and often unrecognized issue in communication.*

*As you read this chapter, think about anti-comforting messages you have experienced and ask yourself this question: Why did these attempts at comforting fail, and what might better have been said or done?*

### Reference

Burleson, B. (2003). Emotional support skills. In J. O. Greene and B. R. Burleson (Eds.), *Handbook of Communication and Social Interaction Skills*. (pp. 551–594). Mahwah, NJ: Lawrence Erlbaum Associates.

\* \* \*

I've always really liked baseball, and I played slow pitch softball in a church league until I was nearly 50. I'm a right-handed hitter, but had realized many years ago that people like Ozzie Smith play on the left side of the diamond, and people like me play on the right. So I learned to hit to right field, and was pretty consistent at it. A couple of games into my final season, I decided to quit at the end of the summer. I hit a line drive between the first and second basemen, and as I trundled to first, the right fielder threw to the first baseman. I've always been pretty slow-footed, so the play was close. As the ball arrived, the umpire threw up his hands, but didn't call me out or safe. He shouted, "No play." Several of us were confused, so the umpire explained. Before the season had begun, the team captains had met and had decided on a new rule: outfielders couldn't throw runners out at first. As I drove home that night, I realized that the rule had probably been put in for me and a player on the Catholic team, who had the same game, age, and athletic makeup as I did. I felt a little embarrassed about it, and at the next game I made a couple of awkward comments about it to my team. I guess I was hoping for some sympathy or encouragement. But it turns out that guys are guys whether they're on a church team or not, and all I got for my trouble was having the rule named after me.

When we think about our lives in the short term, we wish that things would always go smoothly, without crises, disappointments, or humiliation. But in the long term, we often benefit from those stressful or hurtful moments. I got over my short-term feelings about the Dale Rule, and don't really regret having left behind a game that I was getting worse at. My golf game has improved considerably, and I enjoy having my weekend nights back. I have had other experiences that I don't wish to share, and several of those have made me a better person and father, even though the first moments of my enlightenment felt awful. In the episode when the rule got named, I was looking for some comforting. What I got instead was anti-comforting, even though it was intended in a good humored way. It's nice to know that the guys didn't think I was fragile—most of them actually have good interpersonal skills and would have treated me differently if they had thought it was needed—but I actually wanted a little bit of social support. When our lives hit bumps, that's what we all want from those around us, whether we're self-contained or delicate or somewhere in between.

People often find themselves in emotional need. Perhaps the problem is a very substantial one, such as a death in the family or a positive diagnosis of HIV; perhaps it seems huge in the moment but might dissipate with time, such as abandonment by a relational partner; and perhaps it's even more minor than the Dale Rule. But in varying degrees, and with varying justification, people sometimes need the aid of those around them. Those of us fortunate enough to have a supportive social network and to receive good quality comforting from others reap a number of substantial benefits: we are more at peace, we have better health, we find more satisfaction in our relationships, we feel better about ourselves, and we have a generally more positive outlook on life (see reviews in Burleson 2003; Goldsmith 2004). When our emotional needs are not met, either by circumstances or by others, we suffer in some measure.

This essay is about talking to those in emotional need, whether that need is great or small. Forming such messages—deciding what to say and how to say it—is one of the most intricate of all communication skills. Unfortunately, most of what we say to others day to day really isn't consequential, and so we form the habit of simply expressing whatever first comes to mind, without much worry about getting it wrong. When comforting is called for, however, our messages are almost never neutral in their effects, and we have to overcome the routine habit of just talking without reflection. We can make things better, or we can make them worse. And what we say in those moments can reverberate for a surprisingly long time.

Some time ago, I got curious about what I'm calling *anti-comforting messages*. These are things that are intended as emotional support, but are so incompetent that they actually backfire. (The Dale Rule is a mild example.) I expressed my interest on *crtnet@natcom.org*, a discussion list for people (mostly faculty and graduate students) with advanced interests in communication, and invited others to send me examples. Eventually I compiled them and put them on my own website, *www.wiu.edu/users/mfdjh*, where you can see the whole list. (If you have more examples, they will be welcome.) I will use these to illustrate the points I make here.

## Setting the Stage: Basic Principles of Interpersonal Communication

Before plunging into the abyss of communication incompetence, we need to start by seeing why emotional support messages are so hard to accomplish properly. The first thing to notice is that every message has two levels of meaning, content and relationship (Watzlawick, Beavin, and Jackson 1967). Suppose I were to say, "Go back one paragraph, and highlight the definition of anticomforting messages." The content of that statement involves highlighting, paragraphs, and definitions. What the sentence means, more or less on its surface, is the content level of meaning. But the statement also has relational meanings, because it implies who I am, who you are, and what our relationship is. Thus it has several other meanings as well: you need to be told what to highlight, I am entitled to tell you what to highlight, and you have to do what I tell you. If you're annoyed at my statement, we can probably trace your unrest to the relational implications of it, not its content. Every message projects a relationship between the two people. It can be a projection of dominance, as in the highlighting command, or it can suggest equality, caring, contempt, or any number of other things. Routine comments—those that are given and heard as routine, that is—generally don't create any new relational issues. But when people are in emotional need, things can be more labile.

Relationships are composed of people, or more precisely, of identities (Goffman 1959, 1967). Each person has what we call positive face (Brown and Levinson 1987), which consists of the positive things we want others to think about us. Commonly, we want to be seen as smart, friendly, good humored, and so forth, but sometimes we might want to be viewed as cold or dangerous. Even though the identity we want can change, we still intend that others see what it is, acknowledge it, and positively confirm it. The other person is doing the same thing, and there is a kind of unspoken social contract by which we each agree to support the other's identity if at all possible. We also have negative face, which is the desire to be unimpeded. We want to be free to act and think as we please. When events or people impede us, or try to, that is negative, and we resist it (Brehm 1966). The same social contract applies here, too: we each try to avoid interfering with the other's freedoms. When circumstances or accidents result in an affront to either negative or positive face, we often engage in facework to repair things: we apologize, we try to take it back, we give a compliment. All interpersonal communication involves a negotiation of identities, and this is done in part by the relational meanings of what we say, because these bear on face.

Three particular kinds of relational meaning are important (Watzlawick, Beavin, and Jackson 1967). When we become aware of another person's projected identity, we can confirm it, reject it, or disconfirm it. To confirm the other's definition of self is to support it. If the other hints that she is a good student, we immediately compliment her studiousness or grades. Rejecting the other's identity means confronting it and disagreeing. If someone says he is adept at video games, we can refute that projection by suggesting that his little brother is better. Disconfirming a definition of self involves simply ignoring it. A spouse casually sets a new trophy on the dining room table, and the other spouse puts it in a box without comment or eye contact. These three relational meanings, as you might suppose, are in order of supportiveness: confirmation is most positive, followed by rejection (at least the identity was noticed, after all), and disconfirmation is worst (the relational message being "You don't exist"). Notice that there aren't any other possibilities. When you are drawn into a conversation, you have to do one of these three things (or perhaps more than one, in different degrees).

## Applying the Basic Principles to Moments of Emotional Need

Every moment of emotional hurt is unique, and every person is different. Still, there are some likely features that we should be alert to. First of all, the upset person is emotional and perhaps not thinking as clearly as usual. This is not the time to expect him or her to be perceptive about your intentions or feelings. In fact, when people are in the throes of depression or anger, they may well lash out with little provocation or mistake a helpful overture for taunting. For this reason, Burleson (2003, 580) suggests that the support provider actually be explicit about wanting to help (e.g., "I'm on your side in this"). The person in need is likely to be especially sensitive to identity issues, because emotional pain inevitably creates a focus on self. And most of all, it is his or her moment, not yours. The support provider may have to put self in the background, and exclusively feature the other.

Second, different categories of things create emotional stress. A key consideration is whether the problem is manageable, that is, whether it can be fixed with constructive action. For instance, a family member passing away is uncontrollable, and nothing instrumental can be done to reverse this (Davidowitz and Myrick [1984] have studied bereavement support). In contrast, being stressed because of an upcoming public speaking responsibility is open to instrumental advice or assistance. Advice is out of place if the problem isn't manageable, but might be allowable if the problem is potentially malleable. Another consideration is whether the support provider can do something substantial to alleviate the problem. If a friend is late to work and you have a car, offering a ride might be more effective and appropriate than a conversation about feelings.

A third issue is that emotionally hurtful events don't come with obvious labels. Something that bothers one person might pass unnoticed by another. One friend might take a speeding ticket in stride, but another might be extremely upset by it. Whether the instigating event seems justifiable in its emotional effects is really irrelevant to the person who is hurt. It is his or her feelings that are at issue, not your independent judgment about how weighty the circumstances really are. Everything must be seen through the eyes of the person in need, if genuine comfort is to be provided.

Lastly, we should pause for a moment to consider the support provider. As I've implied, giving good emotional assistance isn't easy. As with any voluntary behavior, offering support depends on motivation and ability (Burleson and MacGeorge 2002). If you don't really have a strong impulse to help, you may not be likely to do well even if you have a high level of skill. Adults can generally create a temporary artificial motivation to help others, though. Most of us can force

ourselves to be nurturing, to go through the motions even if we are honestly indifferent, just because it seems to be called for in the moment. Ability deficits are harder to repair. The support provider has to be perceptive about others, has to form the right goals for the interaction, has to be able to think of appropriate and effective things to say, and has to be able to work them into the conversation.

What should the goals be? They need to be chosen with the other person in mind, and his or her wishes should be respected. If the distressed person wants information or advice, give it. If he or she wants to feel better, try to accomplish that. In the absence of reliable signals, though, here are some things to consider.

Identity and relationship issues are permanent considerations. Giving advice usually carries the relational message, "You're not as competent as I am, so I'll help you," which of course affronts both positive and negative face. "Correcting" the other's feelings, perhaps by suggesting that they are unjustified, is an insult to positive face. A great deal of facework is probably going to be necessary in any emotional support effort, and this may involve showing your own vulnerability to make things seem more or less even. But even "This has happened to me, too" might have the implication of devaluing the other's feelings and moving the spotlight to you. The problems that make people upset are rarely one-dimensional. The situation might well call for information, assistance, advice, and identity confirmation, and not just one of them. The support provider's goals should be flexible and adaptable at every moment.

## Anti-Comforting Messages

With these general considerations in mind, let us finally look over some examples of anti-comforting messages and try to understand what went wrong. These were all sent to me with the understanding that one person had actually been trying to help the other, but the effort had backfired. (Some of the contributors were willing to share their names, and those credits are on my website. No one expected their story to be in a book.)

A common sort of episode was being abandoned by a relational partner. Here are some awful things to say.

- Don't take it so hard. She was a slut anyway.
- That's okay. You don't need him anyway.
- Come on, you know you had this coming. You were overdue for payback.
- I think she was a narc.
- He was always a jerk about you behind your back, telling everyone how bitchy you were and how you tried to control him. Who needs that?
- Get over it. Everyone knows college relationships don't really last anyway.

Let's begin by noticing that any of these might have been well intentioned. They really are awful, but they don't necessarily arise from unfriendly intentions.

These remarks are similar in several ways. Consider the identity work they are doing for the upset person. They devalue his or her feelings ("Don't take it so hard," "Get over it") and suggest that they are illegitimate. In fact, the upset person was incompetent to have even been in this position ("She was a slut," "She was a narc"). In other words, not only are the current feelings wrong, but so were the original ones. Rather than having negative feelings, the injured person should be pleased ("You don't need him," "Who needs that?"). All of these are actually damaging to the identity and feelings of the person who is already feeling hurt.

Some other instances of anti-comforting in this same circumstance just seem to miss the whole point, or to distort it.

- That's too bad. Wanna go out Friday?
- Aww, that's nothing! You know how I got dumped?
- Well, at least you are free to go on to graduate school now.
- I know exactly how you feel. My cat ran away from me once. I needed a few weeks to heal after that before I could get another cat.

The first example almost seems like disconfirmation, as though the support pro-vider felt vaguely obliged to say something, but really just wanted to get on with things. The second message is genuinely disconfirming because it changes the conversational focus to the provider. The third one offers consolation of sorts, but does so by implying that the breakup is a good thing, not something to be legitimately mourned. And the last one devalues almost everything: the lost relational partner, the value of being in love (with a human), the stressed person's identity, and the durability of one's feelings.

To this point, we have been concentrating on the relational level of meaning, which bears directly on identities and relationships. But the content of what we say is important, too. If we are offering emotional support, it needs to be sincere. If we are sharing information, it needs to be accurate. If we provide advice, it needs to be wise. Here are some content problems.

- At a funeral home, a women remarked to my father about my grandmother's death that it happened "for a reason." My father, tired and grief-stricken, responded, "And what would it be?"
- Look at it as a growth experience. This way, your first divorce won't hit you so hard.
- Wow, now that it is finally over, I can tell you she's been cheating on you, dude!
- You can't have everything you want in this life.

In the first case, we see a woman trying to give solace in a way that is common in some religious communities. But she mistook the man or his mood, and found herself being asked for proof and elaboration. She could not support her information. He must have seen her comment as superficial, empty, and devaluing. He might have felt that if she had truly cared, she would really have had something to say. The second example offers some advice on how to understand a relational breakup. But the advice is immature and insulting. On top of whatever the upset person was presently feeling, now divorce (and the "first" one, at that) has been piled on. The third message certainly provides information. But even assuming that it's true, it has not been very well adapted to the goal of being helpful. Rather than giving emotional assistance, the information provides other things to be upset about—having been so blind as to date a cheating woman, and having a friend who wouldn't tell you about it. The last example is a cliché. It isn't apparently adapted to the upset person or the circumstances. Aside from having very little content at all, its very commonness suggests insincerity—that the speaker felt he or she had to say something but didn't really care, so said the simplest and quickest thing that occurred. It really doesn't seem to show much interest.

## Conclusions

This has been the opposite of a how-to essay. But often we can most easily see the right way to do things by looking at examples of failure (Petroski 1985). If you would like to read more positive material, I can recommend Burleson's (2003) advice, as well as Goldsmith's (2004) careful studies of supportive conversations.

It is no wonder that people sometimes fail to give useful emotional support, even when they want to. The conversations may be highly charged, and both identities and relationships may be at risk to an unusual degree. A person who is in need is thereby vulnerable and sensitive, too. And the task of navigating through the various demands and goals is so risky that even the provider may feel in danger as well. Perhaps that is one reason why some people try to dodge this basic obligation of close relationships.

## References

Brehm, J. W. (1966). *A Theory of Psychological Reactance*. New York: Academic Press.

Brown, P., and Levinson, S. C. (1987). *Politeness: Some Universals in Language Usage*. Cambridge: Cambridge University Press.

Burleson, B. R. (2003). Emotional support skills. In J. O. Greene and B. R. Burleson (Eds.), *Handbook of Communication and Social Interaction Skills* (pp. 551–594). Mahwah, NJ: Lawrence Erlbaum Associates.

Burleson, B. R., and MacGeorge, E. L. (2002). Supportive communication. In M. L. Knapp and J. A. Daly (Eds.), *Handbook of Interpersonal Communication*, 3rd ed. (pp. 374–422). Thousand Oaks, CA: Sage.

Davidowitz, M., and Myrick, R. D. (1984). Responding to the bereaved: An analysis of "helping" statements. *Death Education*, 8, 1–10.

Goffman, E. (1959). *The Presentation of Self in Everyday Life*. Garden City, NY: Anchor.

Goffman, E. (1967). *Interaction Ritual*. Garden City, NY: Anchor.

Goldsmith, D. J. (2004). *Communicating Social Support*. Cambridge: Cambridge University Press.

Petroski, H. (1985). *To Engineer Is Human: The Role of Failure in Successful Design*. New York: Vintage Books.

Watzlawick, P., Beavin, J. H., and Jackson, D. D. (1967). *Pragmatics of Human Communication: A Study of Interaction Patterns, Pathologies, and Paradoxes*. New York: W. W. Norton.

## Questions

1. One predictable place to find examples of anti-comforting is in televised situation comedies. What makes them so funny in this context? If audiences have seen so many examples of this communication strategy, why do people continue to do it?

2. The general discussions of interpersonal communication and emotionally challenging situations give a number of principles for comforting properly. Identify five anti-comforting messages, and construct appropriate messages to replace the anti-comforting ones. Identify the context for each message.

3. For the most part, comforting actually takes place in a conversation, rather than as a simple message. How would you try to participate in a conversation to give another person emotional assistance?

# 27
# Why Marriages Fail

*John Gottman*

John Gottman, *internationally acclaimed marital researcher, suggests that the quality of communication is the best predictor of a successful marriage. The type of relationship spouses have affects their frequency of communication, their willingness to self-disclose, and their willingness to confront conflict rather than avoid it. Satisfaction is not necessarily created by any of these communication styles per se. That is, different couple types are satisfied with different communication styles. Highly independent couples are satisfied with informational exchanges (self-disclosure, discussion of conflict, etc.), whereas more traditional couples enjoy togetherness, sharing, and similarity.*

*Gottman (1994) argues that couples who maintain a "magic ratio" of 5:1 positive to negative feelings and interaction avoid the risk of marital misery. His research reveals marriages that work are characterized by (1) an overall level of positive affect, and (2) an ability to reduce negative affect during conflict resolution (Gottman 1999, 105). In his popular book,* The Seven Principles for Making Marriage Work *(Gottman and Silver 1999), Gottman suggests that successful couples live by principles such as turning toward each other instead of away, solving their solvable problems, and creating shared meaning.*

*According to Gottman, couples that experience high levels of negativity risk losing their marriages. Such couples face the "Cascade of Dissolution" or moving downward through a pattern of criticism, defensiveness, contempt, and stonewalling that can devastate the marriage. He believes marriages can be restored and repaired if couples will learn and practice new skills, including communication skills. In the following article, he provides an introduction to his research processes and describes the* three very different types of functional marriages: validating, volatile, and conflict avoiding. Partners in these marriages tend to use the 5:1 "magic" interaction pattern of positivity to negativity; each partnership is characterized by highly positive experiences, although the couple may fight actively or avoid conflict. Then Gottman details behaviors he calls "the Four Horsemen of the Apocalypse," or criticism, defensiveness, contempt, and stonewalling. Finally he addresses gender and marital interaction. As you read this chapter, ask yourself about your perceptions of "good" relationships: How willing am I to accept that successful marriages may be characterized by active conflict or avoidance of conflict?*

### References

Gottman, J. M. (1994). *Why Marriages Succeed or Fail*. New York: Simon and Schuster.

———. (1999). *The Marriage Clinic: A Scientifically Based Marital Therapy*. New York: W. W. Norton.

Gottman, J. M. and Silver, N. (1999). *The Seven Principles for Making Marriage Work*. New York: Three Rivers Press.

* * *

Every therapist knows how mysterious marriage can be—witness the apparently incompatible couples who seem to have more fights in a week than most spouses average in a year but still stay together for a lifetime, and even seem to be happy with each other. Or, at the other extreme, consider those couples who approach potential conflict like a fatal virus, dodging and hedging around disagreeable subjects, unable to openly discuss, let alone resolve, what would seem to be critical issues in their marriage. And yet, these same couples—frequently labelled "in denial" or "repressed" by the marital therapy profession—not infrequently raise families and merrily celebrate 30th and 40th wedding anniversaries in spite of doomsday prognoses.

The truth is that, for all our theorizing about how a good marriage coheres and a bad one unravels, few of us can claim to know very much about the mysterious inner workings of this most intimate relationship. The actual daily *stuff* of marriage—the slow accretion over the years of countless small, subtle but deeply telling patterns of interaction that make or break individual marriages—is still *terra incognita* to most of us, married couples and therapists included.

This news may come as a shock, considering the plethora of psychological prescriptions for fixing broken marriages, but until very recently, we did not know much more about the emotional and behavioral processes within marriage than we did about the physiology of sexual behavior before Masters and Johnson. And most of what we still claim to know comes from personal musings based on the idiosyncratic practice of individual therapists; almost none of our theory and practice is founded on empirical scientific research. This is not to say that therapists have not helped countless couples save their own marriages, or have not themselves accumulated a wealth of informal wisdom about marriage over the years. But the reasons that individual marriages succeed or fail remain mysterious, and much of the marital advice—whether it works or doesn't—has only the frailest of empirical foundations. . . .

Twenty years ago, I made my own first forays into this new world of marital research. As a young therapist I felt stymied in my attempts to help a particularly troubled couple, whose therapy sessions inevitably disintegrated into bitter personal fights, over which neither they nor I had much control. On a hunch, I made a series of videotapes of the sessions, then had them watch the tapes with me and tell me what they had been feeling and thinking during certain moments of their filmed interaction.

Both the couple and I were astonished by the vividness and clarity on the tape of the pattern of criticism, contempt and defensiveness they repeatedly fell into—a pattern of which they had been largely unaware and even I couldn't see clearly in session. While I still didn't know what to *do* to help turn them around, not only did the tape act as a kind of positive catalyst for them—it shocked them into working harder at hearing each other and trying to improve the way they spoke to each other—it gave me my life's work. I wanted to develop a science of marital inter-

action, a body of replicable data about the destructive emotional processes between spouses that, unless they were interrupted fairly early on, could reliably predict the dissolution of the marriage. In short, I wanted to be able to see, identify and intervene in these specific and observable patterns before they achieved critical mass.

From this more or less ad hoc beginning, I gradually developed, along with many colleagues, a complex multimethod research model for studying the interstices of marriage. Our data base has been drawn, over the last two decades, from 20 different studies based on the three videotaped conversations of 2,000 couples overall, correlated with electronically measured physiological responses and backed up by questionnaires and interviews. We have used a coding system for relating facial expressions to emotion, as well as measuring other indices of emotional expression, including voice and language, to demonstrate levels of affection, interest, amusement and joy as well as anger, sadness, fear, contempt and disgust at different points during the conversation. We have also watched and listened for specific kinds of verbal and physical behavior that communicated, for example, complaint, blame, criticism, whining, defensiveness, belligerence and domineering. In addition, physiological data—heart rate, blood-flow rate, perspiration during stress, gross motor movement, and sometimes, stress-related hormones in urine and blood—have been synchronized with observed interactions of the couples. We then have interviewed spouses about what they were thinking and feeling (and what they think their spouses were thinking and feeling) during specific moments of the taping. Finally, we have collected questionnaires and oral histories about the state of their marriages, their feelings of loneliness or togetherness, what they think and feel about each other, and what they think the other feels about them.

While we still have a long way to go before we truly understand the complex processes of marriage, we have gathered enough data about the way individual couples interact in marriages to develop a theory of the factors that, if they are not interrupted, put a couple on a trajectory toward divorce, one that grows steeper and slipperier over time. We think there is evidence to show that if these negative patterns of interaction are not reversed in time, there is a point of no return, after which not much can be done to save the marriage.

Even without being able to fully identify and analyze the thousands of factors that go into the subtle and complex communication patterns between a couple, we believe we are still in a position to predict, based on our data, which couples are most likely to be divorced in the future. Of the 2,000 couples in our data base, we have followed 484 couples, many for as long as 10 years, testing four years after the initial interview for the impact of factors we thought might predict divorce and continuing to monitor them after that. We found such strong linkages between the information we had collected originally and the couples' marital status four and more years later—whether they had divorced or not—that we now feel confident about our abilities to predict the potential for divorce in particular kinds of marriages. Indeed, I can now tell from a brief interview with a couple, a few questionnaires and a portion of a videotape what the eventual fate of a particular marriage is likely to be. In fact, from just six variables from our standard Oral History interview, I can predict with 94-percent accuracy which marriages are headed for divorce.

We already have enough evidence to unseat some of the most venerable truisms of marital therapy, including what comprises a "good" marriage. The satisfactorily married couple, according to the conventional therapeutic wisdom, is first of all, deeply *compatible*: the spouses do not necessarily have to come from the same ethnic, religious and class background (though it helps), but they must agree on important things—sex, money, religion, childrearing—and should be able to compromise on about everything else. Not that this couple doesn't argue—they do, but their arguments seldom get lowdown and dirty, or even very heated. When they disagree, they naturally and without prompting do exactly what therapists advise less compatible and more troubled spouses to do: recognize conflicts, ac-knowledge differences openly but address them honestly and calmly before they degenerate into shouting matches. Conventional wisdom says they listen respectfully and empathize with each other's point of view; they don't interrupt much and if neither can persuade the other to do this or that side of the issue, they negotiate a workable compromise. Not surprisingly, these couples look and sound a lot like two psychotherapists engaging in a dialogue.

Undoubtedly, this kind of union—what we call the validating style of marriage—usually works very well. And it is, therefore, not surprising that a wide range of marital theories and therapies—insight-focused, behavioral, psychoeducational—are geared to getting all troubled marriages to approximate this pattern. Certainly, viewing this style of marriage as the ideal has simplified the careers of marital therapists; their fundamental goal has been to help unhappily married couples get back to the bottom-line compatibility they are all presumed to have started with, if the marriage was ever viable in the first place. It followed then that either a lot of fighting or no fighting at all were both signs of a marriage on the rocks, that both indicated hidden agendas and unrecognized symbolic conflicts, which were undermining the marriage. Whichever it was—fighting or no fighting—the couple needed to uncover and "hash out" their differences, then come to a compromise so they could achieve the kind of idyllic balance represented by the validating couple.

But from what we see in the laboratory, the idea that the only truly satisfying marriage is cast in the mold of the validating style is wrong. Likewise, the orthodox belief that compatibility is indispensable to marital happiness and the reduction of conflict is critical to saving troubled marriages is a myth.

Our research shows that it isn't the lack of compatibility that predicts divorce, but the way couples handle their inevitable *incompatibilities*; not whether they fight all the time or never fight at all, but the way they resolve conflicts and the overall quality of their emotional interactions in a marriage that determines its well-being—whether the good moments of mutual pleasure, passion, humor, support, kindness and generosity outweigh the bad moments of complaint, criticism, anger, disgust, contempt, defensiveness, and coldness. In fact, after studying, tabulating, and analyzing probably tens of thousands of marital interactions in our data base, we have concluded that we can actually quantify the ratio of positive to negative interactions needed to maintain a marriage in good shape. And we found that satisfied couples, no matter how their marriages stacked up against the ideal, were those who maintained a five-to-one ratio of positive to negative moments. Whether they fought a lot or not at all, whether they seemed passionately engaged with each other or distinctly distant, and most important, whether or not they were compatible socially, financially, sexually—what counted was the overall *balance* of positive to negative.

This claim sounds entirely presumptuous: how can something with the mercurial, idiosyncratic and labyrinthine dynamics of a marriage be reduced to a simple ratio of interactions? But much to our own surprise, we found that certain kinds of marriages that would seem doomed to failure according to standard therapeutic prognoses, were actually quite successful; what set these rule breaking, good marriages apart from others was their adherence to the five-to-one ratio.

Perhaps the most classic example of the presumably endangered marriage is the volatile type between spouses who apparently live to fight. These Punch-and-Judy couples have intensely emotional marriages, characterized by epic brawls, high levels of jealousy, prickly interactions, petty bickering, sarcastic asides and hair-trigger tempers. Unlike the "compatible" couples that are the marital therapist's dream, these excitable couples do not fight fairly. When they argue, they go for the jugular, rarely listen to or empathize with their mates during the course of battle, and attempt to steamroller each other to their respective points of view.

And yet, that these couples engage in a lot more *sturm und drang* than most couples (and many therapists) could tolerate does not, of itself, mean they don't have good marriages. In a successful marriage of this type, for every nasty swipe, there are five caresses, so to speak. Indeed, far more than other marriages, however solid and satisfying, volatile marriages are inclined to be deeply romantic and frequently dramatic. And because the spouses tend, as one would expect, to be passionate and intense people, their relationship—when it is satisfying—can be much more exciting and deeply intimate than the marriages of less emotionally engaged people.

Of course, there are pitfalls to these volatile marriages. Neither spouse worries overmuch about hurting the other's feelings, nor do the two believe that discretion is the better part of valor. Thus, for these spouses, who readily wade into controversy and contumely, the five-to-one ratio is more dangerously vulnerable to shifting downward than for more cautious couples. And when they fly at each other without forethought, as they often do, they can inflict unforgivable wounds. Under external stresses—the birth of a baby, for example—the normally argumentative style of their marriage can deteriorate into endless bickering and quarreling, even violence.

At the opposite end of the spectrum of presumably "dysfunctional" marriages, at least according to received wisdom, are the imperturbable couples who cannot stand fighting—the conflict avoiders. When a potential disagreement raises its serpent's head, these conflict-avoidant or conflict-minimizing couples are more than likely to step around it, eyes averted. Interviewing these couples, we found it extremely difficult to even find a subject of continuing disagreement between them, and had to settle for relatively trivial problems that may have caused an occasional twinge of discomfort. (One couple admitted that they disagreed once on whether to have chicken or pizza for dinner.) When differences cannot be smoothed over or ignored—sexual incompatibility, for example—they are likely to resolve them by *not* resolving them, concluding that although they recognize the conflict exists, they don't consider it as important as the many areas of common agreement they do share. In a sense, all of their conversations (they couldn't be called arguments) with us about differences between them ended in standoffs; they agree that they disagreed, but make no attempt to persuade each other. They simply agree to continue disagreeing, and then drop the subject.

According to standard theories of marital therapy, the union of this couple, even more than the first, is doomed. Compatibility seems to have become too much of a good thing, as it were, and they are terrified of disagreement. Their unacknowledged conflicts, while "repressed" and "denied," so goes the standard theory, feed a deep, toxic undercurrent of hostility and rage. The prognosis for these couples is that either the spouses will become quietly antagonistic strangers living separate parallel lives in the same household, or, according to the "volcano" theory of marital interaction, the repressed fury (which, it is often assumed, must be there) may explode into outright violence.

Our research shows these "doomed" marriages survive. The reason is that these couples, just like the volatile spouses, share an interactive ratio of five positive to one negative moment. While they have fewer negative interactions, they also have fewer positive ones. The difference is that their relationships are less emotional than the volatile marriages. They are less likely to fight passionately, but also less likely to love passionately. Instead of a marriage that resembles a raging torrent, theirs looks like a calm lake. They are likely to be *truly* compatible, as well paired as matching bookends. Often they come from the same social and economic background, hold similar beliefs about religion, values, childrearing practices, financial issues and the like. They share a sense of their marriage as a kind of secure bastion, a solid fortress of "us," so strong a bond that they can afford to overlook disagreements. Probably for centuries, traditional marriages resembled this type; the married couple, as unbudgeable a social institution as church and state could make them, didn't require romance, or even active companionship, to shore up a union considered by nature, law and religion undissoluble.

Of course, these marriages also have their weaknesses. Because these couples allow so little negativity into their interactions, they may not be able to deal effectively with disagreements that cannot be ignored or evaded, in which case they may live with a good deal of unresolved misery and frustration. In an effort to avoid any confrontation

at all, they also tend to undermine intimacy and, as a result, they may see their marriage become rather cold and distant. While they have fewer negative interactions, they also have fewer positive ones. Nonetheless, like the volatile couples, these conflict-minimizing pairs also have a very good shot at making and keeping a good, solid marriage for life—in spite of the fact that they, too, do not follow the marital "rules" of the therapeutic trade.

In fact, we found such consistency of success for all three types of marital unions—validating, volatile and conflict avoiding—if they maintain the five-to-one ratio that we are inclined to consider it a universal constant. Like any other living thing, the marital relationship must sustain a kind of emotional ecological balance in order to survive. Marriages seem to thrive on, proportionately, *a little* negativity and *a lot* of positivity. The total amounts vary substantially from style to style, but the proportion between the pluses and minuses must remain the same. One couple's successful marriage exhibits a lot of both negative and positive affect, another shows moderate amounts of negativity and positivity and the third, small amounts of each—but all will show the same ratio.

Just as striking, however, is the strong possibility emerging from our studies that *only* couples from one of these three affective styles seem able to maintain the necessary ratio for a satisfying marriage. It seems, in short, that lasting marriages come in three discrete types, and that there are no in-between types that work well or last very long. The fighting styles of each individual spouse probably reflect deeply entrenched personality traits and worldviews; a conflict between styles may well represent fundamental disagreement on the very constitution of happy versus miserable marriages. So, if a validator (temperamentally disposed to calmly and rationally work problems out) or a conflict-minimizer (content to let problems remain unresolved) marries a volatile type (who thrives in the heat of passionate battle), serious problems in the marriage are almost foreordained. Typically, the volatile spouse (often the wife) first feels puzzled and impatient, then patronized and frustrated, finally frustrated and maddened by her validator or conflict-minimizing husband's refusal to go *mano a mano* with her. The more moderate and reasonable he is, the more irritable, insulting and furious she becomes, driving him to defensive retreat, silent contempt and cold hostility. It seems from our studies that one or the other spouse would have to make a very concerted and probably difficult attempt to change his or her style of fighting, which might mean transforming some very basic personal attitudes, as well.

Paradoxically, successful couples *are* compatible—but not in the way traditionally suggested by marital therapy theory. As it turns out, the spouses within each different style are compatible fighters; they do implicitly agree on the way they will disagree, on how they will traverse the rough terrain they inevitably cross on their trek through marriage.

Our research suggests that while disagreements and fights are not pleasant, and no couples except the volatile seem to enjoy them, they are necessary in some degree to all good marriages. Recognizing disagreement and engaging in it, even if it is never settled or no compromise is reached, helps couples cope with difficult issues, while enriching and stimulating both of them. We speculate that the function of negativity, including anger, in marriage is to create a dynamic rather than static equilibrium between spouses; certain forms of negativity are like spice that keep relationships from going flat. Anger, when directed at a particular issue and expressed without contempt or global criticism, is healthy, perhaps even necessary. We have found in our studies that while angry exchanges made both spouses unhappy during the period when they were happening, they correlated with long-term marital satisfaction. Blunt, straightforward anger seems to immunize marriages against deterioration.

Not all forms of negativity are equal, however, in the ecology of marriage, and we have observed that some are clearly more dangerous, more toxic than others. The five-to-one ratio is a measure of a satisfying marriage; that couples experience it at one point in

their marriage is no guarantee that they can count on it forever. From what we can see, no marriage of any type—even one exhibiting a healthy five-to-one ratio of positive to negative interactions—can long sustain itself once four particularly corrosive personal exchanges have insinuated themselves into the relationship. These four processes—criticism, defensiveness, contempt and stonewalling—I call the "four horsemen of the apocalypse" because they seem to have the inherently destructive power of a virus or a cancer; if they are not checked, they can colonize and ultimately destroy a relationship.

Although every couple engages in the terrible four from time to time, they need to be aware lest they begin gradually to occupy a growing proportion of normal fights and disagreements. Therefore, both couple and therapists need to understand the sometimes subtle, but always critical, difference between less damaging forms of negativity and the terrible four. Anger and disagreement, for example, are quite distinct from criticism and contempt. In the former, a husband might say, "I'm upset that you didn't balance the joint checkbook. The bank called today about two bounced checks, and I was very embarrassed." In the latter, his remarks would be less specific, more global, aimed less at his spouse's actions, more toward her very being. "As usual, you screwed up our checkbook and humiliated me. You're no rocket scientist, but I'd think you could learn to do some simple addition and subtraction." It is not the anger that makes this attack destructive, it is the derision and gratuitous insult added to it. She not only made a mistake, she *always* makes mistakes and is kind of stupid, to boot.

Clearly, the walls are already closing in on these two, leaving no room for maneuvering into a more tolerable mutual exchange. Typically, they would trade attacks until one or the other, probably the wife, started screaming and the husband would engage horseman number four—stonewalling. He would "remove himself" emotionally or physically—refuse to answer or look at her, or storm out of the room.

Stonewalling is a characteristically male thing to do; in one of our samples of couples, we found that 85 percent of our stonewallers were male. And, in the course of our research, we have made some startling discoveries about the physiological differences between men and women that account for this disproportion.

Marital strife has a significant physiological as well as psychological component, which shows up differently between men and women during arguments. At the onset of a fight, men become more intensely upset physiologically than women—measured in terms of higher heart rate and blood pressure—and they remain distressed for a longer time—long after their wives have calmed down. Probably this difference in wiring had evolutionary survival benefits: the prehistoric male of our species, to protect the female and her young, had to be more alert and physiologically responsive to external danger than she did—more ready to attack and fight or flee in the face of environmental danger. In modern life, this propensity to higher arousal is not nearly so adaptive; it feels terrible, and to avoid the acute distress it causes, men are likely simply to shut themselves down, refuse to respond, try, as much as possible, to turn themselves into unfeeling stone. But this pain-reducing strategy is terrible for marriage. The stonewalling, as it turns out, increases the woman's feelings of unpleasant physiological arousal more than anything else her spouse does, much more than shouting back, for example.

This physiological gender difference may help explain some of the truisms about male and female styles of fighting in marriage—why women are more likely to be "emotional" during a fight and pursue their mates with complaints, criticisms and demands, while men tend to engage in rationalizations, avoid the subject, withdraw into silence and impassivity, or physically retreat. In fact, our research confirmed that men engage in such maddeningly avoidant behaviors (to their wives, at least) precisely because they are much more unpleasantly physiologically aroused by a fight than their wives.

On the other hand, we also found that in happy marriages, the widely touted theory that men are less emotionally expressive than women was *not* confirmed in our research; in fact, we found that, by and large, in satisfying marriages, there are no gender differences in emotional expression: men are as likely to share their most intimate emotions as women. Surprisingly, in happy marriages, men are more likely to reveal personal information about themselves—dissatisfaction with the self, hurts, dreams, aspirations, reminiscences—than their wives. And when these men are angry, they don't stonewall, but openly let their wives know what they are feeling—which, again, is much less stressful for their wives than stubborn withdrawal. Unfortunately, marriage is still about the only outlet for emotional expression in the lives of most men. Whereas wives usually have a fairly wide support network outside the marriage of friends and relatives, husbands, in essence, only disclose to their wives—and nobody else. It is not surprising, then, that unhappily married men are deeply lonely.

What is surprising is that we found that men who did housework were likely to be more happily engaged and involved in their marriages than men who did not, and less lonely, less stressed *and* less likely to be sick four years after the initial meeting with them in the laboratory. Tested as a separate factor in men, doing housework, by itself, was related to lower heart rate, less physiological arousal in general and better health four years later. Clearly, what is measured here is not the fabulous, curative powers of housework, but the mutual and supportive engagement of spouses in good marriage—not such a startling fact on its own, but astonishing in that it is expressed so clearly in physiology, in the very life and well-being of the body.

Unhappy marriage is not physically good for either spouse, though the actual effects differ according to gender. Men are inclined to withdraw from marital interaction to buffer themselves from physically stressful feelings of arousal—to a certain extent, this mechanism protects them. But years spent warding off emotional and physiological feelings of being flooded by their wives' anger—the use of enormous stores of energy for continual stonewalling and withdrawal—take a very high toll on men's physical health.

Conversely, women actually become sick after too many years of figuratively knocking their heads against a stone wall—trying to get a response from someone who relentlessly refuses to respond. In fact, we found that the husband's contempt in marriage predicted, over time, a wife's susceptibility to illness; for example, by counting the number of a husband's facial expressions of contempt for his wife, we could correctly estimate the number of infectious diseases she would have over the next four years.

It is an unpalatable, but unescapable, truth that some marriages cannot and should not be saved. Not only do patterns of toxic marital interaction keep the body in a state of unhealthy physical arousal, they create a psychological climate of helpless misery—neither spouse *can* surmount the negativity and hostility that have seeped into virtually every shared marital interaction. Our study shows a physiological linkage between spouses—in the laboratory, physiological responses of each spouse can be predicted by those of the other. In other words, in negative interactions, something like a complex feedback loop occurs between spouses, which includes the back-and-forth exchange of negative physiological arousal, psychological misery and destructive behavior. The repeated trauma of the marital interactions has not only become, in a sense, "hard-wired" into the physiology, but these bone-deep states of arousal can no longer be willfully controlled. Couples at the end of these marriages are unable to muster the cognitive and social abilities that, in less damaged relationships, could see them through to better times.

In good marriages, couples can readily repair the damage done during fights and the inevitable fallow periods (there are times, probably, when every spouse secretly wonders if the marriage hasn't been a terrible mistake) just in the mutually soothing exchanges that make any relationship flow. But these repair mechanisms no longer work in badly ailing marriages; there is literally nothing the couple can talk about, no subject, no common interest that is not fully colonized by the all-absorbing state of their mutual contempt and defensiveness. The range of available positive exchanges has so shriveled, and the negativity grown so cancerous, that both spouses have literally lost the ability to breathe and move normally in each other's presence; their muscles tense, their hearts beat harder, they feel they are suffocating.

At this point, we believe efforts to save the marriage are more likely to be disastrous than helpful. The partners are overwhelmed by a sense of failure, hopelessness and mutual alienation; they have been at war so long that there is no common ground left between them. Not only is it fatuous to suggest that they just "try harder" at this juncture, it may be bad for their health—witness our data suggesting that staying in a hostile, distant marriage actually compromises the immune system, increasing susceptibility to illness.

Furthermore, while divorce is never desirable, the research of Andrew Cherlin, Mavis Hetherington and others suggests that it is probably better for children, as long as coparenting tasks are well-managed, than a marriage reduced to a vicious intermingling of mutual hostility and loneliness. The evidence from research I am currently doing reinforces this position. It appears that a well-managed divorce, in which both spouses were helped therapeutically to separate with some degree of calm and dignity and make reasonable mutual childcare arrangements, is better for children than forcing them to live in the donnybrook of their parents' terrible marriage. . . .

The conclusions that have emerged from this large body of research show that "what everybody knows" is not always true—attempts to turn perfectly good, conflict-minimizing or volatile marriages into the validating-style marriages that therapists prefer are unsuited to the real spouses in those real relationships.

A good theory of marital dissolution—why it happens—must accurately predict which couples are most at risk long before the ultimate slide. Until recently, it would have seemed foolish to think that anything as complex, personal and idiosyncratic as marriage adhered to predictable patterns.

And yet, it seems to be so. When we ask enough questions, when we deeply and carefully observe the smallest piece of behavior, we find in the most apparently chaotic marriages an intricate, but ultimately predictable, web of patterns at work. As we study marriage with the same respect and the same attention to detail that natural historians apply to the apparently inchoate confusion of nature, we come up with the same amazing discovery—human relationships, like other natural processes, are not random and unknowable, but appear to obey certain laws. Science, which might be called the study of natural laws, will not compromise the fundamental mystery of the heart, any more than science will eliminate the mystery of spring because the processes of germination and photosynthesis are understood. But with every new bit of knowledge about the couples who come into our laboratory, we increase our ability to help them and ourselves fulfill in all of our lives the original promise inherent in love's beginning.

## Questions

1. Select a personal peer relationship that you consider highly successful. How are positive and negative messages managed in this relationship? To what extent does it reflect a 5:1 positivity to negativity ratio?

2. What would communication in your "ideal" marriage be like? Compare your ideal with that of a classmate of the opposite sex.

3. Does the 5:1 ratio make sense to you? Why or why not?

# Part VII

## *The Dark Side of Relationships*

In recent years, relationship scholars have begun to focus more actively on the negative or painful aspects of relational life. Although a significant number of studies have addressed issues of conflict and relational decline, few have addressed topics such as betrayal, deceit, violence, stalking, or manipulation. In the first major communication-oriented work on the subject, *The Dark Side of Interpersonal Communication*, Cupach and Spitzberg (1994) argue, "To fully understand how people effectively function requires us to consider how individuals cope with social interaction that is difficult, problematic, challenging, distressing, and disruptive" (p. vii). These authors refer to such behaviors as the *dark side of communication*.

Dark side scholarship represented a breakthrough in relational communication research. Previously most scholars represented an optimistic view on relational life, focusing on the positive and affirming features of interpersonal interaction. Yet, as you know, everyday life is also filled with relational hostility, aggression, deception, or anger (Duck 1994). Certain acts considered to be dark occur at some point in most long-term relationships; jealousy rears its ugly head, white lies cover mistakes, name calling surfaces in arguments, or trusted secrets are revealed. In certain relationships the dark side emerges as predictable and dangerous; physical fights become the pattern, stalking replaces questioning, manipulation characterizes everyday interaction, and verbal abuse substitutes for discipline.

Before you imagine the dark side as totally negative and undesirable, consider that the outcomes of dark side communication are not always horrendous. Certain communication acts reflect opposite sides of the same coin within relationships. For example, Felmlee (1998) describes the light and dark sides of interpersonal attraction suggesting that the light side might include nurturing, spontaneous, flattering, and sweet or sensitive behavior, whereas the dark side might include smothering, irresponsible, superficial, and saccharine behavior. Over time romantic partners may experience movement between these light and dark experiences of attraction. Low-level dark side behaviors are predictable and may even, paradoxically, strengthen the ties. Such everyday behaviors include expressions of jealousy, belittling, insincerity, lying, gossip, or avoidance; the odds are that you encounter examples of these on a daily or weekly basis. In certain cases, serious relational conflicts, characterized by dark side behaviors, have been strengthened by these experiences. Relational partners may use deception to keep from devastating the other, hurtful words may be the only way to get a friend's attention on a critical issue, and jealousy may convince another of the importance of the relationship. On occasion, dealing with dark side communication may force some individuals to grow stronger, more realistic, or better able to take care of themselves and others. Duck (1994) argues that "the 'dark side' is integral to the experience of relationships, not separate from it" (p. 9).

Although certain behaviors are problematic rather than horrendous, the dark side must not be taken lightly. Spitzberg and Cupach (1998) suggest, "The juxtaposition of investigating topics such as gossip and embarrassment next to rape, violence, and deadly activities (e.g. unsafe sex) trivializes the notional of darkness in general, and the seriousness of the darker topics therein" (p. xvi). As fear enters a relationship, destructive processes follow.

Examples of the horrors of the dark side may be found in the communication research related to physical and verbal abuse, obsessive relational intrusion, or sexual coercion. In some cases the behavior is linked to physical and/or psychological health issues. In their study of male batterers, Jacobson and Gottman (1998) studied violent marriages by directly observing the arguments of severely violent couples and the emotional experiences of male batterers and battered women during these arguments. As part of the study they assessed emotional arousal at the physiological level, an approach that led to their famous distinction between types of batterers: Cobras and Pit Bulls. Cobras represent the 20 percent of the batterers who experienced a decrease in heart rate as they became more verbally abusive, a very startling finding of the study, whereas Pit Bulls' heart rates increased and they exhibited anger as a slow burn. Cobras demonstrated evidence of severe antisocial, sadistic behavior and exhibited violent responses to a range of people in their lives. Pit Bulls tended to be more emotionally dependent on their partners, prone to fits of jealous rage, and aggressive only to their partners. If you have ever lived with a violent person, you have seen the dark side of interpersonal interactions in a very personal way.

Recently obsession in its many forms has received extensive scholarly attention. In their studies, Cupach and Spitzberg (1998) define obsessive relational intrusion (ORI) as "repeated and unwanted pursuit and invasion of one's sense of physical or symbolic privacy by another person, either strange or acquaintance, who desires and/or presumes an intimate relationship" (pp. 234–235). Stalking represents a severe form of ORI and has received the most research attention. ORI behaviors range from mildly annoying acts, such a pestering someone for a date, leaving constant messages, or providing unwanted gifts or favors, to threatening acts, such as home invasion, physical abuse, verbal threats, or stalking. Sexual coercion represents a type of threatening act often experienced by young adults. In a world of "hookups" or "friends with benefits," desired personal boundaries may be ignored or misinterpreted, resulting in date rapes. In other cases, predatory stalkers "strategically plan sexual attack or coercion" (Cupach and Spitzberg 2004).

Your interpretation of dark side behavior is tied, in part, to your gender, culture, and family experiences. If you grew up learning that deceit was the way to survive in your family, you may view it as functional and protective; if your upbringing stressed openness and truth at all costs, deceit might lead you to end a significant relationship. You may have learned that certain dark side behaviors, such as gossiping, swearing, yelling, or maliciousness are gendered in nature or tied to cultural patterns. Thus, your interpretation of the level of darkness inherent in certain behaviors reflects your past experiences.

In this section you will find an elaborated overview of the dark side, including its "seven deadly sins," as well as treatments of two dark side communication practices, lying and serial arguing. Finally, the communication ties to child abuse will be addressed.

## References

Cupach, W. R., and Spitzberg, B. H. (1994). Preface. In W. R. Cupach and B. H. Spitzberg (Eds.), *The Dark Side of Interpersonal Communication* (pp. vii–ix). Hillsdale, NJ: Lawrence Erlbaum Associates.

Cupach, W. R., and Spitzberg, B. H. (1998). Obsessive relational instrusion and stalking. In

*The Dark Side of Close Relationships*. (pp. 233–263). Hillsdale, NJ: Lawrence Erlbaum Associates.

Cupach, W. R., and Spitzberg, B. H. (1998). Preface. In *The Dark Side of Close Relationships*. (pp. vii–x). Hillsdale, NJ: Lawrence Erlbaum Associates.

Cupach, W. R., and Spitzberg, B. H. (2004). *The Dark Side of Relationship Pursuit*. Mahwah, NJ: Lawrence Erlbaum Associates.

Duck, S. (1994). Strategems, spoils, and a serpent's tooth: On the delights and dilemmas of personal relationships. In W. R. Cupach and B. H. Spitzberg (Eds.), *The Dark Side of Interpersonal Communication* (pp. 3–24). Hillsdale, NJ: Lawrence Erlbaum Associates.

Felmlee, D. H. (1998). Fatal attraction. In W. R. Cupach and B. H. Spitzberg (Eds.), *The Dark Side of Close Relationships*. (pp. 3–31), Hillsdale, NJ: Lawrence Erlbaum Associates.

Jacobson, N., and Gottman, J. (1998). *When Men Batter Women: New Insights Into Ending Abusive Relationships*. New York: Simon & Schuster. ✦

# 28

# A Struggle in the Dark

*Brian H. Spitzberg*

After a decade of growing attention to interaction patterns described under the label of "the dark side," most communication scholars address these types of interactions in their teaching and writings. Yet the concept of the dark side is quite fluid, reflecting its complexity and development over a limited period of time. Although individual scholars addressed many topics currently considered to fall under the dark side label, it was in 1994 that William Cupach and Brian Spitzberg produced their groundbreaking book, The Dark Side of Interpersonal Communication. This work challenged communication faculty and students to consider seriously a wide spectrum of problematic, challenging, and disruptive communication patterns; thus, topics ranging from sexual abuse to name calling gained prominence in the communication literature. The book's title established the overarching reference point for future studies of problematic topics that became known under the rubric of "dark side of communication" studies.

Yet these authors and subsequent writers address this topic in a highly nuanced manner, recognizing the difficulty in interpreting motives for certain seemingly negative behaviors as well as the possibility of unpredictable and potentially beneficial outcomes from dark side communication interactions. The dialogue regarding how to conceptualize this issue continues. In the following article, Spitzberg continues to address the question "What is the dark side?" by exploring what he calls the "seven sins" of the dark side. As you read these, the complexities of this topic will become apparent. You may find yourself rethinking positions you hold, such as how you view lying. Spitzberg provides a model for categorizing specific behaviors as presumptively/normatively constructive or destructive that reinforces the nuanced nature of the dark side. Finally, he summarizes a range of current dark side research topics currently being studied by communication scholars. As you read this article, keep the following question in mind: Under what conditions might I view a problematic interaction as having potential benefits for both communicators?

## Reference

Cupach, W. R., and Spitzberg, B. H. (1994). *The Dark Side of Interpersonal Communication*. Hillsdale, NJ: Lawrence Erlbaum.

* * *

The dark side of human possibility makes most of our history. But this tragic fact does not imply that behavioral traits of the dark side define the essence of human nature.

> S. J. Gould, *Eight Little Piggies* (1994)

This essay is about the dark side of human behavior. The dark side is an integrative metaphor for a certain perspective toward the study of human folly, frailty, and fallibility. It is also a window into the realm of evil, corruption, and baseness. In the process of pursuing this metaphor, we find that the dark sides of our nature are integral to understanding the human condition, and perhaps even to being human. Along the path that these pursuits take, it is not uncommon to experience a sense that we are peering from the wrong side of the prison bars. Our crimes and misdemeanors sometimes seem wholly just and necessary, and our acts of goodness often inadvertently murder the very morals they were intended to serve. Such are the paradoxes of the dark side.

The dark side has fascinated humans and scholars of the human condition at least throughout all of recorded history (see Pratt 1994; Watson 1995). But what is the dark side? Recently, Spitzberg and Cupach (1998) took up the question, and suggested an initial, if yet incomplete, answer in the form of the "seven sins" of the dark side.

First, and perhaps most obvious, the dark side is about the dysfunctional, distressing, and destructive aspects of human interaction. Evil is mostly about violence (Baumeister 1997), the intentional harming of someone or something valued by others. But at levels less than evil, we consider things dark when they impair the ability of someone to function (Charny 1996). From grand failures to the malfunctioning of everyday plans to the grinding destructiveness of dysfunctional family interactions, we find frustration and pain in activities that are so impaired.

Second, the dark side can be found in deviance, betrayal, transgression, and violation. Morals and social conventions may be arbitrary, but they serve to preserve an order that is comforting if nothing else. Thus, rebellion against normative culture is viewed as a threat to the integrity of society, family, relationship, and the self's place in this order.

Third, the exploitation of the innocent is another of the shadows of the dark side. Child abuse, coercion, manipulation of the ignorant, and constraint of basic freedoms strike at our assumptions of individual autonomy and the social contract. Those who cannot help themselves must be protected from those who can. But human nature is not always so cooperative.

Fourth, the dark side is concerned with the unfulfilled, underestimated, and unappreciated endeavors of life. From the unborn to the unloved, from blemishes to blight, we decry the repression of what that might have been, especially when the potential for the positive is apparent.

Fifth, the dark side thrives in the presence of the physically unattractive, the ugly, the distasteful, and the repulsive. The loneliness of rejection, and the seductiveness of self-superiority sought through alienating others, are hallmarks of intergroup conflict, enemyship, and simple neglect. We make the enemy ugly in our eyes, and often, through social isolation and scape-goating, we make the ugly our enemies. In such manner, enemies may be created less by *their* own actions, and more by *our* own actions.

Sixth, objectification in humans represents the darkness wrought by dehumanization. We demean ourselves when we treat people through our symbols as things. There are some ways in which such symbolic reduction of people to objects is more damaging to our spirits than actual physical torture and violence. Bombadiers and warplane pilots drop bombs on "the enemy" rather than on families and villages. A thing is easier to exploit, to neglect, to abuse, and to kill, than is a kindred spirit.

Finally, the dark side reflects a fascination with the paradoxical, dialectical, mystifying aspects of human action. Time and again, our studies of topics on the dark side have revealed that those things we presume to be healthy and moral have their destructive forms and applications. Conversely, those shadowy insinuations of evil that appall our collective and individual senses often function in surprisingly positive ways.

Two simple examples can illustrate. Honesty, and its cousin clarity, are generally accepted as valued and moral goals. Yet, most people lie, even to their best friends and partners (DePaulo et al. 1996; Rodriquez and Ryave 1990). Simple politeness requires considerable deviation from the truth (Bavelas et al. 1990). Leaders employ fundamentally ambiguous symbols (e.g., freedom, pride, and prosperity) because they cannot hope to gain widespread consensus without them (Eisenberg 1984). In stark contrast, everyone *knows* that child abuse is intrinsically dark. Yet, research has shown that some people find silver linings to this dark, invidious cloud (McMillen, Zuravin, and Rideout 1995). Some victims of abuse find themselves more cautious, more resilient, more appreciative of life, or more responsible in child-rearing. This in no way is intended to justify activities such as child abuse or deception. Instead, it is intended to suggest that the human experience is far, far more complex in its functions than our simplistic moral paradigms typically permit us to admit, much less see.

These sins of the dark side illustrate that these shadows are probably far more prominent in our everyday lives than we often realize. One way of thinking about this is to consider two criteria of darkness: functional versus normative. A communication process is functionally dark if it detracts from the ability of a person, relationship, or group to survive and thrive. Violence is a good example, because violence almost by definition threatens the victim's ability to survive, much less thrive (although see Spitzberg 1997). In contrast, a communication process is normatively dark if groups, societies, or cultures generally view the behavior as immoral, prohibited, or dysfunctional. Of course, both of these criteria have their opposite (i.e., functional brightness and normative brightness). If we cross these two criteria, there are three possible territories of the dark side, as displayed in Figure 28-1.

Evil incarnate is the most obvious domain of the dark side, and yet, in some ways, it is among the most difficult to populate. That is, there are few communication activities that are *purely* evil, both functionally and normatively. Perhaps the closest pure example would be rhetorical campaigns that incite terror or genocide. Next are behaviors that are productively bright, yet normatively dark. These are behaviors that a society or culture may consider wrong, but that serve important functions. Obscenity might be a good example; it is generally considered inappropriate in everyday discourse, and yet it serves a variety of expressive and regulatory functions in how we define our relationships with others. The third territory is the productively destructive but normatively productive domain. These are behaviors that groups consider appropriate, but that have destructive effects on other people or other groups. For example, many gang-related communication activities are viewed as vital to their own group, but are destructive to the larger societal or community group in which they exist. Finally, there is the territory beyond the dark side, consisting of behaviors that are both functionally productive and normatively approved. As an interesting exercise, you may try to come up with a communication activity that is inherently "bright."

There are many potential applications of the dark side metaphor to the larger domain of human communication activity. A few illustrations that follow are provided merely

**Figure 28-1**
*A Map of the Dark Side*

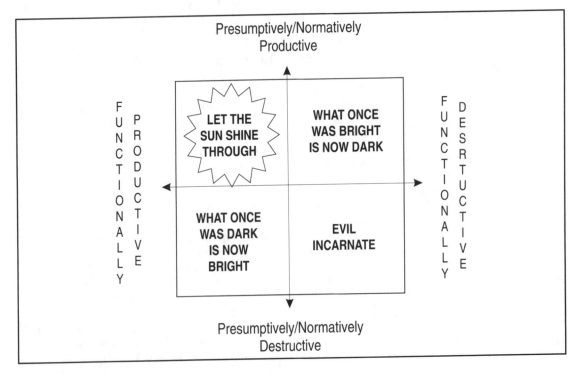

to "whet the appetite" of scholars to take seriously the import of the dark side in their studies and creative pursuits. My reason for offering these illustrations is not to cast a morbid shadow upon our scholarly landscape, but instead to suggest avenues for bridging unrecognized connections among the communication arts and sciences.

The topics of concern to the dark side are often the same topics of interest to the media. I have been involved in research on the following: gossip, obscenity, double binds, mundane incompetence in communicating, equivocation, misunderstanding, failures of social support, unrequited love, relationship break-ups, loneliness, depression, co-dependency, embarrassment, privacy violations, jealousy, envy, infidelity, conflict, deception, hurtful messages, revenge, intimate violence, sexual coercion and rape, fatal attractions, stalking, and the pathology of normal families. These topics litter the talk show circuit and self-help literature, and one would be hard pressed to find newscasts or entertaining movies. Deception, for example, is a major topic of screen characters, of rhetorical scholars studying political deception, of professionals studying ethics of public relations practitioners and advertising campaigns, and of scientists studying the accuracy of deception detection. Crime, criminality, and the dark sides of human behavior, therefore, are "seductive" (Katz 1988; Twitchell 1989) in their ability to evoke curiosity and fascination. Collectively, however, we seem to have little sense about how all these dark and bright sides of our human condition fit together to make us human.

Traditionally, textbooks of human behavior have tended to recommend the virtuous aspects of action and belief. Thus, we are advised by most self-help and undergraduate communication textbooks to be honest, open, clear, articulate, attractive, trustworthy, trusting, cooperative, loyal, nonviolent, confident, assertive, fair, equitable, tolerant, empathic, and optimistic. We are encouraged to be humorous, to be leaders, and to develop heterosexual nuclear families. Yet, honesty can be destructive; openness embarrassing; attractiveness a curse; articulateness inefficient; trust, cooperation, and loyalty exploited; nonviolence a formula for failure; confidence and assertion unlikable; fairness and equity unreciprocated; tolerance taken advantage of; empathy abused; and optimism disappointed with dire consequences (Baumeister, Smart, and Boden 1996; Bochner 1982; Cupach and Spitzberg 1994; Fillion 1996; Goldberg 1993; Levitt, Silver, and Franco 1996; Parks 1995; Ray 1993; Rook and Pietramonaco 1987; Spitzberg 1993, 1994b). Leaders are not necessarily valuable in a world without followers (Conger 1990; Gioia and Longenecker 1994), humor and laughter can be employed in terribly demeaning and corrupting ways (Jenkins 1994; Keough 1990), and some of the most horrific crimes occur in ostensibly nuclear heterosexual families (Blount 1982; Charny 1996; Poster 1978). In essence, the bright side is often darker than it seems.

For example, in the 1960s and early 1970s, assertiveness training became a craze. Researchers, mainly in the areas of counseling and clinical psychology, started conducting considerable scientific research to validate the value of such training. For about a decade everyone in the self-help, scholarly, and lay publics seemed impressed with assertiveness as a key to interpersonal health and self-actualization. Then some scholars decided it would be a good idea to ask the student confederates and "recipients" of the assertion what they thought. It turns out that people on the receiving end of assertion tend to view it as effective, but not very likable or appropriate. In essence, thousands, perhaps tens of thousands, of people were being trained to *lose* friends and influence people. And yet, everyone *knew* that assertion was one of the bright sides of social behavior. Are the risks of social engineering any less any time Dr. Phil advises millions of viewers on television how to respond to a given personal situation?

Similar lessons can be derived from many other realms of the dark side. For example, we constantly are told the importance of reducing conflict, despite the fact that sometimes what is most needed is to know how to start a conflict. We are told that empathy is an essential ingredient for good relationships. But empathy is probably destructive for negotiators and surgeons. We are told to be nonviolent, but we rarely begrudge someone violence in self-defense. We are told to be disclosive and open in relationships, even though such openness can be abused. We are told to be optimistic, and yet lonely persons are those who expect more intimacy than they receive. Thus, the elderly tend to be less lonely than college-age populations, who expect too much in the way of intimacy (Russell 1996). We are told that mutual understanding is essential to a good marriage. However, the research thus far is very qualified. The extent to which husbands and wives *think* they are understood, the more satisfied they are with their marriage. To date, there is very little evidence that *actual* accuracy of understanding and being understood are related to marital satisfaction. Indeed, there is even a tantalizing tidbit of evidence to the contrary. Spouses who *really*, accurately, understand each other may be *less* satisfied, presumably because they find more details over which disagreement and conflict can arise.

The point is that popular press, media, public, and scholarly opinion seem fascinated by the dark side because it reflects those aspects of our lives we collectively want to avoid (Putney 1992). The irony is that the dark side is often not so dark, and the bright side to which we aspire is often darker than we care to believe. Thus, a question such as "Does violence in the media cause violence in society?" is only part of the relevant question. The other questions include issues such as: "Why do people seem drawn to or entertained by violence?" "Under what conditions is violence in the media harmful to society, and under what conditions is it helpful?" "How should the darker sides of our nature be theoretically and artistically integrated into our broader conceptions of ourselves?" Schoenewolf (1991) speaks of the "art" of hating, Spitzberg (1997) about the "competence" of violence, Katz (1988) about the seductions of crime, Sabini and Silver (1982) about some of the functional ambiguities of life (e.g., flirtation), Volkan (1988) about the need to have enemies, and Coser (1956) and Gilmore (1987) about the important social functions of conflict; and several authors have noted the many values of ambiguity (e.g., Bavelas et al. 1990; Spitzberg 1993, 1994a).

The field of communication has a long tradition of studying topics on the dark side, although it has seldom explicitly viewed these topics as possessing common threads of connection with one another—threads that collectively define the nature of the dark side of human communication. There are many examples that illustrate the richness of the discipline, including research on ethics in public relations, advertising, and political communication; the impact of stereotyping, objectification, and paradoxical images of women portrayed in the mass media; Internet addiction; the rhetorical strategies of terrorists and groups such as the KKK; the study of interpersonal conflict, sexual harassment, sexual coercion, safe sex (or the lack thereof), sexual assault, intimate violence, and stalking; as well as dozens of everyday types of communication on the dark side, such as deception, infidelity, rejection, relationship breakup, embarrassment, shame, guilt, anger, loneliness, depression, conversational dilemmas, hurtful messages, criticism, obscenity, and communicative aggression. Finally, many scholars are attempting to anticipate the role that communication media will have on our future. Will the new communication media provide the utopia so many advertisers seem to promise, or will they create a *dystopia* in which the colder media of screens and keyboards and artificial intelligence make relationships less intimate and satisfying? Will the advent of an information economy mean that the information haves will exploit the information have-nots? Is it a brave new world in which privacy is a scarce commodity, or will communication media permit the creation of information islands in which people secure themselves in the telecommuting wombs of their homes? In short, the dark side is integral to the work that communication scholars do, but it has yet to be recognized as such.

The dark side offers tangible opportunities to understand the human condition (Duck 1994; Duck and Wood 1995). To date, we have tended to be too simplistic ideologically. Artistically, we tend to construct characters who are good or evil, but only occasionally do we get a really good characterization of someone capable of, even adept at, both. Scientifically, we tend to treat the bright side as intrinsically moral and the dark side as something to extricate from society, rather than seeking the many ways in which the dark side is an ally to desirable individual and social relations. We have reasonably elaborate understandings of serial killers and crimes of passion, but we have relatively little understanding of the wish to kill that may be in all of us. We have extensive programs of research on deception, but know almost nothing about how hurtful or dysfunctional honesty can be. Until such questions are taken seriously by artists, professionals, and scholars, the answers will continue to elude us, and we will be less able to make legitimate choices in our public policies, much less our daily lives, in regard to social behavior.

## References

Baumeister, R. F. (1997). *Evil*. New York: W. H. Freeman.

Baumeister, R. F., Smart, L., and Boden, J. M. (1996). Relation of threatened egotism to violence and aggression: The dark side of high self-esteem. *Psychological Review*, 103, 5–33.

Bavelas, J. B., Black, A., Chovil, N., and Mullett, J. (1990). *Equivocal Communication*. Newbury Park: Sage.

Blount, F. (1982). *The Subversive Family: An Alternative History of Love and Marriage*. London: Jonathan Cape.

Bochner, A. P. (1982). On the efficacy of openness. In M. Burgoon (Ed.), *Communication Yearbook 5* (pp. 109–124). New Brunswick, NJ: Transaction/International Communication Association.

Charny, I. W. (1996). Evil in human personality: Disorders of doing harm to others in family relationships. In F. W. Kaslow (Ed.), *Handbook of Relational Diagnosis and Dysfunctional Family Patterns* (pp. 477–495). New York: John Wiley & Sons.

Conger, J. A. (1990). The dark side of leadership. *Organizational Dynamics*, 19, 44–55.

Coser, L. (1956). *The Functions of Social Conflict*. New York: Free Press.

Cupach, W. R., and Spitzberg, B. H. (Eds.). (1994). *The Dark Side of Interpersonal Communication*. Hillsdale, NJ: Lawrence Erlbaum Associates.

DePaulo, B. M., Kashy, D. A., Kirkendol, S. E., Wyer, M. M., and Epstein, J. A. (1996). Lying in everyday life. *Journal of Personality and Social Psychology*, 70, 979–995.

Duck, S. (1994). Stratagems, spoils, and a serpent's tooth: On the delights and dilemmas of personal relationships. In W. R. Cupach and B. H. Spitzberg (Eds.), *The Dark Side of Interpersonal Communication* (pp. 3–24). Hillsdale, NJ: LEA.

Duck, S., and Wood, J. T. (1995). For better, for worse, for richer, for poorer: The rough and the smooth of relationships. In S. Duck and J. T. Wood (Eds.), *Confronting Relationship Challenges* (pp. 1–21). Thousand Oaks, CA: Sage.

Eisenberg, E. M. (1984). Ambiguity as strategy in organizational communication. *Communication Monographs*, 51, 227–242.

Fillion, K. (1996). *Lip Service: The Truth About Women's Darker Side in Love, Sex, and Friendship*. New York: HarperCollins.

Gioia, D. A., and Longenecker, C. O. (1994). Delving into the dark side: The politics of executive appraisal. *Organizational Dynamics*, 22, 47–58.

Goldberg, J. G. (1993). *The Dark Side of Love: The Positive Role of Our Negative Feelings—Anger, Jealousy, and Hate*. New York: G. P. Putnam's Sons.

Gould, S. J. (1994). *Eight Little Piggies: Reflections in Natural History*. New York: W. W. Norton.

Jenkins, R. (1994). *Subversive Laughter: The Liberating Power of Comedy*. New York: Free Press.

Katz, J. (1988). *Seductions of Crime: Moral and Sensual Attractions in Doing Evil*. New York: Basic Books.

Keough, W. (1990). *Punchlines: The Violence of American Humor*. New York: Paragon House.

Levitt, M. J., Silver, M. E., and Franco, N. (1996). Troublesome relationships: A part of human experience. *Journal of Social and Personal Relationships*, 13, 523–536.

McMillen, C., Zuravin, S., and Rideout, G. (1995). Perceived benefit from child sexual abuse. *Journal of Consulting and Clinical Psychology*, 63, 1037–1043.

Parks, M. R. (1995). Ideology in interpersonal communication: Beyond the couches, talk shows, and bunkers. In B. R. Burleson (Ed.), *Communication Yearbook 18* (pp. 480–497). Thousand Oaks, CA: Sage.

Poster, M. (1978). *Critical Theory of the Family*. New York: Seabury Press.

Pratt, A. R. (1994). *The Dark Side: Thoughts on the Futility of Life From the Ancient Greeks to the Present*. New York: Carol Publishing Group.

Putney, M. J. (1992). Welcome to the dark side. In J. A. Krantz (Ed.), *Dangerous Men and Adventurous Women* (pp. 99–105). Philadelphia: University of Pennsylvania.

Ray, E. B. (1993). When the links become chains: Considering dysfunctions of supportive communication in the workplace. *Communication Monographs*, 60, 106–111.

Rodriquez, N., and Ryave, A. (1990). Telling lies in everyday life: Motivational and organizational consequences of sequential preferences. *Qualitative Sociology*, 13, 195–210.

Rook, K. S., and Pietromonaco, P. (1987). Close relationships: Ties that heal or ties that bind? In W. H. Jones and D. Perlman (Eds.), *Advances in Personal Relationships* (vol. 1, pp. 1–35). Greenwich CT: JAI Press.

Russell, D. W. (1996). UCLS Loneliness Scale (Version 3): Reliability, validity, and factor structure. *Journal of Personality Assessment*, 66, 20–40.

Sabini, J., and Silver, M. (1982). *Moralities of Everyday Life*. Oxford: Oxford University Press.

Schoenewolf, G. (1991). *The Art of Hating*. Northvale, NJ: Jason Aronson.

Spitzberg, B. H. (1993). The dialectics of (in)competence. *Journal of Social and Personal Relationships*, 10, 137–158.

———. (1994a). The dark side metaphor. *International Society for the Study of Personal Relationships Bulletin*, 11, 8–9.

———. (1994b). The dark side of (in)competence. In W. R. Cupach and B. H. Spitzberg (Eds.), *The Dark Side of Interpersonal Communication* (pp. 25–49). Hillsdale, NJ: Lawrence Erlbaum Associates.

———. (1997). Intimate violence. In W. R. Cupach and D. J. Canary (Eds.), *Competence in Interpersonal Conflict* (pp. 174–201). New York: McGraw-Hill.

Spitzberg, B. H., and Cupach, W. R. (1998). Dusk, detritus, and delusion: A prolegomenon to the dark side of close relationships. In W. R. Cupach and B. H. Spitzberg (Eds.), *The Dark Side of Close Relationships* (pp. xi–xxii). Mahwah, NJ: Lawrence Erlbaum Associates.

Twitchell, J. B. (1989). *Preposterous Violence: Fables of Aggression in Modern Culture*. New York: Oxford University Press.

Volkan, V. D. (1988). *The Need to Have Enemies and Allies: From Clinical Practice to International Relationships*. Northvale, NJ: Jason Aronson.

Watson, L. (1995). *Dark Nature: A Natural History of Evil*. New York: HarperCollins.

# Questions

1. Under what circumstances do you regularly encounter dark side interactions of a particular type? What are the costs to at least one participant in the interactions? What, if any, possible benefits might this participant experience?

2. Describe a situation in which you, another person, or a fictional character enacted problematic, difficult, or destructive communication behaviors. What appeared to be the reason for this choice? What was the effect of the choice?

# 29
# Lying

*Mark L. Knapp and*
*Anita L. Vangelisti*

Lying appears as one of the most complicated relational interaction patterns. Often thought of as deceitful, devious, or unethical, lying has also been considered the lesser of two evils—less painful than the truth. A complication of lying is the distinction between lies of commission (deliberately telling a falsehood to another) and lies of omission (neglecting to tell the whole story or telling selected information while withholding the most critical parts). Many people decide whether to tell the whole truth and nothing but the truth, based on the possible outcome of that choice. In their writing on deception, O'Hair and Cody (1994) discuss the valence or positive to negative directions of relational motives. They suggest, "Positive relational deception strategies are termed utility and usually focus on tactics intended to improve, enhance, escalate, and repair relationships" (p. 196). Often the goal is to promote intimacy or maintain a relationship. Messages may include agreeing with or complimenting other people, even when the message is a fabrication, in order to foster liking. In contrast, regress implies a goal of creating stagnation in or damaging a relationship. Messages may include indications of disinterest in others in order to protect oneself from multiple romantic involvements. In countless cases, deception has started with good intentions but eventually creates painful upheaval when the truth is revealed. Many communicators use a social exchange model when considering deception, weighing the costs and benefits of equivocation or deception in the short term and long term. These complexities confound labeling lying as strictly a dark side behavior.

Frequently romantically involved partners will attempt to establish an expectation of total truthfulness, a goal that frequently puts the partners in conflict with other relational goals such as politeness, positivity, or supportiveness. Partners struggle with minor decisions about whether to respond honestly to the risky question "How do I look?" or whether to report that dinner was "Terrific" even if the meat was overcooked and the sauce was burned. Sometimes they struggle with major decisions about whether to reveal fears of serious illness or the reality of a gambling problem. Often the perceived state of the relationship, as well as the possible costs and rewards of such a disclosure, determine the level of truthfulness provided.

The choice to enter certain occupations may consign one to continuous deception-oriented struggles. Police officers often mask the possible risks of certain assignments when talking with family members; doctors may find themselves downplaying the severity of certain illnesses in order to leave patients with some hope. Historically, many adoption workers refrained from telling prospective parents certain negative information about a potential child's background in order to foster a match. Educators may try not to discourage students' dreams even if they view them as highly unrealistic. As O'Hair and Cody so directly state it: "The person who is brutally honest will be a very lonely person" (1994, 196).

In the following article on lying, Knapp and Vangelisti address lying in established relationships as well as the verbal and nonverbal processes of lie detection in these relationships. Wisely, they warn of the dangers of extreme levels of suspicion on any relationship. As you read this piece, ask yourself the following question: What did I learn about lying in my family of origin, and how does that influence my behavior in close friendships and romantic relationships?

## Reference

O'Hair, H. D., and Cody, M. J. (1994). Deception. In W. R. Cupach and B. H. Spitzberg, (Eds.), *The Dark Side of Interpersonal Communication.* (pp. 181–214). Hillsdale, NJ: Lawrence Erlbaum Associates.

\* \* \*

# Lying

At first glance, it may seem strange that we include lying as a behavior involved in maintaining a close relationship. After all, honesty and close relationships go hand in hand. And some people report that honesty and trustworthiness are more desirable traits in a partner (for long- and short-term relationships) than almost any other—including an exciting personality, a good sense of humor, adaptability, dependability, kindness/understanding, and others.[1] And, as expected, people in close relationships report telling fewer lies to each other.[2] But most people realize that satisfying relationships somehow learn to appreciate and accommodate behavior that falls short of "the whole truth and nothing but the truth."[3] Decisions about truth-telling and lying are at the very heart of what constitutes a close relationship. For many, the familiar promise, "We won't lie to each other" is viewed as a covenant that will lead to and sustain greater intimacy. It is, however, worth noting that each partner may have different referents for what "agreeing not to lie" means. For instance, does it mean I have to tell you things that I know would hurt you and you probably wouldn't find out anyway? Does it mean I have to tell you I hate your outfit (if that's the way I feel) when you ask for my opinion? If I tell you I went to bed with another person, is it lying not to tell you the details? If acts of omission, exaggeration, vagueness, evasiveness, and substitution are all a part of the act of lying, then everybody lies. If we can't avoid lying, then what is the kind of behavior we are trying to avoid with the "we won't lie to each other" promise?

For most couples, the real issue is whether a lie will have a damaging effect on the relationship and whether the motivation for lying was well-intended or not. Thus, when contemplating a lie, the following questions seem to be key: (1) Will this lie help both of us? If the lie is solely for the benefit of one partner, it is more likely to be viewed negatively and incur more relationship damage. Liar motivation is at issue here. The couple's short- and long-range mutual goals are the focus. From this perspective, we would expect most of the lies of people in close relationships to be motivated by a desire to help their partner. And that seems to be the case.[4] Lies designed to protect their partner from hurt, to help them build or maintain their self-esteem, to assist them in accomplishing their goals, and to show concern for their physical and mental states are the most common lies told by the most committed partners. This doesn't mean that self-oriented lies don't occur in close relationships. In fact, sometimes "closeness" itself facilitates or prompts self-oriented lying when the fear of losing it is high and when one's partner makes it clear that there is a high probability that such lies will be forgiven.[5] (2) Is the lie consistent with the rules of fairness in the relationship? That is, does one's partner operate by the same rules you do? Liar intentions are the concern now. If both partners agree that certain classes of lies are okay but others are not (e.g., lying about one's sexual prowess may be okay, but lying about having lunch with an ex-lover may not), then lies in the forbidden categories will incur more relationship damage. Sometimes, of course, a couple either assumes the other knows what categories are okay and what are not or they have not discussed the issue specifically. Thus, when an intentional lie in a category one partner believes is not acceptable occurs, the liar may argue that he or she was not aware of the rule and that it won't happen again. This is one way fairness rules about lying are negotiated. (3) Does your partner (the lied to) believe you have his or her best interests at heart—both generally and in this specific situation? If the answer is yes, the lie is likely to have less damage to the relationship. Even in situations where the liar clearly violates the couple's agreed-upon norms for lying (e.g., lying about an affair), the damage to the relationship will be offset if the offender can convince his or her partner that the lie was consistent with other instances that indicated a concern for the partner's welfare.

The best predicator of relationship termination as a result of a discovered lie is the perceived importance of the information lied about. This explains why those people who are more involved/committed to their relationship are going to have a greater emotional reaction to lies that impinge directly on the relationship.[6]

The way that a liar and a lie detector behave in a close relationship is strongly influenced by certain conditions that are unlike those conditions which characterize less intimate relationships.[7] The first characteristic has to do with the kind of *mutual influence* exerted by the partners to a close relationship. Even in lies to non-intimates, we may be more involved in the lie than we care to admit. It is easy to condemn lies that we feel we had no part in. but we can influence a person's decision to lie, and we can give tacit approval to it once it occurs. A familiar behavior of this type is the hostess who knows a guest is lying about "what a nice party this has been" but recognizes the intent is to avoid unpleasantness, so she cooperates in the deception. In other instances, a person may make it so clear that he or she is intolerant and inflexible regarding a certain behavior that this person's partner feels the necessity to lie when experiences with that behavior occur. Thus, we may be well advised to reflect on our own role in another's decision to lie before we determine how much punishment is deserved. Additionally, the role of the deceived in the deceiver's behavior is likely to affect the deceived person's motivation and accuracy in detecting the deception as well as the way the liar performs the lie. In close relationships, partners constantly negotiate interaction norms with the knowledge that each will play a role in the outcome. Lying is no different. When the outcome is an undesirable one, however, responsibility is frequently attributed to one's partner.

The second important characteristic of lies in close relationships concerns the increased possibility of *multiple exposure* to the lie. Lies to people we don't see that often do not require the same kind of development and/or repetition. This will surely affect the extent to which the liar will want to engage in lies of omission.

The third characteristic of intimates is that they are quite *familiar* with one another's behavior. This raises the question of detection accuracy. Most of the research on detection of liars has been done with people who don't know each other very well. This research indicates that an untrained observer, looking at and listening to a stranger without the aid of any mechanical equipment, will be able to identify liars about half or slightly better than half the time. the percentage of accurate identification is, in reality, probably lower due to the fact that it is easier to deceive a person who has no reason to suspect that he or she is being lied to, and much of the research conducted asks subjects to "identify this person as a deceiver or nondeceiver"—an instruction which immediately forewarns subjects of possible deception.

## Lie Detection

Although research on detecting lying among friends and intimates is sparse, Comadena found intimates generally more accurate than acquaintances. Friends, however, may exhibit more accuracy than spouses.[8] Spouses are committed to a relationship that may last a long time and involves daily contact. As a result, they may be more likely than good friends to develop a desensitization to behavior associated with lying. People in close relationships don't expect their partner to lie, and there also may be a strong desire not to be an accurate detector, as this wife attests:

> Little by little things were happening that didn't make sense, but I can remember making excuses for them myself . . . I didn't want to believe there was anything to find out . . . so I was being deceived from two angles . . . I was deceiving myself . . . I didn't sit there when it was happening saying "I am just fooling myself." You know, I, I, as I said, I made up a lot of excuses, and really believed them . . . I didn't confide in anyone, too, because I was afraid of what they would tell me. I wanted to believe everything was going to be fine and I wasn't being deceived. If I told someone else they might tell me I was being deceived and I didn't want to hear that. . . . But as much as I wanted to be a detective and find him out, I didn't want to either. Because the truth, I was afraid more of the truth than living in the lie kind of.[9]

If intimates do want to detect the lies of their partners, they have several advantages. For example, in more intimate relationships the partners have a mental record or backlog for verbal checking and verification; further, they have a history of having observed the other in many different emotional situations. Hence, intimates should have a better idea of what behavior exceeds the boundaries of normality for their partner. Changes in behavior or activity patters often trigger partner alertness if not suspicion. In addition, intimates have considerably more motivation to look closely for clues than acquaintances or mere observers. Although greater intimacy may give one an advantage in being able to perceive a partner's lies, greater intimacy may also make partners less attentive to the possibilities of lies.[10] Thus, unless intimates have a reason for expecting a lie, they may be less apt to notice it. The first lies to intimate partners are likely to be the easiest to get away with. After all, the relationship was built on trust, so there is no reason to be suspicious. Even if lie goes undetected, it may still have a significant impact on the relationship.[11] For example, a person who has engaged in an important deception in a close relationship may get mad at him or herself and take out their anger on their partner. Perceptions of their partner as being easily duped or as no more honest themselves may begin to take hold and alter feelings and discourse.

Although lie detection is no doubt an important skill on some occasions, there is always the danger of engaging in such acts too often. Those who go on a search-and-destroy mission for their partner's lies may find they have created more harm than good for the relationship. Suspicion can create suspicion to the point where neither person trusts the other and the lie detector has created the very thing he or she set out to destroy. In addition, it is likely that such a campaign against lies may only drive the worst offenders underground so they can refine their strategies. Besides, relationships often rely on certain kinds of deceptions for sustenance. To wipe out any ability to deceive another may wipe out some important structural foundations for the relationship. This doesn't mean we shouldn't probe, question, and investigate situations in which a lie seems to harm the relationship; it simply means we should try to preserve the assumption of truthfulness rather than replace it with an assumption of deceit. If you're like us, there are some things you'd rather no know the "truth" about.

Are there any behaviors that are always associated with lying behavior and nothing else? No. There are behaviors that liars in nonintimate relationships regularly exhibit, such as speech errors, higher pitch, more hesitations, fidgeting, etc., but intimates may attend to more idiosyncratic cues.[12] We know one person whose wife listens for a barely audible gulp after a statement that is already suspected of being an untruth—e.g., "I dropped by the office to do some work," whereas "I stopped by the jeweler to check on your ring" would be the true statement. It is usually wise to look for clusters of behavior rather than a single cue. To say, "I knew he was lying because he didn't look at me" is just as risky as saying "I knew he didn't have a large vocabulary because he used the word *liar* instead of *deceiver*." In order to increase the probability that we are accurate in detecting deception, we should look for clusters of cues—does his or her lack of eye contact fit with other things you've observed such as nervous movement and speech errors?

Some data are known on what seems to be stereotyped categories for lying behavior. Liars, for instance, will sometimes be observed exhibiting a cluster of *anxiety responses* due to guilt or psychological distress. These may include such behaviors as blushing, shaking, gulping, perspiring, voice tremors, speech errors, using fewer different words, and sending shorter messages. Sometimes observers key their observations on what they consider to be *excessive responses*. As noted earlier, excessive responses go beyond the boundaries of normal behavior for the individual being observed. It may be that the person is too inactive or too active; it might be that he or she talks excessively or engages in pronounced pauses and silences; it might be that he or she makes excessive eye contact (staring) or no eye contact at all; or it may be that he or she answers seemingly nonthreatening questions with extremely defensive remarks—"You're a little late this evening, dear. Where have you been?" "CAN'T I HAVE ONE PEACEFUL MOMENT BEFORE I GET THE THIRD DEGREE! IF YOU WANT TO KNOW MY WHEREABOUTS EVERY MOMENT OF THE DAY, HIRE A PRIVATE DETECTIVE!" Another category people sometimes observe in liars is *incongruous responses*. Liars sometimes have a hard time keeping their stories straight. Verbally, a person may contradict some known fact the receiver is aware of, or contradict his or her own earlier statement. Sometimes, incongruity is shown when a person is being very careful and trying to maintain control in a situation that doesn't call for such behavior. Nonverbally, we might see . . . inconsistency . . . —saying "I've always liked you" but exhibiting a host of nonverbal cues that attest otherwise. Finally, sometimes observers detect what might be called *indirect responses*. Verbal indirectness will take on the characteristics of some . . . evasive tactics mentioned . . . [such as] answering a question with a question, changing the subject. A person could also show verbal indirectness through vagueness—fewer verifiable factual assertions, fewer references to a verifiable past, fewer self-oriented statements for which a person could be held responsible, and more broad, sweeping generalizations. Nonverbally, indirectness may be seen, among other things, by not maintaining a direct body orientation when talking to another person or simply by increasing the distance between oneself and the listener. It should be clear from the preceding that many of the behaviors typically associated with liars are also manifested by people telling the truth. Thus, it is advisable to gather as much information about the situation as possible before charging the other with lying.

Of course, lie detection in close relationships is not always wholly dependent on observing the behavior of one's partner. Some of the most common methods involved obtaining information from third parties and finding evidence which contradicts the liar's story.[13] . . .

## Notes

1. S. Stewart, H. Stinnett, L. B. Rosenfeld, "Sex Differences in Desired Characteristics of Short-Term and Long-Term Relationship Partners." *Journal of Social and Personal Relationships* 17 (2000): 843–853; H. LaFollette and G. Graham, "Honesty and Intimacy," *Journal of Social and Personal Relationships* 3 (1986): 3–18.

2. B. M. DePaulo and D. A. Kashy, "Everyday Lies in Close and Casual Relationships," *Journal of Personality and Social Psychology* 74 (1998): 63–79.

3. S. D. Boon and B. A. McLeod, "Deception in Romantic Relationships: Subjective Estimates of Success at Deceiving and Attitudes Toward Deception," *Journal of Social and Personal Relationships* 18 (2001): 463–476.

4. DePaulo and Kashy, 1998; S. Metts, "An Explanatory Investigation of Deception in Close Relationships." *Journal of Social and Personal Relationships* 6 (1989): 159–179; B. M. DePaulo and K. L. Bell, "Truth and Investment: Lies Are Told to Those Who Care." *Journal of Personality and Social Psychology* 71 (1996): 703–716.

5. T. Cole, "Lying to the One You Love: The Use of Deception in Romantic Relationships." *Journal of Social and Personal Relationships* 18 (2001): 107–129.

6. S. A. McCornack and T. R. Levine, "When Lies Are Uncovered: Emotional and Relational Outcomes of Discovered Deception," *Communication Monographs* 57 (1990): 119–138.

7. D. E. Anderson, M. E. Ansfield, and B. M. DePaulo, "Love's Best Habit: Deception in the Context of Relationships." In P. Philippot and R. S. Feldman, eds., *The Social Context of Nonverbal Behavior* (New York: Cambridge University Press, 1999), pp. 372–409.

8. M. E. Comadena, "Accuracy in Detecting Deception: Intimate and Friendship Relationships." In M. Burgoon, ed., *Communication Yearbook 6* (Beverly Hills, CA: Sage, 1982), pp. 446–471. Also see S. A. McCornack and M. R. Parks, "Deception Detection and Relationship Development: The Other Side of Trust." In M. L. McLaughlin, ed., *Communication Yearbook 9* (Beverly Hills, CA: Sage, 1986), pp. 337–389.

9. L. F. Werth and J. Flaherty, "A Phenomenological Approach to Human Deception." In R. W. Mitchell and N. S. Thompson, eds., *Deception: Perspectives on Human and Nonhuman Deceit* (Albany, NY: SUNY Press, 1986), p. 296.

10. T. R. Levine and S. A. McCornack, "Linking Love and Lies: A Formal Test of the McCornack and Parks Model of Deception Detection," *Journal of Social and Personal Relationships* 9 (1992): 143–154.

11. B. J. Sagarin, K. v. L. Rhoads, and R. B. Cialdini, "Deceiver's Distrust: Denigration as a Consequence of Undiscovered Deception," *Personality and Social Psychology Bulletin* 24 (1998): 1167–1176.

12. B. M. DePaulo, J. J. Lindsay, B. E. Malone, L. Muhelbruck, K. Charlton, and H. Cooper, "Cues to Deception." *Psychological Bulletin* 129 (2003): 74–118.

13. H. S. Park, T. R. Levine, S. A. McCornack, K. Morrison, and M. Ferrara, "How People Really Detect Lies." *Communication Monographs* 69 (2002): 144–157.

## Questions

1. What criteria do you use to decide whether, and to what extent, you will tell the truth in friendships or romantic situations? How did you develop these criteria for yourself?

2. Think about a person who you interact with regularly. What are the nonverbal cues, sometimes called *leakage*, that tell you the individual is equivocating or lying? How do you respond when faced with those cues?

3. Imagine you are socializing a young child (age 5–7) regarding honesty. What would you tell him or her about lying to other people? What kinds of situations might you discuss with this child?

# 30

# Irresolvable Interpersonal Conflicts

## Students' Perceptions of Common Topics, Possible Reasons for Persistence, and Communication Patterns

*Courtney Waite Miller*

**O**ngoing conflicts strain relationships. Revisiting an issue over and over again challenges partners, friends, and colleagues who find themselves caught up in difficult or unpleasant patterns in which they feel trapped. However, such conflicts are not unusual, especially in long-term committed relationships or in involuntary relationships, such as those found in the workplace. In studying ongoing conflicts in marriages over four years, marital researcher John Gottman writes, "In looking at the videotapes of most of the cases, it was as if the couple had changed clothes and hairstyle, while continuing to talk about the same or analogous issues in precisely the same ways" (1999, 56). His research team found that 69 percent of the time, these couples were disagreeing about a "perpetual problem" that they had struggled with for many years. The majority of these problems had to do with differences in personality or needs related to a core aspect of self-definition. When couples cannot find a way to dialogue with their perpetual problems, Gottman says the conflict becomes gridlocked and the partners experience emotional disengagement. You may have experienced or observed such painful circumstances, when people you cared about got caught up in destructive continuous conflict cycles. Such struggles may be considered part of the dark side of communication because they impair the ability of the relationship to function, or, as Brian Spitzberg writes in the opening of this section on the dark side, the couples experience "the grinding destructiveness of dysfunctional family interactions."

Although friends and colleagues' ongoing, repetitive conflicts tend to be less dramatic and painful, they also drain positivity and support from the relationship, creating tension and frustration for the parties involved. Less energy is directed toward sustaining the relationship as people regularly find themselves defensive and angry. Such battles impact their social circles of other friends or co-workers, who learn to dread witnessing these encounters. If you find yourself in ongoing, repetitive conflicts, you know the frustrations of this experience.

In the following article, Courtney Waite Miller examines a specific type of ongoing conflict, one she refers to as irresolvable conflict. Such conflicts are based on the perception of at least one person that the issue will never be resolved. In other words, there is no way to bridge the differences, now or forever. If one party believes this, then that person sees no value in revisiting the issue. Miller provides her definition of irresolvable conflict and relates this to other descriptions of ongoing conflicts. Based on a study of undergraduate students, she discusses the types of issues that may be considered irresolvable, the reasons why they are perceived as never resolvable, and, finally, the related communication patterns. The three primary communication patterns are avoidance, argument prevention, and withdrawal.

As you read this chapter, decide if you can identify any issues you would consider irresolvable and ask yourself, "What strategies have I used or observed to manage irresolvable conflicts or other ongoing, repetitive conflicts?

### Reference

Gottman, J. M. (1999). *The Marriage Clinic: A Scientifically Based Marital Therapy.* New York: W. W. Norton.

* * *

"Uncle Jack, I really wish you and Grandma would patch things up so that you can both come to my wedding. It would mean a lot to me to have you both there and know that you're close again."

"Sabrina, this isn't ever, *ever* going to be patched up. Do you understand me? Never. I'm not budging and she's not budging and that's just the way it's going to be. Aunt Lisa and I have already planned on not attending your wedding."

\* \* \*

"John, there has to be a middle ground somewhere. I don't want to have a disagreement with you. Can't we work this out somehow?"

"You and I are never going to see eye to eye on this issue, Anne. No amount of talking is ever going to make me agree with you. Just save your breath [laughing]. Where do you want to go for dinner?"

\* \* \*

Have you ever experienced a situation similar to those above? If you are like me and a lot of people I've talked to, you probably have. When I discuss my research with friends and family, almost everyone responds with stories that are similar to those above.

As I'm sure most of you know from experience, conflict is a common occurrence in interpersonal relationships. Thankfully, many interpersonal conflicts are short in duration (e.g., Vuchinich 1987). However, sometimes we have arguments that seem to last forever. When we have an argument that ends with statements such as those above or experience multiple arguments about the same issue without getting any closer to a resolution, many of us may conclude that the argument is impossible to settle. I call these arguments *irresolvable interpersonal conflicts*. In irresolvable conflicts, at least one of the individuals involved believes the argument is impossible to resolve. In many cases, opposing parties may agree that a conflict is impossible to resolve. However, both parties do not have to agree on a conflict's resolvability for it to be considered irresolvable. One may view a conflict as resolvable and another may view it as irresolvable. In this way, the definition of an irresolvable conflict is a personal judgment.

In addition, an individual does not have to state explicitly that he or she believes a conflict is irresolvable. An individual may decide to share his or her belief of irresolvability with an opposing party, or he or she may keep this belief private. It is an individual's *perception* of irresolvability that defines an irresolvable conflict for him or her.

This perception of irresolvability is what separates irresolvable interpersonal conflicts from other types of interpersonal conflicts such as serial arguments or perpetual problems. A serial argument "exists when individuals argue or engage in conflict about the same topic over time, during which they participate in several (at least two) arguments about the topic" (Johnson and Roloff 1998, 333). Some serial arguments may become irresolvable conflicts. Johnson and Roloff (1998) reported that after repeated argumentative episodes with little or no progress toward achieving resolution, interactants may determine that neither of them will change. This may lead one or both interactants to perceive the argument as irresolvable. However, not all serial arguments become irresolvable conflicts and not all irresolvable conflicts involve repeated arguments. It is possible, albeit unlikely, for an individual to argue about an issue once and declare the conflict irresolvable.

Irresolvable conflicts also are different from perpetual problems in several ways. First, John Gottman (1999) studies perpetual problems in the context of marriages. He defines perpetual problems as "issues with no resolution that the couple has been dealing with for many years" (Gottman 1999, 96). Irresolvable conflicts can occur in any type of relationship. Second, a married individual may or may not believe a perpetual problem is impossible to resolve. However, if a married individual does perceive a perpetual problem as impossible to resolve, there may be no difference between an irresolvable conflict and a perpetual problem.

As you can see, each individual defines his or her own irresolvable conflicts. It is your perception that matters for you. It does not matter what the opposing party thinks or even what your best friend thinks about your conflict. It's your perception of your conflicts that matters. In my opinion, once you believe that a conflict is impossible to settle, you're experiencing an irresolvable conflict . . . and you will communicate accordingly. Your relational partner's perception of irresolvable conflict also will impact how he or she communicates with you. Experiencing an irresolvable conflict is certainly a walk on the dark side of interpersonal relationships, as described by Spitzberg and Cupach (1998).

I will now describe common topics of irresolvable conflicts, possible reasons why irresolvable conflicts persist, and the communication patterns that commonly occur in irresolvable conflicts. I also will address the relational impact of irresolvable conflicts. My research indicates that it is not just the presence of an irresolvable conflict that affects a relationship. Instead, it is the way in which individuals manage the conflict (Waite 2004a). All of my findings are based on a study of students' conflicts in their dating or parental relationships. I will start with examples of common topics of irresolvable conflicts.

## Common Topics of Irresolvable Conflicts

When I first started researching irresolvable conflicts, I reasoned that only very important issues would become irresolvable. I assumed that a compromise could be reached for less important issues or, at the very least, individuals would believe that they could reach an agreement on less important issues if they were forced to do so. However, when I asked undergraduate students to describe an irresolvable conflict in their romantic or parental relationships, their descriptions were similar to those provided by individuals who described resolved conflicts or conflicts they believed they could resolve in the future.

Students perceived the issues at the heart of their irresolvable conflicts as not any more important than the issues involved in resolvable or resolved conflicts (Waite 2004a). Some students described their issues as very important, and some said their issues were not important at all. In reading students' descriptions, I identified serious issues and issues that were more routine. The following are examples of serious

issues involved in irresolvable conflicts (Waite 2004b):

- The topic is religion. I am a Christian and he [romantic partner] is Jewish. While we both believe in one God, we will never agree about his abilities or works in the lives of humans. This has also led to other debates such as evolution versus creationism.

- My mother is extremely closed-minded on the subject of homosexuality. I have a man in my family who was my uncle by marriage. He divorced his wife because he is gay. My mother is convinced that he and his life partner are going to hell, and she's not shy about that opinion at all.

- My parents are divorced and my father is currently dating someone who is considerably younger than he is and was a graduate student of his at one point. While she's very nice, I have issues with their age difference (57 versus late 30s) and the way their relationship began, as a teacher and student. My father does not see anything wrong with him dating someone younger and a former student, and doesn't understand my issues with it.

As you can see, these individuals described difficult conflicts centered on religious and other personal beliefs. Religious/personal beliefs was the most common topic of irresolvable conflict described in both romantic and parental relationships. However, as I mentioned previously, not all irresolvable conflicts involved serious issues. Here are examples of less serious issues:

- The topic is habits and sleep patterns. I sleep late at night and get up late in the morning. My parents think I should sleep early, get up early.

- The disagreement is about how I manage my money. My mother is very meticulous about saving all her receipts and balancing her checkbook. I just don't have the time to do it and I don't see why it's important if I check my bank and credit card statements.

- My boyfriend pressures me to go out on weeknights and he doesn't agree that the fun should be saved for after the school week.

In these cases, the topics are more routine, everyday issues. Nonetheless, the individuals involved did not believe they would ever be able to resolve these conflicts. These examples show that even an unimportant issue may be perceived as irresolvable.

In addition to thinking that only very important issues would become irresolvable, I also thought that arguments on certain topics would evolve into irresolvable conflicts more so than others. I reasoned that it would be more difficult to resolve issues on differing beliefs, different personality traits, or other issues that are important to one's sense of identity. For example, perpetual problems often occur as a result of fundamental personality, cultural, or religious differences, or the essential needs of each spouse (Driver et al. 2003).

Contrary to my predictions, the topics of irresolvable arguments were very similar to the topics of resolvable and resolved conflicts. Students responding about conflicts in their dating relationships described conflicts about religious/personal beliefs, trust, and commitment. These three issues produced the most conflict. It did not matter whether students were describing irresolvable, resolvable, or resolved conflicts. Students reporting on conflicts in their parental relationships described conflicts about financial issues, religious/personal beliefs, and independence struggles. Again, it did not matter what type of conflict students were describing. These results show that arguments on just about any topic can be perceived as impossible to settle. So, if it's not the issue itself that determines perceived resolvability, then why are some disputes perceived as irresolvable when others are not? The answer may be in our beliefs about conflict.

## Possible Reasons Why Irresolvable Conflicts Persist

To research this idea, I asked undergraduate students why they believed they would never be able to resolve the conflict they described. More than half of the students thought that the conflict would remain unresolved because they believe individuals do not readily change their personal beliefs or personalities. The following are examples of students' beliefs:

- This is an issue of values and personal beliefs. Religion is something that is deep-rooted and personal. Opinions about it rarely change.
- Our conflicting views are a result of the differences in who we are as people; we would have to radically change ourselves in order to resolve the conflict.
- What we want in life is strictly personal, so if we think differently about something and at the same time are very set on that goal, it is impossible to change the way the other feels.
- This is a values/morals question, and people rarely budge on those issues.

From reading these examples, we can see that many students think people do not easily change their beliefs or who they are as people. And, as a result, many students believe that irresolvable conflicts will remain unresolved. It is interesting to note that it's not the topic of conflict itself that makes a conflict irresolvable. Instead, students' beliefs about human nature lead them to conclude that a conflict is impossible to resolve.

These beliefs also reflect a sense of hopelessness. Many students seemed quite certain that the conflict was never going to be resolved. Would you continue to try to resolve a conflict you viewed as hopeless? Many of us would just throw up our hands and decide there is nothing we can do. We'd probably decide it's just not worth our time or stress to attempt resolution. However, if we don't even try to resolve a conflict, there is a pretty good chance that it is going to remain unresolved! In this way, it is a self-fulfilling prophecy.

On the bright side, knowing this information may help us avoid irresolvable conflicts in the future. We should remember that negative beliefs inhibit conflict resolution by discouraging resolution attempts. We may have a better chance of resolving a conflict if we maintain positive thoughts during the resolution process. This is related to the way we communicate in irresolvable conflicts.

## Communication Patterns in Irresolvable Conflicts

Think about the two scenarios described at the beginning of this essay. In the first one, it is clear that Uncle Jack and Grandma are no longer on speaking terms. Their ties to each other as parent and child are present, but their day-to-day relationship and communication appear to be overshadowed by their relationship as opponents. This is one way irresolvable conflicts occur in relationships (e.g., Coleman 2000, 2003).

In the second scenario, Anne and John are ending an argument—an argument John is convinced they will not be able to resolve. He makes his opinion clear to Anne and then asks where they should go for dinner. We see that John would rather focus on his day-to-day relationship with Anne than work on resolving the conflict. This is another way that irresolvable conflicts exist in relationships (e.g., Gottman 1999). So far, my research has focused on this type of irresolvable conflict—those that exist within an ongoing relationship.

I am particularly interested in the communication patterns involved in irresolvable conflicts within ongoing relationships. Gottman's (1999) research on perpetual problems in marriages suggests that it is not the presence of a perpetual problem that has an impact on relational quality. Instead, it is how a couple handles a perpetual problem that may have a strong impact on relational quality. Although Gottman's research studies married couples, I believe this finding is applicable to other interpersonal relationships. My research indicates that it is not just the presence of an irresolvable conflict that affects a relationship. Instead, it is the way individuals manage the conflict.

Students who described irresolvable conflicts reported moderate levels of relational damage associated with the irresolvable conflict. In other words, students who described irresolvable conflicts also said that the irresolvable conflict moderately damaged their relationship. Students who described resolved conflicts also described relational damage, but they described a bit less damage than students who reported on irresolvable conflicts.

More interestingly, students also exhibited communication patterns that likely help them endure the irresolvable conflict and resist attempts to resolve it. Individuals may believe that the relational costs of resolving a conflict are greater than the costs associated with continuing a conflict (Putnam and Wondolleck 2003). Thus, they work to preserve the relationship despite an irresolvable conflict. Several communication patterns may help individuals tolerate the irresolvable conflict.

The first communication pattern I noticed was **avoidance** of the irresolvable conflict. On average, the irresolvable conflicts in my investigation had persisted for 20 months at the time of my survey. One student reported an ongoing irresolvable conflict that already had lasted 10 years! Another student reported on an irresolvable conflict that had persisted for only 10 days at the time she completed my survey. However, on the whole, students did not continually argue about their irresolvable conflicts. Students reported an average of 13 arguments over the life of the conflict and reported that an average of seven weeks passed in between arguments regarding the irresolvable conflict. This indicates that individuals only sporadically argue about irresolvable conflicts (Waite 2004a). One or both individuals may engage in avoidance strategies in order to keep arguments from occurring more frequently. Here are some descriptions of avoidance that students provided:

- My parents avoid the topic as much as possible, but I am able to tell when they become angry about it.
- We both try to avoid the issue.
- This issue hasn't come up for some time.

The second communication pattern I noticed was **argument prevention**. Students indicated using moderate-to-high levels of preventative strategies such as purposefully avoiding situations or circumstances that might provoke another argument and actively trying to stop an argument from occurring. The following are examples of students' preventative strategies:

- I try not to bring it up because it's over. My girlfriend makes a small comment and then it gets bigger and bigger.

- As time passed, I learned to pick my battles. Generally, I just shut up now.

- My partner tries to end the conversation immediately while I try to confront the issue.

The third communication pattern I noticed was **withdrawal**. From reading students' open-ended responses about what happens when they argue about an irresolvable conflict, I saw that a large portion of the arguments ended with one party leaving the scene or refusing to continue discussion of the issue. This pattern is common in interpersonal conflicts. Benoit and Benoit (1987) reported that approximately 40 percent of the everyday argumentative episodes described by college students ended when the interactants stopped arguing or when one interactant left the scene. Similarly, Lloyd (1987) reported that 32 percent of disagreements described by dating couples ended when one partner left the scene or refused to continue discussion of the issue. Furthermore, Montemayor and Hanson (1985) reported that 50 percent of adolescents' arguments with parents or siblings ended with the interactants withdrawing without resolution. Here are some examples of withdrawal from my research:

- I state my points, then they [parents] provide their side. We argue rather intensely for a few minutes and then either party ends the argument by leaving.

- We both lay out our reasons for why we want our side of the issue, and then drop the subject when it becomes frustrating.

- We try to rationally discuss it until one of us just quits and says, "Whatever."

It appears that individuals recognize the conflict is harmful to their relationships and, at some point, decide not to engage in a prolonged argument. It seems that individuals decide to "agree to disagree" rather than to continue arguing. Leaving the scene or refusing to continue arguing is a quick method of enacting such an arrangement.

Do you notice any commonalities between the avoidance, prevention, and withdrawal strategies I observed? All are aimed at limiting or containing communication about the irresolvable conflict. And, in fact, this may help individuals endure the presence of an irresolvable conflict in an important relationship. These strategies may also limit the amount of relational damage associated with an irresolvable conflict. However, *none* of the strategies is aimed at resolving the irresolvable conflict. As a result, all of these strategies may actually contribute to prolonging irresolvable conflicts. In other words, the communication patterns individuals engage in during an irresolvable conflict in an ongoing relationship focus on relationship preservation at the expense of conflict resolution. It appears that many individuals would rather maintain a satisfying relationship than resolve the conflict.

Are these strategies successful? My data do not allow me to establish a causal link between these strategies and relational satisfaction. It is impossible to say with certainty that these strategies increase relational satisfaction during an irresolvable conflict. However, I can say that relational satisfaction for individuals experiencing irresolvable conflicts was very similar to the satisfaction levels of individuals who described resolvable and resolved conflicts. This shows that individuals are able to tolerate the presence of an irresolvable conflict and maintain relational satisfaction. This is good news when we consider that these strategies likely will not lead to conflict resolution.

## Conclusion

In thinking about these results, it is important to emphasize that the students in my study were college undergraduates. Most were 18–22 years of age. In addition, I asked students to report on conflicts in romantic or parental relationships, so this study did not include irresolvable conflicts that occur in other relationships. Conflicts in other types of relationships may vary.

Even with those limitations in mind, I hope that this study has given you a greater understanding of irresolvable conflicts in ongoing relationships. Irresolvable conflicts may be about issues that are very important to the individuals involved or may occur as a result of differences in everyday issues. Our beliefs about conflict may encourage the existence of irresolvable interpersonal conflicts by discouraging resolution attempts. However, communication techniques such as avoidance, prevention, and withdrawal may allow individuals to tolerate the presence of an irresolvable conflict while maintaining high levels of relational satisfaction. Hopefully, considering these issues will help you to see your experiences of irresolvable conflicts with a new perspective.

## References

Benoit, W. J., and Benoit, P. J. (1987). Everyday argument practices of naïve social actors. In J. W. Wentzel (Ed.), *Argument and Critical Practices: Proceedings of the Fifth SCA/AFA Conference on Argumentation* (pp. 465–473). Annandale, VA: Speech Communication Association.

Coleman, P. T. (2000). Intractable conflict. In M. Deutsch and P. T. Coleman (Eds.), *The Handbook of Conflict Resolution: Theory and Practice* (pp. 428–450). San Francisco: Jossey-Bass.

———. (2003). Characteristics of protracted, intractable conflict: Towards the development of a meta-framework—I. First paper in a three-part series. *Peace and Conflict: Journal of Peace Psychology*, 9(1), 1–37.

Driver, J., Tabares, A., Shapiro, A., Nahm, E. Y., and Gottman, J. M. (2003). Interactional patterns in marital success or failure: Gottman laboratory studies. In F. Walsh (Ed.), *Normal Family Processes: Growing Diversity and Complexity* (pp. 493–513). New York: The Guilford Press.

Gottman, J. M. (1999). *The Marriage Clinic: A Scientifically-Based Marital Therapy*. New York: W. W. Norton.

Johnson, K. L., and Roloff, M. E. (1998). Serial arguing and relational quality. *Communication Research*, 25(3), 327–343.

Lloyd, S. A. (1987). Conflict in premarital relationships: Differential perceptions of males and females. *Family Relations*, 36, 290–294.

Montemayor, R., and Hanson, E. (1985). A naturalistic view of conflict between adolescents and their parents and siblings. *Journal of Early Adolescence*, 5, 23–30.

Putnam, L. L., and Wondolleck, J. M. (2003). Intractability: Definitions, dimensions, and distinctions. In R. Lewicki, B. Gray, and M. Elliott (Eds.), *Making Sense of Intractable Environmental Disputes* (pp. 35–59). Washington, DC: Island Press.

Spitzberg, B. H., and Cupach, W. R. (1998). Dusk, detritus, and delusion: A prolegomenon to the dark side of close relationships. In W. R. Cupach and B. H. Spitzberg (Eds.), *The Dark Side of Close Relationships* (pp. xi–xxii). Mahwah, NJ: Lawrence Erlbaum Associates.

Vuchinich, S. (1987). Starting and stopping spontaneous family conflicts. *Journal of Marriage and the Family*, 49, 591–601.

Waite, C. (2004a). *Intractable interpersonal conflicts*. Unpublished doctoral dissertation, Northwestern University.

———. (2004b). [Irresolvable interpersonal conflicts]. Unpublished raw data.

## Questions

1. What verbal or nonverbal cues emerge in ongoing conflicts that help you distinguish them from conflicts that are not repetitive?

2. Describe the use of one or more of the communication patterns described above in an ongoing conflict with which you are familiar.

3. In your experience, what are three issues that are likely to be considered irresolvable? Explain why they are considered irresolvable.

# 31
# Child Physical Abuse

## The Relevance of Communication Research

*Steven R. Wilson*

**A**buse, both verbal and physical, represents one of the great tragedies of family life. Although most marriages and families regularly experience differences leading to arguments and anger, such conflicts may help resolve issues or release tensions. In some families, however, conflict is characterized by patterns of violence. Domestic violence is thought to occur when one family member imposes his or her will on another through the use of verbal abuse or physical force. The violent member intends to inflict pain, injury, or suffering, either psychological or physical, on other family members. Until recently, few communication scholars focused on this painful and challenging aspect of family life.

Although often overlooked, verbal aggression can serve as abuse or as the instigating agent for physical abuse. Abusive couples exhibited significantly more reciprocity in verbally aggressive exchanges than distressed nonabusive couples. For a majority of couples, verbal aggression does not lead to physical aggression, yet those who are verbally aggressive often see it as a catalyst for physical abuse (Roloff 1996).

The research on family violence indicates that parent-parent and parent-child abuse become a part of role relationships. Children begin to accept it as part of parental rights. Similar to many issues addressed under the label dark side, research in the area of child sexual abuse is confounded by the lack of a commonly accepted definition, an issue that inhibits research, treatment, and advocacy efforts (Haugaard 2000). There are disagreements on what is to be considered abuse; sexual intercourse with a child is

clear, but varied types of parental touching of a child can lead to controversy. Child physical abuse presents its own set of definitional concerns, although it is considered a serious societal problem. Today, "Physical child abuse is a societal tragedy of immense proportions" (Wilson and Whipple 1995).

*In this provocative piece, Wilson attempts to demonstrate the relevance of communication research for creating responses to child abuse. He describes five links between family interaction and child physical abuse, and calls for an understanding of how communication scholars can contribute to understanding and changing this devastating problem. In each case, Wilson cites existing research that makes relevant contributions. More research is needed to understand patterns of destructive family conflict in order to develop ways to intervene and change these patterns. As you read this chapter, consider this question: What communication concepts should researchers explore as they address child abuse?*

## References

Haugaard, J. (2000). The challenge of defining child sexual abuse. *American Psychologist*, 55, 1036–1039.

Roloff, M. (1996). The catalyst hypothesis: Condition under which coercive communication leads to physical aggression. In D. Cahn and S. Floyd (Eds.), *Handbook of Communication Science*, pp. 484–534. Thousand Oaks, CA: Sage Publications.

Wilson, S. R., and Whipple, E. E. (1995). Communication, discipline and physical abuse. In T. Socha and G. Stamp (Eds.), *Parents, Children and Communication: Frontiers in Theory and Research*, pp. 299–317. Hillsdale, NJ: Lawrence Erlbaum.

\* \* \*

**C**hild abuse is an immense, persistent problem in our society. There is no uniform law that defines what constitutes child abuse in the United States; rather, each state has its own definition. Many states recognize four types of child maltreatment: physical abuse, sexual abuse, neglect of basic needs, and psychological abuse (Barnett, Miller-Perrin, & Perrin 1997). My focus here is on child physical abuse, which, according to most states, occurs when a child sustains a physical injury as a result of the nonaccidental act of a parent or caretaker.

Reports of suspected child abuse are made to Child Protective Service (CPS) agencies in a person's city or county. During 1999, CPS agencies across the United States received more than 3 million allegations of child maltreatment (Peddle & Wang 2001). Nearly one-third of these allegations were confirmed by CPS staff, for an estimate of over 1 million maltreated children in 1999, or 15 out of every 1,000 children in our society. Child physical abuse was the second most common form of child maltreatment after neglect. CPS agencies also confirmed that an estimated 1,396 children died as a result of child abuse and neglect. Eighty percent of these children were under 5 years of age at the time of their death. These official statistics underestimate the real prevalence of child abuse, as many instances are never reported (Gelles 1997).

Despite the scope and severity of this problem, communication researchers have been slow to turn their attention to interaction patterns within abusive families. There are several reasons why this has occurred. First, scholars and the general public alike often have fallen prey to the myth that "only sick people abuse their children," when in fact the vast majority of parents who physically abuse their children do not suffer from any psychiatric disorder (Gelles 1997). Second, the root causes of child physical abuse are complicated. Explanations for child abuse must account for many contributing factors, including individual factors (e.g., a history of abuse in the parent's own childhood), family factors (e.g., social isolation, partner violence), community factors (e.g., poverty, unemployment), and cultural factors (e.g., societal attitudes about corporal punishment) (Belsky 1993). Despite this complexity, communication scholars can help with interdisciplinary efforts to understand child physical abuse. Patterns of parent-child interaction often reflect, and in some cases help account for, the effects of factors at other levels on risk for child physical abuse. In what follows, I propose five links between family interaction and child physical abuse. By doing so, I attempt to demonstrate the relevance of communication research for developing responses to child abuse.

# Links Between Face-to-Face Family Interaction and Child Physical Abuse

Face-to-face interaction is the immediate precursor to most episodes of child physical abuse. Parents typically do not strike their children at random moments but rather at recognizable moments that unfold as part of larger conversations (Davis 1996; Reid 1986). Child physical abuse also reflects persistent patterns of negative and positive parenting behaviors that occur during everyday family interaction. Physically abusive parents pursue different interaction goals with their children than nonabusive parents, experience different thoughts and feelings during interaction, and hold distorted perceptions of their child as an interaction partner.

## Linkage #1: Patterns of Parent-Child Interaction Differ in Abusive and Nonabusive Families

A number of studies have compared parent-child interaction patterns in physically abusive and nonabusive families (see Cerezo 1997; Wilson 2002). As one example, Bousha and Twentyman (1984) compared interactions in three groups of mothers (abusive, neglectful, and comparison; 12 mothers per group) and their children (average age = 4.5 years). Dyads were observed at home, on three consecutive days for 90 minutes each day, by two trained observers, who recorded the occurrence of 11 different behaviors during these interactions. Results indicated that physically abusive mothers differed from demographically matched comparison mothers on how frequently they performed 10 of the 11 behaviors: Abusive mothers performed significantly more acts of physical aggression (grabbing, hitting, kicking) and verbal aggression (swearing, threatening), whereas comparison mothers initiated more topics and gave more verbal/nonverbal instructions and verbal/nonverbal affection. Some differences between abusive and comparison mothers were pronounced; for instance, abusive mothers, on average, performed 23 physically aggressive acts and 12 verbally aggressive acts during the observation period, whereas comparison mothers performed less than 1 act of each type during the period. Most observational studies find that physically abusive parents, relative to nonabusive parents, enact a larger percentage of negative behaviors, as well as fewer positive parenting behaviors. These same studies, however, classify the majority of parental behaviors in both abusive and non-abusive families as positive or neutral rather than negative (Wilson 2002).

Perhaps more important than sheer frequency is the duration, intensity, and sequencing of negative parenting behaviors. Physically abusive parents, in comparison to nonabusive parents, display more noncontingent (i.e., negative) behavior following their child's prosocial behavior; for example, they are more likely than nonmaltreating parents to scold their child in the conversational turn immediately after the child has complied with one of their commands (Oldershaw, Walters, & Hall 1986). Whether parents respond appropriately to positive child behavior is a key factor that distinguishes abusive from nonabusive parents (Cerezo, D'Ocon, & Dolz 1996). Physically abusive parents, in comparison to nonabusive parents, also are more likely to direct negative behavior at their children for long periods of time (i.e., 20 seconds or more), and escalate the intensity of their negative behavior to higher levels during long episodes (Reid 1986).

## Linkage #2: Child Physical Abuse Is Associated With Verbally Aggressive Communication

Verbal aggression can be defined as "a communication intended to cause psychological pain to another person, or a communication perceived as having that intent" (Vissing, Straus, Gelles, & Harrop 1991, 225) and as an attempt "to inflict psychological pain, thereby resulting in the receiver feeling less favorable about self" (Infante, Chandler, & Rudd 1989, 164). Examples of parental verbal aggression include attacking a child's character, competence, or physical appearance; threatening abandonment or physical

punishment; and name-calling and swearing (Vissing & Baily 1996). As already noted, physically abusive parents, on average, direct verbally aggressive messages at their child more frequently than nonabusive parents.

Verbal aggression and child physical abuse, however, are linked more intimately than by simple co-occurrence. In a two-year observational study at shopping malls, Davis (1996) found that 50 percent of the parents who used threats of physical punishment eventually struck their child in the *same* episode. According to Infante et al.'s (1989) argumentative skill-deficiency model, parents who use verbal aggression often do so without responding to the content of their child's assertions or demands and hence end up encountering greater child resistance. These parents in turn rely more on corporal punishment, which places them at greater risk for being physically abused. Aside from being a risk factor for physical abuse, frequent verbal aggression by parents itself has long-term negative effects on children's social and emotional well being (Morgan 2001).

## Linkage #3: Child Physical Abuse Reflects How Abusive Parents Form/Pursue Interaction Goals

Clark and Delia (1979) propose that communicators often pursue three types of interaction goals: instrumental goals related to completion of a task; interpersonal goals such as achieving desired levels of power and trust; and identity goals such as maintaining a positive self-image. Child physical abuse reflects attempts by parents to accomplish all three types of goals (Cahn 1996). In terms of instrumental goals, child abuse often escalates from parental attempts to correct perceived child misbehavior and keep the child focused on the parent's agenda. Based on a survey of CPS files, Gil (1970) estimated that 63 percent of abusive incidents grew out of disciplinary action taken by parents or other caretakers.

Perhaps not surprisingly, abusive and nonabusive parents differ in how they go about seeking their child's compliance. Oldershaw et al. (1986) compared 10 physically abusive and 10 matched-comparison mother-child dyads engaged in 40-minute free-play and mealtime interactions. Abusive mothers made more initial requests; issued more commands without any accompanying rationale; and used more power-assertive techniques (e.g., threats) both before and after child resistance. When their child did comply, abusive mothers were more likely than comparison mothers to scold the child or to continue seeking compliance in the next conversational turn (presumably because they failed to notice that their child had complied). According to Reid (1986), children are at the greatest risk of physical assault during an extended episode in which an abusive parent attempts, but fails, to gain their compliance.

Child physical abuse also may reflect parents' attempts to accomplish relational and identity goals. Ade-Ridder and Jones (1996) argue that child physical abuse is a form of "political communication," in that abuse represents a parent's attempt to reinforce or regain power and control over his or her child (also see Patterson 1986). Physical assault can be a form of "impression management" as well; that is, abusive parents may retaliate physically when they perceive that a child intentionally has attacked their authority or competence, especially when the "attack" occurs in front of other family members (Felson 1978).

### Linkage #4: Abusive and Nonabusive Parents Think and Feel Differently During Family Interaction

Physically abusive parents may pursue different goals than nonmaltreating parents because they tend to experience more negative thoughts and feelings when talking with their child. Milner (2000) has proposed an information-processing model that highlights numerous differences between the thoughts and feelings that physically abusive and nonabusive parents experience during parent-child interaction. In the model, physically abusive parents are assumed to hold inaccurate pre-existing cognitive schemata (i.e., pre-existing beliefs about parenting behavior and about children) that affect how they perceive and evaluate parent-child interactions. For example, physically abusive parents, in comparison to nonabusive parents, report lower self-esteem and self-efficacy as parents. Abusive parents also believe that they have less control, and their child has greater, over negative interactions in comparison to nonabusive parents.

Partly because of such pre-existing schemata, abusive and nonabusive parents may differ in four stages of information processing (Milner 2000; Wilson & Whipple 2001). At Stage 1, *perception*, physically abusive parents may be less attentive to and aware of their child's behavior. For example, abusive parents appear less accurate than nonabusive parents at accurately recognizing children's emotional states, and less likely to distinguish positive from negative child behavior. At Stage 2, *interpretation and evaluation*, physically abusive parents may hold inappropriate expectations and make harsher judgments about their child's behavior. Abusive parents, in comparison to nonabusive parents: have greater expectations that their child will stop minor transgressions if they are punished; often assume that their children misbehave on purpose and hence view misbehavior as reflecting internal, stable qualities of their child; and evaluate misbehaviors by their child as being more wrong. Given these interpretations, it is not surprising that physically abusive parents also report being angered more by child misbehavior. At Stage 3, *information integration and response selection*, abusive parents may fail to adequately integrate child-related information and may lack knowledge about a range of parenting techniques. Abusive parents are less likely than nonabusive parents to alter their attributions for child misbehavior even after they are provided information suggesting their child was not responsible for the misbehavior. Abusive parents also rely more heavily on physical punishment regardless of how their child has misbehaved. At Stage 4, *response implementation and monitoring*, abusive parents may lack skills and/or attentional capacity needed to monitor and modify their responses as interactions unfold. For example, abusive parents are more likely than nonabusive parents to display noncontingent responses to their child's prosocial behavior (see preceding). Milner's (2000) model also recognizes that differences between the information processing of abusive versus nonabusive parents may be most pronounced when children or other events (e.g., job loss) create high levels of parenting and life stress.

### Linkage #5: Abusive Parents Hold Distorted Perceptions of Their Child as an Interaction Partner

Physically abusive and nonabusive parents experience different thoughts and feelings during interaction, in part because children in abusive families often are challenging interaction partners. Several observational studies show that children in abusive families perform a larger number of aversive behaviors, such as temper tantrums, verbal aggression, and whining, and also are less compliant with their parents' initial commands than are children who are not physically abused (e.g., Bousha & Twentyman 1984; Oldershaw et al. 1986). Debate has ensued about whether behavioral problems by children lead to or are the result of physical abuse (see Patterson 1986, for one explanation that incorporates both ideas).

Regardless of the origins of aversive child behavior, several studies document that physically abusive parents hold more negative perceptions, in comparison to most other adults, of their child as an interaction partner (see Milner 2000). For example, Reid, Kavanagh, and Baldwin (1987) had 21 physically abusive and 21 demographically-matched comparison parents complete three separate measures of their child's behavior. Within a week of collecting these measures, observers visited the homes of all participants six times in a period of between 11 and 24 days, observing interactions 45 to 60 minutes in length. Abusive parents rated their children as significantly more aggressive, conduct-disordered, and hyperactive than matched-comparison parents, but observers detected no significant differences between abused and nonabused children for the frequency or the severity of their negative or positive behaviors.

In sum, children in abusive families do display higher rates of aversive behavior compared to children in nonmaltreating families, but abusive parents also hold exaggerated perceptions of how difficult their children are as interaction partners. As a result of incompetent discipline practices and inconsistent responses to positive child behavior, abusive parents also help create many of the behavioral problems that they perceive in their children (Wilson 2002).

## Summary

Child physical abuse is an interactional phenomenon. The study of interaction in abusive families raises several issues about which communication researchers have special expertise, including: (a) mutual and reciprocal influence between parents and children; (b) the simultaneous occurrence of interactional and psychological processes; (c) differing perspectives on interaction between participants and observers; and (d) the dynamic nature of interaction goals. By exploring linkages between family interaction and child physical abuse, communication scholars can help shape more effective responses to this major societal problem.

## References

Ade-Ridder, L., & Jones, A. R. (1996). Home is where the hell is: An introduction to violence against children from a communication perspective. In D. D. Cahn & S. A. Lloyd (eds.), *Family violence from a communication perspective* (pp. 59–84). Thousand Oaks, CA: Sage.

Barnett, O. W., Miller-Perrin, C. L., & Perrin, R. D. (1997). *Family violence across the lifespan: An introduction*. Thousand Oaks, CA: Sage.

Belsky, J. (1993). Etiology of child maltreatment: A developmental-ecological analysis. *Psychological Bulletin*, 114, 413–434.

Bousha, D. M., & Twentyman, C. T. (1984). Mother-child interactional style in abuse, neglect, and control groups: Naturalistic observations in the home. *Journal of Abnormal Psychology*, 93, 106–114.

Cahn, D. D. (1996). Family violence from a communication perspective. In D. D. Cahn & S. A. Lloyd (eds.), *Family violence from a communication perspective* (pp. 1–19). Thousand Oaks, CA: Sage.

Cerezo, M. A. (1997). Abusive family interaction: A review. *Aggression and Violent Behavior*, 2, 215–240.

Cerezo, M. A., D'Ocon, A., & Dolz, L. (1996). Mother-child interactive patterns in abusive families: An observational study. *Child Abuse & Neglect*, 20, 573–587.

Clark, R. A., & Delia, J. G. (1979). Topoi and rhetorical competence. *Quarterly Journal of Speech*, 65, 187–206.

Davis, P. W. (1996). Threats of corporal punishment as verbal aggression: A naturalistic study. *Child Abuse & Neglect*, 20, 289–304.

Felson, R. B. (1978). Aggression as impression management. *Social Psychology*, 41, 205–213.

Gelles, R. J. (1997). *Intimate violence in families* (3rd edition). Thousand Oaks, CA: Sage.

Gil, D. G. (1970). *Violence against children: Physical child abuse in the United States*. Cambridge, MA: Harvard University Press.

Infante, D. A., Chandler, T. A., & Rudd, J. E. (1989). Test of an argumentative skill deficiency model of interpersonal violence. *Communication Monographs*, 56, 163–177.

Milner, J. S. (2000). Social information processing and child physical abuse: Theory and research. In D. J. Hersen (ed.), *Nebraska symposium on motivation. Vol. 45. Motivation and child maltreatment* (pp. 39–84). Lincoln, NE: University of Nebraska Press.

Morgan, W. (2001, November). Verbal abuse by any other name . . . : A look at definitional issues across existing constructs. Paper presented at the annual meeting of the National Communication Association, Atlanta.

Oldershaw, L., Walters, G. C., & Hall, D. K. (1986). Control strategies and noncompliance in abusive mother-child dyads. *Developmental Psychology*, 57, 722–732.

Patterson, G. R. (1986). Performance models for antisocial boys. *American Psychologist*, 41, 432–444.

Peddle, N., & Wang, C. T. (2001). Current trends in child abuse prevention, reporting, and fatalities: The 1999 fifty state survey. Retrieved on May 9, 2002 from *http://www.preventchildabuse.org/learn_more/research_docs/1999_50_survey.pdf*.

Reid, J. B. (1986). Social interactional patterns in families of abused and nonabused children. In C. Zahn-Waxler, E. M. Cummings, & R. Iannotti (Eds.), *Altruism and aggression: Biological and social origins* (pp. 238–257). Cambridge, UK: Cambridge University Press.

Reid, J. B., Kavanagh, K., & Baldwin, D. V. (1987). Abusive parents' perceptions of child problem behaviors: An example of parental bias. *Journal of Abnormal Child Psychology*, 15, 457–466.

Vissing, Y., & Baily, W. (1996). Parent-to-child verbal aggression. In D. D. Cahn & S. A. Lloyd (Eds.), *Family violence from a communication perspective* (pp. 177–198). Thousand Oaks, CA: Sage.

Vissing, Y. M., Straus, M. A., Gelles, R. J., & Harrop, J. W. (1991). Verbal aggression by parents and psychosocial problems in children. *Child Abuse & Neglect*, 15, 223–238.

Wilson, S. R. (2002). *Seeking and resisting compliance: Why people say what they do when trying to influence others*. Thousand Oaks, CA: Sage.

Wilson, S. R., & Whipple, E. E. (2001). Attributions and regulative communication by parents participating in a community-based child abuse prevention program. In V. Manusov & J. H. Harvey (eds.), *Attribution, communication behavior, and close relationships* (pp. 227–247). New York: Cambridge University Press.

## Questions

1. What do you consider to be child physical abuse within families? Do you consider verbal aggression to be potentially abusive?

2. How might physically abusive parents differ from nonabusive parents across stages of information processing?

3. In understanding abuse patterns, why is it important to recognize patterns of noncontingent parent behavior?

4. What do you believe is the impact of growing up in a family characterized by verbal and/or physical abuse?

# Part VIII

## *Ending Relationships*

The life of each ongoing relationship is challenged by developmental changes of the individuals, pressures of competing commitments, as well as efforts expended to maintain multiple relational ties. At any given point in time, you may be building one or two relationships and loosening the bonds of a similar number. You have witnessed and experienced the fallout from friendships that became disappointing or destructive. Geographic mobility separates friends, often dissolving the relationships. Even close friendships undergo many changes, frequently shifting to a more distant level of connectedness.

As the current divorce rate suggests, many relational partners opt to terminate their first or second marriages. Workplace mobility works against developing long-term friends at the office. Most relationships come apart through a process; dissolution is seldom the result of one major event.

Unlike the movie images of a huge fight followed by silence and distance, the majority of relationships end through a coming-apart process; other people or commitments take priority, differences reduce the pleasures of togetherness, and familiarity reveals critical points of tension. In her poem "Simple-Song," Marge Piercy (1982) captures the essence of relationship dissolution, suggesting that when we are leaving a relationship, we have come to believe that the other individual is strange, we cannot communicate, and being together is hard. These words stand in stark contrast to what was said and felt as the relationship developed.

Relationships are terminated for many different reasons, some of which include lack of openness and intimacy, lack of similarity, sexual incompatibility, need for autonomy and independence, money, boredom, and disagreements regarding their social network (Guerrero, Andersen, and Afifi 2001). When long-term relationships end, the sense of loss is acute. You may grieve the loss of a romantic partner or close friend for a long time.

Many models of relational dissolution exist. The stages of grief and mourning, originally conceived by Dr. Elizabeth Kübler-Ross (1970) to account for the experiences of dying patients and their families, have been applied to the death of relationships. These stages include (1) denial, (2) anger and blame, (3) bargaining, (4) depression, and (5) acceptance. For example, friends may deny that there are any really small or large issues that may lead to great anger or threats. Discussions of "Let's try to do better" or "I'll never say that again" represent bargaining. Sadness at the loss of a good friend is followed by a sense of acceptance. Although listed in linear form, the feelings evoked by these stages may be experienced in many different ways.

According to Knapp and Vangelisti (2000), a relationship that is coming apart reflects (1) a recognition of differences, (2) an experience of constricted interaction, (3) a sense of stagnation or marking time, (4) a pattern of avoidance, and (5) the immediate or protracted experience of termination. Duck (1982) described four dissolution stages as Breakdown (dissatisfaction), Dyadic Phase (confrontation and negotiation), Social Phase (move to public level), and Grave-Dressing Phase (getting-over-it activities). You may remember that stage models are linear but that dialectical tensions operate as the "background noise." At periods of clear decline, the dialectical tensions that serve as background move to the foreground as the struggles become overt and intense.

As a relationship comes apart, friends or partners gradually withdraw affection or comfortable contact and are less likely to deal with each other. The high self-disclosure, predictability, and spontaneity that characterize well-functioning relationships disintegrate. Risk taking and effort disappear. Sometimes friendships experience a breach period or hiatus because of time demands, other relational involvements, or a personal choice (Rawlins 1994). These are ambiguous situations that may result in dissolution or reinvigoration, but the future depends heavily on the mutual definition of the relationship.

Miller and Parks (1982) detail numerous communication markers of dissolving relationships. These include verbal markers such as a decrease in the use of future tense references to the relationship, a decrease in pronouns implying mutuality, an increase in conflict encounters, and a decrease in time spent on topics. Nonverbal communication characteristics include less touch and greater distance between persons.

Although this section will not address issues of death and dying, communication scholars are studying interactions with dying persons or, as entitled by Keeley (2004), "final conversations." Keeley's interviews with persons about their final conversations with a loved one reveal three overarching themes that emerged in those conversations—affirmation of love, love and reconciliation, and altruistic love. Such conversations represent the most dramatic examples of ending relationships.

In the readings that follow, the authors discuss various aspects of relationship endings. As you read these articles, think about the relationships in your life that have ended. To what extent do these authors' statements reflect your experiences?

## References

Duck, S. (1982). A topography of relationship disengagement and dissolution. In S. Duck (Ed.), *Personal Relationships 4: Dissolving Relationships*, pp. 1–30. New York: Academic Press.

Guerrero, L. K., Andersen, P. A. and Afifi, W. A. (2001). *Close Encounters: Communicating in Relationships*. Mountain View, CA: Mayfield Publishing.

Keeley, M. (2004). Final conversations: Messages of love. *Qualitative Research Reports in Communication*, V, 34–40.

Knapp, M., and Vangelisti, A. (2000). *Interpersonal Communication and Human Relationships*, 4th ed. Needham Heights, MA: Allyn & Bacon.

Kübler-Ross, E. (1970). *On Death and Dying*. New York: Macmillan.

Miller, G., and Parks, M. (1982). Communication in dissolving relationships. In S. W. Duck (ed.), *Personal Relationships 4: Dissolving Relationships*, (pp. 127–154). New York: Academic Press.

Piercy, M. (1982). Simple-Song. From *Circles on the Water*. New York: Alfred A. Knopf, Inc.

Rawlins, W. K. (1994). Being there and growing apart: Sustaining friendships during adulthood. In D. J. Canary and L. Stafford (Eds.), *Communication and Relational Maintenance*, pp. 275–294. San Diego: Academic Press. ✦

# 32
# Relational Decline

*Mark L. Knapp and*
*Anita L. Vangelisti*

Earlier in this volume (Chapter 15), you read Knapp and Vangelisti's stages of relational "coming together." Using the same theoretical perspective, these authors also discuss stages of "coming apart." The same generalizations that applied to the "coming together" stages apply to the stages of "coming apart": (1) movement through stages is generally systematic and sequential, (2) movement may be forward, (3) movement may be backward, (4) movement is always to a new place, (5) movement may be rapid or slow, and (6) dialectical tensions serve as a background to each stage.

Relationships experience decline, permanent or temporary, by choice and by inertia. Advice columnists regularly respond to readers' questions regarding how to end a relationship. Such explicit desire usually results in statements indicating a lack of interest, a major fight resulting from the less-involved individual's frustration, or significant efforts to disconfirm or ignore the other, such as not returning calls or e-mails. In partnerships, such explicit desire usually results in separation or divorce. Relationships beset by inertia find themselves drifting as major time commitments, geographic separation, or serious personal concerns cause one or both to be unavailable. Thus, lack of ongoing connection renders the tie weaker and weaker.

Most models of relational decline follow similar patterns. Canary, Cody, and Manusov (2003) adapted Steve Duck's original work (1982) in this area to develop a model of relational repair that attempts to explain how to intervene as the relationship disintegrates. For example, they suggest that during "The Breakdown Phase: Dissatisfaction with the Relationship," partners might try to focus on the attractions in the relationship and try to reduce turbulence in the interactions. During "The Social Phase and Beyond," they might enlist public support by asking others to help them understand the breakup or enlist the aid of others to help save the relationship. Even in these painful circumstances, most people follow rather predictable patterns.

In this chapter, Knapp and Vangelisti describe five stages involved in relational decline: differentiating, circumscribing, stagnating, avoiding, and terminating. The discussion of each stage includes the types of communication (or lack of communication) involved throughout the decline of the relationship. Conversations and expressions that are characteristic of each stage are offered as examples throughout the chapter, along with corresponding behaviors (like arguing or ignoring) that are commonly seen as relationships come apart. For example, in the Terminating Stage, communication is characterized as more narrow, stylized, difficult, rigid, awkward, public, and hesitant, with overt judgments suspended. In the Differentiating Stage, communication is characterized by more breadth, efficiency, uniqueness, flexibility, smoothness, and spontaneity, and overt judgments are given. In other words, people communicate within a prescribed range of content, style, and language at different levels of intimacy.

As you read the following article, think about the relationships in your own life that have declined significantly or ended. Ask yourself: To what extent did they follow the stages discussed by Knapp and Vangelisti?

## References

Canary, D. J., Cody, M. J. and Manusov, V. L., (2003). *Interpersonal Communication: A Goals-Based Approach*. (3rd ed.) Boston: Bedford/St. Martin's.

Duck, S. W. (1982). A typography of relationship disengagement and dissolution. In S. W. Duck (Ed.), *Personal Relationships 4: Dissolving Personal Relationships* (pp. 1–30). New York: Academic.

* * *

## Differentiating

Literally, to *differentiate* means to become distinct or different in character. Just as integrating is mainly a process of fusion, differentiating is mainly a process of disengaging or uncoupling. While individual differences are of some concern at any stage in the developing relationship, they are now the major focus and serve as a prelude to increased interpersonal distance. A great deal of time and energy are spent talking and thinking about "how different we really are."

Joint endeavors formerly described by "we" or "our" now assume a more "I" or "my" orientation. Previously designated joint possessions often become more individualized—"my friends," "my daughter," or "my bathroom." Communication is generally characterized by what distinguishes the two persons or how little they have in common. Differences may be related to attitudes, interests, personality, relatives, friends, or to a specific behavior such as sexual needs or picking one's nose. Individuals who persist in interaction at this stage perceive these differences as strongly linked to basic or core values. Hence, we would expect to see less conversation about certain central areas of personality that may reflect these basic values. Persons who move in and out of this stage develop a history of expectations for the manner in which such difficulties will be settled, even if it is simply an agreement to seal off the areas of potential conflict.

When an unusually intense siege of differentiating takes place following bonding, it may be because bonding took place before the relationship achieved sufficient breadth and depth. It may also be due to some unplanned individual or social changes that altered the data upon which the original commitment was made. Advocates of renewable-term marriage argue that couples would be more likely to face, discuss, and work out unexpected changes in their lives if the marriage bond was not a lifelong commitment—if "till death do us part" meant the death of the relationship rather than the death of the participants.

The most visible communication form of differentiating, or affirming individuality, is fighting or conflict, although it is possible to differentiate without conflict. . . .

## Circumscribing

At almost any stage of a relationship we can see some evidence of communication being constricted or circumscribed. In decaying relationships, however, information exchange qualitatively and quantitatively decreases. The main message strategy is to carefully control the areas of discussion, restricting communication to safe areas. Thus, we find less total communication in number of interactions as well as depth of subjects discussed, and communications of shorter duration.

Communication restraint applies to both breadth and depth. As the number of touchy topics increases, almost any topic becomes dangerous because it is not clear whether the new topic may in some way be wired to a previous area of static. When communication does take place, superficiality and public aspects are increasingly the norm. Communications related to one's basic values and hidden secrets may have a history of unpleasantness surrounding them; hence, we see a lot less information exchanged about "who I am and what our relationship is like." A corresponding decrease in expressions of commitment may be seen. When one person ventures such an expression, the echo response may not be so prevalent. "In spite of our differences, I still like you a lot." (Silence)

Familiar phrases typical of this stage include: "Don't ask me about that"; "Let's not talk about that anymore"; "It's none of your business"; "Just stick to the kind of work I'm doing and leave my religion out of it"; "You don't own me and you can't tell me what to think"; or "Can't we just be friends?" The last example is a suggestion that prescribes a whole new set of ground rules for permissible topics in the interaction.

When circumscribing characterizes the relationship, it may also have an impact on public social performances. Sometimes mutual social circles are also circumscribed, sometimes the presence of others is the only time when communication seems to increase—an effort to avoid being seen as not getting along. The following routine is not at all uncommon for some couples at this stage: Driving to a party, the two people exhibit mutual silence, empty gazes, and a general feeling of exhaustion. While playing out their party roles we see smiling, witticisms, and an orientation for being the life of the party.

The trip home becomes a replay of the pre-party behavior.

## Stagnating

To stagnate is to remain motionless or inactive. Rather than orally communicate, participants often find themselves conducting covert dialogues and concluding that since they "know" how the interaction will go, it is not necessary to say anything. At this stage, many areas are closed off, and efforts to communicate effectively are at a standstill. Even superficial areas have become so infected by previous communicative poison that they are generally left untried. In a sense, the participants are just marking time.

Some of the messages that are sent reflect unpleasant feeling states through the medium of nonverbal behavior. Other messages are very carefully chosen and well thought out. Language choices and message strategies seem to come even closer to those used with strangers, and the subject of the relationship is nearly taboo. . . . While there may be many convert judgments made, overt judgments are generally avoided.

Extended stagnating can be seen in many relationships: between alienated parents and children, just prior to divorce, just prior to the termination of a courtship, following unproductive small talk. The main theme characterizing this stage is "There is little sense bringing anything up because I know what will happen, and it won't be particularly pleasant." Experimentation is minimal because the unknown is thought to be known. It is during this time that each partner may engage in "imagined interactions."[1] These imagined dialogues will either take the form of narratives (e.g., "I'll say this and then she'll say this, and then . . .") or perceived actual dialogues (e.g., "I'll do it." "You don't have to." "Ok." "Ok, what?" "Ok, I won't." "Your typical attitude." "And *Your Typical Attitude!*" . . . ).

You might legitimately question why people would linger at this stage with so many apparent costs accumulating. Most don't. But when persons continue interacting at this stage they may be getting some rewards outside of the primary relationship, through increased attention to their work or in developing another relationship. They also avoid the pain of terminating the relationship, which they may anticipate will be stronger than the current pain. Others may have hope that they can still revive the relationship. Still others may spend time at this stage because of some perverse pleasures obtained in punishing the other person.

## Avoiding

While stagnating, the participants are usually in the same physical environment and avoiding attempts to eliminate that condition. The rhetoric of avoidance is the antithesis of the rhetoric of initiation. Here, communication is specifically designed to avoid the possibility of face-to-face or voice-to-voice interaction. The overriding messages seem to be: "I am not interested in seeing you; I am not interested in building a relationship; and I would like to close the communication channels between us." In this sense, then, avoiding suggests a much more permanent state of separation than that communicated by most people in their everyday leave-taking.

When the need to communicate avoidance results from an intimate relationship gone sour, the particular messages may contain overtones of antagonism or unfriendliness. They are more likely to be direct and to the point. "Please don't call me anymore. I just don't want to see or talk to you." This bluntness may naturally evolve from other conditions as well, such as when one person wants to pursue the relationship and ignores the more subtle avoidance cues. These subtle or indirect cues may take the form of being consistently late for appointments or preceding each encounter with, "I can't stay long." Here the avoiding tactics are not motivated so much by dislike of the other as a lack of desire to expend time and energy pursuing a relationship. Sometimes an inordinate number of conflicting engagements can make the point: "I'm so busy I don't know when I'll be able to see you. Friday? I'm going home for the weekend. Monday? I have a sorority meeting. Tuesday? I have to study for a test," etc. etc.

Any of all forms of "distancing"[2] may occur at this stage:

1. Avoidance—preventing an interaction episode from happening and reducing interaction during an encounter.

2. Disengagement—hiding information about self; using a disengaged communication style; and interacting less personally.

3. Cognitive dissociation—disregarding messages; derogating the other person; showing cognitive and emotional detachment.

Cognitive dissociation occurs when physical separation cannot be achieved. It is a form of avoidance in the presence of the other. It is as if the other person doesn't exist. Not surprisingly under such conditions we find the recipient of this behavior participating less in what interaction is available, not evaluating the other highly, and being less inclined to provide a reward to the other when an opportunity arises. The less obvious result of being ignored is the possibility of a lowered self-concept.[3]

## Terminating

Relationships can terminate immediately after a greeting or after twenty years of intimacy. Sometimes they die slowly over a long period of time. The bonds that held the pair together wear thin and finally pull apart. The reasons behind such deterioration may be something obvious like living in parts of the country separated by great distance; or termination may just be the end result of two people growing socially and psychologically at different rates and in different directions. At other times, the threads holding two people together may be abruptly cut. It may be the death of one partner, radically changed circumstances, or an effort by one person to spare both of them the anticipated agony of a prolonged termination period.

Naturally, the nature of the termination dialogue is dependent on many factors: the relative status held or perceived between the two communicators; the kind of relationship already established or desired in the future; the amount of time allowed; whether the dialogue is conducted via the telephone, through a letter, or face to face; and many other individual and environmental factors.

Generally, however, we would predict termination dialogue to be characterized by messages of distance and disassociation. *Distance* refers to an attempt to put psychological and physical barriers between the two communicators. This might take the form of actual physical separation, or it may be imbedded in other nonverbal and verbal messages. *Disassociation* is found in messages that are essentially preparing one or both individuals for their continued life without the other—increasing concern for one's own self-interests, emphasizing differences. Obviously, the amount of distancing and disassociation will vary with the kind of relationship being dissolved, time available, and so on. . . .

We would also predict that the general dimensions of communicative behavior reviewed earlier in this chapter would polarize more than ever around narrow, stylized, difficult, rigid, awkward, public, hesitant, and suspended judgments.

Finally, we would like to take a finding derived from the study of conversations and apply it to relationships. Thus, we would predict that termination dialogue would regularly manifest: (1) a summary statement; (2) behaviors signaling the impending termination or decreased access; and (3) messages that indicate what the future relationship (if any) will be like.[4] A summary statement reviews the relationship's history and provides the rationale for the imminent termination. Decreased-access messages clarify what is happening. Addressing the future avoids awkward interactions after parting. Even when dissolving a long-term relationship, the subject of being future friends or enemies must be addressed. "I'll always respect you, but I don't love you anymore," or "I don't ever want to see you again!" Saying good-bye to a long-term relationship may take longer, especially if one party does not want to end it and seeks to delay the final parting. . . .

## Notes

1. Imagined interactions may occur at other points in the relationship as well—and for different purposes. For example, a person may construct an imagined dialogue relative

to a date or marriage proposal. See J. M. Honeycutt, K. S. Zagacki, and R. Edwards, "Intrapersonal Communication, Social Cognition, and Imagined Interactions." In C. Roberts and K. Watson, eds., *Readings in Intrapersonal Communication*. Birmingham, AL: Gorsuch Scarisbrick, 1989.

2. J. A. Hess, "Distance Regulation in Personal Relationships: The Development of a Conceptual Model and a Test of Representational Validity," *Journal of Social and Personal Relationships* 19 (2002): 663–683.

3. D. M. Geller, L. Goodstein, M. Silver, and W. C. Sternberg, "On Being Ignored: The Effects of the Violation of Implicit Rules of Social Interaction," *Sociometry* 37 (1974): 541–556.

4. M. L. Knapp, R. P. Hart, G. W. Friedrich, and G. M. Shulman, "The Rhetoric of Goodbye: Verbal and Nonverbal Correlates of Human Leave-Taking," *Speech Monographs* 40 (1973): 182–198.

## Questions

1. Analyze a segment from a play, film, or TV show that deals with relationship termination. How does the communication of the relational partners progress through the stages of "coming apart" designated by Knapp and Vangelisti?

2. Using the stages of "coming apart," analyze a relationship that has terminated in your life. Could you tell it was ending before you heard the news? Try to remember the exact words used at each stage as well as the nonverbal cues. Be specific.

3. Using the circumscribing and stagnating stages, create a list of 5–10 phrases that typify the type of interaction that occurs at that stage. Note predictable nonverbal messages that might accompany some of these phrases.

Adapted from Mark L. Knapp and Anita L. Vangelisti, "Stages of Relationships." In *Interpersonal Communication and Human Relationships*, 5th ed., pp. 43–47. Published by Allyn & Bacon, Boston, MA. Copyright © 2005 by Pearson Education. Reprinted with permission. ✦

# 33
# Dialectical Process in the Disengagement of Interpersonal Relationships

*William R. Cupach*

The process of relational decline provides a counterpart to the dialectical struggles experienced as friends or romantic partners develop their relationships. The relational disintegration process involves dialectical tensions similar to those that operated in the relational development stages. In the following piece, author William Cupach succinctly captures this concept, saying, "To the extent that dialectical tensions drive change and evolution in relationships they may account for their quality and success and, conversely, their erosion and failure." As no two people are alike, dialectic tensions are predictable in relationships. However, the saliency of these tensions will vary from relationship to relationship, as will the couple's ability to manage their differences, which, according to Cupach, can serve as indicators for relational difficulty and potential breakdown. As relationships enter troubled waters, partners may experience powerful tensions, which are increasingly difficult to manage.

Frequently, partners and friends are not willing or able to acknowledge the increasing tensions until the stress is so great that it affects all aspects of relational life. Just as each relational culture develops uniquely, each disintegrates in its own way. As you might imagine, it is hard, but not impossible, to reverse the process of decline once the relational culture has been dismantled (Phillips and Wood 1983). Although there are identified stages of relational decline (Knapp and Vangelisti 2005; Duck 1982), each relational culture goes through the stages and encounters the dialectical tensions in a slightly different way. Most people experience a sense of struggle and frustration as an important relationship dissolves. According to Guerrero, Andersen, and Afifi (2000), "Regardless of why a relationship ends, research has shown that people usually experience a host of negative outcomes following relational termination, including emotional and financial distress" (p. 431).

In this chapter, Cupach opens with an overview of how dialectics serve in all relationships: as markers of relational stages, which often cause contention within the relationship and require management. Without effective management, the patterns of dialectical opposition may reflect difficulties in the relationship and lead toward decline and disengagement, a process that Cupach discusses for the final two sections of the chapter. A brief synopsis of the dialectical perspective wraps up this section.

As you read this article, think back to earlier discussions of dialectical tensions. You should recognize certain mirror images of the tensions that occurred as a relationship built resonating through the decline process. Ask yourself this question: What are the dialectical tensions that I have watched or experienced in the development and decline of one relationship?

## References

Duck, S. (1982). A topography of relationship disengagement and dissolution. In S. Duck (Ed.), *Personal Relationships 4: Dissolving Relationships*, pp. 1–30. New York: Academic Press.

Guerrero, L. K., Andersen, P. A., and Afifi, W. A. (2001). *Close Encounters*. Mountain View, CA: Mayfield Publishing.

Knapp, M., and Vangelisti, A. (2005). *Interpersonal Communication and Human Relationships*, 6th ed. Needham Heights, MA: Allyn & Bacon.

Phillips, G., and Wood, J. (1983). *Communication in Human Relationships: The Study of Interpersonal Communication*. New York: Macmillan.

\* \* \*

Interpersonal relationships are inherently paradoxical. They afford simultaneously the opportunities for both ecstasy and agony. They create dilemmas, double binds, quandaries, and contradictions for relational partners. Individuals want to be open and honest, but they also want to protect their partner and preserve their own self-image. They want passion and abandonment but not without security and order. Recognition of these various contradictory phenomena has led scholars to import dialectical principles to provide a more complete understanding of the dynamic construction and erosion of relationships (e.g., Altman, Vinsel, and Brown 1981; Baxter 1988; Cissna, Cox, and Bochner 1990; Conville 1988; Masheter and Harris 1986; Rawlins 1983a, 1983b; Rawlins and Holl 1987, 1988; Wiseman 1986). In the spirit of this line of work, this [article] is based on the premise that the negotiation of dialectical tension between relational partners is central to the conduct and interpretation of relational life (and death). . . .

## Dialectics as Markers of Relational Phases

Development approaches to interpersonal relationships typically identify stages of relationship growth and decline (e.g., Knapp 1984; Levinger 1983; Wood 1982). Such approaches have been criticized for delineating relationship stages in an atheoretical or tautological fashion (e.g., Bochner 1984). Alternatively, as Baxter (1988) argues, a dialectical framework provides a theoretical grounding for identification of developmental stages or phases of relationships. In her application of a dialectical perspective to the strategic management of relationships, Baxter (1988) has identified four potential phases of the autonomy-connection contradiction. Using extant literature on communicative strategies, she illustrates that each phase is characterized by the negotiation and management of the secondary contradictions, novelty-predictability and openness-closedness. Importantly, the nature and function of each dialectical con-

tradiction is qualitatively different in each development phase.

Phase 1, autonomy to connection, is characterized by novelty in the form of psychological uncertainty. At the same time, behavioral predictability is afforded as individuals largely follow familiar and ritualistic scripts that govern appropriate behavior in initial interactions (e.g., Berger and Bradac 1982). Openness and closedness are balanced through gradual, reciprocated self-disclosures and affinity-seeking behavior that is generally indirect in nature. In phase 2, autonomy and connection, predictability is engendered by the mutual creation of private idioms, rituals, and other symbols that characterize the evolving relational culture, while novelty stems from the emergence of nonscripted behavior, the development of idiosyncratic rules for behavior, and the attendant conflict. Openness-closedness is reflected in the continuing self-disclosure necessary for relationship advancement, as well as the identification of taboo topics, and the use of indirect "secret" tests to gain more information and predictability in the relationship. Phase 3, labeled autonomy-connection synthesis, is marked by constructive efforts to invigorate and revitalize the relationship through various maintenance and repair strategies. Phase 4, connection to autonomy, identifies relationships in decline. . . .

In a therapeutic application of dialectical thinking, Sarnoff and Sarnoff (1989a, 1989b) have identified six stages of marital relationships based on six dialectical challenges occurring over the lifespan of a marriage. Each stage represents a mutual goal for expanding the relationship, as well as the concomitant opposing defensiveness that potentially thwarts the goal. For example, stage 1—coupling and concealing—depicts newlyweds faced with desire to share intimacy, checked by the fear of vulnerability. Stage 2—reproducing and retreating—identifies the potential for expanding the relationship by having children, which can evoke envy by the husband who cannot give birth and resentment for the wife who is constrained by pregnancy.

Unless they realize the dialectical nature of their relationship—the constant struggle between the deep need for love and the equally deep fear of it—spouses are likely to blame each other for the conflicts and tensions no couple can avoid (Sarnoff and Sarnoff 1989a, p. 57).

Thus, the authors identify each marital stage and its attendant contradiction with the intent of making spouses aware of such tensions and the behavioral options of managing them.

## Dialectics and Relationship Breakdown

To the extent that dialectical tensions drive change and evolution in relationships, they pay account for their quality and success and, conversely, their erosion and failure. Because all relationships, by definition, possess dialectical opposition, it is not the mere presence of dilemmas that determines relational quality. Rather, it is the ability to successfully cope with inevitable contradictions.

## Management of Dialectical Tension

Cupach and Metts (1988) surveyed college students involved in romantic relationships to assess the occurrence and impact of dialectical forces in relationships. They discovered that the frequency with which dialectical tension was perceived was negatively associated with relational satisfaction. In addition, the degree of personal anxiety and the amount of overt conflict produced by dialectical forces were negatively related to relational satisfaction. These data suggest that when the oppositional nature of dialectical forces becomes particularly salient to relational partners, it can be problematic for the health of the relationship. Moreover, the recurring salience of a contradiction (and its attendant stresses) in a relationship likely suggests the inability or unwillingness of one or both partners to successfully cope with contradictions.

Presumably, the competence of partners to strategically manage dialectical tension is critical (e.g., Baxter 1988; Bochner 1984). Baxter (1988, 1990) proposes four general strategic responses to dialectical opposition: selection, separation, neutralization, and reframing.

The strategy of selection involves choosing actions consistent with one horn of the dilemma or one pole of the contradiction. Individuals may choose openness over closedness, for instance. Separation involves either temporal cyclic alternation or topical segmentation of oppositional forces. Cyclic alternation includes responding to each pole of the contradiction at different points in time, such as being open for a time, then being closed, then being open again. Segmentation deals with each pole of the contradiction with mutually exclusive activity, such as disclosing on some topics but being private about others, or by maintaining relational predictability while incorporating interactional novelty. Neutralization entails compromise between opposing tendencies by diluting their intensity. This is accomplished in one of two ways: moderation is the use of neutral messages, as in small talk; disqualification uses ambiguous or indirect communication that avoids explicit reference to either polarity. Reframing involves transcending the contradiction by redefining the poles as non-oppositional. Viewing autonomy as enhancing rather than impeding connection would be an example of reframing.

Baxter (1990) conducted retrospective personal interviews with individuals involved in romantic relationships to explore the presence of dialectical contradiction across various stages of relationship development and the strategic responses employed by individuals to manage the contradictions. Her results indicated that relational satisfaction was positively associated with the use of reframing in coping with autonomy—connection, and negatively associated with the use of disqualification in coping with openness—closedness. In coping with the novelty—predictability contradiction, the use of reframing and segmentation were positively correlated with relational satisfaction while the use of selection was negatively associated with satisfaction.

The management of dialectical tensions is likely to be influenced by the manner in which relational partners perceptually frame the circumstances surrounding the contradictions. Cupach and Metts (1988) conducted interviews of individuals in both married and dating relationships to explore how dialectical tensions were managed on a day-to-day basis. Management was found to be a function of whether dialectical pulls were viewed as cyclical or static. A cyclical view of dialectical tension sees the imbalance as temporary though possibly recurrent. Such a view was associated with proactive and constructive attempts to deal with attempts to revitalize the relationship by changing behavior (e.g., periodically performing an unexpected behavior to inject excitement into the relationship). A static view of dialectical tension implies a change from perceived balance to perceived imbalance with little hope for future change. Individuals expressing this view of their dialectical tension typically reported being acquiescent (i.e., giving up or giving in to accommodate their partner) or selecting one pole and subverting the other.

Although this study was exploratory and based on a small sample, it suggests an important direction for future research. It would be useful to consider how individual differences in attributional tendencies pertaining to the perception of dialectical contradictions affect dialectical management practices over time and in turn ultimately affect the trajectories and outcomes of relationships.

## Dialectical Patterns Symptomatic of Breakdown

Certain observed patterns of dialectical opposition may signal difficulties in the relationship and perhaps may reflect the inability of partners to effectively manage dialectical opposition. For example, Altman et al. (1981) speculate that a relationship in crisis might first be characterized by high frequency and amplitude of openness-closedness in which individuals engage in a rapid succession of intense confrontations and withdrawals. Then, as the relationship continues to decline, so do amplitude and frequency of openness-closedness as individuals interact less frequently and more superficially. Of course, the determination of whether this pattern reflects crisis in a particular relationship would depend on the subjective judgment of the relationship participants and an examination of the baseline pattern of openness-closedness during a "healthy" phase of the relationship.

Another manifestation of relational breakdown is dissynchrony or incongruence of partners' dialectical cycles or temporal profiles. Altman et al. (1981) discuss two kinds of synchrony in interpersonal interaction: temporal and substantive. Extending their discussion of openness-closedness cycling, they indicate that temporal synchrony occurs when the relational partners are matched in terms of their accessibility to one another. When one partner is accessible, so is the other partner; when one is closed, the other is similarly closed. Thus, temporal dissynchrony involves mistiming, such as when one partner seeks interaction but the other person is "not receptive to contact" (Altman et al. 1981, p. 152).

The substantive synchrony of openness-closedness cycles refers to the matching of content. Matching depicts an instance in which partners are coordinated not only in terms of intimacy but in terms of degree of intimacy in interaction. It could also represent openness on the same subject, such as mutual willingness to discuss particular relational problems.

Mistiming and mismatching probably occur in all relationships to some degree. Research could investigate the consequences and differences of various patterns of cycling: For example, how viable are relationships with long histories of matching or mismatching and timing and mistiming? Do members of viable relationships exhibit better timing and matching than those in unstable relationships? Does continual good timing and matching result in boredom or a stagnating relationship? To what extent do different relationships progress over time toward greater or lesser synchrony? (Altman et al. 1981, p. 154)

## Dialectics and the Accomplishment of Disengagement

Dialectical phenomena pervade relationships, produce and symptomize change, and play a role in the breakdown of relationships. They also are ubiquitous in the strategic phases of accomplishing uncoupling. The individual initiating disengagement is faced with several dilemmas surrounding the process of intentionally changing the definition of the relationship. The initiator's primary goal seems to be termination (or negotiated decline) of the relationship, that is, a desire for more autonomy, but continued connection may be desired until the comparison level of alternatives is sufficient to make leaving the current relationship a safe choice (Sprecher 1988). Moreover, it is typically the case that the initiator still likes some aspects of the partner. This, along with other barrier forces such as guilt and the perceived costs of termination, produces ambivalence (Levinger 1979; Vaughan 1986). Indeed, ambivalence can occur even after the final separation when the initiator has had time to actually experience relational life without the former partner (Vaughan 1986). Alternatively, if the relationship is renegotiated to a friendship, the partner may still be covertly trying to win the initiator back, and the initiator may be tempted because the relationship is running more smoothly. The initiator must inevitably balance the fear of failing again with the same partner, with the fear of failure by defaulting on an opportunity to reconcile the relationship.

The autonomy-connection dilemma is also manifested in behaviors that seem to contradict the goal of termination. Vaughan remarks that "Some initiators feel an obligation to fulfill their role as caretaker at the very moment that they are trying to put that role behind. They face the competing demands of leaving the partner, while at the same time preparing the partner for the loss" (1986, p. 174). This, of course, also can create a dilemma for the partner as he or she is faced with the competing goals of reconstituting a relational identity versus reconciling with the partner. Hope springs eternal in the presence of a partner who continues to be present and accommodating.

Both the initiator and the partner are faced with openness-closedness dilemmas, specifically regarding disengagement. The initiator faces the challenge of the extent to which the partner should be forcefully and explicitly confronted. To be blunt is effortful and accrues numerous possible drawbacks. The initiator may feel guilty for hurting the partner, and forcing the issue may cause the partner to become angry and to retaliate in some way. Being direct without regard for the partner's face can also undermine the goal of maintaining a friendship with the partner and can make the initiator appear cruel in the eyes of others. To be indirect to avoid confrontation with the partner is to protract the difficult process of disengagement. This not only prolongs the initiator's agony, but also gives false hope to the partner (assuming the desire to disengage is not mutual). The ambiguity regarding the status of the relationship stemming from indirectness leaves both partners vulnerable to embarrassment in future encounters with each other and with their social networks.

The partner wishing to maintain the relationship is also faced with the confrontation-avoidance dilemma. On one hand, she or he will want to engage in self-disclosure with the initiator in an effort to maintain intimacy with the initiator (Baxter 1979). At the same time, the partner will often avoid confrontation with the initiator regarding disengagement because it may act as a catalyst in producing termination.

## Conclusion

Interpersonal relationships are inherently dialectical phenomena, characterized by contradiction and process. A dialectical perspective can enhance the understanding of disengagement in at least three interrelated ways. First, dialectical contradictions are the impetus for change in interpersonal relationships. Because disengagement cannot be extricated from relationship development and transitions in general, understanding change yields insight into what we call disengagement. In particular, plotting patterns of change over time provides a temporal profile of relationships. Such profiles may be instrumental in establishing the types of developmental relationship trajectories that coincide with crisis, repair, reconciliation, and redefinition of relationships. Additionally, differences in the characteristic nature of dialectical functioning can be used to delineate phases and stages of relationship development—including those marking breakdown and disengagement.

Second, dialectical contradictions are implicated in the breakdown of interpersonal relationships. The ability to manage oppositional tendencies is critical to relationship satisfaction and is reflected in the synchrony of partners' dialectical cycles.

Finally, dialectical contradictions are manifested in the interactions and ruminations involved in strategically accomplishing relationship disengagement. In addition to reconciling ambivalence about disengaging the relationship, initiators must strike an appropriate balance between openness and closedness that simultaneously permits achieving the goal of disengagement and preserving the face of both the partner and the self. The partner, too, experiences contradictory impulses of trying to maintain the disengaging relationship versus attempting to save and reconstruct a different relational identity.

The chief value of the dialectical approach presented here is that certain processual features of disengagement are revealed and emphasized. Much lip service is paid to studying the dynamic aspects of relationships and disengagement. Although the development of methodological innovations permits increasingly sophisticated research, we also need to more clearly conceptualize what "process" is and means. A dialectical perspective assists us in modifying the way we think about relationships and their disengagement.

## References

Altman, I., Vinsel, A., and Brown, B. (1981). Dialectical conceptions in social psychology: An application to social penetration and privacy regulation. In L. Berkowitz (Ed.), *Advances in experimental social psychology* (Vol. 14, pp. 107–160). New York: Academic Press.

Baxter, L. A. (1979). Self-disclosure as a relationship disengagement strategy: An exploratory investigation. *Human Communication Research*, 5, 215–222.

———. (1983). Relationship disengagement: An examination of the reversal hypothesis. *Western Journal of Speech Communication*, 47, 85–98.

———. (1988). A dialectical perspective on communication strategies in relationship development. In S. Duck (Ed.), *Handbook of personal relationships: Theory, research interventions* (pp. 257–273). London: Wiley.

———. (1990). Dialectical contradictions in relationship development. *Journal of Social and Personal Relationships*, 7, 69–88.

Baxter, L. A. and Wilmot, W. W. (1983, February). An investigation of openness-closedness cycling in ongoing relationship interaction. Paper presented at the Western Speech Communication Association, Albuquerque.

Berger, C. R. and Bradac, J. J. (1982). *Language and social knowledge: Uncertainty in interpersonal relations*. London: Edwards Arnold.

Bochner, A. P. (1984). The functions of human communication in interpersonal bonding. In C. Arnold and J. Bowers (Eds.), *Handbook of rhetorical and communication therapy* (pp. 544–621). Boston: Allyn & Bacon.

Cissna, K. N., Cox, D. E., and Bochner, A. P. (1990). The dialectic of marital and parental relationships within the stepfamily. *Communication Monographs*, 57, 44–61.

Conville, R. L. (1988). Relational transitions: An inquiry into their structure and function. *Journal of Social and Personal Relationships*, 5, 423–437.

Cupach, W. R., & Metts, S. (1988, July). *Perceptions and mangement of dialectics in romantic relationships*. Paper presented at the Fourth International Conference on Personal Relationships, Vancouver, Canada.

Knapp, M. L. (1984). *Interpersonal communication and human relationships*. Boston: Allyn and Bacon.

Levinger, G. (1979). A social exchange view on the dissolution of pair relationships. In R. L. Burgess and T. L. Huston (Eds.), *Social exchange in developing relationships* (pp. 169–193). New York: Academic Press.

———. (1983). Development and change. In H. H. Kelley, E. Berscheid, A. Christenson, J. H. Harvey, T. L. Huston, G. Levinger, E. McClintock, L. A. Peplau, & D. T. Peterson (Eds.), *Close relationships*, (pp. 315–359). San Francisco, CA: Freeman.

Masheter, C. and Harris, L. M. (1986). From divorce to friendship: A study of dialectic relationship development. *Journal of Social and Personal Relationships*, 3, 177–189.

Rawlins, W. K. (1983a). Negotiating close friendship: The dialectic of conjunctive freedoms. *Human Communication Research*, 9, 255–266.

———. (1983b). Openness as problematic in ongoing friendships: Two conversational dilemmas. *Communication Monographs*, 50, 1–13.

Rawlins, W. K. and Holl, M. R. (1987). The communicative achievement of friendship during adolescence: Predicaments of trust and violation. *Western Journal of Speech Communication*, 51, 345–363.

———. (1988). Adolescents' interaction with parents and friends: Dialectics of temporal perspective and evaluation. *Journal of Social and Personal Relationships*, 5, 27–46.

Sarnoff, I. and Sarnoff, S. (1989a, October). The dialectic of marriage. *Psychology Today*, pp. 54–57.

———. (1989b). *Love-centered marriage in a self-centered world*. New York: Hemisphere Publishing.

Sprecher, S. (1988). Investment model, equity, and social support and determinants of relationship commitment. *Social Psychology Quarterly*, 51, 318–328.

Tolhuizen, J. H. (1986). Perceived communication indicators of evolutionary changes in friendship. *Southern Speech Communication Journal*, 52, 69–91.

Vaughan, D. (1986). *Uncoupling: How relationships come apart*. New York: Vintage Books.

Wiseman, J. P. (1986). Friendship: Bonds and binds in a voluntary relationship. *Journal of Social and Personal Relationships*, 3, 191–211.

Wood, J. T. (1982). Communication and relational culture: Bases for the study of human relationships. *Communication Quarterly*, 30, 75–83.

# Questions

1. Analyze a relationship you have observed coming apart, and identify two dialectical tensions the individuals appeared to confront. Give examples of the communication you witnessed that captured these tensions.

2. Identify a relationship that encountered difficulties, but in which the partners reversed the decline process. Give an example of how a dialectical tension was managed and of a strategy that helped reverse the decline.

3. Describe 2–3 communication strategies you believe to be valuable in managing dialectical tensions and slowing or reversing the relational decline process.

# 34

# 'The Worst Part Is, We Don't Even Talk Anymore'

## Post-Dissolutional Communication in Break Up Stories

*Jody Koenig Kellas*

**T**he phrase "And they lived happily after" does not capture the experience of most romantic pairs who break up. Even the phrase "Can't we just be friends?" has it limits in real life. Most adults have experienced a number of romantic breakup conversations and the aftermath of these discussions. There are many possible outcomes, ranging from the experience of developing a close friendship to stalking or threatening action (Harvey and Weber 2002). Little is known about talk after a romantic breakup; however, a great deal is known about divorce and long-term interactions among ex-spouses (Hetherington and Kelly 2002).

Much of the existing research relies on personal narratives because they demonstrate the meaning of the experience for the respondents. According to Wells (1986), "Constructing stories in the mind—or storying, as it has been called—is one of the most fundamental means of making meanings . . . stories are one of the most effective ways of making one's own interpretation of events and ideas available to others" (p. 194).

Although extensive attention is given to breaking up in popular magazines and in television and films, only a limited number of studies have examined the follow-up experiences of young romantic relationships that have broken up. Everyone is familiar with the "classic" break-up story: The couple fights, then they break up, go their

separate ways, and never speak again. Nevertheless, while most have witnessed or experienced this kind of break-up, it is certainly not the way that most couples end their relationships, especially regarding the ceasing of communication.

As Jody Koenig Kellas demonstrates in this chapter, there are many couples who continue speaking to one another after their romantic relationship ends, and according to her research, this communication has a great impact on how well the couple adapts and heals from relationship dissolution. The author uses her foundation in studying break-up stories as a basis for much of the discussion in this chapter, as she first explains types of post-relationship communication and how each type impacts adjustment to the new definition of the relationship. She then describes the role of anger in post-dissolutional communication, and other ways in which couples struggle with communicating after a break-up. Finally, the long-term patterns of communication wrap up the chapter, as Koenig Kellas discusses how post-relationship communication either continues to grow or subsides with time, using a narrative paradigm to examine 90 college-age students' communication with former partners.

As you read this chapter, think about this question: What are the advantages or disadvantages of continuing to talk to one another after ending a romantic relationship?

## References

Harvey, J. H., and Weber, A. L. (2002). *Odyssey of the Heart*, 2nd ed. Mahwah, NJ: Lawrence Erlbaum.

Hetherington, E. M. and Kelly, J. (2002) *For Better or for Worse: Divorce Reconsidered*. New York: W. W. Norton.

Wells, B. (1986). *The Meaning Makers*. Portsmouth, NH: Heinemann Press.

* * *

**W**hen I was 16, I fell in love for the first time with a boy named Justin. It had all the great attributes of a first love—it was fun and exciting, and the feeling of butterflies in my stomach occurred every time I knew I was going to see him. The best part was that we had been best friends before we started dating, so we easily moved into a more intense closeness and into the kind of rich talks that accompanied our new bond. At the time, we—and our friends—saw us as a pair that would be connected forever, and in many ways we did a lot of growing up together. Eventually, however, as many young relationships do, ours came to an end when my family's cross-country move separated us and we discovered that maintaining a long-distance relationship at 16 was too difficult. Justin met a girl who lived in his own zip code, ended our relationship, and in the process gave me my first broken heart.

I could end my story here, leaving a neat and packaged, albeit sad, conclusion to a narrative about my first love and first "real" breakup. That would be, however, simplifying the complex set of communicative interactions that ensued immediately following the breakup and the many interactions that have continued over the years between Justin and me.

I share with you my own story as an exemplar of the idea that people's relationships—and the communications that constitute them—do not simply end with the words "I think we should break up" or "I don't think we should see each other anymore." Instead, many relational partners continue communicating after the "state-of-the-relationship-talk" that ends the romantic relationship in an effort to understand what happened and/or construct a new sense of what the relationship will be now that they are no longer romantically involved. Indeed, even though it may have been easy in some ways for Justin and me to stop talking—we did live 3,000 miles apart after all—both of us made a concerted effort to continue calling one another. During many phone calls and visits, we attempted to make sense of why what seemed like a lasting relationship had to end and to repair the damage that our relationship had encountered so that it could continue in friendship form.

Despite the fact that many people do continue communicating with their former partners, the current models used to explain relationship dissolution concentrate primarily on the communication that leads up to and culminates in the "official" termination (Knapp and Vangelisti 1992). Other researchers look at the post-breakup commu-

nication that takes place outside the relationship (Duck 1982). Some of my research on narratives of relationship dissolution, however, indicates that *whether or not* and *how* people continue talking after they break up matters to them and may affect how well they deal with the relationship's end. More specifically, in a study I conducted with Valerie Manusov (Koenig and Manusov in press), we found that people used "current communication status" as a conceptual yardstick to evaluate the breakup process and/or to describe their present emotions. This seemed to be an integral part of the stories provided by a majority of the people in our study. In this essay, I will share with you what I found when I looked deeper into those stories to explore the importance of what I call *post-dissolutional communication*, or the interaction that takes place between former partners after the breakup of a romantic relationship.

## The Importance of Studying Post-Dissolutional Communication

Relationship dissolution, particularly for young adults, is a regular and often difficult part of the relationship life cycle. Models of relationship development and dissolution document the centrality of communication in the process of leading to, negotiating, and confirming relational dissolution (Duck 1982; Knapp and Vangelisti 1992). Duck's (1982) model of relationship dissolution, for example, explains that people go through four phases when ending a relationship. First, during the *intrapsychic phase*, individuals weigh the strengths and weaknesses of the relationship in an effort to make decisions about whether to break up or stay together. Second, individuals confront their partner with their dissatisfaction in the *dyadic phase*, and, together, they discuss options of repairing or ending the relationship. In the third, or *social phase*, individuals either share with friends and family their unhappiness with the relationship and seek counsel from them, or announce the decision to break up to members of their social networks. Finally, in the *gravedressing phase*, individuals create accounts and stories that explain why the relationship ended. Communication models of relationship dissolution such as Duck's, as well as a large body of research that examines the reasons why relationships end (Metts and Cupach 1986) and the tactics people use to end them (Baxter 1982; Cody 1982), all present communication as integral to the process of relational decline and eventual dissolution. We know less, however, about the role that communication plays between partners after the breakup has occurred. It is worthwhile to learn more about the way people communicate with partners after the deterioration of a romantic relationship for a few other reasons.

First, the ending of a romantic relationship does not necessarily constitute the end of the relationship between partners altogether. Few would suggest, for example, that once the couple ends the romantic relationship, the relationship in all aspects ceases to exist. If nothing else, the storytelling literature suggests that the relationship lives on through the stories about it or the dissolution process (Weber, Harvey, and Stanley 1989). Even when they end, relationships may continue to live in the communication and memories about them.

Terminated romantic relationships do not, however, only continue to exist in the memory of the partners. Experience and research suggest that former partners communicate after the breakup in a variety of ways. Some remain friends (Metts, Cupach, and Bejlovec 1989), and some continue to argue long after they have officially ended their bond (Weiss 1975). Some people might try to remain civil, whereas others try to reconcile. Romantic relationships may cease to be romantic, but the relationship between the two partners may continue in a different size, shape, or form. Weiss (1975) demonstrates this variety in his research on the accounts that people provide for why they got divorced. He argues that "separation is an *incident* in the relationship of spouses, rather than an ending of that relationship. It is a critically important incident, to be sure: an incident that ushers in fundamental changes in the relationship. But it is not an ending" (p. 83, emphasis added). In other words, relationship dissolution does not necessarily constitute the "death of the dyad." Commu-

nication facilitates the relationship that emerges afterward. For example, although not all couples put the same amount of time and effort into maintaining a friendship as Justin and I did (in fact many people I have talked to find it much too difficult or downright strange), communication is central to understanding the relationships that still exist after the breakup. These might be surviving, struggling, dwindling relationships or relationships that only exist in the memories and stories of individual members. Whatever the case, examining this process offers an even more detailed picture of the relational life cycle.

A second reason that understanding communication in post-dissolutional relationships is important is because for most people, the ending of a significant romantic relationship is a difficult and sometimes traumatic experience. How people communicate about traumatic experiences, such as relational loss, may help to explain how they adjust to the experience. One of the reasons it may be difficult to adjust and to come to terms with the relationship ending is loss of the companionship and attachment the relationship offered. *Attachment* is an enduring feature of love, providing the security of no longer feeling lost and lonely in the world (Weiss 1975). Following a breakup, however, people struggle with losing a companion and, sometimes, with feelings of being alone. People may even experience "separation distress," or the anxiety and loneliness associated with the lost attachment (Weiss 1975).

When people end a significant attachment, they have to renegotiate a sense of how they communicate with their former partners and renegotiate a sense of themselves. Stephen (1984) argues that "everyday conversation between couple members, about their past, about the affairs of the day, and about their hopes and plans for the future, is thought to gradually form a basis for the development of a highly integrated 'couple reality'—that is, an intimate, dyadic world view" (p. 4). Breaking up threatens, if it does not destroy, the continuation of this world view and the conversations that help to create what he calls "symbolic interdependence" (Stephen 1984, 4). After a breakup, some people wish to maintain a sense of identity that keeps them close to the couplehood. Others "battle toward an autonomous self" (Weiss 1975, 73). Either of these extremes, or what lies between them, gets negotiated in the processes associated with post-dissolutional communication. Different types of communication between former partners might significantly influence a person's breakup experience and his or her ability to cope with the loss of self and other in the process.

In sum, communication often continues between former partners, and communication between partners may play a hand in how people adjust to relationship loss. With these reasons in mind, and with a desire to better understand communication in this aspect of the relationship life cycle, I conducted a study on the type and quality of communication that people report in their post-dissolutional relationships.

# Post-Dissolutional Communication in Stories of Relationship Dissolution

One place to investigate post-dissolutional communication is in the stories that people tell about their breakups. Narratives have been shown to be important and consequential forms of explaining and understanding the dissolution of romantic relationships among both married and non-married populations (Metts and Cupach 1986; Harvey, Orbuch, and Weber 1992; Weber et al. 1989; Koenig and Manusov in press; Weiss 1975). The ability to construct and tell the story of a breakup enables the teller to make sense of the events (Weiss 1975); increases self-esteem and control over the events (Weber et al. 1989); and has been linked to tellers' adjustment to the relationship's end (Koenig and Manusov in press). Narratives of relationship dissolution allow people to create plot, develop characters, and assign responsibility in a way that communicates for themselves and others how and why the relationship ended. These types of stories are good sites for understanding how communication factors into the disso-

lution process, and what happens between partners after the breakup has occurred. For example, one individual who laments about missing the talks that he and his girlfriend used to have (e.g., "I really miss talking to her, but she won't return my calls") might have more difficulty coming to terms with the breakup than an individual who is on "good terms" with his former partner or someone who is happily out of contact with that person (e.g., "We don't talk anymore which is the best thing for both of us").

## Types of Post-Dissolutional Communication

In order to better understand post-dissolutional communication, I conducted a research study that looked at the types of communication people used with former partners and whether these types of communication related to adjustment. In the study, 90 college-age participants were asked to provide a written narrative describing the dissolution of a romantic relationship. Specifically, participants were instructed to "Please tell the story of a breakup of one of your significant romantic relationships." After completing the story and some questions about who had initiated the breakup, how long it had been since the relationship ended, and current relationship status, participants completed a measure of post-relational adjustment. Adapted from the Fisher Divorce Adjustment Scale (FDAS), this 100-item self-report questionnaire measures individual adjustment (including feelings like anger, self-worth, disentanglement from the former partner, and grief) to relationship dissolution.

After the data were collected, I examined the narratives to see how tellers addressed the issue of communication with their former partners following the breakup. I found that people engaged in several different types of communication with their former partners, including (1) positive communication, (2) occasional/circumstantial communication, (3) rare, awkward, or negative communication, (4) absence of communication, and/or (5) no mention of communication.

*Positive communication*. Despite the fact that people were writing about a relationship that they or their partner had decided to end because the romantic side of it wasn't working, many of them reported that they not only continued to communicate with their former partner but also communicated with him or her in positive ways. One type of positive communication was *friendly post-dissolutional communication*. A number of people described wanting to stay friends with their ex-boyfriend or ex-girlfriend. For example, one person said, "I guess we actually pulled off that whole . . . 'let's just be friends thing.'" Staying friends and communicating positively with the partner after the breakup might depend on what the relationship was like before the two people started dating. For example, Metts et al. (1989) found that both disengagers and disengagees claimed to have stayed friends with their former partner if they had been friends prior to becoming romantically involved. Certainly for Justin and me, salvaging our friendship was the biggest motivation for continuing to talk after we broke up. Other people's positive communication went beyond remaining friends; they communicated with former partners in ways that revitalized the romantic relationships. Those engaging in *rekindled romantic communication* said things like "For the next three months we dated other people and meanwhile maintained our friendship. We came to realize we were meant to be together." Stories describing this type of communication often described an important conversation, realization, or instance of forgiveness as being essential to rekindling the romantic relationship.

***Occasional/circumstantial communication***. Many people, in their stories, explained that communication continued with their former partner although only occasionally. This type of communication was often determined or motivated by routine, or common activities. Many described their interactions with their former partner in ways that can be characterized as *circumstantial communication*. One woman said, "We are friends, but I am not in contact with him unless he is home [from school]," indicating that she only communicates with him when it is convenient. People engaging in circumstantial communication reported not putt-

ing much effort into communicating with their ex-boyfriend or ex-girlfriend. Other people did make an effort to talk to the other person, but not with the same regularity as when they had been dating. People engaging in *occasional communication* tended to say things like "We talk maybe once a week, or every other week." There was a sense that people using this type of communication felt the need to maintain some kind of connection but that it was a muted version of the communication that existed before. Finally, a number of stories characterized post-dissolutional communication in terms of *sexually motivated communication* (e.g., "This summer we went with friends to the beach and again had sex, which happens about every two weeks now"). A number of the people in our study reported that although the romantic relationship had officially ended, couples continued to interact through regular sexual encounters. One woman ended her story by saying, "Afterward, we had flings where we would go out on weekends and kiss and play 'dating couple' again for about six months." This type of communication tended to be characterized by casual and occasional connection.

***Rare, awkward, or negative communication***. A third type of post-dissolutional communication involved rare or negative interactions. Some people, for example, reported *one-sided or unsuccessful attempts at communication*. This type of communication was often characterized by one person's desire to maintain a friendship or rekindle the romance and another person's refusal to accept his or her attempt. One woman, who was particularly hurt by her boyfriend's actions leading to the breakup, said, "He called me every night for a month . . . I stopped returning his calls and eventually the pain went away. Another woman acknowledged her own unreturned attempts at maintaining contact by saying, "the 'trying to be friends thing' never actually worked. Once in a while, I try to reach him to see how he is doing, but it just seems as though he is not interested in pursuing a friendship at this time." These stories suggest the importance of both parties' willingness to continue communication. When both parties of a couple agreed to continue communicating, it was often with *awkward or superficial communication*. In these types of encounters, people described a need or obligation to continue talking, but they also acknowledged the difficulty associated with reframing communication in the new relationship. For example, one man said, "We tried to stay friends after, but it was just too awkward, so we stayed away from each other . . . We talk occasionally, but it is still hard to know what to say." Other types of rare/awkward/negative communication included *rare communication* (e.g., "Since then, we hardly talk"), *ambiguous communication* (e.g., "We haven't remained very close"), and *harassing communication* (e.g., "he threatened me, would drive by my house, and wouldn't come near our friends"). These types of communication occurred often in the breakup stories written by participants in our study. People seemed to struggle frequently with wanting to, or feeling obligated to, continue communicating with the former partner, but they also experienced the awkwardness or potentially harmful ramifications of doing so.

*Absence of communication.* It may be that people who were unwilling to endure awkward feelings or rare or negative encounters were those who reported no longer communicating with their former partners. Some people simply stated at the end of their stories things like, "We haven't talked since." Others described the events that led up to the breakup in ways that conveyed them as motivators for not talking anymore. For example, one woman told a story about breaking up with a man because he had started dating someone else while she was away on vacation. She ends her story with: ". . . we ended up having a fight and ended the relationship on bad terms. I went off to college and all I know about him is that he is now a dad and lives with the girl he was seeing while I was on my trip." Some people reported never talking again but communicating through other mediums, such as e-mail, that were less threatening but allowed closure. One man explained that "because of the way I left the situation, we didn't talk again (ever). Behind her back I took some slanderous shots

at her which I now regret saying, and have since written her letters of apology."

*No mention of post-dissolutional communication.* Finally, others in their stories made no mention of whether or not they still communicated with their ex-boyfriend or ex-girlfriend. These stories did not necessarily seem qualitatively different in content than the other stories, but they did seem to end differently, making less sense about how, or if, post-dissolutional communication affected the breakup experience.

## Post-Dissolutional Communication and Adjustment

The five types of post-dissolutional communication illustrate that people deal with relational termination in different ways. As I mentioned before, one reason it is important to study post-dissolutional communication is that it might help us understand how people adjust to the decline of romantic relationships. In the study I did, I wanted to know if these different types of communication helped to explain how adjusted people felt about the breakup. I found that it was not the type of post-dissolutional communication (e.g., positive, occasional) that seemed related to overall adjustment but rather whether people mentioned communication in their stories. In other words, there was a significant trend toward higher adjustment for people who mentioned post-dissolutional communication in their stories that was absent in those who did not mention it. Thus, although adjustment did not differ according to *how* one communicates with one's former partner, it did differ based on *whether or not tellers mentioned post-dissolutional communication* within their stories.

From a communication perspective, this trend is important. It suggests that meta-communication—or communication about communication—matters in the process of adjusting to a relationship. People who talked about how they communicated with their former partner were more likely to be adjusted than those who did not discuss post-dissolutional communication. This may be explained in several ways. First, Pennebaker and his colleagues suggest that talking about traumatic events relates positively to health. For example, Pennebaker and O'Heeron (1984) found that people who talked about their problems experienced fewer health problems than those who ruminated about them. It may be that the participants in my study, consciously or unconsciously, recognized the value of communication in their relational lives and, by mentioning postdissolutional communication in their stories, demonstrated an acknowledgment of its potential impact. Those who did not mention communication may not value its potential for helping them adjust to the dissolution and thus may not have included this part of the breakup in their stories.

Second, communication seemed to be an important part of sense-making in the story. In other words, a writer's acknowledging the fuller relationship life cycle from development to dissolution and beyond seemed to reflect a fuller understanding of the overall process. Some research has argued that stories help people make sense of events, gain a sense of control, and search for closure and understanding (Weber et al. 1987). Explaining post-dissolutional communication in the story probably provides a more complete account (Koenig and Manusov, in press) of the process and may help tellers gain more control and understanding over the events.

## Post-Dissolutional Communication and Anger

The study results also showed that there was a link between how people reported communicating with their partner and how angry they felt at that person. Specifically, people's anger went down as the amount and quality of the communication with their former partner went up. In other words, the more positive the communication they had, the less anger people felt with their former boyfriend or girlfriend. The biggest difference existed between people who didn't talk to their former partner any longer and people who were on "good terms" or engaged in positive communication with their former partner. Intuitively, this is not surprising. Those who engage in positive communication likely have little reason to be angry, whereas those who don't talk to their former

partners might very well have chosen not to because of the anger they felt toward that person. For example, one woman described the fact that she and her former partner no longer talk *in terms of* his infidelity and her anger:

> He kept telling lies and I could never catch him in them. One day a girl who I knew he was once involved with confronted me. We mapped out numerous times he had given one of us an excuse to see the other. She thought that it was all my fault and blamed me. I got very angry with him and ended our relationship in an angry yelling match. We haven't talked since.

Alternatively, individuals might be angry *because* they don't speak. Another woman describes her "perfect" relationship with a boy she considered to be her best friend. She depicts their relationship as very close but complicated by the fact that she had gone off to college while he was still in high school. She explains the breakup and the lack of communication as motivated not by anger but rather by confusion, and she seems upset *because they no longer communicate*:

> . . . Paul and I talked for a long time. We both cried. He said 'Pam, I love you so much. But this is so hard for me because I'm so confused. I think you're the one I want to marry but I need to make sure. We just need some time apart so that when we get back together we'll have no doubts.' So anyways, we talked every few days for a week. Then we just stopped talking. I always hear him asking about me from friends. I think someday he'll come back to me. But right now he's confused. . . . This has been so hard for me. I did terrible in school last quarter because I was so depressed. . . .

These stories differ significantly in tone from those of tellers who maintained positive communication with the former partner.

## Struggling With Post-Dissolutional Communication

Despite the fact that those who engaged in positive communication felt less anger toward the other person, most of the stories that depicted positive communication indicated that it was not "all roses" from the beginning of the breakup. Ultimately, participants in this study described a number of struggles associated with breaking up in which post-dissolutional communication played a starring role. These included struggles with forgiveness, guilt, concern for the other person, and freedom. Although breaking up was fairly seamless for some people, for many others negotiating post-dissolutional communication was a difficult, *and* important, part of the process.

Many of the people in the study described post-dissolutional communication in terms of *guilt, regret* over the circumstances of the breakup, and *concern* for the other person. After struggling in his relationship for some time, one man described his breakup and his feeling of regret for how his behavior influenced their interactions afterward. He said:

> I was in a bad mood that day to begin with and practically blew up over the phone without thinking. She hung up. To this day, I still regret that one thing I did. I've moved on but still wish we could be good friends. Even though we still see each other when I go home, it's just not the same anymore. Oh well, that's life I guess.

This young man seems to accept the awkward nature of their communication as part of the breakup process but also acknowledges the regret associated with how he acted and the ramifications for post-dissolutional communication with his ex-girlfriend. Other people expressed the tension between feeling relieved about the breakup and feeling concerned for the other person. A woman who felt trapped by her boyfriend described post-dissolutional communication in terms of that tension by explaining:

> I felt very free but did feel some guilt because I did care about him very much, just no longer romantically. We've been able to, after time, move our relationship toward friendship. There seems to be no tension between us as far as hard feelings go, but if I spend prolonged periods of time with him I get that same stressed and trapped feeling.

This woman, and many others who wrote about their breakups, experienced tensions between feelings of *freedom* and *guilt*, as well as uncertainty about the role that post-dissolutional communication plays in mediating that tension.

Several other stories revolved around the complicated process of becoming friends or maintaining positive communication following the breakup. For example, two of the stories reflected themes of *forgiveness*, with one man talking to his former girlfriend because she admitted she was wrong and another woman reporting being friends after she forgave her partner for harassing her at the beginning of the breakup. Some people vacillated between romantic and platonic relationships, breaking up and getting back together before deciding to be friends. Still others report rekindling the romantic relationship. At times, many of the struggles associated with post-dissolutional communication accompanied stories that ended in positive communication or rekindling the romantic relationship. One woman describes the complexities associated with breaking up, getting back together, and eventually becoming friends:

> . . . so we broke it off. . . . We did not speak to each other for a while and it was uncomfortable seeing him at times, though once we started talking, the tension would die down a bit. A few months after we broke up, we got back together and then broke it off for good not long afterwards. After this second breakup it was more mutual, but it was still hard. We didn't communicate for about a month and then we would talk about once a month on the phone just to keep in touch. We ended up being friends.

The stories of positive communication indicate that the categories of post-dissolutional communication are not mutually exclusive and that the process of communicating on good terms with a former partner does not appear to be an easy one.

Finally, in addition to feelings of guilt, concern, forgiveness, freedom, and the complications associated with staying friends or getting back together, people reported that post-dissolutional communication can also be just generally *painful* for some people, particularly when there is a feeling that it is out of one's control. For some people, continuing to communicate is painful. For example, one woman said, "I am okay today if I don't see him. But that is almost impossible considering we are in the same major and end up with at least one class together. Every day it gets a little easier, but there will always be that pain. When I see him, I have to get past that initial attraction and think of why we can't be together." For others, not communicating is painful. This was the case for a woman who lamented, "Now we've lost our closeness. I used to be able to confide all of my emotions and feelings in David. Now he only answers my letters superficially. I feel very sad to think about him."

## Post-Dissolutional Communication and Time

After reading about the adjustment, anger, and struggles associated with post-dissolutional communication, you may be thinking, "I bet time plays a big role in determining the ways in which people communicate." If so, you're right! Different types of post-dissolutional communication were associated with different amounts of time since the breakup. People experience breakups differently according to a number of situational factors. Weiss (1975) suggests that time often plays a determinant role in the continuing relationship of former partners, whereby immediately following the dissolution, people maintain feelings of obligation toward the former partner or a need for that partner's companionship.

For our participants, significant differences existed between people who no longer talked to their former partners and all other types of post-dissolutional communication. In other words, those who occasionally talked, engaged in rare/awkward communication, or didn't mention whether they communicated had been apart for significantly less time than those who no longer talked at all. The biggest difference existed between those who no longer talked and those who continued to talk occasionally or circumstantially. This suggests that as time passes, fewer people talk to their partners, whereas the beginnings of dissolution seem to be characterized by occasional communication.

One man, who reported breaking up with his girlfriend just two and a half months prior to telling this story, explains their ensuing occasional communication:

> . . . Since we broke up, I feel like I am free and that I can do whatever I want. I still care for her, but feel that I made the right decision for me, and what I need to do. We talk maybe once a week, or every other week, but it is definitely hard for her though. I wish her the best and for some reason, I know she will hang around and wait for me to come back. If I do, I do, but things will have to change, and she will have to have lived life and experienced some more things.

This excerpt reinforces the idea that post-dissolutional communication is a complex process, influenced by the tensions of guilt and freedom, satisfaction and concern for the other person. It also supports Weiss' (1975) contention that people often stay in contact with their former partners from feelings of guilt and a sense of loyalty to the partner. This young man expresses happiness with his decision but concern for his former girlfriend. The results of this study may suggest that as time goes on, these feelings of guilt and obligation diminish—perhaps as a result of new experiences, lovers, and/or communication—in a way that may explain why people who have been apart for the longest amount of time no longer speak to their former partners. Interestingly, those who report positive communication with their former partners had been apart for an average of 22 months, second only to those who don't talk anymore (an average of 36.12 months). It seems as though, in the long run, people either tended to stay friends or stop talking altogether.

## Conclusion

In this essay, I have described the complex process of post-dissolutional communication. People engage in a variety of different types of communication with their former partners, and the study I conducted indicates that post-dissolutional communication does in some ways relate to or reflect the process associated with adjustment to relationship dissolution. Those who mentioned communication in their stories tended to be more adjusted than those who did not; those who don't talk tended to be angrier than those who do talk, at least in some capacity; people struggle with how to communicate with their former partner and often vacillate among feelings like guilt, concern, freedom, and regret. Finally, time helps to differentiate between the types of post-dissolutional communication. An examination of specific stories indicates that the process of communicating with former partners following a breakup can range from simple to complex. In some cases, partners end communication altogether with the breakup. Others fluctuate between different types of communication before arriving at a comfortable relationship.

Further understanding the stages and/or tensions associated with the progression or regression of communication following a breakup may add detail to models of relationship development and dissolution and, moreover, may help people to better understand the processes and functions of post-dissolutional communication. Stories provide rich sites for viewing the sense-making process associated with relationship disengagement. This essay provides an initial examination of how post-dissolutional communication is described and helps to facilitate that sense-making process.

## References

Baxter, L. A. (1982). Strategies for ending relationships: Two studies. *Western Journal of Speech Communication*, 46: 233–242.

Cody, M. J. (1982). A typology of disengagement strategies and an examination of the roles intimacy, reactions to inequity, and relational problems play in strategy selection. *Communication Monographs*, 49: 148–170.

Duck, S. (1982). A typology of relationship disengagement and dissolution. In S. Duck (Ed.), *Personal relationships, vol. IV: Dissolving personal relationships*, pp. 1–30. New York: Academic Press.

Harvey, J. H., Orbuch, T. L., and Weber, A. L. (1992). Introduction: Convergence of the attribution and accounts concepts in the study of close relationships. In J. H. Harvey, T. L. Orbuch, and A. L. Weber (Eds.), *Attributions, accounts, and close relationships* (pp. 1–18). New York: Springer-Verlag.

Knapp, M. L., and Vangelisti, A. (1992). *Interpersonal communication and human relationships*, 2nd ed. Boston: Allyn & Bacon.

Koenig, J., and Manusov, V. (in press). What's in a story? The relationship between narrative completeness and tellers' adjustment to relationship dissolution. *Journal of Social and Personal Relationships*.

Metts, S., and Cupach, W. R. (1986). Disengagement themes in same-sex and opposite-sex friendships. Paper presented to the Interpersonal Communication Interest Group, Western Speech Communication Association, Tucson, AZ.

Metts, S., Cupach, W. R., and Bejlovec, R. A. (1989). 'I love you too much to ever start liking you': Redefining romantic relationships. *Journal of Social and Personal Relationships*, 6: 259–274.

Pennebaker, J. W., and O'Heeron, R. C. (1984). Confiding in others and illness rate among spouses of suicide and accidental-death victims. *Journal of Abnormal Psychology*, 93: 473–476.

Stephen, T. D. (1984). Symbolic interdependence and post-breakup distress: A reformulation of the attachment construct. *Journal of Divorce*, 8: 1–16.

Weber, A. L., Harvey, J. H., and Stanley, M. A. (1987). The nature and motivations of accounts for failed relationships. In R. Burnett, P. McGhee, and D. D. Clarke (Eds.), *Accounting for relationships: Explanation, representation, and knowledge*, pp. 114–133. London: Methuen.

Weiss, R. S. (1975). *Marital separation*. New York: Basic Books.

## Questions

1. To what extent are Koenig Kellas' categories of experience similar or different from what you have experienced or observed in post-breakup interactions? What category, if any, would you have expected to be included that did not appear in this article? Explain the interactional dynamics of that category.

2. Analyze a film or television program that depicts post-breakup interaction, and describe it according to one or more of the categories included in this article.

3. What links would you expect to find between dialectical theory and the experiences of the college-age respondents?

# Part IX

## *Contexts*

## A. Family

Family life is a universal human experience, yet, because of the unique communication patterns in each family system, no two people share the exact same family experience. Even siblings have different family experiences due to the transactional nature of communication. The combination of the personality, experiences, age, and gender of each child and each parent impacts their relationship. Because family is such a powerful influence in each person's life, it is important to examine family interaction patterns in order to understand the communication dynamics of this powerful life-shaping entity. Members' communication patterns serve to construct as well as reflect familial experience; essentially, you create your families just as you are created by these families.

As family members and teachers, we hold certain basic beliefs that reflect our backgrounds and have given us particular perspectives on families and their communication. These are as follows:

1. There is no "right" way to be a family. There are many types of families and numerous ways to relate within each family type. Each family must struggle to create its own identity as it encounters positive and negative experiences.

2. Communication serves to constitute as well as reflect family life. It is through talk that persons construct their identities and negotiate their relationships with each other and the rest of the world. This talk also serves to indicate or reflect the state of family relationships.

3. Communication is the process by which family members work out and share their meanings with each other. Members create a family relational culture as well as individualized relational ties with parent(s) and any siblings.

4. Families are part of multigenerational communication patterns. Family members are influenced by the patterns of previous generations as they create their own patterns, which will influence future generations.

5. Well-functioning families work at managing their communication patterns. Such families develop the capacity to adapt to and create change, to share intimacy, and to manage conflict.

There is no single, widely agreed upon definition of the term *family*. Traditionally, blood and legal ties determined family membership; currently, families may be viewed more broadly as "networks who share their lives over long periods of time bound by ties of marriage, blood, or commitment, legal or otherwise, who consider themselves as family and who share a significant history and anticipated future of functioning in a family relationship" (Galvin, Brommel, and Bylund 2004, 6). Given the multiple variations of family structures, members are defining themselves for themselves through their interactions. At the same time, issues such as longevity, legal flexibility, personal choice, ethnicity, gender, geographic distance, and reproductive technology are impacting traditional biological and legal conceptions of the family. Therefore, we dismiss the "traditional" versus "nontraditional" family distinction. Today scholars are concerned with how family members define themselves as families to outsiders as well as how they use communication to explain their family to themselves. This constitutive approach to creating a family challenges old conceptions (Whitchurch and Dickson 1999). We take a broad, inclusive view of families, encompassing countless variations of family forms and numerous types of interaction patterns.

It is important to distinguish between two types of family experience—current families and families of origin. Families in combination beget families through the evolutionary cycles of coming together and separating. Thus, each person may experience life in different families, starting with his or her family of origin. *Family of origin* refers to the family or families in which a person is raised. Noted family therapist Virginia Satir (1988) stresses the importance of the family of origin as the blueprints for "peoplemaking." She suggests: "Blueprints vary from family to family. I believe some blueprints result in nurturing families, some result in troubled ones." Multigenerational patterns, those of more than two generations, are considered part of the blueprint (Hoopes 1987). Family of origin and multigenerational experiences are crucial in the development of communication patterns in current families.

The systems perspective provides insight into family functioning and family communication. This perspective maintains that individuals do not exist in a vacuum; rather, individuals are linked in ways that make them interdependent. Each individual is part of an overall *family system*, affecting and being affected by that system. You cannot fully understand a person without knowing something about his or her family. An individual's behavior becomes more comprehensible when viewed within the context of his or her family system. For example, an individual's behavior may appear strange to you, but, if you understand the whole family context, your perceptions may change. What may be viewed as problematic behavior in one setting may be functional in another context.

Within any system, the parts and the relationships between them form the whole; changes in one part will result in changes in the others; as events touch one member of the family, other members are affected by the change. From the systems perspective, you analyze families by paying attention to the relationships among members, as opposed to paying attention to one individual. Ways of relating, making decisions, sharing affection, or handling conflict may vary slightly or greatly among different families. Yet each family finds its own way to establish communication patterns reflecting their identity.

As you read this section, think about the families you know well or about fictional families, and try to identify key communication patterns that seem to contribute to the family's identity and to its members' ways of relating to one another as well as to people outside the family.

## References

Galvin, K. M., Brommel, B. J., and Bylund, C. (2004). *Family Communication: Cohesion and Change*, 6th ed. Boston: Allyn & Bacon.

Hoopes, M. (1987). Multigenerational systems: Basic assumptions. *American Journal of Family Therapy*, 15: 196–205.

Satir, V. (1988). *The New Peoplemaking*. Mountain View, CA: Science and Behavior Books.

Whitchurch, G., and Dickson, F. C. (1999). Family communication. In M. B. Sussman, S. K. Steinmetz, and G. W. Peterson (Eds.), *Handbook of Marriage and the Family*, 2nd ed., pp. 687–704. New York: Plenum Press. ✦

# 35
# Family Ground Rules

*Elizabeth Stone*

It is likely that you can recall being told stories about your family as you were growing up. It is very likely you heard the same stories over and over again. Family stories bind the family members together. These stories provide your history, indicate what is expected of you as a family member, and give you an identity. According to Elizabeth Stone, they exert an influence on the listeners' lives, revealing "what we owe and to whom, what we can expect and from whom, in time or money or emotion."

Family stories serve the following functions as they carry important messages to family members: (1) to remember, (2) to create belonging and reaffirm family identity, (3) to educate current members and socialize new members, (4) to aid changes, and (5) to provide stability (Galvin, Bylund, and Brommel 2004). These stories may be told on holidays, at special family occasions, or when a family or member is facing adversity. They serve as keys to understanding what it means to be a member of your family.

You might wish to gather your own family stories. Zeitlin and his coauthors (1982) suggest that every family has its heroes, rogues, mischief makers, survivors, saints, and sinners. And each of these characters has an interesting story. Stories of courtships, feuds, lost fortunes, and immigrations are all "grist for the mill." An example of the beginning of a story-collecting process is found in the following quote:

> My child's fifth-grade class had just finished a Grandparents Day celebration and the teacher asked my parents to attend school and be interviewed by all my child's class. I was amazed at the questions the children asked—all the way from "How did you meet?" to "What did you do in World War II?" My father told the story of selling his colt to

get the money for my mother's diamond engagement ring. The horse sold for $75, which at that time was a lot of money. I learned more about my parents that day than I had ever known.

*In the following excerpt from her book* Black Sheep and Kissing Cousins: How Our Family Stories Shape Us *(1988), Stone discusses the impact of family stories—particularly on relationships in the family. Through an analysis of several family narratives, including a few of her own, the author explains how stories convey a family's rules and expectations to its members. She elaborates on "types" of family stories in general, what they mean, whom they are about (usually men), and who conveys them (usually women). The importance of such stories and their prevalence in all families as the "cornerstone of family culture" is the key point maintained throughout the chapter. As you read this excerpt, think about this question: How have the meanings of your own family stories influenced your life?*

### References

Galvin, K. M., Bylund, C. L. and Brommel, B. J. (2004). *Family Communication: Cohesion and Change*. Boston: Allyn & Bacon.

Stone, E. (1988). *Black Sheep and Kissing Cousins: How Our Family Stories Shape Us*. New York: Times Books.

Zeitlin, S., Kitkin, A. and Baker, H. (1982). *A Celebration of American Family Folklore*. Washington, DC: Smithsonian Institute.

\* \* \*

In 1890, my grandfather, Gaetano Bongiorno, came to New York from the Lipari Islands off the coast of Sicily. He was a young man of eighteen, serious and somewhat stolid, but also big and hardworking. Like many Southern Italian men of the time, he was a "bird of passage," a man who had come here to work so he could earn money for his family back home, rather than to settle down here. Over the years, he had a variety of jobs, among them piloting a barge and working as a longshoreman loading and unloading the ships that came into Brooklyn harbor. After work, he would go home to Union Street, where he lived with the two married sisters who had preceded him here. It was even cozier than that; Gaetano's two sisters had married two brothers and those brothers also happened to be first cousins.

The years went by, and Gaetano showed no sign of returning to Italy or marrying and settling down here, either. By 1905, he was already thirty-three. One day in the mail, however, a letter came. Along with it was a photograph of his cousin Annunziata, the youngest sister of Gaetano's sister's husbands.

Gaetano was taken with the photograph of this young woman, and as his sisters had been badgering him to marry, he decided to try to arrange a marriage with her. And so Gaetano sailed to Sicily, went to his uncle, Annunziata's father, and asked for permission to marry her. My grandmother was agreeable to marrying Gaetano. She was fifteen. The idea of marriage seemed very grown-up to her, and the prospect of coming to live in America was exciting. Besides, my grandfather was tall and redheaded, and his looks appealed to my grandmother. So the betrothal was arranged and the marriage soon followed.

In 1905 my grandfather and his bride returned to Union Street and his two sisters and two brothers-in-law, and there they *all* lived until Gaetano and Annunziata could find a place on Union Street of their own. And thus it was that two sisters and a brother married two brothers and a sister and all lived right on top of each other on Union Street in Brooklyn.

The story of how my grandparents had come to marry was often told in my family, and what it said to me was that family was so important that one should even try to marry within the family. I remember at four or five having already decided which of my male first cousins I would eventually marry. The whole story, including my grandfather's Union Street living arrangements, also told me that the essential unit was the extended family. The nuclear family—a couple and their children—tucked itself into the larger unit.

While my conclusions about whom I ought to marry were unwarranted, there was no doubt that the story implicitly laid down other rules about what family members should do for each other. The fact that my grandfather had lived with his two sisters

and their families for years on end was expressed without comment. There was nothing extraordinary about it, nothing even especially laudatory. That was what family members did for each other.

And yet this story could so easily have been told another way, with another meaning. My grandmother was the youngest of twelve children, almost all of whom had left Sicily in the hopes of better prospects elsewhere. A few had come here, a few had gone to Australia, and still others to South America. The story, with a twist in tone, could have become a lament about the Bongiorno *diaspora*, the disintegration of family. Perhaps the insistence on family unity and the belief in Bongiorno closeness was an implicit defense against—and emotional denial of—the fragmentation which had left my great-grandparents alone in one place while their children were scattered elsewhere around the world. But the facts of a family's past can be selectively fashioned into a story that can mean almost anything, whatever they most need it to mean. Homage to family unity was apparently what my family needed, and so that's the story the Brooklyn Bongiornos made for themselves out of selected bits of their collective experience.

By the time I was four or five I was convinced that the bulwark of family could protect me from death itself. There was a little boy my age named Vincent who lived next door to my East Fifth Street cousins. One hot August day, he had come to a family birthday party. Within a week of the birthday party, Vincent was dead of spinal meningitis. I remember that my aunts thereafter decided that only cousins could come to our birthday parties. Though everyone remembered Vincent's death, no one else remembered my aunts' decision to close the birthday party ranks. Perhaps I invented it. Just a few weeks after Vincent died, I was hospitalized myself with polio and certainly needed to think that I could find in my family a magical protection. I was also sure that my full recovery was due to my aunt's *novenas*. In fact my gratitude went entirely to her and not at all to the doctors or whomever she addressed in her prayers.

There is no doubt that we learn about the idea of family and how to be a member of a family from our families. Much of our instruction is mute: the experience of living in a family tells us what we can expect from relatives and what we owe them. But family stories are one of the cornerstones of family culture; they throw what may be mute and habitual into sharp relief. By their presence, they say what issues—from the most public and predictable to the most private and idiosyncratic—*really* concern a given family.

Family stories in fact are not just second-hand accounts of someone else's experience. To the listeners, the stories can be experiences in themselves, and as such they exert a force and influence of their own, sometimes so that the listeners are quite conscious of what's going on, but usually more subliminally. But one thing is certain: given that a story is told in the context of family life, its meaning is circumscribed; when there are clusters of stories gnawing on a given theme, the meaning is more limited, even if no explicit gloss is ever given.

The family, of course, doesn't invent itself or its concerns but is sculpted by class, by the times, and by ethnicity as well as by the combination of individual personalities that comprise it. My family's conviction that the collective welfare of the family is more important than the goals of any one individual—which is the subtext of the story of my grandfather in America—may be unusual in American culture but is, or was, typical of Italian-American culture. There was once a study, done among schoolchildren of varying ethnic backgrounds, that asked whom they would share with if they were given a million dollars. The children named friends as well as charitable organizations as beneficiaries. It was only the Italian-Americans who distributed their hypothetical gift entirely within the family.

Family stories reach into even more private realms of experience to warn and instruct, however subliminally. They tell us about the decorum and protocol of family life—what we owe and to whom, what we can expect and from whom, in time or money or emotion. From the stories we hear, we learn matters of both substance and style.

## Home Is Where, When You Have to Go . . .

I want right at the outset to talk about an imbalance in family stories about the family. There is no lack of men in family stories at all. They appear plentifully—as returning soldiers or prosperous lens grinders or guileless immigrants, as errant schoolboys or black sheep or heroes who save the townspeople from drowning in the flood. But men do not feature prominently as family members acting in their familial role. And they often do not tell their own stories. Instead, their stories come down the generational pike riding sidesaddle, via their sisters, mothers, wives, or daughters.

Family stories—telling them and listening to them—belong more to the women's sphere. When I interviewed married couples, it was not unusual for the woman to know more of her husband's family stories than he did, usually because she'd heard them through her mother-in-law. In this way, despite the convention of patrilineality, the family is essentially a female institution: the lore of family and family culture itself—stories, rituals, traditions, icons, sayings—are preserved and promulgated primarily by women.

On a statistical level, women's prominence in the family is apparent. The number of female-headed families has grown dramatically in our time. In 1983, 5.7 million families were headed by women, which meant that 22 percent of all children were growing up with just one parent, usually the mother. The increase in such families is usually attributed to the increase in divorce, the American inclination to self-fulfillment at the price of commitment and self-sacrifice, and the greater number of women in the work force.

But it seems to me that men's hold on the family and the family's hold on men first began to be challenged with the beginning of the Industrial Revolution. Industrialization was responsible for creating the first widespread division between the public world and the world of home.

Men inherited the world, and when they came home they told stories of work and identified themselves essentially in that fashion, while women were left to keep the family going. Family stories, telling them and listening to them, grew out of the way people lived and to some extent still live. Family stories are often told in an almost ritual fashion, for instance at holiday family dinners, but they are also told incidentally, because someone says something that sparks someone else's memory in the course of daily living, while both are making the beds, cooking the meal, or folding the laundry, and these tasks remain essentially although not exclusively women's work. As a result, through the universe of family stories, we glimpse a world in which women play a more substantial role than men and come through far more untarnished. Thus family stories are the obverse of more public and codified cultural genres in which men invariably play the more dominant and flattering roles.

I didn't begin this research by thinking of family stories as a women's genre, but the men I interviewed first alerted me. Says twenty-six-year-old B. C. Heinz, who grew up in Indiana, "From everything I've studied or seen, I would expect the men to be the storytellers. In tribes the *griots* who tell the family genealogy are always men, but that's not my experience. If I want family history, I go to the women. I want to hear about men, I still go to the women. It's my aunts who tell stories about my father. Never my father himself."

Ben Rindt, an Illinois businessman in his fifties, observed that in his family the storyteller was his great-uncle and almost all his stories were about men and their adventures—on the prairies, in the farmyard, in the stock market. After telling me a particularly dramatic story about his great-grandfather's experience in a wagon train attacked by Indians, he concluded that these were not really *family* stories at all. "If you only see men on a wagon train, that's an expedition, an adventure," Rindt mused. "But women are necessary to represent us as people. If women are there, it means families are there, and it means people are really suffering."

The first and cardinal rule of family life, as embodied in family stories, is that when people are *really* suffering, you can count on the family. Family stories about the Depression that exist in every American family survive not because they're dramatic (they're usually not) but because they're exemplary—the family's celebration of itself for coming through.

Then there's the matter of sickness, affliction, and death. As a nation, no matter how mobile we are and no matter how often we've heard that the family is defunct, we do seem to live with the legacy of the stories we've heard—that it's the responsibility of family to come to the aid of those in trouble.

In family stories, as in practice, the responsibility falls more heavily on the women, who probably are listening more closely anyhow. Whatever details, the flavor of our narrative legacies is not very different now from what it was fifty years ago when Ma Joad in John Steinbeck's *Grapes of Wrath* took her aging mother on the road westward to California, ministering to her as she grew weaker and frailer and finally died.

The ideal of caring for aging parents is sufficiently strong that even the most undeserving aging parents can ride its coattails. Rowena Court, born and raised in Texas, tells a story about her grandmother and her great-grandfather that makes the point. "My great-grandfather," she begins, "abandoned his family when his kids were still young. He disappeared, and the family thought he was dead. One day when Nanny was about thirty years old, her father showed up at her front door. She was married and had kids of her own by then. She said 'Who are you?' And he said, 'I'm your father, and I need some place to stay. I'm dying and I need someone to take care of me.' And she did. First she nursed him, and when he died, she buried him." Home is where, when you have to go there, they have to take you in.

Family stories such as this continue to exert a force on the way we live now. They establish the ideal that we depart from only at the price of our own guilt. Only 5 percent of the nation's elderly are in nursing homes. Even among the very old—eighty five and over—77 percent remain outside institutions. For aging family members who live on their own, family bonds do seem to hold up. According to the National Institute on Aging, 80 percent of the elderly see "a close relative" every week. Equally consistent with the family stories, the emotional responsibility continues to fall on the women in the family, usually the daughters, but occasionally the daughters-in-law as well.

Such loyalty is by no means automatic or the inevitable consequence of propinquity. It's based on a deep stratum of belief which the family works unceasingly to instill. After all, it is rarely the case that unrelated people who spend enormous amounts of time together at work or in the neighborhood will continue the connection if their circumstances change.

Family members may have no more in common with each other than they do with neighbors or coworkers, so the fact that family members almost always keep their connections no matter what, means somebody's been doing something to make sure that these connections survive. It is a relationship supported by an idea that kinship matters profoundly.

Of all the family bonds that we expect to hold up under duress—mother or father to child, child to mother or father, sibling to sibling—the mother-child bond is, for reasons of both biology and social practice, the most invincible, the most mythic. Anthropologist Robin Fox believes the essential irreducible family unit is nether extended nor nuclear but just the pair of a mother and her child.

Indeed there is a "Pieta" genre of family stories involving a suffering child (usually a son) and a ministering mother that appears in family after family. In Irene Goldstein's story the most striking motif is maternal sacrifice, and indeed a whole family's sacrifice, at a very, very high cost. The mother is Irene's grandmother Irena, and the son is Kurtzie, her father's younger and slightly retarded brother.

This is a big story, and it's about how my grandmother was basically the reason that my father's whole family didn't get out of Austria at the start of World War II. The story was that the whole family had gotten visas to go to Palestine in 1935—everyone, that is, except Kurtzie. They wouldn't give one to Kurtzie because he was retarded. My grandmother said if Kurtzie didn't go, she wasn't going, and as a result the entire family said that

they weren't going. And so the whole family died. That's seven people—my grandmother, my grandfather, my father's oldest brother, his wife, my father's oldest brother's son, my father's fiancee, and Kurtzie. Only my father survived.

That story is certainly about loyalty, blind loyalty. I know that one of the things that was told to me was that my grandmother loved her retarded youngest son most of all and could not bear to leave him behind. In this story, my grandmother Irena also seems a totally mythical character, at least in the sense that she didn't seem to be in touch with the kinds of things that other mothers were in touch with like cooking or dirty diapers. What comes through is a totally idealized notion of the maternal, the maternal perhaps as envisaged by a Victorian. Loving, sacrificing. For my father, she was no ideal, and I think he tried to integrate some of what he imagined her qualities to be into himself.

What is so striking about Irene Goldstein's story is that it makes clear how willing family members are to sacrifice—or repress—their own point of view in favor of the collective familial point of view. Irene's father lost an entire family, a fiancee, and almost his own life because his mother was steadfastly loyal to her young retarded son. Somewhere he must have questioned whether it was worth it, somewhere he must have felt enraged at his own losses. It is inconceivable that this same scenario could have played itself out as it did with a group of unrelated individuals. But day by day and story by story, the family teaches us that such extremes of altruism and self-sacrifice are, if not customary, at least not astounding.

If the mutual bonds between mothers and children are the hardiest, then perhaps the most fragile are the ones between siblings, especially brothers, since they are often beset with both emotional reserve and rivalry. If there is any twosome in a family likely to drift apart, it is a pair of brothers.

And so the family stories that are meant to emphasize the extreme importance of family connections and coming through for one another often focus on brothers. The most common celebrates the ideal, those occasions when brothers under siege act as they ought to. From her mother, Jane Gilbert often heard the story of a long-dead ancestor who fought for the South during the Civil War.

> His name was Hubert and he was a prisoner of war, or maybe he was just in a hospital, with his brother. Both of them were soldiers and both were wounded and put in the same bed. The brother died and Hubert spent two days lying in bed with the corpse of his brother. On the surface this is a horrible story, but it was never told as something to make you shudder or go ugh. To me it had something to do with closeness and sticking with your family, even if they're not alive anymore. They told this story with a kind of pride, or strength—that they lay there in that bed and one of them was dead and one was alive. The way I always envisioned it was that the live one, Hubert, even though he was feverish, he didn't want anyone to know his brother was dead. He wanted to keep his brother with him.

The chafing part of family loyalty, of course, is that it often involves delaying or forsaking one's own individual wishes. In fact the tension between individual desire and collective weal is present in almost all realms of human life. The family, as an inherent partisan of the good-of-the-many, mostly offers stories in support of its own interest, though paradoxically these stories are told by the very individuals who may have had to subordinate themselves.

## Proximity

All families agree that when someone's life is on the line, the family has to do something, but in other realms there are more differences between one family and the next. What about how close to one another grown family members should live? As one man I interviewed put it, "One of the messages was 'Don't go too far.' "

What rules, however veiled, do other families have about such matters? Erik Erikson, in *Childhood and Society*, believes that in nineteenth-century American frontier families, the young, sons especially, had to be raised in a way that wouldn't keep them from pursuing their manifest destiny. Better, then,

to have rather elastic family ties that wouldn't bind, because one way or another, the value of exploring, getting up and going, had to be instilled and take precedence over staying huddled together on the same acreage.

Margo Henson, a poet in her forties, is a New Yorker born and bred, but her interior life and her poetry are filled with her maternal ancestors, the Lugers, a prairie family such as Erikson had in mind. Small and pale, with thick, loosely plaited red hair and green eyes, she sits with me over lunch one day and talks these ancestors back to life. She speaks of their bombazine dresses and their fascinators so intimately that one could almost imagine she herself had worn them just yesterday.

The issue of sons moving on is very much a theme in her stories, and its urgency, especially as it relates to the economic survival of the nuclear family, comes through strongly in the first story she tells.

> My mother's family were the Lugers. A bunch of the Luger boys came from somewhere outside Vienna, where they already had a furniture store, to Minneapolis to start another one. The other brothers all had boys but my great-grandmother proceeded to produce six girls—Anne, Olivia, Clare, Julia, Amelia, and Elizabeth—before she got to the two boys, Peter and Fred. So then my great-grandmother said to her husband, 'What is going to happen to our girls? When we die, what is going to happen? Your brothers have nothing but boys. Are they going to take care of our girls, because our girls can't work in the store? We have to do something!'

> What they did was to pack the whole family into the back of the Conestoga wagon, leaving the other Luger boys and their families behind, and to head across the Northwest Territory to Fargo, which was just a beginning town at the time. And they set up their own store. Somewhere along the line, they also lived in Wabash and in Reed's Settlement on the Mississippi.

It's clear that in the Henson scheme of things, family proximity, for the sons at least, is not a major value, and even more, that the nuclear family must take precedence over the extended family.

What about the daughters? Are they free to get up and go? The beginnings of an answer lie in two other "traveling" stories Margo Henson tells.

These are both traveling stories. One is that my great-aunt, when she was three or four, decided to leave home. She made up her mind to run away and she just packed herself up and left. When she got to the edge of town, she found a little boy who was wandering around, not knowing what he wanted to do that day. So my aunt picked him up and the two of them went off across the prairie together. They weren't picked up till about five or six hours later. There's a newspaper photograph of the two of them that I have which is entitled 'The Runaways.'

The other story is about another one of my great-aunts. This is when they were living on the Mississippi and my aunt was about ten. She had read about New Orleans and had been fascinated by it. And there she was living on the Mississippi River and knowing that New Orleans was at the end of it! It was winter and the Mississippi was frozen. So my aunt talked three friends into skating down the Mississippi to New Orleans. They took off and weren't discovered until rather late that night, very cold and extremely frightened on the banks of the Mississippi.

Are these just "cute" stories of failed and foiled runaway daughters? Margo Henson thinks not. "This is the matriarchy telling its own story. There were a lot of women in that family, and they all lived very constricted lives, especially because only two of my great-aunts married. They were better than middle class. My great-grandfather made quite a bit of money and raised his young women very well. They were all given artistic educations.

"Great-aunt Anne was the painter in the family and, so the story goes, wanted to go to Paris but was not allowed to. She was quite a good painter, too. Maybe not brilliant, but well above the maidenly average in the 1800s. My great-aunt Clare played the harp, and she always wanted to go to Ireland and travel around on the back of a cart and play in villages."

"Instead, they spent their lives working at the family store—Olivia was bookkeeper for

near fifty goddamn years. The others did various things—taking stock, selling in the store. I felt they had these little cameo lives, but there was all of this enormous energy that never got used, that was waiting for some kind of release. I feel that very strongly."

So the initial family ground rule, which gave sons permission to move on but kept the daughters at home, thwarted, with nothing to look back on but childhood runaway foibles, became transformed so that the succeeding generations—Margo and her mother—would receive a very different instruction.

As Margo says, "I have a very strong feeling of imperative. My opportunities in life have this push behind me from these women who never had the chance. In fact I feel a responsibility to go and do what they had not done." And Margo Henson has acted on that "imperative" persistently. Every summer she sets off for somewhere, sending postcards the way Hansel scattered bread crumbs.

She has also drawn on the ground rule that one *must* get up and go when the issue is the economic well-being of the family. She married in her twenties and had one son. But when he was eight or nine, Margo and her husband divorced. For a while she taught writing in various New York City colleges, but in the late 1970s, when colleges were tightening their belts and reducing their faculty, the jobs dried up.

Since she had primary financial responsibility for her son, by then a senior in high school, she found a solution—an unconventional one, but one her great-aunts would probably have approved of. She found a live-in tenant to stay with her son in their brownstone in Brooklyn, and for herself she found a series of artist-in-residence positions at colleges around the country, six weeks here, six weeks there, a weekend at home in Brooklyn whenever possible.

In Rachel Kalber's family, the issue of how near family members must stay or how far they can go is also a vital one, and so the family has a small cluster of stories that huddle around the theme, worrying it and examining it.

The first story has to do with her father, a Russian Jew by birth, who, says Rachel, came from a long line of rabbinical scholars and teachers. Like his male antecedents before him, he was as a young child sent by his family to a distant village to study Talmud. In the context, the importance of becoming a Talmudic scholar is so great that it supersedes the value of staying geographically close to the family.

At the time that this story takes place, Chaim Kalber had been away from his family studying Talmud for eight or nine years. Says Rachel Kalber:

My father left his home in the Ukraine when he was nine years old. He was the child chosen to be sent away to study. So he went and studied at the yeshiva and slept in the synagogue on the floor and ate meals on charity.

Then when my father was seventeen or eighteen, he was conscripted into the czar's army. This was World War I, and he was a corporal or a sergeant. At one point he was told there were a bunch of soldiers that had run away—AWOL—and that he had to take them back to be jailed. Walking along with the group, he realized that one of them was a Jew. He began talking to this man, asking what had happened, why he had run away. The man said that his father was sick and close to death and that, since he had not been granted a leave, he had to run away. My father started to ask him where he came from, and it turned out that the man was my father's brother!

What I felt when I heard this story was, 'Oh, the things I take for granted—the family closeness, knowing what's happened in the family.' These things were denied my father. To be so far away that you couldn't recognize your own brother and would have to find out in this horrible way that your own father was dying—it was a very brutal world that my father was telling me about, and it made me feel my good fortune: the fact that I'd always know that I'd always know who my father and mother were, that I'd always know how my brother looked.

While on the face of it, the story seems to underscore the fragmentation of the family, it is to the Kalbers a cautionary tale, describing how dreadful—but not how forbid-

den—it is to be so separated from family. As Rachel hears the story, it has a mystical cast to it, demonstrating that, miraculously, family members will somehow find each other, no matter what.

The subtlety of the Kalber family instruction is that it insists that family members be closely involved—telepathic becomes the ideal—but it does not insist that they live geographically in one another's midst. The additional point is that Judaism and, by its extension, education are so important that it is permissible to sacrifice immediate family closeness for undertakings related to either.

A second Kalber family story reiterates the instruction that its members share in an almost telepathic intimacy. Again, this is a story that Rachel first heard from her father.

The year was 1918 or 1919, the year of a terrible pogrom in the Ukraine. My father, by then working for the Central Jewish Organization, had been sent to collect all the children orphaned by the pogrom and to bring them to a central place.

He came back to his home village to discover that the cossacks had tried to hang his mother and sister, but that they had been cut down in time to save their lives. [After an episode in which Rachel's father was almost killed by the cossacks, he collected the orphans and traveled with them to a town about one hundred miles away.]

An aunt of his was living there. She said, 'How is your mother? Is your mother all right?' She said she'd had a dream two weeks before in which she saw my father's father running. [He had in fact died at the start of World War I.] In the dream, my father's aunt said to him, 'Yakov, why are you running?' And he said, 'I'm running to save my wife. I have to save her. And the children.' My father then told his aunt the story about how his mother and sister had been hung and then cut down. My father always cried when he told this story. He was very moved.

This story was a staple in the Kalber repertoire. "I first heard this story as a child," says Rachel Kalber, "and have heard it often since then. What I got from it was that the Jews were always in danger, and that there was some way in which our family would rescue us. Even my father's run-in with his brother was a miraculous reunion. There was no way you could really lose the family, even if they died. Family was all, and you couldn't break that connection."

The constellation of values that these stories promulgate has guided the family for several generations now. When Rachel's parents came to this country, they settled in Florida for a while, where Rachel and her brother were born. When Rachel was fourteen, she was allowed to go to New York to attend a school superior to those in Florida. "Like my father, I was the child chosen to study," she says. Now Rachel Kalber is the mother of a daughter of her own, who is on the verge of entering college. Though Rachel is divorced and has full responsibility for child support, there is no question in her mind that her daughter will go away to college. For an education, even a secular one, she knows that her parents will contribute.

In *Habits of the Heart*, sociologist Robert N. Bellah and his colleagues coined the phrase "communities of memory" to characterize those groups whose members' affiliation was based not only on current similarities but on a more rooted historical affiliation. Among these "communities of memory" they included the family. "Families," they wrote, "can be communities, remembering their past, telling the children the stories of parents' and grandparents' lives, and sustaining hope for the future. . . ." Family stories certainly do this. In fact the implication of what Bellah and his colleagues had to say is that the mere existence of family stories—whether happy or unhappy—exerts a binding cohesive force.

But family stories do even more. For good and for ill, they delineate the rules and the mores that govern family life, rules that succor and support as well as rules that chafe uncomfortably; rules that are out in the open as well as those that operate only by stealth. Indeed, family stories go a step further and define the family, saying not only what members should do, but who they are or should be.

## Questions

1. In your own family, who are the primary storytellers—men or women? How do you explain this?

2. Think about your family stories. What are the rules embedded in them?

3. Begin your own collection of family stories. You will need a tape recorder or video camera. Simply find relatives to interview and begin. It is best to prepare a list of questions before the interview. Open-ended questions are best because they stimulate ideas and trigger memories. At the beginning of the interview, record the date, location, and names of the people. Once you start asking questions, let the conversation develop on its own. Below are some sample questions.

- What is your birthdate? Where were you born?

- What were your parents' grandparents' names? What did they do for a living?

- What one special thing do you remember about each of them?

- Where did you go to school? What did you like most about school? What did you like least?

- What was your favorite activity as a child?

- Describe the house (or town) you grew up in.

- What was your most memorable birthday?

- What made you afraid when you were a child?

- How did you meet your spouse? Describe your first date.

- What has changed most in your lifetime?

- If you could live your life over, what would you do differently?

Adapted from Elizabeth Stone, "Family Ground Rules." In *Black Sheep and Kissing Cousins*, pp. 15–31. Copyright © 1988 by Elizabeth Stone. Reprinted by permission of Times Books, a division of Random House. ✦

# 36
# Claiming Family Identity Communicatively

## Discourse-Dependent Families

*Kathleen M. Galvin*

In the twenty-first century, fewer families can be described by discrete categories such as stepfamily, biological family, single-parent family, or adoptive family due to overlapping complexities of connections. Family interactions patterns are increasingly unpredictable due to the diversity of family forms.

People continue to marry across their lifespan, with many in their second or third marriages. Stepfamilies, formed through remarriage or cohabitation, generally reflect divorce and recommitment, although an increasing number are formed by single mothers marrying for the first time. Little is known about ex-stepfamily relationships, although increasing numbers of children live in second or third stepfamilies.

Single-parent families continue to increase. Today, women under 30 who become pregnant for the first time are more likely to be single than married. Increasingly, single women and men become parents through adoption and new reproductive technologies. Gay and lesbian committed couples and families are becoming more visible due, in part, to a greater willingness of same-sex partners to identify their lifestyle. A growing number of same-sex couples report children present in their home: about 21 percent of partnered lesbians and 5.2 percent of partnered gays (Black et al. 2000).

More families are being formed, in part, through adoption. The practice of international adoption continues to expand; over 20,000 children a year are adopted internationally (Kreider and Simmons 2003). Many of these families become transracial through the adoption process. Open adoption is emerging as the common domestic form, creating an ongoing adoption triangle—the adoptee, the birth parent(s), and the adoptive parent(s), with variable contact among members.

Intentional families, families formed without biological and legal ties, are maintained by members' self-definition. These "fictive" or self-ascribed kin become family by choice, performing family functions for one another. The next-door neighbors who serve as extended kin, the best friend who is considered a sister, and other immigrants from the same homeland may develop fictive kinship relationships.

The processes by which intentional families are formed reflect a transactional definition of family, that is, "a group of intimates who generate a sense of home and group identity and who experience a shared history and a shared future" (Koerner and Fitzpatrick 2002, 71).

Currently fewer people report membership in families fully formed through lifelong marriages and biological offspring; many experience multiplicities of connections. The complexities are captured in a discussion of the label gay and lesbian families: "Should we count only families in which every single member is gay? . . . Or does the presence of just one gay member color a family gay?" (Stacey 1999, 373). The same question must be asked about labeling families as adoptive, blended or step, single parent, and so on.

The current diversity of family presents communication challenges for its members who must manage their family identity communicatively. Members find themselves explaining their family to outsiders who challenge their claims of relatedness; sometimes members have to reaffirm for themselves what makes them a family. In the following article, Galvin presents a number of communication strategies used by family members to manage their identity both outside the family as well as inside the family. She suggests that members of families formed outside of full biological or adult legal ties will be called upon to address their family's identity. When addressing outsiders, the family members may rely on strategies of labeling, describing, legitimizing, and defending; when talking with each other, family members may rely on naming, discussing, narrating, and creating rituals. As you read this article, consider this question: What *strategies have you used, or observed others using, in an attempt to address family identity, and how effective were these attempts?*

## References

Black, D., Gates, G., Snaders, S., and Taylor, L. (2000). Demographics of the gay and lesbian population in the United States. *Demography,* 37, 139–154.

Koerner, A. F., and Fitzpatrick, M. A. (2002). Toward a theory of family communication. *Communication Theory,* 12, 70–91.

Kreider, R. M., and Simmons, T. (2003, October). *Marital status: 2000.* (C2KBR-30). Census 2000 Special Reports. Washington, DC: U.S. Census Bureau, U.S. Department of Commerce.

Stacey, J. (1999b). Gay and lesbian families are here; All our families are queer; Let's get used to it. In S. Coontz (with M. Parson, and G. Raley) (Eds.), *American Families: A Multicultural Reader* (pp. 372–405). New York: Routledge.

*\* \* \**

Although all societies and cultures have webs of kinship relationships, the structures of which change across time and cultures (Garey and Hansen, 1998), U.S. families represent the forefront of familial redefinition due to the multiplicity of emerging, ever-changing, kinship patterns. As families become increasingly diverse, *their definitional processes expand exponentially rendering their identity highly discourse-dependent.* Family identity depends, at least in part, upon members' communication with outsiders, as well as with each other, about how they make sense of themselves as family.

All families engage in some level of discourse-driven family identity building; less traditionally formed families are more discourse-dependent, engaging in recurring discursive processes to manage and maintain identity. A growing number of U.S. families are formed through differences, visible or invisible, rendering their ties more ambiguous to outsiders as well as to themselves, whereas in other cultures, families are still identified by similarities. Circumstances such as ongoing connections to a birthmother and adoptive parents, visual differences among members, siblings' lack of shared early childhood experiences, same-sex parents, a solo parent and a "seed daddy," or ties to ex–step relatives create ambiguity necessitating active management of family identity. These definitional concerns surface as members face outsiders' questions or challenges regarding the veracity of members' claims of relatedness, or experience a need to revisit their familial identity at different stages of individual or familial development. The greater the ambiguity of family form, the more elaborate the communicative processes needed to establish and maintain identity.

High discourse-dependent families engage regularly in external as well as internal boundary management practices. Times of stress and/or boundary ambiguity challenge family boundaries because expectations of inclusion and support are less clear in self-ascribed or ambiguous relations than in families formed and maintained through traditionally recognized biological and adult legal ties.

What serves as the basis of family? Minow (1998) identifies the key question as "Does this group function as a family?" arguing that the issue is not whether a group of people fit the formal, legal definition of a family, but "whether the group of people function as a family; do they share affection and resources, think of one another as family members, and present themselves as such to neighbors and others?" (p. 8). Communicative practices contribute to family functioning, especially in families formed, fully or partly, outside of traditional means.

## Family Diversity

Families in the first half of the twenty-first century will alter irrevocably any sense of predictability as to what "being family" means. These families will do the following:

1. Reflect an increasing diversity of self-conceptions, evidenced through structural as well as cultural variations, which will challenge society to abandon any historical, nucleocentric biases, unitary cultural assumptions, traditional gender assumptions, and

implied economic and religious assumptions.

2. Live increasingly within four and five generations of relational connections. Escalating longevity, changing birth rates, and multiple marriages or cohabitations will reveal long-term developmental patterns, ongoing multiple intergenerational contacts, generational reversals, and smaller biological-sibling cohorts.

3. Continuously reconfigure themselves across members' lifespans as choices of individuals or subgroups create new family configurations through legal, biological, technological, and discursive means, impacting members' family identity (Coontz 1999; Galvin 2004).

Further examination of these claims provides a picture of current family life.

Fewer families can be depicted validly by discrete categories or unitary terms, such as stepfamily, biological family, single-parent families, or adoptive families, due to overlapping complexities of connections.

## Discourse and Family Identity

We need richer concepts and tools both to make sense of increasingly complex family forms, as well as to address questions such as: "How are we to characterize the most important relationship processes in such families?" and "When do we need to expand our lexicon to address the new relationships and issues challenging such families?" (Grotevant 2004, 12). From a social construction standpoint, "Our languages of description and explanation are produced, sustained, and/or abandoned within processes of human interaction" (Gergen, Hoffman, and Anderson 1996, 102). Discourse processes are relevant to families because, through interaction and language, individuals within their family context collectively construct their familial identity and the realities in which they live (Stamp 2002).

Family communication scholars claim families are based on, formed, and maintained through communication, or "our families, and our images of families, are consti-

tuted through social interaction" (Vangelisti 2002, xiii), necessitating studies that "employ definitions of the family that depend on how families define themselves rather than definitions based on genetic and sociological criteria" (Fitzpatrick 1998, 45). Over time, as diversity increases, communicative definitions of family will be privileged over structural definitions, requiring new models for talking about and studying families (Whitchurch and Dickson 1999). Discourse-dependency is not new; what *is* new is that discourse-dependent families are becoming the norm.

Discourse-dependent family members manage identity across external boundaries through practices such as labeling, explaining, legitimizing, and defending familial identity. Concurrently they manage internal boundaries through practices such as labeling, discussing, narrating, and ritualizing. Usually the necessity for such practices depends on the degree of difference reflected within the family form.

## External Boundary Management Practices

When families appear different to outsiders, questions and challenges arise. Family members tend to engage in a process of managing the tensions between revealing and concealing family information on the assumption that they control access to their private information (Petronio 2002). Yet little is known about how families with differences manage their boundaries. For example, researchers have not yet examined the strategies that gay and lesbian parents use "to shelter their children from negative experiences, to help children cope with instances of prejudice, to build resilience in their children" (Peplau and Beals 2002, 244). Moreover, the practices of parents who build families through new reproductive technologies remain invisible. The following section describes a set of communication strategies commonly found in popular literature as well as academic and professional sources.

### Labeling

Titles or positions provide an orientation to a situation or problem; for example, identifying the familial tie when introducing or referring to another person. The constitutive approach invites questions such as: "What do we want a familial relational label to communicate?" "To whom?" and "How will others view that label?"

Relational labels orient familial ties such as *brother* or *step-grandmother.* When transitions occur, the specific meaning of certain names must be linked to the person-in-relationship. For example, among the many communicative tasks a man faces in becoming a stepfather is negotiating a definition of the stepfather/stepchild relationship (Jorgenson 1994). Frequently this involves overt or covert negotiations about whether to refer to him as "my mother's husband," "Brad," "my stepfather," or "my other Dad"; each choice reveals a different sense of connection (Galvin 1989). Because language serves as a constituent feature of cultural patterns embedded within a relationship, changing the language alters the relationship (Gergen, Hoffman, and Anderson 1996).

Titles and labels establish expectations. When a stepmother looks the same age as her stepson, two siblings represent different races, or "Grandma Carl" is male, creating a relational definition becomes challenging. Today's families are confronted with circumstances unimaginable to earlier generations: How does one reference his sperm donor or the surrogate mother who carried her?

## Explaining

Explaining involves making a named family relationship understandable, giving reasons for it, or elaborating on how it works. When someone's nonhostile curiosity seems to question the stated familial tie, explanation is a predictable response. Remarks such as "How come you don't speak Korean?" or "How can you have two mothers?" are commonplace for some individuals. An explanation for an international adoptee's lack of facility in her native language may include "My parents are Irish, so I didn't learn any Korean" (Galvin and Wilkinson 2000, 11). When a playmate challenged her young son because he did not have a "Daddy," Blumenthal (1990–1991) explained the concept of a Seed Daddy to the boys—"a man

who is not really a parent, but one who helps a woman get a baby started" (p. 185). Finally, negotiating parenthood within a heterocentric context creates issues for same-sex partners faced with educating others about their family but who are often frustrated by the task (Chabot and Ames 2004).

## Legitimizing

Legitimizing invokes the sanction of law or custom: it positions relationships as genuine and conforming to recognized standards. Legitimizing occurs when one's relational ties are challenged, creating a need to provide information that helps another recognize the tie as a genuine, familial link. Adoption agencies regularly prepare parents of families formed through transracial and/or international adoption for questions such as "Is she your real daughter?" Adoption Learning Partners (2004), an online adoption education community, provides new parents with alternative responses to such an intrusive question. These include: "No, she's my fake daughter," "Yes, she's really mine," or "Yes, we're an adoptive family." The response is chosen on the basis of the parent's interaction goals and/or the child's age and ability to understand the interaction. Gay or lesbian parents make reference to outside sources that legitimate their family, such as books that depict their family as genuine (*Heather Has Two Mommies* or *Daddy's Roommate*) or well-known figures who represent gay male or lesbian parents.

## Defending

Finally, *defending* involves shielding oneself or a familial relationship from attack, justifying it, or maintaining its validity against opposition. Defending is a response to hostility or a direct challenge to the familial form. For example, Garner (2004), the daughter of a gay father, depicts the difficulty of listening to constant messages from media, politicians, religious leaders, teachers, and neighbors claiming that gay people are bad or sinful. She describes the specific complications for her nephew when a teacher or friend asserts, "That's impossible. You can't have grampas in the same house. Which one is REALLY your grampa?" (Garner 2004, n.p.). Parents who adopt transracially must be prepared for questions such as, "Couldn't you get a White child?" or "Is she one of those crack babies?" (Adoption Learning Partners 2004). Defending responses may arise from sheer frustration. Annoyed by hearing the question "How can you two be sisters?" a pair of Asian and Caucasian teenage sisters decided, "When we got the question . . . we would respond 'The Mailman' and walk away" (Galvin and Fonner 2003). Children in cohabiting stepfamilies face challenges such as, "He's not your real stepfather if your Mom didn't marry him." Advice columnists regularly respond to questions about how to deal with similar invasive comments or questions.

## Internal Boundary Management Practices

Members of families formed through differences engage in ongoing communication practices designed to maintain their internal sense of family-ness. These practices include: naming, discussing, narrating, and creating rituals.

### Naming

Naming also plays a significant role in the development of internal family identity. Names or titles present issues within family boundaries as members struggle to indicate their familial status. Sometimes names are decided and never revisited; in other cases, the familial ties and labels become a source of ongoing negotiation. Naming a child, especially an older child, or a child adopted internationally and/or transracially, presents a challenge. Children arrive with names reflecting their birth family and/or birth culture. An international adoptee captures the loss involved when her Korean name was replaced by an American one, saying, "That was really all I had when I came to this country: that name. And my parents overlooked it and chose another one" (Kroll 2000, 18).

Open adoption provides a unique set of linguistic challenges, given the lack of terminology for any extended family members in the adoption triangle. Stepfamily members confront the question "What do I call you?" Answers are confounded by the "wicked stepmother" myth, conflicting loyalties between biological parents and stepparents, and the lack of conventional names for a stepparent's extended family. Stepchildren may choose a name honoring a stepparent's parental role, such as a hyphenated last name or biological terms such as "Pop" or "Moms," dissimilar from their name for the biological parent. Gay or lesbian parents confront the issue of inclusive language, or how they wish to be referred to by their children, because linguistic labels do not include the nonbiological parent easily. Some lesbian pairs consider taking one last name, either having one take on the other's name or creating a new name. Those who changed names report it was to establish a public family identity or to strengthen their presence as a couple or family (Suter and Oswald 2003).

### Discussing

The degree of difference among family members impacts the amount of member discussion of their family situation. Lesbian parenting partners encounter decisions regarding how to become parents, who will be the biological mother, and how to decide on a donor (Chabot and Ames 2004). In many cases donors are chosen because of their physical appearance, since "Looking related suggests family, which helps communicate a shared family identity" (Suter et al. 2004). Gay male parents experience variations on these issues such as adoption or gestational carriers.

A blended family must develop its identity and "create a shared conception of how their family is to manage its daily business" (Cherlin and Furstenberg 1994, 370). A study of blended family development found that some of the families "used direct communication, such as regular family meetings, to air issues surrounding the adjustments to becoming a family" (Braithwaite et al. 2001, 243). Concerns regarding belonging result in conversations ranging from grandparent gift-giving, designated space for noncustodial children, signing official school papers, or rights to discipline.

A child's entrance into a family through adoption or new reproductive technologies necessitates an ongoing series of talks across years as the child's ability to comprehend information results in varied depths of explanation. Currently, sequential, age-appropriate discussions of adoption have replaced the earlier "one big talk" as children's informational needs change as they reach new developmental milestones (Wrobel et al. 2003). Transracially adopted children begin to question the physical differences between themselves and other family members at an early age. Parents in families formed through assisted reproductive technology raise questions about how to discuss their children's origins.

## Narrating

Every family tells stories; however, families formed through differences experience more complex storytelling processes. McAdams (1993) suggests that a person's story "brings together the different parts of ourselves and our lives into a purposeful and convincing whole" (p. 12). Over time, "[W]e tell and retell, to ourselves and to others, the story of who we are, what we have become, and how we got there, making and remaking a story of ourselves that links birth to life to death" (Jorgenson and Bochner 2004, 516). Because family stories are "laced with opinions, emotions, and past experiences, they can provide particularly telling data about the way people conceive of their relationships with family members" (Vangelisti, Crumley and Baker 1999). Everyday narratives create a powerful scaffold for a family's identity.

Creation or entrance stories answer the question "How did this family come to be?" They include accounts of how the adult partners met or how an individual chose to become a parent, as well as birth and adoption narratives. In cases of adoption, the entrance story sets the tone for a family's adoption-related communication; it is the beginning of an ongoing dialogue between parents and their children (Wrobel et al. 2003). In addition, "How the (adoption) story is told and retold in the family can have lasting consequences for the child's adjustment and well-being" (Friedlander 1999, 43). Cooper (2004) depicts the development of her stepfamily through three types of stories—stepfamily, blended family, and bonus stories—each reflecting a stage in the family's move toward deeper joining.

Many families formed through differences suppress or lose their narratives. Just as many divorced families and stepfamilies lose the original parental love stories, certain adoptive parents struggle with the extent to which an adopted child's painful birth family background should be told to family members. Uncertain parents may fabricate some pieces of the story to avoid discussing infertility or donor insemination.

## Creating Rituals

Families accomplish their "emotional business" as they enact rituals (Bossard and Boll 1950). A typology of family rituals includes major celebrations; traditions such as reunions, vacations, and birthdays; and mundane routines (Wolin and Bennett 1984). Although most families develop rituals, those formed through differences struggle with what to ritualize, and which rituals from previous family experiences should be continued or terminated.

Family rituals provide opportunities for stepfamilies to define family membership on multiple levels of connection, although they require sensitivity and negotiations. In their study of blended families, Braithwaite, Baxter, and Harper (1998) found members engaged in rituals, or "important communicative practices that enable blended family members to embrace their new family while still valuing what was important in the old family environment" (p. 101). Family members described enacting new rituals not imported from a previous family, rituals that were imported unchanged, and rituals that were imported and adapted. Respondents also reported that some new rituals lasted and some failed, demonstrating that becoming a family is an ongoing process. Gay and lesbian stepfamilies face creating an identity without the traditional courtship and marriage rituals, creating ambiguity about the new family for all members (Lynch 2000).

Adoptive families may celebrate arrival days as well as birthdays; in international adoption, the family may adopt some celebrations from a child's birth culture. Birth family members may be invited to share a holiday or a tradition. Some children report rituals of pulling out adoption papers and looking at them, or attending a summer culture camp (Fujimoto 2001).

## Multiple Identities

As noted earlier, most families cannot be described in unitary terms; many are formed through multiple differences. For example, white lesbian mothers of two African American boys reported the following common (nonhostile) questions from the boy's preschool peers: "Why are you black and she white?" or "Why is he black and you white?" As the boys aged, they encountered variations on the question "Why do you have two moms?" (Fine and Johnson 2004). These authors detail the multiple objectified identities ascribed to them as parents in a family created across race and gender borders. Black lesbians experience "triple jeopardy" by virtue of race, gender, and sexual orientation, with racism as the most stressful challenge (Bowleg et al. 2003).

The concept of family is changing visibly and invisibly, but irrevocably. When family identity is involved, language follows lived experience. This language, managed within and across boundaries, reflects individual's personal or observational experiences. Contemporary families, living in a world of normative instability and definitional crisis, depend increasingly on discourse to construct their identities.

## References

Adoption Learning Partners. Accessed online: *http://www.adoptionlearningpartners.org*.

Blumenthal, A. (1990/1991). Scrambled eggs and seed daddies: Conversations with my son. *Empathy: Gay and lesbian advocacy research project*, 2(2), 185–188.

Bossard, J., and Boll, E. (1950). *Ritual in family living*. Philadelphia: University of Pennsylvania Press.

Bowleg, L., Huang, J., Brooks, K., Black, A., and Burkholder, G. (2003). Triple jeopardy and beyond: Multiple minority stress and resilience among black lesbians. *Journal of Lesbian Studies*, 7, 87–108.

Braithwaite, D. O., Baxter, L., and Harper, A. M. (1998). The role of rituals in the management of the dialectical tension of 'old' and 'new' in blended families. *Communication Studies*, 49, 101–120.

Braithwaite, D. O., Olson, L. N., Golish, T. D., Soukup, C., and Turman, P. (2001). "Becoming a family": Developmental processes represented in blended family discourse. *Journal of Applied Communication Research*, 29, 221–247.

Chabot, J. M., and Ames, B. D. (2004). It wasn't "let's get pregnant and go do it": Decision making in lesbian couples planning motherhood via donor insemination. *Family Relations*, 53, 348–356.

Cherlin, A. J., and Furstenberg, F. F. (1994). Stepfamilies in the United States: A reconsideration. *Annual Review of Sociology*, 20, 359–381.

Coontz, S. (1999). Introduction. In S. Coontz, (with M. Parson, and G. Raley) (Eds.), *American families: A multicultural reader* (pp. ix–xxxiii). New York: Routledge.

Cooper, P. J. (2004, April). Step? Blended? Bonus? Looking back to look forward: Legacies, myths and narratives of stepfamilies. Paper delivered at the Central States Communication Association Convention, Cleveland, OH.

Fine, M., and Johnson, F. (2004). Creating a family across race and gender borders. In A. Gonzalez, M. Houston, and V. Chen (Eds.), *Our voices: Essays in culture, ethnicity, and communication* (pp. 240–247). Los Angeles: Roxbury Publishing.

Fitzpatrick, M. A. (1998). Interpersonal communication on the Starship Enterprise: Resilience, stability, and change in relationships for the twenty-first century. In J. Trent (Ed.), *Communication: Views from the helm for the 21st century* (pp. 41–46). Boston: Allyn & Bacon.

Friedlander, M. L. (1999). Ethnic identity development of internationally adopted children and adolescents: Implications for family therapists. *Journal of Marital and Family Therapy*, 25, 43–60.

Fujimoto, E. (2001, November). South Korean adoptees growing up in white America: Negotiating race and culture. Paper presented at the National Communication Association Convention. Atlanta, Georgia.

Galvin, K. M. (1989). Stepfamily identity development. Speech presented at the annual van Zelst Lecture, Northwestern University, Evanston, IL.

———. (2004). The family of the future: What do we face? In A. L. Vangelisti, (Ed.), *Handbook of family communication*. (pp. 675–607). Mahwah, NJ: Lawrence Erlbaum Associates.

Galvin, K. M., and Fonner, K. (2003, April). "The Mailman" as family defense strategy: International/transracial adoption and mixed siblings. Paper presented at the Central States Communication Association Convention. Omaha, NE.

Galvin, K. M., and Wilkinson, K. M. (2000, November). That's your family picture?!: Korean adoptees communication management issues during the transition to college. Paper presented at the National Communication Association Convention. Seattle, Washington.

Garey, A. I., and Hansen, K. V. (1998). Analyzing families with a feminist sociological imagination. In A. I. Garey, and K. V. Hansen (Eds.), *Families in the U.S.: Kinship and domestic policies* (pp. xv–xxi). Philadelphia: Temple University Press.

Garner, A. (2004). *Families like mine*. Accessed online: *http://www.familieslikemine.com/faq/index.html*.

Gergen, K. J., Hoffman, L., and Anderson, H. (1996). Is diagnosis a disaster? A constructionist trialogue. In F. W. Kaslow (Ed.), *Handbook of relational diagnosis and dysfunctional family patterns* (pp. 102–118). New York: John Wiley & Sons.

Grotevant, H. D. (2004, Spring). Comments. *Relationship Research News: International Association for Relationship Research*, 2(2), 12.

Jorgenson, J. (1994). Situated address and the social construction of "in-law" relationships. *The Southern Communication Journal*, 59, 196–204.

Jorgenson, J., and Bochner, A. P. (2004). Imagining families through stories and rituals. In A. Vangelisti (Ed.), *Handbook of family communication* (pp. 513–538). Mahwah, NJ: Lawrence Erlbaum Associates.

Kroll, M. L. (2000). My name is. . . . In M. W. Lustig and J. Koester (Eds.), *Among us: Essays on identity, belonging, and intercultural competence.* (pp. 18–23) New York: Longman.

Lynch, J. M. (2000). Considerations of family structure and gender composition: The lesbian and gay stepfamily. *Journal of Homosexuality*, 40, 81–95.

McAdams, D. P. (1993). *Stories we live by: Personal myths and the making of the self*. New York: Guilford Press.

Minow, M. (1998). Redefining families: Who's in and who's out? In K. V. Hansen, and A. I. Garey (Eds.), *Families in the U.S.* (pp. 7–19). Philadelphia: Temple University Press. (Originally in 1991 *University of Colorado Law Review*, 62(2), 269–285).

Peplau, L. A., and Beals, K. P. (2002). The family lives of lesbians and gay men. In A. Vangelisti (Ed.), *Handbook of family communication* (pp. 233–248). Mahwah, New Jersey: Lawrence Erlbaum Associates.

Petronio, S. (2002). *Boundaries of privacy: Dialectics of disclosure*. Albany: State University of New York Press.

Stamp, G. H. (2002). Theories of family relationships and a family relationships theoretical model. In A. L. Vangelisti (Ed.), *Handbook of family communication*. (pp. 1–30). Mahwah, NJ: Lawrence Erlbaum Associates.

Suter, E. A., Bergen, K. J., Daas, K. L., and Parker, J. H. (2004, November). Communicative construction of lesbian family through rituals and symbols. Paper presented at the National Communication association Convention, Chicago, IL.

Suter, E. A., and Oswald, R. F. (2003). Do lesbians change their last names in the context of a committed relationship? *Journal of Lesbian Studies*, 7, 71–83.

Vangelisti, A. L. (2002). Introduction. In A. L. Vangelisti (Ed.), *American families: A multicultural reader* (pp. xiii–xx). Mahwah, NJ: Lawrence Erlbaum Associates.

Vangelisti, A. L., Crumley, L. P., Baker, J. L. (1999). Family portraits: Stories as standards for family relationships. *Journal of Social and Personal Relationships*, 16, 335–368.

Whitchurch, G. and Dickson, F. C. (1999). Family communication. In M. B. Sussman, S. K. Steinmetz, and G. W. Preston (Eds.), *Handbook of marriage and the family*. (2nd ed.) pp. 687–704. New York: Plenum Press.

Wolin, S., and Bennett, L. (1984). Family rituals. *Family Processes*, 23, 401–420.

Wrobel, G. M., Kohler, J. K., Grotevant, H. D. and McRoy, R. G. (2003). The family adoption communication (FAC) model: Identifying pathways of adoption-related communication. *Adoption Quarterly*, 7, 53–84.

## Questions

1. What are circumstances in which family members find themselves challenged to communicatively elaborate on their family identity to those outside the family? Explain how one such interaction unfolded.

2. Under what circumstances have you, or others you know, found it important to address family identity with other members of the family? Explain how the interaction unfolded.

3. What strategies do you think are missing from this article? Give some examples.

Adapted from Galvin, K. M. (In press). "Diversity's impact on defining the family: Discourse-dependency." In R. West and L. Turner (Eds.) *Family communication: A reference of theory and practice.* Thousand Oaks, CA: Sage Publications. ✦

# 37
# Sibling Use of Relational Maintenance Behaviors

*Scott A. Myers*

**S**iblings represent the people you are going to know for most of your life and who will share many of your major life events. Safer (2002) eloquently expresses the centrality of this relationship, saying, "No future tie is exempt from their influence; relations with them are the prototype for friendships, romances, and professional connections with coworkers, rivals, and collaborators for the rest of your life. Ultimately they are the only surviving witnesses to your intimate history. Nobody else will remember your childhood" (p. 39).

Sibling relationships change significantly over time as individuals move through developmental stages. Goetting (1986) suggested that these changes occur in three stages: childhood-adolescence, early and middle adulthood, and old age. During these stages, siblings provide one another with companionship and social support.

In childhood the older siblings often function as caregivers and teach social and other skills to younger siblings. The support or nurturing of older siblings reduces the influence of negative life events on children's social adjustment (Conger and Conger 2002). In adulthood the frequency of interaction may decline, depending on geographical distances and the pressures of raising children. A review of the dynamics of siblings across the lifespan reports that even if interaction is infrequent, older adult siblings maintain a symbolic relationship by recalling shared in-

cidents and providing a sense of continuity as well as emotional and instrumental support (Nussbaum et al. 2000). In the final stage, old age, the sibling relationship often takes on greater significance as friends and other family members die. Older siblings help one another review life events and face current ones. Gold (1986) studied older sibling relationships and discovered five types: intimate (14 percent of the relationships studied), congenial (30 percent), loyal (34 percent), apathetic (11 percent), and hostile (11 percent). These percentages reveal the strength and importance of older sibling relationships.

*How do siblings maintain their relationships? In the following article, Myers describes some of his personal efforts to maintain sibling ties, introduces the concept of types of relational maintenance behavior, and then suggests a number of behaviors that siblings employ to stay connected. As you read this article, consider your sibling relationships and the methods you use to maintain them. Ask yourself this question: To what extent do my siblings, or siblings I observe, actively engage in communicative efforts to sustain the sibling tie?*

## References

Conger, R. D., and Conger, K. J. (2002). Resilience in midwestern families: Selected findings from the first decade of a prospective longitudinal study. *Journal of Marriage and the Family*, 64, 361–373.

Goetting, A. (1986). The developmental tasks of siblingship over the life cycle. *Journal of Marriage and the Family* 48: 703–714.

Gold, D. T. (1986). Sibling relationships in retrospect: A study of reminiscence in old age. Doctoral dissertation, Northwestern University, Evanston, Illinois.

Nussbaum, J. E., Pecchioni, L. L., Robinson, J. D., and Thompson, T. L. (2000). Relationships with siblings in later life. *Communication and Aging*, 2nd ed. Hillsdale, NJ: Lawrence Erlbaum.

Safer, J. (2002). *The Normal One: Life With a Difficult or Damaged Sibling*. New York: The Free Press.

\* \* \*

# Sibling Use of Relational Maintenance Behaviors

Take a moment and reflect on your relationships with your siblings. I have three siblings: Michelle, who is three years younger than me; Susan, who is five years younger than me; and Mark, who is seven years younger than me. Some of my fondest memories of my childhood center on the time spent with my siblings. Together, the four of us explored the neighborhood on our bicycles and Big Wheels, starred in talent shows for our parents and grandparents, took turns being cops and robbers as well as cowboys and Indians, formed our own rock band, and forged friendships among GI Joe, Barbie, Donny and Marie, and the Sunshine Family. Holidays always took on a special meaning as we sat around the kitchen table, decorating sugar cookies at Christmas and coloring eggs for Easter. Sad times were equally shared, such as when our gerbil died and our dog Skippy was hit by a car. Everyday tasks, such as walking each other to school and pleading with our parents to be allowed to stay up late on Saturday nights, were completed as a unit of four.

As we grew into adolescence, the activities changed, but our time spent together did not. Instead of spending time playing, we now spent time engaging in household chores, fulfilling school responsibilities, and working. Cooking dinner and cleaning up afterward became a carefully orchestrated routine, equally shared and rotated among the four of us. One of us would clear the table, one of us would put away the leftovers and unused dishes, one of us would wash the dishes, and one of us would dry the dishes. Whoever cleared the table also had to sweep the floor and whoever put away the leftovers also had to wipe off the table and the stove. The completion of other household chores, such as laundry and mowing the yard, was negotiated. At school, we participated in several activities together, in part because there were usually two of us in the same school at the same time and in part because these were activities we mutually enjoyed. In high school, these activities included being on the school newspaper and yearbook staffs (I was editor my senior year; Michelle, Susan, and Mark were, at some point, reporters); participating in the school musicals (Michelle always had a starring role while Susan, Mark, and I were cast as "extras"); and being members of the forensics team. Sports (Susan and Mark were the athletes of the family; Michelle and I were content with watching) and cheerleading (Michelle was a cheerleader all four years in high school; Susan was a cheerleader for two years) were also shared activities. In the summer, it wasn't unusual to find between two and four of us detasseling corn and rouging beans for a local farmer.

Our relationship also reflected our individual personalities, talents, and traits. Being the oldest sibling, I became the family chauffeur once I attained my driver's license. Michelle, who was the first of us to get a job during the school year, was the one from whom we borrowed money if we needed it. She also made the best cheese scrambled eggs, so she was the one we asked to cook the eggs for breakfast. (Her cooking talents did not extend beyond this egg dish, unfortunately.) Susan, who was the most athletic and enjoyed the outdoors, was often tapped to mow the yard because the humid heat seemed to bother her least. Dusting the living room, on the other hand, did seem to bother her. Mark, who spent most of his waking hours with our bulldogs, Muttley and Bubbles, was in charge of making sure they were fed and groomed.

As we graduated from high school and entered and graduated from college, we still managed to spend some time together, but it wasn't as frequent or in the same manner as when we were younger. Relationships with our romantic partners began to dominate our time. If it wasn't a boyfriend or girlfriend who demanded our time, it was our jobs. Today, the role I play with my siblings is different from the roles enacted when we were younger. Because I no longer live in the same geographic area as my siblings, the time spent with them (which is usually over the Christmas holiday) has become more regimented and more routine. For example, when I visit Michelle, the first part of the visit revolves around her daughters. The first thing I do is have Hailey, my 7-year-old niece, show me her room. Inevitably, Hailey and I spend a good amount of time playing with her newest toys. (If you aren't familiar with Polly Fashion, you are missing a novel invention of plastic). Once we have had our fill of Polly and her friends, it's time to hold and coo over Jenna, my niece who is a newborn. Mark and I renew our relationship by going Christmas shopping a few days before Christmas, and we follow the script of picking out our presents for each other in front of each other. The first time I stop by Susan's house, I always give hugs and kisses to her dog Pikachu (a Japanese chin), even though he spends the first 15 minutes barking and running away from me while I incessantly repeat "Come here, Peeky, come here." Eventually, Pikachu remembers who I am, so I then spend the next 15 minutes throwing his ball to him while Susan beams with pride because Pikachu likes me. These are just a few of the behaviors I use to maintain the relationships I have with my siblings. As we grow into middle adulthood, who knows how or whether these behaviors will change.

## Relational Maintenance Behaviors

The aforementioned examples illustrate a concept known as relational maintenance behaviors. Relational maintenance behaviors are defined as the actions and activities used to sustain desired relational definitions (Canary and Stafford 1994). In other words, relational maintenance behaviors are the things people do in order to keep their relationships alive. By engaging in relational maintenance, it is possible for individuals to keep a relationship in existence, to keep a relationship in a specified state or condition, or to keep a relationship in satisfactory condition (Dindia and Canary 1993).

Several assumptions underlie an individual's use of relational maintenance behaviors. Although Canary and Stafford (1994) identified six propositions of relational maintenance behavior use, three propositions are particularly important to the sibling relationship. One proposition is that all relationships require maintenance. Without the use of some maintenance behaviors, a relationship will de-

teriorate and eventually die. Another proposition states that relational maintenance behaviors can be both interactive and noninteractive. An example of an interactive strategy is when my siblings and I sit around the kitchen table and talk about our relatives; a noninteractive strategy is when I wash the dishes after dinner on Christmas Eve because I know my siblings are tired (and perhaps because I feel a little guilty because I don't visit them as often as I should). A third proposition is that individuals use both strategic and routine relational maintenance behaviors. A strategic behavior is used purposely for the conscious intent of preserving and improving the relationship (Stafford, Dainton, and Haas 2000). A routine behavior, on the other hand, takes place at a lower level of consciousness and is not used intentionally for maintenance purposes, although the behavior can serve a maintenance function (Dainton and Stafford 1993). For example, when I visit my siblings over the holidays, I purposely make sure I spend time with each sibling (i.e., a strategic behavior). Making sure I remember Hailey's and Jenna's birthdays, as well as Halloween, Valentine's Day, and Easter by sending a card is a routine behavior I use, although forgetting these special days would probably hurt my sister more than my nieces.

## Relational Maintenance Behavior Typologies

So what behaviors do individuals use to maintain their relationships? One of the most widely recognized typologies of relational maintenance behaviors has been conceptualized by Stafford and Canary (1991). This typology consists of five relational maintenance behaviors believed to be used by romantic partners: positivity, openness, assurances, networks, and sharing tasks. *Positivity* involves interacting with the partner in a cheerful, optimistic, and uncritical manner. *Openness* includes directly discussing the nature of the relationship and disclosing one's desires for the relationship. *Assurances* are messages that stress an individual's continuation in the relationship. *Networks* involve both relational partners interacting with or relying on common affiliations and relationships. *Sharing tasks* requires partners to perform responsibilities specific to the relationship. More recently, Stafford et al. (2000) identified two additional relational maintenance behaviors—conflict management and advice—used by married partners. *Conflict management* refers to behaviors that consist of understanding, forgiveness, and patience. *Advice* centers on providing social support to a partner.

Dainton and Stafford (1993) identified an additional seven relational maintenance behaviors. These behaviors are joint activities, talk, mediated communication, avoidance, antisocial, affection, and focus on self. *Joint activities* consist of activities both partners participate in as a way to spend time together. *Talk* refers to verbal communication that is more centered on topic breadth than topic depth. *Mediated communication* involves any form of communication that is not face-to-face. *Avoidance* refers to the evasion of one partner or a particular topic. *Antisocial* involves the use of behaviors considered to be socially unfriendly or unacceptable. *Acceptance* consists of illustrating displays of fondness for the partner. *Focus on self* revolves around behaviors that are self-directed but are intended for the good of the relationship.

Researchers have found that these relational maintenance behaviors are used in marriages, dating relationships, and friendships. Within each of these relationships, the use of relational maintenance behaviors varies. Among friends, positivity (Messman, Canary, and Hause 2000; Nix 1999) and networks (Nix 1999) are used more frequently than other relational maintenance behaviors. Positivity, openness, assurances, and tasks are used more often by romantic partners and family members than by friends or coworkers (Canary, Stafford, Hause, and Wallace 1993), with tasks emerging as the most frequently used maintenance behavior in both heterosexual (Dainton and Stafford 1993) and homosexual (Haas and Stafford 1998) romantic relationships. Joint activities are used more frequently by dating couples than by married couples (Dainton and Stafford 1993). When romantic relationships increase in intensity, perceived use of openness and assurances increases; when romantic relationships are on the decline, perceived use of positivity, assur-

ances, and tasks decreases (Guerrero, Eloy, and Wabnik 1993). Regardless of the relational maintenance behavior used, the use of these behaviors is generally considered to be rewarding and is positively related to relational outcomes such as liking, loving, and satisfaction (Dainton, Stafford, and Canary 1994).

## Relational Maintenance Behaviors in the Sibling Relationship

The sibling relationship is one area of research in which the study of relational maintenance behaviors has been neglected. Given the pervasiveness of siblingship and the influence of siblings on one another, the study of relational maintenance behaviors among siblings is warranted for three reasons. First, it is estimated that 80 percent of all individuals spend at least one-third of their lives with their siblings (Fitzpatrick and Badzinski 1994). Second, throughout the sibling life span, the sibling relationship serves many functions. During childhood and adolescence, siblings act as teachers, playmates, confidantes, peers, and friends; during early and middle adulthood, siblings act as companions, provide psychological support, and engage in helping behaviors (Goetting 1986). Not only do siblings spend a lot of time together while growing up, but they also compete with one another for shared family resources such as time, money, and affection (Goetting 1986). Third, for most individuals, the sibling relationship is the longest-lasting relationship in their lives (Ponzetti and James 1997) and cannot be terminated. Even when sibling interaction is limited, most adult siblings remain emotionally involved with each other (Bank and Kahn 1975) or keep abreast of each other through third parties (Allan 1977).

One area of research in which I have been involved is sibling use of relational maintenance behaviors. To date, I have conducted two studies on this subject. In the first study (Myers and Members of COM 200), we (my students enrolled in a communication research methods course I was teaching and I) examined the extent to which siblings use each of the five relational maintenance behaviors identified by Canary and Stafford

(1992). We found that although siblings use all five of these relational maintenance behaviors, they do have a preference for using some relational maintenance behaviors over others. Specifically, we found that siblings report using (in order) tasks, positivity, assurances, networks, and openness.

Surprisingly, the most frequently reported relational maintenance behavior used by siblings was *sharing tasks*. Recall that tasks involve both partners participating in and sharing responsibility for tasks unique to the relationship (Canary and Stafford 1992). Interestingly, this finding parallels the results of previous research in that tasks are the most frequently used relational maintenance behavior in some romantic relationships and friendships. What this finding suggests is that tasks are important in all forms of intimate relationships. For siblings, tasks may be an important relational maintenance behavior for two reasons. First, sharing tasks may revolve around participating in family events, helping each other, sharing household chores, or spending time together. Pulakos (1988) noted that the only activity siblings do more with each other than with their friends was sharing holidays together. She found that other activities, such as shopping, studying, and engaging in recreational activities, are reserved for friends. Floyd (1995) reported that two behaviors—doing favors and providing help in an emergency—are more closely associated with sibling relationships than with friendships. Goetting (1986) posited that services such as babysitting, taking care of elderly parents, and helping out in times of illness are additional tasks adult siblings do for one another. Although these tasks may not always be perceived as enjoyable, these tasks may be considered instrumental to siblings. Second, it is possible that siblings consider staying in touch with each other as a task. Connidis and Campbell (1995) reported that sibling contact becomes more of a task as siblings marry and start families of their own. At the same time, siblings tend to stay in greater touch when they live geographically closer together (Lee, Mancini, and Maxwell 1990).

For some siblings, the quality of their relationship may be reflected through the use of the *positivity* relational maintenance behavior.

Positivity, which is defined as communicating in a cheerful, optimistic manner (Canary and Stafford 1992), may explain why siblings are communicatively satisfied in their interactions with each other. Hecht (1978) conceptualized communication satisfaction as the positive affect received from a communication event that fulfilled expectations. When siblings report high amounts of communication satisfaction in their interactions with each other, they indicate that these interactions lack verbal aggression and teasing (Martin, Anderson, Burant, and Weber 1997). Satisfied siblings also report greater feelings of solidarity, trust, and similarity toward each other (Martin, Anderson, and Rocca 1997; Myers 1998). In a study conducted with another group of students (Myers et al. 1999), certain dimensions of relational communication were found to be related to sibling communication satisfaction. We discovered that siblings who are cooperative and supportive are willing to listen as well as speak, act involved in the interaction, share demographic and attitudinal attributes, remain calm and poised, and have a positive impact on their siblings' perceived communication satisfaction. The bottom line, according to Bedford (1995), is that feeling good about a sibling is a rewarding experience. This experience may best be captured when siblings use positivity as a way to maintain their relationships.

The third most frequently used relational maintenance behavior was *assurances*. Assurances center on partners either implicitly or explicitly stressing their desire to remain involved in the relationship (Canary and Stafford 1992). Because the sibling relationship is involuntary, it might be expected that siblings would not utilize this relational maintenance behavior. However, there is evidence that suggests siblings are interested in engaging in communication that stresses their commitment to each other. For example, my students and I found that when siblings establish relational intimacy, they treat each other as equals, establish rapport, engage in self-disclosure, and regard each other as friends during their interactions (Myers et al. 1999). Siblings stress their commitment to each other when they engage in communication that is not only confirming and supportive but indicates an interest in maintaining the relationship. In another study, my colleague Ronda Knox and I (Myers and Knox 1998) studied the use of functional communication skills among siblings. Functional communication skills are eight communication skills that focus on "the management of another person's affect or emotion . . . or [the management of] the activity of communication itself" (Burleson and Samter 1990, 166). We found that regardless of sibling age, siblings use affectively oriented skills (i.e., four skills centered on the management of another person's affect) at a higher rate than some of the nonaffectively oriented skills (i.e., four skills centered on the management of communication activity). Affectively oriented skills, such as providing comfort and ego support, are perceived to be used more frequently by siblings than nonaffectively oriented skills, such as being able to tell jokes and stories. We concluded that siblings use the affectively oriented skills at a higher rate because providing each other with psychological and social support is one way to indicate an interest in remaining emotionally involved in the relationship.

Assurances may also be a by-product of the emotional attachment siblings feel for one another. Siblings who feel closer emotionally confide in each other, talk to each other on the telephone, and see each other in person more often than siblings who are less closer emotionally (Connidis and Campbell 1995). This mutual confiding is also one reason why some siblings consider each other to be close friends (White and Riedmann 1992) and why siblings feel responsible for each other's welfare (Lee et al. 1990). Siblings who feel close to each other also interact more frequently and with a greater breadth and depth of topics (Rocca and Martin 1998).

*Networks*, which involve both partners relying on common affiliations and relationships (Canary and Stafford 1992), may be one relational maintenance behavior that changes over the life span. As youngsters and adolescents, siblings form alliances. Nicholson (1999) interviewed siblings and found that not only do siblings form alliances with each other, but these alliances are considered to be a normal part of family life. He found that there are several reasons why siblings develop alliances. Two reasons—"to improve, develop, or reconcile relationships with someone" and "to do something together" (p. 12)—are particularly relevant to sibling relational maintenance. And not only do siblings have rules for creating an alliance, but they also develop sanctions and penalties for siblings who break these rules. Also during these times, siblings share several activities. Floyd (1996) reported that among brothers, companionship was the most reported reason for perceived feelings of closeness. Companionship emerged in the forms of shared interests, mutual activity, and including each other in conversation. As siblings move into adulthood, the composition of the network may change. For adult siblings, serving in another role (i.e., aunt, uncle, godparent) may affect their interactions with each other. Ultimately, though, when siblings share activities, belong to the same groups, attend the same functions, or have common friends, they spend more time together, which may have a positive impact not only on the behaviors used to maintain the relationships but on how they feel about each other.

The least frequently used relational maintenance behavior was *openness*. Openness, which involves direct discussions about the relationship (Stafford et al. 2000) and allows for the expression of feelings, thoughts, and emotions (Canary and Stafford 1992), may not be as central to the sibling relationship because, unlike romantic relationships, the sibling relationship cannot be terminated. Romantic relationships rely on intimacy and self-disclosure to stimulate and sustain growth, but siblings can (and will) remain siblings regardless of emotional involvement and/or investment. In an earlier study (Myers 1998), I argued that self-disclosure may not occur frequently among siblings because self-disclosure is not regarded as an integral component of sibling communication. Although self-disclosure is considered to be an important behavior in intimate relationships, sibling self-disclosure is used primarily to convey information and to receive information from one another (Dolgin and Lindsay 1999). Pulakos (1988) reported that siblings tend to be more open with their friends than with each other on a number of topics, including money, sex, romantic partners, childhood memories, and important decisions; parents/siblings is the only topic discussed more with siblings than with friends. Openness therefore may not be a frequently used relational maintenance behavior because openness is not essential to maintaining the sibling bond. Although Floyd (1997) discovered that the breadth and depth of sibling self-disclosure is related to perceptions of liking, loving, and commitment, it is possible for siblings to be satisfied with their interactions without engaging in a wide breadth and/or depth of self-disclosure (Myers 1998).

In a more recent study (Myers 2001), I was interested in identifying the relational maintenance behaviors unique to the sibling relationship. (Recall that the Stafford and Canary typology was originally designed to examine relational maintenance behavior usage in voluntary relationships, such as romantic relationships.) Fifty-seven individuals, who ranged in age from 18 to 58 years, were asked to identify three behaviors they used to maintain a relationship with one of their siblings. The examples were then subjected to a typological analysis, in which 14 categories of relational maintenance behaviors emerged. These 14 categories were talk, confirmation, joint activities, mediated communication, aggression, visits, humor, social support, time, affection, antisocial, role model, similarity, and other.

Of these 14 categories of relational maintenance behaviors, eight behaviors have not been identified by previous researchers and thus, may be considered as unique to the sibling relationship. The most frequently mentioned relational maintenance behaviors were confirmation, aggression, visits, and humor. *Confirmation* refers to behaviors that validate a sibling's involvement in an interaction. Examples provided by the participants in this study included "I ask my sibling questions in an attempt to understand him" and "I try not to interrupt my sibling when she is talking." *Aggression* refers to the use of physical and/or symbolic force with a sibling. Examples included "I call my sibling names" and "I fight with my sibling." *Visits* involve one sibling

physically traveling to see the other sibling. Examples included "I visit my sibling at his apartment" and "I stop by my sibling's house periodically." *Humor* refers to the use of behaviors that are entertaining or amusing. Examples included "I joke around with my sibling" and "I laugh at my sibling's jokes."

Less mentioned relational maintenance behaviors included social support, time, role model, and similarity. *Social support* refers to verbal communication that stresses topic depth over topic breadth. Examples provided by the participants in this study included "I ask my sibling for advice" and "I am honest with my sibling about everything." *Time* involves the actual use of time as a way to maintain the relationship. Examples included "I try not to spend too much time with my sibling" and "I spend a lot of time with my sibling." *Role model* involves sibling modeling of appropriate behavior. Examples included "I try to act as a positive role model for my sibling" and "I criticize my sibling in order to help him avoid the same mistakes I've made." *Similarity* centers on common interests shared by siblings. Examples included "I share similar tastes in clothing with my sibling" and "We share similar tastes in music."

Together, the results of these two studies suggest that a variety of behaviors are used by siblings in an effort to maintain their relationships. These findings support the idea that sibling relationships are in need of maintenance just as are other relationships. Bedford (1995) noted that functional sibling relationships provide siblings with positive affect, association, attachment, and well-being. One way in which this may be accomplished is through sibling use of relational maintenance behaviors.

## Conclusion

Through communication, individuals can use a variety of behaviors to maintain their relationships. The sibling relationship is no exception. Although the sibling relationship is involuntary, most siblings have a commitment to the relationship that extends beyond sustaining obligatory familial ties (Cicirelli 1991). By using relational maintenance behaviors, siblings are able to provide emotional, moral, and psychological support; fulfill familial responsibilities; engage in shared activities; and remain involved in each other's lives. As you reflect back on your relationships with your siblings, take a moment and consider the relational maintenance behaviors you have used, continue to use, or intend to use. Your choice of, and use of, relational maintenance behaviors may indeed explain why the sibling relationship is generally considered to be a positive experience (Pulakos 1987).

## References

Allan, G. (1977). Sibling solidarity. *Journal of Marriage and the Family*, 39, 177–184.

Bank, S. P., and Kahn, M. D. (1975). Sisterhood-brotherhood is powerful: Sibling subsystems and family therapy. *Family Process*, 14, 311–337.

Bedford, V. H. (1995). Sibling relationships in middle and old age. In R. Blieszner and V. H. Bedford (Eds.), *Handbook of Aging and the Family* (pp. 201–222). Westport, CT: Greenwood Press.

Burleson, B. R., and Samter, W. (1990). Effects of cognitive complexity on the perceived importance of communication skills in friends. *Communication Research*, 17, 165–182.

Canary, D. J., and Stafford, L. (1992). Relational maintenance strategies and equity in marriage. *Communication Monographs*, 59, 244–267.

———. (1994). Maintaining relationships through strategic and routine interaction. In D. J. Canary and L. Stafford (Eds.), *Communication and Relational Maintenance* (pp. 1–22). New York: Academic Press.

Canary, D. J., Stafford, L., Hause, K. S., and Wallace, L. A. (1993). An inductive analysis of relational maintenance strategies: Comparisons among lovers, relatives, friends, and others. *Communication Research Reports*, 10, 5–14.

Cicirelli, V. G. (1991). Sibling relations in adulthood. *Marriage and Family Review*, 16, 292–310.

Connidis, I. A., and Campbell, L. D. (1995). Closeness, confiding, and contact among siblings in middle and late adulthood. *Journal of Family Issues*, 16, 722–745.

Dainton, M., and Stafford, L. (1993). Routine maintenance behaviors: A comparison of relationship type, partner similarity and sex differences. *Journal of Social and Personal Relationships*, 10, 255–271.

Dainton, M., Stafford, L., and Canary, D. J. (1994). Maintenance strategies and physical affection as predictors of love, liking, and satisfaction in marriage. *Communication Reports*, 7, 88–98.

Dindia, K., and Canary, D. J. (1993). Definitions and theoretical perspectives on maintaining relationships. *Journal of Social and Personal Relationships*, 10, 163–173.

Dolgin, K. G., and Lindsay, K. R. (1999). Disclosure between college students and their siblings. *Journal of Family Psychology*, 13, 393–400.

Fitzpatrick, M. A., and Badzinski, D. M. (1994). All in the family: Interpersonal communication in kin relationships. In M. L. Knapp and G. R. Miller (Eds.), *Handbook of Interpersonal Communication* (2nd ed.) (pp. 726–771). Thousand Oaks, CA: Sage.

Floyd, K. (1995). Gender and closeness among friends and siblings. *Journal of Psychology*, 129, 193–202.

———. (1996). Brotherly love I: The experience of closeness in the fraternal dyad. *Personal Relationships*, 3, 369–385.

———. (1997). Brotherly love II: A developmental perspective on liking, love, and closeness in the fraternal dyad. *Journal of Family Psychology*, 11, 196–209.

Goetting, A. (1986). The developmental tasks of siblingship over the life cycle. *Journal of Marriage and the Family*, 48, 703–714.

Guerrero, L. K., Eloy, S. V., and Wabnik, A. I. (1993). Linking maintenance strategies to relationship development and disengagement: A reconceptualization. *Journal of Social and Personal Relationships*, 10, 273–283.

Haas, S. M., and Stafford, L. (1998). An initial examination of maintenance behaviors in gay and lesbian relationships. *Journal of Social and Personal Relationships*, 15, 846–855.

Hecht, M. L. (1978). The conceptualization and measurement of interpersonal communication satisfaction. *Human Communication Research*, 4, 253–264.

Lee, T. R., Mancini, J. A., and Maxwell, J. W. (1990). Sibling relationships in adulthood: Contact patterns and motivations. *Journal of Marriage and Family*, 52, 431–440.

Martin, M. M., Anderson, C. M., Burant, P. A., and Weber, K. (1997). Verbal aggression in sibling relationships. *Communication Quarterly*, 45, 304–317.

Martin, M. M., Anderson, C. A., and Rocca, K. A. (1997, November). Perceptions of sibling relationships: Verbal aggression, credibility, similarity and relational outcomes. Paper presented at the annual meeting of the National Communication Association, Chicago, IL.

Messman, S. J., Canary, D. J., and Hause, K. S. (2000). Motives to remain platonic, equity, and the use of maintenance strategies in opposite-sex friendships. *Journal of Social and Personal Relationships*, 17, 67–94.

Myers, S. A. (1998). Sibling communication satisfaction as a function of interpersonal solidarity, individualized trust, and self-disclosure. *Communication Research Reports*, 15, 309–317.

———. (2001, November). A typological analysis of sibling relational maintenance behaviors. Paper presented at the annual meeting of the National Communication Association, Atlanta, GA.

Myers, S. A., Cavanaugh, E. K., Dohmen, L. M., Freeh, J. L., Huang, V. W., Kapler, M. R., Leonatti, A., Malicay, M., Schweig, V., Sorensen, H. J., Vang, M. M., and Wise, D. C. (1999). Perceived sibling use of relational communication messages and sibling satisfaction, liking, and loving. *Communication Research Reports*, 16, 339–352.

Myers, S. A., and Knox, R. L. (1998). Perceived sibling use of functional communication skills. *Communication Research Reports*, 15, 397–405.

Myers, S. A., and Members of COM 200. (2001). Relational maintenance behaviors in the sibling relationship. *Communication Quarterly*, 49, 19–34.

Nicholson, J. H. (1999, November). Sibling alliance rules. Paper presented at the annual meeting of the National Communication Association, Chicago, IL.

Nix, C. L. (1999, November). "But a 'real friend' wouldn't treat me that way!:" An examination of negative strategies employed to maintain friendship. Paper presented at the annual meeting of the National Communication Association, Chicago, IL.

Ponzetti, J. J., Jr., and James, C. M. (1997). Loneliness and sibling relationships. *Journal of Social Behavior and Personality*, 12, 103–112.

Pulakos, J. (1987). Brothers and sisters: Nature and importance of the adult bond. *Journal of Psychology*, 121, 521–522.

———. (1988). Young adult relationships: Siblings and friends. *Journal of Psychology*, 123, 237–244.

Rocca, K. A., and Martin, M. M. (1998). The relationship between willingness to communicate and solidarity with frequency, breadth, and depth of communication in the sibling relationship. *Communication Research Reports*, 15, 82–90.

Stafford, L., and Canary, D. J. (1991). Maintenance strategies and romantic relationship type, gender and relational characteristics. *Journal of Social and Personal Relationships*, 8, 217–242.

Stafford, L., Dainton, M., and Haas, S. (2000). Measuring routine and strategic relational maintenance: Scale revision, sex versus gender roles, and the prediction of relational characteristics. *Communication Monographs*, 67, 306–323.

White, L. K., and Riedmann, A. (1992). Ties among adult siblings. *Social Forces*, 71, 85–102.

## Questions

1. Identify the relational maintenance behaviors currently used by you and your siblings. How are these behaviors different from the behaviors used when you were younger? What behaviors do you anticipate using as you and your siblings grow older?

2. Does your use of relational maintenance behaviors depend on the sibling with whom you are interacting? How? Why?

3. Examine the typologies of relational maintenance behaviors identified by Stafford and Canary (1991); Stafford, Dainton, and Haas (2001); and Dainton and Stafford (1993). Which of these these behaviors do you use *strategically* with your siblings? Which of these behaviors do you use *routinely* with your siblings?

4. To what degree is your use of relational maintenance behaviors related to the satisfaction experienced in your sibling relationships?

# 38

# Communicating About Sex With Parents and Partners

*Clay Warren*

**S**exuality, including sexual attitudes and behavior, may be viewed as a topic of communication, a form of communication, and a contributing factor to overall relational intimacy and satisfaction. Troth and Peterson's (2000) research indicates that communication plays a significant role in the development of intimate sexuality. However, in many families and for some relational partnerships, it is a difficult issue to address directly and openly.

Some of today's adults grew up in a home atmosphere of sexual silence and now are living in a world that expects open sexual discussion. They have to overcome the explicit or implicit communication rule they learned, "Do not talk about sex." Others grew up learning to talk about sex in very careful and nuanced ways. Often family communication about sexual issues remains indirect, resulting in confusion, misinformation, or heightened curiosity, although close to 40 percent of parents say they talk frequently with their children about sex (*Family Chats 1998*). Yet, research indicates that girls who talk to their mothers about sexual topics are more likely to have conservative sexual values and are less likely to have engaged in sexual activity than girls who mostly talked to their friends (Dilorio, Miller, and Hockenberry-Eaton 1999). Although mothers have consistently been found to be the primary communicators of sexual topics with children, fathers may play an important role through the discussion of sociosexual issues such as "understanding men" or resisting pressure for sex

with daughters (Hutchinson 2002). Today's young people are exposed to sexuality in the media, music, and other forms of popular culture. If they cannot talk about sexuality with a parent, there is little choice but to turn to peers or media.

Although many partners are able to address sexuality directly, others avoid the topic because their vocabulary for sexual conversation is impoverished. This avoidance has implications for relational intimacy and as well as for sexual health. In this chapter Clay Warren, one of the few communication scholars with a research program devoted to sexual communication, addresses both parent-child and dating partner communication. In this article Warren argues for the importance of sexual communication within the family and makes the case that sex communication is different from sex education. He then addresses parent-child and dating partner interaction on the topic of sex. As you read this piece, consider this question: What did I learn about discussing sex in my family of origin, and how that has changed as I grew into adulthood?

## References

Dilorio, C., Kelley, M., and Hockenberry-Eaton, M. (1999). Communication about sexual issues: Mothers, fathers, and friends. *Journal of Adolescent Health*, 24, 181–189.

Family Chats. (1998, February). *American Demographics*, 37.

Hutchinson, M. K. (2002). The influence of sexual risk communication between parents and daughters on sexual risk behaviors. *Family Relations*, 51, 238–247.

Troth, A., and Peterson C. C. (2000). Factors predicting safe-sex talk and condom use in early sexual relationships. *Health Communication* 12, 195–218.

\* \* \*

**D**uring my first year of teaching courses on interpersonal communication, an unexpected thing happened when the class discussion turned to intimate relationships. Students regularly reported the lack of their family's communication about matters of intimacy.

319

These class discussions served as an early impetus for my program of research aimed at illuminating parent-child communication about sex. One of the central features of this research program was developmental work on a measurement tool called the *family sex communication quotient*. Before you read about the topic of family sex communication, take the inventory (Figure 38-1); it will help you reflect on your own behavior pattern in the family unit (see Warren & Neer 1986, for a full explanation of this questionnaire).

The communication *comfort* dimension was selected as one of the three main FSCQ measures because people positively experience supportive climates, which may be essential to open lines of communication. The *information* dimension was included because the home cannot function as a primary source of sexual learning without sufficient sharing of information. The *value* dimension

### Figure 38-1
### Family Sex Communication Quotient (FSCQ)

Directions: The following statements represent personal feelings about family discussions of sex. Please circle one of the five response categories that best describes your opinion: SA = strongly agree, A = agree, N = neutral (or don't know), D = disagree, SD =strongly disagree. Also, please answer these questions regardless of whether you have ever talked about sex with your parents. Don't spend much time on any one question; make a choice and move to the next. Don't ask others how they are answering their questions, or how they think you should answer yours.

| | | | | | | |
|---|---|---|---|---|---|---|
| I | Sex should be one of the most important topics for parents and children to discuss. | SA | A | N | D | SD |
| 2 | I can talk to my parents about almost anything related to sex. | SA | A | N | D | SD |
| 3 | My parents know what I think about sex. | SA | A | N | D | SD |
| 4 | It is not necessary to talk to my parents about sex. | SA | A | N | D | SD |
| 5 | I can talk openly and honestly with my parents about sex. | SA | A | N | D | SD |
| 6 | I know what my parents think about sex. | SA | A | N | D | SD |
| 7 | The home should be a primary place for learning about sex. | SA | A | N | D | SD |
| 8 | I feel comfortable discussing sex with my parents. | SA | A | N | D | SD |
| 9 | My parents have given me very little information about sex. | SA | A | N | D | SD |
| 10 | Sex is too personal a topic to discuss with my parents. | SA | A | N | D | SD |
| 11 | My parents feel comfortable discussing sex with me. | SA | A | N | D | SD |
| 12 | Much of what I know about sex has come from family discussions. | SA | A | N | D | SD |
| 13 | Sex should not be discussed in the family unless there is a problem to resolve. | SA | A | N | D | SD |
| 14 | Sex is too hard a topic to discuss with my parents. | SA | A | N | D | SD |
| 15 | I feel better informed about sex if I talk to my parents. | SA | A | N | D | SD |
| 16 | The least important thing to discuss with my parents is sex. | SA | A | N | D | SD |
| 17 | I feel free to ask my parents questions about sex. | SA | A | N | D | SD |
| 18 | When I want to know something about sex, I generally ask my parents. | SA | A | N | D | SD |

Scoring: The FSCQ measures a general orientation toward discussion about sex in the family unit along three dimensions: Comfort (items 2–5–8–11–14–17), Information (items 3–6–9–12–15–18), and Value (items 1–4–7–10–13–16). You can give each SA answer a "5", A answer a "4", N a "3," D a "2," and SD a "1." Six of the questions need to be reverse-scored (items 4, 9, 10, 13, 14, and 16). Reverse scoring means the 5 and 1 weights are interchanged, the 4 and 2 weights are interchanged, and the 3 remains the same. It is used in questionnaire design to detect set-response behavior—a tendency of some folks to not think about the questions and, thus, to use the same answers regardless of the question asked. After pairing a number with the 18 questions, you can total them. A strong FSCQ orientation would be 72 or above.

was included because long-range positive values about family discussions will influence the likelihood of discussing sex with one's own children. The FSCQ has proved to be a highly reliable measure of family orientation (its *alpha* score, a statistical estimate measuring reliability, averages above .90).

The score patterns for respondents, whether in the early 1980s or in 2000, has tended to show a moderate to low orientation (between 65 and 36) for family sex communication. Fewer than ten of 100 respondents has reported a strong orientation of 72 or above. The scores on dimensions, however, do not run at the same level. Respondents are apt to score much higher on the Value dimension than on the Comfort or Information dimensions. That means that parents and children are not talking about sex in the family context as much as theoretically or practically desirable, or as valued by the children themselves. You can think about your own score in this context, as we review concepts that have emerged from research studies about sex communication with parents and partners.

## Is Communication About Sex an Important Issue?

Communication about sex is an important issue because youthful sexual behavior is an important problem—a problem some researchers described as epidemic during the 1980s and into the 1990s. A majority of American adolescents have had intercourse before they reach age 19 (around 55 percent of young women and 70 percent of young men); however, condom use is inconsistent at best (Alan Guttmacher Institute 1994). As a result, female teenagers in the United States during the late twentieth century have accounted for between 50 percent and 30 percent of all non-marital births, depending on the year of calculation, and around 40 percent of teen pregnancies are terminated by abortion (Alan Guttmacher Institute 1994). Indeed, among developed countries, U.S. teenage pregnancy and abortion rates are the highest in the world (Warren 1992).

There are many consequences for young people having frequent unprotected sex in ad-

dition to non-marital births and abortions, with the female bearing the brunt. For example, teenage mothers are less likely to finish high school and more likely to have a lower lifetime earning capacity and to apply for welfare than non-mothers in their cohort (Warren 2000). Disease is also a problem, most particularly in the spread of AIDS over the past several decades. Moreover, single-parent families historically have produced around two-thirds of the juvenile offenders (Federal Bureau of Investigation 1998).

There are many other statistics that bear on this problem, but perhaps the above sampling is enough to make the point. The United States has a youth sex problem, and problems deserve communication efforts directed toward effective solutions.

## Sex Communication Is Not Sex Education

Many people have used the terms sex communication and sex education as interchangeable; however, they are not. In fact, they represent distinctly different approaches to information sharing. Sex communication involves people exchanging verbal and non-verbal messages in a mutual effort to co-create meaning about sexual beliefs, attitudes, values, and/or behavior. Sex education, on the other hand, is characterized by senders didactically trying to transfer information about sexuality, sexual intercourse, reproduction, and birth control to receivers. This distinction is important because it helps us understand differences in research results.

By the mid-1980s, summary reviews (Kirby 1984; Search Institute 1985) had been completed on more than 200 institutional sex education studies reported between 1970 and 1984. The news was not what sex educators hoped to hear.

Institutional sex education has not influenced students' frequency of sexual intercourse, birth control attitudes/behavior and corresponding likelihood of producing an unintended teenage pregnancy, satisfaction with social life, and general self-esteem; institutional sex education has increased students' knowledge about sexuality, tolerance toward others' sexual behavior (except for sexual coercion), and communicating with parents in parent-involved programs. (Warren 1995, 179)

In other words, sex education was not proving to be an ideal solution, or at least a solution in and of itself, for the problem of unintended teenage pregnancy. That assessment continues to be a fair descriptor to this day.

Two thorough reviews (Philliber 1980; Fox 1981) summarizing the research on sex communication were completed around the same time as the summaries on sex education. These reviews offered more promise, at least tentatively, in that there was support for the idea that parent-child communication about sex may have an impact on children's sexual behavior by delaying initiation of sexual intercourse and facilitating use of birth control measures. However, as noted by Furstenberg, Herceg-Baron, Shea, and Webb (1986): "[Philliber and Fox agreed] that more research is needed on the way that both direct and indirect sex communication in the family influences adolescent behavior" (p. 220).

Research up to the mid-1980s tended to focus on content and quantitative issues in family sex communication. As one example, Fisher (1986) found that parent-child communication about sex is related to sexual values by frequency pattern—college students and parents in high-communication families have more similar sexual attitudes than students and parents in low-communication families.

Later studies have targeted qualitative issues. For instance, Bonnell and Caillouet (1991) discovered that teens strongly believe that parents should learn how to communicate empathetically and supportively regardless of shared agreement over content-specific issues. Blake, Simkin, Ledsky, Perkins, and Calabrese (2001) recently provided a qualitatively oriented summary:

> The quality of parent-child relationships and parenting style in general, and communications about sex and sexuality more specifically, appear to be strong determinants of adolescent sexual behavior. Relationships to adolescent sexual behavior have been found . . . particularly when parent-child communications were

characterized as being "open and receptive." (pp. 52–53)

During a fifteen-year period between 1980 and 1995, Michael Neer and I conducted a long-running series of studies that explored, in equal measure, the quality and content of parent-child communication about sex. Using the FSCQ as well as questions designed to survey respondents' feelings about sexual behavior (e.g., "Sexual relations with the people I date are very important to me"; "The use of contraceptives should be discussed by a couple before having sex") and to gather objective data (e.g., "Have you had sexual intercourse?"; "Do you use birth control measures?"), we discovered four important umbrella elements of family sex communication (see Warren 1995).

First, *satisfaction with family discussions about sex is dependent on the key factor of mutual dialogue.* Further, children are most satisfied with patterns of family communication about sex when parents help them feel comfortable, or at least free, to initiate discussions. Thus, for best results, parents must move beyond the role of initiators and into the role of facilitators.

Second, *the ability to communicate supportively about sex revolves around an attitude of openness.* Teens want parents to talk with them, not at them, and to avoid preachy messages. Parents who only want to give their children instructions and commands are likely to have little success as communicators in this area.

Third, *for discussions to have the greatest impact, they should become part of the family patterns well before children reach age 16.* Many parents tend to put off talking about sex with their children, and the longer they wait, the harder it is to start. On the other hand, early initiation of discussion tends to facilitate more frequent discussion as well as children's perceptions that their parents are effective communicators.

Fourth, *parent-child communication about sex that is frequent and that is regarded as effective tends to facilitate children's open discussion with dating partners.* The resonance effect is at work here, as children go on to model what they have encountered at home. Also, this communication pattern seems to favorably, if not robustly, influence children's attitudes about birth control measures—a result not achieved by sex education approaches at either the institutional or family level.

## Suggestions for Parent-Child Communication About Sex

An old Ashanti proverb springs to mind: "The ruin of a nation begins in the homes of its people." Perhaps that sounds negative, but it emphasizes the importance of parental roles. These roles extend to the arena of sex. As the National Campaign to Prevent Teen Pregnancy (1998) stated: "Teenagers who have strong emotional attachments to their parents are much less likely to become sexually active at an early age" (p. 3).

Regardless of how a contemporary family is configured, this unit is the principal context in which a child's relationship orientation is formed; among the offshoots of this orientation, in addition to strength of emotional attachment, are communication patterns, including how you approach discussion about sex.

Available research points out three overall principles as appearing sound. Families should talk about sexual issues early, openly, and interactively. With these principles as base, what kind of parent-child communication practices might you try to develop in your own families? (See Warren 2000.)

*Talk with your children.* Such a piece of advice might seem elementary, but I see it as elemental. Some parents don't talk enough, in general. Too many parents may drop into the trap of one-way rather than two-way communication. Two-way communication builds trust that then can be drawn on for sensitive issues. One-way communication builds resentment in children, which can mushroom in their teenage years.

*Talk with your children about sex.* Not talking with your children about sex does not stop them from seeking information; it just sends them to other sources, some of which are unreliable, at best, and often outright misleading. On the other hand, respondents from environments of perceived good family sex communication report holding the following attitudes: Sex should be pursued as a means of genuine caring, not promiscuous pleasure; sex is not the most important goal of dating; talking about contraception does not promote sexual license.

*Begin discussions with your children when they are young.* Younger children are less likely to be judgmental. So, by talking about sex with them at an early age, you are less likely to become defensive and more likely to perceive your role as that of confidante and helper.

*Continue these discussions over time.* A "domino effect" occurs when discussions start early and continue. General communication raises children's expectations for parent-child communication about sex. Similarly, increased frequency of family sex communication raises children's expectations that discussions will become more specific. In other words, talking about sex in general terms (e.g., interpersonal problems with dating partners) will lead children to expect parents to talk with them about sex more specifically (e.g., values about sex, methods of birth control).

*Both parents should talk in a two-parent family.* Recent studies suggest that parents are most effective when both participate in the discussion. In the past, the tendency was for mothers to make more of an effort in this area, particularly in the context of mother-daughter communication. Just as boys have a role in teen pregnancy, however, leaving fathers out of the picture sidesteps half the problem.

*Talk to all children.* Just as both parents should talk, all children should be part of the dialogue. Females in research samples have been more likely than males to value contraceptive use. Parents, however, have been more likely to talk with daughters about sex even when both parents were actively involved in discussion. Such one-sided practice may reinforce the so-called double standard, and, considering the statistics on unintended teen pregnancy, it appears evident that female-directed discussion has failed to achieve its goal. Sons need, and deserve, to be included in family sex communication.

*Establish mutual dialogue.* The heart of the difference between a communication and an education approach to family sex communication revolves around mutual dialogue.

Identified earlier as an umbrella element, parents' ability to facilitate children's initiation of discussion is key. If family discussions degenerate into all-knowing adults prescribing cures to know-nothing children, mutual dialogue is not the goal, and many teens will stop listening.

*Create a supportive environment.* Feeling comfortable when discussing sensitive issues is important, and that feeling usually comes from the practice of good principles. Discussants, particularly parents, must remember a few things about supportiveness as they engage in family communication. Sex communication involves a co-creation of meaning, which means that children's attitudes about sex are equal in importance to parents' attitudes. A parent may have more knowledge to share, but sharing does not happen in a defensive climate. Nonverbal communication is important—how something is said is just as meaningful as what is said.

## Sex Communication Between Dating Partners

Family sex communication, whether quantitatively high or low, and whether rich or meager in effectiveness, is the beginning. Later, children will have good or poor communication about sex with dating partners. Later still, enduring partners may face the issue of parent-child communication about sex.

The last umbrella element of family sex communication, discussed earlier, states that frequent and effective parent-child communication about sex facilitates children's open discussion with dating partners and positively influences, at least to some extent, children's attitudes about birth control measures. Respondents with this kind of background report having a caring, non-promiscuous philosophy about sex.

Indeed, the three basic principles and eight practical suggestions for parent-child communication about sex apply equally to sex communication between partners. Reworked, they might read as follows. In principle, serious dating partners should discuss openly and interactively, sexual issues early in their relationship (even if they are not having sexual relations). Practically speaking, dating partners should try to have good general communication as well as effective communication about sex—begun early in the relationship and continuing throughout its life—that features mutual dialogue created in a supportive environment.

Narrowing the scope even further, one of the most important content items is how dating partners perceive and communicate sexual consent. This issue exploded onto the national scene when the national press brought public attention to the Antioch policy in the fall of 1993. This policy, developed by Antioch College three years earlier, required all Antioch students to obtain consent from their dating partners prior to engaging in sexual activity and, once engaged in that activity, before proceeding to the next level of intimacy. Antioch College (1990) defined consent as "the act of willingly and verbally agreeing to engage in specific sexual contact or conduct" (p. 1). Although the goal of this policy, as identified by various administrators (including the president of the college), was simply to encourage students to communicate openly and honestly about their sexual desires and intentions, it created an international controversy. The Antioch policy was featured on the front pages of major national newspapers in North America and abroad as well as on all the principal U.S. broadcast networks.

The inescapable conclusion, even so close to the second millennium, was this: It is one thing for young people in the United States to have sex when swept away in the heat of the moment, but to premeditatedly, dispassionately, rationally talk about and perhaps plan for sex—how dare you! It is precisely this kind of cultural climate, many argue, that does not help us solve the American youth sex problem.

Although the Antioch policy generated research interest in this area, it is still a fact that researchers believe little is known about consent patterns between dating partners (Hickman & Muehlenhard 1999). What, then, is known? It appears that partners, both men and women, would rather engage in indirect than in the direct communication about sexual consent, because this pattern permits intimate access without the embarrassment of overt rejection (Cupach & Metts

1991). Also, stark statements such as "I consent to sexual intercourse," one of the scripts found in the guidelines of Antioch College, are unlikely to meet the romantic needs of most dating partners.

Nevertheless, the communication of sexual consent remains a targeted research item, in part because of the youth sex problem: "[S]afer-sex negotiation is considered crucial for the implementation of safer sexual behavior in dating partners' sexual scripts" (Buysse & Ickes 1999, 121). Negotiation is crucial because of the inconsistency of condom use among sexual intimates. Using a condom is the method most recommended to practice safe sex. Too often, however, individuals forgo condom use in favor of their perceived ability to distinguish safe from unsafe partners; indeed, partner selection is the preferred method in 70 percent to 80 percent of stable relationships to protect oneself from AIDS (Buysse 1998).

Do three-quarters of the sexually active young people in the United States have a magical ability to select safe partners? The statistics argue otherwise, yet fewer than 30 percent of sexually active individuals discussed sexual history, stance on monogamy, or condom use with their partner prior to engaging in sexual intercourse (Gray & Saracino 1991). Effective perception and communication of sexual consent? Negotiation of safer sex? Current research compels the conclusion that such desirable communication patterns among dating partners are still the exception rather than the rule.

## In the End

Of course I love you,/So let's have a kid/Who will say exactly/What its parents did;/"Of course I love you,/So let's have a kid/Who will say exactly/What its parents did;/'Of course I love you,/So let's have a kid/Who will say exactly/What its parents did—' "/Et cetera.

—(K. Vonnegut 1985, 66)

Kurt Vonnegut captured a lot in this short poem: the power of parents to shape the attitudes and behavior of their children, the ubiquity and perhaps the serendipity of the love urge, and (with just a brief stretch of the imagination) a good reason to become an advocate for effective communication about sex with parents and partners. Whatever your background, it is never too late or even too early to start now.

## References

Alan Guttmacher Institute. (1994). *Sex and America's teenagers*. New York: Author.

Antioch College. (1990). *Sexual violence and safety*. Yellow Springs, OH: Author.

Blake, S. M., Simkin, L., Ledsky, R., Perkins, C., and Calabrese, J. (2001). Effects of a parent-child communications intervention on young adolescents' risk for early onset of sexual intercourse. *Family Planning Perspectives*, 33:2, 52–61.

Bonnell, K. H., and Caillouet, L. M. (1991, April). Patterns and communication barriers between teenagers and parents about sex-related topics. Paper presented at the meeting of the Central States Communication Association, Chicago.

Buysse, A. (1998). Safer sexual decision making in stable and casual relationships: A prototype approach. *Psychology and Health*, 13, 55–66.

Buysse, A., and Ickes, W. (1999). Communication patterns in laboratory discussions of safer sex between dating versus nondating partners. *The Journal of Sex Research*, 36:2, 121–134.

Cupach, W. R., and Metts, S. (1991). Sexuality and communication in close relationships. In K. McKinney and S. Sprecher (Eds.), *Sexuality in close relationships* (pp. 93–110). Hillsdale, NJ: Lawrence Erlbaum.

Federal Bureau of Investigation. (1998). *Uniform crime reports of the United States*. Washington, DC: Author.

Fisher, T. D. (1986). Parent-child communication about sex and young adolescents' sexual knowledge and attitudes. *Adolescence*, 16, 517–527.

Fox, G. L. (1981). The family's role in adolescent sexual behavior. In T. Ooms (Ed.), *Teenage pregnancy in a family context* (pp. 73–130). Philadelphia: Temple University Press.

Furstenberg, F. F., Jr., Herceg-Baron, R., Shea, J., and Webb, D. (1986). Family communication and contraceptive use among sexually active adolescents. In J. G. Lancaster and B. A. Hamburg (Eds.), *School-age pregnancy and parenthood: Biosocial dimensions* (pp. 219–243). New York: Aldine de Gruyter.

Gray, L. A., and Saracino, M. (1991). College students' attitudes, beliefs, and behaviors about

AIDS: Implications for family life educators. *Family Relations*, 40, 258–263.

Hickman, S. E., and Muehlenhard, C. L. (1999). "By the semi-mystical appearance of a condom": How young women and men communicate sexual consent in heterosexual situations. *The Journal of Sex Research*, 36:3, 258–272.

Kirby, D. (1984). *Sexuality education: An evaluation of programs and their effects: An executive summary.* Santa Cruz, CA: Network.

The National Campaign to Prevent Teen Pregnancy. (1998). *Campaign update*, Winter Issue. Washington, DC: Author.

Philliber, S. (1980). Socialization for childbearing. *Journal of Social Issues*, 36, 30–44.

Search Institute. (1985). *The life and family national demonstration project field experiment: Design, measures, analyses, and rationale.* Minneapolis: Author.

Vonnegut, K. (1985). *Galápagos.* New York: Delacorte.

Warren, C. (2000). Talking with your children about sex. In C. G. Waugh, W. I. Gorden, and K. M. Golden (Eds.), *Let's talk: A cognitive skills approach to interpersonal communication* (pp. 292–295). Dubuque, IA: Kendall/Hunt.

———. (1995). Parent-child communication about sex. In T. Socha and G. Stamp (Eds.), *Parents, children, and communication: Frontiers of theory and research* (pp. 173–201). Mahwah, NJ: Lawrence Erlbaum.

———. (1992). Perspectives on international sex practices and American family sex communication relevant to teenage sexual behavior in the United States. *Health Communication*, 4:2, 121–136.

Warren, C., and Neer, M. (1986). Family sex communication orientation. *Journal of Applied Communication Research*, 14:2, 86–107.

## Questions

1. After you took the FSCQ inventory, what were three things you learned about your own upbringing? If you could discuss the results with one of your parents, what would you say?

2. Assume you have, or will have, the responsibility for communicating about sex with an important child in your life. Identify three or four beliefs about sexual communication that you would try to demonstrate in your interactions with the child.

3. In your opinion, what are major factors that influence how well dating partners are able to address issues of sexuality in their own relationship? How can dating partners be persuaded of the importance of discussing sex?

# B. Friends

Friendship is clearly one of the most important contexts of interpersonal communication. Ever since childhood you have depended on friends to be your companions, listen to you, play with you, challenge you with different ideas, and teach you new things. Yet, as the articles in this section indicate, friendships are complicated. They take time, effort, and commitment. Ongoing friendships are characterized by relational maintenance behaviors such as positivity, openness, and commitment as well as by the exchange of relational currencies.

Friendship changes across the lifespan. Peers are extremely important in our early years and during adolescence. Males' development generally occurs in larger groups with changing membership. Females tend to focus on friendships with a few close individuals. As children grow up in the United States, friendship and peer acceptance become increasingly important. Less time is spent with family. High school students and traditional college students find themselves regularly surrounded with friends and potential friends; as people age, they report that it becomes harder to make new friends

In his book *Seinlanguage*, Jerry Seinfeld (1993, 159) captures the difficulty of making new friends after age 30:

> You're not interviewing, you're not looking at any new people, you're not interested in seeing any applications. They don't know the places, they don't know the food, they don't know the activities. If I'm introduced to a friendly guy at a club or a gym, it's like, "Hey look, I'm sure you're a very nice person, you seem to have a lot of potential, we're just not hiring right now."

Of course when you're a kid, you can be friends with anybody. There were almost no qualifications. If someone's in front of my house now, that's my friend, they're my friends, that's it. "Are you a grown-up. No? Great, c'mon in! Let's jump up and down on my bed!" And if you have anything in common at all—"You like cherry soda? I like cherry soda. We'll be best friends!"

Even adults may take friends for granted, but once they move to a new town, change jobs, or lose a friend, they may find it takes great effort to make new friends. A columnist writing about the difficulty of finding friends in her 40s was deluged with letters from readers reporting similar frustrations and a shared sense of estrangement (Paul 1995). Many adults said that their lack of children kept them from community connections; others believed they were outsiders because of snobbishness, their newcomer status, or regional norms. One person wrote, "I've often felt that I'm standing outside looking through a window at a party to which I wasn't invited." From a *social exchange* perspective, connected individuals do not foresee rewards in adding new friends, whereas those without friends feel the costs of being isolated all too keenly. Today many people find and maintain friends through the Internet.

In this society many people depend on their close friends for social support and companionship, whereas the extended family may fulfill these needs in other cultures. Due to the changes in U.S. families, friends are often considered part of the voluntaristic family and, as such, are seen as more important than distant blood relatives.

In his model of friendship development, Rawlins (1981) suggests that a typical friendship moves through six stages:

1. **Role-limited interaction:** Initial interactions are characterized by social roles (sets of expectations that govern how people should behave) and rules (for example, rules of greeting). Communication is extremely stylized to allow people to interact with little knowledge of one another.

2. **Friendly relations:** This corresponds to Knapp and Vangelisti's experimenting stage in romantic relationship development. It is, in a sense, a "testing of the waters."

3. **Moves toward friendship:** In this stage, communication is less role-bound. Invitations to engage are extended by one person and voluntarily accepted by the other. Neither party has the right to place demands on the other. Rawlins suggests that people begin creating "jointly constructed views" of the world. Talk focuses on the similarity of attitudes and values and on the exploration of differences in opinions.

4. **Nascent friendship:** Friendship is crystallized in this stage. People choose to participate in a wider range of activities and topics of conversation as they give birth to a real friendship.

5. **Stabilized friendship:** The key element of this stage is trust. Trusting behavior is any behavior that increases one person's vulnerability to another. For example, when you reveal personal information to a friend, you are engaging in trusting behavior. Trustworthy behavior requires protecting the vulnerability of the other.

6. **Waning friendship:** Friendships may wane because of neglect, major violations of trust, competing demands on time, lack of support from significant others, and numerous other factors. In terms of communication, a waning friendship may be characterized by autonomy rather than by togetherness or by restraint where honesty was once the rule.

As you read this section, consider how your own friendships have developed as you have matured. Has what you value in a friend changed? How have work or school commitments affected your ability to maintain or make new friends? How have factors, such as gender, age, or new technologies, impacted your friendship networks?

### References

Paul, M. (1995, August 20). Lonely? Don't feel like the lone ranger. *Chicago Tribune*, 6: 1, 6.

Rawlins, W. (1981). Friendship as a communicative achievement: A theory and an interpretative analysis of verbal reports. Doctoral dissertation, Temple University.

Seinfeld, J. (1993). *Seinlanguage*. New York: Bantam Books. ✦

# 39
# Being There for Friends

*William K. Rawlins*

In all stages of life, people rely upon their friends for help, support, commitment, love, and acceptance. However, the definition of what makes a good friend changes with age. Children could be best buddies with someone just because they were invited to their birthday party, or shared their chocolate chip cookie at lunch. And although the feelings of affection and bonding are no less important, there are usually much more challenging and complex ways to earn friendships for adults. The maintenance of adult friendships, as discussed in this chapter, depends upon the idea of "being there" for each other.

*Rawlins suggests that "being there for friends" means different things to different individuals. Friendship research indicates individuals have varied goals for their friendships. For example, individuals with a strong focus on intimacy in their same-sex friendships exchange high levels of social support and self disclosure. They are also more likely to engage in constructive methods of resolving conflict (Sanderson, Rahm, and Beigbeder 2005). Those not seeking such strong intimacy are likely to contribute less social support and self-disclosure in their friendships.*

*The following article highlights the distinction between agentic and communal relationships. In general, agentic friendships are begun rationally or conveniently based on joint activities or projects. They are characterized by independence and maintained as long as the benefits outweigh the costs. The term* agentic *characterizes workplace friendships that are pleasant and satisfying but that fade if one member leaves. It also characterizes friendships limited to a particular activity, such as watching ballgames, playing video games, or shopping. Communal friendships, on the other hand, may develop*
 *through convenience or personal attraction and are characterized by mutual responsibilities or obligations, strong emotional attachment, and loyalty. Contact, openness, and cooperation characterize communal friendships. As you might guess, female relationships are more often communal, while male relationships are more often agentic.*

*In the following pages, Rawlins highlights the similarities and differences between male and female friendships, offering examples and explanations for how these relationships begin and are managed throughout adulthood. As you read this article, consider how your friendships have changed since you entered adulthood and ask yourself this question: What does the phrase* being there *for friends mean to you?*

### Reference

Sanderson, C. A. , Rahm, K. S., and Beigbeder, S. A. (2005). The link beween the pursuit of intimacy goals and satisfaction in close same-sex friendships: An examination of the underlying processes. *Journal of Social and Personal Relationships*, 22, 75–98.

\* \* \*

When things are on an "even keel" with family and at work, it is easy to take friends for granted, but when things go poorly or well in life, people want their friends to "be there" to talk to and to help or to celebrate. Reflecting the folk wisdom, "a friend in need is a friend indeed," and "a friend is someone who multiplies our joys and divides our sorrows," being there when needed was the measure of true friendship for these adults. Lamentably, this gift of presence, so vital for friendship, is typically metered within a larger social problematic of coordinating life structures. One's closer friends are persons that one "makes the effort" to contact regularly; one "goes out of one's way" to see them and to "stay in touch"; and they do the same. One pursues other types of friendships largely in conjunction with the common schedules, activities, and role requirements of work, neighboring or in the larger community. Network researchers have called the former type relationships of commitment and the latter, convenience (Feld, 1984).

But what is the nature of the commitment of close friends in adulthood? How is it communicatively and behaviorally accomplished, given two friends' concurrent involvement in their respective, multiple, social realms and their often conflicting needs for independence from and dependence on each other in managing their lives? With some overlap, differing commitment practices composed and expressed agentic or communal tendencies even in these adults' close friendships. And, with a few clear exceptions, the males' accounts of committed and close friendships exhibited agentic themes and the females' communal ones. Whereas both men and women expected close friends to be there to help and talk to them, by and large, they etched these needs differently in time and tangible encounters.

Mutual needs for assistance and discussion are routine matters in communal friendships. "Regular contact" means habitual as well as conscientious attempts to spend face-to-face time together as often as possible, weekly if not more frequently. In the interim, phone calls and sometimes notes or cards keep the friends abreast of evolving day-to-day concerns, moments of self-doubt, and minor or major triumphs or challenges at work or with one's children. Friends' daily lives are always sufficient grist for conversation, and whether a person "just" wants to talk or needs ready advice or relief, a close friend will "be there" for her or him. Commitment in these bonds is special precisely because it reflects a mundane and relatively continuous interweaving of lives.

Although also important in communal bonds, commitment in agentic close friendships is expressed by someone actually or potentially "coming through" when it is "really" needed, "in a pinch," "when the chips are down." Though "regular contact" is also part of such agentic commitment, the words mean something different as the time between interactions specifically devoted to the friendship may vary widely according to its circumstances. Individuals may see each other quite frequently at work, for example, yet have difficulty scheduling "quality time" or discretionary opportunities to speak or spend time together "as friends." The basic independence and separation of lives maintained in agentic friendships usually mean that "regular contact" is more drawn out in time than in communal ones and less organized around everyday concerns. Consequently, the commitment described in close agentic friendships evinces a "heroic" flavor. One feels or learns that one can count on a friend for counsel or help in moments of need, and tacitly indicates reciprocal availability. But these moments are typically conceived as transcending ordinary problems and requiring special effort on the friend's part. Ironically, this very conception may make friends less inclined to seek each other out because they may not want to admit to having such problems or to trouble the friend. Meanwhile, both friends may feel they can count on each other should a "real" need arise.

The differences between communal and agentic senses of commitment are amplified by their usual emphases on the contradictory motives of affection versus instrumentality. Communal friends envision their joint availability and obligations as growing out of caring for each other as intrinsically valued human beings within a shared relationship that comprises a worthwhile end-in-itself. Although both friends benefit from their involvement and efforts on each other's behalf, these actions do not fundamentally derive from a calculation of reciprocal return. Rather, each person views their friendship as a basic existential condition of their ongoing individually yet interdependently conducted lives such that the friend's happiness or sadness directly affects self's well-being.

The allegiance of agentic friends stems more from instrumental needs and reciprocated capacities for practical and emotional relief. Continuing affection and involvement with each other are important, but remain primarily contingent on personal availability and other priorities. Emphasizing individual freedom and rights, agentic friends dislike the concept of obligation in the sense of mutual responsibility applied to friendship. They want to avoid feeling dependent on one another, and they are not comfortable "owing" others, including friends, anything. Ironically, although this mutual stance seems to inhibit sustained integration and interconnection of lives, the intermittent quality of such friendships invokes instrumental assistance at important junctures or "out of the blue" phone calls or letters to attest to their continuity.

Despite variations in agentic and communal emphases in their practices, all of these adults' friendships required time together, either face-to-face or over the phone. Consequently, being there for one's friend usually demanded "making" or "taking time" for him or her. Time constraints were cited throughout the interviews as causing problems between friends. Kathleen's remarks are typical:

> The most trouble? I suppose that it might be time. I would have to say that ever since I had Ginny, having to share time with her and with my husband and with my job, that I find lesser and lesser time to develop or spend time with other people. And so that's probably why I find I spend more time with people like at work and stuff, because they are there, you know, and I can talk to them during the day.

Time limitations compel persons to revise their conceptions or expectations of friendship and/or combine them with work affiliations. But availability due to lack of time can find friends adversely interpreting each other's actions, according to James:

> When we're in a bad mood, it's easy to think that if the other person doesn't have the time or take the time to listen, then that means we're of less value as a friend. And that snowballs to the point where you think this person isn't interested in you.

> Um, the biggest problem I have, I guess, in friendly relationships is making the time away from everything else that we do to, to cultivate it, to make sure the person understands that I care, and that I'm willing to listen. Sometimes you have to schedule that, you know, just like everything else. And if you approach it as an effort and as, I don't want to say as work, but it takes a lot of effort, I think, to make sure that you're maintaining a friendship.

The adult time crunch can make developing or cultivating friendships resemble another job, requiring scheduling and effort to make them "work." Even when one's basic premise is caring, as James implies above, the pressures of larger social configurations convert the words describing friendships into instrumental and cost effective predicates. Consider David's comments:

> Probably competition for time certainly strains commitments, even though I think friends have to understand. I don't think friends demand the time, but I think when you're caught up and getting on with your lives and all the other things that go on around you that take time, the time that you don't have available for your friends I think can eventually become a strain. It's an investment of time.

David's references to "competition for" and "investment of time," coupled with James' previous allusions to a friend's "interest" and "valuing" call to mind a principle of economics that, "The rate of interest is the price of time" (Hicks, quoted in Brown, 1959, p. 273). How much time can someone afford to "invest" in a friend? Might that time be better "spent" elsewhere, in effect, yielding a better return on one's investment? How does one justify "interest" in another person for his or her own sake within such a dominant utilitarian calculus? The prevalence of such language in "accounting for" problems among friends reveals how thoroughly economic assumptions permeate these persons' thinking about friendship, even when attempting communal ones, and ultimately how little control they have over their schedules as enactments of the values of their surrounding social systems.

Consequently, friends must understand their constricted availability to each other throughout adulthood. But resentments persist and dissolve attachments when supposedly close friends "let me down when I needed help," or could not "be there" or "show up" for weddings, anniversaries, reunions, or parties. They also begrudge friends who do not understand why they cannot "make it" to specific activities, events, or functions. People end up judging their friends' availability according to a combination of negotiated expectations, relational precedents, and the priorities and associated schedules of their respective life structures. Even so, because of the definitive anticipations and instances of close friends either being there or not during distressing or joyous moments, crucial events in one's adult life usually involve one's "true" friends and pivotal events affecting friends will rearrange one's own endeavors. . . .

## References

Brown, N. O. (1959). *Life against death*. Middletown, Conn.: Wesleyan University Press.

Feld, N. (1984). The structured use of personal associates. *Social Forces*, 62, 640–652.

## Questions

1. Would you characterize your friendships as generally agentic or communal? Describe one example of each, focusing specifically on how communication patterns reflect the nature of the friendship.

2. Develop a rationale for the importance of communal friendship across the life span.

3. If one person characterizes her or his friendship differently than the other characterizes it (agentic versus communal), how might that affect their relationship? Give an example.

# 40
# Urban Tribes

*Ethan Watters*

**A**t a time in which the age of first marriage is increasing and more individuals are choosing not to marry, the rise of a large group of young single adults is shifting the conception of friendship. No longer do the majority of twentysomethings split off into married couples and romantic pairs, experiencing friendships through a partnered lens; friendship and social life is enacted in groups, frequently a continuation of the collegiate experience. Although some group members may be partnered, the greatest numbers are single. Often these young adults are living in urban areas, great distances from their families of origin, leaving them highly dependent on friends for social life as well as care and support. For most of them, this is life between families; for others, it is the beginning of the rest of their relational life.

This generation of 20–30 year olds is the first to use web-based social networking to make friends and find business associates. They go online to websites named Friendster, Tribe.net, and Linked-Into and encounter opportunities to build networks of friends. In many cases the online connections develop into face-to-face connections. In addition, other opportunities to meet new people appear through speed-dating services, social networking parties, and interest groups formed around interests such as volleyball or wine tasting.

Although this social phenomenon has been evolving for over a decade, it became a recognized reality with the publication of Urban Tribes, a title coined by its author, Ethan Watters. Attempting to capture this group experience, he writes: "We were a curious new breed, those of us treading water in the cities—outside of our families of origin and seemingly unwilling to begin families for ourselves. We were interested in (often devoted to) our careers and avocations, but we stayed strangely off the social map in other ways" (Watters 2003, 19). Moving from analyzing his own personal tribe, Watters moved on to explore this friendship phenomenon in cities across the country. Throughout his travels he uncovered a wide range of very different tribes, but most provided a place to meet the needs of friends, almost like an extended family. Conversations are a primary group endeavor.

Although novel in title, the "urban tribe" is not new in concept. These small societies formed through friendships and mutual interests are common in densely populated urban areas, where people come to find their own community in a sea of diversity. Using examples and feedback from his research on such groups, Watters explains how these societies collaborate, form, and maintain themselves. The establishment of rituals and the creation of individual roles are key elements of each tribe's survival and management, which Watters depicts in great detail. In addition, he highlights the concept of a group's "clustering coefficient" or a way to tell if your friendship circle is diffuse or dense. Finally, Watters summarizes his findings with a discussion of patterns in tribe characteristics and behavior—which proved consistent even across cultures—revealing a fascinating new perspective on the nature of friendship networks in urban areas.

You may or may not have experience with such groups but, as you read this chapter, ask yourself the following question: What communication-related benefits or costs may arise from active social involvement in an urban tribe?

## Reference

Watters, E. (2003). *Urban Tribes: A Generation Redefines Friendship, Family, and Commitment*. New York: Bloomsbury.

\* \* \*

**F**lush with the idea that I had discovered in my urban tribe something true about my generation, I rushed the idea into print. . . .

Fear of being beaten to the punch was not the only reason I worked quickly. I was also anxious to share the idea, because it seemed like good news. The idea that my group of friends comprised more than the sum of the parts represented a dawning realization that my life, which had so often felt like a talentless, improvisational dance, might have more of a structure than I had perceived. To be in your thirties and still be feeling your way along, still figuring things out, was sad and disconcerting, so I held tenaciously to any notion that suggested my life had momentum.

Unfortunately, in my haste to share the idea, I got some things wrong. Writing for the esteemed *New York Times Magazine*, I described the urban tribe as "a tight group with unspoken roles and hierarchies, whose members thought of each other as 'us' and the rest of the world as 'them.'" I was soon to learn that this summary was fundamentally inaccurate. . . .

Through the Internet, my article on tribes had been shared from friend to friend around the world. Although most of the people who contacted me were from the United States, people e-mailed me to tell me about their tribes in India, England, Australia, Canada, and even Karachi. Many of my correspondents expressed surprise that other people were living like they were, in small societies formed by friendships and mutual interests. . . .

Because there were things about tribes that made them hard to see from the outside, they were illusive as a national trend. Tribes did not have membership rolls or official meetings. No parent or mentor had taught or encouraged the formation of these groups. No organization sponsored the national convention of urban tribes. . . . Because there was no recognized social trend toward this behavior, the sensation of being in such a social entity was singular. "We thought we were the only ones" was a common refrain of my correspondents. . . .

While some urban tribes began through specific activities or pre-existing friendships, for most it was a puzzle to figure out why or how they have formed into a group. Many people who wanted to tell me about their tribes had trouble tracing the origins. The beginnings of tribes often seemed to be happenstance—roommate ads answered or acquaintances struck up in cafés. "Outsiders who see our tight bond often ask us, 'How did you all meet?'" wrote Kevin from Dallas. "It's difficult to answer because there was no specific circumstances that led to the formation of our tribe. We became friends through a variety of connections, such as friends of friends. Somehow we were magnetically drawn to each other.". . .

Others also reported that the strength of the bond within the group could not be adequately explained through either the connections that brought them together in the first place or any shared interests or avocations. "No activity or trait defines us," Chuck from Cleveland wrote after I asked him what was unique about his group. "It's just a wonderful collection of individuals who genuinely care about each other. We ourselves are the only cool thing.". . .

Those who wrote to tell me about their tribes were nearly all college educated. I had predicted this, because the marriage delay was greatest among people who stayed in school longer, especially those who went for postgraduate degrees and the demanding careers that lead from them. It made sense to me that the more time one spent outside a traditional family, the more likely it was that one would form a social entity to take its place.

In general the groups that formed from college (or sometimes high school) friendships tended to be more demographically uniform in age, race, and income. The groups that formed later, during the swirl of adult city life, could sometime match the remarkable diversity of those communities. Chris, a graphic designer in L.A., marveled at his group's mix. "When we go out to dinner we look like the UN," he wrote of his group of fifteen. "There are blacks, Italians, Thais, Filipinos, Mexicans, Colombians, Jews, Indians. Nobody seems to care about anyone else's background.". . .

It occurred to me that I might find meaningful commonalities among the tribes by examining the roles people within them took on. At first this appeared promising, for my correspondents identified dozens of roles within their tribes. Interestingly, few of my correspondents identified one person in their groups as the leader, de facto or otherwise. However, there was almost always at least one "organizer" (sometimes called "mother figure," "party planner," or "social director"), who appeared to earn this designation over time by successfully bringing people together or putting in the time to plan the logistics of trips and gatherings. Assuming this person was the chief of the tribe would be wrong. Having held the organizer's role off and on in my own tribe, I knew that from personal experience. The role of organizer commanded little special respect or privileges. If you wanted to be the one to go to the grocery store to gather food, or if you wanted to manage the e-mail list and make the phone calls to tell people where to show up, the role of organizer was yours for the taking. . . .

There was often another group member (usually but not always a woman) who acted as "advice giver" (called by some the group "therapist" or "shoulder to cry on"), who would console and counsel friends, particularly on the subject of romantic relationships. In one case this person was called "Switzerland" because he not only counseled individuals but also had a knack for smoothing rifts between members. Other roles people identified included "innovators," who came up with new projects for the group, and "assistant in charge of details," who followed the directions of the organizer. Other roles identified by those who wrote me included "comedian" and "deal negotiators," who would step forward when someone in the group needed help negotiating a promotion or a home purchase. There was "the worrier," who kept the group from doing dangerous things, and "the chaperone," who, in a slightly different manner, helped individuals make the choices they wouldn't regret the next morning. Women sometimes identified certain female friends as their "guardians" or "bodyguards," who could, usually just by their presence, ward off unwanted advances or make them feel safer when exploring new areas of town or unfamiliar social situations. There was also sometimes a firebrand, or "life of the party," someone other people wanted to be around because he or she could draw people out of their shells and milk the most from social situations.

There were often two or three "children" in a group. These were not literal children, but adults who seemed always in trouble or in need. "The cynic" seemed to be . . . one variation of "the child." The cynic had the disgrun-

tled demeanor of a two-year-old, and other group members seemed to enjoy spending large amounts of time trying to improve the cynic's mood. While you might think that groups would avoid such personalities, these "children" appeared to offer something of a group activity. The "child" would show up on a camping trip having managed to pack only hot chocolate mix. While such habits were exasperating, providing the "child" with food and shelter for the weekend made for a challenging, and ultimately enjoyable, group project. The organizer and the assistants in charge of details would rally and prove their acumen. This challenge was made more meaningful by the stories told later about the weekend. Often it was the boneheaded actions of the "children" that became the groups' most beloved stories to retell.

As I studied people's descriptions of these roles, some enticing patterns emerged. It was clear that there needed to be a certain balance between some roles. There were no groups with all cynics or, for that matter, all organizers or all advice givers. Some general ratios became apparent. The organizers, assistants in charge of details, and advice givers usually outnumbered the children and cynics by at least a four-to-one ratio. Christina, from Raleigh, North Carolina, described such a balance: "Libby is the hostess. Mark always cooks huge dinners. Sylvia is the cruise director, always with an eye on the events calendar to rally the tribe to attend certain cool events. Jenny hosts annual Christmas parties. And then there's Bill, who shows up to everything with his dog and a six-pack.". . .

It seemed to me, however, that the fact people with tribes took on roles at all was something that made these groups of friends distinct. It appeared that taking on a role of some sort allowed each individual to effect a little extra gravity on the group. The gravity manifested by the organizers, those who took the time to pull people together, was the most obvious. But all the other roles functioned similarly. That people took on roles encouraged my suspicion that these groups were not just random collections of friends but functioning social entities.

# Clustering Around the Core

There was another way these groups tended to differ from other, looser groups of friends one might have had in college or at other points in life—they had what social scientists call extremely high "clustering coefficients." This is the idea: You take all the people in your social circle and add up all the possible connections that could exist if absolutely every one of your friends had a personal relationship with everyone else in your social circle. Next you add up the number of people in your social circle that actually do have a personal relationship with someone you know. Your group's clustering coefficient is the number of people who actually know each other divided by the total number who could possibly know each other. So if you have six friends there is a possibility of a total number of fourteen connections within that group. If all fourteen connections actually exist, then you have fourteen divided by fourteen, or one. Your social circle couldn't be more clustered. If ten of those fourteen connections exist, your group has a clustering coefficient of 0.71. The closer your coefficient is to one, the more friends your friends share.

As I learned about tribes across the country, it became clear that their clustering coefficients were quite high. The individual friendships that made up these tribes could not be understood, I came to believe, outside the complexity of these interlocking friendships. Try to examine a single friendship while ignoring the other interlocking relationships the friends share, and the thing you wanted to examine might vanish. It was the high clustering coefficients that kept some of these relationships together. . . .

. . . Many people told me similar stories of maintaining ties through their tribes with people they otherwise would not have had as friends. High clustering coefficients create dense groups that bond friendships—both friendships that would exist outside the groups and many more that would not. Because of intensely high clustering coefficients, friendships in tribes sometimes defy what you'd normally expect of friendships,

namely, that they are always reciprocal, positive relationships which are freely entered into and relatively freely exited from. With highly clustered groups, which friendships you are bound to often becomes as much of a group decision as a personal one. . . .

In describing the dynamics of their groups, many people also talked of tight "core groups" of four to twelve who were surrounded by "affiliate members," "stragglers," or "outliers" who might double or triple the size of the core group. Sometimes groups had ways of clearly stating who was a core member and who was not. Often this communication took the form of who was invited to certain events. . . .

. . . In terms of how membership ebbed and flowed, these groups were not cultish in the least. In fact, they seemed uniquely designed to assimilate new members and to create social situations during which new people could be mixed in with older members. What kept the clustering coefficient high was that new people would almost immediately meet all other members of the group. Over time, most of these groups appeared to have extremely porous borders, with people joining and drifting away frequently. Janice, twenty-two, a part of a thriving Oakland tribe of technoheads, learned that at the outer edges of her group, "most people are not 'forevers.' Most people come to teach us and learn from us and off they go." . . .

## Questions

1.  What do you see as advantages and/or disadvantages of a strong commitment to life within a social friendship network, or urban tribe?

2.  What communication skills would be particularly important if one is to function effectively within a strong friendship network?

Reprinted from Ethan Watters, *Urban Tribes: A Generation Redefines Friendship, Family, and Commitment.* Pp. 40–53, Copyright © 2003 by Bloomsbury. ✦

# 41

# Communication in Cross-Gender Friendships

*Lea P. Stewart, Pamela J. Cooper, Alan Stewart, and Sheryl Friedley*

From the college dormitory to the military training fields to the corporate boardroom, the intermixing of men and women of equal status and similar personal goals has resulted in the development of male-female friendships. Until recently, adult friendships were characterized as same-sex relationships, except in the cases of couple friendships. Today, as men and women study together, plan organizational strategy together, and travel together professionally, their proximity and similar status contribute to the development of cross-sex nonromantic friendship. In addition, as people marry later in life, men and women in their 20s and 30s often socialize in large mixed-sex groups, such as the urban tribes discussed in the previous chapter.

Cross-sex friendships can be very rewarding (Werking 1997) as males and females share their different perspectives and enjoy activities together. Yet, they can be stressful as these friends encounter challenges unlike those they find in same-sex friendships. In addition to the basic sexual challenge, or negotiating expectations about the role of sex in their friendship, they find themselves struggling with managing their emotional bond, given the socialization they received as children regarding male-female relationships. These friends also have to manage their public presentation because such friendships are questioned by others who assume these are romantic ties.

As the following article suggests, little research has examined these types of relationships. When research has been conducted, the emphasis has been on whether cross-sex friendships differ from romantic friendships.

Friendship research suggests that males and females describe friends similarly. That is, both males and females describe a friend as someone who is supportive, encouraging, and trustworthy, someone with whom to share intimacies and who is fun to be with (Duck and Wright 1993; Sapadin 1988). Yet research also suggests that although males and females describe a friend in similar ways, they participate in friendships differently. Thus, cross-sex friendships can be difficult to maintain.

Yet, for those people who beat the odds and manage to establish a cross-gendered friendship, there are, according to the authors of this chapter, unique ways in which they balance communication and behavior to make the relationship work. Stewart and her associates explore why cross-sex friendships occur less frequently than same-sex friendships and have shorter longevity. In examining this issue, they address the communication variables of conflict, intimacy and self-disclosure, and communicator style. The authors then illustrate strategies for change that make such friendships possible, incorporating how to avoid and/or manage the aforementioned problem areas. Finally, a brief summary wraps up the chapter.

Given the complex nature of cross-gender friendships, they take more effort and communication to maintain. As you read this piece, reflect on the male/female friendships that you have witnessed or experienced and ask yourself this question: How might conflict and self-disclosure have contributed to the success or failure of these friendships?

## References

Duck, S., and Wright, P. (1993). Examining gender differences in same-gender friendships. *Sex Roles*, 28: 1–19.

Sapadin, L. (1988). Friend and gender: Perspectives of professional men and women. *Journal of Social and Personal Relationships*, 6, 387–403.

Werking, K. (1997) *We're Just Good Friends: Women and Men in Nonromantic Relationships*. New York: Guilford Press.

*** *

While romantic relationships and same-sex friendships have received considerable research attention, male/female platonic friendships have not (Kaplan & Keys, 1997). This lack of research may result, in part, from the fact that societal norms discourage friendships between females and males. Think of all the movies and television shows in which the main characters begin as friends and inevitably end up in a romantic relationship. Nevertheless, platonic friendships do exist and are worthy of further examination.

As one reads the literature on cross-sex friendships (friendships between women and men), a recurrent theme seems to be the difficulty of these friendships (Rawlins, 1993). As Swain (1992) says:

> Since cross-sex friendship is not a clearly defined or expected social relationship it is often interpreted in terms of heterosexual love relationships. For example, many heterosexual love relationships begin as platonic friendships, thus promoting a view of cross-sex friendships as a stage of development in the coupling process, rather than as a legitimate relationship in and of itself. When an adolescent develops a friendship with a cross-sex friend, family members often tease, hint at, or praise the person for establishing a possible heterosexual dating, sexual, or love relationship. Claims that "we're just good friends" are often viewed as withholding information, or as an indication of embarrassment or bashfulness about the sexual content of the relationship. (p. 154)

In general, cross-sex friendships occur less frequently than same-sex friendships and have shorter longevity (Swain, 1992). Males report more cross-sex friendships than females (Rawlins, 1992). Sapadin (1988) reports that men rate their cross-sex friendships as more enjoyable and nurturing than their same-sex ones, although they rate both similar in perceived intimacy. In contrast, women rate their same-sex friendships as more intimate, enjoyable, nurturing, and higher in overall quality than their cross-sex ones. Further, they feel much more nurtured by their female friends, in both personal and career areas than by male friends (Sapadin, 1988, p. 401).

Why are cross-sex friendships difficult to achieve and to maintain? Several possibilities come to mind. The first one is the one we've already alluded to: society's lack of acceptance of this type of friendship. Rawlins (1993) suggests that cross-sex friendships are socially "deviant." Often others simply don't believe the "just good friends" explanation of cross-sex friendship.

In addition, sexual attraction is often present in platonic friendships, especially for men (Kaplan & Keys, 1997). Because our societal norm for friendship is same-sex friendship, we may have difficulty understanding how a male and female can be just good friends, particularly in light of what we know about the differences between male same-sex friendships and female same-sex friendships.

This brings us to a second possibility, differing attitudes toward friendship. Remember our earlier discussion about same-sex friendships. In terms of intimacy, females tend to show intimacy through self-disclosure, while males are more likely to base their intimate friendships on shared activities. Another difference in attitudes relates to romantic involvement and sexual activity. Women often believe that men's motive for friendship is sexual and are, therefore, reluctant to form friendships with men if they have no desire for a more romantic involvement (Rose, 1985). A final factor influencing cross-sex friendships concerns emotional needs. If, as our research suggests, men look to women rather than to other men to meet their emotional needs (Rand & Levinger, 1979), and women think men cannot meet their emotional needs and so form female friendships (Gilligan, 1982), then a cross-sex friendship may be difficult to maintain.

Closely related to the different perceptions of how best to meet emotional needs, Rubin (1983) finds that males have a more difficult time recognizing the feelings of another person. This is particularly true when the other person is female. Women, on the other hand, are better able to recognize others' emotions. This ability is evidenced by the fact that women use more affectionate touch, expressions of empathy, and feedback after disclosure than men (Buhrke & Fuqua, 1987). As Ivy and Backlund (1994) suggest, differences in the recognition of feelings can create problems for cross-sex friends if an imbalance is perceived in the amount of emotional support one derives from the relationship.

## Communication

Conflict, intimacy and self-disclosure, and communicator style have been studied in cross-sex friendships. We will examine each of these issues.

### Conflict

Every relationship has conflict. However, in some ways, men and women handle conflict differently. If conflict or tension occurs in cross-sex friendships, women are more likely to blame themselves for relational failures and credit others for relational successes (Martin & Nivens, 1987). Also, if problems arise, women are more likely than men to end the relationship. Men are more likely to ignore relational problems by focusing on positive aspects of the relationship.

A recent study on deception (Powers, 1993) sheds some light on why females might choose to end a relationship that is difficult. Women tend to be more sensitive to relational deception than men. In addition, women evaluate the character and competence of a deceiver lower than do men. If a woman discovers deception has occurred, she may decide to end the relationship because deception is so unacceptable to her. (See also Levine, McCornack, & Avery, 1992).

### Intimacy and Self-Disclosure

Dindia and Allen (1992) examined more than 200 studies on self-disclosure and found that women self-disclose more than men. It is important to take into account whether the conversational partners are male or female since women disclose more than men in same-sex dyads but do not disclose more than men when they are talking with a man.

In terms of disclosure in cross-sex friendships, men report that they disclose more intimate information to women than they do to other men. Women, however, claim they disclose more intimate information to other women (Aukett, Richie, & Mill, 1988). In addition, there are some interesting differences in the nature of disclosure in cross-sex friendships compared with disclosure in same-sex friendships (Hacker, 1981). Specifically, unlike self-disclosure in same-sex friendships, there is no significant difference in the amount of disclosure between men and women in cross-sex friendships. Instead, differences emerge in the nature of the self-disclosure between men and women. For example, when talking to female friends, men tend to confide more about their weaknesses while they *enhance* their strengths (Stephen & Harrison, 1985). Women tend to confide about their weaknesses and *conceal* their strengths. . . .

These two different disclosure patterns are reflective of common gender ideology. Men are expected to assume a superior or dominant position through disclosure, so they include and even enhance their strengths when they confide in women about their weaknesses. Women are expected to facilitate the disclosure process by playing a subordinate role in which they confide only their weaknesses and discuss none of their strengths. This superior-subordinate role relationship often found in cross-sex conversation indicates that women may be dominated in cross-sex conversation while men are more likely to dominate the conversation (Rubin, Perse, & Barbato, 1988; Tannen, 1990).

Goldsmith and Dun (1997) asked college students to respond to typical problems encountered by their friends, including failing an exam, registration problems, or being "dumped by a boyfriend or girlfriend." Contrary to the stereotype that women are concerned with emotions while men are concerned with problem solving, when asked to talk about a problem both men and women spent the same amount of time talking about what action to take. Men, however, did use more time to discuss the problem and more of that talk dismissed or denied the other person's problem. Neither men nor women talked much about emotions but focused more on the problem presented.

## Communicator Style

*Communicator style* refers to "the way one verbally and paraverbally interacts to signal how literal meaning should be taken, interpreted, filtered, or understood" (Norton, 1978, p. 99). Such characteristics as dominant, animated, relaxed, attentive, open, and friendly often are used to describe a person's communicator style, and these characteristics contribute to a person's effectiveness in the communication process.

When men and women are asked to describe their own communicator styles, they report minimal differences (Staley & Cohen, 1988). For example, of all the variables that constitute communicator style, women perceive themselves as more animated than men, and men perceive themselves as more precise than women. Both men and women rate themselves similarly on all other aspects of communicator style (Montgomery & Norton, 1981). Thus, both men and women claim they have more similarities than differences in their communicator style. In addition, both men and women report similar self-perceptions concerning stylistic characteristics considered to be indicators of effective communication.

Although men and women claim that they use a similar communicator style, their actual behavior is perceived differently. Women generally use a communicator style that others consider attentive and open, but men are more likely to use a style perceived by others as dominant, relaxed, and dramatic (Montgomery & Norton, 1981; Tannen, 1990). These perceived communicator styles coincide with gender stereotypes. For example, as we discussed earlier in this chapter, females are perceived to be facilitators of communication. Both attentiveness (letting other people know they are being heard) and openness (receptivity to communication) facilitate the interpersonal communication process. Being dominant (taking charge of the interaction), dramatic (manipulating verbal and nonverbal cues to highlight or understate content), and relaxed (anxiety-free) convey control in the communication process—a control often associated with status and power.

Most research that examines the communicator style actually used by men and women in cross-sex friendships focuses primarily on men's use of dominance as a means of controlling the communication. Specifically, this dominance includes men talking more than women, men receiving more positive evaluations for their performance in dialogue from both men and women, and perceptions of greater male influence (Berger, Rosenholtz, & Zelditch, 1980; Tannen, 1990). But dominance may be affected by the other person's level of dominance. Davis and Gilbert (1989) found that when high-dominant women were paired with low-dominant men, the women took a leadership role 71 percent of the time. However, when high-dominant women were paired with high-dominant men, the women assumed the leadership role only 31 percent of the time. Thus, high-dominant men are somewhat more likely to become leaders than high-dominant women.

Language choice in conversations between cross-sex friends also indicates differences in perceptions of male and female communicator styles. In general, there is a tendency for females to judge verbs used in interpersonal communication with friends as more emotional than men do; in contrast, males tend to judge verbs used in interpersonal communication with friends as more reflective of control (Thompson, Hatchett, & Phillips, 1981). For example, a [woman] may characterize her own behavior toward a man as protecting him (intending to communicate positive emotions), but she may be surprised when he responds to her actions in terms of the control he perceives her communication conveys. For a man, protecting may imply that the protector is stronger and the person needing protection is weaker....

## Implications and Consequences of Gender in Friendships

In examining friendship, one observation is apparent: traditional gender ideologies associated with male and female communication remain relatively consistent in friendships. In general, females disclose more and are perceived as using a communicator style that is facilitative and expressive. Males disclose less and are perceived as using a communicator style that is seen as controlling and instrumental.

Within same-sex friendships, women are more likely to focus on topics related to people: self, family, and friends. Female friends encourage disclosure in their interactions and provide a supportive communication climate to facilitate disclosure. Expressive and facilitative behaviors are typically associated with traditional gender stereotypes for women. It is not surprising, then, that these behaviors are prevalent in female interactions and are often the focus for the study of communication among women. Men are more likely to focus on topics related to status, power, and competition. They may avoid rather than facilitate disclosure, usually to control the focus and direction of the interaction. These functions are consistent with gender stereotypes for men.

Many men and women also continue to maintain traditional gender ideologies as communicators in cross-sex friendships. Many men tend to use communication behaviors that reinforce images of power, status, and control, while women tend to use communication behaviors that reinforce images of expressivity and facilitation. Although men both initiate and receive more verbal communication in cross-sex friendships, the participants seem to compromise on certain topics. In conversations among college undergraduates, men tend to speak less about competition and physical aggression, while women tend to speak less about home and family than they would in same-sex groups (Aires, 1987). In cross-sex friendships, women initiate more topics (facilitation), but men decide which of those topics will be discussed at length (control). In cross-sex friendships, men's topics and language choices are more task-oriented (instrumental), and women's topics and language choices are more personal and emotional (expressive). Women generally encourage disclosure (facilitation), and men are more likely to avoid disclosure (control). When men and women do disclose, men disclose strengths and conceal weaknesses (superiority), while women disclose weaknesses and conceal their strengths (subordination).

These communication behaviors reinforce traditional gender stereotypes from both men and women.

# Strategies for Change

Given our changing society, corresponding change in the basic interpersonal relationship of friendship is inevitable. The mobility of our population makes it likely that you will initiate, maintain, and terminate both same-sex and cross-sex friendships many times throughout your life. While these social changes reflect the quantity of friendships you may develop in a lifetime, the quality of those relationships is the far more important issue to consider.

A growing shift away from traditional masculine and feminine gender ideologies is beginning to change the nature of our interpersonal relationships by introducing ambiguity and uncertainty into our friendships. We need to create ways to cope with the evolving roles available to women and men because of changing social conditions, and we should be willing to redefine and renegotiate changes in the roles typically associated with friendship. Effective communication in our friendships will allow us to negotiate changing behaviors that can enhance relationship satisfaction (Petronio, 1982). Consider the following suggestions to facilitate adaptation and change in your friendships.

## Develop a Supportive Climate for Change

Because any change in relationships carries with it an implicit message of dissatisfaction from the one seeking change, it is important that one or both parties in a friendship avoid feeling defensive or threatened by the possibility of change. Using communication that creates a supportive climate establishes a positive context for change. Likewise, viewing change as an opportunity to create a mutually satisfying relationship rather than as an attack or a negative assessment of current definition of the relationship is essential to the process of change. For example, someone who asks a housemate to do more of the housework may believe that their relationship is very positive but that more active participation from the housemate in doing household chores would give them more time to spend in social activities together.

If you find yourself in a relationship that you want to change, try to use communication strategies that encourage your friends to describe their feelings about your relationship and their role in your friendship. Suggest a willingness on your part to cooperate in a mutual problem-solving orientation that will help establish a communication climate supportive of change. Do not judge or evaluate feelings; rather, describe or attempt to understand those feelings. Do not imply your superior ability to define change, but emphasize equal participation by both parties in this process. Do not manipulate or control the defining and negotiation process; instead, approach it as a mutually directed process involving both parties in the relationship. Creating a defensive communication climate rather than a supportive one will only serve as a barrier to negotiating relational change. . . .

### Encourage Effective Disclosure Patterns

Earlier we noted differences in disclosure patterns for males and females. Women traditionally tend to disclose about self and about personal topics for the purpose of serving expressive and affiliate needs. Men tend to disclose about task- or goal-oriented topics for the purpose of serving instrumental needs. Perhaps one of the greatest frustrations expressed by women in cross-sex friendships is that men do not disclose on the expressive or feeling level. While men may find it difficult to alter the nature of their disclosure, they may become comfortable disclosing about self in interpersonal relationships where trust has been established.

Since men appreciate this type of disclosure from women in relationships, men obviously value it. Men may strive to share their feelings more openly with their close friends when increased disclosure is appropriate, and women may facilitate and positively reinforce such disclosure in their relationships.

Women may also respect men's desire to refrain from disclosure. As long as the absence of disclosure is an indication of satisfaction with the relationship and not a control tactic, men's lack of disclosure should not be criticized. Tavris (1992) suggests that women appear to: "be better than men at intimacy because intimacy is defined as what women do; talk, express feelings, disclose personal concerns. Intimacy is rarely defined as sharing activities, being helpful, doing useful work, or enjoying companionable silence. Because of this bias, men rarely get credit for the kinds of loving actions that are more typical of them" (p. 100).

### Communicator Style Awareness

As we examined friendship, we noted some differences between men and women in their communicator styles. Women generally initiate topics in an attempt to facilitate conversation. Men may subtly control interaction because they often choose the topics that will be discussed more fully during the course of the conversation. Women use verbal and nonverbal turn-yielding cues to facilitate the continuation of interaction with men, but men often use avoidance strategies to control the continuation or discontinuation of a conversation. Women tend to be more adept at encoding and decoding the nonverbal cues that are related to expressiveness. Men tend to use a style that enhances the instrumental functions within a relationship.

Although the traditional male-female relationship in most communication situations has reflected male dominance and female subordination, these traditional roles are changing. Any power structure in a relationship may be satisfying if it is negotiated by the people involved. Examine the power structures in your friendships and assess your satisfaction with them.

Relationships that reflect patterns of communication based on inequality and difference are said to be *complementary* in nature. Much like a parent-child relationship, complementary patterns of communication generally imply a superior-subordinate relationship. Relationships that reflect patterns of communication based on equality and similarity are said to be *symmetrical* in nature, such as among peers who form friendships based on equality. For example, one person in a relationship may be responsible for organizing social engagements outside the home while the other is responsible for organizing the daily activities within the home. While the complementary pattern of communication may be closer to traditional gender stereotypes, where men dominate and women are subordinate, the symmetrical pattern of communication is more closely aligned with the independent or nontraditional relationships. In these relationships, all participants are committed to growth and change in the relationship based on the recognition that there will be equal input from everyone into that growth process.

These two patterns of communication establish clearly dichotomous categories of power in relationships. The reality, however, is that most relationships probably reflect both of these power structures at various times and on various issues. Rather than using only complementary or only symmetrical patterns of communication, consider the benefits of using both at given times in your relationship. Consider a variety of communication options so that no person is superior or subordinate all the time. For example, in an apartment, one of the roommates may buy the food and do most of the cooking while another pays the bills and is responsible for cleaning the kitchen. In this instance, both of them serve the instrumental function of decision maker at different times and concerning different decisions. At the same time, symmetrical patterns of communication based on equality in a relationship should become apparent. Relationships that employ a combination of both complementary and symmetrical communication patterns within the relationship are said to be using a *parallel* communication pattern. Again, the key to redefining and changing a friendship is being open to a variety of communication choices, adopting a parallel pattern of communication that is both complementary and symmetrical at appropriate times and in appropriate situations.

## Summary

Interpersonal relationships found in friendships are developed, maintained, and terminated through the process of communication. Because of the intimacy that can develop in these relationships, they may provide us with the ultimate opportunity for personal satisfaction in our communication with others. Men and women, however, may communicate differently in these relationships. An examination of the communication occurring in these interpersonal relationships generally confirms the traditional gender ideologies associated with communication between men and women in other situations. Women may be more likely to use expressive and facilitative behaviors, while men may use instrumental and control strategies.

## References

Aires, E. (1987). Gender and communication. In P. Shaver & C. Hendrick (Eds.), *Sex and gender* (pp. 149–176). Newbury Park, CA: Sage.

Aukett, R., Richie, J., and Mill, K. (1988). Gender differences in friendship patterns. *Sex Roles*, 19, 57–66.

Berger, J., Rosenholtz, S. J., and Zelditch, M., Jr. (1980). Status organizing processes. In A. Inkeles et al. (Eds.), *Annual review of sociology* (pp. 479–508). Palo Alto, CA: Annual Reviews.

Buhrke, R. A., and Fuqua, D. R. (1987). Sex differences in same- and cross-sex supportive relationships. *Sex Roles*, 17, 339–351.

Davis, B., and Gilbert, L. (1989). Effect of dispositional and situational influences on women's dominance expression in mixed-sex dyads. *Journal of Personality and Social Psychology*, 57, 294–300.

Dindia, K., and Allen, M. (1992). Sex differences in disclosure: A meta-analysis. *Psychological Bulletin*, 112, 106–124.

Gilligan, C. (1982). *In a different voice: Psychological theory and women's development*. Cambridge, MA: Harvard University Press.

Goldsmith, D., and Dun, S. (1997). Sex differences and similarities in the communication of social support. *Journal of Social and Personal Relationships*, 14, 317–337.

Hacker, H. M. (1981). Blabbermouths and clams: Sex differences in self-disclosure in same-sex and cross-sex friendship dyads. *Psychology of Women Quarterly*, 5, 385–401.

Ivy, D., and Backlund, P. (1994). *Exploring gender speak: Personal effectiveness in gender communication*. New York: McGraw-Hill.

Kaplan, D., and Keys, C. H. (1997). Sex and relationship variables as predictors of sexual attraction in cross-sex platonic friendships between young heterosexual adults. *Journal of*

*Social and Personal Relationships*, 14, 191–206.

Levine, T. R., McCornack, S. A., and Avery, P. B. (1992). Sex differences in emotional reactions to discovered deception. *Communication Quarterly*, 40, 289–296.

Martin, V., and Nivens, M. K. (1987). The attributional response of males and females to noncontingent feedback. *Sex Roles*, 16, 453–462.

Montgomery, B. M., and Norton, R. W. (1981). Sex differences and similarities in communicator style. *Communication Monographs*, 48, 121–132.

Norton, R. W. (1978). Foundation of a communicator style construct. *Human Communication Research*, 4, 99–112.

Petronio, S. S. (1982). The effect of interpersonal communication on women's family role satisfaction. *Western Journal of Speech Communication*, 46, 208–222.

Powers, W. (1993). The effects of gender and consequence upon perceptions of deceivers. *Communication Quarterly*, 41, 328–337.

Rand, M., and Levinger, N. J. (1979). Implicit theories of relationship: An intergenerational student. *Journal of Personality and Social Psychology*, 37, 645–661.

Rawlins, W. K. (1992). *Friendship matters: Communication, dialectics, and the life course.* Hawthorne, NY: Aldine de Gruyter.

———. (1993). Communication in cross-sex friendships. In L. P. Arliss and D. J. Borisoff (Eds.), *Women and men communicating: Challenges and changes* (pp. 51–70). Fort Worth, TX: Harcourt Brace Jovanovich.

Rose, S. M. (1985). Same- and cross-sex friendships and the psychology of homosociality. *Sex Roles*, 12, 63–74.

Rubin, L. B. (1983). *Intimate strangers: Men and women together.* New York: Harper and Row.

Rubin, R. B., Perse, E. M., and Barbato, C. S. (1988). Conceptualization and measurement of interpersonal communication motives. *Human Communication Research*, 14, 602–627.

Sapadin, L. A. (1988). Friendship and gender: Perspectives of professional men and women. *Journal of Social and Personal Relationships*, 5, 387–403.

Staley, C. C., and Cohen, J. L. (1988). Communicator style and social style: Similarities and differences between the sexes. *Communication Quarterly*, 36, 192–202.

Stephen, T. D., and Harrison, T. M. (1985). Gender, sex-role identity, and communication style: A Q-sort analysis of behavioral differences. *Communication Research Reports*, 2, 53–61.

Swain, S. (1992). Men's friendships with women: Intimacy, sexual boundaries, and the informant role. In P. Nardi (Ed.), *Men's friendships* (pp. 153–172). Newbury Park, CA: Sage.

Tannen, D. (1990). *You just don't understand: Men and women in conversation.* New York: William Morrow.

Tavris, C. (1992). *The mismeasure of women.* New York: Simon and Schuster.

Thompson, E. G., Hatchett, P., and Phillips, J. L. (1981). Sex differences in the judgment of interpersonal verbs. *Psychology of Women Quarterly*, 5, 523–531.

# Questions

1. Think of a cross-gendered friendship that is close to you (either your own or a friend's), and discuss some of the benefits and challenges of that relationship.

2. Analyze your own cross-sex friendships in terms of conflict, intimacy, self-disclosure, and communication styles.

3. Interview two persons, ages 50 or older, and ask them what they learned about having cross-gender friendships when they were young adults. Also, ask them to describe characteristics of a current cross-gender friendship in which they are a participant.

# C. Technology

Every year new communication technologies expand your interaction possibilities for interaction. Personal computers, Palm Pilots, BlackBerries, and cellular telephones serve as lynchpins of everyday business communication. Many friendships are maintained through instant messaging and text messaging. Personal information about acquaintances or friends may be found on their blogs. Family pictures and news circulate on e-mail. Regardless of how impersonal you may believe these technologies are, there is no question that they will continue to have a profound impact on human communication.

Computer-mediated communication (CMC) is critical to any discussion of new technologies and interpersonal interaction. Currently, the following descriptors distinguish CMC from face-to-face communication: it is text-based, primarily linguistic, asynchronous or synchronous, potentially anonymous, and lacking nonverbal and/or standard social cues. These characteristics have made CMC an attractive alternative to interactions that would normally require physical proximity, real time, or a certain amount of risk or money. Users can "talk" without disclosing their names or embarrassing themselves or their families, all on the safety of their screens. Online status, gender, physical appearance, body position, speech patterns, facial expressions, and dress all take a backseat to linguistic expression. Internet "virtual communities" have sprung up, allowing people around the world to discuss anything from alcoholic addiction to wedding etiquette.

As communication technology proliferates, some questions beg a response: How does interpersonal CMC differ from face-to-face communication on a socioemotional level? Which members of different social groups choose to use CMC as an interpersonal medium? Why do they use it and how? Do characteristics of the CMC channel itself promote or give rise to any relational phenomena?

Not only do individuals respond to each other, but entire interpersonal communities are created through CMC. Members may join the community for the sense of connectedness it provides or for the information available through its members.

Communities depend on the regularity and commitment of members. To form a CMC community, "A core of people must believe in the possibility of community and keep coming back to that amid the emotional storms in order for the whole loosely coupled group to hold together at all" (Rheingold 1993, 53). Today communities come together around issues of interpersonal social support and knowledge exchange. Parents of autistic children will find support and informational websites, adult children whose parents suffer from Alzheimer's will find the same.

Concerns are growing about personal dependence on these new technologies as they become increasingly pervasive. Whether by requirement or choice, some people appear unable to separate from their technology. Organizational relationships are changing. Corporate employees report living in a 24/7 world in which they are continuously accessible to a member of their organization; e-mails arrive at 9 P.M. requesting a report at tomorrow's 8:30 A.M. morning meeting, and managers expect employees to carry their company cell phone on vacation "in case of a problem." Teachers and parents e-mail each other, and online grade books and class websites provide parents with continuous access to information about their child's school work and classroom life. As one parent states, "This is much more dependable than hoping your kids bring something home in their backpack" (Guernsey 2001).

The process of making friends is being transformed. Many college students meet new friends in cyberspace rather than in classes or dormitories. For example, Facebook.com has contributed to the development of networks of friends across the country and the globe. Even students on the same campus may interact online for weeks before ever having a face-to-face conversation, meeting only after they have seen their friend's photo, read his or her information profile, and chatted about everything from mutual acquaintances to religion and politics. Sites such as Friendster.com serve the postcollege-age generations in their search for new relationships; members of urban tribes attribute some of their tribes' development to online relationships. Participants in these exchanges interact in "netspeak" translating letter configurations such as CTN, GG, or BBL fluently or relying on EmoteMail to convey affect visually (Angesleva and Reynolds 2005).

Ten years ago such topics would not be included in a text of this nature, but today the key issue is the extent of individual's dependence on such technology. Some experts believe people can become addicted to continuous access to their e-mail, cell phones, or other interactional technologies. For example, some rural campsites report a drop in the number of visitors as well as a reduction of time spent on site because visitors wish to return to their Internet and cell phone access (Canfield 2005).

In her thoughtful essay addressing how computers change the way users' think, MIT professor Sherry Turkle argues that computerization has impacted everything from an understanding of privacy, to taking things at "interface value," to the sharing of feelings. She concludes, "If we take the computer as a carrier of a way of knowing, a way of seeing the world and our place in it, we are all computer people now" (Turkle 2004, B28). As you read the articles in this section, think about your present or future as a member of a CMC relationship or community. What are the advantages and disadvantages of CMC and other information technologies? How have these technologies impacted your interaction with others?

This section contains articles that address the reality of CMC as well as the use of computer-mediated communication by teenagers and by persons joining together to provide social support to grieving families. Finally, an author, raised in an electronic world, reflects on communication theories and concepts in light of her experience.

## References

Angesleva, J., and Reynolds, C. (2005). emotemail. Media Lab Europe and MIT Media Lab. Accessed online May 19, 2005: *http://emotemail.media.mit.edu/*.

Canfield, C. (2005, July 4). Is camping losing outdoors appeal? *Chicago Tribune*, p. 2.

Guernsey, L. (2001, October 18) Please don't e-mail my Dad, Mr. Weatherbee. *New York Times*, D1–D8.

Rheingold, H. (1993). *The Virtual Community: Homesteading on the Electronic Frontier*. New York: HarperCollins.

Turkle, S. (2004, January 30). How computers change the way we think. *The Chronicle of Higher Education*, B26–B28. ✦

# 42

# Internet Interpersonal Relationships

*Susan B. Barnes*

Computer-mediated communication, or CMC, provides opportunities for interpersonal communication that resemble face-to-face interactions in certain ways but that are quite different in other ways. Online interactions are devoid of nonverbal cues that guide much of your interpersonal interaction, although emoticons and other online signals serve this function in some ways. They provide access to others who might be difficult to reach, either by virtue or location or position, through direct personal interaction.

Satisfying Internet relationships require nurturing and reciprocity. You may find yourself engaged in online interactions in order to make new friends or stay in touch with family members, share hobbies or play games, complete homework, solve problems, search for information, or provide social support to others. Many of your ongoing online relationships are characterized by reciprocity or social exchange, although most are asynchronous in nature. Instant messages represent an exception when two individuals are conversing back and forth.

CMC allows you to maintain relationships that might have declined or drifted a decade ago. Although the interactions may not be highly regular, you can maintain contact with a high school teacher, a former workplace colleague, or an old friend who moved away. You may even connect with members of your extended family, the relatives you are unlikely to talk with regularly on the phone. It also allows you to develop new relationships with individuals you are unlikely to meet face to face; chat rooms, friendship-oriented websites, and support groups provide access to such connections.

In addition, your workplace experiences may have involved ongoing online interactions with people across the country and around the world. Those who work for multinational organizations find themselves interacting daily or weekly with many of the same people for many years. On the other hand, some people will regularly relate to colleagues in cubicles 10 feet away through e-mail, thus negating the human moment opportunities that could provide more rewarding and efficient working relationships.

Although these online relationships are both commonplace and significant, there are concerns that constant electronic hyperconnections may have a downside, or the loss of the human moment. Hallowell (1999) suggests, "When human moments are few and far between, oversensitivity, self-doubt, and even boorishness and abrasive curtness can be observed in the best of people" (p. 60). Many online relationships are strengthened by opportunities for face-to-face interactions that support personal nonverbal communication and allow greater ease when discussing highly sensitive topics.

The research on this topic is exploding and, according to Rabby and Walther (2003), the literature has "barely scratched the surface of the specific role that e-mail and other forms of CMC play in relationships" (p. 156). They argue that too little is known about "how people fall in and out of love, manage multiple commitments, obligations and alternative attractions, and deal with their relationships over time to predict the critical success factors for any relationship to succeed, mediated, face-to-face, or mixed" (p. 159). Thus, this is the cutting edge of research on interpersonal communication in a computer mediated world.

In the following reading, Susan Barnes introduces Internet relationships and provides criteria for understanding how computer-mediated relationships are established and managed. She discusses relational development through correspondence over a period of time, the centrality of shared experiences, the mutual desire for security and status, the importance of understanding the other, the online role-plays, and the expectation of reciprocity. In each of these segments Barnes highlights communication concepts and theories that apply directly to online interaction. Clearly there is significant overlap in goals and practices between online *and offline interpersonal interaction. As you read this chapter, consider this question: What is the value of understanding these underlying interpersonal dynamics as you engage in developing relationships in a CMC environment?*

## References

Hallowell, E. M. (1999). The human moment at work. *Harvard Business Review, 77*, 58–66.

Rabby, M. K., and Walther, J. B. (2003) Computer-mediated communication effects on relationship formation and maintenance. In D. J. Canary and M. Dainton (Eds.), *Maintaining Relationships Through Communication: Relational, Contextual, and Cultural Variations.* (pp. 141–184). Mahwah, NJ: Lawrence Erlbaum Associates.

\* \* \*

Building successful relationships using CMC can follow a pattern that is similar to building face-to-face ones. How people meet and the content and the quality of their initial encounter can set the direction of the relationship. Once a relationship is started, the intensity and caliber of the relationship depend on the amount of contact between people (e.g., daily, every few days, weekly, monthly, etc.). In CMC, the pacing of e-mail messages is very important because it reflects what is happening in the relationship. Once a pattern of correspondence is established, psychological reactions can occur when online friends fail to reply to messages at the expected time. Similar to face-to-face friendships, electronic ones are built on regular interaction and reciprocity. According to Chen and Gaines (1998), developing a positive self-image is one motivation for participating in reciprocal CMC relationships. Reciprocity works on the principle of **social exchange** or equity **theory**: An individual attempts to maintain a balance of rewards to costs. Individuals exchanging e-mail messages, participating in discussion lists, and posting personal Web pages must perceive that they receive a benefit from these interactions in order for them to continue. . . .

## Criteria for Examining Computer-Mediated Interpersonal Relationships

Phillips and Metzger (1976) developed a rhetorical framework for understanding interpersonal relationships. The rhetorical position argues that individuals can take action to alter, enhance, or end relationships. . . . [I]ndividuals use communicative strategies to maintain friendships. In addition to strategies, the rhetorical view argues that people have goals that influence the way in which strategies are used. Phillips and Metzger contend that individuals seek goals in their interpersonal relationships and that they approach their goal seeking in an orderly manner, which can be described and critiqued in ways similar to . . . public discourse. The rhetorical framework has six standards for identifying interpersonal behavior: sharing common experience, security and satisfaction, understanding the other, role play, reciprocity, and benefit. . . .

Unlike face-to-face relationships, relationships that form through CMC are built on written rather than spoken words. There are two reasons why written language is an important aspect of online relationship building. First, people who talk over extended periods of time develop a **private language** with their e-mail friends. Private language develops when language is used idiosyncratically by CMC correspondents who share assigned meanings for words and acronyms. Second, e-mail is different from face-to-face interactions because all conversations can be recorded and saved for future reference. Saved messages can indicate milestones in the relationship, for example, a birthday message from an e-mail friend can be printed and saved. Unlike face-to-face conversations, electronic ones can be re-read and can reappear in future messages with comments and reactions. Replying to e-mail, the frequency of contact, and the development of private language all contribute to the building of successful online relationships.

### Relationships Build over Time

The elimination of social information in CMC makes participants communicate in a single verbal/linguistic mode. Consequently, it takes more "real time" for participants to exchange the same number of messages in CMC than it does face-to-face. This approach to CMC is called the **social information processing (SIP) theory**. SIP is built on the following ideas. First, communicators' motives for affiliation with others encourage them to develop relationships and will overcome the limitations of a medium. Second, communicators will adapt their communication strategies to the medium in an effort to acquire social information and achieve social goals. Finally, relationship building takes time and CMC relationship development is slower than establishing face-to-face relationships.

Walther's (1994) research revealed that socioemotional expression was greater when interaction between participants occurred over a longer period of time. He states, "Interpersonal impressions did develop over extended time interaction in CMC, and they developed more slowly than in FtF [Face-to-Face] interaction" (477). Additionally, research has revealed that differences between face-to-face and computer-mediated relationships occur in the initial stage of interaction but tend to dissipate over time. However, a factor that influences the development of relational correspondence in CMC is whether participants expect the relationship to be ongoing and possibly lead to future contact. People who believe their relationships are ongoing will work harder to use CMC to maintain the relationship.

When people come together on- and offline, they often form a type of minisociety, complete with legislative, executive, and judicial components. People engaging in relationships must decide on what to do and believe, they must be able to carry out their decisions, and they must have a way of settling disputes. They must also agree on a common definition of what is being exchanged. . . .

## Shared Experience

Relationships must build substantive meanings for the participants sharing the experience. Montgomery (1996) states, "The meanings associated with partners' communicative acts, both verbal and nonverbal, define relationship events like arguments, lovemaking, flirtation, play, discussions, apologies, and

so forth" (p. 125). It is through the sharing of experiences and events that people develop a sense of the nature of their relationship. Relationships involve two or more people sharing a common experience for meeting some basic human goal.

Short-term goals are generally defined by the situation in which people encounter each other, and goals are negotiated between the individuals. For example, a student contacts his or her professor to get help understanding a homework assignment, or members of a work group use e-mail to coordinate their meetings and activities. Long-term goals require more time and include building one's self-esteem or developing a friendship. The first step in building a shared experience is understanding the situation or context in which the communication occurs. This is particularly important in CMC because individuals can encounter other people from geographically and culturally diverse backgrounds.

When CMC is a supplement to face-to-face encounters, the participants generally understand the context. For instance, when teachers and students communicate through e-mail, they understand each other's roles and the rules of behavior. However, when people first come together in an Internet discussion list, they may not understand the nature of the communication context because the lack of shared face-to-face experiences can make online conversations difficult to interpret. Quoting portions of an e-mail message can help to establish a shared context for the exchange. . . .

Dissimilar external factors, such as linguistic differences, cultural differences, age factors, and gendered discourse can inhibit the building of shared meaning between communicators. However, once participants take the time to understand the different points of view being articulated, group members can share a common experience. Moreover, sharing birthday greetings, births, deaths, and other significant events online can help to create a bond between individuals.

## Security and Satisfaction

Another factor in establishing relationships both on- and offline is security and satisfaction. Security develops from the feeling that one fits into society, and satisfaction is ascribed to the awareness that others have verified one's identity. Phillips and Metzger (1976) state, "Security is sought largely through public means, and satisfaction is the product of private and intimate arrangements" (p. 107). Relationship bonding requires a feeling of security because both partners must feel secure in what is going on. For example, for one person to be in charge requires the other to give permission. If on partner gives permission to the other to take charge, who is really in charge? In any relationship, each partner assigns value and the person who assigns the highest value to the relationship will do more to keep it working. In CMC relationships, the person who assigns the highest value to the relationship will write longer messages and spend more time online maintaining the relationship.

In addition to interpersonal correspondence, the medium helps to create feelings of satisfaction. According to Williams and Rice (1983), the interactive characteristic of new media can satisfy interpersonal needs because these media are flexible enough to personalize information. As a result, computer networks can help foster a sense of social presence. **Social presence** is reflected in how participants in a communication exchange would evaluate the medium that is being used on the following criteria: unsociable-sociable, insensitive-sensitive, cold-warm, and impersonal-personal. . . . For example, people generally expect a business letter to have less social presence than a face-to-face meeting.

Two factors that relate to social presence are interactivity and the public versus private aspect of the interaction. As previously stated, CMC is interactive and the nature of the interactivity depends on whether the online interaction occurs in synchronous or asynchronous time. Unlike face-to-face encounters, Internet conversations do not obviously occur in a public or private setting. Witmer's study on risky communication . . . revealed that people often consider their e-mail messages to be private. But system administrators at corporations and universities can monitor messages, and e-mail can be forwarded to oth-

ers without our knowledge. People sitting alone at home typing their inner thoughts into the computer tend to perceive the experience as a private one. However, others can read many computer-mediated exchanges.

Despite confusion over the public-private nature of CMC, it can support feelings of both security and satisfaction. For example, Hauben and Hauben (1997) argue that by electronically interacting with others, individuals can begin to feel more secure. They provide the following example:

> When I started using ForumNet (a chat program similar to irc, but smaller—[Now called icb]) back in January 1990, I was fairly shy and insecure. . . . I had a few close friends but was slow at making new ones. Within a few weeks, on ForumNet, I found myself able to be open, articulate, and well-liked in this virtual environment. Soon, this discovery began to affect my behavior in "real" face-to-face interaction. I met some of my computer friends in person and they made me feel so good about myself, like I really could be myself and converse and be liked and wanted (William Carroll, cited in Hauben & Hauben, 1997, p. 17).

CMC enables socially reticent individuals to develop interpersonal skills because it removes the social pressure of immediate face-to-face reactions from others. Moreover, some people seem to feel more secure about expressing their personal feelings to others online. Individuals who are shy and do not like to speak in front of small groups can use e-mail as a way to express themselves. For instance, shy students will often use e-mail as a way to communicate with their professors. A study by Mazur, Burns, and Emmers-Sommer (2000) examined the effects of communication apprehension and relational interdependence in online relationships. They discovered that people who are communicatively apprehensive perceived higher levels of relational interdependence with online partners. These findings support the idea that socially shy individuals could use CMC to build and develop interpersonal relationships.

Additionally, CMC can help individuals who are experiencing professional or personal problems. Sproull and Faraj (1996) state, "Despite the fact that participants in electronic groups may be surrounded by people at work or school, at least some of them feel alone in facing a problem or a situation" (p. 128). The feeling of facing a problem alone can lead a person to believe that he or she is at fault. Online support groups help to normalize experiences and allow people who share similar problems to meet.

Online groups that share common interests are also likely to share common problems, and members of these groups can provide support for each other. Many different support groups can be accessed through the Internet. Moore (1995) says, "America Online, for instance, has Monday meetings for infertility, chronic fatigue, and 'Marital Blisters.' On Tuesday, there is an AA meeting, a support group for depression, one for eating disorders, a meeting of Adult Children of Alcoholics, and a forum for Panic Support" (pp. 67–68). Electronic support groups exist for every topic from breast feeding to people with cerebral palsy. Today, computer networks have developed into a medium that facilitates the person to person sharing of emotional and informational support.

For some individuals, CMC can be a preferred method of communication. For example, Murray (1991), in her ethnographic study of IBM employees, revealed that employees choose e-mail as a medium of communication to express logical, well-argued statements. E-mail is generally followed by a telephone call or face-to-face conversation. Beginning an interaction through e-mail removes personal and emotional matters from the initial conversation and makes discussions more rationally oriented.

Because e-mail eliminates immediate face-to-face reactions from others, some people find it a superior way to present issues and problems that need solutions. Separating the people from the problems enables individuals to discuss their problems in a less emotional context. Moreover, e-mail provides an opportunity for socially reticent individuals to express themselves in ways that can lead to an improved sense of security and satisfaction.

## Understanding the Other

Understanding the other, [is] a basic concept from the writings of George Herbert Mead (1932, 1934). . . . According to Phillips and Metzger (1976), "Each individual in a relationship is able to monitor his [or her] behavior as well as take the position of the other in order to perform an analysis of the situation in which he [or she] finds himself [or herself]. This helps him [or her] find the most effective approach to facilitate goal accomplishment" (p. 182). Unlike face-to-face encounters, CMC can make understanding the other difficult because people can more easily misrepresent themselves. Consider the following e-mail story:

> I started corresponding with a woman I encountered on a discussion network. She had a job at a major university facility and I documented her existence. She lived in the same town as my friend's aged mother, and so I asked her to look in. She did, reported pleasant encounters with the old woman. Then she reports that her daughter is "hooked on drugs," her ex husband is harassing. She reports tales from her past that pass beyond all that is reasonable and reports she is now doing three therapy sessions a week with her psychiatrist. Shall I take this seriously. She is looking in on my friend's mother. I am, frankly, worried, and I know, I hope, I will be more cautious next time (cited in Barnes, 2001, p. 117).

As in face-to-face encounters, our *first Internet impression* of others may prove to be wrong. Initial impressions both on- and offline are often quick, inaccurate judgements. Therefore, most discussion groups recommend **lurking** and becoming familiar with individuals and the group's dynamics before joining the conversation. Eager new members frequently embarrass themselves. For example, a student who joined an academic discussion list sent a nasty message to the group's leading academic, calling this professor a "cranky old man." This student had not done his homework and did not understand the professor's role in the group as a provocative writer or his professional reputation. As a result, the professor first appeared to the student as "cranky" rather than insightful. After reading more messages posted to the group, the student realized his error and apologized to everyone.

Dual perspective is an aspect of relationship building that can influence how we understand other people. **Dual perspective** is a state of mind that takes into account the realization that the other person may see the world through entirely different eyes. Moreover, it is often important to discover exactly how that other person sees the world in order to adjust your own behavior. Through the understanding that an individual has the capacity to influence others, the individual has a responsibility when he or she does so. Dual perspective enables people to monitor their language and address themselves directly to the needs of the rhetorically sensitive person.

With casual acquaintances, we only have a limited view of the ways in which they perceive the world. This also tends to be true about Internet relationships. When we meet someone through CMC, the conversation is restricted to text and people can control their reactions and opinions. Interactions are not always spontaneous. Individuals can use **negative spontaneity** to carefully craft their messages to create the "right" impression. Therefore, it is important in CMC to observe the behaviors and roles of others. Spending time carefully reading messages will help you better understand the perspectives of Internet friends and members of online groups.

## Role Play

Role play both on- and offline is important in the formation of relationships. According to Phillips and Metzger (1976), "Behaviors possible are projected as roles, roles are systematically played and are purposeful. They need to be ratified through the response of the other. Successful ratification enhances self-esteem" (p. 182). People can play a variety of roles in CMC. They can be themselves in discussion lists, create a pseudonym in a chat room, or invent a character to play in an online game.

An online participant's perception of the computer-mediated genre can influence the participant's behavioral roles. Saunders, Robey, and Vaverek (1994) researched status roles in computer conferences and discovered that occupational roles apply to CMC. For instance, in online medical contexts, doctors are viewed as high-status professionals and they "tend to send more sentences to low-status individuals than vice versa" (p. 465). Similarly, in computer-assisted instruction, teachers assume high online centrality. Social roles established in face-to-face contexts are frequently transferred into online encounters. Saunders, Robey, and Vaverek (1994) concluded that "advocates of equalitarian social interaction clearly cannot depend on technology alone to overcome the status differentials inherent in occupations and other social roles" (p. 469).

Unlike roles established in professionally oriented CMC, social roles are more difficult to establish. As in face-to-face situations, social roles emerge as people interact with each other. For example, many discussion groups have a **list guru**, a person who sparks the fires of debate and assumes a leadership position. The leadership role of the list guru will influence the formation of Internet friendships developed through online groups. For instance, a complementary relationship can develop between a list guru and a person who needs information or advice. A well-published academic list guru developed a number of complementary relationships with young scholars who wanted to get published. They exchanged e-mail and instant messages about different book ideas, and the list guru provided advice about dealing with publishers.

A leadership role established in one discussion group does not necessarily transfer to another one. Therefore, some people oppose **cross-posting** messages, or moving e-mail from one online discussion group to a different one. Whittle (1997) contends, "Some participants object to wider distribution of their posts on the grounds that cross-posting of their works might expose them to ridicule or loss of status, or because the original context might easily be lost" (p. 134). Expertise and status on one list do not necessarily transfer to another.

The roles we assume in both professional and social online contexts can influence the nature of relationships that we develop.

Therefore, it is important to clearly communicate these roles to others.

## Relationships are Built on Reciprocity

Both on- and offline, interpersonal relationships are developed through reciprocal exchanges. Phillips and Metzger (1976) say, "Each person, consciously or unconsciously, conducts a review of his ongoing relationships and, following the pleasure principle, acts to maintain those that satisfy and diminish or extinguish those that do not. Since both parties to a relationship have equivalent opportunity, maintenance of a relationship is a reciprocal process. Something must be exchanged" (p. 182). For successful relationships to occur, people must feel that a beneficial exchange is taking place. For example, people can exchange professional information and provide emotional support for each other. The following are examples of beneficial online relationships from the HomeNet study:

> One professional in the sample gets information from and sends information to a group discussing income tax regulation. . . . A woman has joined an on-line support group dealing with her chronic illness. And many of the teenagers in the sample exchange daily electronic mail with other kids in their high school, supplementing the endless conversations they have on the telephone and in person (Kraut, 1995, page 2).

Responding to e-mail messages is the first step in building reciprocal online relationships. Whittle (1997) states, "Although net culture is fairly flexible about e-mail turn-around time, the nature of the communication should factor in your decision of when and how to respond, if at all" (p. 53). However, a distinction is generally made between professional and casual use of e-mail. Professional correspondents usually expect a quick reply to their e-mail unless you are out of town. Casual e-mail messages can be read and answered at your convenience.

Responses to online messages can broaden or narrow the exchange depending on whether the response focuses on portions of the original message, offers new ideas, or asks questions to move the conversation in a different direction. Whittle (1997) provides some examples:

- JaneD comments that abortion is wrong and gives three reasons to support her belief. RichM responds by rebutting each of the three reasons and offers four reasons why a woman's right to choose should take precedence over moral judgements about abortion in making law. (Broadening)

- JaneD responds by pointing out that all four of RichM's reasons are based on the assumption that morality cannot be legislated, and she rebuts that assumption by pointing out that ALL legislation is based on morality—i.e., society's concept of right and wrong. (Narrowing)

- Another participant jumps in and comments that the separation of church and state demands that all morality be kept out of all legislation. (Diverting). (1997, p. 71).

When people divert or make outrageous statements to others, many people respond with silence. Ignoring statements is an easy way to deal with inappropriate messages or behavior. Moreover, silence can be used as an avoidance strategy. "A negative use of silence is to drop out of a discussion without comment rather than face up to the weakness of one's position" (Whittle, 1997, p. 71). Rather than reply to criticism, some people will just not respond. Often, no response is perceived as a negative reaction and the person can lose credibility. Additionally, not responding to e-mail can end an online relationship.

In online communication, it is possible to cultivate skill with reciprocity. A small amount of reflected listening can enable an individual to bring the other person's message to the screen so it can be answered line-for-line. . . . Quoting sections of previous messages encourages online discussion for two reasons. First, it helps readers contextually understand who and what the writer is replying to. Second, it supports the idea of reciprocity by providing direct feedback to the message sender. Reflected listening is a style of interaction that was used by psychologist Carl Rogers, and it was applied to a computer program called *ELIZA*, one of the first bots ever programmed. Reflected listening is an effective technique for developing reciprocity between online correspondents, and the *ELIZA* program shows that it works well in text-only exchanges. . . . Online writers need to learn how to write messages that foster responses. Otherwise, their message will be ignored and the individual will be unable to develop computer-mediated relationships. . . .

## References

Barnes, S. B. (2001). *Online connections: Internet interpersonal relationships*. Cresskill, NJ: Hampton Press.

Chen, L. L., and Gaines, B. R. (1998). Modeling and supporting virtual cooperative interaction through the World Wide Web. In F. Sudweeks, M. McLaughlin, and S. Rafaeli (Eds.), *Network & netplay* (pp. 221–242). Menlo Park, CA: AAAI Press/MIT Press.

Hauben, M., and Hauben, R. (1997). *Netizens: On the history and impact of Usenet and the Internet*. Los Alamitos, CA: IEEE Computer Society Press.

Kraut, R. (1995). The social impact of home computing (Online) 3 pp. Available: *http://homenet.andrew.cmu.edu/progress/ppg.html*. (Downloaded April 10, 1996).

Kraut, R., Lundmark, V., Kiesler, S., Mukhopadhyay, T., and Scherlis, W. (1997). *Why people use the Internet*. Available: *http://homenet.andrew.cmu.edu/progresspurposes.html*.

Mazur, M. A., Burns, R. J., and Emmers-Sommer, T. M. (2000). Perceptions of relational interdependence in online relationships: The effects of communication apprehension and introversion. *Communication Research Reports*, 17 (4), 397–406.

Mead, G. H. (1932). *The philosophy of the present*. La Salle, IL: The Open Court Publishing Company.

———. (1934). *Mind, self and society*. Chicago, IL: University of Chicago Press.

Montgomery, B. M. (1996). Communication standards for close relationships. In K. M. Galvin and P. Cooper (Eds.), *Making connections: Readings in relational communication*. Los Angeles, CA: Roxbury Publishing Company, pp. 124–133.

Moore, D. W. (1995). *The emperor's virtual clothes*. Chapel Hill, NC: Algonquin Books of Chapel Hill.

Murray, D. E. (1991). *Conversation for action: The computer terminal as medium of communication*. Amsterdam/Philadelphia: John Benjamins Publishing Company.

Phillips, G. M. and Metzger, N. J. (1976). *Intimate communication*. Boston: Allyn & Bacon, Inc.

Saunders, C. S., Robey, D., and Vaverek, K. A. (1994, June). The persistence of status differentials in computer conferencing. *Human Communication Research*, 20 (4), 443–472.

Sproull, L., and Faraj, S. (1996). Some consequences of electronic groups. In M. Stefik (Ed.), *Internet dreams: Archetypes, myths, and metaphors* (pp. 125–134). Cambridge: The MIT Press.

Walther, J. B. (1994). Anticipated ongoing interaction versus channel effects on relational communication in computer-mediated interaction. *Human Communication Research*, 20 (4), 473–501.

Whittle, D. B. (1997). *Cyberspace: The human dimension*. New York: W. H. Freeman and Company.

Williams, R., and Rice, R.E. (1983). Communication research and new media technologies. In R. Bostrom (Ed.), *Communication yearbook*, 7 (pp. 200–224). Beverly Hills, CA: Sage Publications.

Witmer, D. F. (1997). Risky business: Why people feel safe in sexually explicit on-line communication. *The Journal of Computer-Mediated Communication*, 2(1) [online], 12 pp. Available: *http://www.ascusc.org/jcmc/vol2/issue1/witmer.html* (August 22, 2001).

## Questions

1. How similar or different are your online relational experiences according to the criteria laid out by the author in this article? Are there criteria you would add? If so, what?

2. If you had to provide advice about online politeness and social norms to another student with limited online experience, what advice would you give that person? How might your ideas differ from those in the article?

3. What do you see as the causes of communication breakdowns in online relationships?

# 43

# Teenage Life Online

## The Rise of the Instant-Message Generation and the Internet's Impact on Friendships and Family Relationships

*Amanda Lenhart, Oliver Lewis, and Lee Rainie*

**M**any of you participate regularly in Internet chats and e-mail as well as Instant Message (IM) each day, in addition to engaging in face-to-face and phone conversations. Your online interactions may be related to building or maintaining friendship ties, completing homework assignments, fulfilling employer expectations, developing skills, playing games, or exploring worlds you do not encounter in everyday life. Whatever your goals, they will differ somewhat by your age cohort. In recent years, there have been numerous studies designed to understand why people in various age groups go online. Although there is a wide "gray gap," those senior citizens who do go online are interested in contacting family members, finding health or hobby information, checking weather, or having fun (Fox 2001). Their motives may differ from persons in other age groups who use the Internet frequently for work purposes. In addition to workplace requirements, parents of children under age 18 report going online to learn new things, connect with friends and family, shop, find health information, and manage their finances (Allen and Rainie 2002).

As the process of reaching out and connecting with others has changed dramatically, those changes have influenced teenager computer users more than any other group. They have grown up in a world of computer-mediated communication, and they are skilled in its relational nuances. Sometimes their interactions are constructive; other times they are problematic. For example, in her article on "mean girls" Talbot (2002) reports on the ways that girls can hurt each other online though "spreading scurrilous rumors by e-mail" or sharing highly personal e-mail messages with a wide group of friends.

In the following report, Amanda Lenhart and her colleagues discuss findings from their study of teenagers' use of online communication to develop, maintain, and end relationships. Although many reports on the subject note benefits for certain teens, there are times when aspects of online teen relationships can be destructive. This article addresses the impact of the Internet on teen friendships, and teenagers' use of instant messaging. In the first section the authors provide an overview of how teenagers manage their friendships online, develop and use of multiple identities, contact strangers, and share passwords. In the second section the authors describe the specialized use of IM, including topics such as user profiles, comparison of phone/IM use, and IM practices.

As you read this piece, think about your own teen years or those of young people you know. After reading this article, consider this question: What are the possible implications of teenagers spending so much of their lives online for their communication in future adult relationships?

### References

Allen, K., and Rainie, L. (2002, Nov. 17). *Parents Online*. The PEW Internet and American Life Project. *http://www.pewinternet.org*.

Rainie, L. (2001, September 9). *Wired Seniors*. The PEW Internet and American Life Project. *http://www.pewinternet.org*.

Talbot, M. (2002, February 24). Girls just want to be mean. *New York Times Magazine*, pp. 24–29, 40, 58, 64.

\* \* \*

## Teens and Their Friends

**M**any American youth say that Internet communication, especially instant messaging, has become an essential feature of their social lives. For them, face-to-face interaction and some telephone conversations have been partially replaced with email and instant message communication. Relationships that once might have withered are now nourished by the ease and speed of instant message exchanges and email messages. Romantic relationships are begun and ended online. Difficult conversations with friends are now mediated by the emotional distance the Internet provides. Intimate conversations sometimes seem easier than those that take place face-to-face. Teens say this can be very helpful, especially in otherwise awkward situations or at times when they are too shy to speak. Conversely, relationships with friends and romantic partners are sometimes hurt or destroyed because of misunderstandings sparked by the very voiceless aspects of Internet communication that make it attractive to youth.

## Strengthens Friendships

About half of online teens (48%) believe that the Internet has improved their relationships with their friends. Frequent users of the Internet are more enthusiastic about the friendship-enhancing quality of the Internet—more than six in ten say that it helps "some" or "a lot." But some teens, while they appreciate the ease of communication over the Internet and its ability to help them keep in touch with a larger group of people, also recognize that it may not be the best medium for starting or maintaining deeper relationships. "Unless you know the person really well, they're just some anonymous typist hiding behind a funny screen name," said one 17-year-old boy from Maryland in an email exchange with the Pew Internet Project. "I don't see people at school and think that's somebody I know from AOL. I would not even recognize them and times that I do . . . it's 'Hey, there's HAPPYKID113.' The Internet has helped me socialize with more people, but at a very unpersonal level."

## Time With Friends: A Modest Impact

America's youth do not believe the Internet takes much time away from friendships. Some 61% of online youth say teens' use of the Internet does little or nothing to detract from the time teens spend together, while only 10% say it takes away a lot of time they think young people would otherwise be enjoying in the company of their friends. Some who say that use of the Internet takes time away from friends argue that this is balanced by the increased level of communication young people have with friends who live too far away for regular face-to-face meetings. "If the Internet did not exist at all, I would probably be out doing things with my friends or getting homework done," maintained one girl, 17, in the Greenfield Online group discussion. "I think that would be better in some ways, but I think I'd miss out on a lot, especially on keeping in touch with far away friends."

***Table 43-1***
*How much do teens think the time kids spend online takes away from time spent with friends?*

|  | A lot or some | A little or not at all |
|---|---|---|
| All teens | 39% | 61% |
| Boys | 38% | 62% |
| Girls | 41% | 60% |
| Ages 12–14 | 36% | 64% |
| Ages 15–17 | 42% | 58% |

*Source: Pew Internet & American Life Project Teens and Parents Survey, Nov.–Dec. 2000. Margin of error is ±4%.*

## Good for Meeting People, Not That Great for Making New Friends

Most teens do not believe that the Internet is particularly helpful in making new friends. Sixty-seven percent of all online teens think it only helps "a little" or "not at all" when trying to make new friends. Younger children are more likely than older children to be enthusiastic about the Internet's capacity to help them make new friends. Some 37% of younger teens say the Internet helps them meet new friends, compared to 29% of older teens who say that. Girls aged 12 through 14 are the most enthusiastic about the Internet's capacity to help them make friends online.

Many teens recognize the difference between casually meeting new people online via chat rooms, or other interactive discussions, and establishing a meaningful friendship. They believe it is easier to make contact with new people online than it is to make friends. "One person I met [online] was about to move to our town, so he IM-ed me [sent an instant message]," said one 16-year-old boy in the Greenfield Online group discussion. "When he moved here I kinda showed him around. It was ok, but I really did not like him. He was a little too shy, a year younger than I and incessantly irritating. I would prefer not to have a repeat."

## A Teen's 'True Self'

Some teens feel that Internet frees them to be more fully their true selves. That makes it easier to make friends online than doing so face to face, they believe, because these relationships begin with assessments that focus on personality and intellect, rather than the attractiveness and "style" of the new acquaintance. "At one time, I had a friend online who I considered a better friend than anyone else in my life," reported a 16-year-old boy in the Greenfield Online group discussion. "Why? Well, online, we have [the] mask of the computer screen. We don't have to worry about what we look like or what other people think of us. Imagine, for instance, meeting a teenager online named Pat. All Pat knows is what you tell Pat. Pat knows what you are feeling and who you REALLY are, based on what you talk to Pat about. Pat doesn't worry about what you look like or what people say about you. Pat cares about you. Of course this could also be a bad thing, because it's easy to manipulate someone online. But I choose to believe in the better of the two situations."

To others, appearance still matters a great deal. "I continued to chat with these two girls for a long time," says one boy, 15, in the Greenfield Online group. "Then when I met them . . . they did not look like what I expected. I thought they would be cute, but they weren't. After meeting our online and offline friendships died off."

Research by Elisheva Gross of UCLA and others suggests that teens with strong social connections tend to look to email and instant messaging as a way to reinforce pre-existing bonds, while teens with smaller or less developed social networks look to the Internet to find new companions and social ties to fill-in

for the ties they lack offline.[1] "I've always been very shy in real life," noted one boy, 16, in the Greenfield Online group. "I'm home-schooled, and have avoided most contact with children my own age. The Internet has, in many ways, replaced real-life socialization for me. This is abnormal, but I don't think its 'bad' by any means. I've become comfortable with socializing both on-line and off and I've made a large number of friends by participating in small on-line communities."

### Table 43-2
*Splitting the self*

| How many email addresses or screen names do online teens use? | | | | |
|---|---|---|---|---|
| | One | Two | Three | Four + |
| All teens | 44% | 25% | 10% | 21% |
| Boys | 39% | 26% | 11% | 24% |
| Girls | 50% | 23% | 9% | 19% |

Source: Pew Internet & American Life Project Teens and Parents Survey, Nov.–Dec. 2000. Margin of error is ±4%.

## Multiple Identities: Experimentation and Self-Protection

Fully 56% of online teens have more than one email address or screen name and most use different screen names or email addresses to compartmentalize different parts of their lives online, or so that they can experiment with different personas. Boys more often than girls report having multiple email addresses or screen names. Sixty-one percent of boys have more than one address—almost a quarter have four or more. Half of online girls (50%) have more than one screen name or email account and nearly one in five girls have more than four online identities. The oldest boys (15 to 17) are the most likely to have more than one address, with two-thirds reporting multiple addresses. The most active Internet users are the most likely of all to have multiple addresses.

Of those teens with multiple addresses, nearly one-quarter say that at least one of those addresses is a secret address that teens use when they do not want their friends to know that they are online. More boys than girls have secret addresses and older teens are more likely to report a secret address than younger teens.

Ann Hird writes in her book *Learning from Cyber-Savvy Students* about a particular student with multiple screen names. "Through his choice of screen names, Colin controls the size of the online space in which he functions at any given time. The name 'Cal Zenkow' exposes him to online interaction with a large number of other individuals. The second screen name 'Doctor Topper,' allows him to maintain a private space accessible only to his five closest friends. Neither screen name has any connection to his offline identity."[2] Says Colin himself, " 'Doctor Topper is a screen name I go to sometimes when I want to be left alone.' "[3] Hird also maintains "The Internet provides adolescents with safe spaces for continual modification of the identities they wish to convey to others."[4]

For some teens, the possibility of exploring who they are, who they might become, and how they present themselves to the world in fairly safe online environments is a valuable opportunity and a primary use of the Internet. For others, identity play is something in which they dabble while they play jokes on others, but it is not a serious aspect of their Internet use.

Almost a quarter of online teens who use email, instant messaging or chat spaces confess to pretending to be someone else when they emailed or instant messaged someone. Older youth, especially boys, are the most likely to report that. "I have [pretended to be someone else] a couple of times, but only to freak my friends out, or to play a trick on them," said one 13-year-old girl in an email exchange with the Pew Internet Project. "Sometimes I say I'm someone they know or like. One time . . . I pretended that I was someone who was in love with my friend. It was actually quite funny, but my friend did not think so."

## Meeting Strangers

Many teens with Internet access have been contacted by strangers and the majority of them respond at least some of the time. Fully 60% of all online teens have gotten an email or instant message from a perfect stranger and 63% of those who have gotten such emails or IMs say they have responded to strangers online.

### Table 43-3
*Fretting about strangers*

| How much parents worry that their teens will be contacted online by a stranger: | |
| --- | --- |
| A lot | 25% |
| Some | 32% |
| A little | 24% |
| Not at all | 19% |

Source: Pew Internet & American Life Project Teens and Parents Survey, Nov.–Dec. 2000. Margin of error is ±4%.

Overall, 50% of those who use instant messaging, email or chat rooms have corresponded via IM or email with people that they have never met face-to-face. However, in many cases, these online conversations involve people who have been introduced by their friends or family members. Still, many are not shy about meeting true strangers online, including those they meet in other places online or the complete strangers who have sent them email or instant messages out of the blue. A 14-year-old girl in the Greenfield Online group discussion reported: "Around half of my buddy list[5] are friends I made online. One girl I met in a chat room, we had a lot in common and talked together for almost 3 months and then decided to meet. We did and it was the best. We talked forever and now we see each other a lot."

Boys and older youth are more likely to have emailed or instant messaged a stranger than girls and younger teens. Fifty-four percent of boys have ever done this compared to 46% of girls. Fifty-seven percent of older teens say they have done this compared to 41% of teens ages 12–14. Predictably, youth who are online every day report doing this more often, with 57% saying they have ever emailed or instant messaged someone they have never met face to face.[6]

When asked, most teens say they do not tell their parents when a stranger contacts them online. One 15-year-old girl from the Greenfield Online group explained how strangers find her: "A lot of people can find you on Yahoo or AOL if you have a profile [public place for listing hobbies and other personal information]. They can enter in different criteria and if you match it, they'll get your User ID." She added "I wouldn't talk about it with my parents, they'd flip out and probably restrict my access to the Internet."

### Sharing Passwords

For some wired teens, a sign of true friendship is for one Internet user to share his screen name and password with a buddy. More than a fifth of our respondents (22%) who use instant messaging, email or chat report sharing their passwords with friends or others that they know. Boys and girls report in equal measure that they do this.

While such behavior might seem strange in light of concerns about online privacy, the teens who share their passwords see it as emblematic of their trust in their friends. "Sharing your password can have its ups and downs," admitted one girl, 17, in the Greenfield Online group discussion. "You know you can trust someone if you can give them your password, but if you ever have a problem with that person, then they have all that info at their fingertips. I am glad that I did [share my password]. It makes me feel closer to people by letting them know I trust them with something as personal as my password." But others would not ever share their passwords or have regretted doing it. "I have shared my password with my two best friends," noted a 15-year-old girl in the Greenfield group. "No, I'm not glad that I did because when we got in this big fight they went into my email and wrote my boyfriend telling him that I don't like him and I don't want to go out with him. Mature, huh?"

## Youth and Instant Messaging

Almost three-quarters of online teens (74%), roughly 13 million youth, have used an instant messaging program that allows those online to hold conversations back and forth with other users instantaneously. In comparison, 44% of online adults have tried instant messaging at one time or another.

Many online teens use IM frequently. More than 1 in 3 of those who use IM services (35%) say they instant message every day, with an-

other third using instant messaging a couple of times a week (34%). No matter how frequently they log on, 45% of online teens who have used instant messaging say they use this online communications form each time they go online. Close to half (46%) of these young instant messagers say they spend between [a] half and full hour on instant messaging each time they do IM, and another 21% say they spend more than an hour on a typical session.

Many report that a major advantage of instant messaging is that they can stay in touch with people who do not live nearby. Fully 90% of instant messagers say they use this Internet tool to stay in touch with friends and relatives who live outside their communities. Camp friends are particularly popular instant messaging buddies. "My buddy list includes friends from school, past teachers, family members or family friends, and friends that I have met that don't go to my school but [who] I like to keep in touch with, especially friends from camp [from] the previous summers," summarized a 16-year-old girl in an email message to the Pew Internet Project.

### Who Sends Instant Messages

A greater proportion of online girls than online boys have ever tried instant messaging—the figures are 78% for girls and 71% for boys. And the percentage of online teens who have used IM increases with age.

In addition, girls latch on to instant messaging at an earlier age, with 72% of girls 12 to 14 using the service, compared to 60% of boys the same age who use IM. However, boys seem to catch up to girls as they get older, instant messaging at about the same rate as girls by the time they are in high school.

More youth from wealthier families use instant messaging than those from lower income families. Experience online also is closely associated with use of instant messaging. The longer a teen has been online, the more likely she is to use instant messaging.

### Instant Messaging Compared to the Phone

Ninety-four percent of online teens in our sample report using online communications tools like email, instant messaging, and chat rooms. Still, a strong majority of online

## Table 43-4
### *The basic IM crowd*

Fully 74% of online teens use instant messaging, compared to 44% of online adults. Below are the percentages of online teens in each group who use Instant messaging:

| | |
|---|---|
| **Sex** | |
| Boys | 71% |
| Girls | 78% |
| **Age** | |
| 12–14 | 66% |
| 15–17 | 81% |
| **Sex and age** | |
| Younger (12–14): | |
| Boys | 60% |
| Girls | 72% |
| Older (15–17): | |
| Boys | 80% |
| Girls | 83% |
| **Family income** | |
| Less than $30,000 | 65% |
| $30,000 to $50,000 | 69% |
| More than $50,000 | 79% |
| **Internet experience** | |
| One year or less | 61% |
| Two to three years | 75% |
| More than three years | 89% |

Source: Pew Internet & American Life Project Teens and Parents Survey, Nov.–Dec. 2000. Margin of error is ±4%; n = 754.

youth (71%) who use these online tools say the phone is still the way they most often get in touch with their friends. At the same time, however, a fifth of these online teens (19%) say that instant messaging is their primary way of communicating with their friends and another 8% report that they use email the most often to contact pals.

When asked why they used one method of communication over another, the teens who cited the telephone say they preferred it because nuances of communication are easier to detect. They like the fact that they can hear emotions on the phone and that means they think they make fewer social mistakes on the phone than they do on the Internet. "Online, it is difficult to convey attitudes or tone of voice, whereas on the phone, there is much more of a human aspect, less austere and sterile than cyberspace," wrote a 16-year-old girl in an email to the Pew Internet Project. Others preferred instant messaging for the way it enables multiple simultaneous conversations, and even multiple activities. "I send/receive instant messages almost every time I am online. I talk to up to 8 people at once," said a girl, 16, in an email to the Pew Internet Project. "I carry on separate conversations with each person. That way, you can talk about more stuff at once."

## The Special Character of Instant Messages[7]

Teens report instant messages do not contain the visual and aural cues that people get in face-to-face or phone contacts. They say this can lead to misunderstandings. "Although it never really starts anything big, I do frequently misunderstand people online, and they misunderstand me," said one boy, 16, in the Greenfield group. "It is hard to convey tone of voice and the manner in which one is saying something online. Sarcasm can be easily misunderstood online." At the same time, though, online teens appreciate instant messaging because they say it gives them a greater freedom to craft arguments carefully or to word an unpleasant message delicately.

Fully 37% of instant message-using teens say they have used IM to say something that they would not have said to somebody's face. They report feeling a measure of protection using IM because writers cannot see the first reaction of the recipient. "It is easier to talk to someone about certain topics online, than to talk about them face-to-face," reported a 17-year-old girl in the Greenfield Online group discussion. "Online you can think things over, and erase them before you look stupid, rather than to their face, where you can't always take things back."

This "distancing" trait in Internet communication also can be an aid in repairing ruptured relationships, according to group discussion respondents. It is easier at times to explain some experiences and feelings online and not have to encounter awkward or confused reactions that sometimes occur during spoken or face-to-face conversation. "I had talked about this person behind their back a bit, and that person became upset by that," noted a boy, 16, in the Greenfield Online group. "Neither one of us knew how to bring it up in person, although we wanted to. Finally, we talked about it [online], I apologized, and we found out how much we mean to each other. Since that discussion, we have become very good friends again."

When online arguments are not resolved quickly, or when strangers or others send irritating or incessant instant messages, IM users often use the tools at their disposal to protect themselves. Fifty-seven percent of instant message users say they have blocked an instant message from someone they did not want to hear from. And 64% have ever ignored an instant message from someone they were mad at or did not like.

## Dating

Significant numbers of teens have used instant messages to conduct relationships: 17% of IM users have asked someone to go out with them with an instant message. Teenage boys, especially those between ages 12 and 14, are the most likely to have used instant messages this way. One quarter of instant message-using boys have asked someone out over an instant message, as have 10% of IM-using girls. "She and I started to talk online and played a game where we could ask each other anything," wrote one 16-year-old boy in the Greenfield Online group discussion. "I eventually asked her out . . . online, of course. It's not the most romantic thing to do, but I was very nervous and it helped to make it a little bit easier."

Some 13% of IM users have broken up with someone via an instant message. There are not gender-based differences in this use of instant messaging. An equal number of girls and boys have used IMs to break up with someone. Younger teens (ages 12–14) are more likely than older teens to use this form of communication to end a relationship. Almost a fifth (18%) of teens in this age bracket have done so.

At times, even the emotional core of a relationship is conducted through instant messages and email. "Sometimes it is easier to say what is in your heart online," noted a girl, 17, in the Greenfield Online group discussion. "You can type the words and hit send instead of freezing up in person. In the mornings I sometimes get love letters and it makes me feel so good. I love hearing what my sweetie is thinking."

## Making Plans

Eighty-two percent of online teens use instant messages to make plans with their friends. "We can check movie times online and get directions for where we want to go and have everyone talking and checking with each other at once," said one 17-year-old girl in the Greenfield Online group discussion. "That's really great because it makes things so much easier."

## Pranks and Deception

Instant messages and emails have become a prime vehicle for playing tricks on friends or others. A little more than a quarter (26%) of instant messaging teens have used the medium to pretend to be someone different. "Unfortunately, a friend and I tricked someone once," reported a 16-year-old boy in the Greenfield Online group discussion. "This person was a friend of mine (I'll call him 'Jim'). We created a new screen name and told 'Jim' that we knew his address and phone number and stuff. It only lasted about 15 minutes, but it really did mess up our friendship. I did it all in fun, but 'Jim' took much offense to it, and I can understand why. I decided not to mess with online trickery any more. Another time, another friend of mine created a new screen name and IM-ed his girlfriend to see if she was being faithful."

Online deception concerns some teens enough that they only use email and instant messaging with people they already know. But many just assume it is part of the online environment and cope in other ways. "I don't think people are always completely honest but it's not a big problem," wrote a 17-year-old boy in an email to the Pew Internet Project. "They're mostly small, white lies that are of little consequence." Added a girl, 13, in another email: "Yeah, I think people give a lot of fake info online all the time. Yeah, I guess I worry about it because of my friends' safety. They talk to people they have no idea who they are and sometime I find myself telling them that it might not be the person who they think it is. Of course, they think I'm a stiff @$$, but its ok as long as they're still living. Some of my friends think they're talking to Justin from N'sync, but I don't think so. There is so much information about him that anyone can impersonate him. I think it's quite scary."

## Chat Room Tricks

Online teens also recognize that chat rooms are places where deception is commonplace. There is a sense among many teens, particularly younger ones, that chat rooms are dangerous places. According to online teens, one of the most common questions [from] a new arrival in a chat will be "ASL?" That is a request from another chat participant asking someone her Age, Sex, Location.

One 15-year-old girl said in an email to the Pew Internet Project that she thought that people online lied about who they were, but that it did not worry her because "people ought to know if they go into a chat room what risks go along with it, and you have to know that you can't trust anything anybody tells you." And another 16-year-old girl added: "I rarely go into chat rooms, if ever, and while there, I'm not looking for a faithful friendship so it's not like I am expecting to trust them completely." A common refrain is highlighted by one 14-year-old girl, who wrote in an email to the project: "I used to go into chat rooms, but I don't anymore."

### Table 43-5
*The less experience online a parent has, the more likely it is that he worries*

| The percentage of parents who are worried "a lot" or "some" that the Internet leads young people to do dangerous or harmful things online, by the parents' level of Internet experience: | |
| --- | --- |
| All parents | 45% |
| Never online | 60% |
| A year or less online | 45% |
| More than three years online | 39% |

*Source: Pew Internet & American Life Project Teens and Parents Survey, Nov.–Dec. 2000. Margin of error is ±4%.*

Six percent of online teens who use email, instant messages or chat rooms confess to sending a prank email or email "bomb." Nine percent of boys 15 to 17 report doing this as do 9% of those online every day. For some teens computer viruses and hacking pranks are a big worry. Others are not too concerned. They figure they will not be victims of such attacks. "I know, however, that there are 'bugs' and spy utilities and viruses and all those bad things out there," stated a

boy, 16, in the Greenfield Online group discussion. "[But] for the most part, I feel safe."

## Notes

1. Elisheva Gross, Jaana Juvonen, Shelly L. Gable. "Internet use and well-being in adolescence." UCLA, 2001.

2. Hird, Ann, *Learning from Cyber-Savvy Students: How Internet Age Youth Impact Classroom Teaching*, Stylus Publishing, Virginia, 2000, pg. 53.

3. Hird, p. 53.

4. Hird, p. 100.

5. A buddy list is an instant messaging address book, collected by an IM user. When she logs on, she can find out how many of her buddies are online at the same time she is.

6. Analysis in the preceding two paragraphs is based on a sub-sample of our panel of teens who use instant messages, email or chat rooms. N = 712. N for teens in the whole survey is 754.

7. Analysis from here to the end of this section, unless otherwise noted, is of teens who use Instant messaging. N = 560.

## Questions

1. Compare your attempts to meet someone new on the Internet with attempts to meet someone new face to face. Did you find one form of interaction to be easier, more satisfying, or more relaxing than the other? To what extent do you believe it was related to your age or the age of the other person?

2. How do you think college students' uses of the Internet differ from those described by the authors of this piece?

3. What concerns, if any, did the article raise for you regarding possible dark side issues emerging from teenagers' life online? Explain the concerns.

Reprinted from Amanda Lenhart, Oliver Lewis, and Lee Rainie, "Teenage Life Online: The Rise of the Instant-Message Generation and the Internet's Impact on Friendships and Family Relationships." *http://www.pewinternet.org/reports/toc.asp?Report=36.* June 20. Copyright © 2001 by Pew Internet & American Life Project. Reprinted with permission. ✦

# 44

# The Development of Communication Norms in an Online Support Group

*Isolde K. Anderson*

**O**ne of the remarkable outcomes of CMC is the development of online support groups through which family, friends, acquaintances, and even strangers come together at times of difficulty and change. Whether the event is the adoption of a child or the hospitalization of a partner, online support opportunities provide ways for the immediate family members or close friends to keep others up to date on developments and for a wide circle of caring others to convey their excitement, concern, prayers, or good wishes to the persons affected. Such a website removes pressure from loved ones to continually engage in one-on-one communication with multiple persons, especially at times of high stress. It also keeps those who are concerned up to date on any changes in the situation. On an emotional level, it provides a powerful source of comfort for persons at the center of a challenging situation; they are aware of the ongoing care and concern of family, friends, colleagues, and others, from their home community or across the globe, as they confront difficulties or changes.

Individuals may create websites for a specific concern, or they may turn to online bulletin board services to provide such a website. These sites may allow interaction among those who post or support unidirectional messages from those who post to the central per-

son or persons. The following article describes a guest book hosted on the CaringBridge website that provides a unidirectional guest book. This means concerned persons can post messages to the affected person or persons, but no direct response mechanism is built in. Contributors or visitors can read the entire set of caring expressions, but they cannot directly respond to a specific message sender. In many cases people visit a site to keep up to date on a concern but do not necessarily leave messages. In 2005 CaringBridge hosted 28,000 sites that received more than 162 million visits and more than 4 million guest book entries (http://www.caringbridge.org/about.htm). Other related online bulletin board organizations provide similar services.

Isolde Anderson is interested in norms for communicating through online guest books. In her article, she reviews the research on communication norms and online support groups, a relatively new area of study. She then details a study of one particular website created by the family of a teenage boy who, over the course of a number of years, battled leukemia and eventually succumbed to the disease. Anderson analyzes the messages posted on the guest book and identifies three communication patterns that emerged. These include the use of politeness, euphemisms for difficult topics, and honoring the patient. She then discusses the message shifts over time as the patient moved from diagnosis toward recovery and then faced a relapse and eventual death.

As you read this article, consider this question: What are advantages and disadvantages of expressing caring though an established website, and how might this affect your decision to communicate with persons experiencing a concern via an online guest book?

### Reference

CaringBridge. *http://www.caringbridge.org/about.htm* (Accessed August 8, 2005).

\* \* \*

**C**ommunication research of online support groups often focuses on interactions between multiple participants and perceived benefits of online support, such as convenience of use, anonymity, and the use of writing as a means of connecting with others (Pennebaker and Seagel 1999; Walther 1992). An understudied area is online bulletin boards and guest books where messages are unidirectional, not interactive, yet still create a sense of group identity among message senders. Given the increased use of the internet and expansion of online bulletin boards and guest books (Jones 1997), additional research of this area is warranted. This research examines in depth one such published (online) guest book, analyzing how group communication norms are established over time through the content and tone of unidirectional messages. Three general questions guide this research: (1) How do communication norms develop in an online guest book? (2) What types of communication norms develop in an online guest book? and (3) How does a sense of "groupness" develop among message senders when posting unidirectional messages in an online guest book?

## Communication Norms Online

In general, communication norms determine what behaviors and messages are considered to be appropriate in specific social situations. Communication norms involve "expectations of behaviors that individuals feel should or should not occur in a conversation" (West and Turner 2004, 499). Extensive research has been done on communication norms in face-to-face communication, including studies on politeness (Brown and Levinson 1987), reciprocity (Cialdini 2001), face theory (Goffman 1973; Cupach and Metts 1994), and speech act theory (Nofsinger 1991). However, these various interpersonal communication norms do not necessarily carry over into computer-mediated contexts. Some of the unique characteristics of computer-mediated communication are that (1) it is textual: message receivers can't rely on nonverbal cues to help interpret the meaning of a message; (2) it may be asynchronous: people can post and view messages "at their convenience rather than in real time" (Porter 2004); and (3) it may be anonymous: senders and receivers are physically isolated from one another and can choose their degree of self-disclosure and (sometimes) online iden-

tities (Huffaker et al. 2005). These characteristics impact communication norms as newly formed online groups "must learn to use a communication medium that they have no experience with and therefore develop their own way of interacting" (Postmes, Spears, and Lea 2000, 364).

One norm that appears to carry over into the computer-mediated context is the norm of reciprocity. According to Tidwell and Walther (2002), "Proactive sharing of information assists in the mutual acquisition of information and the reduction of uncertainty" (p. 324). A new communication norm that has arisen in the textual medium of online communication is the increased use of textual signs, emoticons, and other paralinguistic codes to compensate for the absence of nonverbal cues. Lea and Spears (1995) suggest that the conditions of "visual anonymity and physical isolation" that belong to computer-mediated communication can actually "encourage self-disclosure and trust. In group situations, these same conditions can promote more normative behavior, a greater sense of identification with the group and more positive impressions of group members" (p. 218). These studies are all helpful in developing a larger picture of communication norms in a computer-mediated context. What needs further exploration is to what extent online communication norms are specific to the group in which they emerge and to what extent they are impacted by the interactive or noninteractive format of the computer medium used.

Definitions of *virtual community* vary among researchers. In an attempt to unify the research in this area, Porter (2004) identifies a virtual community as "an aggregation of individuals or business partners who interact around a shared interest, where the interaction is at least partially supported and/or mediated by technology and guided by some protocols or norms" (p. 4). Online support groups are one type of virtual community. "Just as in 'real life,' these 'virtual' social groups not only are concerned with exchanging information or debating the latest hot topic, but also provide shared contexts for social interaction. The situation is superficially similar to a local community interest group, or club, but differs crucially in that these groups exist independently of the normal physical and spatial reference points" (Lea and Spears 1995, 202). Numerous studies have found that the relationships formed in such online groups can be as beneficial, satisfying and "real" as face-to-face relationships (Colvin et al. 2004; Wright 2000). When seeking support for a particular need or problem, an Internet group has an advantage over a face-to-face group because "it vastly increases the 'field of availables' for forming relationships far beyond the limits set by physical proximity—or even the extended horizons offered by other communication media" (Lea and Spears 1995, 206). Within online support groups, a sense of belonging and group identity can be developed in various ways. In Tichon and Shapiro's (2003) study of a group listserv, message senders used self-disclosure to attract social support, to show that coping is possible, and to share companionship. Eaglesham (1996) found that the experience of writing messages was beneficial for group members by creating an "open forum" where messages can be posted and reflected upon. Because "people are not involved in an immediate response dialogue," they can, over time, construct a narrative of their beliefs (Eaglesham 1996, 13). This study explores the extent to which these means of developing "groupness" may still appear when the mode of communication is not interactive, but unidirectional.

## The CaringBridge Guest Book

Online guest books are logs or journals set up on a webpage by a particular party for a specific use. Some examples would be a guest book created by a funeral home for a bereaved family, which allows out-of-town friends and relatives to post messages of condolence to the family, or a guest book on an engaged couple's webpage, inviting friends to send wedding greetings to the couple. Some online guest books are public and can be accessed by anyone; others require a password.

CaringBridge (*http://www.caringbridge.org*) is an Internet service established in 1997 that provides personalized web pages for individuals and families going through an adoption, hospice care, birth, hospitalization, or other type of care situation. "CaringBridge brings together a global community of care powered by love of family and friends in an easy, accessible and private way" (*http://www.caringbridge.org/aboutusHome.htm*). It is a unique service that has "hosted more than 20,000 personalized CaringBridge pages, with over 100 million visits, and more than three million guest book entries" (*http://www.caringbridge.com/docs/mediakit.doc*). The web pages include features such as personal photos, a journal for medical or personal updates for visitors, and a guest book where visitors can post messages. Sites can be set up by individuals for themselves or for others in their family. Information posted on the sites is supplied by the family or individual. Each family or individual decides on who can access the site with two levels of security provided, one requiring only the address (URL) of the web page, the other also requiring a username and password. All messages posted in a guest book appear in chronological order and are visible to subsequent readers. Unlike interactive online support groups, the messages in the guest book are unidirectional. Yet group norms may still develop in this context, influencing the content and tone of messages, and thus the group "climate" of supportiveness.

Two student researchers and I worked on this project over a period of four months. We reviewed the literature of various online support groups, such as chat rooms, newsgroups, listservs, web logs, and website-sponsored online guest books. Next, a CaringBridge guest book was randomly selected that was posted on Google and could be read by anyone without requiring a password to enter the site. The CaringBridge executive director was aware of the study. The site was created by the family of a teenage boy diagnosed with leukemia, and contains a brief journal with information supplied by the family, including photos and key dates in the child's life (diagnosis of leukemia at age 12, relapse at age 14, and death at age 14). Four consecutive years of postings were selected for the sample (including three years of bereavement), totaling 677 discrete messages spread over 5,332 lines of text.

An initial coding scheme was developed to identify: (1) demographic variables such as the gender of the message sender, relationship of the sender to the family, and the intended receiver of the message (child or family); (2) message variables such as content (illness, death, heaven, God, etc.) and goal (to comfort self, others, share information, self-disclose, etc.); and (3) communication norms that were immediately apparent such as euphemisms (for death or illness), politeness (introductions of self), reciprocity (responding to family's posting on their website), and the use of religious speech. As the coding progressed, additional characteristics of messages were observed and added to the coding scheme. QSR 6 was used to analyze the data.

## Results of the Study

First, we will report on the frequency of certain variables in the guest book. There were 309 different message senders over the four-year period. Fifty-six of the message senders sent more than one message, posting a combined total of 392 messages (58 percent). Some messages were in the form of greeting cards, with artwork. The vast majority of the messages were sent by females (557, 82 percent) versus males (59, 9 percent). The remainder were sent by groups such as families, sports teams, or office staffs, or by unidentifiable persons (either anonymous, pseudonymous, or with androgynous names such as Chris, Dana, or Casey). Of the total number of messages, 144 were posted over the three-month period preceding the death of the patient; 533 were posted over a three-and-a-half-year period after the death of the patient. Thirty-four percent of the messages were addressed to the patient, 52 percent were addressed to his family, and 12 percent were sent "generally" to the guest book, with no designated recipient.

We identified 10 common themes in the messages. The most frequent were references to illness, appearing in 19 percent of the lines of text. These included terms such as *cancer, disease, leukemia, illness,* and *sickness* (e.g., "I hear that you are headed back to the hospital for a short stay. I just wrapped up my four

week stay at [name of hospital]. I was undergoing another heavy duty chemo phase due to my relapse."). The next most frequent theme was religion, appearing in 6.1 percent of the text, exemplified by terms such as *God* or *Jesus*, or the inclusion of a Bible verse. Closely related were references to an afterlife, including mainly the term *heaven* or *with God*, such as this message: "I do believe J* is safe and secure and resting in God's bosom." Third most common (4.1 percent) were references to the sender's personal experiences of life and/or suffering (e.g., "Our granddaughter L* is in remission and has approximately 413 days of treatment to go."). The theme of death was expressed in terms such as "dying," "going," "gone," "loss" (e.g., "Very saddened and sorry for your loss."). Another frequent area of message content was "angels." This included phrases such as "Thinking of you and your Angel on his birthday" and "Both our angels must be happy now, away from the sufferings of this world," and poems or song lyrics that referenced angels. Other themes included the patient's experience of illness ("Glad to hear you are back home, resting comfortably."), or the family's experience of illness and/or loss ("I know these are such hard days for your family.") Special days and holidays were also referenced in the messages, such as the patient's birthday ("WOW 18! I bet J* had a blast of an 18th birthday in heaven!"), a holiday ("Our sweet, sweet Angel—Today you would be getting the fireworks out and I would be watching every move you made to see you didn't get hurt. You would be helping me get ready for our big July 4th party we have every year."), or a significant anniversary ("It's been a year today, a really tough time for all of us."). Finally, we noted the presence of compliments and praise (e.g., "Great website," "What a caring family").

Reading the guest book we noted the frequent expression of emotions, through word choices ("I feel so sad"), parenthetical comments ("ha, ha"), as well as textual signs such as "xoxox" for hugs and kisses, and {{{{person's name}}}} as a symbol for "hugs." In general, expressed emotions fell into two broad groupings: happiness and sadness. Under "happiness," 11 percent of the messages expressed emotions through words such as *love/hugs, hope, happy, glad,* and *thankful.* Sadness was expressed in 4.5 percent of the lines, using terms such as *sorry, missing (the person), sad/sadness,* and feeling *pain.* Message senders rarely expressed the emotions of anger (1 line), doubt (2 lines), or fear (1 line), which is notable given the patient's youth, severity of illness, and premature death.

In cases where the message goals were clearly stated, these too were coded. In descending order of frequency, the most commonly identified message goal was to encourage the family of the patient, occurring in 23 percent of total lines. The second most frequent goal was to remember the deceased patient or his family (11 percent of lines). The third most frequent goal was to share one's personal experience with illness, treatment, recovery or loss (9.2 percent of lines). Eight percent of the lines in the text included a statement of the sender's beliefs. About half as many lines expressed sympathy to the family for the loss of their son/grandson/brother (3.8 percent). Message senders frequently shared (3.5 percent) general information with other visitors to the site, including their fundraising efforts for leukemia research and family get-togethers. Next in frequency were comments specifically thanking the grandmother for her acts or words of encouragement (2.5 percent). A similar number let the family know the visitor had stopped by the site (2.4 percent). Only two percent of the messages explicitly stated the goal of comforting the family. Attracting support for oneself, by posting the address of one's own website or encouraging e-mail responses, appeared in 1.4 percent of lines. These message goals indicate that the message senders develop a sense of belonging to a group by sharing their common human experience of illness and loss, and desire to support one another in this experience.

What communication norms did we observe so far? First, a politeness norm manifested itself in three observable ways. Often, when the message sender was a stranger, he or she often would introduce him or herself first to the patient or the family; for example, "Hi J*! I met your Grandma online through a leukemia support group," or "Hi J*, I work with your Aunt L* at the hospital." Another way message senders expressed politeness in

this guest book was by stating they were reciprocating the kindness the patient's grandmother showed to them by posting a message on their child's/grandchild's website: "Thank you for your blessings for our family. Our's [*sic*] too, go out to you in the loss of your precious J*." A third way politeness was shown was when message senders self-identified as parents of a diagnosed child or an "angel"; for example, "I see [my son's] battle with t-cell leukemia started the day J* entered heaven. I am so sorry for your loss and know you are not alone."

A second communication pattern, or norm, that was observed was the prevalent use of euphemisms in posted messages for difficult topics such as death, disease, and the family's experience of suffering. Euphemisms and metaphors for disease or illness ("struggle," "battle," "difficult time," "nightmare") appeared in 109 different lines, or 1.9 percent of the total text. Appearing nearly as often were euphemisms for the family's experience, which involved the hospitalization of a loved one and chemotherapy, (e.g., "all you've been through," "precious memories," and "the strength you have."). Most significantly, over 50 euphemisms for death occurred in 325 lines (6.1 percent of text). In contrast, the actual word *death* only occurred four times in the data, and the word *died* occurred twelve times. Some of the euphemisms for death are listed here: "Passing/pass away," "didn't get the chance," "didn't make it," "homecoming," "a better place," "without his physical presence," "too good for this earth," "he is in good hands," "lost the battle," "won the war," "taken from us," "pain free," "at peace," "with you in spirit," "taken into the Lord's hands," "looking down on you," "on the other side," "walking in perpetual light," "an empty hole," "earned his wings," "God's decision." The prevalence of euphemisms indicates an implicit norm that is understood and followed by visitors posting messages in this guest book.

A third communication pattern or norm that was observed in the guest book messages was the tendency by both intimates and strangers to exalt the patient's character and to attribute great qualities to him as a means of honoring his memory. He was variously described as a "hero," a "super hero," a "warrior," "the King's warrior," "beautiful," "wonderful," "gorgeous," "incredible," and "too good for this earth."

To identify additional patterns in the guest book messages, we next examined the intersection of variables ("nodes"). Most significant were differences in the pre- and post-death messages posted. We've already noted that females posted the greatest number of messages overall (82 percent) in the guest book. The gender ratio of message senders differs notably pre- and post-death. Of the 144 pre-death messages, 60 percent were sent by females, 23 percent by males, and 15 percent by groups. Of the post-death messages, 90 percent were sent by females, 5 percent by males, and 4 percent by groups, indicating males posted more messages during the patient's hospitalization than after his death.

Another difference in pre- and post-death messages is that before the patient's death, 141 of the 144 message posted were addressed to him. But after the patient's death, 91 messages were still sent to him by family members, friends, and strangers. Here is a sampling of those messages:

- "It is hard to believe that 18 months ago today you left us and became one of God's angels. You knew I was there today putting beautiful flowers on your grave. I could feel you close to me." (family member)

- "Happy Birthday, J*. We never met, but I am hoping you have met my son Jonathan in heaven and I hope he is close to you today. I visit your website often and love seeing your beautiful pictures." (stranger)

Two additional pre- and post-death differences are worth noting here. First, as can be expected, there is a shift in the *content* of messages. During the patient's relapse and hospitalization, message senders wrote only 48 lines of text in the guest book about their own experience of illness, whereas after the patient's death they wrote 181 lines referring to their own experience of the loss of a loved one. As might be expected, the ratio of religious references in messages also increased

dramatically post-death. During the patient's relapse and hospitalization, only 1.5 percent of messages included a reference to religion ("Keep your eyes on Jesus Christ."), whereas after the patient's death fully 4.6 percent did so. A second notable shift, pre- to post-death, occurred in the *goal* of messages. Post-death messages were more far more likely to state the sender's personal beliefs (about illness or the meaning of death, e.g., "God is in control") than did the pre-death messages (7.9 percent versus 0.23 percent of lines). This indicates that people vary in their comfort level with the timing and content of discussions of illness.

## Discussion

Because we were able to examine four years of messages, we observed several shifts in purpose of the website, from initially encouraging the patient during his treatment, to comforting the family in its loss, to memorializing the child and ennobling the family's loss. The first shift occurred on the day after the patient died, when the messages became ones of condolence for the family rather than notes of encouragement to the patient. The second shift, from sharing sympathy to memorializing the deceased, was not as clearly delineated, but was indicated by a change in the frequency of certain themes and terms, and in the people who posted messages to the site.

The communication norms of euphemisms, politeness, and self-identification as the relative of an ill or deceased person, appear throughout all "stages" of the guest book. They promote certain "understandings" in these supportive messages—that the patient is not alone, there are others who share this experience, and that dying is very difficult to talk about directly—which create group meanings regarding the patient's illness.

Quite striking are the number of different euphemisms for death (50+) and their frequency in the posted messages (325 lines). Possible explanations include: (1) that the type of computer-mediated communication (a guest book) may suggest some implicit norms for appropriate language; (2) that language choice may be affected by the age of the message receiver; (3) that senders' language choice may be affected by who hosts the website (CaringBridge); (4) that the content of the initial postings (primacy), or some key later postings (recency) may set the tone for subsequent messages; or (5) that the permanence of the posted messages predisposes senders toward using "softer" and less bold terms when talking about death. These explanations may also account for the nearly complete absence of "negative" expressed emotions in the messages.

There are different ways self-disclosure may function as a politeness norm in this guest book. For example, when message senders identify themselves as parents of a diagnosed child or an "angel," it may be a way of compensating for the lack of a relational history with the receiver. Such self-disclosure may help establish credibility for their message and reason for writing. Second, such self-disclosure may be a way of reciprocating the highly personal and uncomfortable information they are privy to concerning the patient, via his web page. Or finally, self-disclosure may be a means of reducing uncertainty between communicators (Tidwell and Walther 2002). As an online communication strategy, self-disclosure may serve to minimize receivers' perceptions of deception in the absence of visual cues and provide information about the sender while maintaining politeness (Brown et al. 1987).

The high level of praise for the deceased may serve various functions as well. First, it is clearly a means of comforting the family and confirming the depth of their loss. Second, praising the deceased's positive attributes and struggles with disease constructs a narrative of innocent suffering. Reiterating key elements of his story (what a good person he was and how unjust his death) helps make sense of this premature loss of life. It may also contribute to a sense of group identity among message senders as fellow warriors honoring a fallen hero.

The development of group identity among the 309 different message senders, reflects two contributing influences. The first is that the message senders are self-selected. Only those with specialized interests (in leukemia treatment, childhood illness, the patient, and his family) are likely to access the site

and post a message. Message senders are thus likely to share more common characteristics with other message senders than with the general population. A second contributing factor is senders' sense of sharing in the basic experience of suffering and death. The high number of messages sharing personal experiences with illness and loss corroborates this. When the group is perceived as sharing similar experiences, certain group norms (such as politeness, self-disclosure, and support) may be inferred by group members. This phenomenon is called *referent informational influence* (Postmes, Spears, and Lea 2000).

The aim of this study was to examine how communication norms and group identity form in an online support group. By starting with open-ended observations, we have begun to flesh out what kinds of questions might be addressed in future research of this area. Our examination of communication norms revealed gender differences in who posted the most messages to the site. We also found three general norms guiding message creation—politeness norms, the use of euphemisms, and the exalting of the deceased. We found two contributing influences to the development of group identity among the 309 message senders: the self-selection of message senders, and referent informational influence (Postmes, Spears, and Lea 2000), where the group is perceived as sharing similar experiences, and caring about one another, thus producing group norms of politeness, self-disclosure, and support. Obviously, the nature of the guest book (for a child's hospitalization and subsequent death) affected the types of messages posted to the site. Other types of guest books (e.g., for the birth of a child) would result in different types of messages being posted by message senders.

Unlike interactive messages that occur synchronously, the accumulated messages that are posted in an online guest book build a text that creates a narrative about the message receiver's experience and how it is interpreted and understood by others. Further research in this area might address the following questions: How does the "permanence" of posted messages in a guest book affect word choice by message senders? Are there key messages in the guest book that set the tone for the rest? Two explanations seem to be in tension here concerning how the textual nature of online guest books impacts message creation. One is the idea that the accumulation of text messages creates a body of work that can be referenced by future message senders and *that it gives more information about the receiver*, thus reducing uncertainty. The other explanation is that with the lack of cues associated with face-to-face communication, message senders may tend to over attribute qualities to receivers *based on the little information* that's available to them (Tidwell et al. 2002), thus creating more desirable images of the receiver. These explanations deserve further consideration.

An additional area for textual study would be to examine the purpose of online messages sent to the deceased. In this case, 91 such messages were posted. What does such a message "do" for the message sender and for others who read the message? How does it contribute to the creation of a "cyber memorial" that will last forever?

In conclusion, online guest books are a rich resource for studying communication behavior. Throughout history, people have found numerous ways to connect with each other in times of crisis as well as celebration. The Internet has now created new possibilities for connecting with others that will shape communication far into the future.

## Acknowlegment

Thanks to student researchers Sara Henry and Emily Shebak for extensive help in coding the data and reviewing the literature of computer-mediated communication.

## References

About Us. *http://www.caringbridge.org./aboutusHome.htm* (Accessed July 29, 2004).

Brown, P., and Levinson, S. (1987). *Politeness: Some Universals in Language Use* (Rev. ed.). Cambridge: Cambridge University Press.

CaringBridge Media Kit. http:///www.caringbridge.com/docs/mediakit.doc (Accessed April 5, 2005).

Cialdini, R. B. (2001). *Influence: Science and Practice* (4th ed.). Boston: Allyn & Bacon.

Colvin, J., Chenoweth, L., Bold, M., and Harding, C. (2004). Caregivers of older adults: Advantages and disadvantages of Internet-based social support. *Family Relations*, 53, 49–57.

Cupach, W. R., and Metts, S. (1994). *Facework*. Thousand Oaks, CA: Sage.

Eaglesham, S. L. (1996). Online support groups: Extending communities of concern. Doctoral dissertation, Virginia Polytechnic Institute. (UMI No. 9724055)

Huffaker, D. A., and Calvert, S. L. (2005). Gender, identity, and language use in teenage blogs. *Journal of Computer-Mediated Communication*, 10 (2), article 1. *http://jcmc.indiana.edu/vol10/issue2/huffaker.html* (Accessed February 9, 2005).

Goffman, E. (1973). *The Presentation of Self in Everyday Life*. Garden City, NY: Doubleday.

Jones, S. (Ed.). (1997). *Virtual Culture: Identity and Communication in Cybersociety*. Thousand Oaks, CA: Sage.

Lea, M., and Spears, R. (1995). Love at first byte? Building personal relationships over computer networks. In J. T. Wood and S. Duck (Eds.), *Understudied Relationships: Off the Beaten Track* (pp. 197–233). Beverly Hills, CA: Sage.

Nofsinger, R. E. (1991). *Everyday Conversation*. Newbury Park, CA: Sage.

Pennebaker, J. W., and Seagel, J. D. (1999). Forming a story: The health benefits of narrative. *Journal of Clinical Psychology*, 55, 1243–1254.

Porter, C. E. (2004). A typology of virtual communities: A multi-disciplinary foundation for future research. *Journal of Computer-Mediated Communication*, 10 (1), article 3. *http://jcmc.indiana.edu/vol10/issue1/porter.html* (Accessed February 9, 2005).

Postmes, T., Spears, R., and Lea, M. (2000). The formation of group norms in computer-mediated communication. *Human Communication Research*, 26 (3), 341–371.

Tichon, J. G., and Shapiro, M. (2003). The process of sharing social support in cyberspace. *Cyberpsychology and Behavior*, 6, 161–170.

Tidwell, L. C., and Walther, J. B. (2002). Computer-mediated communication effects on disclosure, impressions, and interpersonal evaluations: Getting to know one another a bit at a time. *Human Communication Research*, 28 (3), 317–348.

Walther, J. B. (1992). Interpersonal effects in computer-mediated interaction: A relational perspective. *Communication Research*, 19, 52–90.

West, R., and Turner, L. (2004). *Introducing Communication Theory* (2nd ed.). New York: McGraw-Hill.

Wright, K. (2000). Providers: An examination of perceived homophily, source credibility, communication and social support within on-line support groups. *Communication Quarterly*, 48 (1), 44–59.

## Questions

1. If you have ever posted a message in an online guest book—for a wedding, funeral, or hospitalization—what were the benefits or drawbacks for you as the message sender?

2. What factors account for the gender difference among message senders in the CaringBridge guest book we studied?

3. What communication guidelines would you suggest to a friend posting in a guest book for the first time? Why?

# 45
# Thoughts on CMC by an E-mailer, IMer, Blog Reader, and Facebooker

*Katrina Shonbeck*

**W**ithin the past decade, online communication has exploded in terms of users and strategies for interaction. Those in Generation Y (ages 10–27) have experienced increasing opportunities for connecting with others online in ways never imagined before. In addition to e-mail, online directories, blogs, and IM have challenged users to keep updated on the latest ways to stay connected. Younger people who grew up with computers are at the forefront of this communication revolution. Many of those in their 30s and older, although proficient on e-mail, are less skilled in the new mediated opportunities. Yet, change is reaching all online users. Today 74 percent of adults online use a computer to access the Internet as compared to 9 percent a decade ago ("Adults Jump Online" 2005).

Significant personal messages are communicated increasingly online. According to Barker (2005), "Message boards, personal websites, listservs and blogs have become virtual soapboxes for brooding over and boasting about the kind of news—disease and death, cheating boyfriends and new boyfriends, job raises and losses" (p. 2D). In the past such information was communicated through more private channels, such as phone calls, face-to-face interaction, or letters, if it was communicated at all. Part of using these new mediated opportunities involves learning to use not only the hardware

but also the language of relating in a new medium. For example, instant messaging (IM) requires developing a new vocabulary of acronyms for high-speed message delivery as well as an understanding of the etiquette involved in real-time access online. In addition, users must understand how to establish boundaries around their websites or blogs in order to provide access only to desired readers, and must understand the "rules" for operating in online directories such as Friendster. Blogging has exploded as a public means of self expression. In State of the Blogsphere, Sifry (2005) of Technorati Weblog, an authority on blogs, reports that as of July 2005 over 80,000 blogs were created daily and a new weblog is created every second. Thirteen percent of all blogs are updated at least weekly.

Such online involvement requires a commitment of time, energy, and a willingness to learn new approaches. This may account in part for why Generation Y members tend to be the heaviest users of these CMC innovations. In the following article Katrina Shonbeck, currently a 21-year-old college student, reflects on her experiences in the world of online communication and relates her insights to the interpersonal communication theories she has studied during college. She describes e-mail and some of the recently developed opportunities for online communication, including IM, Facebook, and blogging, giving personal examples of how she uses these and how she views them in light of reading communication theories. Finally she examines two issues raised about online interaction, broad reach and permanency.

You could have written a variation on this essay. Issues such as age, gender, collegiate experience, economic status, and computer knowledge would render your essay different from the author's. You also live in a wired world, and, whatever your age and background, this reality impacts your interpersonal interactions with some or most of the significant people in your life. In some cases it brings you closer to certain individuals or groups; in other cases it isolates you from potential connections.

As you read this essay, imagine yourself preparing a companion piece to it. Ask this question: To what extent are my experiences different *from or similar to those of the author, and how might I present my insights regarding CMC?*

## References

Adults jump online. (2005, July 29). *USA Today*, 1.

Barker, O. (2005, August 1), Web spins personal laundry. *USA Today*, 1D–2D.

Sifry, D. (2005, August 2) *State of the blogosphere, August 2005, growth. http://www.technorati.com/weblog/* (Accessed August 12, 2005).

\* \* \*

As a current college student, I represent a group of young people who have grown up during the rapid evolution of computer-mediated communication. Due to the user-friendly nature of CMC and the fact that it was developing during the time that people in my age group were maturing, it's easy to understand why I take much of this computer-mediated world for granted. However, through my studies and conversations with a wide range of other people, it's clear that CMC is revolutionizing both how we interact with many others in our lives—friends, family, colleagues, and even strangers—and how we think about relational communication processes.

Computer-mediated communication is changing the world around us in ways we often don't stop to recognize. When was the last time you checked your e-mail? Checked away messages? Looked someone up using Facebook, Friendster, MySpace, or other online personal directories? Updated your blog or read others' blogs? It is easy to gloss over these seemingly mundane daily activities that have gradually been incorporated into everyday living patterns over the last few years, but the reality is every online interaction has an impact on the way we relate to others. Because of this, it's important to start thinking about how we use CMC and how it fits in with current communication theory and research. Given the relative recentness of computer-mediated communication research, I would like to give a general introduction to CMC before describing four of its different forms and the implications of these internet based communication programs for current communication theories.

Computer-mediated communication both challenges and upholds traditional interpersonal communication theories by virtue of the fact that much CMC is instantly received written communication, therefore lacking nonverbal cues. This is not to say that CMC is impersonal. On the contrary, though a machine is the catalyst for all forms of CMC, this form of communication is encourages interpersonal interactions with others who we may never meet otherwise or with whom we can deepen their existing relationships. CMC is used by all types of people ranging from the extreme social butterfly to the antisocial computer aficionados. Naturally social individuals use CMC to broaden their social network and keep in touch with a greater number of people. Less social individuals find CMC helpful because it allows them the opportunity to try out different communication or interaction approaches with less risk to their face. And for the most publicly shy, CMC provides an outlet for meeting and relating with people in a less anxiety-provoking environment.

Additionally, due to the relative anonymity of the Internet, people use CMC to cope with deeply personal issues in addition to daily, maintenance-type communication. For many, when confronted with a difficult life issue (physical, psychological, sexual), support groups online offer a great deal of solace and act as a safe space where people can speak their mind without fear of being shunned or embarrassed. In this way, social penetration and uncertainty reduction theory are challenged because CMC allows, and even seems to encourage, high self disclosure to total strangers or acquaintances. Please keep these ideas in mind as you judge for yourself the validity of CMC as a form of interpersonal communication and the impact it is having on society.

## CMC: Four Applications

### E-mail

E-mail has completely transformed how we communicate on both a personal and business level. When e-mail started to take hold in our society about two decades ago, the different possibilities for various CMC programs were just being realized. Starting in the mid 1980s, e-mail use started to grow as companies and government agencies realized the practicality of sending queries and information that would be automatically delivered to another's virtual mailbox.[1] Because of the expediency of e-mail, it was quickly adopted for non-business purposes with the advent and popularity of the personal computer in the 1990s. The use of e-mail over the past two decades has grown exponentially and in January of 2005, 90 percent of male and female computer users claimed they had ever sent or read e-mail.[2] People e-mail for a variety of reasons. I find myself using e-mail most often to contact professors, stay in touch with friends who are abroad or at other distant schools, plan meetings for extracurriculars and group projects, as well as to receive chain letters, digital picture attachments, and electronic birthday cards and announcements ranging from "deal alerts" at Travelocity to university events.

Though e-mail has many practical uses, it has been faulted for its impersonal nature. First, what is important to realize in this shift toward instantaneous mailing capabilities is that it is neither a good nor a bad development; it's merely a development. Just as the telephone revolutionized communication in the twentieth century, the Internet has transformed and will continue to transform the way we communicate well into the twenty-first century. Some people favor e-mail as a form of communication due to the increasing speed at which we are able to receive and share information. For example, while at work my boss was able to view her one-hour-old nephew because her brother-in-law has a camera phone, and was able to send a picture of his son via an e-mail attachment.

Second, critics of e-mailing, who worry that people are no longer practicing good writing skills by sitting down with paper and pen to stay in touch, often forget the time and effort many people spend drafting e-mails in the form of love letters, thank you notes to potential employers, letters of intent, apologies, explanations, or queries. In fact, because many business and personal e-mails are drafted with a great deal of thought and care, responding to e-mails often requires you to craft an answer that is equally well worded, whether that means it is brief and pointed or entertaining and witty. This explains, in part, why e-mail etiquette does not require users to respond to personal e-mails immediately. Like traditional written communication, e-mailing differs from face-to-face and telecommunications which is often much more fluid and which, despite our best efforts, cannot often be drafted ahead of time.

And finally, there is a dark side of e-mailing. For example, in a study of women's Internet use, researchers found that 34 percent of those who e-mail siblings and 33 percent of those who e-mail parents find it easier to say unpleasant things in e-mail than in face-to-face communication.[3] Face theory supports this finding because it is less risky to say unpleasant things when you cannot see or hear the personal ramifications of your negative messages, even if you can anticipate them.

## IM

Whereas e-mail is seldom reciprocated immediately, instant messaging takes an entirely different approach. As with e-mail, IM is used both in business and personal settings; however instant messaging programs such as AOL Instant Messenger, Windows Messenger, MSN Messenger, and Gaim are used mostly for near real-time communication leading to their more casual nature. To give you an idea of how widespread the phenomenon of IMing is, in January 2005, 42 percent of all computer users sampled in the Pew Internet and American Life Project said they had ever sent an instant message to someone online at the same time as them, and about 14 percent had sent an IM to someone online at the same time as them the previous day.[4]

Often when someone IMs another person it is to get the answer to a direct question that is time sensitive without having to call or talk face-to-face with someone; for example: "What are you doing tonight?" or "Can you send me those charts you finished?" Also, instant messaging is used in place of a conversation you might have over the phone or in person but don't either due to the fact that oral communication isn't possible, desirable, or feels too personal. I believe most traditional college students would agree with me when I say that IM is a safe way to converse with someone, who you wouldn't call or talk to in depth in person, but who you want to get to know better. In fact, many of my friends' current romantic relationships began after a period of instant messaging with that person because it was a less face threatening way to get to know one another before initiating the dating process.

There are several interesting characteristics and features of IM that I would like to highlight, some of which are also pertinent to other forms of CMC while others are specific to instant messaging. First, IM, like most forms of CMC, is faulted for its lack of non-verbals which can lead to misinterpretation and sometimes even conflict. While emoticons and other character expressions, which are used heavily while instant messaging, are a step in the right direction, even these little faces cannot account for tone of voice, indicating a range of meaning from sarcasm to deepest sympathy. Due to the lack of face-to-face nonverbals and the additional absence of auditory cues, many forms of computer mediated communication, not just instant messaging, are often misleading and the cause of interpersonal conflict. Does this mean that we should be more cautious about how we say things online? Or that we should be less sensitive about ambiguous statements? I raise these questions not because they have an answer, but because daily everyone interacting online contributes to the rules and patterns of CMC.

Another interesting feature of instant messaging is the access users have to both the away message and personal profile. In these spaces, users engage heavily in facework, or impression management: deciding what they want others to know about them and how they want to portray themselves online. For example, I have a long list of away messages that I filter through to best capture my current mood, plans, or thoughts. These messages are sometimes in the form of quotations, historic or from movies and songs; questions, "Who wants to see the Acapella show tonight? shoot me an IM"; or straight-out statements, "Working, pls distract me!" Friends quickly become accustomed to how others use IM. Some boycott the away mes-

sage all together so you never know when that person is at their computer, whereas others put up a new away message every time they return to their computer after being "away" for 10 minutes. Next, the profile function of IM serves quite a different purpose for it is a more permanent version of an away message. In the profile sections, many people include their contact information in addition to personal information like extracurricular activities, favorite quotations, links to blogs, digital pictures, funny news stories, top ten lists, etc.

Last, a final impression management consideration of IM is the buddy icon. This allows users to choose an image that they wish be displayed with their half of the dialogue box when talking with others. Some are pictures of celebrities, others are goofy animated cartoons, and still others are serene landscapes—the possibilities for buddy icons are endless. By consciously making choices about how to use away messages, profiles, and buddy icons, people engage in impression management by finding different ways to represent themselves, leading to the incredible consciousness people have of the persona they are conveying online.

## Blogs

Blogs, represent a very different form of CMC from e-mail and IM. A blog is a web log or an online journal that people can choose to update as often as they like with all sorts of information ranging from personal ponderings, rantings and ravings, and political musings along with digital pictures, links to news stories, funny websites, etc. As more people move online, blogs are becoming increasing popular. In January 2005, 10 percent of all computer users sampled in the Pew Internet and American Life Project said that they had created a blog that others could read on the web and 27 percent said they had read someone else's blog online; 7 percent of people said they had a read a blog the day before and 2 percent of computer users had created a blog the day before.[5]

Blogs are changing communication patterns because readers are receiving private information and gaining an in depth look at another's personality, thoughts and feelings without having to talk with that person and sometimes without that person's knowledge. While some readers are able to offer commentary on the information that they are reading, often highly personal in nature, for the most part blogs are one-sided CMC experiences. This means that students can often get to know others by religiously reading their blogs but never once say hello to those persons when they see them around campus. I've found it awkward when I'm able to read seemingly private information that acquaintances wouldn't normally disclose to me and then encounter them without the ability to bring up what they wrote in their posts.

Granted, if the information isn't supposed to be known widely, the author of the blog shouldn't share it, but blogging etiquette is far from established and many users downplay the effect that their words may have on others feelings or perceptions. Relational dialectics are at work when we consider the openness-closedness tension that influences what users chose to post. The decision of who can view the information posted in a blog rests entirely with the person who owns the blog. Many people chose to track who is reading their blogs using others' IM screen names, computer ISP addresses, or blog accounts. While blogging etiquette may not be completely established, it's currently getting a great deal of attention because people are losing their jobs over posts that employers find undesirable, and often unprofessional.

## Online Directories

Online directories, like Facebook, Friendster, and MySpace, have been around in the form of dating services and virtual friend networks for years but have only recently started to dramatically alter how college students interact with one another. In keeping with social penetration, uncertainty reduction, and social exchange theories, people use online directories to gain a wide breadth of information about others before engaging in IM or more personal forms of communication. Also, by using online directories to learn more about someone, you enter communication with that person knowing you have the tools to reduce uncertainty by discussing common in-

terests or similar views, which usually leads to greater liking.

When Facebook reached my school in 2004, the whole campus seemed to be consumed by it. Of course there were pockets of students who refused to join and watch their list of friends grow, but for the majority of us who did join, about two weeks of productivity was lost, or severely curbed, due to the time spent creating and managing our online profiles that contain not only contact information but also personal information such as political views, favorite books, movies, quotes, dating status, and what you are "looking for"—"friendship," "dating," "a relationship," "random play," and "whatever I can get"—along with all the time spent reviewing and confirming some friends while rejecting others.

Even though it is only several years old, Facebook is now established at 839 colleges and universities and is drastically changing college culture. When I entered college 1,000 miles away from all my family and friends, I knew no one at my school and made friends once I arrived. Only three years later, entering college with few interpersonal contacts is a way of the past. For my younger sister, part of getting ready to enter college included joining Facebook as soon as she was issued her college e-mail address. Immediately after uploading a recent photograph of herself, she had seven admitted students request to be her "friend" and during the following months, she continued to be "friended" and to "friend" others. Another interesting facet of Facebook is the ability new roommates or suitemates have to learn about each other before talking to them in person which changes the subsequent interaction that both have with one another. Facebooking others before talking to them and other such experiences challenge theories of initial interaction that presume communicators rely heavily on face-to-face discussion and non-verbal clues to decide whether to pursue a relationship.

Using the social exchange theory as a model, many people, when "facebooked" by others, ask themselves, "What can this person bring to my online character? When people see this person listed as my 'friend' what will that say about me? If it is someone I never talk to, will it be perceived that I am desperate for friends or trying to look like I have a lot of friends?" The same thought process occurs when you have maxed out the number of screen names you can keep in your IM buddy list so that every time you want to add a new screen name you must kick someone else off. The question that you are constantly asking yourself is, "What does it take to keep others on a buddy list, check their away message, Facebook them or friend them back?" As long as the perceived benefits are weighted higher than any perceived costs, you will keep them on the buddy list, check their away message, Facebook them, or confirm them as a friend.

In spite of all the positive aspects of online directories, there are negative aspects to online directories as well. Applications like Facebook can be accidentally misleading, but also intentionally deceptive. A profile can accidentally mislead others in many ways. For example, irony and sarcasm in someone's profile, which may be funny to friends, can easily be taken as the truth by a stranger or an acquaintance. Thus, users of online directories may misinterpret the profiles of another or judge too quickly what a person is really like.

On a darker note, intentionally deceiving others is easier through CMC, including online directories, than it is in face-to-face interactions because you can't see who you are lying to. For example, I have known people that change their interests, political/religious views, or omit certain hobbies in order to match more similarly the profile of someone they are interested in romantically. Aside from straight out lying about yourself, other dark sides of online directories can be more harmful: for example, stalking. While many students make light of this issue by claiming that they "facebook stalk" crushes or acquaintances—a serious issue that has been made simpler by the advent of e-mail, instant messenger, personal blogs, and online directories—it is a serious issue that reminds us to be mindful of the information that we make available for the millions of internet users per day.

## Implications of CMC

I would like to conclude with some general considerations that set CMC apart from traditional forms of communication: namely its broad reach and its permanency. One of the greatest qualities of CMC is that you can increase both the number of people you communicate with and the depth at which you disclose to acquaintances and strangers. Using social exchange theory as a model, CMC allows you to exert less effort to keep in touch with more friends and family in less time than you could in the past, so you are more apt to view rewards of CMC rather than costs. However, if you do not perceive that the other person is reciprocating—replying in an appropriate length of time, staying on topic, responding to your away message, "poking" you on Facebook, sending you e-cards, e-vites, and so on—chances are you will discontinue or greatly reduce the amount of time devoted to that person using CMC.

While CMC saves some time compared to face-to-face and even telecommunications, it also consumes a great deal of time and provides much opportunity for procrastination (a cost depending on the importance you place on CMC and who you allow to contact you via CMC channels). Between checking e-mail constantly, creating away messages, checking away messages, updating blogs, and researching others on Facebook, the amount of time spent investing interpersonally online easily consumes a couple of hours in each collegian's day. In an experiment to see how much time I really spent using CMC, I logged off IM, closed Outlook Express, except to check it three times for group meeting updates, forbade myself from looking up acquaintances on Facebook, and plunged straight into a paper that was due soon. I found I had time to add in a three mile run and watch two episodes of my favorite dramady with friends that evening. I estimate that, when added up, I check e-mail, use IM, and read blogs and online directories a total of about 3–4 hours daily in college depending on my workload.

Finally, I would like to discuss CMC's relative permanency and wide circulation. In general, CMC is a form of communication that can be saved or recorded easily for later viewing and can be forwarded to third parties or linked to by outsiders thus increasing interpersonal interactions. Due to the permanency of CMC and the ease of forwarding or linking to CMC, individuals are finding that they must be more careful with what they say and how they say it online. E-mails, IMs, or blog entries, especially ones containing personal, controversial, or highly emotional content, often get forwarded or requoted by other parties to make a point. Very quickly a white lie can be discovered or a bit of gossip forwarded to an outsider. Once while arguing with a friend via IM, I found myself constantly scrolling up to quote our previous conversation in order to prove that he was contradicting himself and therefore lying to me.

I don't mean to position CMC as a negative technological advance due to its potential permanence and wide audience. In fact, the reverse is often true. People will save positive e-mails, IM conversations, or blog posts because they are uplifting, personally defining, flattering, funny, or generally "feel good" prose. Saving positive CMC messages acts as a reminder that you are thought of, cared about, valued, or maybe going through a similar situation as someone else.

It's important to remember that I represent the traditional college-aged student and because of this, the perspective I have on CMC may differ from yours. But as I see it, computer mediated forms of communication are breaking barriers and challenging the way we are relating to one another. As students leave for college, work, or the military, it is increasingly easier to stay in touch with high school and childhood friends. No longer do people expect to lose as many friends due to distance. Systems theory teaches us that there is no way that CMC can enter our life and not affect every other part of our interpersonal life. How is it affecting yours?

## Notes

1. "E-mail." *Wikipedia: The Free Encyclopedia*. (2005). *http://en.wikipedia.org/wiki/E-mail#Origins_of_e-mail* (Accessed August 21, 2005).

2. "Usage over time." Pew Internet and American Life Project. (2005). *http://www.pewinternet. org/trends/ UsageOverTime.xls* (Accessed August 21, 2005).

3. Raine, L., Fox, S., Horrigan, J., Lenhart, A., and Spooner, T. (2000). *Tracking Online Life: How Women Use the Internet to Cultivate Relationships With Family and Friends*. (2000). Washington DC: The Pew Internet and American Life Project. *http://www.pewinternet.org/reports* (Accessed August 17, 2005).

4. "Usage over time." Pew Internet and American Life Project. (2005). *http://www.pewinternet. org/trends/UsageOverTime.xls* (Accessed August 21, 2005).

5. "Usage over time." Pew Internet and American Life Project. (2005). *http://www.pewinternet. org/trends/UsageOverTime.xls* (Accessed August 21, 2005).

## Questions

1. How do your CMC experiences differ from those of the author? In a page, describe how you would write such a reflection based on your experience.

2. Choose one of the four CMC opportunities (e-mail, IM, online directories, or blogging) or another one with which you are familiar, and indicate the ties to some of the communication theories discussed earlier in the book.

3. How would you explain the interpersonal impact of online directories to relationship building to someone who is unfamiliar with them?

# Conclusion

There is a children's story by Mem Fox entitled *Wilfrid Gordon McDonald Partridge*. It tells the story of a little boy who lives next door to an old people's home. He learns that his best neighborhood friend is now in that home: Miss Nancy Alison Delacourt Cooper, who has lost her memory. So Wilfrid sets out to help her find it. He asks other residents of the old people's home, "What's a memory?" and he receives various answers: "Something that makes you laugh," "Something that makes you cry," "Something that makes you warm," "Something from long ago," "Something as precious as gold." Wilfrid gathers up things: a puppet, his grandfather's war medal, a warm chicken egg, a seashell, and something as precious as gold—his football. He puts everything in a basket and takes it to Miss Nancy. As Wilfrid gives her each article, she remembers something from her past, and when he gives her the football, she remembers Wilfrid and all the fun they had. As a result, their relationship becomes strong again.

The point of this story is the message of this book—the success of relationships lies in creating ways in which both persons feel recognized and connected. Highly functioning relationships are life giving and life affirming. Such relationships contribute to your good health, a strong self-concept, and a sense of connectedness and caring. Through the readings in this text, we hope that you have discovered some new ways to view relationships—their joys as well as their struggles. We also hope that you have come away with a new set of "lenses" to better understand communication in your own relationships and to become more analytical as you observe the relationships of others. May you make deeper and stronger relational ties as you make connections between the thoughts and theories of academic scholars and your own communication experiences. And may these ties be life giving and life affirming for you. ✦

# *Index*